SOURCES OF THE AFRICAN PAST

Case Studies of Five Nineteenth-Century African Societies

David Robinson and Douglas Smith

toExcel
San Jose   New York   Lincoln   Shanghai

Sources of the African Past

This edition published by toExcel Press,
an imprint of iUniverse.com, Inc.

For information address:
iUniverse.com, Inc.
620 North 48th Street
Suite 201
Lincoln, NE 68504-3467
www.iuniverse.com

ISBN: 1-58348-288-1

LCCN: 99-62694

Printed in the United States of America

To Our Families

Contents

List of Maps

List of Plates

ACKNOWLEDGEMENTS

Maps 1.1 and 1.2 are adapted from J. D. Omer-Cooper, *The Zulu Aftermath* (Evanston, Northwestern Press, 1969) and *Cambridge History of Africa*, Vol. 5. The source for Map 1.3 is M. Wilson and L. M. Thompson, eds, *Oxford History of South Africa*, Vol. I (1969).

The maps in Chapter Two are adapted from L. M. Thompson, *Survival in Two Worlds* (Oxford University Press, Oxford, 1976). Map 2.1 is adapted from Omer-Cooper, op. cit.

In Chapter Three, the map of Buganda in 1900 is adapted from M. S. M. Kiwanuka, *A History of Buganda* (Longman, Harlow, 1972), and the plans of the capital area and the royal enclosure are from J. F. Faupel, *African Holocaust* (P. J. Kenedy, New York, 1962).

In Chapter Four, Map 4.1 is adapted from John D. Fage, *An Atlas of African History* (Edward Arnold, London, 1963). The map of Hausaland *c.* 1750 and the two maps showing the main battles and offensives of the *jihād*, 1804–1805, and the Fulani empires of Gwandu and Sokoto *c.* 1812, are from M. Hiskett, *Sword of Truth* (Oxford University Press, New York, 1973). Maps 4.3 and 4.4 are taken from E. W. Bovill, ed, *Missions to the Niger* (Cambridge University Press for Hakluyt), Vol. I.

In Chapter Five, the map showing the great roads of Asante in the early nineteenth century is adapted from I. Wilks, *Asante in the Nineteenth Century* (Cambridge University Press, Cambridge, 1975) and from M. Priestley, *West African Trade and Coast Society* (Oxford, 1969). The map of the Asante Empire is from J. Ajayi and M. Crowder, eds, *History of West Africa* (Longman, Harlow, 1971), Vol. I. Bowdich's map of Kumasi in 1817 is from Kwamina Dickson, *A Historical Geography of Ghana* (Cambridge University Press, Cambridge, 1969). The Fante states map is adapted from J. Fynn, *Asante and its Neighbours* (Longman, Harlow, 1971).

Introduction

As a field of history, Sub-Saharan Africa has grown rapidly since the Second World War under the impulse of decolonization and independence. Educators now face the problem of developing adequate curricular resources both in Africa, where indigenous history is finally finding its rightful place, and abroad, where misconceptions about Africa are still rampant.

Developing these resources is not an easy task. One difficulty is the fragmentation of the subject matter. The continent lacks common institutions and identities; even the colonial territories combined many pre-colonial nations and cultures. Consequently, one cannot find a central tradition, comparable to the growth of the English monarchy or the spread of Islam in the Mediterranean basin, upon which to build a narrative and an interpretation. A second problem is the very high proportion of European and European-filtered materials in the available documentation. This stems in part from the relatively weak traditions of literacy in the pre-colonial period and in part from the Western domination of the last hundred years. Taken together, the fragmentation and the disproportion in the documentation have encouraged the production of microscopic monographs and macroscopic surveys. The middle ground of interpretative literature on the common problems of selected African societies has been neglected.

Sources of the African Past is an effort to confront these issues. As distinguished from surveys, anthologies and specialized documentary collections, it combines a case-study approach with an emphasis on primary and orally transmitted sources to accomplish three objectives: to tell a story in some depth, to portray major themes and to raise basic questions of analysis and interpretation. The case studies are set in the nineteenth century and deal with critical periods in the fortunes of five societies in different parts of the continent. We have assumed that students desire to work with the raw materials of history, and to that end we have provided a workbook for a 'laboratory' experience.

Sources is designed for use in a wide variety of courses and in conjunction with other texts. We have kept our own interpretation to a minimum and invited scrutiny of our decisions of selection and arrangement. We chose the cases on the basis of several criteria: geographical coverage, abundance and diversity of primary sources, impor-

tance in the secondary literature, and relevance to the historical problems discussed below. All the studies emphasize political change. All witness some growth in European influence, ending in three instances with substantial European intervention.

In selecting the documents we sought a balance of perspective without sacrificing accuracy and relevance. This meant, in effect, a conscious effort to present a variety of views: African and European, internal and external, participant and observer, those of the victims as well as those of the victors, those of 'the people' as well as those of the elite. In practice, it was often difficult to give voice to the victims and 'the people', but this is not a problem peculiar to African history. Within the limitations of space, we have tried to make the excerpts sufficiently long to allow the reader to examine the author's style, purpose and other characteristics. Keeping in mind the limitations of libraries, we have attempted to make each chapter self-contained.

The Zulu and Sotho chapters constitute a study in contrast in South Africa. Starting with basically similar forms of social organization, the Zulu created a highly centralized and predatory state under Shaka, while the Sotho developed a more defensively-oriented polity based on consultation through the leadership of Moshweshwe.[1]

The Buganda chapter deals with a period of revolutionary change in East Africa when indigenous Muslims, Protestants, Catholics and traditionalists struggled over power and the identity of the nation. Like the Zulu, the Baganda emphasized military prowess. Like the Sotho, they demonstrated substantial receptivity to the foreign religions and cultures brought to their kingdom. This study ends in 1900 with the full implementation of British rule and consequently offers, together with the South African units, a background for the consideration of European conquest and colonialism.[2]

The study of the Sokoto Caliphate portrays the culmination of a process of Islamic reform in the Central Sudan. Using translations of Arabic works in addition to other sources, we have stressed the life of Uthman dan Fodio, the mixture of planning and coincidence in the execution of the 'holy war', and the ambiguities involved in implementing a vision of a reformed society.[3]

Like the Sokoto chapter, the Asante story is set in the first quarter of the nineteenth century. The Asante Empire controlled the junction of the trading routes north to Sokoto and the savanna with roads leading south to the coast. The sources are principally Dutch and English, while much of the action turns on Asante efforts to control the coast after the British began campaigning against the transatlantic slave trade.[1]

A Reader's Guide

The chapters of *Sources* are organized into several parts. Each case study begins with a brief introduction and maps designed to familiarize the reader with the people and places to be studied. At the end of each chapter, the reader will find several 'Aids to Understanding', consisting of a chronology, glossary, essay of questions and biblio-graphical material. We recommend consulting the essay of questions before as well as after reading the story. In it we have elaborated on the controversies and issues of importance for the historian, subsuming them under the following categories: the use of sources and interpreta-tion; the state and its leadership; trade, diplomacy, technology and the European presence; social, cultural and religious values. The questions encourage com-parisons between the case studies. An index relates the major themes of the various chapters. The bibliographical essay is designed to show the principal secondary sources we have used and to suggest further reading. All the primary and secondary works which have been consulted or cited are found in the bibliography.

In the Documentary Narrative which forms the bulk of each chapter, we have integrated selections from the sources and explanatory remarks to form a coherent story. Before each document we give notes on words and ex-pressions in the text. Expressions which appear in a number of texts are picked up in the glossary. In the docu-ments, all comments in parenthesis are by the original author; our editorial comments are bracketed.

Common Problems and Themes

In what follows we have sought to reflect upon common elements in the five chapters in the hope of assisting those using this material. In terms of sources and interpretation, the case studies share a number of the fundamental difficulties of African history. First, all except Sokoto suffer from a disproportionately large European contri-bution to the documentation. In the East and South African instances, that contribution comes to a great degree from missionaries, whose values and goals often clashed with those of the local society. Second, much of the material deals with the elite and the court. This is perceived most acutely in Asante and Buganda, but it is present throughout. Finally, in the Sokoto and South African examples the founders of the new regimes loom so large in the minds of their contemporaries and succeeding generations that the record is distorted. Such problems are not insoluble and the effort to con-front them can be particularly rewarding for the student of history. The European material is not monolithic.

Much of the distortion can be corrected by comparing Protestant, Catholic and administrative sources in Buganda, Wesleyan and Paris Mission documents in Lesotho, and Dutch and English accounts in Asante. There is good reason to believe that some European texts, such as the minutes of meetings with Moshweshwe between 1848 and 1852, accurately reflect the thoughts of the African actors. The elite bias is more difficult to surmount, but differences within the ruling classes do appear, such as those between Abdullah and Muhammad Bello in Sokoto. Records of the victims of 'holy war', the tribes displaced by Shaka, and the chiefs who revolted against Asante have survived. As for reconstructing the early life of a founding hero like Uthman, the convergence of the accounts of Abdullah and Bello gives some confidence about the broad outlines and chronology. For Shaka and Moshweshwe, the task is to weigh surviving oral tradition against the limited evidence of outsiders.

In relation to the state and its leadership, the five situa-tions offer striking contrasts and comparisons. The Zulu and Sotho chapters describe processes of state formation in societies previously organized around villages or small chiefdoms. Their divergent evolution from similar origins merits examination. In the rise of the movement of Uthman, one also witnesses a process of state formation, but it is set against a more elaborate tradition of statecraft which the movement finally adopted in spite of its com-mitment to reform. Buganda and Asante had already acquired complex and centralized forms of government by the nineteenth century. Like Sokoto, they constituted vast societies of a different order of magnitude (over a million subjects). From the new states of South Africa (a population of perhaps 100 000 in the Lesotho of 1850 and perhaps 200 000 in the Zulu kingdom of the 1820s).

The states faced a number of common problems: suc-cession to the kingship, the recruitment and maintenance of an army and an administration, the integration of conquered areas, and the control of trade and other key resources. The ease or difficulty of succession can be traced to a number of causes. Proximity to the founding hero of the state complicated the situation faced by Dingane in Zululand, whereas Bello benefited from his long association with Uthman in the founding of the Sokoto movement. The adoption of filial as opposed to collateral succession in Buganda probably simplified the succession process, but it certainly did not eliminate con-flict. The Buganda ruler faced in acute form the general dilemma of constructing a new administration loyal to his person rather than to his predecessor. The existence of procedures, such as those directed by the Queen Mother in Asante and the Chief Minister in Sokoto, facilitated the transition. Sokoto experienced relatively peaceful succes-sions in the nineteenth century, a fact which suggests the importance of its grounding in Islamic law.

The emphasis on the army is most apparent in the Zulu and Buganda chapters. Here disputes were often resolved by force and promotion was based on military distinction. In contrast to the Zulu, the Sotho and Asante took pains to integrate firearms into their fighting techniques, which helps to explain their relatively greater success against European encroachment. The Buganda factions also adopted firearms, but they used them in civil war rather than resistance, with a heavy toll in lives and suffering.

Zulu and Sotho administration remained rather simple and personal, consonant with their origins and smaller populations. Sokoto rapidly adopted the complex bureaucratic norms of its Hausa predecessors, despite the principles enunciated by Uthman in the early years. Asante, with its staff of linguists and political agents, was perhaps the most specialized in the tasks of diplomacy and administration. Power in Buganda was extremely centralized, but it is important not to equate this concentration with stability and durability, as the history of that state reveals. In fact, royal authority encountered serious obstacles in all situations, whether from the bureaucracy, the heads of lineages and chiefdoms, or the ruler's own family.

The documents yield insight into the administration and integration of conquered areas. Tighter and more direct control could produce revolt as well as obedience, as the Zulu and Asante leaders discovered, while a more relaxed confederation of vassals under Moshweshwe might prove relatively stable. Much depended on the nature of the regime's demands, its ability to enforce them, the possibilities for the subject group to migrate, and the presence of alternative regimes and sources of support. Shaka's and Sokoto's problems stemmed partly from the availability of land around them, while Asante had to contend with the British alternative in the south and the threat of the Kong state in the northwest. Buganda experienced relatively less difficulty in this regard, but it was none the less sensitive to any activity on its northern and eastern borders.

For Asante and Sokoto, the control of trade was a fundamental dimension of statecraft. Asante had to respond to a basic change in its trading system brought on by the campaign against the transatlantic slave trade, and it compensated for the change by expanding its commerce in kola nuts with the north. Sokoto continued the encouragement and regulation of the long-distance trade of its Hausa predecessors. The Asante selections emphasize deception in trade, while the documents in the Sokoto chapter stress the importance of trust and guaranties in commercial affairs. Readers should examine this apparent difference.

The case studies provide an abundance of data on political leadership. Three pairs of rulers offer intriguing contrasts: Shaka and Dingane in Zululand, Mutesa and Mwanga in Buganda, and Uthman and Bello in Sokoto. Comparisons within and among the pairs should consider the age and background of each ruler, the conditions of his accession, the extent of his consolidation in power, and his relative achievements in the military, political and diplomatic domains. Individual leaders may be tested against their images in the primary and secondary literature; was Mwanga, for example, the 'cruel despot' depicted in the Anglican missionary sources?

Shaka and Moshweshwe benefited from their roles as founding fathers, but this did not protect them against threats from their kinsmen and subjects. Moshweshwe and Osei Bonsu, in spite of the great differences in their regimes, were strikingly similar in their consistent pursuit of negotiated settlements with Europeans, and both encountered increasing impatience with this approach among their followers. Osei Bonsu and the Buganda kings offer an opportunity to examine the aura and institutions of 'divine kingship': to what extent did the rituals of office obscure the personality of the office-holder? To what extent did these rituals enhance or limit the ruler's authority?

The nature of the European presence in the five situations varies greatly. In Sokoto it is confined principally to the visits of a few explorers. The scene was analagous in South Africa in the 1820s, but the number and threat of Europeans escalated rapidly thereafter. A similar escalation occurred in Buganda fifty years later. The situation changed much less quickly in Asante, but British expansion in the coastal region and the campaign against the export of slaves were harbingers of later conquest. One should also examine the widening technological gap between African and European in the course of the nineteenth century, illustrated most dramatically in the military sphere, and compare attitudes of whites towards Africa in the pre- and post-Darwinian periods (Casalis and Clapperton, for example, in contrast to Stanley and Lugard). The roles and goals of Europeans need to be identified in order to appraise their actions; the documents deal with traders, explorers, missionaries, settlers, soldiers and administrators.

From the African side, good information was clearly critical to successful diplomacy. Osei Bonsu kept abreast of events through his complex bureaucracy while Moshweshwe worked through a missionary network. Dingane and Mwanga, however, suffered from the absence of good information about European activities and intentions. Dingane relied too much on the hope of dividing the British and Boer communities, while Mwanga was unable to take advantage of the British–German conflict in East Africa.

The documents suggest frequent difficulties in communication between European and African. An analysis of terms such as 'tribe' in the Zulu chapter, 'boundary' and 'clientship' in Lesotho, 'oathing' and 'human sacrifice' in Asante, 'slavery' in Asante and Sokoto, and 'circumcision', 'polygyny' and 'medicine' in Buganda may cast light on these problems. One should consider to what extent misconceptions, as distinguished from competition for resources, lay at the base of conflicts between European and African. Additional insight into the cross-cultural dimension comes from scrutiny of the narratives of those who moved across geographical and social frontiers: Jacob in the Zulu section, Pasko in Sokoto, and Abu Bakr, Huydecoper and Nieser in Asante.

On social and religious questions, the documents yield a great deal to close reading. Stratification can be perceived at the top of the scale, around the court and ruling class, and at the bottom, in the material on slaves and servants. The situation of the great number of commoners in Buganda is usually less clear. In Buganda, these commoners enjoyed an unusual degree of upward mobility, and a concomitant degree of vulnerability, through the page school. Among those groups which began on a more egalitarian footing (the Zulu, Sotho and the community of Uthman), one can detect an increasing stratification with time.

We have also selected excerpts relating to cultural and religious identity. The Zulu and Sotho societies were perhaps more capable of absorbing people of diverse origin, at least in their periods of expansion, but the same process occurred in the other areas. Christianity and Islam were not necessarily incompatible with indigenous citizenship. Some Sotho, including members of the royal family, accepted baptism. Many young Baganda became Protestant, Catholic and Muslim. Subsequently, however, these religious factions became highly intolerant of one another in their competition for control of the kingdom. The Asante king did not consider Christianity or Islam acceptable for his subjects and prevented any proselytization. By contrast, Islam had become an integral part of Hausa society by 1800. The effect of Uthman's preaching was to question the depth of Islamic identity of the ruling classes and finally to equate his vision of reform with the faith. Both the Sokoto and Buganda examples raise the question of what is involved in the incorporation of a 'universal religion' into an African society.

We would like to thank the following for their criticisms of various drafts and chapters: Alison Des Forges of the State University of New York at Buffalo, Richard Elphick of Wesleyan University, Harvey Feinberg of Southern Connecticut State College, Hermann Giliomee of Stellenbosch University, Graham Irwin and Paul Martin of Columbia University, Gerald McSheffrey of McGill University, William Worger of Yale University, and Marcia Wright of Columbia University. We owe a special debt of gratitude to Leonard Thompson of Yale University and to the Oxford University Press for the freedom to use *Survival in Two Worlds* as a guide to the major issues and sources on the life of Moshweshwe.

DAVID ROBINSON
East Lansing, Michigan
DOUGLAS SMITH
Los Angeles, California

Notes

[1] For background to the South African chapters, see the first volume of the *Oxford History of South Africa*, ed. M. Wilson and L. Thompson (1969). An excellent complement to the Sotho chapter is Leonard Thompson's biography of Moshweshwe, *Survival in Two Worlds* (Oxford University Press, 1975).

[2] For background on Buganda, consult D. A. Low, *Buganda in Modern History* (California University Press, Berkeley, 1971) and M. S. M. Kiwanuka, *A History of Buganda* (Africana and Longman, 1972).

[3] An excellent complement to this chapter is M. Hiskett's biography of Uthman, *The Sword of Truth* (Oxford University Press, New York, 1973).

[4] Ivor Wilks has written a helpful summary, 'Ashanti Government', in D. Forde and P. Kaberry, eds., *West African Kingdoms in the Nineteenth Century* (Oxford University Press, 1967), in addition to his monumental work, *Asante in the Nineteenth Century* (Cambridge University Press, 1975).

SOURCES OF THE AFRICAN PAST

tions had allowed a substantial population growth which in turn challenged the old social and political institutions. Among the northern Nguni, with whom we are concerned, this challenge led to the creation of several loose military confederations which in turn gave way to the cohesive Zulu state.

From the limited evidence available for the period prior to these changes, it appears that the northern Nguni lived in clusters of homesteads near rivers or other water sources. A homestead consisted of several beehive-shaped huts grouped around a cattle enclosure or *kraal*. Several homesteads constituted a small chiefdom of perhaps 2000 persons. The chief, chosen from one lineage, exercised some judicial, administrative and religious authority over the people, in close consultation with the senior male representatives of the homesteads. In addition to these vertical divisions into lineages, the Nguni were also organized horizontally into cohorts of persons born within the

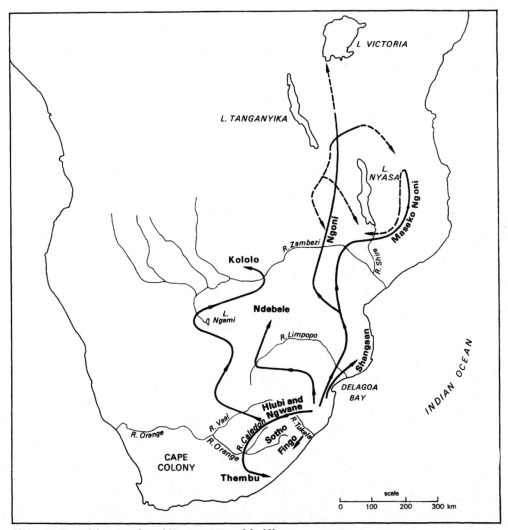

MAP 1.2   *General direction of population movements of the Mfecane*

same four- or five-year period. These age cohorts of males and females learned the tasks and traditions of the society at the various stages of life. The most important stage was the transition to adult status in the late teen years. For the males, this initiation involved circumcision, several months of ritual seclusion, and the formation of very strong bonds of loyalty.

The sources suggest fairly frequent competition between chiefdoms over land, cattle or access to water, and warfare of limited duration and violence. The male members of the homesteads would assemble at the summons of the chief, advance against the foe and throw

their spears while protecting themselves with shields. When the warriors of one group had demonstrated their superiority, they seized their opponents' cattle as spoils. The chief conducted the distribution and kept a portion for himself. In general, the victors did not pursue the vanquished nor bother their women and children.

Conflict also arose within the cheifdoms, especially between competing male members of the ruling lineage. Nguni custom favoured the first son born to the woman designated as 'Great Wife' by the chief after his accession. This son was usually younger than some of the male children of other wives. When the age gap and the ambi-

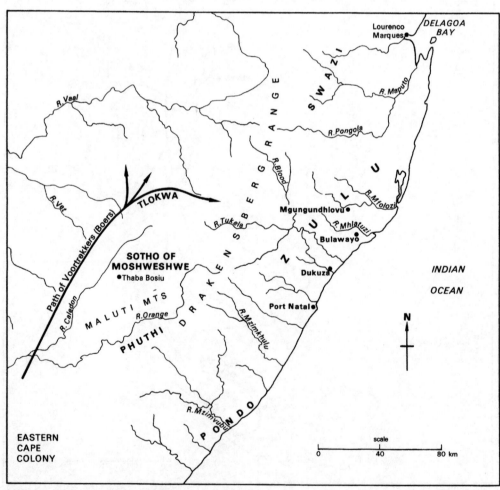

MAP 1.3   Eastern South Africa c. 1836

tion of the sons gave rise to succession disputes, the contenders would mobilize their respective age cohorts and challenge each other in battle. The loser, or the one who sensed he was the weaker party, often took his followers to another area where he might assert himself as the chief.

By the end of the eighteenth century, population growth and land scarcity were making it difficult for unsuccessful contenders to find new areas to move into. Conflict became more intense and violent. Those who succeeded in warfare extended their control and sought to monopolize the trading routes which converged at Delagoa Bay on the Indian Ocean. The northern Nguni chiefdoms now formed three large military confederations: the Ngwane (later to become the Swazi kingdom), the Ndwandwe of Zwide and the Mthethwa of Dingiswayo.

The leaders of the confederations apparently made important innovations within Nguni society at this time. They abolished circumcision and the period of ritual seclusion, which made the homesteads vulnerable to attack by removing many of the men. In their place they created a system in which initiation to manhood occurred within age-regiments and through warfare. They established tight control over these regiments of warriors and used them as the basis for a standing army. When they conquered an enemy, they often absorbed men, women and children, placing the male prisoners in the regiments. Subordinate chiefs might continue to administer their subjects, but they now had obligations to supply tribute and young men for the new cohorts that were constantly being formed.

The extant traditions tend to associate these changes with Dingiswayo. His Mthethwa confederation lay to the south and east of the others and included the Zulu chiefdom of Senzangakona. The Zulu eventually dominated the Mthethwa and transformed northern Nguniland under the leadership of Senzangakona's sons, Shaka and Dingane.

The sources available for the careers of Shaka and Dingane require special comment. They divide into two main categories: accounts by Europeans who visited the Zulu kingdom between 1824 and 1840, and oral traditions collected among the Zulu in the late nineteenth and early twentieth centuries.

The most important sources in the first category are the works of Henry Francis Fynn and Nathaniel Isaacs. Both were about twenty years old when they met Shaka and sought to develop trade between his kingdom and the community in Cape Colony. By this time the scattered settlements of the northern Nguni had already been transformed into the Zulu state. Fynn lost his original journal and later reconstructed it from memory, with the help of others. Isaacs kept a diary and published a book based upon it. He did not, however, enjoy Fynn's close relations with the Zulu, nor was he necessarily concerned to present his observations objectively. In a letter in 1832, he gave the following advice to Fynn (Isaacs to Fynn, 10 December 1832, *Africana Notes and News*, 18, March 1968–December 1969, page 67):

When do you intend to publish? The sooner the better, and endeavour to exhibit the Zooloo policy in governing their tribe. I mean show their chiefs, both Chaka and Dingarns treachery and intrigues ... Make them out as bloodthirsty as you can and endeavour to give an estimation of the number of people that they have murdered during their reign, and describe the frivolous crimes people lost their lives for. Introduce as many anecdotes relative to Chaka as you can; it all tends to swell up the work and makes it interesting.

The Zulu oral traditions are found primarily in the collections made by two Europeans who were fluent in Zulu: the Catholic missionary A. T. Bryant and a Natal official named James Stuart. Bryant collected and synthesized a vast number of traditions of the northern Nguni from 1883 until the early 1920s. Although he apparently interviewed people who had known Shaka and Dingane, he rarely identified his informants. When he published his findings in 1929, he had this to say about his approach to the material and his audience (*Olden Times in Zululand and Natal*, 1929, pages viii–ix):

And, then we are dealing too with a European public to which all history is proverbially insipid; to which that here presented is particularly unattractive, and so alien to its understanding that on that account again, we have been compelled to adopt unusual devices to make our historical reading intelligible and pleasant— by assuming, in general, a light and colloquial style; by creating here and there an appropriate 'atmosphere'; by supplying a necessary 'background'; by inducing a proper frame of mind by an appeal to pathos; by clothing the 'dry bones' of history in a humorous smile; by uniting disconnected details by patter of our own based on our knowledge of Native character and life.

In addition to editing Fynn's *Diary*, Stuart conducted his collecting between 1902 and 1922. His notebooks are being edited by Colin Webb and J. B. Wright and we have quoted several passages from the first volume of their series, *The James Stuart Archive*. As a general rule, Stuart noted the date and setting of his interviews, the social and genealogical position of his informants, and the chain of transmission of the testimony. He recorded some of the material in the Zulu of his informants, some in his own English translation. Consequently, it is easier for the historian to evaluate the material prepared by Stuart.

DOCUMENTARY NARRATIVE

Shaka's Early Life and Career

The nature of the sources makes the reconstruction of Shaka's childhood and early adult career a difficult task. He was probably born between 1785 and 1790 into the small Zulu chiefdom of the Mthethwa confederation. His father was Senzangakona, the Zulu leader, while his mother Nandi came from the Langeni chiefdom. The traditions differ about the nature of Senzangakona's and Nandi's relationship. They tend to agree, however, that the two were not married at the time when Shaka was conceived and that his illegitimate status played an important role in his life. The first two documents give accounts of Shaka's birth and come from the Bryant and Stuart collections.

DOCUMENT 1
'An intestinal beetle'

A. T. Bryant, *Olden Times in Zululand and Natal* (1929), pp. 47–8.

NOTES FOR READING   Bebe = great-uncle of Mbengi who was chief of Langeni at this time; 'fun of the roads' = fondling and sexual intercourse which stopped short of insemination; Mudhli = Senzangakona's cousin and co-regent at the time of the latter's minority.

The youthful Zulu chieftain, Senzangakóna, already some 26 years old, was present. His kindly manner impressed the ēLangeni stranger, who, reaching home, was glowing with his praises. This interested Nandi, daughter of the late king Bébé. Along this selfsame path the ēLangeni girls were then themselves about to go, carrying presents of sorghum beer to their relative married in Qungebeland. So Nandi arranged to accompany them; and, in order to facilitate her effort, she begged the aforesaid messenger to pose as chaperon and, as one practised in the art, to push her suit.

Senzangakóna, still in heart a boy, set blithely forth in company with other youths; and as they larked about the veld in chase of birds, behold a file of damsels four in all, came lilting down the hill,

> Like those fair nymphs that are described to rove
> Across the glades and openings of the grove;
> Only that these are dressed for silvan sports
> And less become the finery of courts.
>
> Ovid, *Metam.*, VI

Having reached the Zulu youths, the chaperon advanced, while the girls sat themselves discreetly distant to rest their weary limbs. Soon the latter were bid to approach, and asked, 'Whence come ye, pretty maidens?' 'From iNgúga kraal,' they said, 'in ēLangeni land, and on our way to eNtuzuma.' 'And which is the daughter of Bébé?' they inquired. 'This here, uNandi.' 'And what will ye here?' Said Nandi, 'Just come to see the child of the king.' 'Why wish to see him?' Said Nandi, 'Because I like him.' 'And can you point him out?' 'There he is,' said she triumphantly; but inconsiderate time then sped the girls away.

On the morrow, from eNtuzuma the ēLangeni girls retraced their steps homewards. While resting, and bathing their tired feet in the gurgling waters of the Mkúmbane, the Zulu youths again espied them, and forsook the birds they were chasing to court the girls. They begged for the 'fun of the roads' and flirting on primitive lines followed. Said Senzangakóna, 'That there is mine; she kneeling on the rock.' And that was Nandi. Then

the lads and lasses, each a loving pair, retired to the privacy of the adjacent bush for the customary intercourse.

The girls went home, and all was soon forgotten—except by Nandi, who, when the third month came, became aware, as did her mother, that something more than fun had happened. Such was the sorrowful fate of Nandi, daughter of Bébé, a former ēLangeni chief, by his great wife, Mfunda, daughter (or sister) of the Qwabe chief, Kóndlo . . .

So a messenger was rushed off bearing a formal indictment against the youthful Zulu chief. But Mudli, Ndaba's grandson and chief elder of the clan, indignantly denied the charge. 'Impossible,' said he; 'go back home and inform them the girl is but harbouring an intestinal beetle' — at that period known as an *iShaka*, but nowadays, owing to the *hlonipá* custom, termed an *iKámbi*, and held, both then and now, a common cause of suppression of the menses. But, in due season Nandi became a mother. 'There now!' they sent word to the Zulu people over the hills; 'there is your beetle (*iShaka*). Come and fetch it; for it is yours.' And reluctantly they came, and deposited Nandi, unwedded, in the hut of Senzangakóna; and the child was named uShaka—the year 1787.

DOCUMENT 2
'She liked the son of the chief'

From the testimony of Jantshi ka Nongila, son of a man who served as a spy under Senzangakona, Shaka and Dingane, recorded by James Stuart in 1903, and published in Colin de B. Webb and J. B. Wright, eds. and trans., *The James Stuart Archive of Recorded Oral Evidence Relating to the History of the Zulu and Neighbouring Peoples* . . . , Vol. I (1976), pp. 178–9.

NOTES FOR READING   Mbengi = chief of the Langeni; Mudhli = cousin of Senzangakona who acted as co-regent during the latter's minority; *isigodhlo* = quarters housing the king or chief and his wives; *impi* = military force.

Italics indicate passages recorded in Zulu by Stuart and translated by the editors. Zulu terms are written in the orthography of the early twentieth century.

In the course of a few weeks Mbengi, finding that Nandi had become pregnant (she had at first stated she was suffering from an illness known as *itshaka* or *itshati*), sent a report to that effect to Mudhli. Mudhli asked why such report had been made to him. The messengers replied, 'He acquaints you of this because the girl stated she liked the *son of the chief*.' Mudhli retorted, 'Is that the case?' 'Yes', they answered. Mudhli then said, 'All right, then please look after that, in case it turns out to be a child. We of the Zulu tribe would be glad if it should happen to be a boy.' The *men from the Langeni* then went off *and there, for the time being, the matter rested*.

Later on, messengers again came to Mudhli to say the girl had been delivered of a child and it was a boy. Mudhli was pleased at this and said, *'On no account let his mother suckle him.'* I think this must have been done because royalty were not allowed, by custom, to be suckled by their mothers.

Mudhli secretly informed Senzangakona's mother of what had taken place. She then used to send a piece of string to where the child was in order to see how big its waist was. All this time the members of the kraal at which Senzangakona's mother lived knew nothing of what had happened. When the child had grown a little, Senzangakona's mother dispatched a man to fetch and bring it to her, which was done. But this act took place at night, and the circumstances appearing to the night guards of the *isigodhlo* of a strange character, they paid special attention. My father said to me, 'I cannot think how the persons referred to came to see that there was a child in the hut.' The persons who saw this belonged to the Zulu tribe. It was the custom to have night guards so as to detect those committing adultery etc. However the incident came to be noticed, the *guardians* of Senzangakona all came to hear of it, and an *impi* was sent to Senzangakona's mother's kraal the next day to kill off the child, seeing that, at that time, Senzangakona had not been allowed to marry. Senzangakona's mother had caused *mats* to be set up at the back of the hut behind which the child was set and where she used to play with it. It was not allowed to sit out in the open in the hut.

Before this *impi* had been sent forth, a report reached Senzangakona's mother to the effect that somehow people had come to hear of the existence of the child there and whose it was. She was advised to have it taken away and sent back to its mother among the Langeni. Senzangakona's mother acted at once on the advice given her.

Two men, on the following day, preceded the *impi* referred to and, making their way to Senzangakona's mother, asked what she had hidden away behind the mats in her hut. The *impi* at this time was close up to the kraal. The two men looked about but found nothing. Whilst they were so engaged the *impi*, in large numbers, arrived and, after searching about the kraal for the child and not finding it, they proceeded at once to destroy the kraal and the members thereof. People were put to death but Senzangakona's mother somehow escaped being killed.... The child was Tshaka.

The traditions agree that Shaka spent a number of his early years with Nandi's Langeni people and that he subsequently went to live at the headquarters of the Mthethwa confederation. For one version of his childhood and adolescence, we return to Bryant.

DOCUMENT 3
'The childhood shows the man'

Bryant, *Zululand*, pp. 62–4.

NOTES FOR READING amaTigulu = Tukela river; Jobe = Dingiswayo's father; Ngomane = Shaka's Mthethwa patron who later became one of his principal advisers (see Documents 4, 20, 22).

Full ten years had passed, and more, since Nandi had been dismissed by the Zulu king and gone home disgraced to ēLangeni-land, 20 miles away.

There, probably because of his disagreeable character, her little boy, Shaka, proved unpopular with his small companions, and no desirable acquisition to the family.

> The childhood shows the man
> As morning shows the day.
> > Milton

His years of childhood in ēLangeni-land do not appear to have been the proverbial 'happy days'. Many little stories are extant of his unsympathetic treatment there, of which the dreadful echo will be heard years hence.

Zulu children dearly like to lick the porridge-spoon—with them an oar-shaped piece of wood for stirring. The bullies of the family would find great fun in thrusting this stirrer into the fire and then, when almost burning, ordering Shaka to peel off the porridge, saying, 'Come, eat this, that we may see whether thou be indeed a chief.' Or, when he would return from herding the cattle for his midday meal, they would force him to hold out both hands, extended side by side like a saucer, into which they would pour boiling collops, and compel him to eat, threatening him with punishment if he allowed the food to drop. And when on the veld they moulded each for himself a little herd of clay cattle and then led forth their respective bulls to fight, each boy pushing his puppet by the hand, they would grow jealous of his skill and, when gone home, make him a theme of constant complaint to mamma and papa. Then his little crinkled ears and the marked stumpiness of a certain organ were ever a source of persistent ridicule among Shaka's companions, and their taunts in this regard so rankled in his breast that he grew up harbouring a deadly hatred against all and everything ēLangeni.

Heretofore, according to Zulu usage, the boy Shaka had paraded *in puris naturalibus*; but now, the period of puberty drawing nigh, he must go home once more to be presented by his father with his first *umuTsha* (loin covering, of dressed skin). This was with every Zulu youngster a great event, corresponding to that auspicious occasion among our own when they are permitted for the first time to assume the glory of a pair of breeches. But Shaka, even at this early age, must have shown himself of a particularly intractable and unlovable nature; for he rejected with disdain the *umuTsha* preferred by his father, and otherwise succeeded in getting himself so generally disliked, that his early return to his mother became imperative.

After Shaka had been some years back in ēLangeni-land, stark famine came to stare him in the face, *c.* 1802. To add to other miseries, Nandi now found herself unable to provide food for her offspring. It was the calamitous famine of Madlatúle (Let one eat what he can and say naught), when people lived on *amaHlukwe* (fruit of the arum-lily), on *uBóqo* roots (*ipomœa ovata*) and other wild plants. The cup of Nandi, with two famished children wailing on her hands, was now filled. So she shook once more the dust from off her feet and, with her family, took the path to Mpapála, at the sources of the amaTigulu river, where, among the emaMbédwini folk (sub-clan of Qwabes), there dwelt a man, Ngéndeyana (or Gendeyana), by whom she had already borne a son, named

Ngwádi. She was affectionately received, and there for a while they all remained.

But even here the boy Shaka, now about 15 years of age, found no sure asylum. In this strange kraal he held no rightful place, and both his father's and his mother's people were pressing for his return. So on his mother's advice he was taken onwards once more, now, some say, to Macingwane, of the emaCúnwini clan, his father's dreaded neighbour. Hearing of this new evasion, Senzangakóna, it is said—though we doubt the report—sent presents to the Cúnu chieftain 'to induce him to betray his trust and destroy his guest. This the chief nobly refused to do, informing Shaka that he could no longer afford him protection.'

As a last resource, Nandi bethought herself of her father's sister, down in Mtétwáland, near the coast, and there Shaka was forthwith hurried. It must not be supposed that either Shaka or his mother was a personage of any consequence at this early period; on the contrary, as destitute vagrants, they were everywhere despised. Jobe was then Mtétwá king; but he knew nothing, and would have cared less, about the arrival amongst his people of a mere homeless woman. But headman in charge of the district in which they settled was Ngomane, son of Mqombólo, of the emDletsheni clan, and with him they soon became acquainted. He treated Nandi and her boy in a friendly manner, and his kindness then Shaka never forgot, and in the day of his greatness elevated him to the very highest position in his realm next after himself. There in a real 'home', surrounded by sympathy and kindness, Shaka at last had come to anchor in a haven of rest. Henceforth happy and glorious were his days, and he never again quitted his adopted country for his own, until that auspicious day arrived when he returned there in triumph to ascend its throne and wreak vengeance, swift and awful, on all his former tormentors.

When Shaka reached his early twenties, he joined his age-mates in an Mthethwa army regiment. He soon distinguished himself as a warrior and was chosen to lead his division. He gained Dingiswayo's attention, rising to become one of his most important advisors, and served the Mthethwa in a series of difficult confrontations with the rival confederation of Zwide.

In Document 4 Fynn describes his impressions of Shaka's early manhood, based on observations made at the Zulu court in the 1820s.

DOCUMENT 4
'Dingiswayo's hero'

H. F. Fynn, *The Diary of Henry Francis Fynn*, ed. J. Stuart and D. Malcolm (1950), p. 13.

When Dingiswayo heard of Shaka he invited him to come under his protection, saying that, as he had been driven from his father, and had become an outcast wherever he went, Shaka should be under his especial care. Shaka accordingly went, when he was put under the care of Ngomane, commander-in-chief of Dingiswayo's army.

He distinguished himself at an early age, by his courage and self-command, being always the first in attack, and courting every danger. He was known by the name of Sikiti, also by that of *Sidlodlo sekhanda* (the honour of the heads of regiments). Various were the acts by which he signalized himself in action, much against the express wish of Dingiswayo, who objected to his taking an active part in battle, considering it unnecessary for a prince to expose himself to that extent. On such occasions, in consequence of his keenness to fight, Dingiswayo would order his shield to be taken from him. Shaka, however, always managed to steal another from one of his companions. He soon became known among the neighbouring tribes as 'Dingiswayo's hero'.

In 1816 Senzangakona died and Shaka became chief of the Zulu. The sources disagree on three subsidiary questions: (1) whether Shaka returned to the Zulu chiefdom before or after his father's death; (2) to what degree Dingiswayo supported his bid for the chieftaincy; and (3) the degree of resistance which Shaka faced. Documents 5 and 6 present different perspectives.

DOCUMENT 5
'No one was ousted by Tshaka'

Excerpts from the testimony of Jantshi ka Nongila, recorded by Stuart in 1903 and published in Webb and Wright (eds), *The James Stuart Archive*, I, pp. 181, 199.

NOTES FOR READING   *giya* = to dance; Dingana, Sigujana, et al. = Shaka's half brothers of whom Sigujana was in line to succeed Senzangakona; Mkabayi = Shaka's aunt; Ndukwana = another informant who accompanied Jantshi. For italics, see notes for Document 2.

After some years Senzangakona decided to go down to Dingiswayo's to *look for a new wife*. When Dingiswayo saw him he specially invited him to come at a later time and join in festivities he was going to bring about in the shape of a public dance. Senzangakona proceeded home and informed his brothers Zivalele and Sitayi, and also the important men Mudhli and Menziwa (father of Mvundhlana) and other people, of the invitation.

Senzangakona thereupon went back to Dingiswayo's with the heads of his tribe and many ordinary members, including my father Nongila. Nothing took place on the day of his arrival. It was arranged that the dance should take place the day following. The next day Senzangakona and his party *danced* first. After he had concluded, Dingiswayo's people *danced*. Whilst Dingiswayo's party were dancing, Tshaka was shut up in the *calf pen* out of sight of the Zulu people. This had been arranged by Dingiswayo. When dancing had been going on some time, Dingiswayo came forward and said, 'Where is the hoe that surpasses other hoes?' He thereupon directed someone to go and open the *pen* for him and, as the messenger proceeded to carry out the instruction, Dingiswayo sang out his praises. Tshaka then *came out of the pen carrying his war shield of one colour. It had* pieces of skins of various wild animals placed in those holes in the shield caused by assegai thrusts. In Tshaka's shield the following skins were used for this purpose: *meercat* (like *a mongoose*, but smaller), *mongoose*, and *genet*. Tshaka came out and then began at once to *giya*. As he did so, Dingiswayo *shouted his praises*. Whilst *giyaing*, he ran round and round in circles and eventually ended off in front of Senzangakona where he stood still. He then said to his father, *'Father, give me an assegai, and I shall fight great battles for you!'* His father directed assegais to be fetched from the huts. A pile was accordingly brought. Senzangakona said, *'Take one yourself.'* Tshaka replied, *'No, let it come from your hand; I cannot take it myself.'* Senzangakona thereupon felt a number, one by one, and deciding on one, gave it to Tshaka. Tshaka, after getting the assegai, resumed his *giyaing*, and when he had finished he walked off in a certain direction in which it appeared Dingana, Sigujana, Mhlangano, Ngqojana, Mpande, and Maqubana were seated. He then went up to Sigujana and, tapping him on the head with his assegai, said, *'Greetings, my brother.'* Sigujana *responded*. They conversed a little, after which Tshaka went off and joined the dancing party, taking part in the dance.

When Tshaka arrived *in the Zulu country*, Senzangakona was certainly dead. I have not heard that Senzangakona declared Tshaka to be his legitimate son.

I do not know if Tshaka became an *induna to Dingiswayo*. Probably not. He was a favourite there because he was a great *warrior*.

It was general knowledge that on Tshaka's dying Mhlangana would *rule*. Ndukwana says this. Ndukwana has heard that Mkabayi *ruled* a little after Senzangakona's death, so she may have done so to allow Tshaka to come up.

Senzangakona had no one who stood armed by his grave as his successor. Sigujana did not stand thus, for when Tshaka got up, people accepted him without a fight. No one was *ousted* by Tshaka. It is probable then that Tshaka was offered the position of king.

DOCUMENT 6
'Resolved to dethrone him'

Nathaniel Isaacs, *Travels and Adventures in Eastern Africa*, 2 vols. (1836), Vol. I, pp. 264–5.

NOTES FOR READING   Zovecedie = Zwide; Umtatwas = the Mthethwa; Tingiswaa = Dingiswayo; Umgartie = Ngwadi, Shaka's maternal half-brother. Isaacs arrived in Zululand in 1825.

At the death of his father, a younger brother took possession of the Zoola crown; Chaka at once resolved to dethrone him, and place himself at the head of the nation.

After several attempts the king succeeded in driving him (Chaka) away to a distant and formidable chief, called Zovecedie, who was then at war with the Umtatwas; this induced Tingiswaa to assist Chaka in obtaining possession of the Zoola kingdom.

Meeting, however, with many obstacles in the way, he formed a sure plan of destroying the young king, which was

very soon carried into execution. Umgartie, his younger brother, and companion in exile, repaired to the residence of the young monarch with a story, that Tingiswaa had killed Chaka, that he was obliged to fly for his life, and throw himself at his brother's feet for protection. This important and wished-for information was readily believed, and Umgartie was soon installed in the office of chief domestic; being now constantly about the king's person, he took an early opportunity to effect his bloody mission.

It was his province to attend him every morning while bathing. On a chosen occasion he sent two of his friends to conceal themselves in the long grass by the river-side, and at a signal given, while the king was in the act of plunging into the water, they rushed forward and speared him to death; the news soon reached Chaka, who marched at the head of the Umtatwas, and took possession of the throne.

The first act that marked his bloody reign, was his putting to death all the principal people of his brother's government; those who were suspected to be inimical to his becoming king, were also speared.

From Chiefdom to Kingdom

As chief of the Zulus, Shaka transformed his army on the basis of his experience fighting for Dingiswayo. He organized his soldiers by age-regiment, housed them in barracks and required them to remain celibate. He introduced the short 'stabbing' spear to Zulu weaponry, thereby emphasizing hand-to-hand combat in place of spear throwing, and designed the 'chest and horns' battle formation, in which the two wings of the army surrounded the enemy while the centre attacked. He increased the mobility of his warriors by having them go barefoot and relieved them of the responsibilities of carrying their own baggage. Finally, Shaka broke with Nguni tradition by commanding his men to kill all who resisted—even the women, children and elderly associated with such resistance. In the following selections, Bryant and Isaacs describe these radical changes.

DOCUMENT 7
'His first real fighting force'

Bryant, *Zululand*, pp. 123–5.

NOTE FOR READING   head-ring = sign of adulthood.

Things having thus been brought into order at home, Shaka turned his attention to pressing needs of state. The most urgent of these was the provision of an adequate defence—and still more, offence—force. Plainly, he could not spend the rest of his life 'doing nothing'. And what had he been doing all his life hereto but fighting? He looked around for the Zulu army, and found none. Obviously the Zulu state was as deplorably organized as the Zulu kitchen. Nothing but a lot of guild-boys, circumcised and otherwise, to fight its battles. So he gathered them all together, the manhood of the clan, and sorted them out. There is good reason for believing that the Zulu regimental names that have come down to us were all of Shaka's coining at the time of his reorganization of the clan's manhood. All such of his father Senzangakóna's men as were of no further use as soldiers, Shaka scornfully rejected as beneath his notice—unhonoured and unnamed they passed out of Zulu history forthwith. Of those whom he regarded as nearing the border-line of senile decay (born c. 1775–1785)—most of these were little older than himself, about 30–40 years of age—he banded together and labelled, irrespective of their former guild-names, the amaWombé (sing. iWombé). He observed that all these were both head-ringed and married; so he permitted them to retain both head-rings and wives, and built for them on the Nolele stream a new headquarters kraal, which he named the Ever-lasting Pest (umBelebele, loc. emBelebeleni), and placed it and them in charge of his maiden aunt, Mkabayi, a virago well calculated to keep the old boys in order.

Next in approach to the army age-limit was a group (born 1785–90) which he called uDubintlangu, alias inTontela. These, though head-ringed, were not yet wived, and he peremptorily ordered them to cut off their head-rings and to renounce all further aspirations to the married state, and become boys (izinTizwa) again. He barracked them in his father's isiKlebé (loc. esiKlebéni) kraal, overlooking the right bank of the Mkúmbáne, under the presidency of his 'mother', Senzangakóna's first love, Mkabi (with Langazana as an able coadjutor). There they became henceforth known as the uJubingqwanga (They of the head-ring ukase). Along with Senzangakóna's unringed men (now grouped together as the umGàmule or úDlambèdlu, born 1790–1795, and barracked in the same kraal), they all together formed the izimPohlo (or Bachelors' Brigade).

Finally, Shaka summoned before him the crowd of idle boys of about 20 years of age. These were better raw material and would bear some knocking into shape. He banded them together as his first real fighting-force, the first genuine 'regiment' in his embryonic military system. He named them úFàsimbà (the Haze), and installed them as the garrison of his new Bulawayo capital. So grandly did they respond to his effective training, that they became henceforth his favourite regiment, 'Shaka's Own'.

DOCUMENT 8
'They fought to avoid being massacred'

Isaacs, Travels, I, pp. 267, 281–2.

His soldiers, (his warriors, as they are designated) without any inherent courage, were ever and anon eager for battle, and shouted for war from the love of plunder; they knew full well that their renown was enough to make their enemies crouch before them, and they gained more by the terror of their name, than they achieved by their prowess in arms. They have this alternative in the field, either to return triumphant and participate in the spoils, or to be deemed cowards and suffer an immediate and cruel death. In the troops of Chaka there was no moral courage; they fought to avoid being

massacred, and triumphed more from the trepidation of their opponents, than from the use of their spears. But cowards are said to be cruel, and the troops of this despot are an illustration. The war at Ingoma, in which I was engaged, convinced me that those whom we conquered were equal in capacity to the troops of Chaka, and that the latter possessed no innate courage.

The numerical force of the Zoola monarch was great at this time, and he took especial care to make his armies as effective as possible; for this purpose they were inured to every species of unnatural abstinence. They were prohibited from marrying, and forbade all sexual intercourse, under the idea that it deprived man of his physical strength and his relish for war; and that in the field his thoughts were apt to be directed towards home, instead of towards his enemy. In this, however, Chaka certainly set the example. He had no queen, although he had at each of his palaces from 300 to 500 girls, who were denominated servants or sisters. If any of these became pregnant, they were immediately taken away, and some imaginary crime alleged for putting them to death.

It was an invariable rule of war with him never to give his troops more cattle or provisions than would barely suffice to support them till they arrived in the country of their enemy. They had strict injunctions to fight or die, to quarter on their enemy, and not return but as victors, bringing with them the fruits of their triumph.

He was exceedingly wary, and used great precaution in concealing even from his generals or chiefs, the power or tribe with whom he designed combating; nor until the eve of marching did he make known to them the object of their expedition. By this he evinced some discretion, and precluded the possibility of his enemy being apprised of his intentions. In this particular, Chaka showed a judgment not common with the native chiefs, and peculiarly his own.

When all was ready for entering upon their march, he confided to one general his design, and to him he entrusted the command, should he not head his army in person. He, however, never confided in one man but on one occasion; upon no occasion whatever did he repeat such confidence. He made it an invariable rule always to address his warriors at their departure, and his language was generally studied to raise their expectations, and excite them in the hour of battle. He particularly detailed to them the road his spies had pointed out, inducing them to believe that they were going to attack any party but the one actually designed, and known only to the general-in-chief. This was judicious, because it kept his real object from being known, and, at the same time, prevented any treacherous communication to his enemy, who might get early intimation of his intended attack.

DOCUMENT 9
'Stout spears'

Isaacs, Travels, I, p. 270.

He next proceeded to introduce a new system of warfare. It had hitherto been the practice to carry several iron spears, and throw them at the enemy, besides the assegai or common spear (bows and other implements of war are not known to them), which he forbade under penalty of death.

For the purpose of proving his superiority and consummate judgment in military tactics, he determined that a sham fight between his regiments should take place in the presence of his whole nation. Reeds were accordingly substituted for spears; one regiment was to pursue the accustomed manner of throwing, and the other, who were allowed but one reed, were permitted to charge. The latter, covering themselves with their immense shields (six feet long and of an oval form), soon beat off their adversaries, and thus decided that Chaka's new regulation was the best. All the superfluous spears were then ordered to be destroyed, stout ones made in their stead, and each warrior was supplied with one: if he lost it in battle he was to suffer death. Thus his warriors had no alternative; their fate was inevitable; the fear of a horrid end by impalement made them fight, when otherwise they would have saved themselves by retreating in the event of being overpowered. The poor wretches were therefore doomed to conquer or die.

Shaka remained under Dingiswayo's authority until 1818, when the Mthethwa leader was killed by Zwide. Shaka then moved quickly to take over the confederation, thereby beginning the transformation of the Zulu chiefdom into the Zulu kingdom. The next document describes his takeover and gives impressions of Shaka's younger half-brother, Dingane.

DOCUMENT 10
'He soon found a pretext'

Fynn, *Diary*, pp. 15–18.

NOTE FOR READING   Mondisa = Dingiswayo's successor as head of the Mthethwa.

He soon found a pretext for attacking Mondisa and that part of the Mthethwa tribe that had remained with him. The tribe was still in confusion from the loss of its chieftain, and in fear of retaliation from the tribes which, having been conquered by Dingiswayo, were now left at liberty. With only a comparatively small force, Shaka succeeded in conquering them, killing half of those left and inducing the remainder to place themselves under his authority. They had no sooner done this than he put to death their chief, Mondisa, brother of Dingiswayo, appointing one of his own choice in his place.

With this additional strength he meditated greater conquests, and fought over again Dingiswayo's battles, but now they were attended with greater slaughter.

Dingane was at this time in disgrace in consequence of an amour with a girl. He was on the point of being killed when he effected his escape to the Qwabe tribe. It was at about the same time that Shaka prohibited his soldiers from marrying wives or engaging in amours of any kind.

Having received a quantity of beads from Delagoa Bay, a market he kept open after the death of Dingiswayo, he sent a present of some of them to Phakathwayo, chief of the Qwabe tribe. Phakathwayo, however, immediately returned them, saying they had been bewitched by Shaka, who wanted to put him to death. This accusation Shaka made a pretext for immediate hostilities. He attacked Phakathwayo in two different directions. Phakathwayo, on being closely pursued, fell dead from fright, whilst his tribe, after a short conflict, fled to the Entumeni forest near by. On the news of Phakathwayo's death being reported to Shaka, he pretended to be very sorry at what had happened. He sent two oxen as an offering to his (Phakathwayo's) family spirits, with prayers to bring about his resurrection. He, moreover, assured the Qwabe tribe of his regret, adding that his intention in coming at all was merely to demand an apology for the way in which Phakathwayo had insulted him. As, however, their king was dead, for the spirits did not seem inclined to raise him up, they would now stand in need of a protector; and seeing that Phakathwayo had no heir, and his brother Nqetho was too young, they had better put themselves under his protection. This they agreed to do, which considerably increased the size of Shaka's army, making it quite formidable. Dingane, by making an abject submission, was allowed to return to the Zulu tribe.

Zwide watched Shaka take over the Mthethwa leadership. Sensing a threat, he moved his Ndwandwe army against Shaka. The Zulu, badly outnumbered, lost many cattle but managed to keep their forces intact. When the Ndwandwe returned a few months later, Shaka was better prepared.

DOCUMENT 11
'The omens having been proven favourable'

Bryant, *Zululand*, pp. 204–9.

It was now about the year 1819, and prospects were beginning to grow ever more gloomy for Zwide: all indications portended an early eclipse as imminent . . . With all his wonted energy and resource Shaka was pulling the strings of fate to his own advantage. He had invoked or inveigled into his service all the past-masters of knavery in the land.

His victories heretofore had been generally attributed to the wondrous magic of his War Doctor, Mqalane, of the Nzuza clan, inheritor of the marvellous medicines of his clansman, Nondumo, son of Mgidi. One of the feats now accomplished by this remarkable wizard was to raise up—whence, unknown—a plague of rats. These he despatched *en masse* into Ndwandweland, where they not only demolished the stores of grain, but even nibbled away the fastenings holding together the assegai blades and shafts, thus weakening the enemy in his most vital parts, his food supply and his weapons.

At the other end intrigued Noluju, of the emaNqayini clan who enjoyed Zwide's confidence on the one side and conspired with Shaka on the other. Regular consignments, furnished to order, were forwarded to the latter of every variety of Zwidean 'body-matter'—doorway-grass (*ama-*

Kòtàmo), hair-shavings, nail-clippings, shreds of raiment and the like—as were required by the Zulu War Doctor to furnish the base essential for his deadly charms.

While plotting thus with Shaka, Noluju was equally busy manoeuvring Zwide into the trap. On the plea of making secret-service observations in the enemy's camp, he paid a visit to Shaka, and while there made final arrangements as to the trick of starving and wearing out the Ndwandwe army by leading it into an endless chase on an empty stomach. Leaving Shaka thus in perfect preparation, he hastened back to Zwide to report that now or never was his opportunity to 'catch the Zulus asleep'.

Zwide was far too business-like to miss a promising chance. He would plunge heavily and at once, as his trusty counsellor had advised. Millet bread was accordingly boiled for the march, shields were prepared, spear blades sharpened. Then the famous amaNkayiya regiment and the gallant amaPéla cantered away to conquer.

Shaka had the Dlamini news-carriers in such perfect order, that the Ndwandwe host had hardly got into motion before the danger signal was received. The alarm was spread like wild-fire through the land. Women, cattle, warriors, children, all bearing what grain they could—the rest destroyed—swarmed in hurrying masses up the Mtónjaneni heights, then along the ridges towards their old fastnesses, the countless kranses and abysmal kloofs about enKandla. Down to the Ntsuze river they fled, over the Túkela and up the heights of kwaNtunjambili beyond, in every kraal as they passed clearing out the grain-pits, replenishing their supplies of millet and scattering or concealing the rest.

The Ndwandwes followed quickly, lured onwards by Zulu decoys (*iziNtsaba*) left straggling behind. Zwide himself had not accompanied the expedition ...

By the time the Ndwandwes reached the Tukela they were, as Shaka had anticipated, thoroughly worn out. Rather than be lured on indefinitely in this wearisome fashion, they deemed it time they should play decoy. So they turned right about and reclimbed the steep Nkandla slopes they had just descended, expecting the Zulus would do the same, whereafter they might easily catch them.

And the Zulus *did* the same. The hunted now became the hunters. They eventually discovered the Ndwandwes encamped by ŏSungulweni hill, seawards of the Nkandla forest. Here the Zulu warriors, with the quarry before them, grew restless and called on Shaka to let them loose. During his inspiriting harangue, a feather fell from his headdress to the ground and fixed itself upright in the soil. This portentous incident unnerved his troops, who regarded it as an unpropitious omen. Not so Shaka. With logic as convincing as that displayed at the snake-bite he reassured them. 'Let it stand!' he shouted, when they rushed to pick it up. 'This one will not fall. There is *another* that will fall'—implying, of course, Zwide.

The omens having been proven favourable in this convenient manner, Shaka forthwith selected certain of the younger regiments of the umBelebele brigade, to wit, the izinTenjana (ezākála ŏNgóye), the uKángela and others, then unloosed the leash and shouted, with the Duke of Wellington, 'Up, braves, and at 'em!'

The ardent young warriors made the welkin ring with their terrifying yells as they rushed on the weakened Ndwandwes. When tired with their vigorous execution, the Zulus, according to plan, beat an orderly retreat. After a short respite, back they charged on the foe, and repeated the assault all day long till evening, their instructions having been simply to harass the enemy and so to reduce his resistant strength. That was the first day's work.

With the dawn the Zulus were back to the fray. They had already discovered the enemy's weakness, and were themselves after yesterday's practice in the best of mettle. Overnight the Ndwandwes had withdrawn down into the Mhlatúze valley, near the confluence of the Mvuzane, thereby to gain the advantage of the river. To-day Shaka proposed to alter his tactics. With the Ndwandwes well worn down from yesterday's tiring ordeal, he would launch so fierce an attack as would bring the battle to a decisive finish. He would throw upon the enemy the whole weight of his strength—the energetic youths who had already battered down the ramparts so well, together with his older and more practised troops held yesteday in reserve ...

So irresistible was the initial impact of the Zulu isiKlebé division that the Ndwandwes were compelled to yield and retire across the Mhlatúze river. But no sooner were they across than they turned upon the pursuing iziMpohlo with such vehemence that they in turn were forced back to the other bank. These river fords, 25 to 100 feet in breadth, corresponded to our bridges in European warfare ...

Upon this rebuff, Shaka ordered his amaWombé veterans to effect a crossing. But they too could secure no permanent foothold on the farther bank. The fight swayed to and fro amidstream, till the waters of the Mhlatúze ran reddened with blood and on each bank so thickly were the corpses strewn that the combatants stumbled and tumbled over them to their mutual peril.

At this stage Shaka hurried a strong detachment of his younger troops up the river to effect a crossing over the Mvuzane, then over the Mhlatúze, so to take the enemy in his flank. This stratagem drawing elsewhere the enemy's attention, reduced the pressure at the ford-head and the amaWombé succeeded in gaining and retaining the farther bank. Thereupon the mass of the Zulu army followed. So great were the confusion and excitement now prevailing that, it is said, the Ndwandwes, distraught from sheer fatigue and desperation, struck out indiscriminately right and left, even at their own comrades, thus hastening their own destruction: and they were soon in disorderly retreat. That was the second day's work.

Under cover of the night, Shaka hurried off his lads of fleetest foot, the umBónambí regiment and the isiPézi, on a flying march to Ndwandweland to secure the person of the king, Zwide, before his battered army should arrive. These were instructed, upon approaching the royal kraal under cover of darkness, to prevent alarm by chanting the Ndwandwe national song (*íHúbo*). This tragi-comedy they acted so successfully that upon nearing the emFakuceba kraal ... where Zwide chanced then to be, the mothers and children from an adjacent kraal, attracted by the good old refrain wafted to them on the breeze, but seeing the singers only dimly, trooped gaily out to welcome back their victorious boys. With clapping of hands, they raised the lusty cry, rousing the inmates of em-Fakuceba, 'Hurrah! for the hosts of Langa come home!'... But when, as the boys approached, the women beheld them suddenly charging in upon them with brandished spears and heard the awful cry of *Nga-dla!* ('I strike home!'), their disillusionment was sharp and cruel.

This premature act of impetuous youth, however, defeated the whole purpose of their mission. For one of the women, with a wound in her shoulder, fled towards the royal kraal proclaiming aloud the presence of the enemy. That was enough: Zwide made a headlong dive down into the nearest reed-bed, where he concealed himself. The frustrated Zulus could now do nothing other than vent their ire on the deserted kraal itself, which they burned to the ground over the corpses of its inmates.

Ignorant of all these happenings, the remnant of Ndwandwe survivors, cheered onward by the hope of finding at last in home and family rest and comfort from all their miseries, trudged laboriously back, famished and footsore, to behold smouldering ash-heaps where once stood their homes, and mothers and wives putrid corpses on the veld—their children, their property, their king, all alike vanished, and not a soul left to tell the tale ... But no moment was left them to grieve over their sorrows. Hard on their heels followed the relentless Zulu army, giving no respite. It overtook and attacked them again near the ëDumbé hill, and left them not till it had chased them into the foreign lands beyond the Póngolo river.

The victory gave Shaka freedom to consolidate his control and absorb most of the northern Nguni. He destroyed many small chiefdoms, put the people to flight, and sped up the process of transformation that had begun in the late eighteenth century. This process and period came to be known as the *Mfecane*, the 'crushing' and 'explosion' of peoples. The impact of the emigrations from Nguniland was felt as far away as the Cape Colony and Tanzania. The next document describes what happened to a few of the many northern Nguni chiefdoms.

DOCUMENT 12
'The Mfecane'

From an account of the ninety-four 'tribes' written in 1864 on the basis of oral testimony by Lt. Governor Scott of Natal. John Bird, ed., *The Annals of Natal: 1495 to 1845*, 2 vols (1885), Vol. I, pp. 128–9, 132

---

4. Tribe of Amasomi

Unkuna—Amasomi—originally occupied the country from twelve miles inland on the Umvoti, both banks, from the Izidumbe to the sources of the Nonoti: were attacked by Chaka, driven from their country, and followed by Chaka's army to the Mona River, where they were surrounded, and nearly the whole tribe destroyed—man, woman, and child.

6. Tribe of Amandhlovu

Unzala-ka-Mangeatshi—Amandhlova—anciently occupied from the Umhloti opposite Verulam to the Tongati low down, on both sides, but not so far as 'Compensation Farm', which was part of the Amacele country. This tribe was dispersed by Chaka, and became principally absorbed by the Amacele, Unzala having married a daughter of Dibandhlela. There is no longer any distinct tribe under this name.

7. Tribe of Amakanywayo

Unhlebende, *alias* Umwahleni—Amakanywayo—originally occupied left bank of the Umgeni up to the lower part of the Little Umhlanga and Seacow Lake. Were dispersed by Chaka's army, turned cannibals from necessity, and continued so from choice.

13. Tribe of Amadungwe, or Abakwa Mkateni

It was one of the tribes which returned from the Umkomazi, and attempted to occupy their own country. Boiya was attacked by Sihlanhlo; the tribes became so dispersed by fear of Chaka that, to protect themselves, they attacked every man his neighbour. Bands of men traversed the country in search of food. Where they found cultivation they, if strong enough, destroyed the cultivators, and were in turn destroyed by stronger parties; until, at length, to cultivate the soil was to ensure destruction. No tribe was strong enough to defend itself, and cultivation ceased; famine reigned everywhere, and destroyed thousands. First, dogs were eaten; they did not last long. At length Umdava, of the Amadunge tribe, commenced the eating of human beings, and soon collected a band of men which became a scourge to the whole country.

The Zulu state which emerged from this destruction was far more cohesive and centralized than Dingiswayo's confederation. Shaka was the supreme commander exercising direct, personal control over affairs throughout his reign. He consulted with a number of advisors at the court and gave substantial administrative responsibility to military officers, called *indunas*, rather than the traditional chiefs. He established military settlements, each containing several thousand soldiers, in the various parts of the kingdom, and used some of these settlements as his capitals. The troops depended upon him for food, arms, cattle, social position and even wives when they retired from active military duty. One result of this centralization was the forging of a new identity. Henceforth the northern Nguni would be called Zulu. The next two extracts describe the new state. Document 14 presents one example of mobility within Shaka's regime.

DOCUMENT 13
'King's kraals and private kraals'

Fynn, *Diary*, pp. 283–6.

Villages or, as they are termed, kraals are of two kinds, those of the King being used as barracks for the several regiments, at which the nation collects on requisite occasions.

Each regiment is divided into battalions, each having two or three captains, over which there is a general who has the entire management. He is responsible for the cattle and the conduct of the soldiers committed to his charge, receiving his orders from the King, who is despotic. Nevertheless the generals, on most important occasions are collected together to discuss the joint questions. Such meetings are merely nominal, as no chief would dare to propose anything in opposition to the King, as such conduct would be detrimental to his future safety. To each of these kraals are attached three or more matrons or dowager queens, who have equal power with the general in taking away the lives of those under them. The people under their immediate care are the females of the King's seraglio, they being formed into regiments in the same way as the men, only not for the same purpose.

Each kraal is supported by the King's cattle, these being in the same manner formed into regiments, assorted to each regiment agreeing with the colour of the shields worn by them. When the cattle arrive from an enemy, they are assorted and sent to their respective regiments. At such a time each individual drives away one or two, or as many as he can in the general scramble. This entitles him to their milk which is for his support while he remains with the regiment. Sometimes they are allowed to take these cattle to their private kraals. In such case they may be called together at a moment's notice to be given to individuals or to be slaughtered without the knowledge of the possessor, the milk being the only remuneration for their services during their lives. The whole of the cattle taken in war are the sole property of the King, who gives away tens, fifties or hundreds to chiefs, favourites and private servants. The common soldiers have little or no expectations of such favours.

Their war trappings are mostly provided by the King, each regiment being differently accoutred, the lightest coloured shields belonging to the men and the darkest to the young lads. The dress worn by the men is a turban of otter skin round the forehead, stuffed with bull-rush seed or dry cowdung. In front stands a feather nearly three feet in length, which is obtained from the gigantic Kaffir crane. From the turban, hanging down the cheeks, are two pieces of monkey skin, and in the upper parts, are bunches of feathers, having been stripped of the quills, which makes them light, neat and airy. Round the neck is hung a necklace of pieces of wood which are worn as medals of bravery. One is added for every one they kill in battle till there is no room left.

Round the arms and legs are ox and cow's tails; across the breast are two cords to which is suspended the skin of the genet and monkey cut into strips about six inches long and half an inch broad, which are so neatly twisted that a stranger without untwisting it would be assured that they were the tails as cut from the body, merely the bone having been taken out. The *umcubulu* or dress worn round the waist, is made in the same manner, only so long as to reach within an inch of the knee. They generally contain from 15 to 20 skins in a dress, sometimes 50 or 60, putting an astonishing value on them, which if it is ever offered, will not induce one to part with it. The warlike appearance of a man in his full dress, certainly exceeds anything of the kind that any savage tribes wear in South Eastern Africa. On Shaka coming to the throne, he compelled the old superannuated chiefs to wear a petticoat similar in shape to those worn by women, only that they were made of monkey skins with the fur left on. The shields are cut nearly in an oval shape, strips of a contrary colour being laced up and down, which makes a finish to the shield. There are a handle and a vacancy for the shield stick, at the top of which is the tail of a genet neatly sewn round. One ox-hide only produces two shields, as they are supposed to reach from the feet to the chin in length and nearly twice the body's breadth. One of the regiments of boys wear hats which Shaka introduced from seeing me wear a Malay hat. Their shields are black, and round the waist is a band of hide behind, as Mr. Thompson says, the girdle of hunger, for the purpose of slackening or tightening as hunger may require, to which is attached a piece of hide as ornament. Various are the dresses, some having their heads covered with feathers, others with pieces of ox-hide, all being inferior to the above full dress.

Their manner of attack, in which they generally follow the track of the spies, is to take the enemy by surprise if possible. A regiment being, previous to leaving home, pointed out for attack volleys down, spear in hand, on the enemy, shielding off the showers of thrown assegais from the enemy as well as they can. Always they come to close quarters, which prevents the enemy from making use of their weapons, not being acquainted with any other method than that of throwing. From so repeatedly conquering in their attacks, they have become daring, though not brave, as I firmly believe that one repulse would so completely throw them back as to dispossess them of their remaining courage.

Private kraals belong to individuals who, having sufficient cattle, are sure of getting sufficient people to establish a kraal either from the regiment or stragglers in distress. Those belonging to regiments are obliged to attend, whenever called on, to their respective divisions. Every chief of a kraal possesses despotic power in his kraal, only that he must not presume to imitate the King in any plans he may adopt, under pain of death. In fact the people in his kraals are slaves at his command whom he can drive away or kill as his caprice may lead him. Although on important occasions the people are collected to give their voice, it is, as with the King and chiefs, merely nominal, as their whole welfare depends on him with whom they reside.

They are supported by the loan of his cattle to milk, only planting their own fields of corn. The cattle are herded by one or more boys as the number may require, which they take to grass at daylight, bringing them home to milk about ten or eleven o'clock. When milked they return to grass and are brought home an hour before sunset, when they are again milked. The cattle altogether are quiet and tractable, more particularly so than those of the Cape Colony, and are never tied up to milk. In cases of their being wild, a hole is bored through the nose in which a cord is put through and fastened round the horns, and while being milked a stick is put in the cord which by twisting round holds the cow on the spot.

DOCUMENT 14
'From inceku to induna'

From the testimony of Dinya ka Zokozwayo, son of a former soldier of Shaka, recorded by James Stuart in 1905. Webb and Wright (eds), *The James Stuart Archive*, I, pp. 101–3.

NOTES FOR READING *inceku* = servant; *isigodhlo* = royal quarters for housing the king or chief and his wives. For italics, see notes for Document 2.

Dinya speaks: The Ncwane is the section to which Zulu ka Norgandaya belongs. This section seems to have come from the north say the Mtetwa tribe. This Zulu became *a warrior of Tshaka*. This name was moreover not his; it was given him by Tshaka. This man Zulu was *born among the Qwabe*, his proper name was Komfiya. He was an *inceku*. When a fight was about to take place between Zulus and Ndwandwes, Tshaka, at Bulawayo, one day took *a long staff* and stuck it into the ground *in the council place* and challenged anyone from among his regiments to seize it, this meaning that he equalled Tshaka's bravery while he was among the Mtetwa and so would be entitled to his praises. Komfiya came forward through an *opening in the isigodhlo fence*, with cowdung on his hands, for he had been smearing floors, and took the stick, to Tshaka's and everyone else's surprise.

When the battle with Zwide came on, Komfiya took part, and in a most heroic manner, until they stabbed him between the shoulder-blade and the arm, thereby causing him to drop his shield. Though he had lost his shield he continued to fight, and he did so in so determined a manner that his own side took hold of him and prevented him from needlessly exposing himself. When later on Tshaka came to *discuss the battle* and he came to hear of Komfiya's deeds of valour, he formally spoke of him as 'Zulu' and said he was entitled to praises Tshaka himself had earned among the Mtetwa. Zulu ka Nogandaya subsequently became *induna* at *the Black Hlomendhlini kraal* under Nongalaza ka Nondela (*at the place of Mngunyana of the Qwaba tribe*) . . .

Komfiya, being an *inceku*, may have been advised by Tshaka to take the *stick* as Tshaka wanted to raise him to a position of rank. It is difficult to see how a mere *inceku* could have dared to take Tshaka's place, and no one else in all the regiments could be found of equal pluck. He must have been encouraged by Tshaka himself for the act of extraordinary daring. And yet as the man was one of courage he may have done it of his own accord after full opportunity had been given to the regiments.

Zulu was of the Mgumanqa regiment.

I have seen Zulu. He was of medium height, black, had *a headring, and was induna of the Mpohlo regiment at the Black Hlomendhlini kraal.*

The chiefs under Shaka contributed cattle, maize and warriors to the king. They had considerable autonomy in their internal affairs, unless they seemed to pose a threat to royal authority. The next two documents describe the fortunes of men who combined chiefly credentials with military prowess.

DOCUMENT 15
'Shaka's intelligence department was supremely efficient'

Bryant, *Zululand*, pp. 422–3.

NOTES FOR READING izimPohlo and umBelebele = two of Shaka's regiments; Mzilikazi eventually settled north of the Limpopo where his Kumalo people became the Ndebele of Rhodesia (Zimbabwe).

Shaka . . . soon made acquaintance with the young Kumalo chieftain, Mzilikazi, and recognized in him a kindred spirit. So much so that, about the year 1822, he entrusted him with the leadership of a small campaign in his master's service. His commission was the common one of raiding cattle and his objective was the Sutu clan ruled by Ranisi near the Zulu border in the Transvaal. The campaign proved eminently successful and the loot was great. So great, indeed, was it that Mzilikazi felt he could pinch a goodly quantum of the proceeds without his royal employer being one whit the wiser. A most disastrous error of judgment; for never yet had anybody caught the Zulu weasel sleeping. Shaka's intelligence department was supremely efficient, and Shaka's police were on the spot within a trice of the event.

The messengers proudly marched into Mzilikazi's kraal and demanded to know, in the name of his most august majesty, the king, where were those stolen cattle. To which Mzilikazi replied by impudently cutting off the plumes that waved so proudly above their heads and sending them back home with their tails between their legs.

Then the izimPohlo boys were sent up in force with instructions to receive the ill-gotten goods and incidentally to receive also the person of the youthful robber, and to bring all home together. The unexpected happened; for it was they who were received, and withal so warmly, by the youthful robber, that they were glad to get back home with their own hides intact; but sans robber and sans cattle.

Mzilikazi dug himself in forthwith. But not there in the open kraal. With all his clan and stock, he executed a forced march up the esiKwébezi valley, till about the river's sources he reached his pet stronghold, an afforested hill called enTubeni. Thereupon the Zulu punitive expedition appeared to retrieve their kaiser's honour—and cattle. But with like results: Mzilikazi was impregnably entrenched. So they sat down and waited. What was now to be done?

At this opportune moment a traitor determined to get back his own. A certain Kúmalo man, Nzeni by name, harbouring a grudge against his chief, stole off to Shaka and gave the show away. Supplied with the umBelebele lads as escort, he guided them round by a circuitous path inland and quietly led them into the stronghold by the back door—over the hilltop from behind. Taken unawares between two fires, Mzilikazi did not capitulate; but a sanguinary massacre took place. Practically all the elders of the clan were butchered, and as many women; but Mzilikazi and two or three hundred of the younger fry, had by the afternoon effected a precipitate escape. Away they scurried to the north, launched on their great adventure of conquering inner Africa and building there a new empire.

DOCUMENT 16
'A chief makes himself'

From the testimony of Dinya ka Zokozwayo, recorded by Stuart in 1905 and published in Webb and Wright (eds), *The James Stuart Archive*, I, pp. 115–16.

NOTES FOR READING *inkosikazi* = the 'great wife'; Pakatwayo = chief of the Qwabe (see Document 10); *insizwa* = youth approaching manhood; *lobola* = bride price; *konza'd* = given allegiance to; Mande and Magaye were each sons of Dibandhela, hence 'Mande *ka* Dibandhlela'. For italics, see notes for Document 2.

Another story about Tshaka refers to his *settling the case of Mande . . .* and Magaye ka Dibandhlela.

Mande belonged to Emfakuceba kraal. Magaye belonged to Nikela kraal, both kraals being Dibandhlela's. Each kraal had a large territory attached to it. Dibandhlela appointed Siwetu (Magaye's mother) as the *inkosikazi*. Emfakuceba is sometimes called simply Emfeni—short form of the word. Mande *exercised authority* at Emfakuceba.

Dibandhlela then took Magaye and *hid* him *among the people of his mother's brother,* Pakatwayo. Magaye grew up. He was fetched and came back when an *insizwa*. He was then installed as chief of Nikela kraal. Mande roused himself and resisted his portion of people being swallowed up by Magaye. Mande gained as adherents many large kraals of Dibandhlela's. The result of this separation was that only three of Dibandhlela's kraals remained with Magaye . . .

Mande took to arms, having *the men of many kraals* to fight for him, whereas Magaye had those of only three kraals. Dibandhlela *became angry*. He *fetched back* two kraals from Mande . . .

They were *senior sons* of Dibandhlela's. Mzipi ka Dibandhlela was another *senior son* of Amabola kraal and under Mziboneli. Sokanjiswa (*of the people of Jokazi* of Nkungwini kraal) was also *a senior son*. Mande said, 'I should have had no objection if my father had appointed Mzipi the *successor*. I refuse to have appointed as chief over me a mere child.' They failed to see that the reason for this appointment was because Magaye's mother was Dibandhlela's *inkosikazi*, who at her marriage was *danced for (with genet tails tied to sticks)* and she was *lobola'd* with tribal cattle, thereby indicating she was the *inkosikazi*. These ceremonials had not occurred in regard to any other of Dibandhlela's wives.

Ill-feeling sprang up between Mande and Magaye, and civil war was fought. Magaye was treated with contempt by Mande. He looked on him at first as not having a *force* which could in any way compete with his. The Nkunga and Amabola (kraals) came over, and then the forces to some extent became equal to one another.

Whilst fighting was still going on Tshaka *crossed over* to Dukuza. He then *mediated* by calling all the [principal chiefs of the region]. All of these had *konza'd* Tshaka; all had *paid tribute*.

All these *assembled* at Dukuza. All the Celes arrived at Dukuza too. Dibandhlela was still living but too feeble and old to attend. The meeting took place *on the flat outside the kraal*. They became very anxious, wondering what was to happen.

Mazangane ka Mfaniswa ka Dibandhlela ka Mkokeleli said, 'I was present when this *case* was *heard*.' I heard this from him. He said that the chiefs all arrived and sat down. Tshaka then came forth, dragging his *kaross* on the ground, accompanied by Mdhlaka ka Ncidi. A seat was placed. He sat. He had no sooner seated himself than he said, '*I speak not to you, Nodokwana ka Dibandhlela; I speak to Mande ka Dibandhlela of Mfakuceba, and to Magaye ka Dibandhlela of Nikela.* 'He said, '*I shall put questions to Mande ka Mfakuceba; let this man Magaye remain silent. I make enquiry*, seeing that you are always fighting. I want to know who is the chief of you two.' Mande replied, 'I am far older than Magaye. His mother was appointed *inkosikazi*, but I object to his youth.' Tshaka said, 'Were you present when (she) was *appointed*?' 'Yes,' replied Mande. 'What did you say, Mande, for at that time, of course, Magaye had not been born and you were already a man. What did you say?' Mande answered, 'What could I say, Sir?' 'But what, then, do you say today? How do you account for your fighting in this way?'

Tshaka then looked towards [the chiefs] and called on them to speak. Before they *answered* he said, '*Let me speak first. Has a chief ever been made? A chief is not made; a chief makes himself. It is the calf of the cow which is picked out and has its place assigned to it.*' When he had said this he said, '*Let the matter of the fighting be discussed. I call on you, Mande; I say, "Let the matter of your fighting be discussed".*' Mande said, 'On the first occasion on which we came into conflict with one another I *defeated* my brother; I got the better of him. (We) again clashed, and again I defeated him.' 'What do you say, Magaye?', said Tshaka. Magaye said, 'My brother is right but I had but few followers, for my brother had *deserted* with the majority of the tribe. I fought nevertheless. The Nkungu and Amabola (kraals) deserted and joined me. I *called up the men attached to our home kraal* . . . 'We fought. Let my brother say if he still *defeats* me.'

Tshaka then said, '*Now answer, Mande; your younger brother has spoken.*' Mande then said the boy was right. 'Strength had not accrued to him when I got the better of him.'

Each of these chiefs . . . had a hut set apart for his occupation in the royal kraal, Dukuza. '*Go away, Mande; go back to your hut*' (i.e. in Dukuza). Mande left. Tshaka then said, after Mande had gone, '*Let us talk confidentially as to how I shall decide this case.*' [The chiefs] said, 'The king has heard what the young chiefs have said. The course is clear enough. Let the king give his decision.' Tshaka then said, '*See now, children of the king! I stand in awe of this man Mande; he is a chief indeed. When he looks at me, though I am Tshaka, my eyes drop to the ground and give way before him. My decision in this case is this: Let me and Magaye rule alone.*'

I shall remove this man Mande of Mfakuceba [and] take [his] followings and join them to Magaye, and we shall hold dances together.'

That was the end. Mande [was] thereupon put to death.

The Apogee and Fall of Shaka

As king, Shaka in theory possessed all the cattle, ivory, animal hides and other products of the realm. Trade in all of these commodities, especially ivory, had existed for some time. Dingiswayo had attempted to control the commercial routes to the European factories at Delagoa Bay. When a handful of British traders and adventurers—including Henry Francis Fynn and Nathaniel Isaacs—landed at Port Natal (modern Durban) and established contact with the Zulu court, Shaka gave them a cautious welcome. As long as they respected his authority, they could hunt elephants, obtain cattle, and conduct themselves as subordinate chiefs. The king enjoyed receiving their exotic presents, questioned them about their customs, and sought to make use of their military technology. The next three documents describe Shaka's relations with the Europeans, his fascination with firearms, and his efforts to include the British traders in his expeditions.

DOCUMENT 17
'No difficult matter to conquer us'

Isaacs, *Travels*, I, pp. 93–4.

NOTE FOR READING   Jacob = Shaka's interpreter (see Document 29).

Early this morning we saw the king sitting outside his kraal with his warriors. Their conversation was mainly on the power of firearms. Chaka desired us, when we approached him, to go and shoot some vultures that they might see the effect of our arms. Jacob, having his musket with him, on hearing the command went out instantly and shot one of these carnivorous birds; the effect which this produced was astounding—they were at once, in a measure, paralysed. Jacob's fire had made the birds wild, and therefore, determining not to be outdone by him, we pursued them, but were stopped by a messenger from the king, who required our presence. We perceived him following, accompanied by a body of his people, and we soon found that his object was to try the effect of our firearms on another species of the animal creation. By this time a body of from 4000 to 5000 people had congregated, when the king halted, and the warriors formed a circle round him, at the same time enclosing us.

Chaka addressed us, and asked 'if our nation were as numerous as the body of men now about him?' We told him that it was, which he doubted, and then inquired 'why we came so few at a time?' We replied that we were perfectly aware of his friendly disposition towards us, and consequently did not require to be numerous. He laughed, and asked me our

mode of warfare, and said 'he thought it would be no difficult matter to conquer us, as our muskets, when once discharged, took some time to reload, during which they might make a rush, and the losing a few men by the first discharge would be nothing to him who had so many.' We now showed him the position of the square, one of us kneeling in front, and the other two in their respective positions, which proved to him that, according to the system of firing in that manœuvre, the position was invulnerable to an irregular force. He saw it, but his warriors being inclined to flatter his military genius, observed that by charging in a body, in the way to which they usually resorted, especially under his bold and judicious command, they thought it would more than overbalance the strength of our position, and the force of our arms.

DOCUMENT 18
'Victory and purification'

Fynn, *Diary*, pp. 126–8.

NOTES FOR READING   Jacob = Shaka's interpreter (see Document 29); Sikhunyana = Zwide's successor as ruler of the Ndwandwe.

The hill from which we had first seen the enemy presented to our view an extensive valley to the left of which was a hill separated by another valley from an immense mountain. On the upper part of this there was a rocky eminence, near the summit of which the enemy had collected all his forces surrounding their cattle, and above them the women and children of the nation in a body. They were sitting down, awaiting the attack.

Shaka's forces marched slowly and with much caution, in regiments, each regiment divided into companies, till within 20 yards of the enemy, when they made a halt. Although Shaka's troops had taken up a position so near, the enemy seemed disinclined to move, till Jacob had fired at them three times. The first and second shots seemed to make no impression on them, for they only hissed and cried in reply: 'That is a dog.' At the third shot, both parties, with a tumultuous yell, clashed together, and continued stabbing each other for about three minutes, when both fell back a few paces.

Seeing their losses were about equal, both enemies raised a cry and this was followed by another rush, and they continued closely engaged about twice as long as in the first onset, when both parties again drew off. But the enemy's loss had now been the more severe. This urged the Zulus to a final charge. The shrieks now became terrific. The remnants of the enemy's army sought shelter in an adjoining wood, out of which they were soon driven. Then began a slaughter of the women and children. They were all put to death. The cattle being taken by the different regiments were driven to the kraal lately occupied by Sikhunyana. The battle, from the commencement to the close, did not last more than an hour and a half. The numbers of the hostile tribe, including women and children, could not have been less than 40 000. The number of cattle taken was estimated at 60 000. The sun having set while the cattle were being captured, the whole valley during the night was a scene of confusion. Parties of three, four, and five men each went about killing cattle and cutting off the tails of others to form part of their war dress. Many of Shaka's wounded managed to crawl on hands and knees in the hope of getting assistance, but for the enemy's wounded there was no hope.

Early next morning Shaka arrived, and each regiment, previous to its inspection by him, had picked out its cowards and put them to death. Many of these, no doubt, forfeited their lives only because their chiefs were in fear that, if they did not condemn some as being guilty, they would be suspected of seeking a pretext to save them and would incur the resentment of Shaka.

No man who had been actually engaged in the fight was allowed to appear in the King's presence until a purification by the doctor had been undergone. This doctor gave each warrior certain roots to eat, and to everyone who had actually killed one of the enemy an additional number. To make their bravery as public as possible, bits of wood are worn round the neck, each bit being supposed to reckon for an enemy slain. To the end of this necklace are attached bits of the root received from the doctor, part of which has been eaten. They then proceed to some river to wash their persons and, until this had been done, they may not eat any food, except the meat of cattle killed on the day of battle. Having washed, they appear before the King, when thanks or praise are the last thing they have to expect; censure being loudly expressed on account of something that had not been done as it should have been, and they get off well if one or two chiefs and a few dozen soldiers are not struck off the army list by being put to death.

DOCUMENT 19
'Seized and ravished by force'

Fynn, *Diary*, pp. 129–30.

NOTES FOR READING   Messrs Francis Farewell and James S. King were both involved in the effort to build trade between Port Natal and the Cape Colony; Hottentot = Khoikhoi.

Beje's capabilities of defence were equally good. He, too, had a strong position among the rocks, and succeeded in cutting to pieces one of Shaka's regiments, raised only two months previously, and numbering two thousand men. This regiment had the name of the regiment of 'Warmth', or in the Zulu 'Motha'. A few escaped and came to the army, now on its return homeward; but orders were given to put them to death at once, as men who had dared to fly.

Shaka now started on his return journey, leaving the regiments to attack the above-named chiefs. We accompanied him. When we had almost reached the place where we had left Mr. Farewell, news arrived of a vessel having anchored at Port Natal. We accordingly left Shaka and went to Natal, where the vessel that had arrived on 6th October, 1826, from Algoa Bay, proved to be the schooner *Anne*, with Mr. King and Mrs. Farewell on board.

About this time, Michael and John, two of the Hottentots in the service of Mr. King, were sent by him elephant and sea-cow shooting. They had not been long absent when we heard that they had committed a crime likely to endanger the whole of our party. The laws of the Zulus are so severe against the crimes of adultery and rape that, up to this period, we had not heard of a single violation of them. These Hottentots had seized and ravished by force the daughter of a Zulu chief, who, dreading the result of connection with a European—all persons wearing clothes (as our Hottentots did) were deemed by the Zulus to be Europeans, for as yet our race was not regarded as earth-born, but as animals that had sprung out of the sea—reported the crime to Shaka. This incensed him against the whole of our race, and Mr. King, who arrived at this critical moment, was placed in an extremely awkward position. After Shaka had vented his rage on him, he demanded satisfaction, as the culprits belonged to us. Had his own people been the offenders they would have suffered death the instant the deed was done.

Mr. King acknowledged there was sufficient cause for his anger, assuring him that such crime was also punishable by death under the laws of our country. This had such an effect on Shaka's mind as completely to avert what he intended in the event of Mr. King attempting to palliate their crime. He then demanded that the whole European party, then at Natal, should join him in an attack on Beje, whom he was unable, without the assistance of our muskets, to drive out of his stronghold, except by sustaining great losses. Mr. King saw the necessity of acceding to his wishes to prevent his avenging himself on the whole of us. After some deliberation, Messrs. Cane and Isaacs, together with part of the crew of the *Mary*, also two Hottentots, and several natives (with guns) volunteered to go. They succeeded in completely defeating Beje's tribe and killing the chief himself. On our side, Mr. Isaacs was severely wounded. Shaka did not as much as thank them for their services; on the contrary, he took every opportunity of depreciating what they had done and minimising the value of fire-arms in the estimation of his people.

The images of Shaka in many sources have suggested obsessions and other psychological interpretations. These interpretations emphasize a sense of sexual inferiority (see Document 3), the fear of having a son only to be killed by him, and a general preoccupation with death. The next two documents provide some of the basis for such views.

DOCUMENT 20
'Impressions from Jantshi ka Nongila'

From the testimony of Jantshi recorded by Stuart in 1903 and published in Webb and Wright (eds), *The James Stuart Archive*, 1, pp. 187, 189, 195, 198, 201–2.

NOTES FOR READING *izinduna* = used for both chiefs and military officers; Ngomane ka Mqomboli = the Ngomane of Document 3; *izangoma* = diviners; *bula* = to divine; *tefula'd* = spoke in the Qwabe fashion. Stuart added the bracketed remark below attributing the vulture story to Dingane instead of Shaka. For italics, see notes for Document 2.

Tshaka also attacked and defeated Mvenya, father of Dumisa, who is the father of the late Saoti. Mvenya was not killed. As a matter of fact, Tshaka did not put to death the kings or kinglets he defeated if, when he proceeded against them, they ran away and did not show fight. He made them *izinduna.*

Kutshwayo, *chief of the Dube,* is another of those conquered by Tshaka. This man, like many others, was *attacked* merely to *make him pay tribute,* i.e. reduce him to become a subject and then instate him as an *induna.*

Sotshangana ka Zikode was also *attacked* by Tshaka. He was living in Zululand, I believe south of the Mkuze. The only king who was *not* attacked by Tshaka was Mtshwetshwe of Basutoland. He, hearing Tshaka was so powerful, *payed tribute* with *elephant tusks* and acknowledged allegiance . . .

Tshaka was a man of dark colour, not yellowish. He was tall, not very tall. When he came from Dingiswayo's he had not *put on the head-ring.* He *did so among the Zulu.*

His buttocks were *broad,* so that one could see that he was a *chief.* He belonged to the Wombe regiment. He was powerfully built and had a bad temper. His strength was remarkable, for he could, when examining a beast, lift up its leg by one arm and stoop to look under it. Only Ngomane ka Mqomboli ever dared to answer him back *among the Zulu.* Even his own relations were afraid of doing so . . .

I know Tshaka once wanted to see if *izangoma* were able to find out the truth or not. He would call them up in a body to *bula* and see who had sprinkled blood about his *isigodhlo* (an act done by himself), and such 'doctors' as smelt out other persons as being the cause of this, he had put to death. That doctor who rightly guessed by saying, '*It was done by the heavens above.*' was allowed to go free . . . .

Amongst Tshaka's extraordinary acts was his causing a pregnant woman to be cut open in order to see what position the child took up in its mother's womb. He did this more than once. He would also cut off a man's ears, giving as his reason for doing so that 'they do not hear'. He would say, '*The vultures are hungry; they have come to attend the assembly,*' when he saw vultures hovering about, and then give orders for them to be fed with human corpses. (No, it was Dingana did this.) He would direct that people be killed to satisfy their appetite.

My father formerly had his kraal at Eshowe near where the chiefs Sikonyana and Ntshingwayo live. He also *built* at the Nseleni, across the Mhlatuze, north side.

Tshaka spoke the Mtetwa dialect when he became king. He consequently always *tefula'd.* He is said to have lisped or stuttered, or pretended to do so . . .

At Dukuza, while Tshaka was sitting in company, he pointed to the cattle in the kraal and said, 'No ordinary man will inherit those cattle; none but a great man will get them. The day I die the country will be overrun by locusts; it will be ruled by white men. The stars will be bright in the sky. While I am still taking care of you, you alone will smell one another out. Afterwards, men will be smelt out as umtakati by their own wives; wives will smell out their husbands.'

Just as he finished speaking thus, he suddenly exclaimed, *'There is Sotobe',* seeing a ship sailing on the sea. Those with Tshaka then looked and saw the ship holding its course at sea. Sotobe had, as a matter of fact, just left and was on his way towards the Cape. My father was present when Tshaka spoke as stated, and he added that, as he spoke, Tshaka was seated in the cattle kraal and pushed the *manure dust* about slightly with the fingers of each hand when moving backwards and forwards as if to emphasize his words.

Tshaka also said, in conclusion, 'No man dare *pala inhlonze yazo lez' izinkomo, a yi ti xwe, xwe, xwe.'* He thereupon got up and left the *cattle kraal* by the *small opening* and entered one of his huts, leaving those present wondering at the words he had spoken.

My father said Tshaka was *a great king, and very clever,* because he defeated all the *chiefs* in every direction. He was very resourceful in his plans for overcoming his rivals. Dingana and Mpande *came on the scene after he had subdued the whole country,* and therefore my father did not have very much to say about them. He says he *had a hard time* in the days of Tshaka by always having to go out to *spy.*

Tshaka had no children; he did not wish to have any, for they would have been *chiefs.* In the old days if a king had a child, it, when it grew up, might drive its father from home. This once happened, the instance being quoted by my father. Tshaka was afraid of the same thing happening to him. I do not know if Tshaka ever *was circumcised* . . .

Tshaka *assembled* those *from the old Zulu heartland* to select from them spies. My father was called with others and went up to Tshaka's kraal. Tshaka expressed his wish several times before Nongila would come forward. My father was created *induna* of all the *spies* . . .

Tshaka said *cowards* must be *picked out from the regiments* . . . If Tshaka saw *wounds* behind, (the man) was killed because (Tshaka) said he must have been running away.

DOCUMENT 21
'A few grey hairs'

Fynn, *Diary,* pp. 141–3.

NOTES FOR READING Sikhunyana = Zwide's successor as ruler of the Ndwandwe; umGeorge = King of England.

One day, after the defeat of Sikhunyana, Shaka saw me writing a letter to Mr. Farewell. He asked me if the ink would wash off the paper. On my replying in the negative, he asked if it would stain a shield. I told him it would not, but the hair and the skin might appear slightly tinged. He thereupon threw a bottle of ink over a white shield to observe its effect . . . In the evening he asked how it was that Europeans had different coloured hair, and if there were no preparations to change its colour.

I told him Macassar oil was said to produce that effect. On arriving where we had left Mr. Farewell, he asked Mr. Farewell the same question and received the same reply. When Messrs. King and Isaacs arrived they were asked, and understanding what we had said, agreed with us. Shaka, finding us all agreed as to its virtues, called us into his hut and, ordering all his attendants to go out, made us swear by him that we would not mention what had taken place concerning the oil, and went on to say he would collect ivory in great quantities and give the tusks to whatever person produced the oil. He said he wanted it for his mother- and father-in-law, who were grey-headed, which did not look well in such great personages. We, however, saw that he wanted it for himself, having a few grey hairs on his chin.

We now endeavoured to assure him of our having great doubts as to its powers, fearing should it not prove what we had led him to believe it was he would be displeased; but the more we attempted to deprecate it, the more he thought of its value. He said he could plainly see it was an oil used by umGeorge and that none of his people were allowed to touch it. Seeing the improbability of our procuring any in the immediate present, we attempted, though in vain, to lessen it in his esteem. He had, however, set his mind on this invaluable oil. It was his constant theme and induced him to take the whole of his force elephant hunting . . .

When he presented Mr. King with the 86 tusks, on the latter's departure for the Colony, he told his people that he, Mr. King, would bring back immense quantities of such things as they required. Afterwards, however, in his hut, he told Mr. King to bring nothing but Macassar oil. His people were dogs, he would give them nothing. All he wanted was Macassar oil and medicine.

Shaka maintained a close relationship with his mother who resided at the capital. In 1827 she died, apparently by natural causes, although a few traditions state that the king killed her in anger because she had protected a child conceived by him. Her death led to a long and enforced period of mourning in the Zulu kingdom. Shaka ordered his armies to go to the extreme southern and then the extreme northern frontiers of the kingdom under very difficult conditions. The next two documents describe the events of 1827–28.

DOCUMENT 22
'I saw large tears fall'

Fynn, *Diary*, pp. 132–6, 144.

NOTES FOR READING   For Ngomane see Documents 3, 4 and 20; 'the great female elephant with small breasts' = Nandi; Fynn was trained as a physician's assistant.

After travelling slowly for two days, we passed his usual residence, Bulawayo, closely adjoining which was the kraal of Nandi, his mother, and, proceeding forward, arrived about nine at night, at the place Shaka intended to fix his residence, that is, the one he had come purposely to rebuild. This work was begun on the following morning. Messengers now arrived to announce that Nandi was very unwell. Doctors were immediately dispatched, and also some European medicines which Shaka had been made a present of, and had by him, having first asked their uses. As messengers continued to arrive with accounts of the invalid getting worse, Shaka decided to return to her kraal accompanied by his forces.

We started at nine o'clock at night and arrived at Bulawayo about three in the morning. Shaka now requested me to visit his mother. I went, attended by an old chief, and found the hut filled with native doctors and nurses, and such clouds of smoke that I was obliged to bid them all retire, to enable me to breathe within it. Her complaint was dysentery, and I reported at once to Shaka that her case was hopeless and that I did not expect that she would live through the day.

The regiments, which were then sitting in a semicircle around him, were ordered to their barracks, while Shaka himself sat for about two hours in a contemplative mood, without a word escaping his lips, several of the elder chiefs sitting also before him. When the tidings were brought that she had expired Shaka immediately arose and entered his dwelling, and, having ordered the principal chiefs to put on their wardresses, he, in a few minutes, appeared in his.

As soon as the death was publicly announced, the women and all the men who were present tore instantly from their persons every description of ornament. Shaka now appeared before the hut in which the body lay, surrounded by his principal chiefs in their war attire. For about 20 minutes he stood in a silent mournful attitude, with his head bowed upon his shield, and on which I saw large tears fall. After two or three deep sighs, his feelings becoming ungovernable, he broke out into frantic yells, which fearfully contrasted with the silence that had hitherto prevailed. This signal was enough. The chiefs and people, to the number of about 15 000, commenced the most dismal and horrid lamentations.

I expected, on seeing the old woman in her last agonies, that I should again witness a scene like to those at which I had been present on two similar former occasions. Not for a moment did I anticipate the extent to which the proceedings were now to be carried. The people from the neighbouring kraals, male and female, came pouring in, each body, as they came in sight, at the distance of half a mile, joining to swell this terrible cry.

Through the whole night it continued, none daring to take rest, or to refresh themselves with water, while at short intervals fresh bursts were heard, as more regiments approached.

The morning dawned without any relaxation, and before noon the number had increased to about 60 000. The cries now became indescribably horrid. Hundreds were lying faint, from excessive fatigue and want of nourishment; while the carcasses of 40 oxen lay in a heap, which had been slaughtered as an offering to the guardian spirits of the tribe. At noon the whole force formed a circle with Shaka in their centre, and sang the war song, which afforded them some relaxation during its continuance. At the close of it, Shaka ordered several men to be executed on the spot, and the cries became, if possible, more violent than ever. No further orders were needed. But, as if bent on convincing their chief of their extreme grief, the multitude commenced a general massacre. Many of them received the blow of death, while inflicting it on others, each taking the opportunity of revenging their injuries, real or imaginary. Those who could not force more tears from their eyes—those who were found near the river panting for water—were beaten to death by others who were mad with excitement. Toward the afternoon I calculated that not fewer than 7000 people had fallen in this frightful indiscriminate massacre. The adjacent stream, to which many had fled exhausted, to wet their parched tongues, became impassable from the number of dead corpses which lay on each side of it; while the kraal in which the scene took place was flowing with blood . . .

The ceremonies of his mother's burial were the subject of much deliberation between Shaka and his favourite counsellors. On the second day after her death the body was placed in a grave, in a sitting posture, near the spot where she died. At this part of the ceremony I was not allowed to be present, and, if what was related to me at the time by several of the attendants be true (and I believe it to be true, knowing to what extent superstition will carry this people), it was fortunate for me that I was not present, to witness the horrid spectacle of ten of the best-looking girls of the kraal being buried with her alive.

All who were present at this dreadful scene, to the number of 12 000, drafted from the whole army, were formed into a regiment to guard the grave for the next 12 months, and during that time were prohibited from all intercourse with the tribe or any of their nearest relatives. About 15 000 head of cattle were set apart for their use, which were contributed by all the cattle holders of the country, as offerings to the spirits of the departed queen and her ill-fated attendants. Had I been present on this occasion I should have had to keep guard with the rest.

Hitherto, the proceedings had been local. But now the chiefs, anxious to show further proof of their attachment, proposed that further sacrifices should be made. And Ngomane, Shaka's principal favourite, made a speech proposing the following resolution:

'That, as the great female elephant with small breasts, the over-ruling spirit of vegetation, had died, and as it was probable that the heavens and the earth would unite in bewailing her death, the sacrifice should be a great one; no cultivation should be allowed during the following year; no milk should be used, but, as drawn from the cow, it should be poured upon the earth; and all women, who should be found with child during the year, should with their husbands be put to death.'

On the day of the army's departure the regiments assembled to the left of my place, drawing up in such a way as to form three sides of a square. The doctors having performed the usual ceremonies of strengthening them for the attack, Shaka came into their midst, and, in a speech, began to explain to them that the necessity of the expedition was to erase his wounded feeling for the mother he had lost. To make the loss more memorable, it was necessary that regret should be felt

by other tribes in addition to his own. They must, therefore, exterminate the whole of the tribes between him and the Colony. He wished, he said, to open a road, and, for that purpose, had already sent chiefs in order that he might be on good terms with the white people.

DOCUMENT 23
'Ominously murmuring'

Bryant, *Zululand*, pp. 625–6.

NOTES FOR READING Manyundela = Mdlaka, Shaka's commander-in-chief (see Document 26); Soshangane = an Ndwandwe leader; Balule = Limpopo River; Mhlangana and Dingane = two of Shaka's half-brothers; Swazi = an area to the northeast of Zululand.

Then the upper army, fresh from operations farther inland, trooped in, and turned the merriment into horror. Their general, Manyundela, had been left on the field! For this outrage and disgrace, nothing less would mollify Shaka than the instant slaughter of numberless warriors, expediently arraigned for cowardice.

At length the call was given to break camp and march back home. And after that? Shaka, feverishly active himself, could not and would not tolerate an indolent and effeminate entourage; he would not degrade himself into a king of muffs. Already at the Mzimkúlu he had discussed the problem and decided that, without even one instant for idle breathing-time at home, his army, from the extreme south, shall now proceed direct to the extreme north. That arrant cur, Soshangane, now, they say, posing as a Tónga potentate, will furnish them with an eminently suitable objective. Arrived at the Mngéni, he promulgated the ukase—'Off with you, all and straightway, to Shanganeland!'

It was at the Mngéni that Shaka at last overreached himself—and fell. His rule had latterly, and notably during the year 1827, become so recklessly brutal, that his Zulu subjects, most docile and long-suffering of peoples, for the first time commenced to kick. The sufferings of the Bálule expedition, immediately succeeded by the massacre at Nandi's burial, then by the distant Mpondo campaign, now by the general order at the Mngéni to depart once more, without rest or respite, into the famished and pestilential wilds of Soshananeland— these incessant hardships had at length combined to goad his people to the verge of rebellion and his army to the verge of mutiny. 'Eat?' he yelled; 'why, as for food you shall live on locusts; and when locusts fail, you shall pluck the stink-plant (*umSuzwane* or *Lippia asperifolia*) and plug therewith your nostrils, for the stench of putrid corpses that will assail them.'

Ominously murmuring, they marched away at the end of July, 1828. But yet not all of them. Large parties of the stronger-minded openly deserted, preferring vagabondage to such cruel bondage. Others, like Mhlangana and Dingane, made a semblance of submission; and concocted schemes of vengeance as they went.

The route they took was, not that along the fever-stricken coast, but that which offered better hopes of health and plenty, along the inland Swazi border. Yet hardly were they two days on the march, when the chafing hand of tyranny again overtook them—messengers arrived ordering that each and every one, officers and men, should henceforward carry his own baggage and all bearer-boys return to the Dukuza capital, the elder of them to be drafted into a new regiment to be named the *iziNyosi* (the Bees).

Shaka's half-brothers and his principal servant took advantage of the discontent to plot against the king. The next two documents describe the death of Shaka in September, 1828.

DOCUMENT 24
'That you may live in peace'

Isaacs, *Travels*, I, pp. 257–9.

NOTES FOR READING Mataban = a Zulu messenger; Toogoosa = Dukuza, a Zulu capital; Boper = Mbopha, Shaka's principal servant; Umslumgani = Mhlangana; Essenzingercona = Senzangakona; Umnante = Nandi.

After our morning repast, however, and as we were starting for the river Umsegas, Mataban came from Toogoosa, nearly exhausted from exertion, and, with a countenance betokening something of mighty import having been done, told us tremulously that Chaka was dead! We were not so much astonished as anxious to ascertain the cause, and importuned him to tell us as soon as he could, when he said, 'that there was a long tale to relate'. After recovering himself from the effects of his great exertion, having left Toogoosa only the evening previously, he informed us, that while Chaka was sitting the night before, with two or three of his principal chiefs admiring the immense droves of cattle returning to the kraal, and probably contemplating the deaths of innocent people, he was surprised at the boldness and presumption of his principal domestic, Boper, who approached him with a spear with which they usually kill bullocks, and, in a voice of authority, asked the old chiefs, who were humiliating themselves in the presence of the despot, 'what they meant by always pestering the king with falsehoods and accusations?' The audacity of Boper, who had been always an humble suppliant, excited Chaka's surprise, nor were the exasperated chiefs without their apprehensions, and made an effort to secure Boper, but they were foiled; for, at that moment, Umslumgani and Dingàn, the two eldest brothers of the king, stole unperceived behind him and stabbed him in the back. Chaka had a blanket wrapped round him which he instantly threw off, and made an ineffectual attempt to escape that death to which, by his blood-thirsty decrees, he had consigned many of his innocent and unoffending subjects. He was overtaken in his flight by his pursuers, when the domestic Boper pierced him through the body with his weapon; he fell at their feet, and in the most supplicating manner besought them to let him live that he might be their servant. To this, however, no heed was

given, they soon speared him to death, and then left him to execute a similar deed on the chiefs who were with him, and who had attempted to escape, but were arrested in their flight, and put to death in the same manner as their ferocious master. One of them was an old grey-headed man who had, but a short time before, put to death his seven wives with their children, for not having mourned for the death of Chaka's mother. The assassins now returned to the dead body of Chaka and danced round it, as much elated as though they were rejoicing at the death of a tiger, an animal they greatly dread.

The people of the kraal fled in great consternation, except the chief Sotobe, and one or two others, who seized their spears as if designing to attack the assassins; but they were deterred by their opponents' menacing attitude, and by their address. 'Don't you know it is the sons of Essenzingercona who have killed Chaka for his base and barbarous conduct, and to preserve the nation of the Zoolas, the sons of our fathers, that you may live in peace and enjoy your homes and your families; to put an end to the long and endless wars, and mourning for that old woman Umnante, for whom so many have been put to a cruel death?' Thus saying, they went to the palace, where they dared not enter an hour before; and Sotobe went to his kraal. It appears that the death of Chaka had been long premeditated by the brothers, by whose hands he fell; and that the late savage massacres had hastened a resolution, which might, otherwise, have been stayed for a time.

DOCUMENT 25
'The king was no longer there'

From the testimony of Baleka ka Mpitikazi, who received most of her information from her Langeni grandmother; recorded by Stuart in 1919 and published in Webb and Wright (eds), *The James Stuart Archive*, I, p. 6.

NOTES FOR READING amaMpondo = people of the south of Zululand; Faku = the Mpondo ruler; Balule = Limpopo River; *inceku* = servant; Ndhlela ka Sompisi = one of Dingane's principal advisers (see Documents 27 and 28); *umdhlebe* = a tree, the scent of its flowers was believed by the Zulu to cause death; Malamulela = the Intervener.

The death of Tshaka. Father said an army went out against the amaMpondo. The amaMpondo came and defeated them, so they retreated. Tshaka became angry, for he himself had not been there. He was a great warrior and performed great deeds. He cried, 'So Faku does not know me?' He took his crane feather and stuck it in the ground, where it stood swaying. He then armed, taking his war shield, which was black with a white patch at the side. The army went down along the coast and attacked the amaMpondo. Some of the amaMpondo cattle were 'eaten up', while others where left behind. The Zulu then returned, driving the cattle. The army arrived home. He ordered it to move on to campaign away at Balule.

Then his brothers, Gqugqu, Mhlangana, and Dingana, hid. Tshaka's *inceku*, Mbopa ka Sitayi, saw them and said, 'Hau! So you are here, children of the king? You are troubled by the madman. As soon as you returned from Pondoland the order was given to move on. Are you not going to stab him?' They said, 'What should we do to him?' To which he replied, 'Stab him to death. He is a madman.' They then said, 'How could we overcome him? You stab him' (Mbopa).

Mbopa stabbed him. After stabbing him he ran to Mhlangana alone and said, 'Dingana has overcome Tshaka and has taken the chieftainship,' He then went to Dingana and said, 'Hau! Mhlangana is going to kill you', then back to Mhlangana and said, 'Dingana is going to kill you. Cut short an assegai and hide it in your clothing.' Mhlangana did so. Mbopa then rose up and went to Dingana and said, 'Mhlangana is carrying an assegai against you; he is going to kill you.' Mhlangana was caught, and indeed an assegai was taken from his clothing. He was then killed. Mhlangana said, 'Nhi'! Son of Sitayi, have you done this to me?' He died.

Dingana then ruled. He killed all the children of his father Senzangakona. Mpande remained. He was saved by Ndhlela ka Sompisi, who said to Dingana, 'Surely you are not going to kill Mpande, one who is just a simpleton? You are not going to kill this idiot, Nkosi?' So Mpande was left. All the children of the chief Senzangakona died.

The warrior regiments were not there; they had been laid low by fever. They had camped in a forest where there were *umdhlebe* trees. They breathed in the scent of the *umdhlebe*; they got terrible headaches, passed blood, and died.

Others came back, for not all had died. They arrived to find that the king was no longer there, and that Dingana had now stepped into his place, calling himself Malamulela, because he had intervened between the people and the madness of Tshaka. But he himself then killed all the children of his father. Tshaka, though, did not kill the children of his father.

Dingane's Reign

Dingane inaugurated his reign with promises of amnesty, peace and prosperity for the weary Zulu people. Lacking some of the self-confidence of his predecessor, he allowed his advisers and subordinate chiefs to assert more authority. He did, however, eliminate some of Shaka's counsellors and resumed the practice of executions at the capital. He was obliged to follow in the military traditions established by his brother but could not inspire the same demonstrations of bravery in battle (cf. Document 10). His armies, in fact, performed rather poorly and compensated for it by turning on Zulu subjects. The next three excerpts give impressions of the new king's conduct in office. Fynn, the author of Document 26, did not have a close relationship with Dingane and left Zululand in 1832. Note his suggestion that Dingane actively influenced the traditions about Shaka.

DOCUMENT 26
'Only a show of justice'

Fynn, *Diary*, pp. 162–3, 165–6, 174–5.

NOTE FOR READING   For Mzilikazi, see Document 15.

In the circumstances there were few who did not bless the spirits of their forefathers for allowing them to enter their huts and rest themselves, few who did not contemplate their late sad position and compare it with the present and that which the promises made them led them to expect. For Dingane not only behaved towards them in their distressed state with liberality and kindness, but promised to set the minds of his people at ease in the future by not imitating the conduct of Shaka, in such matters as he considered to be hurtful to them.

He composed or caused to be composed national songs, containing denunciations against the former state of things; his general conversation was, moreover, directed against the severe character of Shaka's government. He adopted mild measures, and thought that he was establishing himself firmly, when obstacles occurred which showed him the true state of things, and the motives that had driven his predecessor to such extreme lengths of severity and cruelty. I shall not be in the least surprised to see repeated by Dingane the very acts for which he and his confederates assassinated Shaka.

The deep impression Shaka had made on his subjects, as well as the numerous cunning devices he had from time to time resorted to, caused many to suspect that he, Shaka, was still alive and that, in order to be quite satisfied as to their loyalty, he had conspired with Dingane to the effect that the latter should temporarily pose as king. Dingane knew of these prevailing suspicions, also that a large section of the nation deeply deplored the death of Shaka. He consequently decided to allow Shaka's favourites to retain their respective positions for the time being, a policy which seemed to hold out prospects of a better future. The favourites, however, remained in office only until he had firmly secured the sovereign power, when he found an excuse for putting to death Mdlaka, Shaka's commander-in-chief, a man who had held that position from the commencement of Shaka's reign, had had the entire management of the army and who had rigorously and successfully fought his many and famous battles, conquering every nation or tribe he attacked. He had given great satisfaction to Shaka, though it was never acknowledged. But as his protector was no longer living his days were numbered. Such a man had to be removed if room was to be found for creatures of Dingane's own choice, by means of whom he could then inaugurate his own despotic career.

The person appointed to take Mdlaka's position was Ndlela, a man who, as it happened, was greatly respected by the people. The remainder of Shaka's favourites were removed one by one from their positions, and a body of chiefs selected by Dingane himself were appointed in their place. On such chiefs, therefore, was laid full responsibility for dealing with and settling all the disputes of the people. It appeared at first as if Dingane did not and would not interfere with this tribunal, so much so, that persons accused of having committed crimes might expect to be tried fairly, instead of their fate depending, as had formerly been the case, merely on the King's own decision. This, however, proved to be only a show of justice, for all cases, prior to any proceedings in connection therewith, were reported to him. If trivial he disposed of them himself; if important they were referred to the chiefs for adjudication, steps, however, being taken in each instance to acquaint the judges beforehand with the King's private opinion. And so it happened that all these decisions were invariably biased to the extent of being made to conform to the King's will, pleasure or personal caprice.

Not three months after the return of the army from Soshangane's, the people became convinced that Dingane's promises were nothing but words. Numbers were put to death for the most trivial offences, and many for having expressed disappointment at non-fulfilment of the promises he had made. Then did the destruction of human beings begin to go on as a matter of daily routine, as it had done in Shaka's day, and many of the former objectionable customs were retained, contrary to the expectation of the people in general . . .

Nqetho, heir apparent to the chieftainship of the Qwabe tribe, had just married two wives. One of these was the widow of his deceased brother, but in accordance with custom automatically became his, Nqetho's, wife. Since Nqetho's brother's death she had lived in Shaka's seraglio, but as that vast establishment had now almost entirely broken up, to make room for the smaller one of Dingane, she claimed Nqetho as her husband. In consequence of this he sent to Dingane that only one woman had come to him to be married, alluding only to the other girl. But Dingane, having heard of the other (i.e. the spinster), handed Nqetho's messenger over to the chiefs, by whom he was to be tried for attempting to impose on the King.

The chiefs decided in favour of Nqetho, giving it as their opinion that he was not obliged to report his having taken to wife a woman who was already married to him by an ancient custom. Dingane was of a different opinion, pointing out that his orders were that no marriage of any kind was to be entered into. When Nqetho received this information, he concluded that his life was in danger, real and immediate.

He forthwith collected a few of his tribe and revolted. He made his way into the centre of the tribal area by night, using the general cry of rebels. He proclaimed liberty to the oppressed, was lavish of promises of good, and quickly appointed people in different parts to call the Qwabes together. In three days he had managed to collect a large body without interference of any kind by the Zulus. The outrages committed by this tribe, and the cattle they seized in various directions, induced many to believe that Dingane's not acting promptly in repressing the lawlessness arose from a sheer sense of fear, brought on by the suddenness and energy of the rising, which resulted in many more joining Nqetho than would otherwise have been the case . . .

Pushing on, the Zulus overtook the Qwabes about 25 miles from the sea, on the River Embokodweni, which enters the sea about 15 miles from the port. The Qwabes boldly stood their ground in anticipation of attack. As soon, however, as the Zulu force came up, although each army got ready for action, neither side felt disposed to attack the other; the Zulus then contented themselves with capturing such cattle as they found in Nqetho's immediate possession, without being interfered with in any way by Nqetho, and then withdrew . . .

Several attacks have since then been made on various other tribes living both far off and near by, the last being against Mzilikazi, but in each case without any success. Within the limits of his own dominions he has not spared the lives of his subjects. He has massacred numbers with the same unsparing hand as his predecessors, though in a more treacherous and crafty manner.

Few of the many tribes tributary to the Zulus during the reign of Shaka, who was always more partial to foreigners than to his own countrymen, were spared by Dingane, who had no difficulty in inventing reasons for destroying them one by one, so that he might derive from the conquest of people already his subjects that glory which he was incapable of winning in wars against admittedly hostile neighbours—incapable because of the Zulus having, when under his control, lost that daring and prestige for which they had been so conspicuous in the reign of Shaka.

DOCUMENT 27
'You have removed the blanket that covers you'

From the testimony of Jantshi ka Nongila, recorded by Stuart in 1903 and published in Webb and Wright (eds), *The James Stuart Archive*, I, p. 196.

NOTES FOR READING   *isigodhlo* = quarters housing the king and his wives; *konza* = pay allegiance; Mgungundhlovu = Dingane's principal capital. For italics, see notes for Document 2.

Dingana said, '*I do not want an isigodhlo. That is what is destroying the people.*' Nzobo said, 'You can't be called a king if you have no *isigodhlo*. How, without one, can you be a king?' Dingana replied, 'It is the *isigodhlo* which is the cause of people always being put to death. It is a bad institution.' Nzobo: 'The killing of people is a proper practice, for if no killing is done there will be no fear.' Dingana then concurred and the *isigodhlo* continued to exist. Dingana then *retained an isigodhlo during his reign.*

After a time Dingana *removed the restrictions imposed on* all his regiments, and said they were to go and *have premarital intercourse* with the girls. The great men, his brothers and others of importance, thereupon entered his *isigodhlo* and *sported* with the girls there. Dingana saw this but said nothing. After a time the regiments came back to *konza* at his kraal. When he found they were all there, one morning when the sun was rising a man was heard to shout, '*Let all the people of Mgungundhlovu assemble!*' All came out and were *all present.* Dingana then directed all to *proceed outside the kraal.* They did so and sat down there. The Dhlambedhlu regiment remained. Dingana then left his hut, and *came out through the narrow gateway of the isigodhlo.* As the Dhlambedhlu saw it was he, they *went out.* When Dingana came to where the people were, he stood with a black blanket on. He said at once '*Seize that fellow Mfihlo!*' They caught him. Dingana said then, 'Catch *that fellow Ngqojana! Catch Mqubana!*', and so on in regard to all his brothers, and all were arrested. He then mentioned the names of ordinary men. He caused all those people to be at once killed with straight, thick, short sticks— not so long as *fighting sticks*. Ndhlela *rebuked him* here, saying, '*You have removed the blanket that covers you. How will you cover yourself now?*' Some say Ngqengelele said this but my father says it was Ndhlela. These executions took place between sunrise right up to sunset when the remark just referred to was made. My father said he was present and very many men were singled out from the *company* he was in, and when the men carrying out Dingana's orders wanted to take my father, Dingana would *stop them and point to those next to him.* Only my father remained in his *company*; all the others were killed.

DOCUMENT 28
'Dingane, Ndhlela and Jobe'

From the testimony of Lunguza ka Mpukane, son of an official of the chief Jobe, recorded by Stuart in 1909, Webb and Wright (eds), *The James Stuart Archive*, I, pp. 313, 329–30.

NOTES FOR READING *inceku* = servant or attendant; *tefula'd* = spoke in Qwabe fashion; *sisa'd* = entrusted livestock to a dependent; *isicamelo* = part of king's bodyguard and its location within the kraal; *takata'ing* = using supernatural forces for evil purposes; *bula* = to divine. For italics, see notes for Document 2.

I remember *Jojo of the Masikane section of the Makabeleni*, who lived at Pisweni at the place of Makaya, and who escaped although apparently condemned to be killed. An *inceku* shouted, *'Let the man you caught be brought forward!'* He was brought to Dingana who said, *'Fellow, what thing that you prize do you leave here on earth?'* He replied, *'I leave my king who, like a child beginning to talk, can only grow in greatness.'* *'What else do you leave?'* He said, *'Nkosi, I leave my child.'* The king said, *'What is it?'* He answered, *'It is a boy.'* Then the king said, *'O Zulu! Let him be, for he says that he leaves two things of value, his child and his king.'* He was thereupon spared, and eventually died a natural death. This happened at Mgungundhlovu. He had been caught on the right side of the kraal (looking towards the gate), but had not been removed to Nkata. I do not know what offence he was said to have committed . . .

Ndhlela was *dark-complexioned*, about six feet high, rather stout, not *bewhiskered*—slight beard, smaller than mine. He carried an *ilunga* shield, i.e. white with *two markings* . . . He *tefula'd* slightly in the ordinary Zulu way.

He was a kindly man. He could speak well, was a good orator, *clear-headed*, i.e. no fool. And when he had occasion to admonish anyone he did so in a temperate way. He sometimes *upbraided* people, but generally speaking had no *temper*. His praises were: *'Fighting stick that points out to us the Ngwane; he who crosses to the other side; hornbill that is slow to move.'* He sometimes said to me, *'Here boy, are my goats still doing well with your father Dhlodhla?'* meaning my 'grandfather', to whom he had *sisa'd* them. I would answer, 'Yes.' Dhlodhla was my father's uncle.

Ndhlela was the supreme *induna*, older than Dingana. Next to him were Nzobo (Dambuza) and Mapita ka Sojiyisa. Nzobo was slightly shorter than Ndhlela—same size as Ndhlela—but portly. He had a *headring*. He was *dark in colour*. These *izinduna* inspired awe; they were chiefs. And if one spoke to an *induna*, others would wonder whatever there was which you could require to talk to the *induna* about. He had a temper,

and would rebuke people angrily. He lived *in the isicamelo*, on the left side of the kraal.

The doors of the huts at Mgungundhlovu did not all face one way; some faced the *cattle enclosure*, others looked towards the gates at the lower end, and so on. The huts were generally smaller than those of Natal natives . . .

Ndhlela seemed to me the great or principal *induna*. All affairs seemed to centre in him. Mapita came and consulted him. I cannot discriminate as to what class of affairs the one *induna* attended to, and what the other, for they dealt with them in their own quarters.

Ndhlela and Nzobo used to try cases, and when they found anyone had *done wrong* they would have him killed without reference to the king, though the king would be told afterwards what they had done.

Our chief Jobe put many people to death. He did this frequently, even more than Ndhlela. Jobe killed them for *takataing*, as he said. He made reports of those he killed to Dingana. Where any death had occurred under suspicious circumstances, doctors would be called together to *bula* and *smell out*, then Jobe would kill off those smelt out. If anyone was ill and there was any doubt about his illness, Jobe used to warn people that if he died others would have to die along with him. If he then got well, well and good, but if he did die, numbers might be killed off. Jobe exercised this power by virtue of his being regarded as Dingana's 'father', just as he had been Tshaka's 'father', and there was a tradition to the effect that he was always to be treated with the utmost consideration—'be helped to (drink) milk', meaning that (it was wanted that he should) grow to an advanced age.

Dingane's difficulties with his African subjects and neighbours were matched by problems related to the European community at Port Natal. The king initially pursued Shaka's policy of treating the whites as subordinate chiefs with special standing and autonomy. However, Port Natal became a haven for refugees from Zululand—over 2000 by 1835—and Dingane grew increasingly concerned about the Europeans' loyalty and military potential. His suspicions were fed by a resourceful interpreter named Jacob who had developed a deep distrust of whites.

DOCUMENT 29
'Jacob's story'

Fynn, *Diary*, pp. 180–4, 188–9, 208.

NOTES FOR READING Dutch farmers = Boers; Hottentot = Khoikhoi; Robben Island = famous prison; for Francis Farewell and James S. King, see Document 19; Cane = John Cane, a Port Natal settler. The last portion of this selection, beginning 'After Shaka's assassination', was written by James Stuart, Fynn's editor.

Jacob originally belonged to a tribe under the chief Ndiambe that occupied land on what was once the borders of Cape Colony. At an early age he was captured by Dutch farmers during one of the numerous incursions they were at that time making among the tribes with the object of recovering stolen cattle. He was named Soembitchi by his master and remained in his service long enough to acquire a fair knowledge of the Dutch language.

He then ran off to his own country, being thereafter frequently employed to interpret for his countrymen in their dealings with the Dutch. When, later on, the former organised parties for stealing cattle in the Colony, he used to accompany them as guide. In one of these raids, after capturing a drove of cattle in the neighbourhood of Bushman's River, the party he was with entered a bush and killed an ox. While busy skinning it they suddenly heard the trampling of horses, and Dutchmen crying out 'Vang hom! Vang hom!' i.e. Catch him, catch him. When the natives emerged from the bush and looked to see what number of Boers were coming after them, they were observed, then closely pursued, which ended in Jacob and two others being arrested.

Some argument ensued as to whether the prisoners were or were not to be shot. One was actually set up as a mark, and several shots fired at him before he was killed. The other, however, and Jacob, owing to their knowledge of Dutch, were spared. They were each then tied to a horse and the horses made to canter to a Dutchman's farm, whilst a Hottentot riding behind flogged them with a sjambok as often as they failed to keep up. Owing to the severe sjamboking they received, Jacob's companion died. Shortly after this Jacob managed to escape, once more running back to his own country.

He was now taken by Major Frazer, commandant of the Frontier, and used as an interpreter. Jacob, however, remained only a short time, when he again returned to his country. At that time a law was in force prohibiting Kaffirs from crossing the Fish River boundary. In company with several others, Jacob one day conveyed an elephant's tusk to the missionary station at Theopolis with the view of selling it. After finding a purchaser, a Hottentot, and after concluding a bargain with him, the latter called Jacob's attention to the existing law, and recommended him to make off as soon as he could, at the same time refusing to pay what he had promised to do. Jacob was determined to recompense himself in some way, so on the way back he stole and made off with a number of cattle. He was pursued and arrested. He was then sent under escort to Grahamstown, where, as it happened, the notorious Kaffir chief Lynx was in custody. The two were then transported to Cape Town and directed to undergo their sentences on Robben Island.

When in 1822 Captain W. F. W. Owen, R.N., arrived at Table Bay with his squadron, for the purpose of surveying the south-east coast of Africa, Jacob was placed on board his ship, H.M.S. Leven, by direction of the Governor, and told he would have to act as interpreter. It so happened that his services were not required in that capacity, the reason being that Capt. Owen did not visit any country south-west of Delagoa Bay, where the man's services might have been useful, but only places beyond or northward of that bay, where the native dialects differ widely from the Kaffir language.

Owen extended his voyage to several ports in that part of Africa, e.g. Madagascar, Mozambique and the Isle of France (Mauritius), after which he returned to Algoa Bay. It so happened that Farewell and Thompson had already reached Algoa Bay with two chartered vessels, the Salisbury, Capt. King, and the Julia, and were making final preparations for a voyage to St. Lucia. Jacob asked Capt. Owen to allow him to join Farewell's vessel as interpreter. Owen agreed and after paying him such wages as were due to him and making such arrangements as were necessary in regard to his services in the future he passed him over to Farewell on loan, upon which the latter sailed off to St. Lucia.

Owing to the coast about St. Lucia Bay being dangerous, great difficulty was experienced in landing. In one case the boat was upset, when two sailors lost their lives. Jacob, who happened to be in the same boat, managed to save himself by swimming to shore. Shortly afterwards he was punished by Thompson for some offence, upon which he ran away. As no more was heard of him, Farewell concluded he had been killed, and continued to be under that impression until our arrival at Shaka's residence.

It appears that, when he deserted, he was taken to Shaka, who, from the fact of his having escaped drowning by swimming, nicknamed him Hlambamanzi. Shaka, with his accustomed liberality, then gave him ten head of cattle and placed him under the protection of a chief to find him a wife. In view of the statements he no doubt made to Shaka about the conduct of Europeans in general towards him, it is remarkable that Shaka was not unfavourably disposed towards us, though it is evident Thompson himself would not have met with a pleasant reception had he been of our party.

Our arrival on the scene in 1824 brought Jacob's qualifications as an interpreter into request. Shaka took him into favour, and, that he might always be near at hand, appointed him one of the night guards of the isigodlo (royal harem). Owing to the general information acquired in the Colony as well as among the Dutch in his various disasters, owing also to what he had learned during his voyages with Capt. Owen, when the scenes were so often and greatly varied, all this, added to a naturally observant and intelligent disposition, also to his extreme craftiness and capacity for deception, made Jacob particularly acceptable to Shaka in the execution of his various purposes.

When I had been about 12 months in the country, most of which time I had had but little opportunity of conversing with Europeans, the knowledge I gained of the Zulu language enabled me to follow his interpretations closely, and to check him in the false renderings which he had long been in the habit of giving without danger of refutation. Owing to his docile manner, he always remained in favour with Shaka. In his conversations with the King he used to praise or disparage our country and manners so long as Shaka was inclined to listen to him.

In consequence of the gifts of cattle repeatedly made to him by Shaka, he became a man of some importance; he was the owner of several kraals, and a number of followers, whose lives he used not to spare when he wished to kill any of them. Among his followers was one who was constantly in attendance on him, called Hlomula. This youth's manners had so captivated several Europeans that they, in turn, tried to persuade

Jacob to give them the lad, but without effect. One night Jacob fell asleep, though at the time on duty guarding the King. Shaka happened to wake, called Jacob, and finding him asleep ordered Hlomula to beat him. Jacob woke on being called and then apologised to Shaka. Shaka asked Jacob if he had heard the boy refuse to beat him as directed. He admitted having done so, whereupon Shaka exclaimed "Kill the boy at once, he fears you more than he does me!" The boy was seized by Jacob and there and then put to death.

After Shaka's assassination Jacob transferred his residence to Port Natal. When Dingane directed Cane to make a visit (his second) to the Colony Jacob was ordered to accompany him. Jacob, however, went only as far as the amaMpondo, when, under the pretence of being afraid of proceeding further, he parted company with Cane. In consequence of this Cane was obliged to go on alone.

On his return to Zululand he reported to Dingane the loss and inconvenience he had been put to on account of Jacob's desertion, whereupon Jacob was ordered to forfeit ten head of cattle. This he refused to do. However, two cattle were surrendered, though much against his will. After this he was again ordered to proceed with Cane to the Colony. It was only the fear of being put to death that made him obey; he went off breathing vengeance against Cane for forcing him to go against his will.

This time he went the whole way. On his return to Natal with Cane, the two remained some time in the vicinity of the port on account of the rivers being swollen. Whilst waiting, one of Dingane's messengers happened to arrive at Natal, when Jacob took the opportunity of whispering to him, for the information and warning of the King, that the Europeans of the Cape Colony, on the advice of Cane, where about to attack the Zulus.

When this report reached Dingane it was already clear that Cane had been unnecessarily dilatory about continuing his journey to its natural end in Zululand, and instead of going himself with the goods purchased or otherwise procured for the King in the Colony he had contented himself with forwarding them by irresponsible native carriers.

The false information maliciously communicated by Jacob to Dingane produced a remarkable change in the King's attitude towards the European settlers. At first it appeared as if only Cane was the person affected, it being generally known that Jacob had openly quarrelled with him only. But whilst having every reason to be dissatisfied and angry with Cane, who had certainly been negligent and dilatory in the execution of his duties, the nature of the rumours was such as to make Dingane suspect not only Cane but every other white man in the country of being actively disloyal towards him.

Jacob was executed in 1832 when Dingane became convinced that he had lied. Despite Jacob's death, a number of the whites who had enjoyed good contacts with Shaka —including Fynn and Isaacs—no longer trusted Dingane and soon left Port Natal.

The Zulu king wanted to improve relations with the European community but lacked a trustworthy intermediary. He found an opportunity in 1835 when the Port Natal settlers commissioned Allen Gardiner, an ex-naval officer turned missionary, to seek a trade agreement with the Zulu. The next two documents describe Gardiner's conversations and agreement with Dingane.

DOCUMENT 30
'True Englishmen never broke a treaty'

From Gardiner's diary for May 1835.
A. F. Gardiner, *Narrative of a Journey to the Zoolu Country in South Africa* (1836), pp. 126–7.

NOTE FOR READING   Indoonas = *indunas*, i.e. chiefs, advisers or military officers.

The ridiculous part of the ceremony being over, Dingarn commenced the business by observing that he had not before asked me respecting the news I had brought, as the Indoonas were absent, but that now they were come he wished to hear it. A meeting of the white people at Port Natal, I informed him, had lately taken place, to consider what was the best method to prevent his people from deserting and coming down to us in future. The advice I had given, and which was unanimously adopted, was then stated, as also the request that I should communicate it to him, which I was glad to undertake, being desirous at all times to be the King's friend. In reference to the proposition to send deserters back, provided he agreed to the arrangement, he asked, 'Would you send them bound?' 'We could do nothing.' I replied, 'unless he agreed to guarantee the lives and property of every individual now residing at Port Natal. The white people were but few, while the natives were comparatively numerous; and as the greater part were deserters from him, they would never (being themselves in similar circumstances) be induced to lend their aid to secure a single individual who sought refuge among them; and, however desirous the white people might be to second the views of the King, it would be quite beyond their power, as the natives would contrive to harbour and secrete them in defiance of all their vigilance. On the other hand, once assured of their pardon and security, the black people would, I had no doubt, assist us; and it would then be difficult for any deserter to make his escape.' Dingarn at once entered into the plan, which he considered equitable; and after picking a little of the fence, and considering a minute or two, he turned round and with some energy said, 'he granted all; that he would never molest any of his subjects now at Natal for past offences; that he should keep fast his word; but that he knew the white people would be the first to break the treaty.' I observed here, that 'true Englishmen never broke a treaty; that it had always been our boast to adhere to them; and that, if he had met with white people who had deceived him, he had been unfortunate—they were not the right sort of Englishmen.' Dingarn replied, 'I believe you. I am glad, very glad, and thank you much for the word you have brought. I have seen many white people, but now a great chief is come among us, to whom I can speak my heart.' I told him that 'I needed no thanks; that it was only my duty; that I feared God, and therefore he might rely upon all I told him, for I dared not speak what was not true.

In God's word we were told to do to others as we would be done by; and, therefore, while in his country, I should study his interest as much as I should that of my own sovereign.' Here he pointed his finger at me in the usual style of recognition and satisfaction when animated, and again thanked me for the good word I had brought.

DOCUMENT 31
'Chief of the white people'

From Gardiner's diary for July 1835.
Gardiner, *Narrative*, pp. 212–15.

NOTES FOR READING   For Thomas Halstead, see Document 37; Issibubulungu = area in the Port Natal region.

On being requested to commence the conversation, I said that I was desirous to know on what account two of the traders (mentioning their names) had been sent out of the country; that I had already heard their own statement, but, as there were always two sides to every case, it was necessary to know what charges he brought against them before we could decide what ought to be done in the matter. 'Now,' he said, 'it is my turn to speak'—and related the whole circumstance; from which it would appear that they had given him just cause for offence. The allegations were, that John Snelder, as before stated, had returned with some young men, whom he had induced to accompany him to Port Natal, about the time that the treaty was arranged; and that Thomas Halsted had falsely used his name, by informing the Indoona of the town where he was trading, that it was the King's order that he should dispose of his cattle to him. He likewise complained of the general conduct of the traders in inducing his people to desert, and conveying them out of his country in their waggons. On this latter point I questioned him closely, in order to ascertain whether, since the negociation of the treaty, so serious a charge could be substantiated.

No positive proof was adduced—but so little reliance were they disposed to place upon the professions of any of the traders, that Dingarn plainly avowed he could not depend upon them, since they had so often deceived him before. On this, I assured him that the white people at Port Natal were agreed to observe the terms of the treaty; and that he might rely upon it no deserters had been received there since that period. That I did not know they were there, he said, he was quite certain, or they would have been sent back; but he had often spoken on the subject to them, without effect. The word, I replied, which had passed between us should not fall to the ground; if deserters were found at Port Natal, he might rely upon their being sent back. Dingarn then said, that he considered me as the Chief of the white people there; and that he should look to me to keep things right. I told him that as far as I was able this should be done, but that beyond persuasion I had no power. His reply was, 'You must have power. I give you all the country called Issibūbūlūngu—you must be the chief over all the people there.' I said, that I did not wish for power; that my object in coming into his

country was only to be a teacher; but, since he had said that he should look to me alone to regulate all matters relating to the white people, I would accept it. . . .

Thinking it would be more satisfactory to both parties, I offered some advice respecting a guarantee; which, if required of all traders entering the country, would tend to establish mutual confidence. To this, however, Dingarn would not listen —saying, that all such matters must be regulated by me at Port Natal; and that from this time he should not receive any trader who had not previously obtained my consent; thus throwing the whole responsibility upon me. I inquired if he would not make some exceptions, particularizing one who was well known to him. 'No,' he replied, 'there must be no difference; those who wish to trade must first obtain leave from you; a message must then be sent, signifying the same to me, and I will send an answer to Port Natal. This is the place to which they must come; and when they arrive I will send round to all who wish to sell to them, and the things shall be brought here.'

Gardiner subsequently left for the Cape Colony and London to seek British authorization for his agreement with Dingane. The Europeans at Port Natal repudiated Gardiner's claims to represent them, helping to undermine his efforts. Gardiner returned with an appointment only as Justice of the Peace and thereafter confined his activities to his mission station. The next document gives the views of Port Natal settlers on Gardiner's initiative, especially on the question of returning 'deserters'.

DOCUMENT 32
'The natives were delivered up'

A letter from the Port Natal settlers to the *Grahamstown Journal* in 1837. Bird, *Annals*, I, pp. 322–3.

NOTES FOR READING   U'Tugela = Tukela River; Umzimvubu = Mzimvubu River; Faku = Chief of the Mpondo; Kafir = pejorative term for Bantu-speaking African.

Sir,—We have read with surprise a letter in the 'South African Commercial Advertiser' of 19th April, 1837 (copied from one in the 'Record'), purporting to be written by Capt. Gardiner, wherein he states distinctly three courses to be taken in treating with Dingaan. There is a fourth; but we must confess we do not understand it, as he does not clearly specify what it is.

We have now consulted, and are unanimously of opinion that by Capt. Gardiner's own words at the time, also from his interpreter, George Cyrus, who we think is at Graham's Town, and by what we have heard from Dingaan since, that it was upon the third course that the natives were delivered up, that is to say, *unconditionally*.

He states that a weak and timid policy might be contented with the third alternative. We answer: 'So it was.' We are not aware of any other policy having been pursued until the late slaughter by Dingaan of Dubo's people, and the desertion of the Amapisi, when we all agreed to reject the treaty, as most cruel and utterly impracticable, and to protect the people; and though we by no means wished to come into collision with Dingaan, yet if he molested us to offer resistance.

Such a message was conveyed to Dingaan; and though before that he had stopped the trade, and even taken the guns from one of the hunters (as he says, by the advice of Capt. G.), yet we had no sooner assumed this firm attitude than he immediately declared the trade open, and expressed a wish to be on closer terms of friendship and alliance with us than ever. How long it may last, now that Capt. G. has arrived again to carry out his 'energetic and humane policy,' we cannot say. We know that Dingaan expressed disappointment upon Capt. G.'s recent visit to him, no doubt expecting Capt. G. to fulfil his treaty, the impossibility of which we need not point out.

But to return to the letter. Capt. Gardiner states that he has received the thanks of many, both black and white, for his interference in the treaty. Possibly he may have received thanks from Dingaan, who thirsted for their blood; but that he received thanks from the majority of the white residents here, we most positively deny. Many of the whites, of course all the blacks, were not parties in the treaty, and always disapproved of it. Still, when entered into, the Europeans would have kept it had it not been for the sanguinary measures of Dingaan.

So much repugnance did the whites feel to this treaty that H. Ogle, when compelled by its terms to take and deliver up to certain slaughter the mother and two infant sisters of Nontabula, one of his headmen, gave the son and brother of these victims a cow as some atonement for his conduct.

We also see by Capt. Gardiner's evidence, as given in your paper at various times, that he has stated that Dingaan gave him the country from the U'Tugela to the Umzimvubu River, of course comprehending Natal and the country of the Amapondas.

We beg through the medium of your journal to point out to those who may feel interested in our affairs, that Chaka gave at several times, and to several different parties, the same tract of country, and that Dingaan has often confirmed the same 'gift' to the predecessors of Capt. Gardiner; and also that Capt. Gardiner has treated with and received a country from a man *who has not, nor ever had, the slightest title to it.* If desolating a wide extent of country by fire and sword, if murder of the inhabitants in cold blood as well as in battle, if cruelties the most unheard-of to the aged and defenceless, the women and the children, could give such a right,—such a right had Chaka, and none other; he never having occupied it, excepting upon his return from his first marauding expedition against Faku, when the worn-out and knocked-up cattle were left at different places upon the route until recovered.

Unluckily for the validity of such a gift, there lives at Natal a chief, named Umnini, whose ancestors have, as far back as Kafir tradition reaches, been the legal and rightful chiefs and owners of the country around, and who has never abandoned it. After a knowledge of the above, who will argue for the justice or the necessity of receiving such a grant; in fact, receiving from Dingaan the property of Umnini?

We remain, etc.,

(Signed)	R. Biggar,	D. C. Toohey,
	T. D. Steller,	W. B. Blanckenberg,
	G. White,	J. Stubbs,
	J. Duffy,	R. Russell.

In appreciation of Gardiner's efforts in 1835, Dingane had permitted several missionaries, including the Anglican Francis Owen, to establish mission stations in the kingdom. Owen arrived at the royal capital of Mgungundhlovu in 1837; in the next document he describes his mission and the expectations of his host.

DOCUMENT 33
'Guns or God?'

From the journal of Owen for October and November 1837. F. Owen, *The Diary of the Rev. Francis Owen*, ed. Sir George Cory (1926), pp. 40, 64–5, 67–8, 71, 72–3.

NOTES FOR READING 'He' in the first sentence = Dingane: Unkunginglovo = Mgungundhlovu, Dingane's capital.

He then gave orders for all the boys that could be found in the town to come forward: about a dozen appeared: the rest he said were all gone to a distance to get wood which I believed. He said that I might begin to teach them today. What followed I shall relate very minutely, as different opinions may possibly be formed of the propriety of my conduct. The king asked me to give him some gunpowder. I said I never gave gunpowder away and that I had none to spare, having only a little to shoot birds. He asked me if I could not give him a little as he wanted to shoot elephants. Being convinced that this was his real object and in order to save myself from the unpleasant office of giving him an article of this nature, I told him it was sold at Port Natal and he could get it there if he pleased. But I hereby got myself into another dilemma, for he now wanted *me* to purchase some and give it to him; and he said he would give me an elephants' tooth to purchase it with. This I declined, saying, I was not a trader but a teacher and that he had better speak to Mr. King, the driver of my waggon, who was returning to Port Natal and give him the tooth instead of me, and that he would get him gunpowder. He however renewed his request so earnestly that on reflection I thought proper to grant it him, being quite satisfied in my own mind that the object for which he wanted the powder was an innocent one. What his reasons were for not making the bargain in his own name he did not state. Either he did not wish to have any dealings with the Port Natal people, with whom he is not on very good terms, or he was afraid of a refusal, or it is against his dignity to offer anything for the sake of an equivalent, tho' he will readily give an equivalent for anything offered him. Most probably he was afraid the Port Natal people would not supply him with powder tho' they have with guns. I may also observe that

I have the strongest reason for believing that tho' the letter goes in my name the destination of the gunpowder will be known by the Natal people. He seemed well pleased that I granted him his request and immediately told the children that they were to go with me to be taught to read. . . .

Nov. 9th.—Dingarn sent in the evening to borrow a bullet mould of me, as his own was not large enough. Having received intelligence from Capt. Gardiner that the gunpowder which I procured for Dingarn would not have proceeded from Mr. Maynard's store had it been known that it was for Dingarn, and it having been also represented to me by Capt. Gardiner, that the sole purpose for which Dingarn wants powder and other warlike stores is to do mischief, I resolved to act upon his testimony and advice, considering this as the safest and wisest course, from which I should not have deviated in the first instance, if the least suspicion had crossed my mind either that the settlers at Port Natal were unwilling that Dingarn should have powder, or that Dingarn would use it improperly. Accordingly I desired the messenger to tell the king that I could not lend him the bullet mould, but that I would explain the reason when I saw him. . . The same act which appointed Capt. Gardiner declared it illegal to supply native chiefs with arms or powder: consequently he declined sending any, tho' he would detain the teeth for further orders from Mr. Norden.

I may observe here that I was not in the slightest degree aware of any such act as that just alluded to, when I got a supply of powder for Dingarn, or when I wrote the second letter (Nov. lst) in his name for the same article: otherwise I should not have interfered in either case. I acted for the best, and, the Lord helping me to resist the importunities, or even to incur the displeasure of Dingarn, I shall never again assist him in any sort of way to obtain either arms or ammunition, whatever may be his motive for desiring them. The letter which was addressed to me being read, and which contained several palliatives from the writer, as the announcement of a few presents and an expression of confidence in Dingarn's integrity with regard to the use of the powder, the king made no observation, but his mind was evidently disturbed. At length he called 'the speaker' (the name by which my Interpreter goes) to his side and told him that he wast *cast down*, because the Port Natal people supposed he intended harm by the powder. I reminded him that the letter did not say so, but they were obliged to keep the law which our king had made. He asked 'do they then think beyond the sea that I intend evil?' I said, the law was not made in reference to him in particular, but to all black kings. As this did not satisfy him I asked what would he think of us, if we broke the laws of our king! Would *he* (Dingarn) not be displeased with his people if they were to disobey *his* word. But I said we ought to be subject to kings and magistrates not only for wrath but for conscience sake: not merely for fear of punishment, but because God in his word commanded us. He did not however pay much attention to this, but abruptly appealed to his people (who were present) whether the Port Natal people had treated him well. They trade with us (said he): we are all as one, and why do they suspect me of evil. His people assented to all their chief said, crying out with

one accord 'Yearbo baba' (Yes, Father). I endeavoured to soothe him as well as I could, but to little purpose, apparently, tho' he said he was not displeased at *me*, but at them at Port Natal. He however at length said that I must come again in the morning to write for the teeth: I was glad at his determination to have the teeth back, as if they had waited for orders, Mr. Norden would have been reduced to the painful dilemma, either of sending the powder or of giving a further provocation to Dingarn's anger, who would in that case have been yet more displeased than if the teeth had been returned at once. I left him heavy and displeased. He did not recognise me when I took my departure, either in the native style of pointing the finger, or in the English way which he had adopted of smiling or nodding the head, and I really feared that by brooding over the subject during the night, his wrath would wax hotter and hotter. . .

Nov. 22nd.—Dingarn has just stopped the trade with Port Natal. His people having declined purchasing some cloth which Capt. Gardiner sent the other day to Unkunginglovo at Dingarn's request, he professed to be so angry that he swore by his Father, that whosoever should sell another head of cattle to any person, either for cloth or beads should be put to death. Under this pretence, tho' probably to wreak his vengeance on the people of Port Natal for not selling him gunpowder, he has virtually stopped the trade without *appearing* hostile to the Europeans themselves, of whom he is doubtless afraid, and of whose services to *himself* he is anxious to avail himself. My Interpreter and I are both included in this interdict. Neither of us can purchase cattle. . . Dingarn having in vain endeavoured to extract from my Interpreter what my sentiments were on his message this morning, called me to him, and told me he was *very sore*. The white people, he said, were not *one with him*. They granted him some things, but other things they withheld (alluding to the gunpowder): yet he was ready to do all the white people asked him: first one teacher asked to instruct his people, then another, and he granted all! Yet he could not have his wants supplied in return! He said, moreover, that I was like the rest: that I was one with the white people; for when he asked me only to *lend* him a bullet mould, I refused, this shewed that I was like them. I told him that I was ready to do him every service in my power, consistently with my duty to my God, my king, and my country. He said it was no use for me to 'twist myself out' of the charge that he brought against the white people, for it was evident that I opposed his having fire arms as much as they did. I told him I did not mean to twist myself out of this charge, that I desired his good, chiefly the good of his Soul, which I had come in the first place to promote, and that I was ready to teach him anything else besides God's word consistently with my duty to my country. He said it was in vain for me to shelter myself under the pretence that I desired his good, because I did not lend him the bullet mould. He repeated over and over again the substance of what he had said, addressing himself to his servants, all of whom acknowledged, and then he said he would tell me plainly that *he was offended*. When I asked if he was offended at me, he told me *not to ask that question*. I must infer it from what he had said.

Dingane's Day and Blood River

In 1837 Dingane learned that another group of Europeans, seeking land rather than trade or converts, had crossed the Drakensberg and entered Zululand. They were the Boer or Afrikaner migrants known as Voortrekkers, descendants of predominantly Dutch ancestors who began settling in Capetown in 1652. During the eighteenth century descendants of the original Dutch settlers pushed progressively eastwards. When the Cape Colony was annexed by the British in 1806, they already occupied its eastern edge.

These Boers were a pious conservative people accustomed to large landholdings and a pattern of using African labour for menial tasks. In the thirty years following British annexation they grew frustrated at a number of infringements upon their way of life. They could no longer expand because of the proximity of the Drakensberg Mountains and Nguni and Sotho farming communities. They chafed at new laws imposed by the British, laws abolishing slavery, repealing the pass laws which restricted the movement of Africans, and providing minimal rights to African workers. In 1835 many of them left the eastern Cape for the north-east. By 1837, a group led by Piet Retief had reached the Vaal River, pushed Mzilikazi (see Document 15) to the north, and entered the realm of Dingane. The next document describes the sentiments of the Voortrekkers.

DOCUMENT 34
'The Retief Manifesto of 1837'

John C. Chase, ed., *Natal Papers*, 2 vols (1843), Vol. 1, pp. 83–4.

MANIFESTO OF THE EMIGRANT FARMERS

Numerous reports having been circulated throughout the colony, evidently with the intention of exciting in the minds of our countrymen a feeling of prejudice against those who have resolved to emigrate from a colony where they have experienced for so many years past a series of the most vexatious and severe losses; and as we desire to stand high in the estimation of our brethren, and are anxious that they and the world at large should believe us incapable of severing that sacred tie which binds a christian to his native soil, *without the most sufficient reasons*, we are induced to record the following summary of our motives for taking so important a step; and also our intentions respecting our proceedings towards the Native Tribes which we may meet with beyond the boundary.

1. We despair of saving the colony from those evils which threaten it by the turbulent and dishonest conduct of vagrants, who are allowed to infest the country in every part; nor do we see any prospect of peace or happiness for our children in a country thus distracted by internal commotions.

2. We complain of the severe losses which we have been forced to sustain by the emancipation of our slaves, and the vexatious laws which have been enacted respecting them.

3. We complain of the continual system of plunder which we have endured from the Kafirs and other colored classes, and particularly by the last invasion of the colony, which has desolated the frontier districts, and ruined most of the inhabitants.

4. We complain of the unjustifiable odium which has been cast upon us by interested and dishonest persons, under the cloak of religion, whose testimony is believed in England to the exclusion of all evidence in our favor; and we can foresee as the result of this prejudice nothing but the total ruin of the country.

5. We are resolved, wherever we go, that we will uphold the just principles of liberty; but whilst we will take care that no one shall be held in a state of slavery, it is our determination to maintain such regulations as may suppress crime and preserve proper relations between master and servant.

6. We solemnly declare that we quit this colony with a desire to lead a more quiet life than we have heretofore done. We will not molest any people, nor deprive them of the smallest property; but, if attacked, we shall consider ourselves fully justified in defending our persons and effects, to the utmost of our ability, against every enemy.

7. We make known, that when we shall have framed a code of laws for our future guidance, copies shall be forwarded to the colony for general information; but we take this opportunity of stating that it is our firm resolve to make provision for the summary punishment of any traitors who may be found amongst us.

8. We purpose, in the course of our journey, and on arriving at the country in which we shall permanently reside, to make known to the native tribes our intentions, and our desire to live in peace and friendly intercourse with them.

9. We quit this colony under the full assurance that the English government has nothing more to require of us, and will allow us to govern ourselves without its interference in future.

10. We are now quitting the fruitful land of our birth, in which we have suffered enormous losses and continual vexation, and are entering a wild and dangerous territory; but we go with a firm reliance on an all-seeing, just, and merciful Being, whom it will be our endeavour to fear and humbly to obey.

By authority of the farmers who have quitted the colony,

(Signed) P. Retief

Retief and his party hoped to settle in the vicinity of Zululand. To that end they visited Port Natal, where they received a friendly welcome, and contacted Dingane. The next document gives portions of the correspondence between Retief and Dingane. Missionary Owen served as the king's scribe.

DOCUMENT 35
'Retief and Dingane'

Excerpts from the correspondence of Retief and Dingane in October and November 1837. Bird, *Annals*, I, pp. 359-60, 361-4.

NOTE FOR READING Umsilikazi = Mzilikazi.

Port Natal, 19th October, 1837.

To the Chief of the Zulus.

I take the opportunity of the return of your messengers to inform you that my great wish is to have an interview with yourself personally, in order to remove the impressions made by certain vague rumours which may have reached you respecting the intentions of the party who have quitted the colony, and who desire to establish themselves in the country which is uninhabited and adjacent to the territory of the Zulus.

Our anxious wish is to live at peace with the Zulu nation. You will, doubtless, have heard of our last rupture with Umsilikazi, resulting from the frequent and ruinous robberies committed habitually by his tribe; in consequence of which it had become absolutely necessary to declare war against him, after having in the first instance failed in every attempt to arrange our differences.

I shall set out in a few days for the country of the Zulus, in order to settle with you our future relations. The hope of always living on terms of peace and amity with the Zulu nation is the sincere wish of your true friend,

(Signed) Retief, Governor, etc.

Umgungundhlovu, 8th November, 1837.

To Pieter Retief, Esq., Governor of the Dutch Emigrants.

Sir,—This is an answer to your letter of 24th October, and will inform you of the conversation that has taken place. I regret to hear that you have suffered such heavy losses by the acts of Umsilikazi. I have taken from Umsilikazi a great number of your sheep.

Now, as regards the request you have made to me as to the territory, I am almost inclined to cede it to you; but, in the first place, I desire to say that a great number of cattle have been stolen from my country by a people having clothes, horses, and guns. The Zulus assure me that these people were Boers: that the party had gone towards Port Natal; the Zulus now wish to know what they have to expect.

My great wish, therefore, is that you should show that you are not guilty of the matters alleged against you: for at present I believe that you are. My request is that you recover my cattle and restore them to me; and, if possible, hand over the thief to me. That proceeding would remove my suspicions, and will give you reason to know that I am your friend: then I shall accede to your request. I shall give you a sufficient number of people to drive the cattle that you may re-capture for me: and they will remove all the suspicions that the stolen cattle are in the hands of the Dutch. If any cattle have been taken that were not mine, I pray you to send them to me.

(Signed) Mark + of the Chief Dingaan.

Witness: (Signed) F. Owen.

Port Natal, 8th November, 1837.

To Dingaan, King of the Amazulu.

It is with pleasure that I recognize your friendship and justice in the matter of the flocks taken by you from Umsilikazi. I thank you also in regard to the skins that you have so obligingly offered to return to me; but I wish you to keep them for your own use and advantage. I have no difficulty in believing, as you say, that so small a number of my cattle should have been taken by your army from the possession of Umsilikazi, since, having seen a number of yours at the different villages, I found none of my own among them. Umsilikazi, I have no doubt, has fled to a distance, for he must think and feel that I shall punish his misconduct. Have I not already reason to complain that I have been constrained to kill so many men of his nation because they had been bound to execute his cruel orders?

That which has just befallen Umsilikazi gives me reason to believe that the Almighty, that God who knows all, will not permit him to live much longer. The great Book of God teaches us that kings who conduct themselves as Umsilikazi does are severely punished, and that it is not granted to them to live or reign long; and if you desire to learn at greater length how God deals with such bad kings, you may enquire concerning it from the missionaries who are in your country. You may believe what these preachers will tell you of God and His government of the world. Respecting such things, I advise you frequently to discourse with these gentlemen, who desire to preach the word of God to you, because they will teach you how justly God has ruled and still rules all the kings of the earth.

I assure you that it is an excellent thing for you to have given permission to preachers to establish themselves in your country: more than that, I certify to you that these preachers have come to you because God instilled into their hearts the idea of doing so; and they are able to show you, by reference to the Bible, that what I am now saying to you is the truth.

As a friend, I must tell you this great truth, that all, whether white or black, who will not hearken to and believe the word of God, will be unhappy. These gentlemen have not come to you to ask for land or cattle, still less to cause you trouble in any way, but only in order to preach to you and yours the word of God. . .

As to the thieves who have taken your cattle, and what they have said, namely, that they were Boers, it was a skilful artifice to induce you to regard me as a robber, in order that they themselves may escape with impunity. I confidently believe that I shall be able to prove to the king that I and my people are innocent of the crime. Knowing my innocence, I feel that you have imposed a severe obligation on me, which I must fulfil, in order to show that I am not guilty. As for the proceeding which you require from me, accompanied as it is by expense, by trouble, and risk of life, I must be responsible for it to you, to the world, and to God, who knows all.

I go now, placing my trust in God, who gives me hope that I shall be able to carry out this undertaking in such manner as to give a satisfactory answer. That done, I shall look forward to being satisfied that I am dealing with a king who keeps his word. I hope that some of your men, and especially those of the kraals from which your cattle have been taken, will be ordered to accompany me, as has been agreed; and, moreover, that they obey my orders with precision. I thank you for the friendly reception you have given me, in return for which I shall always endeavour to show you equal good-will.

Yours obediently,

(Signed)   P. Retief.

Dingane received Retief at the capital but asked that the Boers prove their trustworthiness by capturing the 'people having clothes, horses, and guns' who had taken his cattle and insulted him. The culprits were the Sotho of Sekonyela who lived west of Zululand. Retief accepted the challenge but only fulfilled part of the king's mission.

DOCUMENT 36
'He had told a lie'

From Owen's journal of January 1838. Owen, *Diary*, pp. 100–01.

NOTES FOR READING Sinkoyella = Sekonyela, the Sotho chief who is an important figure in Chapter Two.

Jan. 22nd.—In the evening I was sent for by the king to read a letter he had received from Mr. Retief, the Gouverneur of the Dutch Farmers. It stated that the affair with Sinkoyella (the native chief of the Basootoos or Mantitees, against whom Dingarn sent the Boers to recover his cattle which had been stolen) had happily been settled without bloodshed: that he had very easily got him into his hands and bound him hand and foot, after which he confessed that he had stolen 300 head of cattle from the Zooloos, and began to pray earnestly for his life. Mr. Retief then released him, after he had made many humble confessions of his wickedness in not having attended to the advice of his Missionary. He endeavoured to impress Dingarn with the obligation of God's Law, which required him to release the prisoner, and in a separate letter requested me also to press this point. To punish Sinkoyella he had made him deliver up 700 head of cattle and also 63 horses and 11 guns, for without these he could not have accomplished the theft. The cattle were to be sent to Dingarn, but the horses and guns were distributed amongst Mr. Retief's own people. Sinkoyella's cattle had been stolen by the Bastards, so that his people were obliged to aid him in furnishing the stipulated number. In his letter to me, Mr. Retief informed me of the great relief his

arrival afforded the Missionaries in Sinkoyella's country, for they were in great fear of a Zoolu army coming to avenge the wrong done to this nation. Dingarn made no observation to the letter, but by *his manner* gave me strong reason to suppose that he was disappointed at the relief of Sinkoyella, and that the guns were to be given to *him*. I impressed upon him the duty of releasing Sinkoyella according to the law of God, but he made no reply.

Jan. 23rd.—Early in the morning I was sent for to reply to the above letter, when my suspicions of Dingarn's cruelty were but too fully confirmed; for he requested me to write to Mr. Retief to say that he had told a lie in *promising* to send Sinkoyella a prisoner, if he should succeed in taking him, for he had seized him, bound him and then let him go again. The best way to avoid writing such matter as this, I thought, was mildly to remonstrate and tell him that I was sure Mr. Retief would be displeased with him, if he sent him such a message and that I did not wish to be in any way the means of creating dissatisfaction between them. I said that I knew Mr. R's reason for not delivering the prisoner up, meaning that it was against the law of God, but he interrupted me, saying 'And I know it too: it is because he thought I should have put him to death: but no such thing: I only intended to talk to him and then I should have let him go', but as he evidently was afraid of displeasing the Dutch, he changed the tone of his language and said that *he* was not angry, *he* did not say that they had told a lie, but he could not stop his people's mouths, who would be sure to say so, therefore in order to satisfy them it was necessary that Mr. Retief should send *him* the guns and horses along with the cattle. I said that Mr. R. had distributed these amongst his own people, and he could not take them away again. But Dingarn said that Mr. R. had told *his* people that if he wished to have them they should be sent. When the cattle, guns and horses arrived he promised to assign the Dutch some land. The whole communication was indicative of the cruelty, artfulness, trickery and ambition of the Zoolu chief, who I have too much reason now to fear is induced by the example of other native chiefs to make himself strong by the 'isibani' or musket, the power of which he dreads on the one hand and covets on the other.

Dingane was disturbed not only by the release of Sekonyela and the refusal to hand over the guns and horses. He was also anxious about the continuing arrivals of Boer settlers in Zululand. By the time Retief appeared at the Zulu capital in February 1838, the king had decided on a new approach to the Voortrekkers. For several days, the Boers and their hosts celebrated; Dingane even agreed to give land to his guests. Then came the sixth day of February.

DOCUMENT 37
'Dingane's day'

Owen, *Diary*, pp. 106–8, 109–11.

NOTES FOR READING   Thomas Halstead was the Boers'
English interpreter; Mr Venable = a missionary;
Umthlela = Ndhlela.

Feb. 6th.—A dreadful day in the annals of the mission! My
pen shudders to give an account of it. This morning as I was
sitting in the shade of my waggon reading the Testament,
the usual messenger came with hurry and anxiety depicted in
his looks. I was sure he was about to pronounce something
serious, and what was his commission! Whilst it shewed consideration and kindness in the Zoolu monarch towards me, it
disclosed a horrid instance of perfidy—too horrid to be
described—towards the unhappy men who have for these
three days been his guests, but are now no more. He sent to
tell me not to be frightened as he was going to kill the Boers.
This news came like a thunder stroke to myself and to every
successive member of my family as they heard it. The reason
assigned for this treacherous conduct was that they were
going to kill him, that they had come here and he had *now*
learned all their plans. The messenger was anxious for my
reply, but what could I say? Fearful on the one hand of
seeming to justify the treachery and on the other of exposing
myself and family to probable danger if I appeared to take their
part. Moreover I could not but feel that it was my duty to
apprize the Boers of the intended massacre whilst certain
death would have ensued (I apprehended) if I had been detected in giving them this information. However, I was
released from this dilemma by beholding an awful spectacle!
My attention was directed to the blood stained hill nearly
opposite my hut and on the other side of my waggon, which
hides it from my view, where all the executions at this fearful spot take place and which was now destined to add 60
more bleeding carcases to the number of those which have
already cried to Heaven for vengeance. There (said some one),
they are killing the Boers *now*. I turned my eyes and behold!
an immense multitude on the hill. About 9 or 10 Zoolus to each
Boer were dragging their helpless unarmed victim to the
fatal spot, where those eyes which awaked this morning to see
cheerful light of day for the last time, are now closed in death. I
lay myself down on the ground. Mrs. and Miss Owen were
not more thunderstruck than myself. We each comforted the
other. Presently the deed of blood being accomplished the
whole multitude returned to the town to meet their sovereign,
and as they drew near to him set up a shout which reached
the station and continued for some time. Meanwhile, I
myself, had been kept from all fear for my personal safety,
for I considered the message of Dingarn to me as an indication
that he had no ill designs against his Missionary, especially
as the messenger informed (me) that the Boer's Interpreter,
an Englishman from Port Natal was to be preserved. Nevertheless, fears afterwards obtruded themselves on me, when
I saw half a dozen men with shields sitting near our hut, and
I began to tremble lest we were to fall the next victims! At
this crisis I called all my family in and read the 91st Ps., so
singularly and literally applicable to our present condition,
that I could with difficulty proceed in it! I endeavoured to
realize all its statement and tho' I did not receive it as an
absolute provision against sudden and violent death, I was

led to Him who is our refuge from the guilt and fear of sin,
which alone make Death terrible. We then knelt down and I
prayed, really not knowing but that in this position we might
be called into another world. Such was the effect of the first
gust of fear on my mind. I remembered the words, 'Call
upon me in the day of trouble and I will hear thee.' But of the
Boers, Dingarn, the Mission, the Providence of God, I
had other thoughts. Dingarn's conduct was worthy of a
savage as he is. It was base and treacherous, to say the least
of it—the offspring of cowardice and fear. Suspicious of
his warlike neighbours, jealous of their power, dreading
the neighbourhood of their arms, he felt as every savage
would have done in like circumstances that these men were
his enemies and being unable to attack them openly, he
massacred them clandestinely! Two of the Boers paid me
a visit this morning and breakfasted only an hour or two
before they were called into Eternity. When I asked them what
they thought of Dingarn, they said he was good: so un-
suspicious were they of his intentions. He had promised to
assign over to them the whole country between the Tugala
and the Umzimvubu rivers, and this day the paper of transfer
was to be signed... At present all is still as death: it is
really the stillness of death, for it has palsied every tongue
in our little assembly. Since writing the above Mr. Venable
has arrived from Temba station on the Umhlatoosi. His coming
was unexpected, as it was peculiarly seasonable for his
presence administered comfort, and mutual conference
under present circumstances was much to be desired. The
occasion of his coming to the king was, however, very
painful. Mungo, the principal Indoona of Congela had called
about half a dozen of his men and enquired of them the
reason why they had attended the teaching of the Missionaries.
He then gave an order, that no one in future, neither man nor
woman should go to be taught, and that the children should
not go and learn to sew. Mr. Venable intended coming to see
the king in this business, but yesterday morning about 10,
four messengers arrived who had been travelling all night
from the capital, in order to bring James Brownlee, the
Interpreter, to interpret for the king. They said that William
as well as Mr. Hally, my own Interpreter, were not here and
that Thos. Halstead, the Boers Interpreter, was at Capt.
Gardiner's, a palpable lie, for he was here when the messenger
left on Sunday evening, and I tremble to say is now amongst
the number of the slain: so the natives to say tho' Dingarns
servant this morning informed me he was not to be killed.
The reason for this call from James Brownlee is mysterious,
he is a boy and the king likes him; for what end he should
have sent in so unaccountable a manner and with such
haste is surprising. On Mr. V's arrival he was surprised to see
the Boer guns under the trees and the natives handling them
freely, but they themselves not to be found, but described as
having gone a hunting, etc. At length Umthlela the Indoona
told him that the Boers were killed. Mr. Venable made no
reply, and the savage, remorseless Indoona asked him if he
did not *thank* the king for having killed them. Before this
conversation, Mr. V. had told him for what purpose he had
come to see the king, and Umthela had asked him what they
wanted to teach. Being told the 'Book', he asked, cannot you
teach us to shoot, or to ride? At length our friend left and

came to the station where as he saw no one about as usual he expected to find *us* also gone. Our conversation has been partly on the wisest course to be adopted in the present exigency. We agree that we have no security for life. The man who brings our milk informs us that the army went out to-day against the Boers. We tremble for the result. In the evening the king sent to me for some medicine to heal a man who had been wounded by a spear in a quarrel with another Zoolu.

Feb. 7th.—In the morning two Indoonas with an attendant called. One of them patted his breast, a common gesticulation of friendship. No Indoona had ever been to the station before and they asked to see the hut, waggon, etc. They were remarkably civil. They had been sent by the king to inform me that it was not his intention to kill either me or the other missionaries, for we had come into his country by *fews* and *fews*: he could live in peace with us, for we were his people. All George's people, meaning the British were his, i.e., he liked them, but the Amaboro were not his people: nor were they George's. He said that all the *armies* that came into his country should be killed, that the Amaboro (Boers) were going to kill the king: they had come like an army and had fallen into a passion with him. Many other causes were then assigned for their slaughter, as that they had not brought Sinkoyella and his people prisoners. Some of the other reasons I could not well understand nor did I trouble myself about them as there was but one true reason, the dread of their power and that the whole was a premeditated preconcerted plan of Dingarn who was anxious to see in order that he might butcher them all at once. I cannot now have a reasonable doubt, tho' I could not imagine previously that his designs were so treacherous.

Dingane had hoped to eliminate both Retief's party and the Boers who had settled in the Tukela Valley. The second part of his plan failed when the Zulu army ran into stiff opposition. Moreover, the king's hopes of winning the support of the Port Natal community did not materialize. Most of the British settlers supported the Boers in an expression of white solidarity, while the missionaries, including Owen and his family, fled from the kingdom. The next document gives Owen's perception of the king a few days after 'Dingane's day'.

DOCUMENT 38
'Their real intention was to kill'

From Owen's journal for 10 February 1838. Owen, *Diary*, pp. 113–17.

NOTE FOR READING Umselekaz = Mzilikazi.

Feb. 10th.—The smoothness of Dingarn yesterday instead of satisfying me, only excited my apprehension and I slept under a painful foreboding of something evil to follow. God be praised who has taken away my fears. Early this morning the chief sent for me to tell me the words which I was to speak at Port Natal. On my arrival he called several of his great Indoonas about him and having (with my Interpreter) taken my seat in the midst of them he began to acquaint them with my determination of leaving, saying he did not know the reason whether it was that I was fretting for the Boers or for some other cause. However, he said he had no objection to my going and he would wish me a pleasant journey. His tone and manner more than his words gave me reason to apprehend that something was still in his mind, and as he went on speaking his manner became more vehement, so that I knew not whereunto it would tend. He entered into a long account of Capt. Gardiner's first arrival in the country, and his request for Missionaries and having railed at him with much contempt, he concluded by saying that instead of bringing on his second visit, as he had promised (so Dingam pretended) a ship load of goods, he brought *this man*, pointing to me. He said it never was his wish that white people should build houses in his country: he had no objection to their coming on a visit and then returning, but he had told them again and again, it was not his mind that they should build houses: however, they would not believe him: they would not take his No: they were determined to come and live here, and that when I came to Nobamba, I asked him to build another house for a future teacher at Congela: but he now would ask me one question. Who was it that sent for me? Did he send for me? As far as his impetuosity would allow me to speak, I told him that I had come with Capt. Gardiner by his permission, and that he had apparently given me a hearty welcome. He said that Capt. Gardiner had *forced* him to build a hut for me, he had been so pressing in his solicitations, that he could not for shame refuse, but now he wanted to know who sent for me? for he heard reports continually from that place pointing to the station, that I had said he sent for me here only to kill me. He referred to our native servants, who he said reported that I spoke evil of him: that we praised God, but when we did so always had him in our hearts: we praised God (he said) but reviled him: and to shew this was the case he would send for the girls who were at my house that they might speak in my presence all that they had heard us say against him, for this charge did not apply to me only, but to my wife and sister also, and to every member of my establishment, except my Interpreter, who he said was the only one of us that had not told lies of him. Accordingly he despatched two messengers for the servants. It was in vain for me to tell him that they could not understand the language which I spoke, he would not hear reason, nor would he have credited my testimony if I had told him that they spoke lies. Indeed I could not say that we had not in our own language spoken to one another of his vices, but never as I remember in the presence of our servants, before whom we were careful never to mention the king's name. His own conscience, however, I saw to be at work, he knew in himself that he was guilty of such and such crimes; he would naturally suspect that I also would be ready to condemn him and would therefore readily hearken to any reports to this effect ... Like a prisoner awaiting the sentence of his judge, I was in a measure pacified when I heard the despot declare that he had *sworn* he would never kill his missionaries. However, my confidence was not placed either on the word or oath of the Zoolu monarch, but on him who has said, 'Lo, I am with you always,' at the same time as I had no absolute provision in the word of God against violent death, I composed my mind whilst the chief was speaking to think of another world to which I hoped my spirit would fly. In the meantime, I felt the alarm which the sudden call for the servants would occasion Mrs. and Miss Owen, and the rest of our little establishment. Presently the messengers returned with the two girls and the boy. One of the former had attached herself to us by her good conduct, good humour and the hope of doing good to her soul. Of all persons I should least have suspected her of propagating a false rumour against us. Nevertheless, when required to speak, she lifted up her voice in condemnation of her master and mistress, she who had been the peculiar subject of our united daily instructions. Faultless hitherto she now openly declared with special reference to Mrs. and Miss Owen, that the king was the subject of our discourse all the day long: that she did not hear half what we said, but only when we mentioned 'his name', she knew the purport of our observations: she said they had called him an evil doer, a murderer and a rogue, and that when the king had sent to say he would not kill us, Mrs. Owen had said he was deceiving us: that when I received a kind message from the king, I did not believe him, but took my book and walked about, that I did not trust the king's word when he sent to say he should spare us, but that I prayed to God to deliver us from him: and that I prayed to God to condemn the king. She said that I looked thro' a telescope when they were dragging away the Boers, and that thereupon I fainted with horror. The boy and the other girl corroborated her evidence. The king then said to his Indoonas, 'you hear what they say.' It pleased God, however, to restrain their passions and they said nothing. As I now did not so much fear immediate violence, as destruction on the road by connivance of Dingarn without his express sanction, whereby he would shelter himself from the odium of our death as in the case of Thos. Halstead, I directed my Interpreter to give him a hint that if mischief were to befall us on the road, the blame would certainly be laid on him. Indeed I could not tell him what evil might not result from this manifestation of his anger, even if no evil were designed or thought of at present. It was impossible to tell what consequences might not follow from the zeal of his captains and people, who are not influenced by those restraints which in some measure tie up the hand of the monarch himself, or how they might not influence him against me. For the present, however, appearances were favourable and I felt an unspeakable relief. Dingarn said that he was not angry with me, but only wished to shew me my faults. He had before said that if I had not asked to go he should soon have sent me away because I spoke evil of him. By degrees the storm subsided, and at length he told me to write a letter to the Governor of the Colony, to give his reasons for killing the Boers, viz., that they had laid claim to his cattle, saying they belonged to them, for he had taken them from their common foe Umselekaz, who had stolen them from the Boers: that they fell into a passion with him about this: that they wanted before they left to fire a salute with blank cartridge as they did on their arrival, but that their real intention was to kill him, as a proof of which when their guns were examined after their death, hey were found to

be loaded with ball. He told me also to write that he would not allow white people to build houses in his country. This letter will not go without a suitable P.S. from myself. In the warmth of his anger at the beginning of the interview, he gave me this message to take home to my countrymen, which I now deliver; that his people are not such fools as I expected, I had thought to come here and blind them, but they would not be deceived by me . . . We immediately commenced packing our waggons: when however, the oxen arrived it was found that their feet were sore: many of them were in other respects sick and all exceedingly poor, nevertheless, we determined to proceed as we could. It was impossible, however, to get ready the same evening, and one more night we slept at the station. It was an anxious, trying day, but we closed it by a refreshing season of worship at which I expounded the vision of Jacob's ladder.

The conflict between Boer and Zulu was not resolved until December 1838, when a Voortrekker force led by Andries Pretorius encountered Dingane at Blood River. The following account by one of the Boer commandos describes a Zulu attack on the author's family, the battle of Blood River and the new arrangements in old Zululand.

DOCUMENT 39
'Blood River'

An account by Daniel Pieter Bezuidenhout, published in Afrikaans in the *Orange Free State Monthly Magazine* (December 1879), translated by Bird, in *Annals*, I, pp. 371–2, 374–6.

NOTES FOR READING   Kafir = pejorative expression for black Africans; Umpanda = Mpande; Sapusa = Sobhuza, the Ngwane ruler.

The third attack was on my father's bivouac, consisting of five wagons and three skin tents; and there were three men with it—namely, my father, Roelof Botha (my brother-in-law), and myself.

It was about one o'clock in the night, and there was no moonlight. We stood on a rough hillock, near thorn trees. We had three or four bold savage dogs, that would tear a tiger to pieces without difficulty. I heard the dogs bark and fight, and thought that there was a tiger. I got up, having no clothes on my person except a shirt and drawers, and went to urge on the dogs: and, when I was about 300 yards away from the wagons, I heard the whirr of assagais and shields, and perceived we had to do with Kafirs, not tigers; and with the Kafirs the dogs were fighting. I shouted to my father: 'There are Kafirs here, and they are stabbing the dogs;' and I ran back towards the wagons to get my gun, for I was unarmed. But the wagons were already encircled by three rows of Kafirs. Still I strove to push with my hands, and struggle, in order to pass through the Kafirs to get at my gun. When I had in this way got through the three lines of Kafirs, I found that there was still a number within the lines closely surrounding the wagons. As I was still advancing, I heard my father say, 'O God!' and I knew from the sound that he was suffocated by blood. He had a wound in the gullet, above the breast. Roelof Botha had fired three shots, and there lay three Kafirs, struck down by his shots: then he, too, cried 'O Lord!' I heard no more, and then I tried to make my way back, away from the wagons, through the three rows of Kafirs. Then I received the first wound from an assagai on the knot of the shoulder, through the breast and along the ribs. A second assagai struck the bone of my thigh, so that the point of the blade was bent, as I found afterwards when I drew it out. The third struck me above the left knee—all the wounds were on my left side. A fourth wound was inflicted above the ankle, through the sinews, under the calf of the leg. Then I found myself among the cattle, and stood a moment, listening. I heard no futher sound of a voice—all were dead; and the Kafirs were busy, tearing the tents, and breaking the wagons, and stabbing to death the dogs and the poultry. They left nothing alive. Of the women and children murdered at my father's wagons, there were: my mother, Elizabetta Johanna, born Liebenberg; my wife, Elizabetta Cecilia Smit; my mother-in-law, Anna Smit, born Botha; my sister, Susanna Margarita, married to Botha, her little child, Elizabetta Johanna, about five months old; another sister, Maria Adriana Bezuidenhout; also my sisters, Rachel Jacoba and Cornelia Sophia, a little brother, named Hendrik Cornelis, my little daughter, Anna Bezuidenhout (she was eleven months old), who was murdered with her mother. My wife lay in bed with a little one, three days old, also murdered with the mother; and on the following day we found my wife with her breast cut off, and the corpse of my child laid at the blood-stained breast. There was also a brother of mine, Petrus Johannes, fourteen years old. He slept in my father's tent, and when I shouted, 'Here are Kafirs,' he understood me to say that the sheep were running off. He jumped out, and received only an assagai-wound along the skin of the back, and then ran among the thorn trees ... Well, in the following year Andries Pretorius came from Graaff-Reinet, and was chosen as commandant. We were all this time in Gatslager, and there was a camp—Maritzlager—near the Little Tugela. Then Pretorius went as general, with four hundred men. I was one of them. Then we had the battle, on a Sunday, at Blood River, where we killed 3500 Kafirs. We had formed an encampment with our wagons. Between the wagons we had fastened long ladders, and skins of oxen were stretched over the wheels. At the back of each wagon there were little heaps of gunpowder and bullets; and when the battle was fought, and the Kafirs in thousands were no further than ten paces from us, we had scarcely time to throw a handful of powder into the gun, and then slip a bullet down the barrel, without a moment even to drive it home with the ramrod. Of that fight nothing remains in my memory except shouting and tumult and lamentation, and a sea of black faces; and a dense smoke that rose straight as a plumb-line upwards from the ground. From Blood River we marched upon Dingaan's city. When we arrived, Dingaan had fled; and we found no one. We then held a sale at Dingaan's city of elephants' teeth, beads, and other valuable

articles which we found there. Amongst other things there was a silver goblet, which Andries Pretorius bought for £60. I believe Marthinus has it still.

From Dingaan's city we held our course upwards along the White Umfolosi (Umfolosi Mhlopi or White Sand River). Dingaan was at the lower end of the river with his military force. He drove us through the river, and five of our men fell in the fight, amongst others Jan Oosthuizen, Gert Scheepers, and the elder Biggar.

Andries Pretorius then went into the interior to fetch away his own party of emigrants. After the battle on the Sunday at Blood River, all the native tribes whom he had previously conquered fell away from Dingaan. Matoba, Job, Sapusa, Hutsi, and Umpanda, all came to us to sue for peace. This Pretorius granted them. Umpanda was the most important amongst them, as the half of the people of Zululand recognized him as their captain.

After Pretorius had returned with his family, he was again chosen to be the commandant, and we again marched against Dingaan, with four hundred men. Pretorius had granted peace to Umpanda on condition that his (Umpanda's) forces should advance against Dingaan along the coast. When we had begun our advance, old Sapusa, the father of Umswazi, sent three of his captains; and Pretorius said: 'Well, I grant you peace, but on condition that you bring me Dingaan's head!' Umpanda moved forward along the coast, and we along the upper country with four hundred men. Our wagon encampment remained at the other side of the White Umfolosi, and the mounted force went forward and drove Dingaan through the Pongola. He continually fled, till he reached the other side of the Umguza River, at Bamboesberg. There Sapusa took him prisoner. On the first day (according to the statement of the Kafirs), Sapusa pricked Dingaan with sharp assagais, no more than skin deep, from the sole of his foot to the top of his head. The second day he had him bitten by dogs. On the third day, Sapusa said to Dingaan: 'Dingaan! are you still the rain-maker? Are you still the greatest of living men? See, the sun is rising: you shall not see him set!' Saying this, he took an assagai and bored his eyes out. This was related to me by one of Sapusa's Kafirs who was present. When the sun set, Dingaan was dead, for he had had neither food nor water for three days. Such was the end of Dingaan.

After Dingaan's army had in this way been driven over the Pongolo, and he had ceased to exist, our commando and that of Umpanda came together. Umpanda was always near our camp. Thence we went forward, and took as booty a large number of cattle. There were 46000 head, and we shared these with the captains who had forsaken Dingaan. We returned with the mounted force to the Umfolosi. There, Pretorius said: 'Umpanda, Dingaan is driven off; his kingdom is at an end. I now appoint you to be King of the Zulu race that remains. You see that I have conquered the territory as far as the White Umfolosi (mouth of St. Lucia's Bay). Maintain peace with our people as long as you live. Then I give you as a concession—for it is my territory, conquered by my weapons—the kingdom of Zululand.' A salvo of twenty-two guns was then fired by us in presence of Umpanda and his people. We graved the day and date and year on two long large stones. One of them we placed erect in the ground, and buried the other below the soil on the bank of the Umfolosi. Panda withdrew from the spot, became King of the Zulus, and remained in peace with us till his death.

Till we meet again,

(Signed) Daniel Pieter Bezuidenhout

Blood River demonstrated the crushing superiority of European weapons and military technology, implied much earlier by Isaacs in his discussions with Shaka (Document 17). It also helped undermine the fragile unity of the Zulu leadership. As Bezuidenhout noted, the subjects of Dingane soon repudiated his authority. Mpande, another son of Senzangakona, joined forces with Pretorius, defeated Dingane and drove him into the arms of enemies of the Zulu. Mpande then accepted a treaty with Pretorius in which he was confirmed as king of a truncated Zululand and vassal of the Boers. A few years later, when the British annexed Natal and most of the Boers left for the high veld, the new king recovered his autonomy and enjoyed a long, peaceful and relatively prosperous reign over the Zulu. He did not, however, challenge British jurisdiction in Natal nor attempt to revive the military glories of Shaka.

AIDS TO UNDERSTANDING

Chronology

1785–90 Birth of Shaka
c.1790 Emergence of Ndwandwe, Ngwane and Mthethwa confederations
c.1802 Famine in Langeni area
1806 British annex Cape Colony
1816 Senzangakona dies, Shaka becomes chief of the Zulu
1818 Dingiswayo killed by Zwide, Shaka begins to take over the Mthethwa
c.1819 Shaka defeats Ndwandwe of Zwide
c.1823 Shaka forces Mzilikazi to flee to west
1824 British traders arrive at Port Natal
1827 Death of Nandi, Shaka's mother
1828 Assassination of Shaka
1832 Fynn and Isaacs leave Zululand
1835 Voortrekkers begin leaving Eastern Cape; Gardiner negotiates with Dingane
1837 (October) Voortrekkers under Retief reach Zululand.
1838 (January) Retief captures and releases Sekonyela
1838 (February) Retief and his party killed on Dingane's Day
1838 (December) Zulu army defeated by Pretorius at Blood River
1840 (January) Mpande's forces defeat Dingane
1840 (February) Pretorius proclaims Mpande king of the Zulus
1840 (October) Boers proclaim Natal Republic
1845 British annex Natal

Glossary

bula = to divine
Cane, John = British trader and settler
Dukuza = an important Zulu capital
Farewell, Francis = British trader and settler
head-ring = head band signifying attainment of manhood
impi = military regiment or unit
inceku = attendant of a chief or king and responsible for duties in the royal household
induna = civil or military official, usually appointed
isigodhlo = quarters housing the chief or king and his wives
Jobe = father of Dingiswayo and also the name of a local chief (Document 28)
Kafir = pejorative term of Arabic derivation applied principally to Bantu-speaking Africans
King, James = British trader and settler
konza = pay allegiance
Mbopa = principal servant of Shaka
Mdlaka = Shaka's Commander-in-Chief, subsequently killed by Dingane
Mgungundhlovu = Dingane's principal capital
Mhlangana = half-brother of Shaka
Mthethwa = northern Nguni confederation headed by Dingiswayo
Mzilikazi = Nguni chief who served, then fled from Shaka
Nandi = Shaka's mother
Ndhlela = principal adviser to Dingane
Ndwandwe = northern Nguni confederation headed by Zwide
Ngomane = Shaka's patron among the Mthethwa
Ngwadi = Shaka's maternal half-brother
Ngwane = the third northern Nguni confederation
Nqetho = Qwabe chief
Senzangakona = chief of the Zulu and Shaka's father
Sikhunyana = successor to Zwide as head of the Ndwandwe
tefula = to speak the Nguni language in the Qwabe manner

An Essay of Questions

Sources and Interpretation

The student of Nguni and Zulu history faces three major problems: the absence of contemporary accounts before 1824; the preponderance of accounts by Europeans, some of whom lacked sympathy with and knowledge of the Zulu; and the great impact which Shaka and the *Mfecane* had upon the traditions of the northern Nguni people. The process of reconstruction is consequently very difficult. How would you criticize the documents in this chapter as sources for the early life and career of Shaka, Shaka after 1824, Dingane? How would you compare Fynn and Isaacs, or the Bryant and Stuart collections of Zulu traditions? Compare Documents 1 and 2 on Shaka's birth; 5 and 6 on Shaka's accession to the Zulu chieftaincy; 15 and 16 on the chiefs under Shaka; 24 and 25 on the assassination of Shaka; 26, 27 and 28 on Dingane's rule.

The contemporary accounts of Shaka and Dingane were written by a variety of individuals. How would you evaluate the following as factors which contribute to understanding and objectivity: knowledge of the Zulu language; ability to provide medical assistance; vocation of trader; vocation of missionary; Voortrekker identity; British nationality; residence at the Zulu court; adaptability to Zulu custom?

The Transformation of Society

Dingiswayo and Shaka helped bring about radical changes in northern Nguni society. In trying to explain the causes of this transformation would you emphasize demographic pressure; individual leadership; military innovation; new economic opportunities? Do you find indications of continuity with old customs and structures? How important was religious ritual in the new society?

The sources lay great stress on the military and predatory nature of the Zulu state. How would you compare it with Buganda in this regard? What were the channels of social mobility and distinction? Look closely at the careers of Komfiya (Document 14), Magaye (Document 16) and Ndhlela (Document 28).

One problem faced by the Zulu was how to translate conquests into effective administration. How well did they succeed at this task? Did the obstacles stem from a lack of precedent; external pressures; the nature of the military state?

The sources suggest considerable fatigue among the Zulu in 1828 and again at Dingane's downfall. Was this a temporary phenomenon or an accumulated weariness? Is there such a thing as a 'threshold' of violence and fatigue beyond which a leader cannot push his people? Compare Zululand in this regard with Buganda in the period between 1888 and 1893.

Shaka and Dingane

Shaka is clearly the most dominant figure in this chapter as he is in Zulu tradition. How would you estimate his capacities as a military tactician; administrator; diplomat; organizer of an intelligence network; economic strategist? What effect did the possession of great power have on his personality; his judgement?

A number of writers have advanced psychological interpretations of Shaka, based on the stories of illegitimacy, sense of sexual inferiority, and fear of patricide. How solid do you find the basis for such views? What lines of psycho-historical interpretation would you advance? Look closely at Documents 1–3, 7 and 8, 16, 20–2.

What estimates would you make of Dingane's character; his military leadership; his administrative competence? Did he have a foreign policy?

Identity, Technology and Diplomacy

Europeans and their technology became important in Zululand in the 1820s. How did the Zulu conceive of and relate to the whites? What kinds of distinction did they make between Boer and Briton? What information was available to Dingane about them and how useful was it? Did he miss opportunities to utilize the rivalry between the two 'tribes' of Europeans? Is it appropriate to use 'tribe' and 'chief' to designate the Europeans and their leadership and the Africans and theirs? Why was the return of deserters so important for Dingane? Compare him in this regard with Osei Bonsu and Asante.

The case studies offer several instances in which an African ruler endeavoured to use a foreigner to handle some of his foreign affairs. Compare Dingane's plans for Gardiner and Owen with Casalis' role in Lesotho and the use of the Muslims and Europeans in Asante.

The Zulu were fascinated by European guns but did not incorporate them into their military strategy, with disastrous consequences at Blood River. How do you explain this? Would the Zulu have used guns had they been more widely available? Was the refusal of Boer and Briton to sell or give guns to Africans an expression of racial solidarity?

Jacob is one of a number of individuals in the case studies who cross cultural boundaries. Compare his fortunes, perceptions and loyalties with those of Pasko in Sokoto and those of Abu Bakr, Huydecoper, Nieser and Brew in Asante. How objective and how correct was Jacob in his observations about white greed and inevitable white encroachment?

Conclusion

To what extent can one compare the process of state formation in Zululand in the early nineteenth century, involving a population of perhaps 200 000, with the management of an existing system in Buganda, Sokoto or Asante, involving at least one million people? Would you describe the history of the 1820s and 1830s as the story of an inevitable European conquest of an African society, or as the clash of Zulu, British and Boer imperialisms, or in some other way?

Bibliographical Essay and Bibliography

In constructing the Zulu chapter we have relied on the works of Omer-Cooper and Thompson. Marks (1967, 1969 and 1975), Krige and Wilson provide anthropological and historical background on the Nguni people. Morris and Roberts have recently published general accounts of the Zulu in the nineteenth century, while Marks (1970) deals with the 1906 rebellion in Natal. Read Mofolo and Ritter for examples of what an African and a European, respectively, have made of Shaka. For a recent psychological analysis of Shaka, see Gluckman.

In addition to the contemporary and oral accounts we have used, one might consult Champion and Kotze for missionary materials, Delegorgue for a traveller's account, and Cope for Zulu praise poems. Bird and Chase provide collections of material from numerous sources.

Contemporary Accounts and Oral Tradition

Bird, John, ed., *The Annals of Natal: 1495 to 1845*. 2 vols. T. M. Miller, Cape Town, 1885.

Bryant, A. T., *Olden Times in Zululand and Natal*. Longmans, Green & Co., London, 1929.

Chase, John C., ed., *Natal Papers*. 2 vols. R. Godlonton, Graham's Town, 1843.

Cope, T. *Izibongo: Zulu Praise Poems*. Oxford University Press, Oxford, 1968.

Delegorgue, M. A., *Voyage dans l'Afrique australe*. 2 vols. Depôt de Librairie, Paris, 1847.

Fynn, H. F., *The Diary of Henry Francis Fynn*, ed. J. Stuart and D. Malcolm. Shuter & Shooter, Pietermaritzburg, 1950.

Gardiner, A. F., *Narrative of a Journey to the Zoolu Country in South Africa*. W. Crofts, London, 1930.

Isaacs, Nathaniel, *Travels and Adventures in Eastern Africa*. 2 vols. E. Churton, London, 1936.

Kotze, D. J., ed., *Letters of the American Missionaries, 1835–8*. Van Riebeck Society, Cape Town, 1950.

Owen, F., *The Diary of the Rev. Francis Owen*, ed. Sir George Cory. Van Riebeck Society, Cape Town, 1926.

Webb, Colin de B., and Wright, J. B., eds and trans., *The James Stuart Archives of Recorded Oral Evidence Relating to the History of the Zulu and Neighbouring Peoples*. Vol. 1. Pietermaritzburg, University of Natal Press, and Durban, Killie Campbell African Library, 1976. Killie Campbell Africana Library Manuscript Series, Number 1.

Secondary Sources

Burness, Donald, ed., *Shaka, King of the Zulus in African Literature*. Three Continents Press, Washington, D.C., 1976.

Callaway, Canon, *The Religious System of the Amazulu*. Durban, Adams & Co., London, 1870.

Cowley, Cecil, *Kwa Zulu. Queen Mkabi's Story*. C. Struik, Cape Town, 1966.

Gluckman, Max, 'The individual in a social framework: the rise of King Shaka of Zululand'. *Journal of African Studies* (UCLA Press, Los Angeles), **1**, 2 (1974).

Krige, E. J., *The Social System of the Zulus*. University of the Witwatersrand and SOAS, Johannesburg, 1936.

Marks, Shula, 'The Nguni, the Natalians and their history'. *Journal of African History*, **8**, 3 (SOAS, London, 1967).

—'The traditions of the Natal "Nguni": a second look at the work of A. T. Bryant'. In Thompson, L. M., ed., *African Societies in Southern Africa*. Heinemann Educational, London, 1969.

—*Reluctant Rebellion*. Oxford University Press, New York, 1970.

Marks, Shula, and Gray, R., 'Southern Africa and Madagascar'. In *Cambridge History of Africa*. Vol. 4. Cambridge University Press, Cambridge, 1975.

Mofolo, Thomas, *Chaka: an Historical Romance*. Oxford University Press, Oxford, 1967.

Morris, Donald Robert, *The Washing of the Spears*. Cape, London, 1966.

Omer-Cooper, John, *The Zulu Aftermath*. Longman, Harlow, 1969.

—'The Nguni outburst', In *Cambridge History of Africa*. Vol. 5. Cambridge University Press, Cambridge, 1976.

—'Colonial South Africa and its frontiers'. In *Cambridge History of Africa*. Vol. 5. Cambridge University Press, Cambridge, 1976.

Ritter, E. A., *Shaka Zulu*, Longman, Harlow, 1964.

Roberts, B., *The Zulu Kings*. Hamish Hamilton, London, 1974.

Thompson, Leonard M., ed., *African Societies in Southern Africa*. Heinemann Educational, London, 1969.

Wilson, Monica, and Thompson, L. M., eds, *The Oxford History of South Africa*. Vol. 1. Oxford University Press, Oxford, 1969.

Chapter Two

To Build a Nation: The Story of Moshweshwe

PLATE 2.1   *Thaba Bosiu, capital of Lesotho in the days of Moshweshwe*

PLATE 2.2   *Moshweshwe's method of consolidation and expansion. Morija mission (foreground) in conjunction with Letsie's village (middle left) and Molapo's village (centre). See pages 50–55).*

PLATE 2.3   *Moshweshwe in 1833*

PLATE 2.4   *A sketch of a man from Lesotho made in the 1830s*

INTRODUCTION

On the plateau west of the Zulu kingdom, a contemporary of Shaka named Moshweshwe created a state called Lesotho. Moshweshwe and his Sotho people built from small settlements very much like the Nguni; they also had to contend with pressures created by Boer and British expansion. Lesotho, however, acquired a different character from its Zulu counterpart. Forged amid the disruption of the *Mfecane* (Chapter One, Document 12), it grew by re-establishing security and attracting uprooted people to its fold. The documentary record makes it possible for the historian to explore Lesotho's development, examine Moshweshwe's deliberations about custom, change and sovereignty, and make fruitful comparisons with similar themes in other chapters.

The ancestors of Moshweshwe belonged to the southern Sotho, who lived between the Drakensberg mountain range and the Vaal River. Like the Nguni and the other Sotho, they made their living by a mixture of farming, herding and hunting. The plateau or high veld was free of the tsetse fly and thus conducive to raising cattle. Inadequate and irregular rainfall made for small settlements which usually did not exceed several hundred inhabitants.

The sources available to describe the southern Sotho in the late eighteenth century are very limited. The basic corporate unit was the lineage, which usually occupied one section of the village and possessed a courtyard for the arbitration of disputes. The village chief came from the dominant lineage and might also have jurisdiction over some smaller settlements. He exercised a limited military, judicial and religious authority over his subjects. He received a portion of the spoils from raids, and payments for settling problems that could not be resolved at the lineage level. Typically, he accumulated wealth in cattle and entrusted portions of his herd to less fortunate

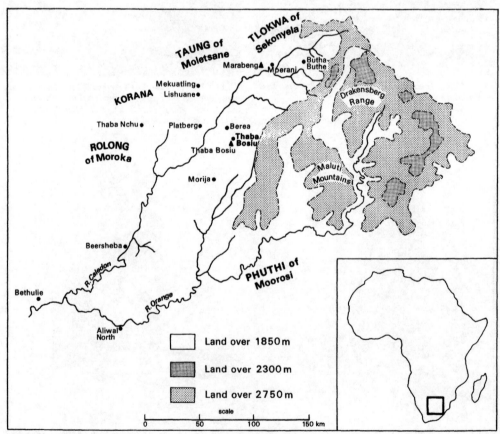

MAP 2.1. Lesotho c. 1840.

villagers, who became his clients. The chief played an important role in religious ceremonies by appealing to his ancestors or bringing in specialists in divining or herbal preparations. The rituals were especially intended to ensure adequate rainfall and harvests. In all of these functions the headman was obliged to work in close consultation with the lineage elders and to convene assemblies in which all the men of the village could subject him to criticism.

The chief was also responsible for overseeing the process of initiation which was critical to social cohesion and the transmission of culture. In the boys' case, he assembled the candidates when one of his sons reached the age of 15 to 20. He named the teachers who conducted the rigorous instruction during several months of seclusion. Circumcision was the most important single event of the period. The chief's son became the head of the initiation group and built his adult career upon the strong bonds forged with his age-mates. In their ranks he found companions, advisers and supporters for his quest to become chief.

As long as the southern Sotho population remained small in relation to the land, unsuccessful candidates for chieftaincy and others seeking autonomy could find space to start a new village. This was the situation in the early nineteenth century when the region felt the impact of the *Mfecane*—the 'explosion' of the northern Nguni which hurled bands of warriors and refugees on to the high veld.

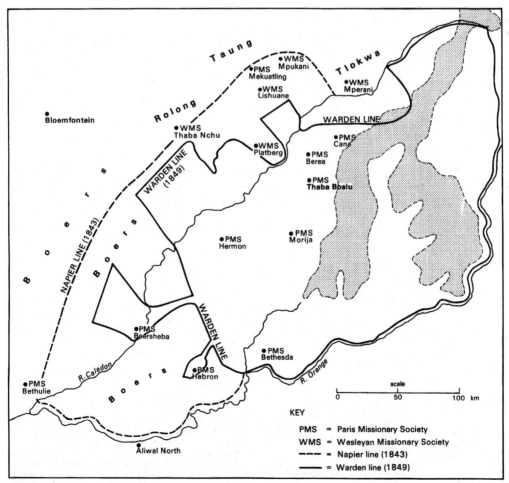

MAP 2.2. Lesotho and the Napier and Warden Lines

This chapter begins with the response of one man and his followers to the resulting disruption.

The tasks of historical reconstruction and interpretation are somewhat easier for Lesotho than for the Zulu state. One rarely finds the intention to distort of an Isaacs or the desire to embellish of a Bryant. Moreover, Lesotho possesses a continuous documentary record beginning in the 1830s, thanks to its constant interaction with the Boers and British and to the presence of sympathetic French missionaries. The perspective of Moshweshwe and his advisers appears in the letters, speeches and other testimony which they have left in this record, as well as in material published in the late nineteenth century by those Sotho who acquired literacy in English and their own language.

DOCUMENTARY NARRATIVE

The Time of Disruption

In the upper Caledon valley of the late 1780s a boy called Lepoqo was born to the first wife of a chief named Mokhachane. Lepoqo joined in the usual play and work of children and was initiated in the customary way. His success in cattle-raiding won him praise and a new name—Moshweshwe. At about the same time he paid a visit to a wise and well-known man named Mohlomi. These events are described below by the Rev. D. F. Ellenberger,

MAP 2.3   Lesotho under British rule

a French missionary who collected southern Sotho traditions in the late nineteenth century. Like Bryant in his work among the Zulu, Ellenberger rarely identified the names and social position of his informants.

DOCUMENT 1
'The heart is the medicine'

D. F. Ellenberger, compiler, and J. C. MacGregor, translator from the original French, *The History of the Basuto: Ancient and Modern* (1912), pp. 106–107.

It was in these humble surroundings that a son was born to Mokhachane. The child was called Lepoqo when it was born, but became known to fame by the name of Moshesh, a name which was given to him later on, as will be described in its place. Lepoqo grew up there at Menkhoaneng, in his father's village, and in those days few could have foreseen the great rôle he was destined to play in the history of his country. He was, however, bright and intelligent, and of a powerful physique, and soon began to show his superiority over the other lads of his age.

He was circumcised rather later than the usual age for undergoing the rite, possibly because no feast and function could take place during the great famine of Sekoboto, which afflicted the land in 1803. Anyhow, it was after this famine that the young man was circumcised at Malaoaneng, at the age of about eighteen years.

When he came out of the lodge, his grandfather Peete took him to see Mohlomi, who at that time was very old. The famous son of Monyane received him with benevolence, blessed him after their manner by brushing his forehead against his own, and, detaching one of his own long earrings, fastened it in the ear of the youth, saying, *'Ke lesala la muso'* ('It is the sign of power'). He also presented him with an ox, a shield, and a spear, and even had a beast slaughtered for him.

Such a reception accorded by a man of Mohlomi's standing to the son of a man of such small account as Mokhachane was very curious, and perhaps it was that which gave the young Lepoqo the hardihood to ask the old chief what medicine he had used which enabled him to acquire the position which belonged of right to his elder brother Nkopane; thinking, no doubt, to acquire hints for his own guidance in future. But Mohlomi answered and said, *'Motse ha o na sehlare: sehlare, ke pelo'.* ('Power is not acquired by medicine: the heart is the medicine').

When he got home, Lepoqo began to distinguish himself. He lifted the cattle of a very important man of the name of Ramonaheng with so much skill and address that the following *lithoko* ('praises') were composed about him: *'Ke eena Moshueshue, Moshaila oa ha Kali, lebeola: o beotse Ramonaheng litelu.'* The name *Moshueshue* is a rhetorical figure in which the sound corresponds with the thing spoken of—an onomatopeia—in this case the sound is made by a scraping instrument, such as a razor or knife in cutting the hair or the beard; *Moshaila* is an abbreviation of *Moshuashuaila* ('a scraping instrument'); *lebeola* is a barber. So that the *lithoko* may be translated in this manner, the word *Moshueshue* meaning to convey the sound made by the operation of shaving: 'The barber of Kali has shorn with his razor the beard of Ramonaheng'—*i.e.* he has swept off his cattle.

From that time forward Lepoqo came to be called Moshueshue, which in English has become abbreviated into Moshesh, by which name we shall henceforth call him, though he had other names as well.

In about 1820 Moshweshwe left his father's village and established his own at Butha-Buthe mountain. The area was dominated by another group of southern Sotho, the Tlokwa of Manthatisi and her son Sekonyela (see Chapter One, Documents 35 and 36). Soon thereafter three groups of Nguni, spun off from the *Mfecane* and led by Mpangazita, Matiwane and Mzilikazi (for Mzilikazi see Chapter One, Document 15), invaded the high veld. The Tlokwa bore the brunt of the first onslaughts and soon turned to plundering others. The results were catastrophic.

DOCUMENT 2
'Butha-Buthe'

An account of the struggle between Moshweshwe and the Tlokwa. T. Arbousset, *A Narrative of an Exploratory Tour to the Northeast of the Colony of the Cape of Good Hope* (1852), pp. 85–6. (First published in French in 1846.) Arbousset was from the Paris Evangelical Missionary Society (PEMS) and arrived in Lesotho in 1833. He wrote this work in 1836.

NOTES FOR READING Buta-Bute = Butha-Buthe; Thaba-Bosio = Thaba Bosiu, the next settlement and eventual capital of Moshweshwe.

Notwithstanding the advantages of its position, Buta-Bute is one of the most sadly celebrated towns in the country of the Basutos, for in that town they sustained, in 1823 and 1824, against the queen of the Mantetis, two sieges, the recollection of which still makes them cower with terror. Mokhachane, it is said, lived in peace and abundance at Leinehuaning, near the sources of the Tlotse, on the spot which had seen the birth of himself, his children, and his grand-children. One of these, Moshesh, was the first who left his father to go and found Buta-Bute. He had scarcely been gone two years when he was attacked, almost unexpectedly, by a hostile horde with a woman at their head. Moshesh, and his Basutos, were sacked, pillaged, and ruined. They went afterwards to settle at Thaba-Bosio, which became the capital of their kingdom.

These wars, the principal events of which we may relate, were very destructive. The recollection of them is by no means effaced from the minds of the natives; and the subjects of Sekoniela, in their daily dealings with those of Moshesh, continually entreat them to forget the atrocities of Buta-Bute. The two nations are still objects of mutual defiance and dread.

DOCUMENT 3
'The trace of it will never be effaced'

An account of the invasions of southern Sotho country. Eugene Casalis, *The Basutos* (1861), pp. 16–17. (First published in French in 1859.) Like Arbousset, Casalis came from the PEMS and arrived in Lesotho in 1833.

NOTES FOR READING Natal = northern Nguniland; Moselikatsi = Mzilikazi; Mateoane = Matiwane; Pakalita = Mpangazita; Fal = Vaal River; Mantatis = another name for Tlokwa, derived from name of Sekonyela's mother.

This state of things lasted until the year 1820; Moshesh was then living at his native place, to the north of Thaba-Bosio, and at a distance of two days' journey from that town. The green pastures of Butabute, and the steep hills where the son of Mokhachane hunted the elk and the wild boar with his companions, are still celebrated in the national songs of these tribes. At a moment when it was least expected, these favourite sports were suddenly interrupted by a disastrous invasion from Natal, whence we have already seen issue the terrible Moselekatsi. The people of this country were groaning under an iron yoke. Chaka, a chief as clever as he was cruel, had subdued them, and held them in subjection, by putting to death, without mercy, any one who would not submit to his authority. One of the most influential vassals of this despot, Mateoane by name, weary of this tyranny, secretly quitted the country, leading with him some thousands of warriors devoted to his person. On his route he met Pakalita, chief of the Fingoes, whom, after several combats, he put to flight. Pakalita, hotly pursued, crossed the chain of the Malutis, and fell upon the Mantatis, whom he found near the sources of the Fal. These latter, favoured by their knowledge of the localities, plunged into the mountain passes, advanced rapidly southward, and carried desolation into the peaceful valleys of Lesuto (as the Basutos call their country). From that time this land became the scene of continual slaughter. Mateoane, thinking himself at a safe distance from Chaka, settled on the banks of the Caledon. Pakalita also took up his abode in the same quarter. The two tribes did not cease to harass each other, and to make the Mantatis and the Basutos, who were always at war with each other, feel the terrible consequences of having them as such near neighbours. This state of things lasted for some years; the fields remained uncultivated, and the horrors of famine were added to those of war. Whole tribes were entirely ruined by this twofold scourge. The ties of kindred and friendship were broken, and were at last entirely forgotten. All gave themselves up to murder and to pillage. At length, associations of cannibals were formed in the mountains, who, belonging to no particular party, went everywhere in search of victims. We have frequently visited the caves where these wretches lived. The ground is thickly strewed with half-roasted skulls, shoulder-blades, and broken bones. Large red spots are still perceptible in the most retired parts of these dens, where the flesh was deposited;

the blood has penetrated so deep into the rock, that the trace of it will never be effaced.

In 1824 the pressure of the Tlokwa induced Moshweshwe to move his people to a less vulnerable location. They migrated fifty miles to the southwest and settled on a mesa-like mountain which could only be scaled at a few narrow passes. The new home, which they called Thaba Bosiu, fell within a region then controlled by the invader Matiwane. The next selection recounts Moshweshwe's efforts to provide security for his people.

DOCUMENT 4
'Submission to Chaka'

Ellenberger and MacGregor, *History*, pp. 170–2.

NOTES FOR READING   Basuto = the Sotho people; Amangwane = Ngwane, one of the Nguni confederations; Mofeli = Mopeli, a half-brother of Moshweshwe; A. Sekese = Azariel Sekese, Ellenberger's informant. It was customary for the patron to entrust cattle to his client.

On the one hand, he [Moshweshwe] was extending his rule and bringing more and more people under his influence; but on the other, he was sore let and hindered by Matuoane, who, after the death of Pakalita in 1825, became the paramount power in the country; and it was only by paying him large and frequent tribute that Moshesh was able to purchase his tolerance. Even Basuto, broken by war and starvation, in their eagerness to find a strong protector, joined Matuoane, and were marked with the distinguishing mark of the Amangwane—that is to say, a short piece of reed was thrust through the lobes of their ears, which served at once as an ornament and a receptacle for snuff. Every three months at least had Moshesh to pay his potentate several head of cattle, in order to be allowed to live. But his exactions did not stop there. He was always inventing pretexts whereby he could extract more and more cattle from Moshesh, by alleging imaginary grievances against him. The following is an instance of his methods. One of his minor chiefs, called Mateleka, incurred his displeasure by entering the house of one of his wives by night, and, fearing the consequences, fled. Matuoane sent the slayers after him to kill him, and they found him in the valley of the Thupa Kubu and slew him there; but Matuoane, hearing that they had not buried him properly, sent them back to do so. When they got there, they were unable to find the body, and Moshesh was accused of having stolen it, in order to make medicine of it. He denied all knowledge of the matter, suggesting that it had been taken by cannibals or eaten by wild beasts. But his denial availed him nothing, and he remained under the accusation; which after all, according to A. Sekese, was not without some element of truth, for Moshesh, hearing that Matuoane was about to attack him, had indeed made use of certain parts of the body for the purpose stated—a practice which was common enough among the Basuto in those days.

Again, about the time of the arrival of a certain Mokuena, Mphutlane, who came to join him from the north, Matuoane sent to Moshesh to say that 'he desired to eat a quail, 'which meant that Moshesh was to send him some cattle. Moshesh sent some, but the Matuoane said he was still an hungered; and a counsellor of his, Khabeko, said, 'How is this, chief, that thy vassal waxes fat on his cattle there on the mountain? Is this thing pleasing to thee? As for me, I think his cattle should all be taken.'

This of course was duly reported to Moshesh, and it did not add to his comfort; but he still persevered, though the demands on his resources became more frequent and exacting, and he began to feel very unsafe in the neighbourhood of such a tyrant. One of the wives of Matuoane, visiting Thaba Bosiu, was received by Moshesh with the utmost honour and hospitality. He gave her presents, put a collar of brass round her neck and bracelets on her arms, gave her red clay powder and perfume for her toilette; and, when she returned, presented her with a fine cow, 'in order,' he said, 'that thy children, my sister, may drink of my milk; and that thou, their mother, may make of the white cream of the milk an ointment wherewith to anoint thy hair, thy hands, and thy feet, after the manner of the daughters of chiefs.

But all these attentions were of no avail. Matuoane was really growing jealous of Moshesh's increasing power, and was only waiting for a suitable opportunity to put an end to this *Mosothoana* ('little Mosuto') who owned so many fine herds of stock.

Moshesh was too shrewd not to see how things were shaping; indeed, some of the many Basuto who were living with Matuoane kept him very well informed of what was going on in the court of the latter. So, driven thereto by a sense of the danger threatening him, Moshesh decided to place himself under the protection of a greater than Matuoane. He accordingly decided to tender his submission to Chaka, the terrible son of Senzagacona, and the only power of which Matuoane stood in awe. With this end in view he took council with his friend Mofeli, chief of the Mahlapo clan, as to what kind of presents would be most acceptable to Chaka. Mofeli suggested ostrich plumes, the feathers of the crane and the finch, and otter and jackal skins. Moshesh at once set about obtaining these commodities, giving cattle in exchange, and when a great quantity had been collected, he sent them to Chaka, by the hands of his faithful messenger, Khoho, and others, with a message of submission and a prayer to be taken 'under the wings' of the great Zulu chief.

The messengers, according to instructions, passed by Mofeli's place, in order that the latter might assist them with his advice, and send two of his men to introduce the mission to Chaka.

Chaka received the mission most favourably, and, addressing his people, said, 'To-day I have received as my subject a Mosuto called Moshesh, who dwells on a mountain. Never more shall I make war against him.' Addressing the messengers, he said, 'Say to Moshesh, that when he sees my armies, he must collect his flocks and herds at the foot of his mountain, and my people will pass them by.' Moreover, Chaka sent fifty head of cattle to Moshesh by the hands of

Khoho, and told him to return without delay to fetch a hundred more, which he had taken from Faku, and which he desired to present to Moshesh.

Shaka sent an expedition against Matiwane in 1827 and seriously reduced his fighting strength. After additional setbacks, including one at the hand of Moshweshwe, Matiwane returned to his original homeland, where he was eventually executed by Dingane. Freed from his clientship to the Nguni chief, Moshweshwe enlarged the number of his own clients. By lending cattle, encouraging settlement and cultivation, and reintegrating people who had resorted to cannibalism (Document 5), he strengthened and expanded his community. At the same time, he had to remain vigilant against attack. One came in 1829 from Sekonyela (Document 6) and exacerbated the enmity between the two chiefs. Another came in 1831 from Mzilikazi (Document 7).

DOCUMENT 5
'Living sepulchres'

Casalis, *Basutos*, pp. 18–19.

NOTES FOR READING   Caffraria = area east of Cape Colony where Matiwane was defeated by a British force.

During the height of the struggle he took refuge at the top of Thaba-Bosio, where the steep rocks secured him from being surprised by the enemy. By degrees his adversaries lost ground; Pakalita died; Mateoane carried his arms into Caffraria, and there sustained a defeat, from which he never recovered. Only the Mantatis now remained, and with them Moshesh endeavoured to come to terms. Two well-concerted expeditions had greatly increased the number of his flocks, so that at the end of the struggle his resources enabled him to rally around him those who were entirely destitute. Thousands of Basutos had taken refuge in the Cape Colony; peace alone was wanting to induce them to return. Moshesh, therefore, endeavoured to restore tranquillity; his first care was to suppress cannibalism. Those of his subjects who were innocent of this horrible practice were disposed to treat the guilty with rigour. Moshesh saw that this would incur all the horrors of a civil war, and tend to depopulate still more a land already almost destitute of inhabitants. He knew also that cannibalism, not being the result of national customs and traditions, must in reality be repugnant to those even who indulged in it. He therefore answered, that men-eaters were living sepulchres, and that one could not fight with sepulchres. These words were sufficient to rescue the wretches whom he wished to bring to repentance. They saw in the clemency of their chief an unhoped-for means of restoration to their former position, and resolved to avail themselves of it. From that time cannibalism was gradually discontinued. There are critical moments in the fate of nations, when a word suffices to introduce a new era.

DOCUMENT 6
'He was naturally very indignant'

Ellenberger and MacGregor, *History*, pp. 193–5.

NOTES FOR READING   'This raid' = raid for cattle against the Xhosa ('Amaxhosa'); Moorosi = leader of the Phuthi, a group of Nguni subjects of Moshweshwe; Letsie = oldest son of Moshweshwe; Motlokoa = one of the Tlokwa; Mamohato and Masekhonyana = wives of Moshweshwe; Batlokoa = the Tlokwa; Mophato = lodge used in the third and last phase of initiation; Azariel Sekese = Ellenberger's informant.

This raid was so satisfactory that a few months later—that is to say, in the beginning of 1829—Moshesh organised another, conducted also by Moorosi, who, from long practice, had become a past-master in the art. At this time Letsie, Mafa, Jobo, Makuai, Morai, Moholise, and Motintinyane, as well as many other lads, were in the circumcision lodge, and there were few left on Thaba Bosiu, save those who were in charge of this business, and some old men who were in charge of the women and children. Moshesh tried to induce Sekonyela to accompany him on the expedition, which he was undertaking in order to 'clothe his son,' as he put it. But Sekonyela declined, whereupon Moshesh sent his messenger, Khoho, to Sekonyela, to request him to supervise the circumcision lodge, as his eldest son was among the initiates, and this Sekonyela consented to do.

Now at this time there dwelt on Thaba Bosiu a Motlokoa called Mokakaïlane. He had fled, so he told Moshesh, from Sekonyela in consequence of an intrigue which he had with one of the chief's wives, but in reality he was a spy of Sekonyela's. Moshesh received him and even gave him a wife. When the expedition started, this worthy, having excused himself from joining it on the plea of sickness, immediately reported to Sekonyela the defenceless state of the place. 'The cattle have been left in the care of women,' he said; and Sekonyela at once left for Thaba Bosiu with an army. Before, however, he reached Thaba Bosiu, word of his approach came to Ratsiu, an uncle and counsellor of Moshesh. The Batlokoa came on in three parties, and at early dawn one of them, with Sekonyela at the head of it, scaled the mountain without any opposition, the traitor Mokakaïlane acting as guide. For greater freedom they had left their clothing at the foot of the mountain, at the spot where, later on, Masopha, son of Moshesh, had his village. Having reached the village of Maqhatseng, they killed an old man, Rataba by name, and took the cattle out of the kraals. They also captured many women, including Mamohato, the great wife of Moshesh, and Masekhonyana, and pillaged the houses. Old Mokhachane saved himself by pure luck, and a presence of mind which enabled him to profit by it. As he had no time for flight, and was physically unable to fly if he had it, he began by throwing all his household goods and medicines, bags, horns, etc., in the courtyard (*lelapa*) of his house, to give the appearance of a hurried departure. Then he hid himself inside the hut, so that when the Batlokoa entered the *lelapa*, and saw everything scattered about, they left, imagining that the place had already been looted and that there was nothing left worth taking. Another band of Batlokoa broke into the circumcision lodge, but the young initiates fled, taking with them the cows which they had been milking. After burning the Mophato, the Batlokoa tried to take these cows, but Letsie and the other initiates attacked them with such vehemence that the would-be raiders were fain to give it up.

Meanwhile Ratsiu had not been idle. As soon as he heard of the approach of the Batlokoa, he spread the alarm on all sides, and by this time those of Moshesh's people who did not live on the mountain had begun to arrive in considerable numbers, and had recaptured the cattle of Makhabane, of which a third band of Batlokoa had possessed themselves.

During this time Sekonyela was taking his ease in Moshesh's chair of state, without any idea of the counter-attack which had already begun. He was, however, suddenly recalled to his senses by the news that many of his warriors had been killed, and that the rest were fighting for their lives. Then, all too late, he hurried down the mountain by the path of Rafutho, causing the cattle and the captured women to be driven before him. At the spot where the mission-station now stands, he encountered the rescue party of Basuto under Ratsosane and Pelea, who, hearing that Sekonyela was carrying off their women, including the queen Mamohato, attacked him with such fury that the Batlokoa began to give way; whereupon the captive women threw themselves upon the ground in order to avoid being carried away in the rush. The Basuto drove the Batlokoa across the Phuthiatsana, right through the herds of captured cattle as far as Sefikeng. From there they returned with the cattle. Others came up with Mokakailane at the cave of Thupa Kubu and slew the traitor there.

Moshesh returned in due course from his raid on the Amaxosa with a fine lot of cattle, which were called '*Khomo-e-Monyatsana.*' He was naturally very indignant at what had taken place in his absence, and sent the following rebuke by the mouth of his messenger Khoho, together with four head of the captured cattle. 'It is a prey which has fallen to my spear, and, though I send it to thee, I marvel greatly that the *mophato* which I left in thy care has been burned. Whence came the fire that burned it? Moreover, I heard that some of thy people have been killed; how came they to be slain? I ask these things of thee, Sekonyela.' Sekonyela bent his head in shame, and answered never a word. (Narrative of Azariel Sekese.)

But although he had suffered no great damage and his raid had been entirely successful, the result of this incident was to cause Moshesh to refrain from distant expeditions for the time being. The Baphuthi, however, had no such anxieties, and continued their cattle-raids with great perseverance. Thus, some months later, Moorosi and Sepere raided the Tembu chief Maphasa. Just before delivering their attack at dawn, they encountered seven girls who had gone to draw water. These they murdered, lest they might alarm the village, and then delivered their attack. They were entirely successful, and returned with a large number of cattle. Later on Bushmen of Moorosi, being fired by his example, stole two horses from a farmer near Dordrecht. One of these Moorosi sent to Moshesh by the hand of Lipholo, with instructions to teach the chief how to ride it. It was the first horse that Moshesh ever owned, and he was delighted with it, though at first he was rather reluctant to trust himself on its back. He got over this, however, and having mounted awkwardly enough, maintained his balance by means of two long sticks which he held in either hand. Lipholo led the horse about gently, having no better bridle than a bit of olive wood for a bit, with reins of plaited grass. Moshesh, however, in due course became an excellent horseman.

DOCUMENT 7
'We will never attack him again'

Casalis, *Basutos*, pp. 22—4.

NOTES FOR READING   Korannas = Khoi raiders; Zulus = Ndebele of Mzilikazi.

Cannibalism was now nearly at an end; those who had never been guilty of it were becoming the stronger party. Moshesh was beginning to breathe again, when he was attacked by other enemies. These were, on one side, the terrible hosts of Moselekatsi, and on the other, the Korannas, well-mounted, and armed with muskets. The former came from the north, the latter from the west; and they arrived simultaneously, as if they had concerted to swallow up a people already weakened by a succession of misfortunes.

At a little distance from Thaba-Bosio is a charming little river, winding its way among willow-trees. On the borders of the stream the troops of Moselekatsi halted, to recover from the fatigues of a march of more than a hundred leagues. From the top of the mountain they might frequently be seen bathing, arranging their military ornaments, sharpening their javelins, and, towards evening, executing war-dances. The Basutos, on their side, did not remain idle. They carefully barricaded the breaches that time had made in their gigantic citadel. The assault was made simultaneously upon two opposite points, and was at first terrific. Nothing seemed able to arrest the rush of the enemy. Accustomed to victory, the Zulus advanced in serried ranks, not appearing to observe the masses of basalt, which came rolling down with a tremendous noise from the top of the mountain. But soon there was a general crush—an irresistible avalanche of stones, accompanied by a shower of javelins, sent back the assailants with more rapidity than they had advanced. The chiefs might then be seen rallying the fugitives; and snatching away the plumes with which their heads were decorated, and trampling them under foot in a rage, would lead their men again towards the formidable rampart. This desperate attempt succeeded no better than the former one. The blow was decisive. The next day the Zulus resumed their march, and returned home to their sovereign. At the moment of their departure a Mosuto, driving some fat oxen, stopped before the first rank, and gave them this message—'Moshesh salutes you. Supposing that hunger has brought you into this country, he sends you these cattle, that you may eat them on your way home.'

Some years after, being at Cape Town, I saw there some deputies from Moselekatsi. On asking them if they knew the chief of the Basutos, they replied quickly, 'Know him? yes! That is the man who, after having rolled down rocks on our heads, sent us oxen for food—we will never attack him again!' And they have kept their word.

In the following documents we quote from an article written by one of Moshweshwe's sons. Sekhonyana was born about 1828 to Masekhonyana (Document 6). He was baptized as Nehemiah, attended English schools and served his father as a letter-writer and negotiator. Here he reflects on the early years of the kingdom and provides a Sotho calendar of significant events described in this chapter.

DOCUMENT 8
'Not right to kill one man for another'

From Nehemiah Moshesh, 'A little light from Basutoland', *Cape Monthly Magazine* (Jan.–June 1880), pp. 221–33, 280–92.

NOTES FOR READING Thaba Bosigo = Thaba Bosiu; Langalibalele = chief of the Hlubi people of Natal; Viervoet = mountain from which Rolong fell in the battle of 1851 (see Document 22); *Fetcani = Mfecane*; Matuana = Matiwane; Mosilikatsi = Mzilikazi; Kafir = pejorative expression applied to Bantu-speaking Africans, derived from the Arabic for 'pagan'.

Moshesh never killed any one by his mere order, or in cold blood, and he only had four people executed by sentence of his court. One was a wife who had fought with another wife of her husband and smothered her in the dung of a kraal wet with rain. She was thrown off the precipice at Thaba Bosigo. There was great discussion in the council when this case was tried, in order to discover how the crime should be punished, as the general idea was that a fine should be inflicted. Some said, 'Let the husband be fined', but it was answered to this that he had done no wrong and had already been deprived of his wife. Others said, 'Let the parents of the murderess be fined', but to this it was objected that they had done no wrong, and at last it was decided that the murderess should herself pay the penalty with her life, as should she escape punishment, wives would be continually quarrelling, and there would be no peace. Two others were two Amahlubi, who refused to abide by a judgment of Langalibalele, between them and another about some picks, and were quarrelling with the other, refusing to submit to Moshesh's decision that they must be bound in that case by the judgment of their own chief in their own country. The other case was that of Makwalla, for the murder of Ramotapé after continued adultery with his wife. Moshesh argued that it was not right to kill one man for another, as it would end in slaughter of the tribe . . .

Kanyapa is the name of the snake which is believed to live in the rivers, and it was said to have been seen in Caledon River, where Mabeling, one of Letsie's men, was drowned when going to a hunt. That year is thus called Kanyapa.

'Kanyapa' was the year of a great rain. *Tihela* is the year of the battle of Viervoet, and means 'throwing off', because the Barolongs rushed over the precipice on that occasion. *Sikiti* is the year 1865, because war was carried on hand to hand when Wepener was killed. Sikiti means butting. *Mamutohani* was the year when my father was circumcised. Mamutohani was a disease among cattle, something like lung sickness. *Tlala ea makhabunyani*, meaning the famine of the beggars, applies to a time when from a drought there were no crops for two years. It was about four years before the Fetcani took place. *Fetcani* means fugitives and alludes to the disturbances caused by Matuana, who was about five years in Basutoland. *Kabukulane* means young locusts. It is applied to the year of Letsie's circumcision, as the young locusts destroyed the crops then. *Intoa ea Bakotu* means 'war with Korannas' (which lasted two years), and is applied to the year of Piet Witvoet's attack, with Makheta. *Intoa ea Mosilikatsi* means 'war with Mosilikatsi,' and is applied to the year of his attack upon Thaba Bosigo by his general Mkoko. *Senekan* is applied to year of Commandant Senekal's war, 1858. *Cathcart* is applied to year of General Cathcart's war. *Intoa ea Umlanjeni* is applied to the time of the Kafir war of 1850, and refers to the prophet Umlanjeni.

Expansion and Innovation

Moshweshwe's victory over the Ndebele in 1831 ended a decade of disruption and pushed his prestige to new heights. He was no longer a chief but the 'Great Chief' or king, who called on his subjects for labour, occasional tribute, and military service. His capital at Thaba Bosiu contained perhaps 2000 inhabitants, while Lesotho embraced perhaps 25 000—much larger than any political entity previously created by the southern Sotho.

He could not, however, let down his guard. The danger that had arisen in the east now came from another direction. The fundamental cause was the expansion of European settlements into the eastern part of today's Cape Province, a process described in Chapter One. The Boers or Afrikaners, descendants of the primarily Dutch colonists of the seventeenth century, moved steadily to the east and northeast, particularly after the British Government annexed the Cape Colony in 1806 and began imposing new laws on its white subjects. As the Boers advanced, they pushed others, particularly the Khoi and the Coloured people of mixed descent, back towards the Drakensberg range. Two of these groups, the Kora and Griqua, began raiding Lesotho villages in the late 1820s. Moshweshwe saw the necessity of adapting Sotho fighting techniques to the firearms and horses possessed by his enemies (see Document 6). By trade, purchase and seizure, he managed to acquire guns and mounts and began training part of his army in the new warfare.

At the same time Moshweshwe sought a more direct and substantial relationship with whites. Traders and Sotho refugees returning from the Cape Colony described the different European groups and their customs. When a

Griqua hunter told Moshweshwe about the work of missionaries in 1832, the king acted with dispatch.

DOCUMENT 9
'Tell the first you meet to hasten here'

Eugene Casalis, *My Life in Basutoland* (1889), pp. 137–8. (First published in French in 1882.) Casalis wrote this account in the 1880s from notes and his recollection of events.

NOTE FOR READING The 'he' of the first sentence is Adam Krotz, a Griqua hunter.

Having learned of our arrival at Philippolis, he came to seek us, and told us the following story: 'While I was carrying on my hunting at a place eight days' journey from here, a chief sent two men to beg me to visit him. I took with me as interpreter one of the natives of the country whom I had received on my farm. He conducted me to a mountain where this chief had fixed his residence, and who was, for this reason, called the Mountain Chief. His true name was Moshesh, son of Mokhatchané.

'He told me that for several years past he had been the victim of incessant attacks, by which three-quarters of his subjects had been destroyed or dispersed. He had asked me there to know if I could give him any good advice, if I could show him any means of securing peace for the country. I thought at once of the missionaries; I spoke to him about Moffat and about our own men. I tried to make him understand the services which such men could render him.

'The idea of having near him permanently wise men, friends of peace, disposed to do all in their power to aid him in his distress, pleased him greatly. He wanted to have some at once. "Do you know any?" said he to me, "who would be disposed to come?" I replied that such men sometimes came our way. "Oh, I beseech you, tell the first you meet to hasten here. I will give them the best possible welcome. I will do everything they advise me to do." I promised him not to forget his prayer.

'Shortly after my return home I found that he, in doubt whether I should have the means of fulfilling my promise, had sent me 200 cattle, in order that I might procure him in exchange at least one missionary. But they had been intercepted and captured *en route* by the Koranas.'

Krotz related Moshweshwe's request to three young French missionaries who had come to South Africa to preach the Gospel: Eugene Casalis (aged 20), Thomas Arbousset (aged 23) and Constant Gosselin (aged 33), members of the Paris Evangelical Missionary Society (PEMS) of the Reformed Church. They grasped the opportunity and arrived at Thaba Bosiu in June 1833. Moshweshwe welcomed them warmly, provided land for their mission (Morija), and sent his two oldest sons, Letsie and Molapo, to learn from them. In 1836 Casalis and his

bride established another station at the foot of Thaba Bosiu, and thereafter he maintained a close relationship with the king. The missionaries learned the Sotho language quickly. Although Gosselin had an 'artisan' vocation and very little education, Casalis and Arbousset possessed some scientific as well as theological training. They became acute observers of events and customs in Lesotho and have left an invaluable record. The next two extracts are from Casalis. In the first he gives impressions of his early contacts with the king. In the second, set a few years later, the missionary engages in far-reaching discussions with his host.

DOCUMENT 10
'My missionaries'

Casalis, *My Life*, pp. 216–18.

NOTE FOR READING Moriah = Morija.

Our labours of installation had not prevented us from going, from time to time, to visit Moshesh at Thaba-Bossiou, and to renewing to him our assurances of friendship and devotion. He received us with evident pleasure, and, spite of the disadvantages of a defective interpretation, he revealed himself more and more to us as a superior man, well meriting the title of *Mothou oa litaba*, 'man of wisdom', which his subjects gave him in one of their songs.

We thought at first he had the intention of coming to establish himself near us, but this illusion was soon dissipated. His plan, carefully thought out, was to allow us to found a new town at Moriah, with his sons and their subordinates, and so encourage his subjects to gradually descend from the heights to which they had retired during the wars, while he would continue himself to reside, with two or three thousand of his followers and his principal counsellors, on the natural fortress where he had been able, in the most critical moments, to defy his enemies. Thaba-Bossiou was thus to remain a rallying-point and a refuge if new troubles should break out.

As the resolution of the chief became more evident, we the more felt the necessity of making him frequent visits. The man who had brought us into the country had the first right to our instruction. We saw also that in order to familiarise ourselves with the customs, the ideas, and the manner of life of the Basutos, we needed from time to time to get away from Moriah. There we were at home, and were, as well as we were able, regulating our life in accordance with our own usages. At Thaba-Bossiou we were obliged, on the contrary, to live like the natives. As soon as the language of the country was sufficiently familiar to us, it was decided that every week one of us in turn should visit the metropolis. The chief strongly approved our resolve. 'Now', said he to us, 'you will be indeed my missionaries, and you shall see if you ever have any lack of auditors. Every time you come to teach us, I shall be there to get my people together, and to see that everybody listens to you with attention.

DOCUMENT 11
'His insatiable curiosity'

Casalis, *My Life*, pp. 219–27.

At night Moshesh made us seat ourselves by his hearth in the house of his chief wife. We supped with him and his children. He himself cut and placed before us slices of beef or of game, taking care to see that some one brought us a dish of curdled milk and a loaf of sorgho. The repast finished, he took great pleasure in repeating what we had said in public, and in asking explanations. It was thus that he discovered, to his great surprise, that our teaching was based on facts, or real history, and was not, as he had thought at first, composed of myths and allegories. 'You believe, then', said he to me one evening, pointing me to the stars, 'that in the midst of and beyond all these, there is an all-powerful Master, who has created all, and who is our Father? Our ancestors used, in fact, to speak of a Lord of heaven, and we still call these great shining spots (the Milky Way) you see up above, "the way of the gods"; but it seemed to us that the world must have existed for ever, except, however, men and animals, who, according to us, have had a beginning,—animals having come first, and men afterwards. But we did not know who gave them existence. We adored the spirits of our ancestors, and we asked of them rain, abundant harvests, good health, and a good reception amongst them after death.'

'You were in darkness, and we have brought you the light. All these visible things, and a multitude of others which we cannot see, have been created and are preserved by a Being all wise and all good, who is the God of us all, and who has made us to be born of one blood.'

This last assertion appeared incredible to the chief's advisers. 'What!' said the boldest, 'that can never be! You are white; we are black: how could we come from the same father?'

To which the chief replied without hesitation, 'Stupids! In my herds are white, red, and spotted cattle; are they not all cattle? do they not all come from the same stock, and belong to the same master?' This argument produced more impression among them than it would have done amongst us.

He was greatly struck when we enumerated the commandments of the decalogue. 'That', said he, 'is written in all our hearts. We did not know the God you announce to us, and we have no idea of the Sabbath; but in all the rest of your law we find nothing new. We knew it was very wicked to be ungrateful and disobedient to parents, to rob, to kill, to commit adultery, to covet the property of another, and to bear false witness.'

He admitted the existence of sin, and indeed went beyond our own statements as to the extent of the evil which reigned amongst men. On this point he was more than a pessimist. He explained evil as a kind of fatality, or at least the result of an incurable weakness. 'To do good', said he, 'is like rolling a rock to the top of a mountain; as to the evil, it comes about by itself: the rock rolls without effort to the bottom.'

The histories of the Old and New Testaments greatly interested him, and he continually made me repeat the more striking of them. The history of Joseph, and that of David in the first part of his life, threw him into veritable ecstacies. Amongst all the parables of the Sacred Book he gave the preference to that of the Prodigal Son. But we did not fail to observe that what struck him the most, as well as those of his subjects who followed our instructions with assiduity, was the person and work of Christ.

Knowing the white men only through us, they accorded them a high place as regards intelligence and virtue, but the life of Jesus seemed to them a superhuman ideal. They so clearly recognised in Him a man-God that they would not have believed the stories of the Evangelists if these had not insisted on His celestial origin and miraculous birth. It was as Redeemer that His mission most appealed to them, and in which they were most interested—a striking proof, surely, of the indestructibility of conscience in all lands. The practice of sacrifice was familiar to them: they had the habit of offering victims as a means of averting domestic or public calamities. From that to the idea that a man such as Jesus was had been able to save sinners by dying for them was to them an easy transition.

Beyond the religious question, which predominated in our interviews with the chief, his insatiable curiosity raised an infinity of others. He wished to know the origin and history of the different peoples whose names he heard us pronounce. It was a great stumbling-block to him when he learned that the nations which recognised Jesus Christ still loved war, and applied themselves to perfecting the military art. 'It was excusable in us', said he, 'who had no other models than wild beasts, but you who profess to be the children of Him who said, "Love your enemies", for you to take pleasure in fighting!'

All that we could say to him about the alleviations which Christianity had introduced, as, for instance, the care which was taken of the wounded, the absence of personal hatred in the heart of our soldiers, etc., only increased his stupefaction.

'Then you work this evil without anger, mixing wisdom with it! I can make nothing of it, except that war must be a rod which God does not choose to break, because He will make use of it still for the chastisement of men.'

There was no pretence in this indignation, for, generally speaking, Moshesh had the greatest repugnance to the shedding of blood, showing it often even to the detriment of his policy. He was not wanting in personal courage, but on almost all occasions when he had taken arms to resist the invader, he drew upon himself the blame of his subjects by the extreme facility with which he gave up the results of a definite success as soon as the enemy sued for peace. In his civil judgments he did not have recourse to capital punishment, even in cases of murder, saying that the execution would not resuscitate the victim, and that instead of one death there would be two. After hearing the history of Cain, he did not fail to observe to his counsellors that the Divine procedure on this occasion fully justified his own views. I confess I did not myself share them without restriction; but it is a fact, nevertheless, that under his *régime* cases of murder were very rare.

On many occasions I have had to repeat with reference to Moshesh the words, 'He who does not sufficiently hate vice, does not sufficiently love virtue.

At the same time it was impossible not to admire (especially when one compared him with other African chiefs) his good nature and his inexhaustible patience. I have seen him endure from some of the most scoundrelly of his subjects invectives and affronts which it would have been very difficult for me to digest. 'Let them alone', he would say, smiling, 'they are mere children.' And his dignity lost nothing by this, for never was chief more respected or more loved. The imbeciles of the country almost all came to seek his protection; they felt instinctively that with him they would be guarded against all ill-treatment, and that he would not allow them to die of hunger.

And polygamy, what did our brave chief think of this: he who was notoriously the greatest polygamist of the country? The subject often came up in our conversations. We never introduced it in a special or direct manner in our preaching, because we well knew that a reformation in this matter could only be the natural and spontaneous fruit of a cordial adoption of the great Christian principles. But Moshesh made no difficulty about discussing it with us.

'You are right', he would say; 'even with us there have been, in all time, men here and there who were content with one wife, and, far from blaming them, they have always been cited as models. Since we do not admit that one woman has the right to several husbands, one does not see why a man should have the right to several wives. And then if you knew what these women make us suffer by their quarrels, and the rivalry which they foment amongst our children!'

'As in Jacob's case, for example,' we would say.

'Precisely; ah! we recognised ourselves perfectly in that narrative when you recounted it. Would you believe it? With all my herds and my stocks of grain, there are days when I am in danger of dying of hunger because all my wives are sulking with me, sending me from one to the other, "until", say they, "you get to your favourite, who certainly ought to have a choice morsel for you!" But there, it is an affair of our manners and of our tastes. Our women age quickly, and then we cannot resist the temptation of taking younger ones. Amongst the older women there are some who become idle, and they are the first to advise us to take another wife, hoping to make a servant of her. For, as chiefs, it is a means of contracting alliances with the chiefs of other peoples, and this helps to maintain peace. And then we have a great many travellers and strangers who visit us. How could we lodge them or board them, if we had not several wives?'

'You could have domestics.'

'Domestics? What do you mean by that? I have warriors, but no domestics. These people, these young men you see around me, recognise my right to punish them if they refuse to obey when I order them to look after my herds, to carry a message, or to bear arms; but there is not one of them who would not laugh at me if I wished them to draw my water, grind my corn, or sweep my cabin. Ah! polygamy;—you are attacking there a strong citadel: I greatly fear you will not be able to shake it, at least in our time. Perhaps our children will be in a better position. Those whom you call the patriarchs were polygamists, you have told us; and it took a long time to get the white men from whom you are descended to content themselves with one wife.'

'No, it did not take long after the coming of Christ; and it is the Word of Christ that we have brought to you, not that of the patriarchs.'

'Very good', said the chief, with a laugh. 'We will talk of this again. It is certainly annoying there should be this difference between you and us. Without that we should soon be Christians.'

Although the missionaries never succeeded in converting Moshweshwe, they did make considerable progress in creating a significant Christian community in Lesotho. The king allowed several of his wives, brothers and sons to join the community. He also made several fundamental changes in Sotho institutions around 1840, when missionary influence was at its height. While he held firm on the customs of polygyny and clientship, Moshweshwe suspended the initiation rites for those under his direct control. Many of his sons did not receive the customary introduction to adult life. He condemned the execution of persons charged with witchcraft, took a position in favour of Christian burial (Document 12) and granted divorces to two of his wives who had converted (Document 13).

DOCUMENT 12
'Would you wish to be buried alone?'

From the entry in James Backhouse's narrative for 11 July 1839. James Backhouse, *A Narrative of a Visit to the Mauritius and South Africa* (1844), pp. 373–6. Backhouse was an English Quaker who visited South Africa in 1838–40.

NOTE FOR READING   Mocatchani = father of Moshweshwe.

11th. In the course of last night, one of the wives of Moshesh, having eluded the vigilance of a person deputed to watch her, threw herself from the cliff of Thaba Bossiou, in a fit of despondency, under which she had been labouring for some time, and which was probably increased by the recent loss of a baby, and the fever of the measles, under which she was suffering. This circumstance prevented the Chief and his people assembling as he had wished, to ask us questions on various subjects, and to receive our answers. The Chief was greatly distressed by the occurrence, the woman having been a favourite wife. Thomas Arbousset visited Moshesh in the morning, on his return to Morija, and it was agreed that we would call upon him in the afternoon; but he sent a message, at an early hour, requesting Eugene Cassalis and ourselves to go to him immediately, for the relatives of the woman were determined to have her buried according to their heathen rites, and he was opposing them. The power of Moshesh was sufficient to enable him to act arbitrarily, but his wisdom led him to prefer overcoming their opposition by argument. Their custom was, to inter the family of the Chief in a cattle-kraal, and to assemble their cattle and slay one of the oxen for a sort of offering and feast.

On arriving upon the mountain, we found a large herd of cattle collected in idolatrous reverence of the deceased. The people had tied the body of the woman, so as to bring her into a sitting posture, and had broken down a place in the wall of one of the cattle-kraals, in which they were preparing for her interment. The Chief, in his undress, a karross, etc. was holding a strong argument with them, on the superior advantages of the mode of burial adopted by Christians. These burials, he said, were seasons of instruction, as he had himself witnessed two days previously, at the interment of a child of Eugene Cassalis, and in them, idolatrous rites to the deceased, which were offensive to God, were avoided. Eugene Cassalis took part in the argument, and when they had concluded, I made a few remarks upon the custom of different nations in regard to their dead, and the universal adoption of the practice of burying them decently in the earth, without heathen rites, wherever the Gospel was received in truth. Moshesh appealed to the social feelings of man, saying, 'When a child is born, it clings around its mother's neck; when it is older, it seeks playmates of its own age; when grown to manhood, man seeks association with his fellow-men; and which of you, even in death, would wish to be buried alone?' No one had previously been buried in the kraal chosen for the interment of the deceased, nor was there a prospect that another would be buried by her side: but about two weeks previously, one of the people of the station applied to Moshesh, for leave to bury a deceased relative according to Christian practice. The chief gave consent, and the woman was interred in a piece of ground, selected for a cemetery, on the top of the mountain, and it was by her side, that the Chief wished that his wife's remains should be buried.

Mocatchani was greatly incensed at this departure from the customs of the nation: he sent several messages to Moshesh, desiring to have the man put to death, who had infringed upon them by burying his wife according to christian practice. When the Chief had concluded his argument, he challenged those who had anything to object, to come forward. Some of them said, they would do so when the Missionary had withdrawn. To this he replied, that to attack a man when his back was turned, was a cowardly practice, and in itself an acknowledgment that he was too powerful to be met to the face; that if they had any better arguments than the Missionary or himself had brought forward, they were prepared to hear and admit them; but if not, he would have his own way; he said also, that he was not himself a converted man; that he had long tried to resist the truths spoken by the Missionaries, but he was convinced, and he could no longer stand against them. He then made a short pause, and there was no answer. He therefore requested Eugene Cassalis to send C. Gosselin, a pious artisan, to prepare a grave. Some of the objectors said, that if Moshesh thus broke through their customs, he should not be their Chief; but threats of this sort he disregarded, well knowing that his people were too dependent upon him to forsake him. For

in one of the wars, in which they were perpetually engaged, for many years before the Missionaries came among them, Moshesh proposed that the flocks and herds of the tribes should be collected, and defended, upon one of the mountains. At that period, his father was in power, and the people declined joining in his plan, thinking they could defend their own cattle, in which they proved mistaken. Moshesh obtained the assistance of such persons as had no cattle, and saved his, and the other people became dependent upon him for milk, which constitutes a principal article of their food. He afterwards lent them cows, but the increase was his; and his stock of milk-cows now amounted to about 20 000; they were dispersed through the numerous villages of his extensive and populous country. When C. Gosselin was preparing to leave, and Moshesh and several of the people were looking round, Mocatchani came up, and inquired how they meant to bury him when he died; Moshesh replied, in the same manner in which they were going to bury his own wife; and he added, that he wished also to be so buried himself, and desired the people to observe how Gosselin made the grave, that in case he died before them, they might know how to bury him.

DOCUMENT 13
'Two of my wives have fallen into Christianity'

Our translation of excerpts from Casalis' journal of 23 April 1841, from the PEMS publication, *Journal des Missions Evangéliques* (JME), vol. XVI (1841), pp. 409–13.

NOTES FOR READING Abraham Ramaseatsane = counsellor of Moshweshwe, Christian and informant of Casalis; Letsie and Molapo = two oldest sons of Moshweshwe; Masekhonyana and Mamosebetsi = the king's two Christian wives; Basuto = the Sotho people.

Abraham Ramaseatsane just told me in detail everything that happened at the assembly. Apparently Letsie and Molapo and the Christian contingent at Morija were not convoked. On the chief's orders, immense containers of local beer circulated among those present before the opening of the session. When Abraham came, everyone looked his way. He was the only Christian present. All the other members of my Church either did not know about the meeting or were not able to go because of the unusual, almost furtive manner in which the convocation was made.

Trusting in God, our brother sat next to the chief, a place which his tribal rank accorded him. Moshesh had already started speaking. He said: 'My children have fallen into Christianity, and two of my wives as well; what can I do? I sense hesitation in myself and could easily soon fall the same way. Would that God had made this religion into something to drink! I would have all of you drink it. But we have not had missionaries. You are still ignorant and you constrain me, knowing that my body belongs to you and that a chief is the servant of his people. I have to inform you that Masekhonyana and Mamosebetsi have left me. They are no longer my wives in the way they were before, although their residence is still my responsibility. When the sowing season comes, you will gather as usual to cultivate the fields which I have assigned them.'

One of those present suddenly interrupted the chief: 'No, it must not be so! We know only one death which can separate wives from their husbands, the death which takes us all to the tomb. That death has already taken away Letsie's mother and several others whose milk has fed us. We submitted to those blows which no shield can defend against. But what is this new death, invented by whites, which takes away our wives while they are yet vigorous and young? We will have none of it! Moshesh, speak frankly. Either Masekhonyana and Mamosebetsi are still your wives, and we are ready to serve them as before, or they no longer belong to you and we no longer recognize them.'

The word of Jesus Christ', responded the chief, 'otherwise so beautiful, would upset me if it permitted these women to remarry. That would make me angry.' At this critical moment tempers flared and the rest of the meeting was a frightful display of disorder. Someone from Thaba Bosiu cried out for the death of Abraham: 'He's the one who took advantage of his chief's trust and dared join the new religion.' The assembly turned as one body toward the humble witness of Jesus Christ. A sinister hissing spread, then the rattling of shields created that mournful rumbling which for the Basuto is the signal for combat. One voice emerged above the others: 'I have a handsome herd', repeated this madman to make himself heard; 'it belongs to whomever will pierce the breast of the first person who dares to read the Christian book to these women who have lost their minds and left their chief' . . .

Moshesh pretended to be unaffected by it all. What a role to play at a critical moment! It is said, however, that after dismissing the assembly, he took his main vassals aside and told them; 'In spite of all this noisy protest, you must realize that it is useless to oppose the word of God—sooner or later it will triumph.'

. . . In several places where I am well known the people refused to welcome me. The word is that a verdict was rendered on the Gospel at the national assembly. It is clear to me, however, that this deplorable rejection owes more to ignorance than ill will. We are thought to be crafty conspirators, capable by our prayers, our books and songs, to change everything in the country. . .

A word on Moshesh's behaviour. I would only call it equivocal for now, letting events make it more clear to me with time. Here's the explanation which he gave me. I transcribe it without comment.

'The people I govern are crude, noisy, undisciplined; they utter violent things they don't mean. Scenes like these happen at all our assemblies, it's the custom. It is all meaningless unless the chief participates. The Basuto consider this freedom of speech as one of their rights. They would have suspected me of wanting to snatch it away if I had imposed silence on them. As for the beer, it is one of those pernicious habits that the Gospel will bring to an end. My people know that I never drink fermented alcohol, but they require it of me. You know yourself how it is called the nourishment of men. I ordered the

people to farm the fields of Masekhonyana and Mamosebetsi because they are distinguished wives who have given the tribe children who will one day have some authority, and they deserve to be taken care of. But I gave this order not as their husband. On this matter you know what we have decided between the two of us, and I will not go back on what I have signed. True, I said that the idea of remarriage causes me pain, but I did not say that with the idea of preventing what the Gospel allows. We are still in darkness on many matters, but I pray to God to enlighten me and convert me. I hope he will have mercy on me, then all will go well. For now, judge me by my acts and not on what I may be led to say.'

The relationship between Moshweshwe and the missionaries went beyond discussions of custom and change. The king utilized the PEMS representatives as agents of his own consolidation and expansion. Between 1833 and 1847 he supervised the location of nine mission stations in areas over which he was establishing control. Typically he placed a son, son-in-law, brother or close ally near the station. He correctly assumed that the missionaries would develop strong loyalties to Lesotho and support the kingdom against encroachments by Africans or other Europeans. One alliance between missionary station and indigenous African settlement developed across the Caledon on the northwestern frontier of the kingdom. The Taung community, led by Moletsane, had just emerged from a long troubled period occasioned by the Mfecane.

DOCUMENT 14
'With the consent of Moshesh'

An account of how Moletsane and his Taung community settled at Mekuatling. Casalis, *Basutos*, pp. 73–7.

NOTES FOR READING   The Barolong or Seleka-Rolong, another Sotho people, were enemies of the Taung (Bataungs'); Zulu = Ndebele of Mzilikazi; Beersheeba was another PEMS station, established in 1835.

To the north of the Caledon, toward the centre of the country comprised between that river and the Fal, another tribe, that had long been a prey to misfortune, awakened our sympathies. The *Bataungs* closely resembled the subjects of Moshesh in features, manners, and language, but they had a distinct government; their chief town was called Entikoa, and there resided their chief Makoana, and his nephew, Moletsane, an enterprising man, who enjoyed great renown among the warriors of that country.

The invasion of the Zulus of Natal had been no less disastrous to the Bataungs than to those dwelling on the banks of the Orange and Caledon. Moletsane finding himself ruined, invaded the territory of the Barolongs, and advanced to the banks of the Merikoa, conquering all that lay in his way. Sebetoane, chief of the Bapatsa, was in alliance with him, when an unexpected attack from Moselekatsi obliged them both to flee. Sebetoane continued his march northward, till he reached the shores of the Zambesi, where Livingstone found him enjoying great prosperity. Moletsane fled in an opposite direction, and for the time settled on the Fal, whence he contrived, by means of a few fortunate expeditions, to take vengeance for the defeat he had sustained. But he soon found that his adversary was too strong for him. The tyrant of the Zulus sent a formidable armed body against him, who committed dreadful slaughter among the Bataungs, and Moletsane, much enfeebled, withdrew to the Modder, where fresh disasters awaited him. The Griquas robbed him of almost everything still in his possession; and from that time this chief, whose name had been almost as famous as that of Moselekatsi, lived in oblivion on the confines in the land of his fathers; most of his subjects, wearied with reverses of every kind, had deserted him and sought refuge near the Caledon, in the mountains of the country of Moshesh. The privilege of labouring at the restoration of this unfortunate tribe was reserved for Mr. and Mrs. Daumas; they commenced the work about the time that Beersheba had reached that state of prosperity which has been described above.

Our new companion had sojourned for some time at this station to learn the language of the natives, and, accompanied by Mr. Arbousset, had visited the country of the Bataungs, and was convinced that it did not afford sufficient security to a people intimidated by a succession of disasters. With the consent of Moshesh, the seat of the new mission was placed at Mekuatling, in the northern part of the country belonging to this chief, where a great number of Bataungs were already to be found living among the Basutos, there being still room for some thousands more of inhabitants. Makoana was first invited to come and see the place which the Missionary had chosen.

Many eloquent speeches were made on this occasion, which we will take the liberty of submitting to the reader, as a specimen of African rhetoric. 'My lords', said the chief on his arrival, 'when you passed through Entikoa in the moon of May, and assured me that you intended to instruct me, I said to myself, "These white men may lie as well as ourselves", and I did not believe you, especially when I saw you depart soon afterwards. Now I think otherwise. This place shall be mine—it is good—I will remove to it with all my family.'— 'Makoana', answered the white men, whose veracity was thus acknowledged, 'our hearts are rejoiced to see you, for we are attached to you and your subjects. We acknowledge you as the eldest son of Taung, the king of the tribe of the Bataungs.'—'Ah!' interrupted the chief with emotion, 'every one knows that I am the son of Taung, but seeing me poor, my subjects no longer rally around me!'—'You live', continued the Missionaries, 'three days' journey from here, in a fertile country, it is true, abounding in game, but exposed to the attacks of numerous enemies. When we passed through your towns you said to us, "I will go and build on the river Tikuane, and live there in peace." We did not oblige you to speak thus; we believed you, and you see we are come ourselves to build near the river you mentioned; the place is already peopled with many of your subjects, who come daily

to seek a refuge from hunger and the attacks of their enemies. Look at the beautiful fields they have cleared! Is not this a spacious and fertile valley? In these mountains wood for fuel may be found in great abundance. This is, besides, a retired corner, sheltered from those unexpected attacks which are so formidable to men buried in sleep; from whichever side the enemy may come, we shall have warning of his approach. We are on the territory of King Moshesh, who wishes well to the Missionaries.' An old man, in the suite of Makoana, addressed the company in his turn, and ended with this exclamation, worthy of a counsellor of the shepherd-kings: 'I have carefully examined the country, and have seen that it is a land of rain and of corn. We will come and dwell here when we have got in the harvest. Why am I not a young man? I would be shepherd to the white men.'

Immediately after this important meeting heralds were sent in all directions to announce that the following day was called the day of God, and that the inhabitants of the country, old and young, were invited to prayer. The next day the natives assembled in great numbers, and listened with profound attention to some remarks on those words of the forerunner of Christ: 'Repent ye, for the kingdom of heaven is at hand.' By dint of attention and goodwill they managed to follow, without many digressions, the modulations of the voices of the Missionaries in singing a hymn, the first verse of which commenced with these words, 'Chaba tsotle tsa lefa se, li thla thla Sioneng' (All nations of the earth shall come to Sion).

These prophetic words were not to be realised concerning poor Makoana. In spite of the promises he had made in such fine language, he feared to lose a measure of his independence by approaching Moshesh, and preferred vegetating in a country almost uninhabited.

Moletsane, wiser than he, did not hesitate to accept the shelter offered to his tribe. He established himself near Mekuatling, with some thousands of Bataungs, amongst whom Mr. and Mrs. Daumas have, from that time, continued to propagate the cause of Christianity and civilisation.

The alliance between the missionaries and Moshwesh-we became very close in the 1840s. During that time Eugene Casalis served as the king's minister for 'foreign' or European affairs. They shared a deep concern about the growing pressures on Lesotho: the raids of Griqua and Kora, the steady movement of Boer farmers across the Orange River, and the rivalry of other Sotho like the Tlokwa (Documents 2 and 6) and the Rolong (Document 14). Against such pressure they sought the protection of the group of foreigners who seemed least hungry for land and most inclined to respect Lesotho's autonomy—the British. The British encouraged the missionary work of societies like the PEMS, controlled the Cape Colony Government and claimed jurisdiction over the Boers. Casalis put Moshweshwe in touch with George Napier, the British Governor of the Cape Colony. The result was a treaty of mutual respect which recognized a broad interpretation of Lesotho's boundaries and served as the basis for the king's land claims for the rest of his life.

DOCUMENT 15
'The Napier Treaty of 1843'

G. McC. Theal, ed., *The Basutoland Records*, 3 vols, Vol. I (1883), pp. 55–6.

NOTE FOR READING   Gariep = Orange River.

1. The chief of the Basutos engages to be the faithful friend and ally of the colony.

2. He engages to preserve order in his territory; to restrain and punish any attempt to violate the peace of the frontier of the colony by any people living within his country, or by any people from the interior who may attempt to pass through the territory for that purpose; and to seize and send back to the colonial authorities any criminals or fugitives from the colony.

3. The territory of the chief Moshesh is bounded from the west, from the junction of the Caledon with the Gariep rivers to the sources of those rivers near the Bouta Bouta; on the south, by the Gariep River, from the junction aforesaid; on the north, by a line extending from about 25 to 30 miles north of the Caledon River, excepting near to its source, and at its junction with the Gariep, where the lands of Bethulie and the territory of Sikonyela come close upon its northern bank.

4. He also engages to assist the colonial authorities in any enterprise which they may find it necessary to undertake for the recovery of property, or the apprehending of banditti, who, having been pursued from the colony, may have taken refuge in any part of the country under his jurisdiction.

5. And, generally, he engages to apprise the colonial authorities of any intended predatory or hostile attempt against the colony which may come to his knowledge, and to co-operate cordially, and in all good faith, with the Colonial Government, in preserving peace and extending civilisation among the native tribes.

In consequence of the above engagements, the Governor, upon his part, engages:–

To make the chief a present from the Colonial Treasury of not less than £75 annually, either in money or in arms and ammunition, as the chief may desire.

And in order to facilitate a due observance of these mutual engagements, and to secure the benefits which they are intended to afford to both parties, the Chief Moshesh will correspond direct with the Government on all subjects mutually concerning his territory and the colony; and he also engages to receive and protect any agent whom the Government, in course of time, may think necessary to appoint, at his residence, and confidentially communicate with such agent upon all matters concerning his territory and the colony.

Thus done at the Government House in Cape Town, this fifth day of October, in the year of our Lord One Thousand Eight Hundred and Forty-three.
                        (Signed)   George Napier, Governor.
Signed and sealed in our presence:
        (Signed)   John Montagu, Secretary to Government.
                    John Philip, D. D.
This done at Thaba Bosigo, on the thirteenth day of December, in the year of our Lord One Thousand Eight Hundred and Forty-three.
                        Mark X of Moshesh.

Conflict and Negotiation

In the late 1840s an expanding Lesotho came increasingly into conflict with its neighbours. The Napier Treaty provided no guaranties of protection and the Cape Colony Government could not effectively control the growing population on the other side of the Orange River. From Moshweshwe's vantage point, there were two major areas of concern. In the northwest he and his ally Moletsane (Document 14) faced a hostile array of predominantly Sotho settlements, led by Sekonyela of the Tlokwa, whose capital was Marabeng, and Moroka of the Rolong, whose headquarters was at Thaba Nchu. Moroka had close ties with the adjacent stations of the Wesleyan Missionary Society (WMS). These Methodists established a series of posts among Moshweshwe's enemies and fulfilled for them the same functions of protection and advocacy performed by the PEMS representatives for Lesotho. Moroka and the Methodists took strong exception to the territorial claims in the Napier Treaty.

DOCUMENT 16
'Never his vassals'

From a letter written by the Rev. W. Shaw, head of the Wesleyan Missions in South Africa, to H. Hudson, Acting Secretary to the Cape Colony Government. Theal, *Records*, I, pp. 57–9.

NOTES FOR READING   Moroko = Moroka; Mantati nation = the Tlokwa.

Platberg, Bechuana Country, 15th December, 1843.

Sir,—I have just learned from the Chiefs that the Colonial Government is now forming Treaties of Alliance with the Griquas under the Chief Adam Kok, and also with the Basutos under the Chief Moshesh.

As the terms of these Treaties are now become public, and the chiefs of the tribes connected with the Wesleyan Missions are aware of them, I am requested by Moroko, chief of the Barolongs, Peter Davids, chief of the Griquas, Carolus Baatje, chief of the Newlanders, and Gert Taaibosch, chief of the Korannas, to state that they are willing and anxious to enter into similar treaties with the British Government, and I am to express their earnest hope that in this respect the Government will afford to them the same powerful support and protection which by these treaties are now afforded to the Chiefs of the neighbouring Tribes.

It may be proper that I should state for the information of His Honour that the tribes enumerated above reside in a compact district of country situated on the north side of the Caledon River and extending from a branch of the Modder River upwards in the direction of the source of the Caledon near the great road that crosses the Drakensberg towards

Port Natal. These tribes have long been in close union with each other, having migrated together from the Vaal River to the country which they now occupy at a time when the country in which they now reside had been entirely depopulated by the native wars with the Zulu tribes, and in consequence of which the Chief Moshesh residing on the opposite bank of the Caledon River gladly entered into arrangements with them, recognizing their title to these lands, in consideration mainly of the protection which he hoped to receive from the residence of a powerful body of people friendly to him, and who had already become possessed of firearms, for at that time he was living in great fear from the hostility of the Zulus.

It is equally necessary that His Honour should be apprised that these tribes when combined are more powerful than Moshesh and the Basuto nation. For besides a very large body of native warriors who are armed with native weapons, these chiefs and their adherents can muster at least 2000 men who are already armed with muskets, in the use of which they are quite as expert as the Dutch Boers, and they have the means of mounting on horseback not less than 1500 men, while from the superior knowledge and intelligence of the Griquas and Newlanders, they are far more powerful for good or evil than the Basuto nation under Moshesh.

It is to be hoped therefore that the Government will extend the principle of forming Treaties with the Native Tribes to the Chiefs who have authorized and requested me to make this communication in their behalf, since already their jealousy is not unnaturally aroused that neighbouring Chiefs of no greater rank or power, and certainly possessing no more friendly feeling towards the British Government than themselves, should have been selected as the objects of this honour and benefit, while they seem to be entirely overlooked.

His Honour will remember that these chiefs have been recognized in a Proclamation issued last year by the Colonial Government, whereby the Emigrant Farmers were forbidden to disturb them or take possession of their lands, etc. And they likewise entered into an agreement of friendship, which has never been broken by any act of theirs, with Dr. A. Smith, who was authorized by Sir B. D'Urban, at that time Governor of the Colony, to form alliances of this nature with them, and from whom they received medals and staffs of office in testimony of their recognition by the Colonial Government as Chiefs in friendly alliance with us.

At the very urgent request of the Chiefs I am also to state to you, for the information of His Honour the Lieutenant Governor, that on one very material point His Excellency the Governor has been seriously misled by the person or persons who have described the boundaries of Moshesh's territory. In consequence of the incorrect information given to the Government on this point, the boundary, as now acknowledged in the Treaty just concluded, is so described as actually to include the *far greater and more valuable part of the territory now and for years past occupied by the Chiefs and Tribes in whose behalf I write, and include likewise a valuable portion of the country of the Mantati Nation under the Chief Sikonyela.*

These chiefs are at a loss to understand on what principle the Colonial Government has been induced, by a single stroke of the pen, to deprive them of their right to all that is valuable in the territory in which they are now actually residing. But being fully convinced of the justice and even benevolence of the British Government towards the Native Tribes, they willingly believe that this step is the result of erroneous information conveyed to Government through some channel with which they are unacquainted. Seeing a manifest disposition on the part of Government to protect them from the encroachments of the Emigrant Farmers, they cannot believe that anything but incorrect and misleading information could have induced His Excellency on the part of the British Government to consent to a treaty with Moshesh, which inflicts a far more ruinous stroke of injustice upon them than any they were ever likely to suffer from the Emigrant Farmers.

I am therefore to request that His Honour the Lieutenant Governor will have the kindness to take this very serious matter into early consideration, and convey with his own powerful recommendation, the prayer of the Chiefs to His Excellency,——that the Treaty with Moshesh *may not be finally ratified and confirmed, so far as refers to that portion of it which fixes the Boundaries,* until the Government can with greater precision, and with due regard to the rights of all the independent chiefs concerned, determine the limits of their several territories.

In consequence of His Honour's knowledge of the Tribes, acquired at Colesberg last year, I need hardly state that if the Government will only assume the principle *that the Territory as now occupied by the several chiefs is to be taken and regarded as their own,* then the question of boundaries to be recognized in these treaties will be settled without difficulty and cavil. But if the Colonial Government assume the right of settling *disputed* claims to land arising out of past occurrences among the native tribes by means of treaties with the Chiefs, the path to be trodden will be found most tortuous and thorny, and nothing but confusion and dissatisfaction can be the result. Indeed in the case now under discussion, should the Colonial Government confirm the Treaty as made with Moshesh, it requires very little acquaintance with the native tribes to foresee that much bad feeling will be generated betwixt Moshesh and these chiefs, and probably war and bloodshed will speedily follow. They were never his vassals, they do not even belong to his nation, they are governed by very different laws, and most of them do not even speak the same language,——it will therefore not surprise His Honour to learn that they declare they can never submit to become his subjects.

The second focus of concern was the west and southwest, where the Boer and Coloured population was steadily expanding. In the next document, Moshweshwe reflects on the problem of Boer settlement within Lesotho and the general question of land rights.

DOCUMENT 17
'Passers-by'

A letter from Moshweshwe to the Secretary of the Cape Colony Government. Theal, *Records*, I, pp. 85–6.

'The selling or renting of land', says he, 'has been hitherto a practice wholly unknown to us and I believe to all Bechuana nations. The subject has never yet been made a question for discussion or enquiry. Our system is that whenever people wish to establish themselves on unoccupied spots, they apply to the principal chief of the country for permission and he entrusts to the principal man among them the care of dividing the ground fit for cultivation. If the ground is not sufficient, a fresh application is made. As long as the people choose to remain on the spot it is considered as theirs; but whenever they move, another party may come and take possession, provided they previously make due application to the chief. I could not, according to the custom of my tribe, alienate any portion of my territory without the consent of my people. It would be on my part introducing an unprecedented practice. The people I govern look upon me as being entrusted with the preservation of their country, and I could not forfeit or cede my right to any part of it without being considered as having robbed the community. Besides, I would remark in a general way that the custom of the tribe forbids the chief to do anything important, without assembling the people and giving them the opportunity of expressing their opinion.

'I cannot, without exposing my answer to too great a delay, ascertain the exact number of the Boers now within my territory. It is considerable and certainly not under three hundred families. From their first appearance till now I have never ceased to warn them that I viewed them as passers-by, and although I did not refuse them temporary hospitality, I could never allow them any right of property. I have rented no place to them, and I have abstained from receiving any remuneration for the use they had of parts of the land, fearing lest such remuneration might be considered or construed into a purchase. Last year, finding that many disposed of places by sale among themselves, I published a notice to annul all such acts and to warn them (the Boers) more generally not to consider any part of my country as their own. Two copies of that document were sent to the Civil Commissioner of Colesberg, being for the information of the Government.

'Notwithstanding my protestations against it, many of the emigrants have transferred their supposed rights to others without my knowledge or consent. The Boers are, however, very cautious in concealing the papers of transfer which they make among themselves.'

In 1848 Governor Harry Smith of the Cape Colony took a bold step: the annexation of the entire area between the Orange and the Vaal Rivers as the Orange River Sovereignty. The British Resident in Bloemfontein (about a hundred miles west of Thaba Bosiu), Major Henry Warden, was given the responsibility for keeping peace among the competing African, European and Coloured communities. Warden had a small staff and military detachment and consequently relied on local white settlers and the British WMS missionaries to help him carry out his tasks.

In his effort to draw boundaries, Warden convened meetings to hear the rival claims. When he tried to settle the thorny issue of who controlled land, cattle and people in the northwest, he found little agreement. In Document

18 Moshweshwe argues against establishing any boundary lines.

DOCUMENT 18
'These boundary lines are bad things'

Proceedings of the second meeting of Moshweshwe, Sekonyela and their representative allies. Theal, *Records*, I, pp. 242–4.

NOTES FOR READING   Mantati = the Tlokwa people of Sekonyela; Molapo = second oldest son of Moshweshwe who controlled a post in northern Lesotho and came into frequent conflict with Sekonyela; Platberg = site of Coloured community and WMS station northwest of the Caledon.

15th June, 1849.

British Resident: Chiefs and you, headmen, I am glad to see you. As you all know, the day named for this meeting was Monday last, the 11th instant, but Moshesh and Molitsane did not appear; they kept us waiting here five days. I expect His Excellency will require these two chiefs to pay the additional expense caused by the long detention of eleven waggons with the troops.

Moshesh: I should have been here sooner but for my Missionary, Mr. Dyke, who refused to accompany me.

Molitsane: I was on the other side of the mountain with my people waiting for Moshesh.

British Resident: Molitsane, your Missionary, Mr. Daumas, was here on Monday, and he tells me that he advised you to attend on that day.

Molitsane: It is true, but I wished to accompany Moshesh.

British Resident: My letters to you will have explained the object of this meeting. I now again repeat that His Excellency commands that peace be restored to this part of the country. This quarrel between Moshesh and Sikonyela, and in which Molitsane has lately taken a part, has cost the lives of many of your people. Cattle, horses, and sheep have been carried off, and we now find the Mantati people so reduced, from the heavy losses they have had in cattle and sheep, that half the women and children of the tribe are without food. I have taken some pains to learn the number of cattle the Mantatis have lost, and I find it amounts to 11 570, besides sheep and goats. More than 300 Mantatis do not at this moment possess twenty head of cattle among them. I made a list of what each man has lost, and I will send it to the Governor. We will not go back into grievances, real and imaginary, between Moshesh and Sikonyela in years long past, but it may be well to remind them that they were parties to the agreement at Platberg in the month of February, 1846, wherein they bound themselves to live in peace and keep their people on the lands they then occupied until the boundary lines were made. It is well known that the Basuto people only are now to be found on lands they did not occupy two years ago. This spreading out of the Basutos and making new kraals near to Sikonyela's mountain brought on a quarrel between the Chiefs. Sikonyela warned the new comers to quit his country; they refused to do so, their huts were then destroyed, and the following day a Basuto commando was on the ground. Blood was shed, and collisions between the two tribes have continued to within a few days of our meeting here. I now ask the Basuto Chief whether he is ready to make peace with Sikonyela.

Moroko: I hope all of us will obey the Governor's commands. Government is our best friend, and we all need its support. Immediately I heard that Molitsane had taken many cattle from Sikonyela, I rode over to the Mission Station and recommended Molitsane to restore the cattle, but he would not listen to me. Now the time has come that he must do so, or quarrel with Government.

Moshesh: I wish to have peace with Sikonyela, but you want me to give up the cattle. All the chiefs know that it is our custom to distribute among the people all we take in war. How can I rob my people of cattle to give to the Mantatis?

Sikonyela: When you talk of peace, Moshesh, you mean war. You sent to me a man named April to ask if I desired peace. I replied, yes, and what followed? Your son Molapo attacked the Mission Station, killed two of my people, and carried off more than 1000 head of cattle.

British Resident: This attack on the school place will make His Excellency very angry. All the chiefs must have heard, and more particularly Moshesh, not only through his missionaries but his sons, who can read both English and Dutch, that missionary institutions are all under the special protection of the Queen of England, and this attack was made after Moshesh received my letter inviting him to this meeting.

Moshesh: When I heard what my son Molapo had done I was much grieved and ordered him to give back the cattle.

Sikonyela: Molapo only returned the missionary's cattle and two or three head belonging to the man who accompanied Mr. Daniels to Molapo's kraal.

British Resident: Moshesh, what say you to His Excellency's commands about peace?

Moshesh: I should like to talk alone with Sikonyela, but the other chiefs may be present if they wish.

Sikonyela: I would rather talk with you in the hearing of all the chiefs.

The chiefs were left to themselves for several hours, and at sunset Moshesh and Molitsane with their people, about 800, rode off to some neighbouring kraals for the night. The Chief Moroko informed me that Moshesh refused to give up any cattle, unless Sikonyela would agree to there being no line of boundary between the two tribes. Moshesh said, 'These boundary lines are bad things for all of us, and we do not want the British Government to interfere in such matters.' All the other chiefs, however, were of a different opinion, particularly Sikonyela, who declared that without a boundary there was no peace for the Mantatis.

Despite Moshweshwe's arguments, the Resident soon promulgated the 'Warden Line', a boundary which cut deeply into the Lesotho defined by the Napier Treaty (see maps). It removed a triangle of territory at the confluence of the Caledon and Orange Rivers, where a number of Boers had settled, and also excluded Moroka's Rolong

and Moletsane, the ally of Moshweshwe. The king was not represented at the final hearings; he only consented to the arrangement under pressure and subject to certain conditions.

DOCUMENT 19
'Do now as you have promised'

Moshweshwe's letter to Warden accepting the new boundary. Theal, *Records*, I, pp. 286–7.

NOTES FOR READING Letsie = oldest son of Moshweshwe; Beersheba and Hebron = settlements of PEMS missionaries and Lesotho subjects. For Moshweshwe's description of his predicament at this time, see Document 34.

Thaba Bosigo, 1st October, 1849.

Major Warden,—My son Letsie has brought to me your letter of the 20th ultimo. You mention in it that I have been 'so long regarded as a most faithful ally of the British Government.' This is a pleasing acknowledgment made to me. The proofs I have given to you of my fidelity are many, and to-day you will require another from me. To this also I consent, since you beg of me to accept the limit you have lately laid down for the Caledon district. I accept of it. I have respected the English Government since I have made a treaty with it, and at the present day I respect it still on account of that treaty.

On your part, Major, do now as you have promised my son Letsie and those who were with him at your meeting of the 25th ultimo at Riet Poort, viz.:

1st. That those of my people on the other side of the limit shall not be driven away from their pasturages, but any one of them who may choose to live under your rule shall be protected by British law, and that any who may prefer to leave will be allowed to sell their places and leave, but will not be driven away, for their villages amount to more than a hundred in number, and no one will contest that they have ever forfeited their lands. Those villages I refer to are included within the limits north of a line running from Commissie Drift to the junction of Cornet Spruit with the Orange, and are intermixed with twenty or twenty-five Dutch farms. I entreat the Government to take well care of that people, without there being any difference made between white and black, that they may not grieve and mourn, and that I be not brought into trouble on account of any of them.

2nd. That you will make proper limits for Beersheba and Hebron.

3rd. and lastly. That there will be an outlet or free space of at least two miles wide from these parts to those places.

Thus I have written and agreed to, subject to His Excellency's approval. I am,

Mark X of Moshesh

Witness: Paulus Matete.

Attached to this letter is a list of villages, comprising 98 names, and ending with 'and a few others'.

The Warden Line solved nothing. Sekonyela, Moroka and others continued to harass Moshweshwe's subjects. The king's sons, brothers and allies, some of whom lived outside the newly-defined Lesotho, responded in kind. In 1850 serious fighting broke out between Moroka and Moletsane.

DOCUMENT 20
'War began again'

From the testimony given to a British Commission in 1852 investigating the troubles within the Sovereignty. Theal, *Records*, I, pp. 536–9.

NOTES FOR READING Molapo served as Moshweshwe's representative and spokesman at the hearing; Moseme and the Baramokheli remained subjects of Moshweshwe; Archbell = WMS missionary; Maitland = Governor of Cape Colony after Napier; Taaibosch and Carolus Baatje = Kora and Griqua leaders on the northwestern side of the Caledon; Paulus Moperi = Mopeli, half-brother of Moshweshwe (see Document 4).

Molapo, in answer to a question from Major Hogge, states that Moseme is a Chief of the Baramokheli, a tribe of the Basutos, and under Moshesh. Moseme and his people acknowledged Moshesh as their Chief, and in 1833 resided at Thaba Nchu, before Moroko came into that country. At that time, before ever they saw a white man, they brought their tribute of lion skins and ostrich feathers, as was customary with tributaries. In 1833 Moroko and the Barolongs arrived at Thaba Nchu with Mr. Archbell, and were told by Moseme that Moshesh was their Chief, and that he had no power to allow them to settle there as was desired. Moroko sent two of his chief men to Moshesh, who gave him permission to settle at Thaba Nchu. Moseme's people at that time might number about 2000 on the mountain alone, and the total population might be 3 to 4000 souls. Moshesh went in person to Thaba Nchu and located Moroko, and received a number of cattle from Moroko, and told Moseme and Moroko to live together in peace. Moroko was shown where to build his town. The following year Moroko did not send any present of cattle to Moshesh, but sent some karosses. Such presents, whether made in cattle or other things, are an acknowledgment of superiority. Moroko at Touw Fontein claimed as far as the Caledon, and was angry with Molitsane for opposing his views. As soon as the British Government came in Moroko altered his manner towards Moshesh, and thought to make himself independent. *He was no longer as before.* Before the arrival of Sir P. Maitland the Barolongs had attacked Moshesh, whilst tributaries. Moroko went straight to Moshesh after an attack made by his people upon Moshesh's people across the Caledon, praying Moshesh not to take notice of it, that it was done without his knowledge entirely. Moshesh went to Thaba Nchu according to Moroko's request, and the matter was settled amicably. An attack was also made on one occasion by Moroko and Taaibosch against Sikonyela, and Moshesh protected Sikonyela's cattle. Moroko seems to have sought opportunity

through the British Government to acquire his independence, fearing some day or other to have to answer for these aggressions. When the Governor was at Winburg in January 1848 previous to declaring the Sovereignty, he did not talk so long with the Chief Moshesh as they have talked to-day. They were ready at that time to have talked as they have done to-day. When Mr. Casalis represented that as some Boers were living among the natives, disputes might be expected if they were not separated, Sir Harry exclaimed, 'not one shall be removed.' Moshesh fully comprehended that every man was to stay where he then was, and was perfectly satisfied with the Governor's declaration 'that no man should be removed.' Moshesh declared his submission to the Queen as his superior, that he was only a child under her, and hoped she would take care of him. Sir Harry said to Moshesh, 'you are Chief of your people under the Queen, and the Queen is over you as this house is over us.' The greatest difficulty is about the making of lines. Moshesh understood the Governor literally, and never expected that Lines would be made, but, as promised by His Excellency, that every one would be permitted to live where he lives. Having found subsequently that lines were made, and the original words of the Governor departed from, they submitted; but they have never been satisfied. They agreed to His Excellency's proposals, but these proposals have been departed from. Moshesh gave the line at the Koesberg to Sir P. Maitland with his whole heart.

Major Hogge stated that whatever might have been Moshesh's views in acknowledging Her Majesty's authority as paramount, he had subsequently consented to the line.

Molapo stated that Moshesh's consent was given; but it was given by him under compulsion and intimidation. Major Warden made first one Line, and then another, and would not hear a word said against the last. Major Warden threatened them with letting loose Taaibosch and Sikonyela upon them with their Commandos. Letsie, who was deputed by his father, consented, trusting that war would be put a stop to; but it was not so. Months afterwards war began again, and although Major Warden had promised to prevent it if Moshesh signed the Line, he did not do so. Letsie, who signed the Line for Moshesh, said, 'I am in the situation of a dog with a riem round his neck.' Moshesh performed what was required of him in signing the line, but Major Warden did not perform his part by keeping Taaibosch and Sikonyela quiet.

Major Hogge admitted that there were some reasons for dissatisfaction on the part of the Basutos, otherwise he could not have met them to-day; but that there was no justification for the length they had gone. He thought British interference in native quarrels was a mistaken policy, and said that he would recommend its discontinuance in the future.

Molapo stated that Major Hogge showed that he had well considered the state of the country, in expressing the opinion he did. Moroko, Taaibosch, and Carolus Baatje were all sitting just where Moshesh had allowed them to sit. Their petty squabbles were nothing. Sikonyela *is* a Chief, another man, and is sometimes at peace, sometimes at war with Moshesh. Moroko being placed in the position of the only ally of the Queen has made Moshesh very sorry, as he has been considered an enemy . . .

Molapo allowed that the attack of the Baramokheli upon

Moroko's posts in September 1850 was unfortunate; but was in some measure justified by the expedition against Molitsane, the ally of Moshesh, not having been communicated to him (Moshesh), and warning given him to remain quiet. But this not having been done, the people thought it was a general war over the country, and went and took Moroko's cattle. . .

Paulus Moperi stated that when the cattle of Moroko were taken in September 1850, knowing nothing of the causes of the war, and hearing the firing, they thought it was to be a general war, and knowing that Moroko's forces were out, they attacked his posts and took his cattle. That owing to the drought it was impossible to collect the cattle all at once and to return them as required by Major Warden, and the herds which were sent as instalments were sent back, some dying on the road, some getting lost. Moshesh wished Moroko to send his principal men into his country to seek the cattle, as his Chiefs would not give them up, but were concealing them. Moshesh did his best, but it was not easy to get the cattle. When Moshesh found that Moroko would not send anybody, Moshesh made a subscription, and got an instalment together, which together with the cattle found belonging to Moroko amounted to 2600.

Molapo states that Moroko's cattle that year were dying in hundreds by the drought. That Moroko refused the instalments because he wanted an excuse for going to war. That the cattle, owing to the drought, were not so good as could be wished; but if Moroko had really wished for peace he would have taken the instalments, and asked for further payment. The whole cause of the attack of Moroko's posts arose out of the circumstance of Major Warden's expedition being secret. No one knew what was going to be done. All was confusion. Molitsane having been very much plundered by Sikonyela, aided as he supposes by the Fingos, was the cause of his sons and people attacking Umpukani.

The situation in the southwest was also in turmoil. In February 1851 Resident Warden took the side of the Boers in the disputed triangle by attacking two Lesotho subjects: the Phuthi of Moorosi (see Document 6) and the Thembu. One contingent in Warden's force was led by Poshuli, the brother of the king who lived outside the recently drawn boundaries of the kingdom. The next document describes the conflict and indicates the difficulties Moshweshwe faced in controlling some members of his family.

DOCUMENT 21
'They do not know whom Poshuli acknowledges'

From testimony given to the 1852 Commission. Theal, *Records*, I pp. 541–2.

NOTES FOR READING Moperi = Mopeli, Moshweshwe's half-brother (see Documents 4 and 20); Umlanjeni = Mhlanjeni, a Xhosa diviner and prophet who urged the killing of yellow cattle as a means of purification and of driving the whites out of the country; Baillie = Englishman who led some Mfengu refugees in the attacks.

Moperi: With respect to the Tambookie case, an old Tambookie petty Chief, who had been a convict or prisoner somewhere for some act or crime, came about 1835 and settled near the Orange River by permission of Moshesh. He is now a very old man. He was the first man who ever brought them a gun. The man's name was Danster, and no complaint has ever been made against him or his people. They were settled in a good sowing place. Danster had killed a black and white cow of his own, and some boers came and said it was their cow which was killed. Some time afterwards some 20 boers came and accused Danster's people of having killed the yellow cows. Danster's people got frightened and fled with their cattle towards the Orange River. There was a universal belief that yellow cattle must be killed. When the boers saw them flying they pursued them, and one man, who had remained with the cattle when the others fled, fired upon the boers. The boers fired again and killed him. The other Tambookies then came back and fired, when one boer was killed and one wounded. They then retreated, and the Tambookies retained possession of their cattle. The boers then fled, and reported the case to Major Warden. There were about 40 Tambookies, some armed with guns, some with assagais. There were about 20 boers. Major Warden soon came into that part of the country. The Tambookies, when pursuing the boers, had taken Mr. Read's cattle and some property from his house. Before Major Warden came, Posuli informed his brother Moshesh of what had happened. Moshesh sent a message to Posuli, that as they knew nothing of the case he must sit still and do nothing. The first thing Moshesh heard afterwards was that Major Warden had come, forced Posuli to go with him, who had treacherously murdered three Tambookies whom he had inveigled to him. Major Warden then wrote to Moshesh that he had driven those Tambookies across the Orange River, and was about to cross in pursuit. He had taken all their cattle. Women and children had been taken and sold. Some of the latter were orphans, some had parents alive. Three chiefs were killed by Posuli, one son of Danster was killed in the fight. They know of nothing done by Danster beyond killing the yellow cattle. Moshesh's people killed no yellow cattle. Moshesh sent two men to see what was the meaning of the killing the yellow cattle, but they had to return home. They could not get so far as Umlanjeni. They have heard much about him through the White People, and wish to know if there is really such a man as Umlanjeni.

Major Hogge gave a short account of the rise of Umlanjeni, and how he obtained his influence. He asked whether these Tambookies have been driven away, or have they become robbers in Smithfield District?

Moperi states that on Moshesh receiving Major Warden's letter, he wrote immediately to say: 'be gentle; I will go with you, because there are some of my people (Morosi's people) there, and we will see who is wrong.' When Major Warden went across the Orange River, Morosi sent to ask what was wanted with him, and whether Moshesh was present; because if it was a question relating to the ground he could do nothing.' Mr. Cole, the messenger, said, 'if Morosi do not come tomorrow I will come to Morosi's kraal, he shall see me with his own eyes.' The people of Morosi turned out, and when Mr. Cole made his appearance near the kraal next morning, he was attacked and lost nine men. Mr. Cole retreated to Major Warden's force, which attacked Morosi's people and killed 8 men. Another engagement took place subsequently on the flats, when Major Donovan killed a number of Tambookies. Morosi was sitting still when he was attacked by Mr. Cole. He had sheltered the Tambookies. Those Tambookies who were attacked by Mr. Cole had never been engaged in the war in Kaffirland.

Major Hogge wished to know whether any of those Basutos who had been furnished with Land Certificates had sold them to any parties.

Moperi did not know anything about this.

Moperi states that Posuli is not at present with Moshesh. He went with Major Warden, and has not returned to Moshesh. They do not know whom he acknowledges. When Posuli was with Major Warden, Baillie's Fingos attacked him, and they cannot understand why one Englishman should attack another, for Posuli was then also an Englishman. On account of these attacks of Major Warden on Morosi, and these lines which separated Moshesh's subjects from him, the thieving took place, notwithstanding all he could do to prevent it. He has also returned all the cattle he could possibly find, although he is made responsible for the acts of people who were cut off from him. They (Moshesh's people) cannot think why Baillie should have attacked Posuli. They never knew why he did so. Various cattle thefts were made by Baillie's Fingos. There were 5 attacks by Baillie, of which one was upon the Missionary Station of Hebron. The natives believed that Baillie's Fingos were under the orders of Major Warden and paid by him, and the thefts committed by Moshesh's people were in reprisal.

The once amiable relations between the British Government and Lesotho continued to deteriorate, culminating in a battle in June 1851 when Moshweshwe's eldest son Letsie responded to an attack on Moletsane.

DOCUMENT 22
'Warden's War'

From the diary of Arbousset.
Robert C. Germond, compiler and translator, *Chronicles of Basutoland* (1967), pp. 189–92.

NOTES FOR READING   Arbousset was at the Morija station; see the reference to the battle of Viervoet in Document 8.

1st June
'An order is issued by the Bloemfontein authorities, directing the farmers to hold themselves in readiness for an attack against the Basuto.

'The local chiefs had simultaneously been summoned to a general assembly on the fourth of the month. It is to be held in Bloemfontein under the eyes of the British Resident, Major Warden, with the avowed object of inquiring into the causes of the present disturbances in the Orange River Sovereignty.

2nd June
'Moshoeshoe sends a representative armed with a letter in which he begs to declare that, in so far as his tribe is concerned in the disturbances of the Sovereignty, there can be no cause other than the limits which have been fixed in the very heart of his country . . . This was his last dispatch to the British Resident.

8th June
'The Major replies unfavourably and states his grievances. These concern the violation of the limits of which Moshoeshoe is accused, and acts of plunder by Basuto against the Boers and the natives, their neighbours.

21st June
'Major Warden proceeds to establish a camp at Platberg, the Wesleyan Station situated six to seven miles from Bosiu. His forces consist of a detachment of British infantry, another of Hottentot dragoons, a large party of Barolong from Thaba Nchu, Bastards of Philippolis and Platberg, a few Bahlaping of Bethulie, Korannas, Boers, Fingos, and a number of Batlokoa.

22nd June
'A letter from Major Warden invites Moshoeshoe to a conference at Platberg, but the chief does not reply.

23rd June
'Actuated by a spirit of conciliation and accompanied by a son of Moshoeshoe, Messrs. Casalis and Dyke visit the Resident in order to attempt, by every means at their disposal, but on their own private responsibility, to prevent a complete rupture and to spare the Sovereignty, the tribes, and the missions a war which they consider as highly detrimental to the true interests of all the parties involved.

24th June
'The brethren return from the camp to their station, their hearts moved with the sweet sense of having fulfilled their duty as ministers of peace, their consciences soothed and, moreover, authorized to encourage the chief to accept a private interview between himself and the Major on the Caledon, for the following day but one.

'Nevertheless, on the 25th, Mr. Warden writes to Moshoeshoe, enumerating his grievances and demanding of him the restitution at Platberg of six thousand head of cattle and three hundred horses on the 4th July next.

'This was his last communication with the chief and it reached Bosiu on the morning of the 29th.

25th June
'Throughout these last days bands of Basuto can be seen passing by, armed with rifles, assegais, war axes, and clubs. The majority were mounted on horses and heading for Kheme where Letsie has recently established his observation camp. On my arrival, I find the camp on the move, setting out for Mekoatleng, whither Major Warden has directed his march since early morning. The breaking up of the camp is a tide of voices which sound and echo, clash and interclash, in the confusion, the noise, the clatter of arms, the neighing of horses. . . The next moment, dead silence, self-bewildered.'

. . . .

'On June 28th, Major Warden marched his troops in our direction. Moletsane encamped on a high mountain opposite the station; he placed his footmen, his cattle, the women and children out of harm's way, and held himself in readiness with all those of his warriors who were mounted, numbering about fifteen hundred to two thousand.

'It was on the 30th June that Major Warden launched his forces against a section of Moshoeshoe's people who had pitched camp on our mountain. How can I describe our feelings when we heard the rumbling of cannon?'

. . . .

'On June 30th last, a considerable army corps, composed of Barolong under the command of chief Moroke, Korannas subject to the authority of Gert Taaibosch, various other allies, a Boer detachment, a few Cape Mounted Rifles, a company of English soldiers, trailing two cannons behind them, launched a simultaneous attack on the Bataung under chief Moletsane and the Baramokhele, subjects of Moshoeshoe, in the vicinity of the station of Mekoatleng. At the first shock, the Baramokhele were worsted, and all their cattle fell into the hands of the Barolong and the Korannas, but soon a large body of warriors, led by Moshoeshoe's eldest son, arrived on the battlefield, retrieved the captured cattle and cut to pieces a large number of Barolong and Korannas who had attempted to resist him. This last engagement took place on the summit of a mountain with perpendicular cliffs. The Basuto, after killing a large number of their adversaries on the plateau, drove the rest towards the edge of these precipices. There a desperate struggle ensued. The assegai, the battle axe, and the rifle wraught terrible havoc in the ranks of the Barolong and Korannas, who fought bravely. Those who did not fall under the blows of these arms, were hurled into the awful gaping abyss around them. At the same time the artillery, supported by the Cape Rifles and a considerable body of natives, was repelled by Moshoeshoe and forced to retire in great confusion towards the camp. On the following morning the British Resident began his retreat in the direction of Thaba Nchu.'

The defeat of Warden and the Rolong helped discredit the aggressive policies which he and the Cape Governor had pursued. An investigating commission (see Documents 20 and 21) came to the Orange River Sovereignty and reported its findings early in 1852.

DOCUMENT 23
'The Government has committed grave errors'

Assistant Commissioner Hogge's statement to Moshweshwe in February 1852. Germond, *Chronicles*, pp. 194–5.

NOTE FOR READING farmers = Boers.

'On the 22nd of the same month, a final conference is convened between Major Hogge and Moshoeshoe at Bolokoane, on this side of the Orange River, in the presence of a thousand Basuto and Tembus.

'The Major frankly acknowledges that, after hearing all the parties (to the dispute) and reading the various documents submitted to him, having fully considered and carefully weighed the whole evidence, they find that the Government has committed grave errors against the Basuto and the Bataung.

'He affirms that, on this account, the English will forthwith cease all hostilities;

'That the British Resident in Bloemfontein (Major Warden) has just been dismissed from his functions;

'That Captain Bailie, whose conduct in the Caledon District has been so inhuman, will immediately be placed under arrest;

'That the Tembus' children, about sixty in number, whom the Boers have reduced to slavery, will be restored to their parents;

'That the boundary of the Caledon Province which is so detrimental to the interests of the Basuto, will be reconsidered and altered;

'That there will no longer be limits between the various tribes;

'That the Government will cease to intervene in their disputes;

'That Chief Posholi, Moshoeshoe's younger brother, will henceforth be acknowledged as the latter's subject;

'That the same will apply to Chief Moorosi and the Tembus established in his vicinity and who profess allegiance to the Basuto king.

'On the other hand, His Excellency the Commissioner demands that the cattle and horses taken by the Basuto and the Barolong from the Boers who had remained faithful to the Government be restored within a fortnight;

'That a border be drawn between the farmers and the Basuto;

'That compensation be paid to the Barolong chief of Thaba Nchu for losses which he sustained at the hand of the Baramokhele and the Bataung before the affair of Kononyana, but deducting therefrom whatever he may since have retrieved by way of reprisals.

'Mr. Owen will remain for a time at Winburg with the mission, amongst other things, of ensuring that everything is decently carried out and duly concluded.

'The chiefs agree to the proposed arrangement.'

The Commission's findings vindicated Moshweshwe but did not resolve the fundamental problems. In 1852 British–Lesotho relations changed again for the worse. Moshweshwe had not returned the Boers' cattle, as he had promised (see Document 23). The new Governor, George Cathcart, issued an ultimatum to the king to deliver 10 000 cattle and 1000 horses within three days. Moshweshwe tried to explain his situation to Cathcart.

DOCUMENT 24
'Peace is like the rain'

Minutes of a discussion between Cathcart and Moshweshwe, held in December 1852. Theal, *Records*, I, pp. 618–19.

NOTE FOR READING   Owen was the other member of the 1852 Commission.

15th December, 1852.

The next day the chief himself came to talk. The ultimatum was repeated to him. He returned home the same afternoon, professing and promising to endeavour to collect the cattle within the given time. His sincerity was, however, doubtful.

The following is a minute of the conference which took place on the occasion:

Governor: I am glad to see you and to make your acquaintance.

Moshesh: I am glad to see the Governor, as since his arrival in this country I have been expecting a visit from him, which his letter to me in October has led me to expect.

Governor: I told you in that letter that I hoped to meet you in peace, and I still hope so, as I look to you as the great chief in this part.

Moshesh: I hope so too, for peace is like the rain which makes the grass grow, while war is like the wind which dries it up. You are right in looking to me, that is in accordance with the treaties.

Governor: I will not now talk much, but wish to know whether you received my message yesterday, in which I made the demand of cattle and horses. I have nothing to alter in that letter.

Moshesh: Do you mean the letter I received from Mr. Owen?

Governor: Yes.

Moshesh: I received the letter, but do not know where I shall get the cattle from. Am I to understand that the ten thousand head demanded are a fine imposed for the thefts committed by my people, in addition to the cattle stolen?

Governor: I demand but ten thousand head, though your people have stolen many more, and consider this a just award, which must be paid in three days.

Moshesh: Do the three days count from yesterday or to-day?

Governor: Today is the first of the three.

Moshesh: The time is short, and the cattle many. Will you not allow me six days to collect them?

Governor: You had time given you when Major Hogge and Mr. Owen made the first demand, and then promised to comply with it, but did not.

Moshesh: But I was not quite idle. Do not the papers in the Commissioners' hands show that I collected them?

Governor: They do, but not half of the number demanded.

Moshesh: That is true; but I have not now control enough over my people to induce them to comply with the demand, however anxious I may be to do so.

Governor: If you are not able to collect them, I must go and do it; and if any resistance be made it will then be war, and I shall not be satisfied with ten thousand head, but shall take all I can.

Moshesh: Do not talk of war, for, however anxious I may be to avoid it, you know that a dog when beaten will show his teeth.

Governor: It will therefore be better that you should give up the cattle than that I should go for them.

Moshesh: I wish for peace; but have the same difficulty with my people that you have in the colony. Your prisons are never empty, and I have thieves among my people.

Governor: I would then recommend you to catch the thieves, and bring them to me, and I will hang them.

Moshesh: I do not wish you to hang them, but to talk to them and give them advice. If you hang them they cannot talk.

Governor: If I hang them they cannot steal, and I am not going to talk any more. I have said that if you do not give up the cattle in three days I must come and take them.

Moshesh: I beg of you not to talk of war.

Governor: I have no more to say. I must either leave this in peace in three days, or go to Thaba Bosigo. I therefore advise you to go and collect the cattle as quickly as possible.

Moshesh: Do not talk of coming to Thaba Bosigo. If you do, I shall lay the blame on the Boers, from whom the cattle were stolen, and whom I requested to come and point out to me their cattle, that I might restore them. I will go at once and do my best, and perhaps God will help me.

After leaving His Excellency's tent, but before returning home, Moshesh sent to request that the day on which the interview took place might not count in the three. This request His Excellency acceded to; and on the 18th instant, the appointed day, Moshesh's son Nehemiah came in with three thousand five hundred head of cattle, which were received.

The 3500 cattle which the king gathered did not satisfy the Governor. Cathcart's men started rounding up cattle near Thaba Bosiu, whereupon the Lesotho forces counter-attacked and drove them back to the Caledon. Moshweshwe quickly dispatched a note to Cathcart, urging him to accept the cattle already offered. This helped the Governor save face and he withdrew. Lesotho marked the events as the 'year of Cathcart' (Document 8).

Cathcart's reports confirmed the findings of the 1851–52 Commission: effective rule of the Orange River Sovereignty would entail considerable expense. A budget-conscious British Government began making plans to withdraw in 1853. When Moshweshwe learned their intentions, he decided to consolidate his kingdom in the north by attacking the capital of his long-time antagonist Sekonyela.

DOCUMENT 25
'You will offer it to me as a stool'

Arbousset's account of the defeat of Sekonyela in October 1853. Germond, *Chronicles*, pp. 216–22.

NOTES FOR READING   Arbousset is writing to the PEMS headquarters; the Bushman's arrow refers to the deadly poisoned weapons of the San used in war and hunting.

'A political event has just occurred in this country concerning which I owe you a detailed account; I refer to the destruction of the Batlokoa nationality by the Basuto. Glancing through my *Relation*, you will doubtless have noticed that for the last thirty years, these two tribes have been very hostile to each other. The former having invaded the latter's territory at this period, forcibly deprived it thereof. Under the leadership of the Queen Mantati ('m'a-Nthatisi) and her son Sekonyela, they besieged Moshoeshoe in Boutaboute (Botha Bothe) for about two months and ultimately compelled him to migrate to Bosiu, where he has ever since remained. Another, less powerful but none the less famous chief, Abraham Khoabane, likewise found himself obliged to abandon the fine mountain of Mara-beng to the conqueror, and to seek refuge in the Maloti, whence he eventually proceeded to establish himself on our station of Berea.

'At this time the Batlokoa tribe may have numbered fourteen thousand souls; it revealed itself intrepid and courageous; to-day its insatiable and ferocious chief is a striking proof that audacity and ambition do not suffice for a man to found any-thing durable. He has always been a hard task master to his people and has forfeited their sympathy. He has never ceased to plague his neighbours, and not one of them has remained his ally or even his friend. Moshoeshoe, on the contrary, gentle and humane by nature, has seen his power grow from year to year, and he may be described to-day as stronger and, at the same time, more influential and wealthy than any other chief in Southern Africa.

'Last year in the month of May, he made his adversary feel the weight with which he could crush him and forced him to conclude a treaty of peace.

'We had hoped that, on either side, they would remain faith-ful and that we would at last enjoy greater tranquillity. We argued that Sekonyela had everything to lose by renewing hostilities; Moshoeshoe, on his side, had no inclination, had never had any, to destroy him. Nevertheless, it was not long before a Koranna named Gert Taaibosch hastened to Mara-beng from the banks of the Vaal, followed by a band of brigands no less irresponsible than himself. Their presence once more kindled the fire of revenge and ambition in the heart of the Batlokoa chief; he resumed his predatory incursions in Basuto territory and among the Bataung; for seven to eight months these were tolerated; but at last, yielding to necessity, Moshoeshoe mustered an army of ten to twelve thousand men and, on October 24th last, proceeded in the direction of Sekonyela's capital.

'"To what purpose am I thitherwards bent?" said he as he was about to depart, and, indicating the window of Mr. Casalis' drawing-room, added: "Were I to grasp a cudgel and to rain blows, right and left, on that, what beauty would there be in my deed! And how the wind and the rain would rush in through the wreckage which I would leave!" Never before had the son of Mokhachane seemed more interesting to me than in this moment of intimate struggle which, had it not, however, revealed itself in his features, he alone could describe. It must be understood, besides, that good Mosuto that he is, he had already taken every precaution which his personal credulity or that of his people could demand of a chief on the eve of battle. On the previous day, called upon to pronounce himself, a priest of war had solemnly declared (mistakenly by the way) that the divining bones revealed his enemy prostrate and dead, his

head turned to the setting sun. A witch of sorts who augured more correctly, had for her part declared to the chief: "Go, go sit on yonder rock (on the summit of the plateau of Marabeng); let Posholi (one of the chiefs) precede the army, a quiver bound to his brow, and let him open the combat by discharging an arrow at the mountain which you are to capture; it will be fought in stormy weather; your enemies will perish in deep waters." There remained nothing more for Moshoeshoe to do than to perform a last duty, namely to descend to his father, Mokhachane, whither he religiously betook himself. Once there, he shuts himself up with him in the seclusion of a hut, piously receiving the old man's words, is purified with his hands and forthwith, mounting his horse and accompanied by his escort, repairs to the camp at Sefikeng. This was on Tuesday, October 24th. For the details of the expedition I shall follow a man whom I consider to be as reliable as any other native of my acquaintance, and who barely moved from Moshoeshoe's side throughout the campaign. This is one Elia Mapike, a deacon of the church of Christ in Morija.

'"On the Wednesday", says he, "we reached Motlafouteng" where various general dispositions were taken. Well chosen spies proceeded thence in various directions. A short prayer service was held among the Christians. Heathens who attended it found the hymns so beautiful that they begged us to sing them over again for their own benefit and some of us did so in the light of a fire which was kept burning at the bivouac.

'"Early next morning the spies returned and delivered their report. Thereupon Moshoeshoe assembled his army and addressed it thus: 'My companions in arms! This is the combat you have so long demanded of me. Men of Lesotho, yonder is the limit which Sekonyela formerly imposed on us in our own country. Behold the waters of the Putiatsana; quench your thirst in these waters which the son of Mokocho ravished from us. God sees us from above and protects us. I have told the churches, I have told the representative of the English Queen in this country that I was about to avenge the insults of the Batlokoa. Had he not sworn his faith a year ago? He has broken his troth. Have I not spared his herds? He has taken mine. It is he who besieged us at Botha Bothe in days of yore. I wished to forgive him the ill he did us then; but he defied me to do him this good. I desired the land to resemble a two-horned ox, I wished it to have two chiefs. If the country had had only one, it would have been like a unicorn. Besides, hark, I bear a grudge, but not so much against the Batlokoa; seize me the Korannas, and you will have fought. To-morrow, brothers, you will have reconquered for me this lofty rock, on which the Batlokoa is complacently seated (Marabeng); you will offer it to me for a stool.' Here the army interrupts with loud hurrahs or, to be more exact, rends the air with a deafen-ing whistle and roars: 'Thou shalt sit, sit thou upon the rock, oh King!' The chief continues: 'The women and children shall be respected as if they were my own; you shall take them prisoners. You shall fight in silence, as do the men of Inkhosi Zulu, as do the soldiers of the English Queen, that the mouth of the muskets alone may speak and be the more sonorous. You shall pursue the enemy relentlessly, leaving his cattle behind you, without collecting them, for it is there that his darts would fall upon you. Is it not true that you killed one another at the battle of Kononyana (Mekoatleng) for failing to recognize each other? Take good care of your lives, let every one of you gather white chalk to-day, dilute it in his hand and daub his face with it. Letsie, my son, I have just borrowed yonder men, I commit them to you: this war is your own affair.' Thus concluded the chief. The troops followed his words with thunderous applause mingled with the beating of shields, and everyone returned to his bivouac."

'On that day the heavens were dark and overcast; an oppressive heat stifled the earth; seemingly of gloomier mien than the very Maloti, the clouds massed before a violent wind which blew from the east; thence issued a fearful tempest which shattered the silence and multiplied its terrors; the rain fell in torrents, the lightning flashed through the camp and again and again the thunder crashed in every direction. The more timorous spoke of evil omens; superstition moreover induced many to strip their bodies of every shiny object or anything of a whitish tinge.

'Moshoeshoe now assembled his council, on the summit of a mountain which offered a view of the greater part of the Batlokoa territory. There he fixed his plan of attack and explained it to his lieutenants in every detail. It would be simultaneous, and the plateau of Marabeng together with that of Joala Bogolou were to be taken by storm. "Tonight", quoth he to his brothers Posholi and Mohale, "you will proceed to the west to encircle the villages of Matio-a-Magolou. The booty which may fall into your hands is pre-awarded as your own and exclusive portion. As for me, I shall hide with my sons and the army corps on the southern flank, at such a distance from Marabeng and Joala Boholo as not to be discovered. Small bands, each of ten to fifteen herdsmen, will place themselves in ambush in the immediate vicinity of each locality and lie in wait until the enemy's cattle come out to graze. Then the companies stationed by Moletsane will pounce on their herds and seize them. The enemy will sally forth to recover them and will be fired upon. From the summit of Marabeng the Batlokoa and the Korannas will likewise hasten to the rescue in which event, finding the plateau but poorly defended, I will invest and capture it while, to the north, Maoutse will be attacked and, in the middle, the mountain of Joala Boholo."

'The night was bitterly cold; an exceedingly violent and icy wind blew from the south, in spite of which the order was not to light a single fire; those in ambush endeavoured to keep warm by huddling together with their mouths under their furs, while the others relied on a forced march to defy the cold.

'On the morning of Friday, October 28th, Moletsane attacks and puts everyone to flight. In the direction of Maoutse, Posholi and Mohale are equally successful. An express is dispatched post-haste and reaches headquarters to warn Moshoeshoe who immediately sets forth and storms Joala Boholo, the residence of Sekonyela's heir. The reputedly impregnable plateau of Marabeng is next surrounded. There is only one narrow entrance and it is made even narrower by a stone wall which the Batlokoa have rudely erected. Before this rampart Moshoeshoe finds a number of tentless wagons in which, armed with muskets, a party of Korannas have posted themselves, while the whole brow of the mountain is black with Batlokoa. Posholi, who precedes the army, discharges a Bushman's arrow, and the battle is on. The Korannas are first attacked, hard-pressed, compelled to retreat to the summit of

the plateau, an initial advantage which exalts the ardour of the assailants; they press on, despite a hail of bullets, of darts and of stones; they indent the cliffs, cling to the rocks and reach the summit... In another and no less precipitous, if lower sector, the Basuto climb on one another's backs and thus scale the mountain. After this second repulse, the enemy flee in every direction; Sekonyela himself steals away furtively, his people reach the bottom, but there the enemy riddle them with their shafts, drive them back mercilessly, forcing them to regain the summit of the plateau; large numbers are now stabbed to death and many prisoners are made; women and a few children tumble down the mountain top or are hurled therefrom by the attackers. Marabeng is taken; the enemy pursue the fugitives, many of whom escape under cover of a heavy rain; some only to conceal themselves in the waters of the Caledon where not a few are done to death.

'On the Saturday, Moshoeshoe visited Marabeng personally in order to inspect the town. He found no one there, with the exception of Sekonyela's maternal uncle, Letlala, who, presenting himself before the king addressed him thus: "My Lord, I am old, put me to death".—"Nay, my father", replied the conqueror, "we do not kill the aged; you shall live on."—"But life is too great a burden for me, my sons are now no more, destroy me too, I implore you.—"My Lord, I may not grant your request; have a nobler courage than to know how to die; live on!"'

'Returning to Joala Boholo, his headquarters, the chief issued orders for the care of the prisoners, but more especially the women and children.

'From Monday to the following Sabbath, the days of the week were filled with multifarious duties. The Boers flocked to Moshoeshoe who, good politician that he is, granted them leave to examine every head and to remove whatever might belong to them. He despatched Elia to the Wesleyan Mission of Oumparana (Mpharane) to protect it. Three looters had just broken into the residence of the missionary in his absence. They were arrested and punished. Wagons then arrived from a neighbouring station and removed the more valuable property from the parsonage, placing it in safe keeping. Several women and fifty-nine children who had fallen into the enemy's hands were released. Elia committed them to the care of a Batlokoa Christian and provided them with millet for their sustenance. "That", said he, "is all I took from the missionary's home with the exception of a little salt with which to cleanse the wounds of the injured."

'On the following Monday, Nguetsi, the chief of a neighbouring tribe, related to the Basuto, and who speak their language and follow their customs, was summoned. Its population is almost as numerous as the Batlokoa. Moshoeshoe assembled his troops and said: "Men of Lesotho, we are about to return to our homes; your respective chiefs will distribute your share of the spoil which they have received. I shall tarry until Sekonyela informs me of his hiding place and what he intends to do. His country reeks of destruction; let none occupy it. The Batlokoa survivors may remain to guard their corn. Nevertheless, their principal men will proceed to Bosiu to confer with me, or else despatch their representatives. The relatives of the women and children whom we are taking with us, will come and fetch them from me. Chief of the Bakolokue

(Oetsi) come hither!" Oetsi approached. "Levela and Matela, present yourselves!" They introduce themselves. Moshoeshoe thereupon bends a copper wire with which he encircles the principal Basuto chiefs of these quarters; next he brings Oetsi inside as well and then proceeds: "You shall all three remain united, even as your heads are within this ring; you shall abide as quiet as you are at present, but each at home, diligently tending your flocks and tilling your fields. When the harvest is over, we shall meet again here and then we shall settle all matters concerning the country which the war has just devastated."

'Thus did this expedition end. Since then, the Batlokoa have ceaselessly demanded asylum of the Basuto; some have remained behind. Prisoners depart daily to return to their homes, which, alas, are desolate and, for the most part, utterly destroyed. We have learned that Gert Taaibosch is dead; that the heir to the Batlokoa succession and other influential chiefs have likewise fallen in battle. As to Sekonyela, he has despatched three deputies to Bosiu, to offer his full and unconditional surrender and Moshoeshoe has granted him peace.'

The experience of the past several years had undermined Lesotho's confidence in British wisdom, integrity and respect for local custom. The citizens of the kingdom discerned that whites were advancing at the expense of blacks and they sympathized with Mhlanjeni and the Xhosa (see Documents 8 and 21), who fought the Cape Colony forces between 1850 and 1853. In this context the fortunes of Lesotho's Christian community declined. Most of the members of the royal family who had approached or been converted to Christianity, including Molapo, turned away from the church. (See Documents 18, 20 and 30.) Initiation ceremonies were restored during a general resurgence of traditional religious practices (see Document 25). In the next selection Casalis expresses the missionaries' lament.

great stumbling-block presented by the selfish policy of nations calling themselves Christian. Our converts thought that war ought to cease entirely where the supreme authority of the Word of God was admitted; they, therefore, imagined they had nothing to fear from the white race, and this feeling had become so strong that military exercises were gradually discontinued. The country of the Basutos furnished the Cape Colony yearly with a large number of workmen, who, owing to the confidence inspired by their reputation for fidelity and honesty, easily found occupation. A writer of the Cape Colony once asked, in an ironical tone, if the French Protestant Missionaries were *Quakers*, that their disciples appeared everywhere unarmed, taking nothing with them on their journey but their staff and a little bag of books.

Alas! cruel disappointments were to bring about a reaction, which soon caused our detractors to change their tone. The encroachments of our race were about to re-kindle the warlike instincts of the natives, and to lead many of them to see in Christianity nothing more than a series of precepts without practice, and theories without application. The demands and pre-occupations of politics would stifle the voice of conscience, and furnish a number of people, especially the chiefs, with a specious pretext for putting off indefinitely those reforms which were distasteful to them. From that day we dated our most serious difficulties.

Moshesh, whose mind had been greatly enlightened, but whose heart had not yet been brought into subjection by the Gospel, appeared from this time to give very divided attention to the instructions of the Missionaries; and several of his sons became entirely indifferent to them.

It is well known with what carelessness the government of the Cape has allowed a number of the families of the colony to escape from its authority, and advance indefinitely beyond the frontiers. It was not, however, difficult to foresee the consequences of this emigration, the cause of which sufficiently explained the object in view. What could be expected from people who exiled themselves, chiefly because they had been obliged to emancipate their slaves?

DOCUMENT 26
'Precepts without practice'

Casalis, *Basutos*, pp. 116–18. Casalis wrote this a few years after his departure from Lesotho in 1855.

It is a sorrowful statement, but truth requires it to be made, that the work of social and religious regeneration among the Basutos seemed to present fewer difficulties and to progress more rapidly twelve years ago, than it has done since. At that time nearly all the family of the chief seemed won over: he himself sometimes appeared only to be waiting for a little more advancement among his people, in order to renounce ancient customs, and regulate his life and government by Christian laws. The Basutos were then still ignorant of the

Preserving the Kingdom

With the defeat of Moroka and Sekonyela (Documents 22 and 25) and the absorption of many of their people into Lesotho, Moshweshwe reached the height of his power. He controlled most of the territory demarcated in the Napier Treaty of 1843 and a diverse population of perhaps 100 000. Lesotho was now the most powerful single state between the Orange and Vaal Rivers.

During the 1850s the economy prospered and became more closely integrated with the Cape. Moshweshwe encouraged the planting of wheat and potatoes to supplement the existing diet of millet and maize. European traders established retail outlets for tools, clothing, sugar, coffee and tea. Some complications arose in the wake of this interaction. The next two documents illustrate Moshweshwe's efforts to control them by legislation.

DOCUMENT 27
'Spirituous liquors'

A law promulgated on 8 November 1854. Theal, *Records*, Vol. II, p. 133.

Ordinance against the introduction and sale of Spirituous Liquors in the territory of the Basutos.

Whereas the spirituous liquors of the whites were unknown to former generations of our Tribe, *Matie*, and *Motlomi* until *Bomonageng*,—and our father *Mokachane*, now very advanced in age, has never used any other drink than water and milk; and whereas we deem that a good Chief and Judge cannot claim to be competent to execute his duties, if he make use of any thing of an intoxicating nature; and whereas spirituous liquors create quarrelling and strife, and pave the way to the destruction of society, (for surely the spirituous liquors of the whites are nothing else than fire):

It is therefore hereby made known to all, that the introduction and sale of said spirituous liquor within Basutoland is henceforth prohibited, and provided any person, whether white or coloured, contravene this order, the spirits shall be taken from him and poured out on the ground, without excuse or indemnification.

And this order shall be printed in the Basuto and Dutch languages, and posted up at the places of public meetings, and in the villages of the Basutos.

Given with the advice and concurrence of the great men of our Tribe, by us the Chief of the Basutos, at Thaba Bosigo, the 8th of November, 1854.

(Signed)   Moshesh, Chief.

DOCUMENT 28
'Sale and Debt'

A law promulgated on 6 September 1859. Theal, *Records*, II, pp. 536–7.

The Law for Trade

I, Moshesh, write for any trader, whoever he may be, already in my land, and for any who may come to trade with the Basutos; my word is this:

Trade to me and my tribe is a good thing, I wish to promote it.

Any trader who wishes to establish a shop, must first obtain permission from me. Should he build a house, I grant him no right to sell it.

Further, I do not grant him liberty to plough the fields, but only to plant a small vegetable garden.

The trader who fancies that the place he is sojourning in belongs to him, must dismiss the thought, if not, he is to quit; for there is no place belonging to the whites in my land, and I have granted no white man a place, either by word, or by writing.

Further, any trader who leaves a debt there from whence he comes, and he who contracts any whilst in my land, any such debt, if brought to me, I will enquire into, in our Court of Justice, that I may settle it; and the debt will be paid up in the manner the Basutos pay their debts. But the suer is to

appear before me, and the debtor likewise, that justice may be done.

Further, the law that I issued on the 8th day of November, 1854, I renew this day, that people may be reminded of it, and conform themselves to it . . . [See Document 27.]
I am,   Mark X of Moshesh, Chief of the Basutos.
[Literal translation]   (Signed)   Ths. Arbousset, V.D.M.
Bethesda, 6th September, 1859.

Moshweshwe's authority and Lesotho's prosperity had fragile foundations. The king was approaching seventy years of age. In 1854 he suffered the first of several illnesses which eventually sapped his strength. He found it increasingly difficult to control the subordinate chiefs, particularly members of the royal family such as Poshuli (see Document 21). They took more and more initiative without consulting him and their cattle-raiding exacerbated relations with the Boers. The next two documents provide impressions of Moshweshwe's eldest sons.

DOCUMENT 29
'Letsie, the eldest son'

Our translation of the impressions of Arbousset in a letter of 21 January 1848, *Journal des Missions Evangéliques* (1848), pp. 291–2. For other references to Letsie, see Documents 22 and 25.

Dear gentlemen and most respected brothers,

Our letters have often described Mosesh, king of the Basutos, but rarely his oldest son and successor Letsie, chief of Morija. He is a man of about thirty-six years of age, tall, well built, but unfortunately he has had only one eye since birth. As regards morality, I find him sensual and not very favourable to the progress of religion and hard work. This unfortunate disposition can be explained in various ways. First of all, his main counselors have all converted—that humiliates and discourages him. Then he is too attached to polygamy to embrace the pure and exacting teaching of the Gospel on that question. Finally his natural nonchalance makes it easier for him to govern his subjects by the erroneous customs of the past rather than to search for new rules more appropriate to the time . . . The son is much less popular [than his father]. He has a firm, determined quality, but is too independent, autocratic, sometimes cruel. More than anyone, I am disturbed by Letsie's faults since his education has been entrusted to me for almost fifteen years. Imagine, gentlemen, what pain I had in seeing him, despite the ascendancy which circumstances have given me over him, and despite especially the influence of Moshesh, put to death most unjustly one of his subjects. . .

DOCUMENT 30
'Molapo, the next eldest son'

Impressions from 1854 by Joseph Orpen, administrative officer of the Orange Free State. Joseph Orpen, *Reminiscences of Life in South Africa from 1846 to the Present Day* (1964), pp. 257, 258–9.

NOTES FOR READING field-cornet = part-time official working for the landrost (administrative and judicial officer); Louis Fourie = Boer farmer; Hottentot = pejorative term for Khoi. For other references to Molapo, see Documents 18 and 20.

We rode on the morrow to Leribe, just over the Caledon River; Molapo had just settled there and was having a large village built, but had a temporary residence overlooking this; it was under the high overhanging precipice, at the top of the flat-topped mountain Leribe. Molapo received us, as he always did, with great courtesy and kindness. I explained that I had come because his father had delegated the principal authority in that part to him, and had referred me specially to him about promoting good relations, and that this had to be accomplished principally by the prevention of thefts and trespasses. We had much conversation on these subjects. With regard to thefts, I said, and he agreed, that the best way to prevent them was that we should work so heartily to discover and punish them that they would be found bad for the thieves, and for this object they must in each case be reported quickly and directly to him, followed up and discovered at once and be severely punished.

Molapo always worked well with me and the field cornets in these matters; thefts became rare and were traced up and well punished when they did take place . . .

When we had finished our business of inspection, Mr. Louis Fourie asked Molapo and all of us to his farm house, a couple of miles further on. When we arrived there, Molapo's retinue saddled off at a little distance and he and his interpreter were asked to the house. When we entered it, we were given chairs and presently asked to lunch at the table, while Molapo was given a little stool to sit on against the wall near the door, and his interpreter was left standing. While we white people ate, plates of food were handed to Molapo. He was a proud and wealthy man and had sat at table with Government officers of the highest rank. Louis Fourie was a very respectable and wealthy man and had his sort of pride too, and the colour difficulty obtruded itself. I could see that Molapo was uncomfortable. At the table was a Boer named Daniel Pietersen, commonly called Daniel Hakkelaar (stutterer). Presently Molapo said to him, 'Mr. Pietersen, the last time I met you, I gave into your custody a bastard Hottentot named Kieviet Witbooi, and you promised me that you would take that man and deliver him to the magistrate at Colesberg for trial. Will you please tell me what became of him?' Daniel Pietersen answered never a word, but went on eating and looked sullen. No one else spoke and we naturally looked alternately at the two. Molapo caught my look and said, 'Mr. Orpen, I asked that question because Mr. Daniel Pietersen soon afterwards shot that Hottentot dead, bound as he was and lying on the ground.' Absolute silence continued till we left the house.

Equally troublesome for Moshweshwe was the British decision to abandon the Orange River Sovereignty. By the Bloemfontein Convention of February 1854, Special Commissioner George Clerk handed over the Sovereignty to the local whites and provided for the sale of arms exclusively to them. The agreement said nothing about boundaries between Lesotho and the new Boer-dominated Orange Free State. Moshweshwe grew alarmed and journeyed to Bloemfontein to see Commissioner Clerk.

DOCUMENT 31
'The delicate question of the frontiers'

An account of the king's visit by PEMS missionary Pierre-Joseph Maitin. Germond, *Chronicles*, pp. 225–7.

NOTES FOR READING Maitin accompanied Moshweshwe because of the illness of Casalis; the 'president of the provisional government' of the Orange Free State was Josias Hoffman, who knew Moshweshwe and had constructed houses and a church in Lesotho; Clarke = Clerk.

'On the 9th, Moshoeshoe having engaged Moroke to accompany him, we resumed our march towards the capital of the Sovereignty. I remarked to Moshoeshoe that so large a company of men might alarm the inhabitants, whereupon he requested me to precede him with two of his men, in order to proclaim the pacific object of his visit. There was much excitement on account of the rumour which had spread in the last few days concerning the chief's hostile intentions. This was promptly calmed by what I was able to announce on his behalf.

'Although he was annoyed to hear that Moshoeshoe was coming under the existing circumstances, Sir George declared that the chief was his friend, that he would always be pleased to receive him, whatever the situation. The president of the provisional government expressed great satisfaction at the honour of Moshoeshoe's visit. It was almost dark, but, prompted by a feeling of delicacy and lest he should alarm the residents by entering the town at night, the chief spent it in the open at a certain distance from Bloemfontein, after sending one of his sons to inform Sir George of his intention. Everyone expressed regret that he had not come in directly, and a messenger was dispatched to beg him to sleep in town, but it was too late.

'On the following day, the tenth, he arrived and halted close to the house of the British Resident at six in the morning. He was received with every demonstration of confidence and esteem by the representatives of the old and the new governments. Four oxen were handed over to him to feed his people. Having been invited to breakfast with the British Resident, I was requested to act as interpreter. Various members of the provisional government were present. Naturally, the topic of conversation was the change in the government. In the course of this conversation, the president of the provisional government having remarked that it was best to forget the past and to begin afresh, the chief replied: "I share your opinion, but only half-way. Yes, let us forget all that was painful (under the English Government), but let us not forget the good. I wish you to understand my thought: when a man weds, what he expects to find in his mate is not bad, but good qualities. As usually happens, his wife will have both good and bad qualities and it is very likely that the latter will strike him far more than the former. But if his wife should chance to die, when he buries her, at the same time he buries whatever may have appeared evil in her and remembers only her good qualities. Peradventure he should wish to marry again, what will he expect of his second partner? Only the good qualities of the first. If he finds them, if he finds new ones, he will be happy."

'Moshoeshoe expressed the satisfaction which he felt to see that the men chosen to represent the Government were among his old friends. "But", he added, "you have saddled yourselves with a very heavy burden. May God give you the wisdom and the insight which you will need, in order that you may not be crushed under its weight."

'Sir George Clarke afterwards invited Moshoeshoe to meet him. The chief requested as a favour that Moroke and the members of the new government be present at the conference. Her Majesty's commissioner replied that he wished to meet Moshoeshoe first, after which he would grant the chief two more interviews, one with Moroke and the other with the new government. The conference with Moshoeshoe was long and friendly. His Excellency informed Moshoeshoe that he had been acknowledged as a faithful friend and that it was because of the unjust treatment which he had received that the British Government was withdrawing; that he must rest well assured of the great interest which the Government bore him; that, besides, his co-operation would always be needed for the preservation of peace in the country; that Basutoland and the Colony would continue to share a common frontier in one direction, and that what inspired confidence for the future was the presence of a wise and enlightened chief, such as Moshoeshoe, as neighbour.

'The chief then touched on the delicate question of the frontiers. Sir George said that everything had been arranged; that the farmers wanted peace; that they would settle matters amicably with Moshoeshoe as they had done before the British Government took possession of the country, etc. As Moshoeshoe expressed some doubt, Sir George reminded him of all that he and Governor Cathcart had done on his behalf ever since they had become acquainted with his affairs. Moshoeshoe finally requested that it should be well understood that, while they accepted the Sovereignty from the hands of the British Government, the frontiers on the Basutoland side had not been fixed. But this question would be debated at the conference with the new government which was due to meet at four o'clock.

'Evening came without the interview taking place. Moshoeshoe begged me to write to His Excellency to request him to have it arranged for the morrow. Sir George replied that his numerous commitments had not allowed him to hold this session, but that, on the next day, at seven o'clock, he would have the pleasure of meeting Moshoeshoe with the members of the new government. At the agreed hour, Sir George was ready to leave for the Colony. When he came to greet the chief, he handed me a letter containing documents for him which stated that the farms given by the agents of the British Government and situated in Moshoeshoe's territory, would be paid for by this government to the occupants, who would then have to quit. Sir George requested me to explain the document and its contents to Moshoeshoe, adding that he hoped that the

latter would be satisfied; that, in any case, he would always be glad to meet Moshoeshoe in his just demands. Finally, as it was time for him to go, Moshoeshoe, his sons, and I accompanied His Excellency. As we entered the town, the troops were all lined up, ready to march.

'In the afternoon, Moshoeshoe had an interview with the members of the new government. Addressing the President, the Chief expressed the satisfaction he felt to see him at the head of affairs, reminding him that he had lived among the Basuto for several years. Moshoeshoe then said how keenly he desired to see Blacks and Whites living together in good harmony. After which he added that it was not for him to advise the members of the Government, he, poor ignoramus, who knew nothing but what experience had taught him, while they, thanks to their books, could know the experience of all nations and be instructed not only by the evils produced by a given cause, but also by the good which had resulted from another given cause; but at least he wished to remind them that there is a book of God which must form the foundation of their laws, and to entreat them to be just in all their dealings with the Blacks as well as the Whites. Suddenly, he exclaims with fervour: "Fear drink! let the drunkard be tolerated by none, whether Black or White!" He then concluded with these words: "May God bless you! May he lead you in whatever you do! May He be your light, your wisdom, your strength! May it be given you to do His will and to be agreeable to Him! Amen." The members of the new government replied in chorus: "Amen". The President thanks Moshoeshoe and assures him of the good intentions of the farmers towards him. At the Chief's request, he was informed that a deputation of two members of the Government would be sent to Thaba Bosiu to reach an understanding with him on various matters, after he had consulted his tribe.

'The session had ended when Sekonyela (chief of the Batlokoa) who, after the war of the Basuto against his tribe had taken refuge in Bloemfontein, entered the room. Immediately, Moshoeshoe rises and holds out his hand. The two withdraw together, to a seat in the courtyard to converse.

'The members of the Government were astounded at the speech of the chief. One of them enquired of me: "Moshoeshoe is a Christian, is he not?"—"I wish I could reply in the affirmative, but I cannot."—"Is he then a hypocrite? Does he not believe what he told us?"—"Moshoeshoe has told you nothing but what he believes to be the truth."—"If that is so, he will be saved, do you not think so?"—"I trust he will, for I hope he will be converted, but he is not yet so." I concluded by saying that, heathen though he may still be, I believe that Moshoeshoe is nearer to the kingdom of heaven than many who call themselves Christians. Everything I had to say was listened to in a serious and friendly manner.'

President Hoffman sought to reassure Moshweshwe by sending a special envoy to Thaba Bosiu in April 1854. Joseph Orpen (see Document 30) had come from Britain to South Africa in 1846. In the next selection he gives his impressions of Moshweshwe before and after their encounter.

DOCUMENT 32
'Old man, great is thy faith!'

From Orpen's account of his visit. Orpen, *Reminiscences*, pp. 208, 209, 210–12.

NOTES FOR READING battle of Berea = Moshweshwe's victory over Cathcart in 1852; for Nehemiah, see Document 8; Giddy = son of a Wesleyan missionary from the Platberg station.

During the last day or two of the session, Mr. Hoffman asked me, as I have stated, to do him the favour of going to Moshesh as a sort of ambassador for a few days. On the 19th, the day after the prorogation, he furnished me with a letter of credence. He had promised Moshesh that he would depute such an officer to give him information of the manner in which the new Government would be formed. I was to do this, promote good relations and transact some business . . .

The opinion which I had up to this time entertained of Moshesh is quite clearly laid down in a 'Summary of occurrences in the Orange River territory since the annexation to the British Dominion' which had been adopted by the committee of the Assembly of Delegates of which I had been a member. We had forwarded it to Sir G. Clerk to send to the Imperial Government. It was drafted by my brother Frank and agreed to by me, even before it was submitted to the committee. It was published with the other records of the assembly of delegates in a supplement of the 'Grahamstown Journal' of the 27th May, 1854, besides appearing, I believe, in an Imperial Blue Book, and it calls for the consideration of any person professing to write a history of those times. It is a strong ex parte statement, containing what we all believed at the time to be the truth. It represented that Moshesh had, during the last two wars of the Cape frontier, rendered assistance to the Gaikas, Tamboukies and rebel Hottentots. It is an indictment against Moshesh throughout and it stated that he was not properly punished at the battle of Berea and that the Basutos considered the issue of that battle to have been a defeat of the British forces and that they would, especially since that battle, look upon abandonment as an act of pusillanimity on the part of the British Government. It is remarkable, however, how, even with this strong denunciation of Moshesh, the committee added 'whatever the result of the Berea affair be called, Moshesh at least deserves credit for the moderation with which he has since conducted himself.'

I refer to the above statement of my deliberate opinion up to 1854, because Dr. Theal, in his history of the period 1854 to 1872, on page 10, states that, at the time when I was appointed to this mission, my opinion of Moshesh coincided with that of Mr. Hoffman, whom he had described on page 7 as a philanthropist of the school of Wilberforce and Buxton, and one who maintained that in dealing with Moshesh nothing but moral force was needed . . .

As for me, I had volunteered against Moshesh in 1851, and my opinions up to 1854 were recorded as above stated . . .

The next day we swam the Caledon river and reached the French Protestant Mission House at the foot of Thaba Bosio, where we were very kindly entertained by the Rev. Casalis and Mrs. Casalis, who asked us to stay with them during our visit. Word was sent to Moshesh of our arrival and a meeting was arranged for us next day on the mountain.

Next day I was led up the mountain by Nehemiah Moshesh, who had been sent to welcome and bring me. Mr. Casalis did not attend this meeting, which was of a preliminary and private nature nor did he attend any other meeting, nor did he talk of politics at all with me during this visit. Nehemiah could speak and read and write English fairly well, having been at school at Capetown and had much practice since his return. He used generally to translate for his father. Moshesh's 'great wife' was dead. Nehemiah's mother was Moshesh's wife next in rank; she had charge of his European house and was greatly trusted by him. Moshesh came forward from his European house and met us in a very warm and cordial manner and took us inside, where Mr. Giddy and I sat on a sofa near a table and he in a chair on the other side of the table with Nehemiah and a few others around. His wife brought in a tea tray with white china tea cups and plates and tea and sponge cake, made by herself. She had long before got the wife of a respectable German trader, Eberhardt, to teach her, so that she might entertain European guests properly. We were introduced by Nehemiah to her. She was a very kindly old lady. After telling Moshesh the news and reading Mr. Hoffman's letter to him and having some chat, he told me, as I knew he would, that he wished me to oblige him by staying some days, for the business was serious and important, and he wished to call together a number of his chiefs and people to hear me.

To this, I, of course, agreed. I then spent some days at the mission house, rode about with Nehemiah and was shown over the mountain and told stories of the attacks that had been made on it and battles fought below it. I found that Mr. Casalis had been intimately acquainted with two grand-aunts of mine in Paris . .

In a few days, Moshesh sent to inform me that he was prepared to receive me in public. I went up the mountain with Mr. Giddy and found Moshesh seated in a great circle of his chiefs and people, who called out a greeting as we entered the circle and were given seats near Moshesh. After he had introduced me, I delivered to him Mr. Hoffman's letter, which was read, and then I gave him the information which I was requested to give, as to the formation of a new Government and who its officers were as well as the messages which I had been requested to give and some of the principal pieces of news, with my explanations.

Moshesh then asked me would I allow him to ask a question or two which he would like to put to me. I said I should be happy to answer any questions of his.

'Mr. Orpen', he said, 'Will you please tell me what is your native country.'

I told him it was England.

He then said: 'Supposing now that you were to go home to England, would Queen Victoria receive you?'

'Yes', I replied, 'I have the honour to hold Her Majesty's Commission as a justice of the peace in the Cape Colony and on a proper occasion I would be admitted to the presence of Her Majesty.'

Moshesh then addressed his people and said: 'You see now. This is what I have been telling you. Here is now an Englishman who is now a member of the Government Council of the Free State. If he went to London, Queen Victoria would embrace him. The Queen has not left us for ever. No Sovereign ever did throw away subjects. The Queen is sitting on the top of a high mountain, looking down at us, her children, white and black, who are playing below and sometimes quarrelling too. She is watching us and trying us. Some day, Queen Victoria will come back among us. On that day I shall rejoice as I rejoice at the rising of the sun.'

As he went on with his speech, I thought, 'Old man, great is thy faith!' I did not know, till he now mentioned it before his people, of Sir George Clerk's promise to him that Government would continue to watch over him and appoint an agent to aid him in maintaining peace, or how these promises must have tended to strengthen his confidence that Government would eventually do justice. I hardly dreamed that his words would prove prophetic . . .

Moshesh then went on to explain the different matters on which I had spoken and sketched the history of the country during the last few years. Speaking of the British Government, he said that if it had made mistakes, still its general desire was to be just and generous to all. He spoke of the emancipation of the slaves, and of the safety and justice meted out to all in the Colony and, coming down to the time of Cathcart, he dwelt on the fact that he had let them off, easily, out of generosity, reminding them of the relief and gladness they had then felt and how impossible it would have been for them to have resisted the great power of England.

The relations between the Orange Free State and Lesotho remained cordial until 1855 when the Boers forced Hoffman's resignation because he had broken the arms embargo by delivering a keg of powder to Moshweshwe. The new president, Jacobus Boschof, pressed the Boers' land and cattle claims. He adopted the Warden Line as the effective boundary between the two states, while Moshweshwe used the territorial definitions of the Napier Treaty. In 1858 the growing tension erupted into war. The king allowed Boschof's forces to advance towards Thaba Bosiu and then ordered his commandos to attack Boer farms. Demoralized by the news of the raids and their failure to take the mountain fortress, the Boers petitioned High Commissioner Grey of the Colony to mediate a settlement. Grey intervened and drew a new boundary which followed the Warden Line in the north but was more favourable to Lesotho in the southwest. Moshweshwe accepted the terms. Document 33 presents the Boer complaints prior to the attack while Document 34 gives the king's views three months prior to the settlement.

DOCUMENT 33
'Moshesh has refused to give us any satisfaction'

Boschof's letter to Sir George Grey. Theal, *Records*, II, pp. 320–2.

NOTES FOR READING   Landdrost = administrative and judicial officer; for Nehemiah, see Documents 8 and 32; field-cornet = part-time official working with the landrost.

Bloemfontein, 16th March, 1858.

Sir,—As Your Excellency will have perceived from the communication made to you by Mr. Sauer, the Landdrost of Smithfield that he had reason to believe that an attack on that district was premeditated by the Basuto Chief Posuli, brother to the Chief Moshesh, I think it right in consideration of the interest which you have on former occasions shown in the welfare of this State, to inform you that I have been obliged to call out the Burghers in defence of the rights of this State, violated by the Basutos, and that we are at this moment on the point of a war with all the tribes that acknowledge Moshesh as their head.

This Chief has, notwithstanding his solemn engagements to compensate for robberies from time to time committed on our frontier farmers, failed to comply therewith. Several hundred horses are not yet given up; the few delivered up by him are miserable Kaffir horses and mares, whilst the best horses stolen from our farmers are still retained and ridden by the natives, even before the eyes of their owners. It is true that Nehemiah, for a while, took measures which gave a considerable check to horse and cattle stealing on the Smithfield side; but it now appears that the Basutos have been advised to annoy our farmers in another way to a still greater extent.

Pretending that we occupy a considerable portion of the Basuto country, and wilfully misinterpreting the treaty entered into by Moshesh and myself at Smithfield in October, 1855, they have from time to time, in defiance of our laws to the contrary, entered far into the State in numerous armed bands, hunting and riding about, and there disturbing the peace of our farmers and their families: but never have they done so more daringly than since the publication in the *Cape Argus* of the reports and misrepresentation of certain so-called Basuto Commissioners employed by the Editor of that paper.

To the meddling and misstatements of those men we have good grounds for ascribing the conduct of that people, who have latterly gone to such extremes that they have settled on several farms not formerly occupied by natives, entered the State in strong armed bands, and destroyed dwelling houses, orchards, and gardens, alleging that such farms are their property, that they have a right to occupy them, and cannot be expelled except by an order from Moshesh.

That this Chief encourages them in such proceedings is evident, as no satisfaction can be got from him, and as he has, in fact, informed me that he claims a very considerable part of the Smithfield district, many years ago occupied, built upon and improved by our people; and is prepared to support his claims, if need be, by support of arms.

Under such circumstances it cannot be wondered at that our borderers, expecting an attack from the Basutos, have gone into lagers. Whilst this was being done and measures were being taken for the security of our whole frontier line, cattle stealing has been carried on by the natives on the borders of the Winburg district, amounting within the last ten days to three hundred head of cattle and forty horses, whilst five of the thieves have been shot and two wounded, and one man on our side wounded.

Moshesh has refused to give us any satisfaction. This I ascertained beyond a doubt, on meeting his son Nehemiah at Fieldcornet Fouché's on the 10th instant. The Chief pretends that the complaints of our people are frivolous; that they occupy lands which he only lent them; that they are in fact his subjects, and ought to have looked to *him* for redress if they had any ground of complaint; that he found no fault with Posuli; that his people had a right to settle down on the same farms with our Boers, and that he was even surprised that they, the Boers, should go into lagers on his, Moshesh's, territory.

Mr. Joseph M. Orpen had, on the invitation, as it appears, of Nehemiah, come over from Aliwal, where he now resides, attended the meeting which Mr. Sauer, the Landdrost of Smithfield, held with that Chief on the 3rd instant, and acted as Nehemiah's secretary and adviser. On the last occasion, at which I was personally present, Mr. Orpen, accompanied by one of the French missionaries, again attended, and requested to be allowed to assist Nehemiah, which I positively refused, telling him that I have reason to suspect him of advising the Basutos to take the hostile attitude lately assumed by them, that his reports to the *Argus* are of themselves enough to excite a rupture between us and the Basutos, and that I could not allow him (who styles himself a justice of the peace of the Aliwal district) to interfere in our disputes with the natives. I had him placed under arrest till the meeting was over, and then ordered him to quit the State.

I mention this circumstance in the hope that Your Excellency may see cause to order such men to remain within the colony, and not to meddle in matters which can only bring ruin and bloodshed on hundreds of innocent people, particularly when, by the office they hold in the colony they can easily persuade the natives that they act on the authority of the Colonial Government.

A war with the Basutos seems now unavoidable, and whether the Griquas and the native tribes over the Vaal will keep out of this quarrel remains to be seen. The Free State has many enemies, and the natives are easily excited and urged on to mischief by villainous white men. God only knows what will be the result of this struggle; but it is clear to me that it cannot be avoided; and I would only beg as a favour of Your Excellency that you will not prevent the colonial farmers from voluntarily coming to our assistance, to prevent the ruin and destruction of their relatives and fellow countrymen, should they be inclined so to act. I have, etc.,

(Signed)   J. N. Boshof, President Orange Free State.

DOCUMENT 34
'I will speak of many Basutos who were . . . then killed, most cruelly'

From Moshweshwe's letter to Grey. Theal, *Records*, II, pp. 384–8.

NOTE FOR READING   Beersheba and Morija = two PEMS stations with adjacent Sotho settlements.

Thaba Bosigo, June, 1858.

Your Excellency,—It may scarcely appear necessary to lay before Your Excellency any lengthened details of what has taken place between the Orange Free State and myself. I know that you have followed with interest the transactions which have led to the commencement of hostilities, and you have heard with pain of the horrors occasioned by the war, at present suspended in the hopes that peace may be restored by Your Excellency's mediation.

Allow me, however, to bring to your remembrance the following circumstances:—About twenty-five years ago my knowledge of the White men and their laws was very limited. I knew merely that mighty nations existed, and among them was the English. These, the blacks who were acquainted with them, praised for their justice. Unfortunately it was not with the English Government that my first intercourse with the whites commenced. People who had come from the Colony first presented themselves to us, they called themselves Boers. I thought all white men were honest. Some of these Boers asked permission to live upon our borders. I was led to believe they would live with me as my own people lived, that is, looking to me as to a father and a friend.

About sixteen years since, one of the Governors of the Colony, Sir George Napier, marked down my limits on a treaty he made with me. I was to be ruler within those limits. A short time after, another Governor came, it was Sir P. Maitland. The boers then began to talk of *their right* to places I had then lent to them. Sir P. Maitland told me those people were subjects of the Queen, and should be kept under proper control; he did not tell me that he recognised any right they had to land within my country, but as it was difficult to take them away, it was proposed that all desiring to be under the British rule should live in that part near the meeting of the Orange and Caledon rivers.

Then came Sir Harry Smith, and he told me not to deprive any chief of their lands or their rights, he would see justice done to all, but in order to do so, he would make the Queen's Laws extend over every white man. He said the Whites and Blacks were to live together in peace. I could not understand what he would do. I thought it would be something very just, and that he was to keep the Boers in my land under proper control, and that I should hear no more of their claiming the places they lived on as their exclusive property. But instead of this, I now heard that the Boers consider all those farms as their own, and were buying and selling them one to the other, and driving out by one means or another my own people.

In vain I remonstrated. Sir Harry Smith had sent Warden to govern in the Sovereignty. He listened to the Boers, and he proposed that all the land in which those Boers' farms were should be taken from me. I was at that time in trouble, for Sikonyela and the Korannas were tormenting me and my people by stealing and killing; they said openly the Major gave them orders to do so, and I have proof he did so. One day he sent me a map and said, sign that, and I will tell those people (Mantatis and Korannas) to leave off fighting: if you do not sign the map, I cannot help you in any way. I thought the Major was doing very improperly and unjustly. I was told to appeal to the Queen to put an end to this injustice. I did not wish to grieve Her Majesty by causing a war with her people. I was told if I did not sign the map, it would be the beginning of a great war. I signed, but soon after I sent my cry to the Queen. I begged Her to investigate my case and remove 'the line,' as it was called, by which my land was ruined. I thought justice would soon be done, and Warden put to rights.

[Moshweshwe then reviewed the Warden War, the 1852 Commission and the British decision to withdraw from the Sovereignty.]

On the Government being withdrawn, it was natural for me to suppose that the grants I had made to it were to be cancelled, for the conditions on which they were made could no longer be fulfilled by the British Government. I told my people the British Resident had taken away the limit in his pocket, and would cast it in the Orange River. I did not, and do not, consider it as existing after Sir George Clerk retired, and I made no new proposal to the Free State Government.

The first head of that Government, replacing the British Resident, was Mr. Hoffman. He had the confidence of my people, and we lived in peace. He was, however, too soon removed, and Mr. Boshof was appointed as President. Things went on quietly for a time, but rumours at length spread through the land that the Boers were again pretending to a right to portions of my country, and especially to that part which I had disputed with Major Warden. I heard of hostile plans being laid to oblige us to yield. I then wrote to Your Excellency, requesting you to come forward and assist us in this vexing question. My prayer to you was not answered.

It is not the custom of Basutos to speak much of their real feelings,—they are wrong perhaps, but they soon show by actions when they are dissatisfied. Seeing the Boers determined to encroach upon the land, they became restless and some took advantage of the angry feeling to carry off cattle and horses. This system I did not approve, when therefore lists were sent to me of stolen property, although very incorrect and unjust, I still ordered a collection to be made, equivalent to the property said to have been lost and the fine imposed upon us in consequence.

The Boers were not satisfied with this, as they said they must have horses instead of cattle. Out of a large number of cattle I sent to them, they took off as many as they liked, and returned me the remainder, ordering horses to be sent instead. I had, however, fully understood that the question of the cattle was a pretext for a quarrel with me, the Boers trusting that they would obtain land if a war was commenced.

I tried my utmost to satisfy them and avert war. I punished thieves, and sent my son Nehemiah and others to watch the part of the country near the Boers, and thus check stealing. In this he was successful, thieving did cease. We were at peace for a time. In the commencement of the present year (1858) my people living near farmers received orders to remove from their places. This again caused the fire to burn, still we tried to keep all quiet, but the Boers went further and further day by day in troubling the Basutos and threatening war. The President (Boshof) spoke of Warden's line, this was as though he had really fired upon us with his guns. Still I tried to avert war.

It was not possible, it was commenced by the Boers in massacreing my people of Beersheba, and ruining that station, against the people of which there was not a shadow of a complaint ever brought forward. Poor people, they thought their honesty and love for Christianity would be a shield for them, and that the white people would attack in the first place, if they attacked at all, those who they said were thieves. I ordered my people then all to retreat towards my residence, and let the fury of the Boers be spent upon an empty land; unfortunately some skirmishes took place, some Boers were killed, some of my people also. We need not wonder at this, such is war! But I will speak of many Basutos who were taken prisoners by the Whites and then killed, most cruelly. If you require me to bring forward these cases, I will do so. I will however speak of the horrible doings of the Boers at Morija, they there burnt down the Missionary's house, carried off much goods belonging to the Mission, and pillaged and shamefully defiled the Church Buildings.

I had given orders that no farms should be burnt, and my orders were obeyed till my people saw village after village burnt off, and the corn destroyed, they then carried destruction among the enemy's homes.

On coming to my mountain, the Boers found I was prepared to check their progress, and they consequently retired. My intention was then to have followed them up, and to have shewn them that my people could also carry on offensive operations, believing that having once experienced the horrors of war in their midst, I should not soon be troubled by them again.

My bands were getting ready to make a descent upon them, when the Boers thought proper to make request for a cessation of hostilities. I knew what misery I should bring upon the country by leaving the Basutos to ravage the Boer places, and therefore I have agreed to the proposal of Mr. J. P. Hoffman. I cannot say that I do so with the consent of my people, for many of those who suffered by the enemy were anxious to recover their losses.

If they have remained quiet, it has been owing to my persuasions and my promises that they might have good hope of justice,—Your Excellency having consented to act as arbitrator between the Boers and Basutos. With the expectation of soon meeting you, I remain, etc.,

Mark X of Moshesh. Chief of the Basutos.

The strength of the king and his state declined after 1858. Moshweshwe was less able to survey his subordinates as they established their own autonomy in anticipation of his death. He no longer had the services of Casalis, who left in 1855, and did not develop the same close relationship with any of the missionaries still in Lesotho. Meanwhile, the Orange Free State was growing in population and power, due in part to the white monopoly on the arms trade. In 1864 the raiding between the two sides almost broke into war. In 1865, under the assertive leadership of J. H. Brand, the Boers moved to the attack.

DOCUMENT 35
'Clouds of vultures'

An account by a PEMS missionary of the invasion of Lesotho in 1865. Germond, *Chronicles*, pp. 271–2, 273, 276–7.

NOTES FOR READING Molapo's country = northern Lesotho (see Document 30); Jousse and Lautré = PEMS missionaries; Government of the Transvaal Republic = another state established by emigrant Boers.

'It is three months ago to-day since the delegates of the Free State ascended Moshoeshoe's mountain bringing the Boer ultimatum to the Basuto chief. Three days later war was declared. The latter is still raging and the future is darker than ever. You are aware of the result of the first attack on Thaba Bosiu. The Boers made a second attempt and with heavier losses. The first assault fell on the south-eastern angle of the mountain, the second was directed against the main entrance, immediately above the mission house. Under cover of a brisk artillery fire, the Boers advanced in good order until they reached the cliffs which crown the mountain. At this point the natives had built a series of superimposed walls and from these ramparts maintained a continuous fire. But, overwhelmed by a hail of shells which reached them behind their fortifications, the Basuto were forced to abandon them one by one. The bravest of the Boers, with Wepener at their head, had already scaled the basaltic ledges which you know and, penetrating beyond the little terrace which surmounts them, were actually entering the winding path which turns to the right and by which the plateau is reached, when Wepener fell, struck by a bullet. At this juncture, the Boers hesitate and, realizing their numerical inferiority, begin to fall back. Soon, under a deluge of stones and boulders which the natives hurl at them, they commence tumbling down the mountain in disorder and confusion. The Boers lost a dozen men killed on that day, including the Commandant, the bravest and most honourable man in the army. Several were severely wounded and a very large number more or less badly bruised.

'The Boers now appear to have abandoned their original plan of storming the mountain; they have invested it and intend to starve the Basuto into submission. It is rumoured that the latter have only enough supplies left to last them a few more days at the most. They will be forced to surrender. And then, what will the result be? The Boers are said to be determined to remain in the field until they have actually captured Moshoeshoe's mountain, and, when they have taken it, to post a garrison of several hundred men on the summit with artillery to overawe the country and to prevent the natives from coming down their mountains to cultivate their fields again. As you will appreciate, this plan aims at nothing less that the complete destruction of the Basuto as a nation and the seizure of their country. It is obvious that the natives could not survive in the Maloti for long and that they would find themselves compelled to seek a new home elsewhere, or to disperse over the whole surface of the Colony and the Free State, as labourers and domestic servants. No doubt too, a certain number would re-main in the Maloti and there become a terror and a perpetual scourge to the new colonists of Basutoland.

'Besides, the war is anything but over, Molapo's country has not yet been invaded. To crown the misfortunes of the Basuto, the Government of the Transvaal Republic has just declared war on Moshoeshoe. During a raid in the direction of Natal, Molapo's men killed several Boers among whom there chanced to be a few Transvaalers. One of the latter was related to Pretorius, the President of the above republic. The offence was too great and the opportunity too good to fail to avenge this crime in spectacular manner and, at the same time, to secure a portion of the conquered territory. What will the outcome of all this be? God knows.

'Two days ago, an Englishman passed through, on his way back to the camp at Thabu Bosiu from which he had been absent but a few days. He had taken part in both assaults against Moshoeshoe's mountain and was able to give us a few details which clarified the somewhat confused account which I had received. The Basuto, he said, had fought well but were poor shots. However, if they are unskilled in the handling of fire-arms, they were on the other hand, most dexterous in throwing darts and stones, a fact which many of the assailants were able to verify by painful experience.

'A white flag was flying over the mission . . . this did not prevent it from becoming a fairly keenly contested strategic point and theatre of engagements concerning which it can be said that we were the ones to pay the cost. Basuto had taken cover in the mission buildings from which they directed a brisk fire against the Boers. It became necessary to dislodge them. The Basuto thrown back, their adversaries entered the house and you may well imagine the damage which they did.

'The future is very gloomy. All those whom I question on the ultimate issue of this war, shake their heads and say it is quite unpredictable.'

'After the abandonment of the siege of Thaba Bosiu by the Boers, the division of their army which had passed here in July is again approaching our quarters.

'Having so far failed to induce the Basuto to submit to the harsh conditions which they wished to impose upon them, the Boers and their auxilliaries have chosen to ruin and to starve them, if they can, by seizing their cattle, destroying their villages and mercilessly pursuing them into the heart of the mountains. There is no doubt that, by this means, they have succeeded in doing considerable harm to the Basuto. Moreover, they have had a free hand, as the Basuto, who are supposed to defend their country, have remained concentrated around Thaba Bosiu from which the enemy have withdrawn' . . .

'After the withdrawal of the besiegers, those of our missionaries who were nearest Thaba Bosiu were able to visit the place. The description which they give of it is heart-breaking in the extreme. Piles of cattle and horses lay on the mountain plateau and all around its base in the last stages of putrefaction. Their numbers were estimated at twenty thousand. The majority of these animals had died of hunger and thirst; the rest were killed by the enemy's shells and bullets. Clouds of vultures gorged themselves on these remains, but the scavengers did not operate fast enough to prevent the foulest miasmas from infecting the country-side. As the missionary establishment was situated in the heart of the battle-field, it has been completely destroyed. There is nothing left of Messrs. Jousse and Lautré's houses, the temple and the school, but cracked and tottering walls.'

These tactics of siege and scorched earth brought the desired result. The Boers forced separate treaties on Moorosi (Documents 6 and 21) and Molapo, who became subjects of the Orange Free State. In April 1866 they imposed harsh terms on the king, who surrendered most of the lowlands where cattle and crops could be raised. The only consolation was the opportunity, for the first time in two years, to plant and harvest crops.

Raiding resumed the next year, followed by a new Boer attack. Moshweshwe realized that he was now no match for his assailants and urgently appealed for British intervention. He stressed his loyalty to the Queen and decried British claims of neutrality by pointing to the arms embargo. Ultimately he succeeded. High Commissioner Wodehouse condemned Boer aggression and stopped the sale of arms to the Free State. In 1868, as Lesotho was on the verge of collapse, he proclaimed the annexation of 'Basutoland'. The next two documents give Moshweshwe's protest against the 1867 attack and the proclamation of 1868.

DOCUMENT 36
'Your wish to exterminate the Basutos'

Moshweshwe's letter to President Brand. Theal, *Records*, Vol. IIIb, pp. 788–9.

NOTES FOR READING   Masupha = third son and a close adviser of Moshweshwe; Volksraad = elected and ruling council of the Orange Free State.

Thaba Bosigo, 9th July, 1867.

Sir, — I have received your letter of the 26th June. I am sorry to hear that some of your people have suffered so much, although I am not sure that the details stand as you have mentioned them. My reason for writing to-day is to remind you that I have already warned you that the great desire you and your people had for war would surely cause mischief between the Basutos and Boers. I beg to know what is the cause of this year's war. Last year it was through the wish to enlarge your country. This year it seems that it is caused by your wish to exterminate the Basutos. That wish has been the real cause of all the mischief of which you have written.

If I were also to expose to you all the sufferings which your people have caused to the Basutos in these latter times, you would see that they are twice as many as those undergone by the people of the Free State, without speaking of the blood shed, both men and women belonging to me having been killed this side of the line made by Sir G. Grey and Sir P. Wodehouse. You might have prevented all these accidents, the more so that the line made by Sir P. Wodehouse

had been favourable to you. Last year we made peace with you. I gave you 5000 head of cattle, but I have not given this country away, it belongs not to me, as you know yourself very well that every country in the world does belong to the people which dwells in it.

If I remove the Basutos, I have nowhere where I can establish them. Although I do not like war and am afraid of its consequent horrors, I cannot consent to buy the lives of my people with the country belonging to them, where they were born, where their forefathers were born likewise; besides I know of no country where they could go.

As to Mr. Bush who has been killed, in what part of the Free State has he been killed? I do not understand what you mean when you speak of Basutoland as if it were Orange Free State ground; therefore I should like to hear where and why and when he has been killed. Was it during the peace of last year, or when? Or is it during that useless war of yours? If it has taken place in Basutoland, white men have no right to dwell in Basutoland, unless they have received the authorization from the Government of Basutoland. Just the same as that the people of Basutoland have no right to dwell in the Free State. Respecting the raid you speak of as being in the intention of Masupha, it is not true. Wars of all kinds are caused by other wars; when you say that there is peace, then it is peace for all.

In case you are a chief liking his people, and knowing what is his duty as a leader who calls himself a Christian, I must beg of you to let the Boers know that they must remain where they are, in the Free State; there is no other way to keep up peace. Another matter is that no missionary station in Basutoland can be ceded to the Free State.

Now I trust that you will consider well all the matters spoken of in this letter, because I also have been ordered by the Government of this country to write as I have done. I have the honour to be yours truly,

(Signed)   Moshesh, Chief of the Basutos
By Nehemiah Moshesh.

P.S.—Another matter which surprises me is that you white men feel no pity for each other. Those who enrich themselves by rearing cattle have no sympathy with those who get rich by trade, and *vice versâ*. If you were men loving each other, you would not hurt each other. By this I mean that it is a long time I have told Mr. Brand that he ought not to arrange matters with the sword, because it is an arrangement which goes forward of its own way and in its own manner.

Again, I am very sad because Your Honour has not consented to listen to my advice. But even now, in case you were willing to listen, it is yet time to set aright all matters which might cause quarrels and other things of the same kind. Again, you said that you would cause my letter to be read in your Council, for I did beg of you that your Council should hear my letter, that it might judge of my intentions and thoughts; but in this you have not given me a satisfactory answer. If indeed you had the intention to take my letter up to your Council, then it is no fault of yours, even if matters have gone worse in these last days.

If I write this, it is that I have been ordered to write in this way by the Government of this country, according to the right which it possesses. I end by saying that I wish you would let me know who it was that said that my advice had no importance, whether it was you, or whether it was the Volksraad.

(Signed)   Moshesh.

Seal of Moshesh.

DOCUMENT 37
'British subjects and British territory'

Sir Philip Wodehouse's proclamation of 12 March 1868. Theal, *Records*, IIIb, p. 894.

Proclamation

By His Excellency Sir Philip Edmond Wodehouse, Knight Commander of the Most Honourable Order of the Bath, Governor and Commander-in-Chief of Her Majesty's Colony of the Cape of Good Hope in South Africa, and of the Territories and Dependencies thereof, and Vice-Admiral of the same, and Her Majesty's High Commissioner, etc., etc., etc.

Whereas, with a view to the restoration of peace and the future maintenance of tranquillity and good government on the Northeastern Border of the Colony of the Cape of Good Hope, Her Majesty the Queen has been graciously pleased to comply with the request made by Moshesh, the Paramount Chief, and other Headmen of the tribe of the Basutos, that the said tribe may be admitted into the allegiance of Her Majesty: And whereas Her Majesty has been further pleased to authorize me to take the necessary steps for giving effect to Her pleasure in the matter:

Now therefore, I do hereby proclaim and declare that from and after the publication hereof the said tribe of the Basutos shall be, and shall be taken to be, for all intents and purposes, British subjects: and the territory of the said tribe shall be, and shall be taken to be British territory. And I hereby require all Her Majesty's subjects in South Africa to take notice of this my proclamation accordingly.

GOD SAVE THE QUEEN!
Given under the public Seal of the Settlement of the Cape of Good Hope, this 12th day of March, 1868.

(Signed)   P. E. Wodehouse, Governor.

By command of His Excellency the Governor.

(Signed)   R. Southey, Colonial Secretary.

In 1869 Wodehouse and Brand gave substance to the proclamation in a convention which established boundaries of British Basutoland. This agreement failed even to restore the lands held by Moshweshwe under the Warden Line. It did, however, preserve a truncated Lesotho from extinction. Annexation came not a moment too soon, for in March 1870, the founder and father of the Lesotho nation died.

AIDS TO UNDERSTANDING

Chronology

1785–90   Birth of Moshweshwe
1806   British annex Cape Colony
c. 1820   Moshweshwe establishes settlement at Butha-Buthe
c. 1821   Beginning of *Mfecane* invasions into Caledon valley
c. 1824   Moshweshwe moves to Thaba Bosiu
1831   Moshweshwe staves off Mzilikazi's attack
1833   Arrival of first missionaries from the Paris Evangelical Missionary Society (PEMS)
1839*ff.*   Period of great missionary influence in Lesotho
1843   Napier Treaty
1848   British annex area between Vaal and Orange Rivers as Orange River Sovereignty
1849   Promulgation of Resident Warden's Line
1850   Fighting between Rolong and Taung
1851 (February)   Warden and Poshuli attack Phuthi and Thembu
1851 (June)   Moshweshwe defeats Warden and Rolong
1852 (February)   Report of the commission inquiring into affairs in the Orange River Sovereignty
1852 (December)   Moshweshwe repels Cathcart's attack
1853   Moshweshwe conquers Sekonyela
1854 (February)   British withdraw from Orange River Sovereignty and give sovereignty to local whites
1854 (March)   Moshweshwe visits Bloemfontein
1854 (April)   Orpen visits Thaba Bosiu
1855   Boschof replaces Hoffman as President of the Orange Free State
1858   War between the Orange Free State and Lesotho
1865   Orange Free State attacks Lesotho
1866   Orange Free State forces treaty on Moshweshwe
1868   Wodehouse proclaims British annexation of Lesotho ('Basutoland')
1870   Moshweshwe dies

Glossary

Beersheba = PEMS station in Lesotho
Butha-Buthe = Moshweshwe's first settlement
Cathcart, Sir George = British Governor of the Cape Colony 1852–54
Clerk, Sir George = British Special Commissioner in 1854 withdrawal from Orange River Sovereignty
Daumas, Francois = PEMS missionary at Mekuatling with Moletsane
Gosselin, Constant = PEMS 'artisan' missionary
Hebron = PEMS station in Lesotho
Jousse, Theophile = PEMS missionary
Kafir = pejorative term of Arabic derivation applied principally to Bantu-speaking Africans

Letsie = Moshweshwe's eldest son
Mokhachane = Moshweshwe's father
Molapo = Moshweshwe's second son
Moletsane = Moshweshwe's Taung vassal at Mekuatling
Moorosi = Moshweshwe's Phuthi (Nguni) vassal
Mopeli = Moshweshwe's half-brother
Morija = first PEMS station in Lesotho
Moroka = chief of the Rolong at Thaba Nchu
Napier, Sir George = Governor of the Cape Colony
                     1838–44
Nehemiah (Sekhonyana) = one of Moshweshwe's sons
Orpen, Joseph = British settler, administrator and dip-
                 lomat in Cape Colony and Orange Free
                 State
Poshuli = Moshweshwe's brother
Sekonyela = chief of the Tlokwa
Smith, Sir Harry = British Governor of Cape Colony
                   1847-52
Warden, Henry = British Resident at Bloemfontein
                1845-52

An Essay of Questions

Sources and Interpretation

The sources for Lesotho's history share many of the problems of the Zulu materials. The data is limited for the period prior to 1833 and a European perspective dominates most of the literature. Keeping the Zulu chapter in mind, how would you qualify the Sotho materials as sources for reconstructing the early career of Moshweshwe and the time of disruption (pages 44–49); for discerning the motivations and priorities of Moshweshwe? Compare the nature and quality of the missionary material in the two chapters. How do you account for the differences? How do the differences affect the interpretation? Compare the oral traditions collected by Ellenberger with those obtained by Bryant and Stuart.

We have consciously organized the narrative around Moshweshwe, his problems and his solutions. How might the same history appear from Sekonyela's perspective; or Moroka's; or from the perspective of the Orange Free State? Compare the king's perceptions about rights over people and land (Documents 14, 17 and 34, for example) with those of Moroka and the Methodists (Document 16). Compare the two accounts of the events of 1858 (Documents 33 and 34).

The European sources come from a variety of individual perspectives. Evaluate the following as factors contributing to the depth of understanding and degree of objectivity in these materials: knowledge of the Sotho language; ability to provide assistance in correspondence, record-keeping and negotiations; role as missionary; role as administrator; Boer identity; British nationality; French nationality; Protestant identity? Do you find some stereotypes in all the European sources?
Examine the excerpts from Casalis (Documents 3, 5, 7,

9–11, 13–14, and 26) and Arbousset (Documents 2, 22, 25, and 29) and evaluate the two men as historical sources, agents of the PEMS and human beings. Do you find significant differences between Casalis' accounts in the *JME* (Document 13) and those taken from his books? If so, how would you account for them?

The documents include several statements of history. Evaluate the perspective and content of Nehemiah's calendar of events (Document 8); Ellenberger's oral traditions (Documents 1, 4 and 6); Moshweshwe's account of past events (Document 34).

How much of an impression of the common people do you gain from the Sotho materials? Compare this chapter with the others in that regard.

Identity and Religious Change

Like the Zulu state, Lesotho absorbed persons of very different origin into a new identity. How would you compare the processes of absorption in the two cases? How compatible was citizenship in Lesotho with conversion to Christianity? Was the position of Abraham untenable (Document 13)? What was the nature and source of opposition to Christianity? How compatible was citizenship with European identity at the time of Casalis' arrival as contrasted with the moment of Molapo's encounter with the Boers (Document 30)? What distinctions did the Sotho make between Boer and Briton? Compare their distinctions with those of Dingane.

Moshweshwe suggested that he had less freedom to adopt Christianity than his subjects (Document 13). How did the customary obligations of a chief affect his capacity to innovate and to convert? How would you compare Moshweshwe's position to the situations of the kings of Buganda and Asante in this respect?

The PEMS missionaries enjoyed substantial success in Lesotho in the 1830s and 1840s. What comments would you venture about the missionaries' expectations of Moshweshwe and of the Christian Sotho? Would you say that these Sotho converted to Christianity? Would you explain the abandonment of the church by many Sotho in the same terms as Casalis (Document 26)?

The Formation of the New State and Society

Lesotho developed more slowly and with greater calculation than the Zulu state. What impact did the *Mfecane* have on the character and priorities of Lesotho; on the assessment of old customs; and on the reception given to the material objects and ideas offered by the Europeans? What was the impact of geography on Lesotho's character? Would you explain Lesotho's survival in the 1820s and again in the 1860s in geographical terms?

What conclusions would you draw about Moshweshwe's policies over the years of his reign: on questions of incorporation and justice (e.g. Documents 5, 8, 11 and 24); on respect for traditional custom (e.g. Documents 11–13); on the influences introduced by Europeans

(Documents 27–28); in relation to his overlords in the early period (pages 44–49); in relation to the European and African challenges of the last two sections? What consistencies and inconsistencies do you observe? Compare Moshweshwe's use of legislation (Documents 27 and 28, for example) with Dingane's (Chapter One, Document 31) and Asante's.

Moshweshwe wielded more power than perhaps any chief in southern Sotho history. To what extent was he still a chief by custom and consent? Do you perceive important changes in the way he ruled over the years? What freedoms and constraints impinged upon him? Compare his interpretations of custom in Documents 5, 11, 12 and 13.

How would you compare Moshweshwe and Shaka as military innovators; military tacticians; administrators; diplomats; political and social innovators; and in their attitudes towards their subjects?

Sovereignty, Diplomacy and Technology

Moshweshwe is usually described as a leader who preferred negotiation to conflict wherever possible. Is this a fair evaluation? Was it as true when he faced a weak rather than a strong adversary? What were the instruments of his diplomacy? What internal constraints affected the conduct of his diplomacy? Do you perceive growth in Moshweshwe's exercise of the art of diplomacy? What were the king's policies on land alienation, boundaries, refugees and resident Europeans? How good was the information upon which he based his decisions? How was it obtained? Compare Moshweshwe as a diplomat with Dingane and with Osei Bonsu of Asante.

What innovations did Moshweshwe make in the military field and how successful were they? Is it fair to say that Lesotho was more innovative militarily than Zulu in the long term? What use did Moshweshwe make of the geographical resources of his kingdom in his military strategy?

Conclusion

What overall estimate would you make of Moshweshwe's career and contribution? Do you consider him a statesman?

Bibliographical Essay and Bibliography

In preparing this chapter we have relied greatly on the work of Leonard Thompson (1975) and on his advice in the selection of documents. For anthropological and historical background, see Wilson's chapter on the Sotho and Thompson's on the High Veld in Wilson and Thompson. Germond and Theal provide collections of documents arranged in chronological order, while the *Journal des Missions Evangéliques* contains a running commentary from the PEMS missionaries after 1833. Ellenberger

provides oral tradition from the turn of the century. For summaries of recent developments in Lesotho, see Halpern and Stevens. For additional bibliography and visual impressions of Lesotho in the nineteenth century, see Thompson (1975).

Contemporary Accounts and Oral Tradition

Arbousset, T., *A Narrative of an Exploratory Tour to the Northeast of the Colony of the Cape of Good Hope*. J. C. Bishop, London, 1852. (First published in French in 1846.)

Backhouse, James, *A Narrative of a Visit to the Mauritius and South Africa*. Hamilton, Adams & Co., London, 1844.

Casalis, Eugene, *The Basutos*. J. Nisbet, London, 1861. (First published in French in 1859.)

— *My Life in Basutoland*. Religious Tract Society, London 1889. (First published in French in 1882.)

Ellenberger, D. F., compiler, and MacGregor, J. C., trans., *The History of the Basuto: Ancient and Modern*. Caxton Publ. Co. Ltd, London, 1912.

Germond, Robert C., compiler and trans., *Chronicles of Basutoland*. Morija Sesuto Book Depot, Morija, 1967.

Journal des Missions Evangéliques, Journal of the Paris Evangelical Missionary Society, Société des Missions Evangéliques, Paris, 1841, 1848.

Moshesh, Nehemiah, 'A little light from Basutoland'. *Cape Monthly Magazine*, 3rd series, ii (J. C. Juta, Cape Town, January–June 1880), 221–33, 280–92.

Orpen, Joseph, *Reminiscences of Life in South Africa from 1846 to the Present Day*. Davis, Durban, 1908. Enlarged edition, 1964.

Theal, G. McC., ed., *The Basutoland Records*. 3 vols. Cape Town, 1883.

Secondary Sources

Halpern, Jack, *South Africa's Hostages*. Peter Smith, Gloucester, MA, 1965.

Omer-Cooper, J. D., 'The Nguni outburst' and 'Colonial South Africa and its frontiers.' in *The Cambridge History of Africa*. Vol. 5. Cambridge University Press, Cambridge, 1976.

Sanders, Peter, *Moshoeshoe: Chief of the Sotho*. Heinemann Educational, London, 1975.

Stevens, Richard, *Lesotho, Botswana and Swaziland*. Pall Mall, London, 1967; Praeger, New York, 1967.

Thompson, Leonard M., *Survival in Two Worlds. Moshoeshoe of Lesotho, 1786–1870*. Oxford University Press, Oxford, 1976.

—ed. *African Societies in Southern Africa*. Heinemann Educational, London, 1969.

Wilson, Monica, and Thompson, L. M., eds., *The Oxford History of South Africa*. Oxford University Press, Oxford, 1969.

Chapter Three

From Autocracy
to Oligarchy in Buganda

PLATE 3.1   *A scene from the court in the early 1860s*

PLATE 3.2   *Mutesa and his chiefs during Stanley's visit
(see Document 8)*

PLATE 3.3   *A naval battle between Buganda and a foe
on the eastern frontier*

PLATE 3.4   *Mwanga in 1893*

INTRODUCTION

In this chapter we probe the history of the East African State of Buganda in the late nineteenth century, beginning with the reign of Mutesa and ending with the establishment of British rule. Here we are not looking at the process of state formation, since Buganda already had a political and military organization similar in its complexity and centralization to Asante. The state had developed in greater isolation than the subjects of the other case studies; nothing in its history compares with the transatlantic, trans-Saharan, or savanna trade networks of West Africa. Buganda does show some analogies with the South African kingdoms: to the emphasis on conquest of the Zulu, to the competition between Christians and adherents of the traditional religion in Lesotho. But here we have Muslims as well, and the rivalry becomes so intense that it finally escapes the control of the king and leads to new forms of authority.

The Baganda were Bantu-speaking farmers living on the northern and northwestern shores of Lake Victoria. In contrast to their neighbours in Bunyoro, Ankole and Rwanda, they did not emphasize cattle raising nor were they divided into ruling pastoral and subject farming classes. Buganda has a rich soil and well-distributed rainfall, an ideal environment for the plantain (type of banana tree) which served as the staple food and the material for building homes. Women assumed the responsibility for cultivating it, thereby freeing the men for hunting, war, public works, and government service.

These men and women were organized into about forty patrilineal clans, most of which had settled in the proximity of today's Kampala by 1500 AD. At that time the dominant leadership in a relatively egalitarian society came from the clan heads, collectively known as *Bataka*. The *Bataka* recognized one chief—the Kabaka—as the 'first among equals', the arbiter of disputes and the recipient of wives from the clans. The clans competed for power, since each Kabaka—in contrast to the normal patrilineal pattern—belonged to the clan of his mother and was buried in its lands. This custom prevented the emergence of a royal lineage. The Kabaka later became one of the most powerful kings in pre-colonial Africa.

Until about 1650 Buganda was quite small and lived in the shadow of its powerful neighbour, Bunyoro. Although Bunyoro rarely exercised administrative control over the Baganda, it did make their lives precarious through frequent raids. Gradually the Kabaka emerged as a military leader who first mobilized the defence and later the expansion of Buganda. At the same time a new religious identity was forged as the people attributed survival or success to some of the old gods of the clans. In particular, they raised the deities of some of the islands and lake shore to a 'national' status and established shrines in newly conquered areas. Foremost among these figures were Mukasa, the high god concerned with health and prosperity; Kabuka, the principal war god whose priest accompanied military expeditions; and Nende, a second god of war. Collectively the deities were known as the *Lubare*, and the clans originally associated with them continued to furnish the officials for each cult. This has made for a very close identification of interest between the clans and religious authorities throughout Buganda history. Since no single clan controlled the position of Kabuka, and since no cult developed around a particular Kabaka until his death, the king had more freedom to challenge the clans and the priests than did many African rulers.

By the nineteenth century the Buganda kingdom controlled over one million people in a substantial area to the west and north of the lake. During this period, analogous to the eighteenth century in Asante, a perceptible shift of power occurred away from the clan heads to the Kabaka, who seized the initiative in distributing to his most faithful followers the spoils of conquest—people, land, crops and cattle. While the clans usually determined the leadership of the heartland counties, the king appointed the governors in the newer ones. These county chiefs (*Bakungu*) collected taxes, recruited soldiers, judged disputes and formed the principal administrative structure of the kingdom. The kings also created another class of chiefs, the *Batangole*, whose jurisdiction cut across county lines. This was part of the Kabaka's continuing search for a means of keeping informed and maintaining loyalty to his person. By pitting *Bataka*, *Bakungu* and *Batangole* against one another, and by preventing most of the *Bakungu* and *Batangole* posts from becoming hereditary, he came to wield immense power.

By the mid-nineteenth century this expansion and centralization produced a large and complex bureaucracy. The Kabaka usually shifted his capital several times during his reign, but always within the old heartland. He required his principal *Bakungu* and *Batangole* to reside there much of the time, in order to prevent them from fomenting rebellion. Consequently, these officials governed their domains through deputies. At the same time these chiefs and other ambitious Baganda preferred staying close to the king and the nerve-centre of the state. In particular, they coveted the opportunity to participate in the military campaigns organized from the palace—campaigns which served as the most important avenue to distinction and promotion. By the time our story begins, the Kabaka rarely led the expeditions himself, but he did mete out praise and blame, thereby determining promotion, demotion and even execution.

The principal civilian administration was vested in the *Katikiro* or Prime Minister, who supervised the judicial and taxing functions of the state. He served as the last court of appeal and, along with the king, could call in the executioners to silence a complaint or end a promising career. He controlled the process of tax collection and sent the Kabaka's portion to the royal treasury, where it was constantly redistributed to successful military commanders and other recipients of royal favour. Next to the *Katikiro* in rank was the *Kimbugwe*, who counselled the king and served officially as the 'keeper' of his umbilical cord and thus of his spirit. Along with the

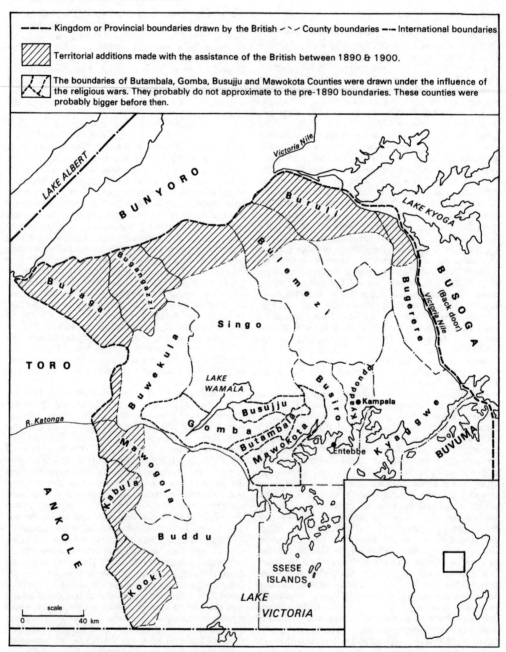

MAP 3.1   Buganda in 1900

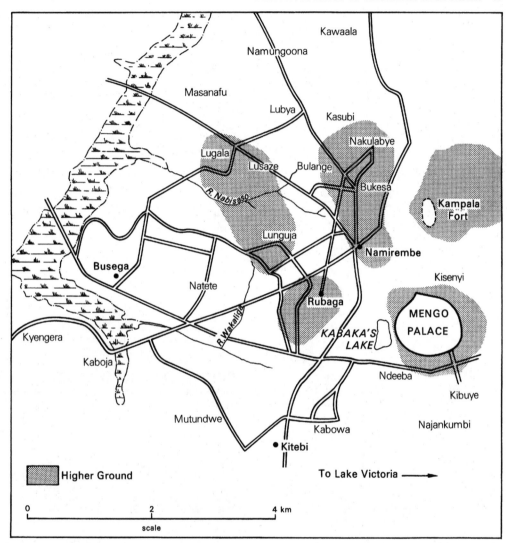

MAP 3.2   The capital area

Katikiro, he could enter the king's enclosure without permission and held title to a number of estates. Another important figure was the Queen Mother, usually the mother of the reigning *Kabaka*. Like the *Katikiro* and the *Kimbugwe*, she lived at the capital.

The palace (*Lubiri*) dominated the capital and housed perhaps a thousand people. Some of the space went to the scores of royal wives. Each had her own thatched hut and attendants. Each hoped to bring honour to her clan and power to herself as mother of the next Kabaka. Much of the rest of the palace was filled by several hundred royal pages ranging in age from twelve to twenty. They served in the private quarters and audience chamber of the king, the royal treasury, and other parts of the palace. They came to the Kabaka on the recommendation of important chiefs and used their experience as pages as

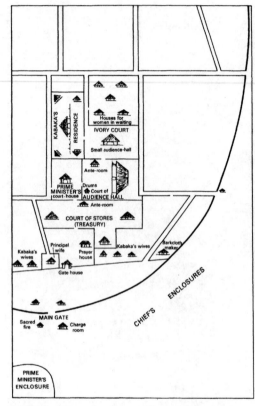

MAP 3.3   *The royal enclosure at Mengo Palace*

civilian administration and competition for office—including that of the Kabaka. The majority of the people lived in the hinterland, had no position within the clan or territorial hierarchies, and went by the unflattering designation *bakopi*, 'peasants' who were considered stupid and uncivilized by their city kinsmen. At the capital two perennial conflicts dominated politics. One pitted the clan heads and priests, who supported the descent principle and the old values, against the Kabaka and his officials, who stood for the territorial and appointive principle. The other struggle matched the older officials, held over from a preceding regime, against the new king who sought to place his own friends and favourite pages in power. In the midst of these conflicts, the main figures of the documentary narrative pursued their careers.

The sources for this chapter are abundant but uneven. Beginning in the 1840s, Muslim traders from Zanzibar made their way to Buganda, followed some years later by European explorers, missionaries, soldiers and administrators. The missionaries, and particularly the Protestants, emphasized literacy and educated an elite who composed accounts in their own language, Luganda, in the late nineteenth and twentieth centuries. These Baganda committed to writing much of the oral tradition of their day. Consequently, much of the material reflects European and Buganda Protestant perspectives. The indigenous Muslim, Catholic and royal perspectives appear in some documents, but the voices of the clans, priests and common people have scarcely survived.

DOCUMENTARY NARRATIVE

The Early Reign of Kabaka Mutesa (*c.* 1856–76)

an apprenticeship in politics, hoping one day to become *Bakungu* and *Batangole*. Many of the key figures in the documentary narrative first entered the political arena in the dangerous but intoxicating atmosphere of this royal page school.

The Kabaka was not always so autocratic as this sketch might suggest. The *Katikiro, Kimbugwe,* and Queen Mother exercised some restraining influence, formed the core of an informal council of advisers, and helped select the new king. Clan heads and priests were quite strong in the heartland. Finally, the ultimate threat which discontented Baganda posed for the king was to supplant him with a brother or son. In this context, the accessions of Mutesa and Mwanga in the late nineteenth century were rather unusual in Buganda history. Each of their predecessors died a natural death and each of them acceded to power without a protracted and violent struggle.

The capital, then, was the centre of decision-making in nineteenth-century Buganda for military expeditions,

On the death of Kabaka Suna in about 1856, an obscure prince named Mukabya took power with the help of Suna's Katikiro. The new ruler eliminated his rivals, consolidated his control with a minimum of violence, and took a new name—Mutesa, 'the one who gives good counsel'. He then embarked on a reign marked by expansion, prosperity, and the appearance of new material and ideological challenges from outside.

With time Mutesa replaced his father's senior officials with persons of his own generation. He proved particularly adept at wielding the power of patronage and acquired a reputation as a prestigious, autocratic and often cruel king in the 'best' Buganda tradition. One of his favourites was a man named Mukasa, whose career illustrates the opportunity—and the dangers—of government service, and who held the post of Katikiro in the last decade of Mutesa's reign. For an account of Mukasa's rise we go to the explorer Henry Stanley, who put this story together from what he heard at the Buganda court in 1875.

DOCUMENT 1
'Am I worthy or not?'

Henry Stanley, *Through the Dark Continent*, 2 vols (1878), I, pp. 386–90, 392–3.

NOTES FOR READING Magassa = Mukasa; Mtongole = singular of Batangole, office-holders; Mkungu = singular of Bakungu, county chiefs; Pokino = title of county chief of Buddu; twiyanzi or yanzi = expression of praise and loyalty to the king. For another version of Mukasa's career, see A. Kagwa, *The Kings of Buganda*, trans. and ed. M. S. M. Kiwanuka (1971), pp. 183–4.

About the time that Mtesa succeeded his father and beheaded the senior chiefs of Uganda, there was observed at the court a smart, clever, cleanly looking lad, assiduous in his attendance on the monarch, and attentive to his smallest wishes. He was the son of a Mtongoleh or sub-chief, and his name was Magassa. To his other desirable qualities might be added a fine set of white teeth, bright eyes, and general good looks. Mtesa became enamoured of him, and made him guardian over the imperial lavatory, an office of great trust in Uganda.

As Mtesa grew to man's estate, Magassa the boy also became a young man, for he was about the same age as his master, and, retaining and improving those qualities which first attracted the monarch's eyes, was promoted in time to be a Mtongoleh of the bodyguard, and a double-barrelled gun was put into his hands, with the power of gunpowder, and a few bullets and percussion caps, which caused the heart of young Magassa to bound with joy . . .

A day came when a Mkungu of the first order, named Pokino, offended Mtesa.

Casting his eyes about for a fit man to succeed him, Mtesa's eyes lighted on the sparkling, bright face of Magassa, and his decision was at once made.

'Here, Magassa', cried the Emperor, and the accomplished courtier fell at his feet to the ground to hear his command. 'Haste, Magassa, take men and eat up Pokino's land and name, for old Pokino has forgotten me.'

'Twiyanzi, yanzi!' he cried and moaned, 'Twiyanzi, yanzi, yanzi!' each time more emphatic, and rubbing his cheeks in the dust; and then, springing to his feet, he seized his spear, and, holding it aloft, as if in the act of launching it, he proclaimed aloud, 'By the Emperor's orders, I go to eat up Pokino. I will eat him clean out of land and name, and Magassa shall become Pokino. Emperor, behold me!' and again he fell to the ground, screaming his thankful Twiyanzis, and loyally abasing himself in the dust.

After the levee was over, Magassa, eager to change his name for Pokino's, beat his war-drum, unfolded his banner, and mustered his followers, and, like the fell leopard, pounced upon purblind Pokino, whom he quickly deprived of life, land, and name, and in place of their former owner became their master. But with even old Pokino's vast estates and large possessions the young Pokino was apparently discontented. Shortly afterwards the Emperor commanded him to 'eat up' Namujurilwa, the Achilles of Uganda.

With the fall of Namujurilwa, young Pokino became Lord of all Uddu, from the Katonga valley to the Alexandra Nile, a district embracing over 3000 square miles, with twenty sub-chiefs recognizing him as their master, possessing two great capitals, Namujurilwa's at Masaka, and Pokino's, hundreds of women-slaves, and thousands of youthful slaves of both sexes, with cattle also by the thousand, and chief of a population numbering over 100 000. What a change this—from the keeper of the lavatory to the Lord of Uddu!

Pokino's life at his capital of Uddu, Masaka, is almost regal. He has 'eaten up' the lands of two great chiefs, old Pokino and the lion-like Namujurilwa, and now out of the eater cometh forth meat, and out of the strong cometh forth sweetness. His sub-regal court is crowded with applicants and claimants for bounties, and slaves requiring to be fed, and good offices are given with a liberal hand, and cattle are slaughtered by hundreds until Pokino's open hand and large heart is published throughout Uganda. By this politic liberality he secures the affection of the natives of Uddu, the friendship of the great chiefs at the court, and the approbation of the Emperor . . .

[A few years later after a successful campaign] Pokino advances, prostrates himself in the dust, and begins to relate his adventures and his doings in Usongora, while the heroes of the great raid are enmassed in view and within hearing of his words.

After the conclusion of the story, the Emperor says briefly, 'Drink, if thou darest.'

Pokino rises, advances to the test-pots, receives the ladle, and dips it into the pombé; then taking it up, he holds it aloft, and, turning to the warriors who followed him, cries aloud, 'Tekeh?' ('Am I worthy or not?').

'Tekeh!' ('Thou art worthy!') responds the multitude with a shout.

Again he asks 'Tekeh?' and again 'Tekeh!' is shouted with renewed acclamation, and, being found worthy, he drinks, utters his grateful Twiyanzis to the Emperor, and retires to permit others to advance and drink the test-beer. Those found worthy are rewarded, those unworthy are doomed to death by popular condemnation.

Soon after this, Myanja, the Katekiro, was found guilty of the overweening pride of appropriating to himself the most beautiful of the female slaves without regarding his master's right to select his allotment first, and the result of this was that Myanja was disgraced and shortly beheaded.

The Premier's place being now vacant, Pokino was appointed to fill it; and thus was the once humble Magassa elevated to be next in power to the Emperor, with the utmost of his ambition fulfilled.

He is now daily seated on the carpet at the right hand of his sovereign, controls all things, commands all men, and, when leaving the presence of his master, he is escorted by all the chiefs to his own quarters, waylaid by multitudes on the road with profound greeting, has the pick of all females captured in war, the choicest of all cattle, and his shares of all cloths, beads, wine, and other gifts brought to Mtesa.

For a more intimate view of the palace and the pages who served the king, we go to the biography of one of the most prominent Catholic chiefs at the turn of the century. Somewhat younger than Mukasa, Stanislaus Mugwanya entered the palace early in the reign of Mutesa.

DOCUMENT 2
'New things were still coming into Buganda'

Joseph Kasirye, 'The Life of Stanislaus Mugwanya', a mimeographed translation at the Makerere College History Department, from the Luganda version published in 1963, pp. 4–6,7,9.

NOTES FOR READING   Speke = British explorer who came to Buganda in 1862 (not 1861) and serves as the source of Document 6; Lubiri = palace; Mberenge = Mugwanya's older brother and head of one branch of the Mushroom clan; one of Mberenge's and Mugwanya's sisters was married to Mutesa. The mistakes in grammar are part of the English translation.

Mugwanya himself thought that by the time he was sent to the Lubiri he was 12 years old. He confirmed it that when John Hanning Speke came in 1861 [1862], the first European to come to Buganda, Mugwanya had only been in the Lubiri for a short time. The people sent [to] the Lubiri were not too young, i.e. under age of 12 or over 15 years of age. The reasons for this were (1) Kabaka to get boys who were well trained as servants, (2) when the boys were still virgin.

By the time Mugwanya went to the Lubiri he was very good at the xylophone and entenga. All the intelligent children took [a] little time to learn those interesting things.

In the past the sending of boys and girls to the Lubiri had two purposes. Some people thought that the child given to Kabaka was to die there and never come back; that is why some sent children who were not their real products. Others thought that unless the child is sent to Kabaka and experience hard life, he/she will never develop into a good, respectable, trustworthy child.

In the Lubiri of Suna Semunya and Mukabya Walugembe Mutesa, there were hundreds of pages (Bagalagala); so that was why it was by chance that a page became known to Kabaka. In most cases such young children suffered great hardships.

Because the Kings were wise people and had to attend many meetings, they learnt most of their men in the meetings (nkiko). On most occasions they did not ask the child's name at once. But first noted his character, traced his father; from that time the child will be called 'child of so and so'. It was very important if a boy or a girl was known and could be called by Kabaka as 'son of so and so' or 'daughter of so and so'. After that the Kabaka could learn the page's name. This chance was called 'Announcement' from this people became widely known, loved and sometimes made chiefs. If a Mukungu [singular of Bakungu] was given a post he liked he would beat the Mubala (drum beat rhythm).

'If you are named, do not be excited. If you are the one do not be infatuated!'

Mugwanya's entrance was different from that of the other pages. His elder brother, Mberenge, did not just send him but brought him in person. And because Mugwanya went after learning to play the musical instruments, and was different from other boys, handsome, brightly coloured skin, he did not experience the Lubiri hardships, he stayed with Kabaka all the time. It was not long before Omutanda (Kabaka) learnt that his page from his father-in-law could play the 'ntenga' and xylophone; and so Kabaka and his slave spent time playing the instruments, sometimes along with other slaves when they were free from Kabaka's work.

At that time, new things were still coming into Buganda. The Arabs were bringing beautiful goods to exchange them for slaves in Buganda. Cloth was one of the most popular goods. Those who brought cloths knew it had to be kept clean and so the Arabs taught the people the art of making soap from fat mixed with the salt of the ash of Matooke peels. Kabaka Mutesa started washing his body with soap. But Kabaka chose Mugwanya as the page to clean his back with soap. This was a trustworthy job and if you think deeply you can see that it was a chance in a million to touch Kabaka's body. It is surprising that this job was not done by women as would have been expected!

When Mugwanya spoke of his stay with his Kabaka Mutesa, he said, 'When you are at the back of the house and looking at Kabaka Lukeberwa (Mutesa) who is extremely perfect on every joint, you may think he was not born!' Everyone who saw Kabaka Mutesa said he was extremely handsome like his father Suna II. If you try to find who was more handsome of the two you will find difficulty. Although Mugwanya did not see Suna, he said once, 'I think the Kabaka of Nnabulagala (speaking of Mutesa) was superior then [than] he of Wamala (Suna) because he was kind, and you could joke with him if he was in a good mood. Men could look at him closely but "he of Wamala" only allowed his in-laws to look at him.

Mugwanya was always with Kabaka at the time when he was playing. We are told Kabaka himself was a good wrestler, challenging his strong brothers and his strong Bakungu. It was real wrestling. He was a strong wrestler, not because others allowed him to be but he was really good and a true sportsman; he is spoken of as having been a wise wrestler. That is why the young people of that time were good wrestlers . . .

When Mugwanya was still in the Lubiri the Arabs in Buganda increased rapidly in numbers. They became well liked by the Kabaka because of the attractive goods they brought, e.g. guns, cloths and others; in return they got ivory and slaves. It was the Arabs who introduced Islam to Kabaka and when Kabaka learnt that there must be a supreme God, he allowed people to study Islam and its books. Kabaka himself because he was very clever was the first to learn Arabic and good pronunciation (like that of the Arabs) and writing; Mugwanya was one of the pages who learned quickly to read and a little writing. Kabaka encouraged his Bakungu to learn the first prayer lessons, used in prayer, to memorize them and also to read letters on a writing tablet. . .

By this time all the intelligent chaps had started speaking Swahili . . .

Mugwanya learnt perfectly but did not become a true Muslim, although he taught Nalinya a princess and slaughtered meat for her like a Muslim. Also Kabaka learnt but was not a true Muslim. He listened to every religion but did not take up any of them.

The Islamic influences which Mugwanya recalls from his childhood go back to the reign of Suna. They originated primarily in Zanzibar, hub of a vast land and maritime trading network built on ivory, slaves and agricultural production. In addition to guns and cloth, the Arab and Swahili traders brought the Islamic faith which began to make an impression at the court. The next selection deals with the interest in the new faith and comes from two Baganda Protestants writing at the turn of the century.

DOCUMENT 3
'Where is there a God greater than I?'

Excerpts from the English translation of a Luganda version of "How religion came to Uganda", by Apolo Kagwa and Henry Wright Duta Kitakule and published in *Uganda Notes*, May 1902, p. 35 (and reprinted in the *Uganda Journal*, 1947, pp. 110–11).

NOTES FOR READING Medi Abraham = Ahmad b. Ibrahim, an Omani Arab whose father moved to Zanzibar in the early nineteenth century; Lubare = traditional gods; Kauta Mukasa = the Mukasa of Document 1. The various capitals (Banda, Nakawa, etc) are all close to today's Kampala. The adherents of Islam were known as 'readers' because of the emphasis on reading the Koran.

During the reign of Suna (the king who preceded Mutesa) he was visited by some Arabs: Medi Abraham, and Kyera, and Amulain, and Mina, and Katukula Mungazija, and Zigeya Mubulusi.

Of these he liked Medi Abraham best, and gave him a great many presents, ivory, women and slaves.

Later on Medi Abraham told Suna, when he saw him killing people, that, although he killed them with so little thought, yet there was a God who created them, and from Him he had obtained his kingdom, and the people he governed, and that he himself was created by Him.

This Suna did not believe, for he said he knew his Lubare gods and they had given him his kingdom, but Medi Abraham repeated his words every time he was called to see him.

Some time afterwards Suna asked Medi, 'Where is there a God greater than I?' And Medi told him that there is a God who will raise up all who believe in Him, and they will go to Paradise.

When Suna understood this, he agreed that Medi should read to him, but only now and then, and he got through the first four chapters of the Koran.

When he had got hold of these, more or less by word of mouth, Medi returned to the coast and did not come again to Uganda, and soon after this Suna died and Mutesa succeeded him, and made his capital at Banda, half way between Mengo and Ngogwe. He also encouraged Arabs

to visit him . . . Mutesa made friends of these and gave them many things just as his father Suna did before him.

King Mutesa asked Katukula what it was his 'father used to talk to them about, when they visited him', and he told him, 'we used to tell him about God, the King of Kings, and that He will raise people from the dead'.

King Mutesa asked him, 'Are you not lying? Is there a resurrection from the dead?' They told him that indeed there was, and that those who learnt the words of God, when they died would rise again.

So King Mutesa said to Katukula, 'Well then, come and teach me to read,' and he brought a Swahili called Makwega, who taught the king every day, and he learned Mohammedanism very quickly. Some others learned with him [including] Kauta Mukasa, who was Katikiro . . .

These were first taught, but afterwards the converts were slow in coming forward.

When the king went from his capital, Banda, and went to Nakawa he persevered with his reading and fasted during the first fast, and he then ordered all his subjects to read Mohammedanism. He also learned to write in Arabic: the Arab Wamisi brought the Mohammedan Kibali who taught the king.

Then Mutesa came from Nakawa to Nabulagala, and thence to Rubaga, where he stayed some time. He again ordered his people to read, but he saw they were not giving their minds to it. So he said to his head district chiefs, 'I want to know if people are learning to believe in Islam well.' His chiefs told him they were.

Many who would not learn were then seized, called infidels and killed. Then every married man fixed up a stone in his yard to pray at, and every chief built a mosque, and a great many people became readers, but were not circumcised, and all the chiefs learned that faith.

As the last paragraphs of Documents 2 and 3 suggest, Islam did not enjoy unencumbered progress in the kingdom. The Baganda were still attached to their traditional religion and shrines; most resisted Mutesa's pressures to practise the new faith. None the less, an earnest indigenous Muslim community did develop at the court and in time it even challenged the commitment of the king.

The next source describes both the forced observance of Islam and the hesitation of the Kabaka. It comes from the only Muslim author quoted in this chapter and points up the paucity of material from an Islamic perspective.

DOCUMENT 4
'Excepting only to be circumcised'

Sheikh Ali Kulumba, 'The History of Islam in Uganda', a manuscript translation at the Makerere College Library of the Luganda version published in 1953, pp. 172–4.

NOTES FOR READING Ramadan = Muslim month of fasting; the jute pipe was for drinking juice; Nakawa = the capital particularly associated with the strict observance of Islam; Kabaka Mukabya Walugembe = Mutesa.

Kabaka Mutesa began to fast in 1867 at Ramadan. He placed a deputy in charge to teach Buganda to fast. The name of this deputy was Kakolokoto. Unfortunately Kakolokoto had not yet learned properly the rules of observing the fast. He experienced severe thirst and asked for a small pipe of jute and put it in his mouth. He had just swallowed one sip when the executioners caught him by the arms to take him back to his master ... From this comes the proverb, that when a Muslim eats during the fasting period, they call him 'Kakolokoto'. The Kabaka observed this fast in his capital at Nakawa. So it was that the ways of religion took hold on Kabaka Mukabya Walugembe for he saw that it is not a good thing for a reader to remain with savage customs and be a Kabaka who does not know God ...

It was the decision of Mutesa to do all these things excepting only to be circumcised. He himself wishes to be circumcised but people frightened him much saying, 'If you are circumcised, the Bataka are going to remove you from the throne, for the Kabaka must not shed blood in Buganda.' During this time, however, the Kabaka continued to lead [in prayer] and they prayed in the Muslim way with him. There were about 30 chiefs who were first to be circumcised and they saw that it is not difficult. In their hearts they began to blaspheme the Kabaka and to abhor that he should lead them in Muslim prayer. The rumor reached the Kabaka that 'these people are abusing you, the Arabs are not trusting in you as the Reader they most trust since they are circumcised and since that is the will of God which they have since the ancient covenant with Abraham.' The Kabaka began to get angry secretly ...

The immediate stumbling block was circumcision, which contravened local custom against any mutilation of the body and against the shedding of the king's blood.

A larger issue was the obedience of all subjects to the sovereign.

By the mid-1870s Mutesa had some second thoughts about his encouragement of the new faith, as the next document—from a page who later became a Protestant—attests.

DOCUMENT 5
'Muslim martyrs'

Hamu Mukasa, 'Do not turn back', Vol. I, pp. 20–2, a manuscript translation at the Center for Research Libraries, Chicago, of the Luganda version, *Simuda Nyuma*, 3 vols., of which Vol. I was published in 1938 and Vol. II in 1942; Vol. III was not published.

NOTES FOR READING   Kaffir = Arabic and Swahili for 'pagan'; Muddawulira = a leading local Muslim; Mbogo = Mutesa's brother; Semajwali = another leading Ganda Muslim; Namugongo = principal place of execution.

Thus all the affairs of this type were happening and multiplying the [Kabaka's] anger upon anger, and his wrath grew. The Bakungu chiefs, when they understood this and perceived how angry the Kabaka had become, and how displeased he was with the readers putting on airs, and no longer trusting them, then the chiefs who didn't like religion cleverly decided to encourage the Kabaka's wrath over the deeds of the readers so that he would clear them out. They had also anxiety lest the Kabaka order circumcision as he had ordered fasting. 'Where could we go? except to die, we the great men who are not young? If they circumcise a great man, it is like dying badly. Furthermore, it is not difficult for the Kabaka to drive us out of office and give [our places] to the readers. So they hit upon the idea that they denounce to the Kabaka the readers, how they abused the Kabaka and everyone who remained 'Kaffir' ... and not circumcised, how they would not eat Kaffir meat, and how they did not like the Kabaka because he refused to be circumcised and prayed without being a circumcised believer.

So the Kabaka became full of anger about all these cases, and a dangerous situation came about. This was the accusation which was made against them [the Muslims], and they [the Bakungu] bore witness to the following crimes ... First, they abuse the Kabaka for non-circumcision, saying he is a Kaffir, and do not agree to his leading them in prayer in the mosque, [preferring to] pray outside; then, they abuse the Kabaka because he eats Kaffir meat, which is not slaughtered by Muslims, and he eats pig; moreover, Muddawulira defied the Kabaka, saying, 'When you kill meat I do not eat it, even if you are Kabaka; and Mbogo and Semajwali were running out of the Kabaka's country, and they called it the land of Kaffirs; and they slandered the mosques, saying that they were built badly in an unholy way. Therefore how have these people been loyal? On the contrary, they are the enemy, enemies of your country. These people, your highness, do not deserve to serve you, nor to remain alive in this land; they will not win [this case] on account [of the way] they are acting.

So the Kabaka ordered all those pages of the palace to be seized, and all those chiefs of the mosque who were reading, and commanded the executioner Mukajanga to take them to Namugongo, next to Kira, to be burned by fire for their crimes, of which you have just heard.

Thus religion was hated, as he favored the Kaffirs, for now the Kaffirs had obtained power over the Readers. The result was a great human sacrifice spreading over the whole land. All who were killed amounted to about 70 pages, slaves and chiefs. The readers were all those burned at Namugongo. But to count all the victims, who were very many indeed, would be probably about 1000 ...

The execution of 1876 did not mean that the practice of Islam was forbidden or that the king ceased to be influenced by the Zanzibari and Ganda Muslims. He did, however, keep a little more distance from the Muslims and did show some attraction to another religion which had been introduced by other foreigners, the Europeans. The person who first campaigned for Christianity in Buganda was Henry Stanley (see Document 1). Other

Europeans had travelled to the lake kingdom some years before and left impressions of Mutesa.

DOCUMENT 6
'To the worthy . . . and to the unworthy'

John Hanning Speke, *Journal of the Discovery of the Sources of the Nile* (1863), pp. 236, 242, 246–8, 323–4. Speke was an English explorer caught up in the search for the sources of the Nile; he spent about five months in and around the capital in 1862.

NOTES FOR READING Speke uses the prefix Wa- instead of Ba- for the plural of some local words (e.g. his Wakungu = Bakungu); *mbugu* = long cloth robe; bark was the source of clothes before the introduction of Zanzibari cloth; Kamraviona = principal attendant; *pombe* = fermented drink made from plantain or grain; *n'yanzigged* = applauded (see notes to Document 1). For Ganda impressions of Speke's and Stanley's visits, see the *Uganda Journal* (1961), pp. 220–3.

The mighty king was now reported to be sitting on his throne in the state hut of the third tier. I advanced, hat in hand, with my guard of honour following, formed in 'open ranks', who in their turn were followed by the bearers carrying the present. I did not walk straight up to him as if to shake hands, but went outside the ranks of a three-sided square of squatting Wakungŭ, all habited in skins, mostly cow-skins; some few of whom had, in addition, leopard-cat skins girt round the waist, the sign of royal blood. Here I was desired to halt and sit in the glaring sun; so I donned my hat, mounted my umbrella, a phenomenon which set them all a-wondering and laughing, ordered the guard to close ranks, and sat gazing at the novel spectacle! A more theatrical sight I never saw. The king, a good-looking, well-figured, tall young man of twenty-five, was sitting on a red blanket spread upon a square platform of royal grass, encased in tiger-grass reeds, scrupulously well dressed in a new mbŭgŭ. The hair of his head was cut short, excepting on the top, where it was combed up into a high ridge, running from stem to stern like a cockscomb. On his neck was a very neat ornament—a large ring, of beautifully worked small beads, forming elegant patterns by their various colours. On one arm was another bead ornament, prettily devised; and on the other a wooden charm, tied by a string covered with snake-skin. On every finger and every toe he had alternate brass and copper rings; and above the ankles, halfway up to the calf, a stocking of very pretty beads. Everything was light, neat, and elegant in its way; not a fault could be found with the taste of his 'getting up'. For a handkerchief he held a well-folded piece of bark, and a piece of gold-embroidered silk, which he constantly employed to hide his large mouth when laughing, or to wipe it after a drink of plantain-wine, of which he took constant and copious draughts from neat little gourd-cups, administered by his ladies-in-waiting, who were at once his sisters and wives. A white dog, spear, shield, and woman—the Uganda cognisance—were by his side, as also a knot of staff officers, with whom he kept up a brisk conversation on one side; and on the other was a band of Wichwézi, or lady-sorcerers such as I have already described.

I was now requested to shoot the four cows as quickly as possible; but having no bullets for my gun, I borrowed the revolving pistol I had given him, and shot all four in a second of time; but as the last one, only wounded, turned sharply upon me, I gave him the fifth and settled him. Great applause followed this *wonderful* feat, and the cows were given to my men. The king now loaded one of the carbines I had given him with his own hands, and giving it full-cock to a page, told him to go out and shoot a man in the outer court; which was no sooner accomplished than the little urchin returned to announce his success, with a look of glee such as one would see in the face of a boy who had robbed a bird's nest, caught a trout, or done any other boyish trick. The king said to him, 'And did you do it well?' 'Oh, yes, capitally.' He spoke the truth, no doubt, for he dared not have trifled with the king; but the affair created hardly any interest. I never heard, and there appeared no curiosity to know, what individual human being the urchin had deprived of life . . .

To call upon the queen-mother respectfully, as it was the opening visit, I took, besides the medicine-chest, a present of eight brass and copper wire, thirty blue-egg beads, one bundle of diminutive beads, and sixteen cubits of chintz, a small guard, and my throne of royal grass. The palace to be visited lay half a mile beyond the king's, but the highroad to it was forbidden me, as it is considered uncourteous to pass the king's gate without going in. So after winding through back-gardens, the slums of Bandowaroga, I struck upon the highroad close to her majesty's, where everything looked like the royal palace on a miniature scale. A large cleared space divided the queen's residence from her Kamraviona's. The outer enclosures and courts were fenced with tiger-grass; and the huts, though neither so numerous nor so large, were constructed after the same fashion as the king's. Guards also kept the doors, on which large bells were hung to give alarm, and officers in waiting watched the throne-rooms. All the huts were full of women, save those kept as waiting-rooms; where drums and harmonicons were played for amusement. On first entering, I was required to sit in a waiting-hut till my arrival was announced; but that did not take long, as the queen was prepared to receive me; and being of a more affable disposition than her son, she held rather a levee of amusement than a stiff court of show, I entered the throne-hut as the gate of that court was thrown open, with my hat off, but umbrella held over my head, and walked straight towards her till ordered to sit upon my bundle of grass.

Her majesty—fat, fair, and forty-five—was sitting, plainly garbed in mbŭgŭ, upon a carpet spread upon the ground within a curtain of mbŭgŭ, her elbow resting on a pillow of the same bark material; the only ornaments on her person being an abrus necklace, and a piece of mbŭgŭ tied round her head, whilst a folding looking-glass, much the worse for wear, stood open by her side. . .

I then took out two pills, the powder of which was tasted by the Wakungŭ to prove that there was no devilry in 'the doctor', and gave orders for them to be eaten at night, restricting her pombé and food until I saw her again. My game was now advancing, for I found through her I should get the key to an influence that might bear on the king, and was much pleased to hear her express herself delighted with me for everything I had done except stopping her grog, which, naturally enough in this great pombé-drinking country, she said would be a very trying abstinence.

The doctoring over, her majesty expressed herself ready to inspect the honorarium I had brought for her, and the articles were no sooner presented by Bombay and Nasib, with the usual formalities of stroking to insure their purity, than she, boiling with pleasure, showed them all to her officers, who declared, with a voice of most exquisite triumph, that she was indeed the most favoured of queens. Then, in excellent good taste, after saying that nobody had ever given her such treasures, she gave me, in return, a beautifully worked pombé sucking-pipe, which was acknowledged by every one to be the greatest honour she could pay me. . .

The road to the palace I found thronged with people; and in the square outside the entrance there squatted a multitude of attendants, headed by the king, sitting on a cloth, dressed in his national costume, with two spears and a shield by his side. On his right hand the pages sat waiting for orders, while on his left there was a small squatting cluster of women, headed by Wichwézis, or attendant sorceresses, offering pombé. In front of the king, in form of a hollow square, many ranks deep, sat the victorious officers, lately returned from the war, variously dressed; the nobles distinguished by their leopard-cat skins and dirks, the commoners by coloured mbŭgŭ and cow or antelope skin cloaks; but all their faces and arms were painted red, black, or smoke-colour. Within the square of men, immediately fronting the king, the war-arms of Uganda were arranged in three ranks; the great war-drum, covered with a leopard-skin, and standing on a large carpeting of them, was placed in advance; behind this, propped or hung on a rack of iron, were a variety of the implements of war in common use, offensive and defensive, as spears—of which two were of copper, the rest iron—and shields of wood and leather; whilst in the last row or lot were arranged systematically, with great taste and powerful effect, the supernatural arms, the god of Uganda, consisting of charms of various descriptions and in great numbers. Outside the square again, in a line with the king, were the household arms, a very handsome copper kettledrum, of French manufacture, surmounted on the outer edge with pretty little brass bells depending from swan-neck-shaped copper wire, two new spears, a painted leather shield, and magic wands of various devices, deposited on a carpet of leopard-skins—the whole scene giving the effect of true barbarous royalty in its uttermost magnificence.

Approaching, as usual, to take my seat beside the king, some slight sensation was perceptible, and I was directed to sit beyond the women. The whole ceremonies of this grand assemblage were now obvious. Each regimental commandant in turn narrated the whole services of his party, distinguishing those subs who executed his orders well and successfully from those who either deserted before the enemy or feared to follow up their success. The king listened attentively, making, let us suppose, very shrewd remarks concerning them; when to the worthy he awarded pombé, helped with gourd-cups from large earthen jars, which was n'yanzigged for vehemently; and

to the unworthy, execution. When the fatal sentence was pronounced, a terrible bustle ensued, the convict wrestling and defying, whilst the other men seized, pulled and tore the struggling wretch from the crowd, bound him hands and head together, and led or rather tumbled him away.

The Europeans who visited Buganda after Speke arrived from the north as part of a process of Egyptian expansion. Nominally subject to the Ottoman Sultan and increasingly under the influence of European advisers and creditors, the Khedive of Egypt sought to extend his control from the Khartoum area south to the sources of the Nile, beginning in the late 1860s. By 1872 his representatives were in correspondence with Mutesa, who briefly considered re-orienting his trading contacts from Zanzibar to the north. By 1876 he had clearly decided against the Khartoum network because of legitimate fears that Egypt might seek to annex his dominions. To the first of the Khedive's agents to reach the capital, the American Chaillé-Long, we are indebted for a description of a scene at the palace in which Mutesa demonstrates his capacity for dealing as decisively with the traditional priests as with the Muslim martyrs of Document 5.

DOCUMENT 7
'The fatal cords of the executioners'

Observations of Colonel C. Chaillé-Long at the court of Buganda in July 1874. Chaillé-Long, 'Itinerary', in Egyptian General Staff, *Provinces of the Equator. Summary of Letters and Reports of H.E. The Governor General.* Part I, Year 1874 (1877), pp. 61–2.

NOTES FOR READING   Kongowee = Commander of the army. The spirit guardians were Lubare priests who were protesting what they took to be Mutesa's decision to allow Chaillé-Long to explore the lake, a decision which was never implemented.

There was an unusual assemblage at the palace, and some great question evidently engaged M'tesa's attention. I leaned feebly against the post behind me, and suddenly there were cries and confusion without, and the fatal cords of the executioners were encircling the necks of seven men, who had just been by turns addressing M'tesa. These were the spirit-guardians of the lake, a terror to all Uganda supposed to exercise control over the lake and the river. The terror they have inspired, the murders they have committed, are a matter of tradition. M'tesa had broken the chain of this superstition in order that his men might take me far out upon the lake. M'tesa said to me: 'It pains my bowels to do this, but they have done me and my people great injury, and I do this for you as well.' This execution was followed by a rush into the palace of a large number of officers of the Army, headed by the Kongowee (General in chief) with clubs in their hands. With wild gesticulations and loud vociferations they rushed towards

M'tesa, shouting: 'You are the great M'tesa, we are your faith-fuls.'

The next and best known European visitor was the journalist and explorer, Henry Stanley (see Document 1). Like Speke, Stanley spent about five months in and around the capital. Unlike both Speke and Chaillé-Long, he received an enthusiastic reception and acquired a positive impression of the king, prompting him to issue a call for missionaries to create a new and powerful 'Zion' on the shores of Lake Victoria.

DOCUMENT 8
'Harvest ripe for the sickle of civilization'

Stanley, *Dark Continent*, I, pp. 192–4, 209.

NOTES FOR READING   Sekeletu = chief of the Kololo living in Barotseland; Muley bin Salim = prominent Zanzibari teacher and trader. Uganda is here synonomous with Buganda; only in the 1890s did Uganda come to mean the entire British colonial territory of which Buganda was the southern part.

The *Kabaka*, a tall, clean-faced, large-eyed, nervous-looking, thin man, clad in a tarbush, black robe, with a white shirt belted with gold, shook my hands warmly and impressively, and, bowing not ungracefully, invited me to be seated on an iron stool. I waited for him to show the example, and then I and all the others seated ourselves.

He first took a deliberate survey of me, which I returned with interest, for he was as interesting to me as I was to him. His impression of me was that I was younger than Speke, not so tall, but better dressed. This I gathered from his criticisms as confided to his chiefs and favourites.

My impression of him was that he and I would become better acquainted, that I should make a convert of him, and make him useful to Africa—but what other impressions I had may be gathered from the remarks I wrote that evening in my diary:

'As I had read Speke's book for the sake of its geographical information, I retained but a dim remembrance of his description of his life in Uganda. If I remeber rightly, Speke described a youthful prince, vain and heartless, a wholesale murderer and tyrant, one who delighted in fat women. Doubtless he described what he saw, but it is far from being the state of things now. Mtesa has impressed me as being an intelligent and distinguished prince, who, if aided in time by virtuous philanthropists, will do more for Central Africa than fifty years of Gospel teaching, unaided by such authority, can do. I think I see in him the light that shall lighten the darkness of this benighted region; a prince well worthy the most hearty sympathies that Europe can give him. In this man I see the possible fruition of Livingstone's hopes, for with his aid the civlization of Equatorial Africa becomes feasible. I remember the ardour and love which animated Livingstone when he spoke of Sekeletu; had he seen Mtesa, his ardour and love for him had been

tenfold, and his pen and tongue would have been employed in calling all good men to assist him.'

Five days later I wrote the following entry:

'I see that Mtesa is a powerful Emperor, with great influence over his neighbours. I have to-day seen the turbulent Mankorongo, king of Usul, and Mirambo, that terrible phantom who disturbs men's minds in Unyamwezi, through their embassies kneeling and tendering their tribute to him. I saw over 3000 soldiers of Mtesa nearly half civilized. I saw about a hundred chiefs who might be classed in the same scale as the men of Zanzibar and Oman, clad in as rich robes, and armed in the same fashion, and have witnessed with astonishment such order and law as is obtainable in semi-civilized countries. All this is the result of a poor Muslim's labour; his name is Muley bin Salim. He it was who first began teaching here the doctrines of Islam. False and contemptible as these doctrines are, they are preferable to the ruthless instincts of a savage despot, whom Speke and Grant left wallowing in the blood of women, and I honour the memory of Muley bin Salim— Muslim and slave-trader though he be—the poor priest who has wrought this happy change. With a strong desire to improve still more the character of Mtesa, I shall begin building on the foundation stones laid by Muley bin Salim. I shall destroy his belief in Islam, and teach the doctrines of Jesus of Nazareth.'

It may easily be gathered from these entries that a feeling of admiration for Mtesa must have begun very early, and that either Mtesa is a very admirable man, or that I am a very impressionable traveller, or that Mtesa is so perfect in the art of duplicity and acted so clever a part, that I become his dupe. . .

In the evening I concluded my letters dated 14th April 1875, which were sent to the *Daily Telegraph* and the *New York Herald*, the English and American journals I represented here, appealing for a Christian mission to be sent to Mtesa.

The appeal written hurriedly, and included in the letter left at Usavara, was as follows:

'I have, indeed, undermined Islamism so much here that Mtesa has determined henceforth, until he is better informed, to observe the Christian Sabbath as well as the Muslim Sabbath, and the great captains have unanimously consented to this. He has further caused the Ten Commandments of Moses to be written on a board for his daily perusal—for Mtesa can read Arabic—as well as the Lord's Prayer and the golden commandment of our Saviour. 'Thou shalt love thy neighbour as thyself.' This is great progress for the few days that I have remained with him, and, though I am no missionary, I shall begin to think that I might become one if such success is feasible. But, oh! that some pious, practical missionary would come here! What a field and harvest ripe for the sickle of civilization! Mtesa would give him anything he desired—houses, lands, cattle, ivory, etc.; he might call a province his own in one day. It is not the mere preacher, however, that is wanted here. The bishops of Great Britain collected, with all the classic youth of Oxford and Cambridge, would effect nothing by mere talk with the intelligent people of Uganda. It is the practical Christian tutor, who can teach people how to become Christians, cure their diseases, construct dwellings, understand and exemplify agriculture, and turn his hand to anything, like a sailor—this is the man who is wanted. Such an one, if he can be found, would become the saviour of Africa. He must be tied to no church or sect, but profess God and His Son and the moral law, and live a blameless Christian, inspired by liberal principles, charity to all men, and devout faith in Heaven. He must belong to no nation in particular, but to the entire white race. Such a man or men, Mtesa, Emperor of Uganda, Usoga, Unyoro, and Karagwé—an empire 360 geographical miles in length, by 50 in breadth —invites to repair to him. He has begged me to tell the white men that, if they will only come to him, he will give them all they want. Now, where is there in all the pagan world a more promising field for a mission than Uganda?'

The Last Years of Mutesa (1877–84)

Stanley exaggerated; Mutesa had certainly not converted to Christianity nor had 'Islamism' been undermined. None the less, the explorer did make a good impression, particularly when he helped the king in a struggle against the Bavuma people of the eastern frontier. He also engaged the king in conversations about Christianity and had passages of the Bible translated. His servant and interpreter remained at the court to provide instruction to the Kabaka. More important was the reception of Stanley's call in Europe, especially in the Church Missionary Society (CMS) of England. By 1877 the first Anglican missionaries—not 'blameless' nor always 'liberal' but certainly 'white' and in this case Protestant—had arrived in the East African capital. In 1879 they were joined by French Roman Catholics belonging to the White Fathers Society. The two sets of missionaries established their respective headquarters close to the palace and began to compete with each other and with the Muslims for royal attention and converts among the pages. Factions soon emerged with ethnic, national and religious labels: the 'Arab' party for the followers of Islam; the Baporostante, Bangereza ('Englishmen'), or 'People of the Book' for the Anglicans; and the Bafransa ('Frenchmen') or 'Bakatoliki' for the Catholics. All were known as 'readers' and all, to some extent, stood opposite a fourth group, the traditional religious authorities. Given a very centralized society and the ambition of the young Baganda who converted to the new faiths, the competition for religious allegiance became an intense struggle for political and ideological domination.

One important reason for the turmoil of this period was the decline in the fortunes of the kingdom and in the energy of its sovereign. A series of epidemics ravaged the population. Military expeditions were less successful despite the large-scale introduction of firearms. The generation of chiefs trained in the page school pressed for promotions that a stagnant state and bureaucracy could not provide. Finally Mutesa himself, although only about forty, became seriously ill in 1879, probably with gonorrhoea. The Kabaka never fully recovered and could no longer control the traders, missionaries, and ambitious Baganda drawn to the court.

By 1879 the hopes of both the Anglican and Catholic missionaries were high. Mutesa received them well, gave them access to the court and allowed them to attract young pages and others to their headquarters. He even sent a delegation to Queen Victoria in the company of CMS representatives. The king was puzzled by the divisions within Christianity, but took advantage of the rivalry, as the following documents show.

DOCUMENT 9
'Courted by the king'

Our translation of White Father Livinhac's comments on Mutesa's methods. Abbé A. Nicq, *La Vie du Reverend Père Siméon Lourdel* (1896), p. 269.

First, through the agency of people who have an air of letting you into confidential secrets, he lets you know that he is delighted at the arrival of his new guests, and wants nothing to do with those who preceded you as they have let him down. He knows, however, that you would never do such a thing, and it is your friendship that he wants. He knows, too, that your religion is the only good one, and this is why he wants to learn all about it . . . and adopt it. His slaves are sent to salute you and to offer presents. He gets you to join in religious discussions with other strangers . . . in the country and decides arguments in your favor.

DOCUMENT 10
'The king wanted to know more'

Our translation of Father Livinhac's account of the debates encouraged by Mutesa. Father J. Mercui, *L'Ouganda, la Mission Catholique et les Agents de la Compagnie Anglaise* (1893), pp. 10–11.

NOTES FOR READING   Mackay was the most important Anglican (CMS) missionary in the early days; Lourdel was the principal Catholic figure. This debate occurred in June, 1879.

The king wanted to know more about the differences between Protestant and Catholic. Addressing himself to Father Lourdel, he said, 'Read me something and give me your prayer.' Lourdel then took the Swahili catechism of the Holy Ghost Fathers and read the first chapters, with Mutesa listening attentively. In effect, he knew that language perfectly. When the Father finished, he slyly asked Mr. Mackay what he thought of the reading. Mackay replied, 'Very good. I did notice, however, that he called the Holy Virgin the Mother of God, which is false: God, having no beginning, can not have a Mother.' 'Excuse me', interjected Lourdel, 'he did not begin as God, that's true, but he began as a man; and, when he became a man, he wished to be born of a mother.' The king indicated that he understood the distinction; Mackay did not persist on that question, but shifted to another point. 'The Catholics say that their leader is impeccable and thus put him in the place of God. That is impossible.' Lourdel responded, 'Distinguish, please, between impeccability and infallibility. We affirm the latter but not the former.' Mackay did not persist.

The optimism of the missionaries faded at the end of 1879 in the face of a reassertion by the traditional religious leaders. As the king's health worsened, they contended that the cause of his illness was the reception of the new religions, and urged him to receive the ministrations of the priest of Mukasa, the god of healing. The king accepted, but not without protests from the CMS missionary, Alexander Mackay.

DOCUMENT 11
'Strongly in favour of the *Lubare*'

From Mackay's diary. J. W. Harrison, ed, *A. M. Mackay* (1890), pp. 160–4. (J. W. Harrison was Mackay's sister.)

NOTES FOR READING the god Mukasa is not to be confused with Katikiro Mukasa of Document 1 or Hamu Mukasa, author of Document 5; Gabunga = head of Lungfish clan and admiral of the fleet; Maandwa = medium; Ramathan = important Muslim at the court; Kago = county chief of Kyadondo; Mufta = Stanley's servant who remained in Buganda; Kitunzi = county chief of Gomba; Mukwenda = county chief of Singo; Suma = Suna.

I began by asking if it was now his pleasure that I should cease teaching the Word of God at court on Sundays. He said, 'No; not by any means.' I said that now he and his chiefs had made up their minds to bring to stay at court the *lubare*, whom he (Mtesa) allowed to me the other day to be a deceiver, that I had no right to interfere with his orders or whom he chose as his guest; only this visitor, for whom preparations were made, was no ordinary guest, but was looked up to by the people as possessed of powers which belonged to God alone; that we could not mix up the worship of God Almighty with the worship of a man who was the enemy of God. Mtesa listened attentively, and then said to his chiefs, 'Do you hear what Mackay says? He says that we cannot bring the *lubare* here without offending God.' One of the chiefs replied that the *lubare* was only coming with medicine to heal the king. I replied that the *lubare* was not merely a doctor, but was looked up to by all as a wizard, and as being able to heal people by enchantment. Mtesa allowed that I was right, and said he knew very well that this Mukasa was coming to use witchcraft. I said further that we should only be delighted if Mukasa could cure the king, and neither I nor any one else could object to his bringing medicine for that purpose. The king went on to say that Gabunga (chief on the Lake) had come some time ago to say that Mukasa was able to cure him. 'Bring his medicine, then,' said Mtesa. Jumba brought some; but said it was of no use unless the *lubare* was present himself to perform the cure. 'This and that other fellow', continued Mtesa, 'says that he is a *Maandwa*, and that the spirit of my ancestors has gone into them; but do you think I believe that?' I said that I believed he had more sense than to believe anything of the kind; for when a man dies, his soul returns to God, so that these fellows were only liars, and deceived the people. The king replied, 'What you say, Mackay, is perfectly true, and I know that all witch-

craft is falsehood.' I thanked him for this statement, but the Katikiro and other chiefs showed themselves very ill-pleased. They saw no harm in the *lubare* being received with all honour. He would make medicine which they would hang up in the palace-houses, as Mukasa was a great medicine-man. I repeated that medicine was an excellent thing, but it was not medicine that Mukasa got so great a name for, or that they regarded him as a *lubare* for; but that he was a great diviner, and wished the people to believe him a god.

The king assented again strongly to this, and called forward one of the coast men—Ramathan—who is said to be an Afghan from Cabool. . .

Ramathan at first saw that the king was assenting to my statements, so he also assented, and said that if this *lubare* were able to cure the king, he should have done so long ago, as Mtesa had now been ill for two years.

After further talk, when he saw that the chiefs were strongly in favour of the *lubare*, Ramathan veered over to their side, and said that, as raw flesh of a day old did not ever corrupt anything, there could be no harm done in letting the *lubare* settle in the palace for a day or two.

I said that I could not hinder the king having the *lubare* as many days at court as he liked, only I found it my duty to tell him that his encouraging this false person would have a powerful effect in the country in confirming the faith of the people in witchcraft, in which he (Mtesa) himself did not believe. I took my stand on the Word of God, which said that all who used witchcraft were enemies of God.

Mtesa said that he did not know what to do, as his mother and her friends were the main advocates of the *lubare*, and it was they who first advised him (Mtesa) being carried to see the wizard; and when he declined, on the ground of sickness, they got him to have the wizard brought here. He did not know how to get out of the fix, for he knew that it was wrong, yet his mother's people wished it. I replied that we were ready to show all honour and respect to his mother and relations, but God was greater than all; and I advised him to choose which he would serve. I had no more to say, and soon after the king dismissed the court.

I left, feeling that I had the king's ear, but that several of the chiefs were strongly opposed to me.

Before court broke up, the king called forward Kago and another chief—both great advocates of the *lubare*—and deputed them to go to his mother and the other old women (aunts, etc.), and say that he (Mtesa) did not wish to have the *lubare* brought to court, but that he wished to hear what they had to say.

In the afternoon, when Mufta was with me, he was sent for by the king, who was holding another court. I believe that Kitunzi was there present, and advising the king strongly against having anything more to do with the white man's religion, as it was only a preliminary step to taking the country that we were now teaching. Ramathan was also present, and was talking much against us.

Mufta was told to leave, and go back to me, which he did. A third *baraza* was held in the evening, but what transpired I do not know.

Tuesday, 23rd.—This morning Mukwenda told Lourdel that

the king had said he would kill any boys who came again to learn reading here. I doubted the truth of the king having said so, for Mukwenda is himself a mere boy, and has no say at court; although some of the chiefs had probably said that they wished no more teaching by us. One or two lads were reading, however, with me this morning, and others last night till after dark.

Soon after eight o'clock a messenger came, saying that the king called us all to court.

When we were seated I was called forward, and Kago and a woman were brought in. The king said that the result of Kago's mission was that this woman, (his aunt, I believe), had been sent to bring me to the council of the king's mother, and others of the family of Suma, that I might explain to them why I refused to allow the king to see the *lubare*.

I replied that I would not go to explain at any other court than this; that I did not refuse to allow the king to see the *lubare*, only as a servant of God I had warned him of the sin of witchcraft; that I used no force, and had told the king yesterday that it was my place to tell him the truth, while he was free to follow or reject my advice.

The chiefs—especially the Katikiro—all set to talking a deal, after which I saw that the king was afraid of acting contrary to them. Mtesa then gave a verdict which pleased them all, for they *nyanzigged* boldly after he said it. He said that now they would leave both the Arab's religion and the Muzungu's religion, and would go back to the religion of their fathers!

One result of the decision to go 'back to the religion of their fathers' was a temporary ban on evangelization by the missionaries. Mutesa also seized this opportunity to stress his desire for guns and other material benefits of the European presence—a theme which he had often repeated in his conversations with the missionaries.

Mutesa could not, however, escape his fascination with the new ideologies, nor did his attachment to the Lubare last very long on this occasion. Six months after he re-embraced the Lubare, Mutesa claimed to be a Muslim again. Throughout this period the king seemed to enjoy the debates among the competing parties.

DOCUMENT 12
'So many religions in the country'

From Mackay's journal for December 1880, *Church Missionary Intelligencer*, (1881), pp. 613–15.

NOTES FOR READING Mr (Charles) Pearson = Anglican missionary; Levesque = Catholic missionary; Katonda = God the Creator; Muzungu = white person of European; Nende = second god of war; Sekibobo = county chief of Kyagwe; Lieutenant Smith = Anglican missionary who came to Buganda in 1877; Baker = Englishman working in the Upper Nile for the Khedive; Singo = county governed by the Mukwenda; Mapera = local pronunciation of 'mon père' and referring to Lourdel.

Wednesday, 22nd.—Mr. Pearson and myself went to court, where we found MM. Levesque and Lourdel. The latter goes every day with some drug for the king. It would be a farce to call his mixtures 'medicine,' for none of their party have any idea of medicine.

After a little the court opened, and, there being many chiefs present, we were seated in the very back corner—i.e. behind them all.

Mtesa began asking his chiefs a host of questions on the gods of the country. Some under-chiefs had returned from plundering in Busoga, and the charms which their sorcerers had taken with them were presented to his Majesty. This was probably the occasion of Mtesa's asking his chiefs, 'Which is the greater—the king or the lubare?' Some said the king was the greater, others said the lubare. Talk continued on the matter for a long time, to little or no purpose, as all the chiefs are profound sycophants, and echo everything Mtesa says, although one moment he said that their own gods were nothing, and Katonda all in all, and next moment that the idols and sorcerers had divine power.

Mr. Pearson then asked if anything would be done to any one who embraced Christianity. Mtesa replied that there were many old people (women chiefly) in the country, who had power, and these would be sure to kill any one who despised the gods of the country. Mr. Pearson replied that he (Mtesa) was King of Buganda, and that if he gave the order that men embracing Christianity were to be let alone, no one could touch them. Mtesa than said that if any one went to the Muzungu to read he surely committed no criminal offence. 'To read,' he said, 'is not robbery, and one could not be condemned for that.' I then explained that merely learning to read was not to embrace Christianity. I said, 'If a man becomes a Christian he will know that the religion of the lubare is false, and hence will not be able to attend court when any of the lubares make a demonstration there. If a man is baptized—either a chief or a common man—will he be punished for refusing to join in the ceremonies of the lubare?' To this no answer was given, but talk was continued on the powers of the gods.

'What is Nende?' asked Mtesa.

Kyambalango replied, 'Nende is a man—Nende is a god.'

Katikiro said, 'Nende is an image.'

'Sekibobo,' said Mtesa, 'what is Nende?'

Sekibobo is one of the three greatest chiefs. He was sitting a little behind, as he was troubled with catarrh, and etiquette forbade him to sit in his usual place. But before Sekibobo could make up his mind, not as to what Nende was, but as to what answer would please the king most, Mr. Pearson, who was sitting behind the chief, called out, 'Nende is a tree! Nende can neither walk nor speak, nor eat.' Mtesa repeated this for the benefit of all, and from many a sycophant came the echo, 'Nende is a tree, and cannot speak or eat.' Some, however, dissented, saying that Nende is a god; when I proposed that Nende should be brought and set on the floor before us all, that we might see what he was. This created some merriment, while others were shocked at the idea of such sacrilege, and Katikiro replied, 'The woman who has charge of Nende will not allow him to be brought.'

Again we asked if people could with impunity come to us to be taught the knowledge of God.

Mtesa replied that before Stanley came he was a Mussulman, then he became a Christian, and when Lieutenant Smith came here Smith used to teach one part of the day, and he (Mtesa) the other. I said, 'Those were happy days; but they are long gone by.' The king laughed, and continued that now he found so many religions in the country, each asserting itself as the true one, that he did not know what to do. He then called M. Lourdel forward as also Babakeri (an old soldier of Baker's, and a heathen, but a favourite counsellor).

We put the question very plainly, repeating it again and again, that there should be no mistake. We said that we did not ask the king to order his people to follow Christianity, we only begged that he would give permission (rukhsa = liberty) to any one in the kingdom, high or low, to accept any religion he chose; if any one liked to continue a believer in the lubare he might do so; if any one chose to go to the Frenchmen to be taught he might do so; if any one chose to become a Mohammedan he might do so; and if any one chose to come to us to be taught the book of God he might do so.

First, the Arabs were asked by the king if he should grant our request. They replied that they had nothing to say, as the elder Arabs were not present that day. One old fanatic, however, commenced a harangue on the absolute truth of the creed, as they stick to the Koran and the patriarchs. I declined to have them consulted in this matter, as, I said, they had come for trade, and not as teachers, and no one wished to take their Koran from them.

Next Mtesa asked Babakeri if he should give the liberty we begged. This fellow, after some hesitation, replied. 'Yes, sir; give liberty.'

Mtesa, too cunning to listen to good advice, which he feared might result in leaving him less absolute than he is at present, tried a new artifice to evade the question. 'Suppose', said he, 'I divide the country, and give Singo (Mkwenda's country) to the English to be taught, and Kyagwe (Sekibobo's) to the Frenchmen, that they may teach every one there—will there not be rows between them?' We replied that in Zanzibar both English and French lived and taught in peace, and in Europe also, and that we should make no trouble with the French teachers.

Mtesa then proposed that the Frenchmen and ourselves should first agree on religious matters, and then he would listen to us both. This was merely a ruse to try to get us to enter on discussion, which he enjoys, especially if it occasions ill-feeling between the disputants. We were silent, however, and his ruse failed.

Before the talk on religion was finished he listened to the report of the plundering batongole just returned from Busoga. A chief was ordered at once to go to bring the women, cattle, and slaves, which they had left a day's march from the capital. One of the returned batongole (being accused, I fancy, of appropriating too much of the spoil to himself) was ordered, without ceremony, to be killed. An executioner of whom there is always a host present at every court, jumped forward with perfect delight in his face, rope in hand, to drag off the delinquent. The fellow bought himself off, however, with the

greatest calmness, for some women and cattle. The executioner stepped back disappointed.

A few moments afterwards, in the discussion, Mtesa said, 'God hears everything I say; He hears when Mackay speaks; He hears when Mapera or the Arabs speak!' Oh, the savour of death unto death, which our teaching seems to have been to him, and to the whole court. Human life and eternal life equally despised—while his conscience has become scared against what he knows, as well as we, to be great sin. Lasciviousness seems to have turned his soul and mind, like his body, into utter subjection to itself. The first chapter of Romans most accurately describes the state of this king's court and country.

After mentioning the solemn fact of all having to answer to God in the next world, Mtesa suddenly asked me if he could get a white princess by going to England. Prudence prompted me to reply. 'I am not an English princess, therefore I cannot give you a reply.'

The conference ended by Mtesa laying the case thus before the court:—'If we accept the Muzungu's religion we must then have only one wife; while if we accept the religion of the Arabs we cannot eat every kind of flesh.'

Thus it is that a trifling restraint on the flesh is balanced against eternal life and peace with God.

Like the Kabaka, most of the pages at the palace were caught up in the ongoing religious debates which challenged their traditional attachments to clan and region. Many of them adopted Islam and Christianity at different times in their lives. In their cases, unlike Mutesa's, the new religious allegiance consistently superseded other loyalties. Stanislaus Mugwanya of Document 2 and Mathias Kalemba, the subject of the following document, exemplify this process.

DOCUMENT 13
'The Baganda did not have the truth'

Kalemba's story at the time of his baptism in 1882, as told to Livinhac in 1882. A translation of Nicq, *Lourdel* pp. 224–6. A complete English translation may be found in J. P. Thoonen, *Black Martyrs* (1941), pp. 50–1.

NOTES FOR READING Kalemba was born in the 1840s and was executed in 1886 (see Document 21); Mapera = Lourdel.

'My father had always believed that the Baganda did not have the truth. He sought it in his heart. He had often said so to me, and before dying he told me that one day men would come to teach the good way. This statement made a profound impression on me, and every time the arrival of some foreigner was announced, I would watch him and try to make contact with him, telling myself that perhaps he was the one prophesied by my father. That was how I began frequenting the Arabs who came for the first time under the reign of Suna. Their beliefs seemed to me superior to our superstitions. I received instruction and embraced their religion with a number of other

Baganda. Mutesa himself, to please the Sultan of Zanzibar, whose power and wealth had been exaggerated to him, declared that he also wished to be Muslim. The order was given to build mosques in the provinces. For a moment it seemed that the whole country would embrace the religion of the false Prophet. But Mutesa had an extreme repugnance for circumcision. Thus, catching himself abruptly, he gave the order to exterminate all those who had become Muslim. Many perished in the massacre; two or three hundred managed to escape and get to Zanzibar with the help of Arab caravans. I succeeded, with a few others, in hiding my conversion and in passing for a friend of our gods; in secret, however, I was still faithful to the practice of Islam.

'So there I was when the Protestants came. Mutesa gave them a good welcome. He had their book read at court and seemed inclined towards their religion, which he called much superior to that of the Arabs. I wondered if I had been wrong and if the newcomers were the true envoys of God. I visited them often and attended their classes. It seemed to me that their teaching was superior to that of my first masters. Thus I abandoned Islam. I did not, however, ask for baptism.

'Several months went by and then Mapera arrived. Mackay, my teacher, was careful to explain that the whites who had just arrived did not know the truth. Their religion was 'the religion of the woman'. They adored the Virgin Mary, he said. He counseled me to avoid them completely. That's why I never came to see you and it's likely that if my superior had not made me responsible for supervision of the construction of one of your huts, I would never have come here. But God showed his love for me. The first time I saw you close-up I was very struck, but I held back. I watched you closely, however, when you were praying and speaking to the people. Seeing your goodness, I told myself: How can it be that men who seem so good could be the envoys of the Devil?

'I began to talk to those who were coming to you for instruction concerning your doctrine. What they taught me was just the opposite of what Mackay had told me. I felt myself impelled to attend your catechetical classes. God was gracious in making me understand that you teach the truth and that you are truly the men of God my father spoke about. Since then I have not had the least doubt about the truth of your religion and I am truly happy.'

The missionary asked Mathias if he were resolved not to return to Protestantism. If you must do it, he added, it would be better not to receive baptism.

'Fear nothing, my father. Two years ago I made my decision, and nothing could make me go back on it. I am Catholic and will die Catholic.'

In his final years, Mutesa continued to vacillate about his allegiance and preferences. He enjoyed more intimate contacts with the Zanzibari Muslims than with the missionaries; he had, after all, known several of them throughout much of his reign. He usually preferred the Catholics to the Protestants, partly because the French did not seem to pose the same threat to his kingdom as the English. Although the White Fathers left Buganda temporarily in 1882, their following, like that of the Muslims and

Protestants, continued to grow under indigenous leadership. But the cohesion of the kingdom was fragile. The princes were fighting one another for the succession, the younger generation of chiefs was pressing against the old, and Mutesa was losing his grip. When he died in October 1884, the air was heavy with anxiety about the future. Even Philip O'Flaherty, an Anglican missionary who had frequently argued with Mutesa, greatly regretted his passing.

DOCUMENT 14
'My staunch and generous friend'

O'Flaherty's impressions, recorded in *Church Missionary Intelligencer* (1885), pp. 241–3.

NOTES FOR READING   Ashe = another CMS missionary; Namasole = Queen Mother; Sekibobo = county chief of Kyagwe; Luekula = area on western border of Buganda which became a county in the 1890s; Mwalima = Swahili for teacher. At the time of writing, Mwanga had just acceded to the throne. The 'governor-generalship' refers to a practice which Mutesa used of giving small chieftaincies to foreign favourites, roughly equivalent to the *Batangole*.

October 10th.—'A month ago the King sent for me and asked me to examine him privately. Some princesses came in, and the examination was postponed. I told his Majesty that I did not wish to prescribe for him, as I was no finished physician, and I was afraid I might be blamed if anything serious happened. He agreed; and an ignorant coast-man guaranteed to heal him. I warned him many times about those coast quacks. The result is that this morning at 3 a.m. the King died. One or two of our Christian young men ran down at that hour to inform me, and said, 'Fortify yourselves, for our habit is mutual and indiscriminate pillage, rapine, murder.'

'We were in expectation every moment that the mob would come and set fire to our house, and set their spears into us, having first plundered and maltreated us. Mr. Ashe and myself, while we loaded our guns and those of our men, to be in readiness for any sudden onslaught of a mob, for then we could disperse them, made up our minds not to fight chiefs, but let them rob on, because we think it is bad policy, and especially we think that our Master would not fight. To defend ourselves against a disorderly, bloodthirsty rabble is another thing.

'It is but a fortnight since the King sent for me at night, to see a princess aged nineteen, who was thought to be dying with the *kawompuli*, or black-plague. She is now all right.

'The last private interview I had with Mtesa he cordially thanked me for my kindness to his daughter. "I know, Philip", he said, "that you love me, my family, and my people; and I love you."

'He all along has been my staunch and generous friend. Many times the Arabs bribed the chiefs to speak against me, accusing me of many things and many evil designs, but they always came off the worst. I remember when Namosoli died, and Sekibobo—then no friend, now a staunch one—was imprisoned in the stocks, having been accused by a powerful faction for having bewitched his royal mother; and every one of the chiefs had something hard to say against him,—I remember getting up, and in a long and warm speech took the fallen commander-in-chief's part, and, in indignant tones and measured terms, said that those very chiefs who joined in condemning him and clamoured for his blood were those whom I often saw at his generous table, flattering him like a King. And I remember Mtesa sending for me next day, and saying, as he pointed to the prostrate chief at his feet, "There, Philipo, you, a stranger, pleaded for him nobly; there he is for you;" and turning to the chief, wriggling on the ground for joy, he said, "See, I have given you the chieftainship of Luekula."

'It has often been said that Mtesa was grasping; that might be so in a few cases, but generosity and hospitality and large-heartedness were the features I remarked most deeply characteristic of him. His love as a father and a husband was delightful to see; and never did he begin to eat himself till he saw that all his pages and numerous household were served first. His pages, princes, and chiefs, he clothed right royally; he enriched his country by encouraging trade with Arabs and others; the stranger he fed, and the foreigner he protected; his chiefs are dressed richly, in gold lace, gold buttons, and the finest cloths of scarlet, crimson, green, blue, saffron, and black, and fine white linen. In pleasant conversation, lit up with a winning dignity of manner, Mtesa was not surpassed in the world; keen and subtle in argument, quick as thought to comprehend, having to a most marvellous degree a command of temper and of language, he was ever fond of the sonorous, flowing cadences of Arabic poetry, in which taste I also share.

'I weep for my constant friend and generous protector. Once, and more than once, he tried to press upon me a governor-generalship; more than once he sent for me, to chide me that I did not go oftener to see him privately, for he gave me a privilege of private *entrée* that the Katikiro and Kimbugwe—the favourites—alone possessed. I mourn for my friend and protector. The last public interview I had with him was when he sent for me to tell me that he had *floored* the great Arab Mwalima (Rabbi) in argument. Thus: "Whom do the Arabs say that Jesus, the son of Mary, is? They say He is the *word* and spirit of God—Kelemet Ulla ve Rúhu hu. Well, I told him thus: Argue no more in my presence with Philipo. You have no leg to stand upon; for the Word of God must come from God, and be God, as a word has intelligence and wisdom in it. It is a Spirit of God; and, secondly, the Spirit of God must be one with God, for is not God a spirit?" And the light beamed in his face as he spake.'

October 11*th and* 12*th.*—'Spent two sleepless nights, waiting hourly to be attacked, robbed, and burnt. We loaded our guns, and resolved to defend our lives against a lawless rabble; but will not fight an organised body bent on booty. This would be bad religion and bad policy.

'The young King Mwanga often came here, though always in fear; and it is not long since I paid him a visit, and he came with me nearly a mile on my way home. And it is most curious that I should have told him then thus: "Mwanga, this illness is wasting your father. He certainly cannot reign long, and most certainly you will reign in his stead. Then remember and be

kind to us." Whether Mwanga makes a good monarch or not, time alone can tell. It greatly depends on the hands he falls into. But I have no great faith in him. He will, I think, be favourable to us. His sister, Rebecca Mugali, the true Christian of sterling character, is appointed Queen of Bu-Ganda or Lubuga. She might have a good influence over him.

"One good thing has happened; yea, two good things. (1) No prince has been yet put to death; (2) there has been no mutual fighting, no murder, rapine, or bloodshed. Such a thing, I am told, was never before known.

The Early Reign of Mwanga (1884–88)

The accession of Mwanga happened quickly and without the bloodshed predicted in O'Flaherty's account. Mutesa had defused the succession struggle by designating Mwanga, while his Katikiro Mukasa (see Document 1) ensured a smooth transition and kept his post until 1888.

Still, it was hardly a propitious moment. Added to the usual uncertainties of a succession were the new internal tensions based on the religious factions and stronger external pressures stemming from European expansion. It was a richer, more open and more fragmented Buganda than the young Mutesa had encountered on his accession. Mwanga, less than twenty years old, did not have the experience to deal with the situation. What follows is a range of assessments of the new king, beginning with the comments of a Catholic missionary written just after Mwanga invited the White Fathers to return to the capital. Document 16 is a statement made in 1888 by Katikiro Mukasa. Documents 17 and 18 represent estimates of the new Kabaka by Anglican missionaries. Roscoe arrived in Buganda in 1890, while Fletcher came in 1893 and lived in the area where Mwanga spent his childhood.

DOCUMENT 15
'Affectionately'

Our translation of Livinhac's account of the Uganda mission written about December 1884. *Les Missions Catholiques* (1885), p. 240. A similar statement appears in Nicq, *Lourdel*, p. 267.

Mwanga is a young man of about twenty years who has always shown great interest in us. He even asked to have religious instruction, but his moody father did not permit him to mix with our catechists and he had to come secretly through the bush to receive the first notions of Christianity. He took special pains to send his friends and servants to listen to our lessons so that they might repeat them to him later. Our departure [in 1882] affected him profoundly. The day I left the capital to go to the embarkation point on the lake, he waited for me on the path to say goodbye. The deepest sadness was etched on his face. He repeated that it was painful for him to see us go. I whispered in his ear: 'If ever you become king of Buganda, you will call us and we will quickly return.' He answered me by affectionately pressing my hand.

Since the successor of Mutesa had to be chosen among many children, we did not dare hope that the choice would fall on the only one who had shown an attachment to us. God has seen fit to answer our prayers and those of our neophytes. May He keep the king in this generous frame of mind!

DOCUMENT 16
'A youth'

M. Wright, *Buganda in the Heroic Age* (1972), pp. 28–9.

The king was still a youth, as his actions and conduct showed. He had not got the skill and wisdom of his father, Mutesa, and listened to the slanders of anyone. He was very greedy, not content with the spoils brought him from other lands, where his armies carry war; but he must rob and spoil his own subjects.

DOCUMENT 17
'Hemp-smoking'

John Roscoe, *Twenty-five Years in East Africa* (1921), pp. 115–16.

NOTE FOR READING   hemp = marijuana.

Much of Mwanga's so-called bloodthirsty nature was doubt-less due to Indian hemp smoking; this vice to which he had become addicted shattered his nerves. The drug had an injurious effect upon him, his moral character was under-mined, and he yielded to the worst passions of nature, while his powers of self-restraint were weakened. There was, how-ever, much good feeling and even tenderness in his character when he could be kept from his bad habits and was free from evil influences. Whenever he fell into habits of vice, he would give way to terrible passions being unable to restrain his lusts towards his page boys. Afterwards he would suffer torture mentally and physically, and be more like an irresponsible person than a sane man . . .

DOCUMENT 18
'Isolation'

T. B. Fletcher, 'Mwanga: the man and his times', *Uganda Journal* (1936–1937), p. 163.

NOTES FOR READING   Mengo = new capital of Mwanga next to Rubaga hill where Mutesa reigned during most of his last years; Natete = Muslim centre in the capital area.

Mwanga . . . was a youth in his late teens or early twenties. Previous to his accession Mwanga had spent the larger part

of his life away from the capital, living at some distance, as distance was accounted in those days, away from the new movements and the new civilization, which were rapidly appearing in and around Mengo [the capital]. As a youth much of his time was spent at Golola in the County of Gomba, fifty miles from Mengo, and for a few years prior to his being called upon to succeed to the throne he lived at Nkanaga in the County of Butambala, which is still more distant. At both places he was entirely surrounded by pagan life and thought. For a short period only was he in contact with the missionaries and Arabs at Natete. So short was the time, and at a period of such unrest in the country, that no good results could be expected.

For much of 1885 the hopes of both the Catholic and Protestant missionaries were fulfilled. As in 1879, they enjoyed access to the court, advanced the work of trans-lating and printing the Bible in Luganda, and attracted more and more young Baganda to their mission stations for instruction, including several hundred pages. They were not, however, without very powerful antagonists, particularly the senior Bakungu and Batangole who had become wealthy and influential from trade and military campaigns. These men grew anxious about the security of the government and their positions. At the court they viewed with apprehension the large number of Christian pages who communicated state secrets to their missionary patrons. Abroad they noticed the progressive encroach-ments of British and German forces, which were 'eating up' the East African coast and moving closer to the Lake. In September and October this concern was directed at the imminent arrival of James Hannington, the first Anglican Bishop for Eastern Equatorial Africa. Hanning-ton planned to reside at the capital and to journey to Buganda through its 'back door' or eastern frontier, rather than the well-established southern trade routes. The next document describes the atmosphere of the palace and Anglican mission on the eve of his expected arrival.

DOCUMENT 19
'Eat the country'

From Mackay's letter to the CMS of 29 September 1885. *Church Missionary Intelligencer* (1886), pp. 99–100, 101.

NOTES FOR READING   bhang = marijuana; the persecution refers to the execution of three young Protestants in January 1885; Mruli = post north of the Buganda fron-tier; Thomson = English explorer; Sematimba = Pro-testant chief; Msalala = CMS station south of the Lake; Ukumbi = White Fathers station south of the Lake.

When I came to Buganda Mwanga was only a little boy. But in all these years a whole generation of little black fellows has shot up into manhood. It would be very hard to describe

Mwanga's character. I have perhaps had more opportunity of knowing him than my brethren have had. He knows how to behave with dignity and reserve when he thinks the occasion requires that; but he soon throws off that assumed air, and chats familiarly. Black men are all very vain, nor is our king free from this defect. But none can fail to see that he is fitful and fickle, and I fear, revengeful. One vice to which he is addicted is the smoking of bhang. I cannot say precisely what are the temporary or permanent effects of the drug, as I have never tried it. I believe that it induces a sensation of temporary delirium, and, if persevered in, causes a peculiar insanity. At all events, bhang smoking was a capital offence in Mtesa's days. The Wanyamwezi are largely addicted to it; but I believe they will not allow their chiefs to smoke it. It is supposed to make them savage or fierce.

This being so one cannot place much confidence in Mwanga's stability. Under the influence of the narcotic he is capable of the wildest and most unpremeditated actions. Recently I have had reason to find him guilty of such. But generally the young fellow is amiable. I only hope that by trying to obtain some personal influence with him some good may be done. These kings and their great chiefs will only listen to admonition when given in the most gentle way, and at a suitable occasion. Otherwise they are very apt to resent any good advice. We sorely need your prayers that this king may be brought to the feet of Jesus. With man it seems impossible; but what is impossible with God? . . .

Since Mwanga came to the throne I am happy to think that we have really had fuller liberty than we had before. Of course the persecution of last spring excepted. It is a good sign that a great number, I may say almost all, of the pages and storekeepers, etc., about the court are pupils, either of ours or of the Papists. Again and again I have seen the various store and other houses at the court literally converted into readingrooms. I have almost feared that such extreme publicity might lead to a sudden check some day. Lads, sitting in groups, or sprawling on the hay-covered floor, all reading; some the Book of Commandments and other texts, some the Church prayers, and others the Kiswahili New Testament. They are, besides, very eager to learn to write, and at all times are scribbling on boards, or any scrap of paper they can pick up. Invariably some one or other of them sends us a semi-legible note containing news of anything said by the king affecting us. We make them pay for any paper or pens they want. Nor do we give them books, large or small, for nothing. The only things we give gratis are alphabets, and little pages of syllables. But that is more in the way of advertisement. When they learn syllables they invariably buy a book.

Our day-school, every forenoon, from eight to twelve, is well attended. Few come every day, yet there is always a fair number. On Sunday the numbers that come far exceed our space. But outside is large enough for all, and when the inside of our chapel is filled with classes, others find a shady corner here and there out of doors.

We have not had any baptisms for some time, and now there are some thirty candidates who have been a long time in preparation, and most of whom we hope to see baptized soon. I am particularly pleased with the earnestness and diligence of some, and I fear I am rather hard to please, being

often more inclined to reject or delay than to agree to the baptism of some.

Of the king's two sisters, Queen Lubuga (Mugali Rebecca) still adheres to us. I cannot say how far she leads a consistent life, except that she wears no charms, nor has, I believe, any in her house. I saw her once or twice, in public only, during the last month, and she sends repeatedly to us here with some small token of friendship.

While we were still [on a journey with Kabaka Mwanga] our mail arrived . . . I read with alarm of the German doings at the coast, as we had telegrams to 17th June mentioning that the German fleet had been ordered to Zanzibar . . . The matter was besides much complicated by the letters from Bishop Hannington informing us of his intention to cross the Masai country and strike the Lake at Kwa Sundu near Busoga.

It is only natural that these Natives be very jealous for their land. In Buganda they look on the Lake as a natural barrier, preventing invasion from the south. When the Egyptians were north at Mruli, Mtesa was ever trembling. From the west they fear nothing. The Congo State may some day alarm them not a little. But the sore point is Busoga. From there they know the solid ground stretches off east all the way to the coast, and an army coming in that direction would find an open road. Mtesa used to twitch me by saying, 'You white men would like much, would you not, to see the country behind Busoga? That I would never allow.'

I could see well how much our deep troubles this last spring owed their origin to the rumour of Thomson's visit to Busoga, although he was home again before they hardly knew here. What would it be now when the report came out that a great man was coming with a large party that very way to Buganda, while, at the same time, the white men were making war on Seyed Burgash? The case looked serious. For it must be remembered that Baganda have no acquaintance with the geography of Europe, and look on all pale faces as of one race. All are called Bazungu. The Arabs have even averred that we are only the pioneers of annexation—spies in fact. When Lieutenant Smith came here, Hamadi bin Ibrahim advised Mtesa to kill him and Wilson, as, he said, 'wherever these English put their foot, the land becomes theirs in time.' From that day onwards Mtesa was ever suspicious, yet prudent. When the Arabs continually reiterated their warnings as to our ultimately eating the country, Mtesa replied. 'Let the Bazungu alone. If they mean to eat the country, surely they will not begin at the interior. When I see them begin to eat the coast, then I shall believe your words to be true.'

Now, the beginning has been made at the coast—Bismark versus Burgash. Who will win? And then, too, the English are coming to the jealously guarded land of Busoga, at the other side of Buvuma. One white man is supposed to be a host in himself.

On Friday (25th inst.) Ashe and myself went to court to congratulate the king on his safe return, taking with us a box of sundry small articles as a present, it being our custom to give both him and the Katikiro something every time the boat brings us goods. His majesty expressed himself well pleased with the gift. We then told him that we wished his permission to let the boat go to Kavirondo to fetch his guest whom we had been expecting for some time. He was our Bishop, a chief of the Church, and our superior. We mentioned that his reason for coming that way was to avoid the Germans (Badutchi), who had some misunderstanding with Seyed Burgash. We did all we could to remove from the king's mind suspicion as to our having any connection with the Germans. We were cross-questioned as to the Germans' quarrel with the Sultan, and as to what they wanted there at all. Our information being very meagre, it was difficult for us to say much definitely. . .

Next morning the king had a council of his chiefs. Present— Kibare, Kangao, Mukwenda, Pokino, Mugema, Nsege, Ngobya, Kyimbugwe, and Koluji—all important personages. The Katikiro was absent. Mwanga made a speech to them on his relations with white men from the beginning. When he came to the throne he wanted Bazungu, and had sent Sema-timba with me to Msalala to bring three Englishmen. They refused to come. He therefore sent for the Frenchmen at Ukumbi. They came at once. He then narrated every word of our conversation with him yesterday, adding what I have omitted to mention above, that we had asked him to build a house for the Bishop, as we were short of accommodation. The chiefs then expressed their opinions on the situation. All seemed to be of one mind, that white men were all one, and that we and the Bishop were only the forerunners of war. We were only waiting for our head-man to come, when we would commence to eat the country.

Mwanga and his advisers had the movements of Bishop Hannington closely watched. When the Bishop entered Busoga, they gave the order to execute him. Hannington's death sealed Mwanga's reputation in European circles as a cruel despot and made him fear British retaliation. The suspicion directed at the British and their missionaries quickly infected the relations of the White Fathers with the palace.

DOCUMENT 20
'The faces of our catechists became troubled'

From Lourdel's letter to Cardinal Lavigerie in November 1885. *Les Missions Catholiques*, (1886), pp. 314–15; reprinted in *Church Missionary Intelligencer* (1886), pp. 634, 635.

NOTES FOR READING   Muganda = singular of Baganda or a Ganda person; Lukonge = chief of area on southern shore of the Lake who had killed two CMS missionaries in 1877; Joseph Mukasa = the Catholic page who kept the Catholic community together during the missionaries' absence and headed the page corps of the inner palace under Mwanga, not to be confused with the god Mukasa, the Katikiro Mukasa, or the author Hamu Mukasa; Namasole = Queen Mother.

About fifteen days ago I learned secretly that the chief minister had said that the three Englishmen living here would be executed if the white man killed in Busoga was really their leader and they were having him brought from the East coast. I informed Mackay and Ashe. The next day these gentlemen

heard the same thing from others. They then decided to make a generous gesture—a gift to the king and two of his counsellors—in order to save their own lives. The king and his minister, astonished that their plans were discovered, demanded of the Englishmen that they tell them who had told them of the plan and who had told them of the order to kill the white man in Busoga. Mackay and Ashe held firm and did not let themselves be intimidated by Mwanga's threats. The king forbid them to allow any Muganda to come to them, under penalty of death. 'Lukonge was wise in having the whites killed and he has suffered no repercussions since,' he said.

When the prohibition was extended to whites in general, I asked the king if he included us also in the ban. He said no, that we could continue to give instruction. At the same time poor Mwanga added: 'I am the last king of Buganda. The whites will take over the country after my death. While alive I will be able to prevent it, but I will be the last of the black kings of Buganda.'

Affairs were in that state when the king, suffering from eye trouble, asked me for a remedy. I took him an eye-wash. On November 13th, two days after starting treatment, his eyes began to improve. That evening I made a second visit and we chatted very amicably for a while. Pleased with his improved health, he complimented me, called me 'father' and made me promise never to leave Buganda. He would take my cap, put it on his head, and then laugh as he looked at himself in the mirror. When night fell I left, leaving him two opium pills and instructing him to take one before going to bed if his eyes were giving him pain. He sent me away with one of his finest goats. I returned home that evening, consequently, thrilled at this reception and hopeful that our mission would be able to overcome the obstacles created by the news of the German invasion and the effort of the whites to penetrate Busoga. But God had decided otherwise.

November 14th, in the morning, Joseph Mukasa, one of our finest Christians and the most trusted of Mutesa's servants who now exercised great influence over Mwanga, burst into the mission to tell me: 'The king slept badly. He may have the fever.'

. . . Sunday the 17th, after performing the Mass for our Christians, I went to see the king. I learned that he was restored to good health, that his eyes had healed and that, during the night, he had spoken a great deal. Soon a young page came up to me and whispered: 'You have refused to baptize me despite my pleas. I made it plain then that soon we would be expelled.'

'What do you mean?' I said.

'The king had only bad things to say about you last night. He thinks that you tried to poison him as revenge for his killing the whites in Busoga, that you wanted to put another prince on the throne because he doesn't practise the religion. In any case, he has decided to expel the whites, or else kill them.'

The faces of our catechists became troubled. The king called his minister and some of the important counsellors. Today I was told to wait until called, contrary to my custom of going in to see the king whenever I wished, even when he was alone with the chief minister.

I sat down, anxiously awaiting the result of the session. After a while a door opened and a young page, one of our catechists, his face distraught, told his companions that Joseph Mukasa, their leader and the one to whom I referred above, had just been bound and carried away to be burned. The king had said that Mukasa had told me to give the king the medicine which had had such bad effects. The real reason is that Joseph had become the enemy of the Katikiro and the Namasole because he consistently tried to prevent the king from going back to the *lubare*.

Mwanga had also decided to execute Joseph because, three days before, the page leader had said to him: 'Why have you begun to kill the whites? Your father Mutesa never did.'

The king took these words as a gross insult and decided to kill the young man in spite of all the services he had rendered. He also accused him of having alerted the Englishmen, through me, about the decisions to kill Hannington and them.

Joseph Mukasa was executed on 15 November. Tension at the capital remained high through the spring of 1886, when the kingdom suffered military reverses and some natural disasters. At that time the king and his senior chiefs took extreme measures against the Christians. The following account comes from an eyewitness, a very young Protestant page at the court.

DOCUMENT 21
'Christian martyrs'

James Miti, 'History of Buganda', Vol. I (no pagination), a typescript translation at the School of Oriental and African Studies, University of London, from the Luganda version written in the 1930s.

NOTES FOR READING Kangawo = county chief of Bulemezi; Banyoro = people of Bunyoro; Munyono = temporary residence of the king in the Kampala area; Apolo Kagwa = prominent Protestant page, author of Document 3; Nyonyintono = prominent Christian page; Dionyzius = Denis, a Catholic page.

After a defeat of the Baganda and the death of their leader Kangawo Kibirango in a war against the Banyoro, the army was led back to Buganda by Nnanutwe Mbula, only to find that the king's storehouse and other houses had been consumed by fire . . . the king had moved to the Katikiro's house . . . Two days afterwards, however, a number of the Katikiro's houses were struck by lightning and great consternation was caused. People began to talk and conjecture as to the probable cause of the two disastrous occurrences. Some people attributed them to the king's cruelty to and murder of Bishop Hannington. . . The destruction of the Katikiro's houses by lightning was due, they said, to the king's presence there and to his minister's having acted as his abettor. The occurrence of shooting stars on two or three successive nights was also interpreted as God's vengeance against the wicked king.

Believing in the truth of the people's interpretation and fearing lest similar misfortune should befall whatever place he would escape to, Mwanga had a new residence built at Munyono whither he afterwards fled and stayed. The Arabs and some chiefs taking advantage of this occasion, pointed out to the king that the Christians were really against him and urged that worse things would happen to him if the king did not punish the Christians for what they had caused. The king, therefore, listening to his evil advisors, resolved from that day to persecute and kill off all Christians in Buganda, irrespective of sect or condition.

The persecution period began with an incident which though trifling in itself and affording little provocation later resulted in a wholesale massacre of Christian converts. It happened on May 25, 1886, when king Mwanga had gone out in the royal canoe for hippopotamus and duck shooting . . . (When Mwanga returned to shore, his pages were not in attendance and the king became enraged. Mwanga rushed to his palace and began heaping abuse upon each Christian who crossed his path) . . . The king's anger was now directed against Apolo Kagwa, who was another Christian convert serving in the palace as one of the pages. Kagwa's punishment was a special one: after being severely beaten he had the whole of his head hacked with a knife in several places and sustained many severe injuries all over his body. Learning what had happened the rest of us were struck with terror and the youngest among us were advised by Nyonyintono to run away and escape the best we could. . . It was only while the executioners were leading Dionizius outside that a number of us, Daniel Sekajija, Lule and the writer, sneaked through the sides of the gates unnoticed and made good our escape. Arrived outside of the enclosure, the prisoner was thrown down and without further ceremony had his head chopped off in the presence of us all, near a thicket upon which the king's enclosure abutted. Dionizius' martyrdom took place on May 25, 1886. Dionizius was the precursor and pioneer of the galaxy of martyrs that soon after followed him.

By the end of June around fifty Christians had been executed and many others were mutilated. About half of those killed were Protestant pages, most of whom were employed at the royal treasury. The Catholic victims had worked in the audience chambers of the king and included a number of highly respected leaders. The Anglican and especially the Catholic Church have subsequently celebrated the faith of those who died.

The persecution ended even more abruptly than it began. After June the surviving pages resumed their labours and their affiliations with the missionaries who were never harmed. The king now began to identify with the younger generation against the senior chiefs and traditionalists. In 1887 he armed regiments of Muslims, Catholics and Protestants and gave them license to police the kingdom and strip officials of their wealth and land. The regiments abused this freedom by widespread confiscation and killing.

DOCUMENT 22
'Blinded . . . to their misconduct'

Miti, 'History' (no pagination).

NOTES FOR READING   Mengo = Mwanga's main capital; Kisalosalo = predominantly Catholic regiment; Munyono = Mwanga's temporary capital; bitongole = batangole.

As for the king, mindful of the good services that some of his surviving chiefs and other servants had rendered to him in the past and apparently casting away all hatred (of Christians), he reinstated some of them in their former chieftainships or positions of honour or employment. Kaggwa Ndikimulaga (a Roman Catholic) was entrusted with the work of completing the lake at Mengo. He was charged with hurrying up the work, and given orders that all Buganda should supply labour and material for this undertaking. Whoever came late to work or missed a day had to be fined a young girl and a servant, several head of cattle and a bundle of bark-cloth. These things had to be paid at once; afterwards the shirker had to pay the foreman whatever the latter demanded of him. The supervision of the repair work that was to be done to the king's enclosure was left to Edward Mukasa, another Christian convert (Protestant) to whom similar full powers were given in the execution of his duties.

Creating a new department (Kisalosalo) the king appointed Henry Nyonyintono to be its head and to administer it in whatever manner he saw fit. This man, it will be remembered, had suffered much while confessing Christ and was one of those who had been castrated at Munyono . . . There were also one Muhammedan (Makolowa) and one pagan (Kiyindiri) upon whom the king conferred lower chieftainships in the new department which he had entrusted to the charge of the Christians. This department rose so rapidly in the king's favour that many servants deserted their masters in other departments for new ones in this. The result was that, as such deserters usually ran away with some of their master's guns, the Ekisalosalo became a most powerful body and considering themselves the best organization in the country, they adopted the name of 'Abapere' whereby they wished to express to all their own unequalled strength.

The people, however, entertained certain grievances against their master in this, that whenever any chief lodged a complaint for the recovery of his firearms from a servant who had run away with it to another chief, no attention was paid to him. Added to this the compulsory labour of digging the lake at Mengo and that of repairing the royal enclosure almost at the point of the spear, were objects of constant complaint among the common people.

. . . These 'regiments' or 'bitongole' had an internal government of a graded chieftainship such as is visible in the Buganda Kingdom Government, but on a much smaller scale; that is to say there was the man in charge of the whole regiment and he had his assistant with other subordinate chiefs. With his regiments well-organized, king Mwanga now began buying more firearms and equipped his men as a precaution against future attacks and as a better means of aggression against rebellious tribes. But his love for his men blinded him to their misconduct, with the result that the more he loved them, the more mischievous did they become and the more they were disliked by the people themselves.

Who Shall Rule Buganda?

In 1888 Mwanga shifted course again. Influenced by popular resentment and the surviving senior chiefs and fearful of the growing power of the regiments, the king moved against the younger generation. What he had managed in 1886 was, however, no longer possible in 1888, which became known as the 'year of the three kings' and the 'three revolutions'. In September, the Muslims and Christians combined to overthrow Mwanga and install his brother Kiwewa as Kabaka. In mid-October, the Muslims ousted the Christians. Finally, in late October, the Muslims drove Kiwewa out, putting another brother—Kalema—in his place. For a description of these events we go to the CMS missionary Ashe, who put together his version on the basis of conversations with Baganda and European eyewitnesses.

DOCUMENT 23
'The first revolution'

Robert Ashe, *Chronicles of Uganda* (1894), pp. 97–9, 101–105.

NOTES FOR READING   the old Katikiro = Mukasa of Documents 1 and 16; Gabunga = head of Lungfish clan and of the royal fleet and in this instance a young Christian; Nyonyi Entono = the Nyonyintono of Documents 21, 22; Omwanika = storekeeper of the palace; Mujasi = head of the king's bodyguard, and in this case an influential Ganda Muslim at the court since the middle of Mutesa's reign.

The result was, that Mwanga and these men hatched between them a diabolical plot, which had for its object the annihilation of all the readers in Uganda, both Christians and Muhammedans. The old prime minister, Mukasa, would have nothing to say to the scheme, affirming that 'the readers' were too numerous to be destroyed.

The conspirators now summoned the Mandwa, or priests of Lubare, who duly proceeded to slaughter cattle, and take the omens regarding the success of the plot. If the blood of the slaughtered animal flows out in several divergent streams the omen is good; but if it pours out in one full stream it is bad. This is called Kulagula (to foretell). For several days the omens were observed with the most satisfactory results, and the Mandwa declared that the issue of the plot would be satisfactory; and in this they were right, though the satisfaction was to be enjoyed by those whom they desired to put to death. The plot was as follows: Mwanga was to give out that he had determined to destroy the worship of Lubare in the country, and that he intended to begin by stripping the Mandwa of all their wealth, and that his first step would be a raid on the Island of Bugala, which belonged to the priests, and on which was much cattle. He was then to summon all the fighting men in the country who had guns, and who were all either Christians or Muhammedan readers. The old heathen warriors still clung to their ancient weapons, spear and shield. The assembled readers were then, on some pretext or another, to be landed on another bare and desert island, and there left to perish miserably. The canoes were to be withdrawn, and the waters of the Lake watched, to prevent any canoe reaching the hapless victims of this outrageous scheme of vengeance. Like everything that Mwanga planned or did, this plot partially leaked out, and the intended victims learnt enough to arouse their worst suspicions.

The king now ordered the Gabunga, who had charge of the canoes, to collect all the boats in Sesse, while he ordered Mujasi, a cruel and fanatical Muhammedan who commanded his bodyguard, to march the soldiers to the point of embarkation on the Lake. Mujasi sent back to say he was dreadfully ill, and his eyes were so much affected that he could not see, while another Muhammedan chief plastered some of the rotten fruit of the banana on his leg, which he exhibited to the king's messenger as a frightful ulcer, affirming the while that he was quite unable to walk. Musalosalo and Omwanika, the two principal Christian chiefs, also received orders to march to the Lake with the Christians. Omwanika, or Kagwa Apolo, was the leader of the Bazungu or English readers, while Musalosalo, or Nyonyi Entono, was chief of the Bafransa or French readers . . .

The king came out of the royal hut, and made his way to the Lake. It was now daylight, and the king saw that only a few of the more timid had entered the canoes; by far the greater number, disregarding his orders, were standing on the beach. Thereupon the king entered his own noble canoe (named *Waswa*), followed by Nyonyi Entono, who came unarmed, whispering to his personal attendants not to accompany him. *Waswa* was now paddled out a little distance into the Lake, none of the other canoes following. The king turned, and ordered Kagwa Apolo to enter another canoe. This he slowly did, whispering to his followers the same order as Nyonyi Entono had given, that they should not embark with him. The king then commanded one of the smaller chiefs to get into a third boat, but he stoutly replied, 'I will not.' Next the king ordered the Muhammedan Lubanga, already referred to, to enter the canoe—he replied that he must first go for his gun, and turning his back walked into the long grass to await what should befall . . .

The king, now seeing how matters stood, . . . sent post haste to tell the old Katikiro that the whole country was in rebellion. The answer he received was that the plan to kill the leaders had been against his, the Katikiro's, judgment and advice. When old Mukasa's messenger had delivered the message the king was silent. Meanwhile the Muhammedan readers sent messengers to the old Prime Minister, and to Nyonyi Entono and Kagwa, the two leaders representing the French and English readers, saying, 'We had better depose Mwanga, since he is certain to renew his attempt upon our lives.' And to this the Katikiro agreed, and it was accordingly determined to place another king on the throne. Then came the question of who should be chosen as Mwanga's successor, and they decided upon Mwanga's brother Kalema, a man who, it appears, was more or less favourably inclined towards the Arabs and the Muhammedan faction, and who afterwards played so important a part in the politics of Uganda.

Two messengers were accordingly despatched to fetch Kalema from the enclosure where the royal princes were guarded by Kasuju, the keeper of the king's children.

The messengers were afraid, however, that their tidings might not be well received by Kasuju, and that they might lose their lives. So they returned, saying it was impossible to reach Kalema, and that it would be better for a strong armed party to go and take him out of his prison palace by force.

On hearing this, Nyonyi Entono suggested that it might be better to secure the king's oldest brother, Kiwewa, who lived in an open enclosure, and whose person was sacred, although it was the immemorial custom of Uganda that the eldest son might never succeed to the throne. Nyonyi Entono argued that as the Christians and Muhammedans were people of '*dini*' (religion), and had turned their backs on heathen customs, they need not regard this old superstition. In this he was supported by a Muhammedan chief named Katabalwa. The others agreed to the suggestion, and forthwith a man named Buga Ekwagala, with three others, were sent to fetch Kiwewa, that he might be proclaimed king. On arrival they found him in his house; but on communicating their message he flatly refused to accompany them, saying that the thing was impossible. But his visitors would take no denial, and actually forced him out of his house, and led him towards Rubaga Hill, doubtless impressing on him as they went the ease with which he might step into Mwanga's great position. The rebels now secured the royal drum, Mujaguzu, on which they beat the royal tattoo in honour of the new king. Mwanga, to his dismay, heard the king's drum booming out on Rubaga Hill, opposite his own enclosure, and the site of the French Mission.

Mwanga fled with a few supporters to the south side of the lake. Meanwhile the Christian Baganda obtained a large share of the spoils of the September revolution: Nyonyintono became a county chief, and many others gained important offices. At this time the Baganda and Zanzibari Muslims grew restless.

DOCUMENT 24
'The second revolution'

Ashe, *Chronicles*, pp. 115–18.

NOTES FOR READING   Baraza = meeting; Nkore = Ankole, a kingdom bordering on Buganda on the west; Kangao = county chief of Bulemezi; Walker = CMS missionary.

But King Kiwewa fell more and more under Muhammedan influence. There were numbers of Arab traders in the country, who naturally threw all their influence into the scale against the Christian chiefs, and eagerly fomented the feeling of jealousy with which the Muhammedan faction saw these Christians occupying so many of the important positions in the country. The Arabs also were much vexed at the appointment of Nyonyi Entono as Katikiro in the place of the deposed Mukasa, for the Katikiro had great interest in the ivory trade of the country, and they were bitterly aggrieved that this important post had not fallen to one of their own co-religionists. There is little doubt that these Arabs, from the first, had planned to seize Uganda for themselves; indeed, without their aid the native Uganda Muhammedans could never have formed the strong faction in the kingdom which their party was soon to become.

The Arabs very soon succeeded in forming a plot to overthrow the Christian chiefs, and sought for a fitting opportunity to put it into execution. They first of all cleverly worked upon the fears of the king, persuading him that the Christians meant to depose him, and put in his place one of his sisters, who was a Christian; 'for', said they, 'is not the chief nation of Europe governed by a woman, Queen Victoria? and therefore the Christians in Uganda are seeking to establish the same custom here.' As the Muhammedans had been chiefly concerned in placing Kiwewa in power, he doubtless felt more or less bound to listen to their counsels, and to wink at the treacherous plot which they had hatched against the Christians. Accordingly in October of this year the Muhammedans in open baraza accused Nyonyi Entono, the Katikiro, of being concerned in a plot to depose Kiwewa. He vehemently denied it, and left the Baraza in great indignation, and repaired to his own enclosure. Certain negotiations were then entered upon, and messengers were coming and going between the Katikiro's enclosure and the lubiri (king's courtyard). An important Muhammedan chief was actually within the Katikiro's fence as a hostage. He had been sent in this capacity to carry assurance that no treachery was intended, and some of the Christian chiefs, not suspecting evil, trusted themselves within the lubiri. A murderous volley was suddenly opened upon them, and one or two of them fell, and the rest fled. Directly the shots were fired outside the Muhammedan hostage was instantly shot dead, and Nyonyi Entono came out with his following, only to meet a thoroughly well-organised attack. The Arabs were there, and personally took part in the encounter. The Christians had been taken unawares, and after making a short, but ineffectual stand, they retreated; and their two leaders, Nyonyi Entono, the Katikiro, and Kagwa Apolo, the Mukwenda, led the more earnest converts in good order out of the country. Their number was not great, and King Entare (lion) of Nkore or Busagara, gave them an asylum at a place called Kabula.

The Muhammedan power was now completely in the ascendant, and a re-distribution of chieftainships took place. A new Katikiro was appointed, while Mujasi, the Kangao, became Mukwenda.

But with the new order of things it fared ill with the European missionaries, who were immediately arrested, brought up to the Katikiro's enclosure, and immured in a filthy prison, where they were kept for a whole week. The two missions were meanwhile sacked and looted, and on the eighth day the

missionaries were brought down to the Lake, and put on board the English mission boat, the *Eleanor*, or *Mirembe*. Walker was even stripped of his outer clothing. The French priests were allowed to take on board some cowrie shells with which to buy food, and then the little party sadly bade farewell to the land of so many sorrows and triumphs of the Gospel.

The missionaries went to their respective stations south of the lake while the Baganda Catholics and Protestants took refuge in Ankole. Within a few days the Muslim party pressed Kiwewa to convert, be circumcised and declare Buganda a Muslim state.

DOCUMENT 25
'The third revolution'

Ashe, *Chronicles*, pp. 118–21.

Having thus got rid of their Christian rivals, the Muhammedans now determined that the whole of Uganda should profess Islam; and in order to accomplish this resolve, they realised that it was necessary to begin by converting the king. The Katikiro (Muguluma), and Mujasi the Mukwenda, with others, accordingly waited upon the king, and broached their ideas to him. Kiwewa now saw that he was in the hands of fanatics of the worst type, and began bitterly to regret that he had suffered these Muhammedan bigots to drive from the kingdom his Christian chiefs, who, at any rate, had not proposed baptism to him, as the Muhammedans were urging upon him the initiatory rite of their religion.

Kiwewa declared point blank that he would never consent to the rite, and that he would rather be deposed, as Mwanga had been, than agree to its imposition, and the baffled chiefs left him to consult as to what was best to be done. They then formed the extraordinary project of seizing the king, and imposing the rite by force, and twelve of their number were appointed to carry out the undertaking, of whom Bugala and Mujasi were the principal men. But, like so many Uganda plots, this scheme leaked out, and Kiwewa got wind of it, and sent to say he had reconsidered his determination, and was prepared to become an out-and-out Mussulman, and appointed a day when he would undergo the initiatory rite at the hands of those whose religion he was about to profess. It is stated that the unhappy king had made an abortive endeavour to poison some of his fanatical chiefs . . .

Mujasi and his assistants accordingly presented themselves at Kiwewa's enclosure, and were admitted with their following, and the outer gates were closed. The king had, meanwhile, made his own preparations, and behind the bark-cloth hangings in the house of reception had placed a large number of his executioners ready with their cords, waiting to spring out and seize the chiefs when the time was come.

The haughty Muhammedans entered, and the King politely received them. 'Mutuse banange' ('You have come, my friends'), he said. Then something of this sort occurred. Suddenly rising, he turned to Mujasi, and said, 'So you have eaten Buganda, and you will make the Kabaka your slave?' Mujasi and the Katikiro were instantly pinioned from behind, and Kiwewa killed the former with his own hand. There was wild confusion. The Katikiro's boy, who was sitting in the doorway, fired a gun at the king. On this the gates were burst open, and the Muhammedans and Arabs who were waiting outside rushed in. Kiwewa ran from his enclosure and fled to his father's tomb, accompanied by a number of the old heathen chiefs.

But neither Mukasa nor the guardians of the grave would give him any countenance or afford him any help. They even showed him violence, and five of his people were killed. He then fled to a place called Kyebango, accompanied by the chiefs still faithful to him; and there he spent the night.

The Muhammedans meanwhile brought Kiwewa's younger brother, Kalema, who, to gain the kingdom, willingly embraced Islam. He was a very different man from Mwanga, and as brave as Mwanga was cowardly. Next day he sent to attack Kiwewa, whose chiefs advised him to give battle. Kiwewa was, however, quickly routed, and some twenty of his followers were killed. He himself was made prisoner, and brought back to the capital, where he was put into the stocks and strongly guarded.

The three revolutions were undoubtedly palace coups which substituted the personnel of one group for another. They also bore witness, however, to profound changes. Factions organized on the basis of loyalty to new faiths had become more powerful than the king, the senior chiefs and other defenders of tradition. These parties had assumed the right to depose Kabakas and choose their successors. The Muslim party had added circumcision as a condition of holding office.

The regiments of 1887 and the revolutions of 1888 destroyed the generation of older officials who expressed the values of the vast majority of Baganda who belonged to none of the 'revolutionary' factions. While this majority may have been ready to accept the leadership of the new Muslim chiefs, they resented the efforts to make Islam the state religion.

Conversion and circumcision were frequently enforced at the point of a sword, while Lubare shrines were destroyed. In addition, the new regime eliminated most of the potential challengers to Kalema, including Kiwewa and the two infant sons of Mwanga, and wrought vengeance on those it deemed to be its enemies. One prominent victim of Muslim zeal was Mukasa, the former Katikiro of Mutesa and Mwanga.

DOCUMENT 26
'With much dignity'

Ashe's account of Mukasa's death. Ashe, *Chronicles*, pp. 133–4.

NOTES FOR READING Emin Pasha = Austrian convert to Islam who worked for the Khedival government and visited Buganda in 1876 and 1877–78.

There remained only the old Katikiro, who had refused help to Kiwewa when he fled to Mutesa's tomb, and who, through all the troubles, had succeeded in keeping on the winning side . . .

Kalema, suspecting his loyalty, sent men to murder him. When the messengers came he behaved with much dignity, and met his death with the greatest courage. He saw that his murder was intended, and made no resistance. He was shot, and his body cast into one of the houses, which was then set on fire, so that all that was mortal of him thus perished in the flames. This man was one of the most remarkable Africans I have ever met. He possessed an astonishing insight into character. He was as courteous and polite as an Arab. Emin Pasha called him the one gentleman in Uganda. When not carried away by the cruel passion of revenge he could take a statesmanlike view of affairs. I have a vivid recollection of his proud and handsome face, which yet was so difficult to read.

But underlying all his suavity and politeness there was a determined and bitter hatred for foreigners; and whether it was consummate acting or genuine feeling, he displayed a touching fidelity to the memory of his old master, King Mutesa. Though he could read a Gospel, and knew something of the Koran, he died as he had lived—an adherent of the old Uganda religion.

The Catholic and Protestant exiles took advantage of the growing dissatisfaction. Never abandoning their hope to recapture the seats of power, they regrouped in Ankole, a kingdom west of the lake and the province of Buddu. Its king had been an arch enemy of Buganda but now welcomed the refugees and established relationships of blood-brotherhood with them. The Christians in turn built roads and bridges and fought for their host while they recruited followers among the discontented of the Buganda heartland. By February 1889 they thought themselves sufficiently strong—about 2000 guns—to begin the counter-attack. They did not have much success in battle or recruitment until they found a royal standard-bearer in early May.

DOCUMENT 27
'Of the royal line'

Miti, 'History', I, p. 330 (this portion is paginated).

NOTES FOR READING Nyonyintono died in battle about the time Mwanga joined the Christians; Kiwewa was already dead.

Yet a continuous influx of Christians increased their power and their influence became recognized throughout the neighboring districts. They had now enough guns to fight with, enough courage and knowledge of the tactics of the time and a sufficient physical strength to marshall an effective force against any enemy, even against the formidable Mohammedan forces who had forced them into flight only a short time back. Their one wish was for someone, preferably of the royal blood, for them to rally round—some person to whom they should all pay their allegiance and to whom they should look up as their supreme leader. But he must be one of the royal line.

Unanimous under their chief Nyonyintono, they needed a royal leader for the realization of their wish . . . They agreed that they must try to recall Mwanga. He was the best of the three (the others being Kalema and Kiwewa) in spite of all his erratic ways and his persecution and murder of Christians. His acts of violence of former days would now be forgotten, and he would be most whole-heartedly welcomed back to his throne, if he could only be reached and be prevailed upon to promise to act as the Christians' central figure in their contemplated struggle for the overthrow of Mohammedan supremacy.

The Christians needed control of the lake in order to monopolize the supply of guns and munitions, ensure their own mobility, and thereby capture the capital. They obtained this control from two sources. Charles Stokes, an English trader and former CMS agent, provided weapons and a great deal of logistic support with his boats. The island inhabitants, who were attached to the Lubare and particularly upset at the enforced Islamization, used their canoes to cut off supplies to Kalema. None the less, the campaign was not an easy one. Religious, generational and personal rivalries plagued the Christian camp. Coordination of Christian and traditionist forces in the east and west was exceptionally difficult. After an initial capture of the capital in October, the coalition lost it to Kalema and his supporters, only to retake it in February of 1890. This time the Muslims suffered severe losses and were unable to mount a serious counter-offensive. They lost Kalema to smallpox and chose a brother of Mutesa named Mbogo as their Kabaka in exile. With the aid of Bunyoro, they continued to pose a threat to the new 'Christian' Buganda.

Years of virtually continuous fighting had ravaged Buganda. Document 28 gives Father Lourdel's impressions of the capital area.

DOCUMENT 28
'Clouds of crows wheel overhead'

Our translation of excerpts from Lourdel's diary of 7 and 8 October 1889, found in Nicq, *Lourdel*, pp. 487–9.

NOTE FOR READING Rubaga hill contained both the last principal capital of Mutesa and the Catholic mission station.

---

7 October. What a change from a year ago! There is no longer any trace of the great road which led from here to the capital. Of the hundreds of reed huts which sheltered the king's wives there is nothing but ashes. The banana plantations, so lush before, have disappeared and given way to bush. Mengo, Mwanga's capital, has also disappeared in the tall grass. There

is nothing more than the base of the lightning rod. Rubaga and Mengo—those two little Sodoms of Uganda—became the prey of flames. Clouds of crows wheel overhead and swoop down on the bodies which no one has taken the trouble to bury.

I took care of almost a hundred wounded, all soldiers of Mwanga. Not one Muslim who was wounded or overtaken in his flight was spared the spears of the *bakopis* (common people). It was impossible to stop the latter from discharging their dreadful mission . . .

Today I found two of the orphans kidnapped by the Arabs last year.

8 October. I'm anxious to see our dear house at Rubaga again. On the road I passed many bodies which gave off a fetid odor. What sadness I felt to see that house which we sweated over, completely in ruins—no more doors, windows, porch, walls pushed over, ceilings bashed in, and high grass and brush over everything. Our groves of eucalyptus, guava and mango trees are hardly visible in the dense growth which fills the space where our garden once was.

As Lourdel indicates, the victors showed no more mercy than their victims had shown in the preceding months. In fact, the Zanzibaris who supported Kalema's cause were put to death, whereas the missionaries had only been expelled. The Christian chiefs also displayed little gratitude towards their 'pagan' allies. The victory belonged to their god and to those who had been diligent in prayer and 'reading' throughout the difficult months of exile. The spoils were distributed accordingly.

DOCUMENT 29
'The list of new appointments'

Excerpts from Miti, 'History,' I, p. 355 (this portion is paginated).

NOTES FOR READING Kagwa, author of Document 3, was now the head of the Protestant faction; Mugwanya, the subject of Document 2, headed the Catholic side after the death of Nyonyintono; Kakungulu and Kintu played important roles in the 1889 campaigns and expressed discontent at their 'relatively minor' positions. Miti does not mention the position of Mugema, county chief of Busiro, which went to the Protestants.

The king, wishing to restore the former constitution of his kingdom, gave instructions that the people themselves should elect their own chiefs, and the following was the list of new appointments.

Protestants:
1. Apolo Kagwa   Prime Minister (or Katikiro)
2. Nicodemus Sebwato   Chief of Buddu (Pokino)
3. Jona Waswa   Chief of Singo (Mukwenda)

4. Lawi Wakibi Sekiti	Chief of Butambala (Katambala)
5. Kamya Lubebe	Chief of Gomba (Kitunzi)
6. Absolom Mudina	Chief Treasurer
7. Semaon Kakungulu	Chief of a frontier district in Kyagwe (Mulondo)
8. Yesiya Kasozi	Chief of the War Fleet

Catholics:

1. Stanislaus Mugwanya	Kimbugwe
2. Alexis Sebbowa	Chief of Kyagwe (Sekibobo)
3. Sematimba	Chief of Kyadondo (Kago)
4. Kityo	Chief of Mawokota (Kaima)
5. Joseph Nsingisira	Chief of Bulemezi (Kangawo)
6. Kasi	Chief of Busujju (Kasujju)
7. Gabriel Kintu	Head of Police
8. Minywakyamagwa	Head of King's Scouts
9. Sepiria Mutagwanya	Head of King's Butchers

Which appointments having been confirmed by all the people in a large assembly it was unanimously resolved that all future appointments to chieftainships should be left in the hands of the people themselves, subject to confirmation by the king.

'The people' of Miti's account were, in fact, the leaders of the Protestants and Catholics, the beginnings of the oligarchy which would dominate Buganda's future. As in the revolution of 1888, the king now simply confirmed the choices made by the factions.

The struggle for control of Buganda was not yet over. Both the Germans and the British were expanding towards the Lake while within the kingdom the Catholic and Protestant Baganda had by no means reconciled their differences. In fact, such differences were exacerbated by an intriguing layered administration. For example, underneath each of the Protestant county chiefs in Document 29 was a layer of Catholic sub-county chiefs, who were themselves served by Protestant subordinates. Loyalty to faction clashed with obedience to superiors and prevented the system from working. Mwanga was more closely identified with the Catholics, and their party consequently grew at the expense of the Protestants through defections and new commitments.

In response, Apolo Kagwa, the Protestants and their CMS allies sought aid from the Europeans most congenial to their cause—the British. Their opportunity arose in the midst of a confusing triangular dispute among Mwanga, an agent of the Imperial British East Africa Company (IBEA) named Frederick Jackson, and a representative of the German Colonization Society named Karl Peters. Mwanga had written to Jackson for support to regain his kingdom in 1889. When the British agent responded with nothing more than a flag, Mwanga sent a second letter. Peters intercepted this message and rushed to the capital in February, 1890, to offer a German treaty of protection. With the support of the Catholic faction and Father Lourdel, the king signed the agreement. Jackson arrived in April and declared the document worthless, since Mwanga had already accepted the British flag. The

Protestants and their missionaries saw their chance and backed Jackson, whereupon both sides wrote to European officials in Zanzibar for clarification.

The dispute was settled in principle in Europe by the Anglo–German Agreement of July 1890 which assigned Buganda to the British sphere of control. The implementation came in December, when a new representative of the IBEA—Captain Frederick Lugard—arrived in the capital. The next two documents give different perspectives on his mission and its impact.

DOCUMENT 30
'To save the country from itself'

Lugard's reflections found in his work, *The Rise of Our East African Empire*, (1893), vol. II, pp. 20-21.

NOTES FOR READING Uganda = Buganda only at this time; Maxim gun = one of early machine guns; Nile = Victoria Nile between Busoga and Buganda.

I judged it best, in the first place, to adopt a firm and independent tone, being convinced that, to such a character as I supposed Mwanga to be, a deferential attitude would be interpreted as fear; and that if we showed too great anxiety to please, and were ready to supplicate for a treaty *in formâ pauperis*, we should only pander to his vanity, and render him the more unamenable and haughty. Such an attitude suited neither my conceptions of my duty nor my own inclinations.

As a result of international negotiation, Uganda and the countries round about had been ceded to the influence of Great Britain. I, myself an officer of the army, had been deputed, as the representative of a great chartered Company, to make a treaty with a semi-savage king noted for his cruelty and incapacity. I sought no unfair advantage, no acquisition of territory, no monopoly of trade, no annexation of revenues. My task was to save the country from itself; and for such a treaty as I proposed to make, I saw no need to stoop to bargaining by presents (of arms, a Maxim gun, etc., as had at first been suggested), and no cause for obeisance or deference. It was for this reason, as well as to hasten my arrival before any crisis between the factions took place, or the expected munitions reached Uganda, that I crossed the Nile without waiting for permission, and, marching rapidly on the capital, selected my own camping-ground. Mackay and Ashe relate how they knelt before the king, when praying for permission to leave the country. Such an attitude seemed to me to lower the prestige of Europeans, and I determined to make my own methods the more marked by contrast.

DOCUMENT 31
'He has chosen Kampala for strife'

Miti's account of Lugard's arrival found in his 'History,' I, pp. 368–9 (this portion is paginated).

NOTES FOR READING   Askaris = soldiers; Snider = gun; for the 'eastern route' see Document 19; Mufransa = 'French' or Catholic; Mungereza = 'English' or Protestant; Kampala = hill just north of Rubaga and Mengo and site of capital of today's Uganda.

Then, on December 18, 1890, another white visitor arrived in Buganda, without previous introduction or even announcement. He came with a large body of African *askaris* of different tribes such as Swahili, Somali, etc., each man armed with a 'Snider'. He also brought with him two Maxim cannons. Like his predecessor Jackson, the new arrival reached Buganda by the eastern [Busoga] route, and similarly, the latter's mission to this country was not the evangelization of its people but purely a diplomatic one. The new man was F. D. Lugard, who later, as Captain Lugard, was to lay the foundation of a protectorate over Uganda out of the chaos and disturbances of the time . . .

Immediately upon his arrival, Lugard's sleeping quarters were arranged among the Catholic party. But they, on discovering that Lugard was certainly not a fellow 'Mufransa' objected to accommodating him among themselves and demanded that as a 'Mungereza' he should be lodged among the people of his sect. At that time the Catholic headquarters were on Kampala hill, where the Kampala Museum now stands. Wishing to satisfy the Catholics, King Mwanga gave instructions that Lugard should change his quarters and live among the Buganda Protestant converts in their own quarters. But Lugard preferred to stay where he was, be it even among a sect of different belief: what did he care for religion as such? He had come for political reasons and not for religious motives.

The people were badly impressed by the white visitor's boldness and defiance of their master's orders. They wondered what kind of man he was and suspected that he would use force rather than gentleness in obtaining what he had come out for. Hence the place where Lugard had chosen to stay was no longer referred to as Kampala but its name was lengthened into 'Kampala Alizala Bigwo,' meaning 'he has chosen Kampala for strife.' Here, having had a fort built on Kampala Hill, Lugard asked King Mwanga to get ready a general assembly of his chiefs, nobles and other people, at which the white man would deliver his mission to the people of Buganda.

Lugard wasted little time. Within days he had forced the reluctant king to sign a treaty offering British protection in exchange for recognition of the suzerainty of the IBEA. While this offered Mwanga some security against the Muslims and Bunyoro in the north, it forced him to relinquish jurisdiction over Europeans resident in his country and to gain Company consent before negotiating with anyone other than the British.

The treaty did nothing to resolve the tensions between Protestant and Catholic which had been built into the distribution of offices in 1890 (Document 29). The burning issue was the relationship between religious affiliation and political office at every level. Lugard spent many hours discussing the issue with the parties in March 1891 and reached a provisional decision.

DOCUMENT 32
'Going over to the religion of the king'

Excerpts from Lugard's diary found in *The Diaries of Lord Lugard* (ed. by Margery Perham, 1959), vol. II, pp. 108-9.

NOTES FOR READING   the thirteen big officers = the first five Protestants and first six Catholics in Document 29, together with the county chief of Busiro and the Kabaka; Shamba = field.

The case is as follows:—My proposition was that there should be absolute freedom of religion; that for the present the 13 big officers of State, under whom is the whole of Uganda, should be selected half from one side, half from the other, and in the event of one changing his religion he should leave his Shambas and be provided for by the other side, his party appointing a new man to his place to keep the balance of parties equal. Any lesser man to follow what religion he pleases, and stay in his own place, and render the produce of the Shamba and the work to the chief in whose estate he lives. The Catholics were strongly in favour of this, and so was the King. The Protestants demurred, because they said that the real Christians in the country were a very small minority, and the rest would go over in large numbers to the religion professed by the King, whatever it might be, (and this is R. Cath.). They had only been deterred so far by fearing to lose their places and Shambas. Now if these restrictions were removed, the Protestant party would be decimated, and then if trouble arose, and the parties turned out to fight, the Catholics would not be restrained but would go for the small residue of Protestants left, and destroy them. At present one reason for the maintenance of peace had been that the two parties were so evenly matched that all knew a war would be a destruction of the whole country. Moreover they now had the ingress into the Shambas of the professing Protestants, but if these became Catholic they would no longer have the opportunity of spreading their religion among them. Further they accused me of breaking the Treaty I have made. For at the time they all signed the Treaty, the Catholics had drawn up a codicil that their old Treaty regarding religion should not be broken, and I had signed this. Now the position was reversed, the Catholics being willing to follow me with full confidence, but the Protestants took the Codicil (a weapon the Catholics had forged) and threw it in my teeth. The question was a difficult one. If their conclusions about men going over to the religion of the King are sound, (and all are unanimous, and the Catholics don't deny it), then by forcing this agreement I should deal a very heavy blow to the Protestant religion. This of course I do not want to do. If the King comes over to the Protestant side, this party will have cut their own throats by the clause they have stuck to.

Having once clearly grasped the point of the matter, I decided in my mind that the better thing was to try and carry the case in favour of the Protestants, for I do not wish to deal a heavy blow to my own creed, or to the party who saved me, and threw in their lot with me when I came here. Moreover I think that just at present a balance of power in the

State is most desirable. So I had a council again of chiefs of each party in the evening. The Catholics behaved really admirably. Tho' strongly in favour of my first proposition, (which they knew to be *mine*), they said that they would leave it all in my hands and act on my decision. I decided in favour of the Protestants on the grounds that I had pledged myself not to break their old treaty, and as this was a clause in it, (unknown to me), I was bound by my own word to respect it. Therefore all the petty chiefs named in that treaty would lose their places if they went over to the other side, but I carried it that this arrangement should only last for two years, after which there should be absolute freedom of religion for all parties, and no-one should lose his place by changing his religion. This was agreed to by all.

A fragile peace prevailed at the capital through the rest of 1891. During much of that time Lugard was in the west extending his Company's control into other parts of what became colonial Uganda. When he returned to his headquarters in late December, he found the two parties at loggerheads and their respective leaders—Kagwa for the Protestants and Mugwanya for the Catholics—struggling to restrain their followers. At the same time Lugard received reinforcements of men and weapons but also the notification that the IBEA wanted to abandon its protectorate within a year. To avoid this, he would need to reduce costs, resolve local problems in some incisive way, and persuade the British government to assume direct responsibility.

The opportunity for one 'incisive' solution came in January 1892. Several minor clashes occurred between the Catholic and Protestant factions. Then Mwanga tried a case concerning the death of a Protestant shot by a Catholic, allegedly in self-defence. The Kabaka decided in favour of the Catholics on the basis of customary law. Lugard demanded a reversal of the decision. The next two documents give opposing perspectives on the events leading up to the Protestant–Catholic confrontation of 24 January 1892.

DOCUMENT 33
'Some guns by night'

Lugard's version written on 27 January 1892 and taken from his *Diaries*, III, pp. 29–32.

NOTES FOR READING Dualla = Lugard's Somali interpreter; the Katikiro = Apolo Kagwa; Mujasi, Kanta and Musalosalo = offices or *Batangole* in the hands of some of the more militant Catholic leaders; Sembera = Sembera Mackay, a Protestant leader. The king was at Mengo hill while Lugard and several hundred of his soldiers were camped around the Kampala fort. The Protestant missionaries, now based at Namirembe, accepted Lugard's invitation to take refuge in the fort, while the Catholic ones remained at their Rubaga station.

After hearing the story the King said to the man, 'Did the Protestant follow after you into your enclosure?' The man

said 'Yes'. 'Oh then' (said the King) 'Bus! You were justified in shooting him, there is no case against you.' Dualla then expostulated. He repeated all the story, and asked if each point was *really* so, and he had made no mistake in hearing it. They said his repetition was all quite right. 'Then do you mean to make no punishment at all', said Dualla, 'that is not the custom of any country in the world. If the man was robbed of his gun he had a perfect right to follow the robber to recover it; is it not so if a leopard seizes your goats, would you not pursue him into his cave.' 'Yes', they said, 'but it is not the law of Uganda.' Dualla argued vehemently saying he was positive I would be greatly vexed at the decision. The King replied he had made his decision and he could not help it if I disliked it. I got the news in the evening this was *Friday 22nd* (my birthday).

Next morning I sent Dualla with a letter saying I utterly disapproved of the decision. I also got a long letter from the King (written by the Catholics) giving a list of their grievances, and saying they could get no justice etc. The greater part of it was written in a haughty uncompromising style, but the latter part was an abject prayer from the King that I would give him time to tie up his goods and run away, and calling me his friend. One sentence was mysterious, he said 'there are also very many other matters which 20 of the Catholics know, but I do not know'. Possibly this may allude to the news of the withdrawal from Uganda which, of course, the Priests know of, and which they may have told to the 20 Catholics. It has occurred to me that the Priests may have thought that I had my orders to evacuate, and was holding on pending reference home, and that if a crisis was precipitated I should under the circumstances be afraid to fight, and would withdraw. This is a mere conjecture to account for the sentence quoted, and for many reports which have reached me. For instance Mafta, Stokes' headman, says one of the Frenchmen insulted me grossly to him saying he could drive us out of Kampala with a stick. Again I hear that the priests spread a report that being a mere trading company, we never could and never would fight. These are mere reports much repeated. I wrote to the King saying that things were very very critical, and the Protestants were exasperated, and I could not but think they had justice and right on their side, and that there would certainly be war unless these matters were redressed.

I called the Katikiro and told him to be ready, as I expected the Catholics to attack. I knew that the Protestants were very greatly outnumbered in Mengo . . . and they had not anticipated this crisis (brought on entirely by the Catholics) and so had not collected all their forces as the latter had. I therefore told him I would give him some guns by night. The utmost secrecy was observed, only five or six men came at a time in the pitch dark night, and took two guns each, and returned. Altogether they took some forty guns, mostly muzzle loaders and a keg of powder.

Next day I got a letter from the King telling me exactly the hour of the issue of the guns, and saying it would be interpreted as permission to kill him. The letter was couched in very humble terms, and on reading it I hoped that my prompt action in arming the Protestants (of course the number of guns given out was enormously exaggerated) would avert the crisis. I sent Dualla with a letter saying I quite disapproved of the decision, and wished the King to reconsider it. Dualla had some difficulty in getting an audience. My letter was read, and I had said, I think, that if no justice was done there would be war. The King had always shown extreme fear when he found war was imminent. A marvellous, almost miraculous, change was now observable. He (Dualla says) evinced no fear or uneasiness, and merely said 'All right. I have made my decision and won't alter it. If the Captain wants war it is his matter, and he is taking a side, and not doing justly.' The Catholics (Mujasi, Kauta, and Musalosalo being present) then said 'all right, if he sends Askari to help the Protestants they will be killed to a man and if there is war, we shall take Kampala, and all the goods, and not only that but all the Europeans will lose their lives.' Dualla was astounded at this open challenge and insult before the King, no less than at the confidence they shewed, and the laughing exultation they exhibited. With many words and instances he proved how in all cases I had acted with extreme impartiality, and that it was *they* who would lose their goods and their lives not I, because *they* not *I* were taking a side. He then asked for his reply to my messages, and they told him that was all ... Later I got a letter to say the War-drums were beating. For several days I had not had off my clothes, and had slept very anxiously and got little real rest. On Sunday morning [the 24th] the Catholics began to collect. I had already warned both missions, and offered them an asylum at Kampala. The King sent down begging me to stop the war. I said I would do so if he sent me the murderer, and asked what apology or answer the Catholics would make to the public insults in the Barza.

Meanwhile the Catholics collected round the King's hill, and the Protestants near Kampala. I issued all the guns I had in store (some 500 or more), mostly muzzle loaders, together with ammunition to the Protestants, but forbade them to fight till they got orders ... The Catholics had repeatedly fired on the Protestants, who had yet refused to fight. The attack was apparently wantonly begun by the Catholics, and poor Sembera (the best fellow in Uganda, and the peacemaker) was shot by these first few shots and killed. The battle now began.

DOCUMENT 34
'The aggressions of the Protestants'

The White Fathers' version in Bishop Hirth's letter to Livinhac on 10 February 1892. *Church Missionary Intelligencer* (1892), pp. 514–15.

NOTES FOR READING Kimbugwe = title of Mugwanya, leader of the Catholic party and subject of Document 2; Unyoro = Bunyoro; Emin Pasha = Austrian convert to Islam who had worked for the Khedive and stayed on in the Upper Nile; Pokino = county chief of Buddu; Gabriel Mysoi = Gabriel Kintu, the Mujasi (head of the king's bodyguard) and a very partisan Catholic (see Document 29). Lugard had 200, not 700 or 800 trained Sudanese soldiers.

You know of the struggle that followed this division of country, and how that struggle from day to day became hotter. Religion and politics were mixed up together, without the missionaries being able to separate the two questions.

The aggressions of the Protestants against the Catholics increased day by day, and were supported at the English fort. The justest decisions of the king remained without effect when they were given against Protestants. Half the Sésé Islands were taken by force from Mwanga by the English, disregarding the indignant protests of the whole country; attempts were made to assassinate the king himself, and the assassins were acquitted by the fort, and rescued from pursuit, etc.

At last, not being able to acquire the important charges confided to the Catholics, they carried war into the provinces. Whole villages were taken, always with the assistance of the fort; threats of death were hurled against all the Catholic chiefs, particularly against Kimbugwé, charged with obstructing their interests. I received also a threatening letter signed by the Katikkiro himself. For a long time our Christians had no access to the English fort, which was occupied night and day by the Protestants.

About January the fort received two consignments of arms and ammunition, the only things that arrived from Mombasa. This coincided with Captain Lugard's return from Unyoro. He had there met the old troops of Emin Pasha, who were sent by Emin on their way to Bukoba. Captain Lugard negotiated with them, left half of them in Unyoro, that they might annoy King Kabarega by their inroads, and led the rest to Mengo, which thus received a force of 700 to 800 trained men. From that time the Captain's plans were laid, although they were still kept secret. The Catholics, who from day to day became more numerous, were to be put an end to. For about a month Mwanga had openly acknowledged the Catholic faith, and once a week at least went with his whole Court to the Mission at Rubaga, to attend the preaching there, and the whole country seemed to be inclined to follow him. The Protestants were greatly exasperated, and it was said that it was they who prompted the Captain to take violent measures. For fifteen days anarchy reigned. Murders and thefts of rifles became more frequent, the Catholics having the disadvantage. Captain Lugard wished to settle one of those disputes himself. It concerned a Protestant chief who had been killed on the estate of a Catholic, against whom he had led a band armed to the teeth, and furnished with firebrands. The case was a perfectly clear one, but the Protestants would not admit it. While at the fort they were negotiating with the king for justice, they were distributing by night hundreds of English army rifles; a like distribution had already been made some days previous in the capital of the Pokino. At last, on Sunday, January 24th, the matter came to a crisis. In the morning a few shots were heard, and again, towards two o'clock, more were fired. The Catholics were obliged to answer. Their first shot hit Sembera Mackay, one of the seven Protestant deacons, just as he was about to aim at one of us. A hand-to-hand combat immediately ensued. The struggle was too unequal; there was no proportion between the arms of the two parties. The Catholics had the whole English fort against them, but they fought for faith and country. They saw themselves being hunted from their country; they did not wish to go without a supreme effort to obtain the victory of justice. In half an hour the fight was waged for life or death. The head chiefs fell first, and had to be carried away, which caused some confusion. But Gabriel Mysoi was to be seen everywhere, encouraging them, and trying to restore order. Five times he forced the Protestants back to the fort. The fifth time he penetrated into it under the fire of two mitrailleuses, but after firing sixty-eight cartridges his ammunition was exhausted, and he withdrew to the king's residence in order to remove him and his court. The Catholics were vanquished.

Lugard had won the battle but he had not advanced his mission to unify Buganda or to separate religion and politics, as he had himself declared upon arrival (Document 30). The British flag was completely identified with the Protestants. Many Protestants wanted to eliminate the Catholic leadership which had gone into exile. Lugard worked diligently in the coming months towards a reconciliation and finally achieved a very limited solution in April 1892. Mwanga and the leading Catholics returned to the capital. The king signed a new treaty of protection while the parties agreed to a new distribution of offices. The layered administration of 1890 was abandoned in favour of a system in which the adherents of the new faiths would occupy different areas. The next two documents describe the negotiations and the settlement, which gave the Protestants the lion's share of territory.

fortunately, our adversaries spend part of the night with him at the fort.

April 4. Our hopes are dashed. The Captain no longer wants to give anything but Buddu, that is, the area south of the Katonga, a natural frontier which will reduce disputes. Our Catholics present the best possible reasons for increasing [their share], praying, begging, promising inviolable loyalty. The Captain will not budge. 'The Buddu is the most beautiful province,' he says; 'it was not ravaged by the Muslims, everyone wants it.' I then wrote to the Captain to remind him that Buddu is only one-seventh of the country, that the north was ravaged by the Muslims while the south is occupied by the hemp smokers and the center by 20 000 Baziba that he forbids [us] to expel. I told him that giving only Buddu is contrary to religious freedom, because over 20 000 catechists will never agree to go to a province which is ten days distant and different from Buganda in custom and language, that is to condemn them to apostasy or unfaithfulness, contrary to the tradition of tolerance which England never ceases to show in her colonies.

April 5. Our envoys return to the fort. They are able to obtain nothing. The Captain tells them that he gave them Buddu in spite of the Protestants, who would rather fight than give any more, that later he will increase it. I plan to inform him that he will not be able to increase the Catholic share without igniting new disputes and that any land he might subsequently give the Catholics will already be Protestant. Everything is useless.

DOCUMENT 35
'The Catholic share'

Our translation of Father Brard's presentation of the debates in his diary. Mercui, L'Ouganda, pp. 272–3.

NOTES FOR READING The negotiations were conducted at the Kampala fort; Katonga = river flowing into the northwestern corner of the lake; Baziba = another Bantu people, on friendly terms with the British.

April 2. The Catholics return to the fort.
The Captain, worked over by the Protestants, does not wish to cede Buddu. He proposes other provinces in the interior, completely ravaged. The Catholics refuse.

I went myself to see the Captain. He is very embarrassed and tried to get me to stay out of the treaty question. I told him that religious interests are very closely linked to this treaty and that I had the duty and obligation to protect them, that the missionaries have never interfered in political affairs but they have always protected their religion. I took the liberty of reminding him that, when he came, he requested on several occasions the support of the missionaries and got their signature on this first treaty. He granted my point and promised, as is his custom, to reflect on the considerations I raised. I had hardly left when the fort was engulfed by the Protestants.

April 3. The Captain calls the Catholics together and agrees to give them Buddu, in spite of the Protestants and the king. He proposes even to increase [the offering] a bit. Un-

---

DOCUMENT 36
'The 10 landed chieftainships'

Lugard's notes for 20 April 1892. Lugard, Diaries, III, p. 188.

NOTES FOR READING barza = meeting; R.C. = Roman Catholic; Mulondo = office in Kyagwe, held in this case by the Protestant Kakungulu (Document 29); shambas = fields.

According to agreement I held a barza to settle the new Chieftainships. After some discussion and twisting the following remain decided:-

1. Katikiro remains Katikiro; this was a Protestant chieftainship and remains so.
2. Kimbugwe. I offer the old Kimbugwe to retain title (an R.C.). Mulondo has the shambas.
3. Mukwenda remains. Protestant chief of Singo.
4. Sekibobo. Sebwato (old Pokino) becomes Sekibobo, was an R.C. now a Protestant.
5. Pokino. Sebowa R.C. (old Sekibobo) becomes Pokino. These two change places.
6. Kangawo. Was R.C. now Protestant; Zachariah appointed.
7. Mugema. Always Protestant and remains so.
8. Kago. Paulo, late Kitunzi, becomes Kago; was R.C. now Protestant.

9. Kaima. Thomasi Mkisi, a leading Buddu chief; *was* R.C. now Protestant.
10. Katambala. *Was* Protestant now becomes Mohammedan.
11. Kitunzi.   „   „   „   „
12. Kasuju.   „   „   „   „   „

These are the 10 landed chieftainships of Uganda. Of these the Protestants hold 6. Mohammedans 3. Catholics 1. Add the two highest of all, Katikiro and Kimbugwe, of which the Protestants hold one, and the best part of the other.

Fully aware that the problem of Protestant–Catholic relations was not resolved, Lugard left in the middle of 1892 to help campaign in Britain for the retention of Buganda. In 1893 the British Government took over from the IBEA. The British Commissioner, Sir Gerald Portal, brought together the Catholic and Protestant parties and their respective Bishops (Hirth and Tucker). In April 1893 they modified the earlier arrangement by providing the Catholics with additional territories (Buwekula, Mawokota, and part of the Ssese Islands) and offices, including their own Katikiro—Stanislaus Mugwanya. As a result, relations between the two factions and with the British improved considerably.

The same cannot be said for the Muslims. Driven to the north in 1890, they continued to harass Christian-dominated Buganda and wait for their opportunity to seize power. Their negotiations with Lugard in 1891 broke down, but in 1892 they accepted an agreement giving them three small provinces west of the capital (Document 36). The Muslim leader, Prince Mbogo, consented to drop the title of Kabaka and recognize Mwanga. The most instrumental mediator in these negotiations was Selim Bey, a Sudanese soldier who had served under the Egyptians before enlisting with the British. The Muslims continued to press for a more equitable land settlement. Governor Portal did not act on their demands during his short tenure of three months; neither he nor his successor, Captain J. R. Macdonald, appreciated the depth of Muslim alienation. When the Muslims protested against working for Mwanga, Macdonald took a hard line.

DOCUMENT 37
'They refused to work'

From the Protestant writer, Hamu Mukasa. 'Do not turn back', Vol. III, pp. 25–34 (see Document 5).

NOTES FOR READING Lukiko = council; Nubians = Sudanese; Juma = a militant Muslim leader; Kakungulu = prominent Protestant military leader (see Document 29); Muzungu = European, in this case Macdonald. Lunguja is both the Luganda word for Zanzibar and also the name of Kalema's capital, just west of Rubaga —the first time it refers to the capital while subsequently it indicates Zanzibar.

When Governor Portal finished making the agreement with the Kabaka, he left for Europe and left Captain Macdonald in charge. He told him that he had left him the Muslim matter and that if they refused to work for the Kabaka he was going to do like this: to note the ring-leaders, call them gradually, arrest them, give them to him, and that they were going to be taken to foreign countries where their pride was going to disappear. Captain Macdonald answered that he would do like that. Then Governor Portal, our first Governor, went back to Europe. . .

Then on June 14, 1893, Captain Macdonald sent to the Kabaka to send for Muslims and Catholics to come and work on the palace. The Kabaka then sent for Muslims and Catholics to come to the Lukiko in which he was going to tell them. They all came and he told them in the meeting. It was a big Lukiko. The Catholics agreed to coming to work. The Muslims told the Kabaka that they wanted to go back and tell their friends so that they (could) get ready. They said they were going to see what their comrades thought and that in two days they were going to say what they had decided. . .

They met and decided to agree while they were making plans with the Nubians [Sudanese]. They did like that, and some went to Kampala to meet the Nubians and some went to the palace to deceive the Kabaka that they had agreed. When they had agreed they were to have each his piece of work to do, and the Katikiro allocated work. When they left they went and told their friends to hurry and their pieces of work had already been given. Their teacher Juma and Kamya Wanyomzita went to meet the Nubians [to propose] that they combine and fight together. The Nubians agreed and Selim Bey told Captain Macdonald that if the Kabaka wanted to fight the Muslims, he was going to help the Muslims. He said that the Muslims had been brought in peace but that the Kabaka wanted to fight and kill them.

When Captain Macdonald came to know this from Selim Bey's speaking out he called all important Muslims to see what could be done. They said they did not want to work. They went on that if they were forced they were going to fight. They spoke in this way after they had made ready for war. Captain Macdonald then ordered the Nubian soldiers to come quickly. They came quickly with their guns thinking that the Muzungu did not yet know they had rebelled and that they could kill him if he said what they did not like. When they came they found the Europeans ready, each with a gun in the hand. All the missionaries had been put behind the fence for fear that they could be killed [in] the houses. He then set the cannon pointing at them and it was already loaded with bullets. The Europeans stood behind the cannon. He then said that he had called them, that those who wanted to could fight, and those who did not want to had to put their guns down immediately. When they saw that they could be destroyed if they refused, they put down their guns. He ordered them to go back to their houses and they did so. . .

On June 24, 1893, our people sent detectives to go and see what they were doing. They found them all going to Lunguju where was their Kabaka Kalema's town. They were getting ready to come and fight. Our Kabaka sent Kakungulu to go and attack them, they met and the guns fired. The Muslims were defeated and some of their leaders. . .were killed. Many others, about 30 or more, were killed on their side. They killed about 6 [of our] people. They were chased a long distance of about 12 miles to Kibalusi, where our people stopped and came back. They [our people] then chose a general to follow them [the Muslims]. They again chose Kakungulu who followed them up to Kinakulya in Bunyoro. Here he stopped and came back. When they had been defeated the Muzungu said to the Kabaka that he had seen it was not good to keep Mbogo in Buganda because he was going to spoil people's hearts. He said that when his soldiers saw Mbogo they regarded him as the Kabaka because he was of their religion. He said they were with Selim Bey when they were coming from Bunyoro and that then he was joining the Muslims ... For this, he said, Mbogo had to be taken to Lunguju and in addition he was old. If he were a young man he would have been taken to a far island.

Now on July 10, 1893, the European told Mbogo that he was going to be taken to Lunguju as it had been agreed with Captain Lugard. Mbogo then answered that he was joking, he did not mean it, he was old and that he could die there. He went on that maybe he would die on the way, he could not manage the food of Lunguju. Mbogo asked why they were killing him although he had agreed to come back. He said he had told the Muslims not to fight and they had refused. The Muzungu then said that he understood all Mbogo had said but that Mbogo had to do what the Government had told him to do. He went on that Mbogo was not going to die, he was going to be looked after, he was going to eat food of rice and meat and that he was going to sleep in a good house. Mbogo cried real tears when people of his clan, princesses and friends came to fare him well ...

They then started to settle anywhere they liked, in the villages of Muslim, Protestant or Catholic chiefs. The Muslim war then ended and they dispersed in every country they wanted. On August 15, 1893 the Muslim rebellion stopped completely, and it was in this month that the Kabaka gave some villages to the Muslims. They were then pleased and settled in peace. They did whatever they were told because they knew how helpless they were.

The Muslims were forced to surrender most of the territory they had obtained in 1892, keeping only Butambala and some scattered villages. With no strong external patron and with little sympathy among the other parties or the British, they had little chance of re-establishing their position as the Catholics had done in a similar situation earlier that year. Mbogo went into exile to Zanzibar for three years, then returned to preside over the bitter but now resigned Muslim community of Buganda.

Buganda now belonged to the British and the Christian chiefs. The vast majority of the Baganda still adhered to traditional beliefs. They received no recognition in the new scheme. Forced to become clients of the Protestant and Catholic officials, many in time adopted the religious affiliations of the new oligarchy, either from conviction or the desire to secure a better future for themselves and their descendants.

Epilogue

After years of strife, the Baganda were exhausted. The British overlords and the Christian chiefs, led by Katikiros Kagwa and Mugwanya, consolidated their control. One casualty of this process was what remained of the Kabaka's authority.

DOCUMENT 38
'Stopped from making visits'

Mukasa's description of the loss of royal tribute, 'Do not turn back,' III, pp. 54–6. (See note on Document 5.)

NOTES FOR READING Gabunga = head of the royal fleet; batangole = officials, chiefs.

In October 1896 the Kabaka visited Gabunga ... He was given many gifts. Gabunga gave him 20 cows and 50 goats. All the gifts from other chiefs put together amounted to 80 cows and 350 goats. It is difficult to tell the number of chickens he was given from Batangole and peasants. They also gave him loads of bark cloth as people of that side were bark cloth makers. When the Kabaka came back there was quarrelling among the chiefs and batangole. This was because some were made to give a certain number of articles. Some chiefs interchanged gifts and accepted the thanks of the Kabaka even though they were not the real people who had given that particular article. Rumors reached the European missionaries who in turn reported to the Government, pleading for the small chiefs for their being forced to give things to the Kabaka in a way which was not good.

The Government officials called the Katikiro and told him that they had heard the rumor and that if the rumor was true, the Kabaka was going to be stopped from making visits in the country. They went on that Kabaka's visits meant havoc to some people and it appeared as though people were still ruled like in the old days. They said that although the act was interpreted as giving gifts to the Kabaka, it was like ruling because they assessed people, cows, goats and chickens and bark cloth and that they (the chiefs) forced people to donate these gifts. They went on that those who refused were fined. They asked what type of gifts these were. They said that they had then warned and if such a thing happened, the Kabaka was going to be stopped from making visits in the country. The Katikiro went and told the Kabaka, and the Kabaka said he had never known that the bigger chiefs forced their juniors to give them things and also that he had not known yet that those who refused were fined. He said he was going to avoid that.

The last major assault on Mwanga's prerogatives came when he personally negotiated a large ivory deal with Zanzibar. The British claimed a monopoly on the ivory trade. Consequently, Mwanga was fined and ordered to expel about a thousand pages from the palace in December 1896.

DOCUMENT 39
'Now to be under surveillance'

James Miti's account, Miti, 'History', Vol. II, pp. 514–17, 519.

NOTES FOR READING George Wilson = Sub-Commissioner in charge of Buganda; the Prime Minister = Kagwa.

Mwanga stated that he never knew that things had come to such a pass that even the king himself had to have permission before he could export any articles from his own country. Nor was he aware that he was also subject to the same customs regulations as the rest of his people in his own country he was king of Buganda and the ivory had been obtained by himself in his own country: who else then had a right to demand export duty from him?

A further accusation against Mwanga was that he kept in his enclosure men of bad character, notorious for their disobedience to the king's ministers and also for offences against nature (sodomy). Thirdly, it was asked whence Mwanga obtained all the means that he bestowed upon his friends. Fear was entertained lest he might be turning public funds to his own use. The king, now angered beyond words, replied to the second charge by asking whether his accusers also did not drink beer in their homes and whether they did not drink it together with their servants and friends. And as to his courtiers' alleged shameful practices and disregard of all authority and contempt of the ministers and other chiefs, as far as Mwanga was aware there had never been any case or cases of that nature brought to his notice by any of his chiefs. He would certainly have dealt most severely with such offences, if any had been complained of by his chiefs or other people in the country. And, concluded the king, it was a matter of great surprise to him that his own ministers and other chiefs should report to Her Majesty's Government things of which they had never seen themselves nor for which they had any proof. Mwanga was greatly disappointed in Her Majesty's Government being so over credulous and acting upon mere hearsay.

After hearing this, Wilson intimated that he would communicate with her Majesty's Chief Commissioner at Entebbe and that he would inform the king of his reply in due course. Not wishing to act without the knowledge of the ministers, Wilson summoned Apolo, Mugwanya and Kisingiri in the month of December 1896 and asked what they considered the best means for keeping their king away from bad company and for restoring the old connection and cooperation between the king and his people. The ministers suggested expulsion of all the king's pages and courtiers and their replacement by a fresh lot of a better class, chosen or approved of by themselves. As to the king's alleged debauchery, Her Majesty's representative was of the opinion that the ministers and other chiefs were equally to blame in this regard, for drums and other signs of excessive beer-drinking were often heard almost all around Mengo and Kampala. This he left entirely in their own hands to take what steps they considered proper.

On the day on which the ministers had proposed to discuss the matter, however, they were again called away to Kampala to have the decision communicated to them in the matter of their king's illegal export of ivory. Mwanga had been found guilty, but it was left to the king himself to see what fine he should pay. Wilson pointed out that Mwanga's fault had been the result of his negligence to ask for the advice of his ministers and his dependence upon his flatterers, for had he disclosed to his ministers his intention of exporting ivory from the country, he would certainly have been advised to apply for permission from Her Majesty's Government. In all likelihood the king might have had his ivory exported duty-free, if Her Majesty's Government had only been informed of it.

Wilson also suggested the following: (1) that the king's escort should henceforth be made up of government officials instead of mere young boys, and that the king should never be allowed to move about without the escort of a number of his chiefs. (2) The king should not attend court in person; the ministers and other chiefs should discuss matters alone in the court, and only after they had made final decisions should they submit such resolutions to him for his approval and signature. Or, if he should wish to be present at the discussion of some important matter or at the trial of some big case, he should attend the court only as a passive member, that is, he should not have any voice in the proceedings. He should only sign what had been discussed and finally decided upon by the court. (3) For the purpose of safer custody, the Buganda Government funds should be taken away from the king's keeping and handed over into Her Majesty's Government's hands, for fear lest Mwanga might use up all the government resources by turning them to his own private use.

Here it has to be said that as to Buganda Government funds, the charge brought against Mwanga was an entirely false one. There had been no government money or property in those days. The king was government, and everything had belonged to him and he had been at liberty to dispose of land and other property in his kingdom as he pleased and to whomever he chose. Where chiefs had property in land, such was invariably the result of a gift from the king. No person could own anything unless it had been given him by the king . . .

After hearing the king's replies to the various charges through the ministers, Wilson gave orders that additional assessors should be called in and asked their opinion about the matter. Their decision being the same as that of the ministers, the next morning Apolo Kagwa led a procession of chiefs to the king's palace and asked to see him with an urgent message. Mwanga suspected some conspiracy and gave orders that all the people should assemble in the court hall and that the alleged message should be delivered there.

At 2 p.m. the Prime Minister spoke as follows: 'Sire, Her Majesty's Government and ourselves have decided, after deep consideration, that your Majesty's palace should be rid of the present lot of servants, courtiers and other royal attendants in Your Majesty's service, or at least of most of them, and that a new and better type of page should be engaged in their place. The reasons that have led to this decision are none other than the corruption and spirit of insubordination which are so much manifest in Your Majesty's servants and which, we fear, may in time affect Your Majesty's private life badly and have disastrous effects upon our kingdom.

'Secondly, it has come to our notice that Your Majesty is now in the habit of preferring the company of young boys and other low type people to that of Your Majesty's chiefs when out on daily walks or on journeys. It is below Your Majesty's dignity to have such company and it has been decided that henceforth Your Majesty's escort shall consist exclusively of Your Majesty's Government officials and that even these shall attend to Your Majesty's person by appointment.'

The king listened with a heavy heart. He had now to be dictated to. He, Mwanga, the king of Buganda, now to be under surveillance!

This punishment crystallized what Mwanga had sensed for some time: the Christian chiefs and British officials had made him a captive in his own court. He reacted by isolating himself from these 'usurpers' and listening to those numerous persons—'low type people,' traditionalists, Muslims and disaffected Christians— who resented the new order. When Gabriel Kintu, one of the military heroes of 1889 (Documents 29 and 34), organized a revolt in 1897, Mwanga joined in. The next three documents recount the flight of Mwanga to Buddu at the beginning of the revolt and assess his character and motivation. Compare these evaluations with those found in Documents 15–19.

DOCUMENT 40
'The king has fled' (I)

Reflections on the Kabaka's revolt and character by Bishop Alfred Tucker, head of the CMS mission in Buganda. Alfred Tucker, *Eighteen Years in Uganda and East Africa* (1911), pp. 81–3.

NOTES FOR READING Munyonyo is the Munyono of Document 21; Budu = Buddu, the province on the western shore of the Lake; Gabrieli = Gabriel Kintu; Mujasi = head of the king's bodyguard; Eldoma Ravine is in the Rift Valley of Kenya.

A fortnight later the storm, which slowly, silently, and almost imperceptibly had been gathering on the political horizon, burst with a great thunderclap upon the country. 'Kabaka aduse' (The king has fled) was the cry which was passed from lip to lip, in half whispered accents, on the morning of July 6th. Not trusting his gate-keepers he had in the darkness of the night cut his way out through the reed fences of his enclosure and, embarking in canoes at Munyonyo, by sunrise was well on his way to Budu, where he at once raised the standard of revolt.

He had chosen his ground well. The chiefs of Budu were disloyal to a man, and as a consequence the whole country governed by them was seething with sedition. It was only necessary for the king to make his appearance for a general rising at once to take place, and in a few days there rallied to his standard all the disaffected and discontented ones in the country south of the Katonga.

The king's ablest lieutenant was Gabrieli, the Roman Catholic Mujasi, who some two months previously had been convicted of disloyalty, but who had managed to evade arrest. His co-conspirators—the Roman Catholic chief of Mawokwata, the Kaima; and the excommunicated Protestant chief of Singo, the Mukwenda—had, however, been caught and deported to the Eldoma Ravine, where some eighteen months later I found them engaged in the humble occupation of sweeping the quadrangle of the Fort.

And what, it may be asked, had moved the king thus to embark on this mad enterprise? Was it injustice or harsh treatment of himself or his people? Nothing of the kind. It was simply and solely his hatred of Christianity and the opposition which, in consequence of its spread, he found on every hand, even within his own household, to the life of unbridled lust which he longed to be allowed to live. Moreover, there is very little doubt but that he was cognisant of Gabrieli's conspiracy, and dreaded some punishment on the fact becoming known to the Administration. The heathen party in the country was entirely with him in his dislike of European control.

But in dealing with this revolt there was another force to be reckoned with, besides those inherent in disaffection and discontent, and that was the loyalty of the great mass of the population to the kingship. Not simply loyalty to Mwanga personally—him they hated—but loyalty to the king as an institution.

Dr. Cook, writing on July 7th, thus described the situation: 'The whole country is very much excited. Men are pouring into the capital with guns (mostly retainers of the various chiefs), and a good many seem to be stealing quietly away to join the king in Budu. The king has immense prestige in the country, where the "Bakopi" (peasants) all implicitly believe in him.' And again writing on the 12th: 'Nearly all the police have deserted. They went off with guns last night to join Mwanga. The Katikiro wrote rather a gloomy letter to Walker, saying he does not realise how serious a matter it is, and that the people hate and detest the conquerors. The king hates the Europeans because they stopped his gross immoralities. The chiefs hate us because a Christian is expected only to have one wife and because no slaves are allowed; and the people hate us because they say they are obliged to carry loads, and to make roads (measures adopted by the Government for the good of the country), and because the old heathen customs are dying away.'

DOCUMENT 41
'The king has fled' (II)

Reflections on the Kabaka's revolt, character and career by James Miti, Miti, 'History', Vol. III, pp. 542–4 (this portion is paginated.)

The King called a big council during which he appointed new men to fill the vacancies created by the deportation of his two chiefs . . . The appointment of these three men was about Mwanga's last official act as King of Buganda. He had no more time for his kingdom, for, by the morrow, he would have renounced the throne and joined his party to fight against what he considered undue usurpation of his powers on the part of the white man and against their policy which to him seemed more that of a conquerer than that of a people who had only asked and had been allowed the task of protection over a smaller state.

To many people King Mwanga's conduct may have been difficult to account for. But his spirit of rebellion was rooted deep in his mind and was something more than a superficial and transient sentiment. Mwanga possessed an in-born antipathy as it were against the white element in his country, this aversion having been fed and nourished by the incessant trouble which he had with Her Majesty's officials of the time. As to his chief ministers, it was their fidelity to their respective religious beliefs and respect for constituted authority that caused their master's dislike of them rather than any breach of confidence with their master by them. Had Mwanga kept the peace and worked for the interests of his people, his ministers would have respected and obeyed him; but because he defied higher authority, led his own people to rebellion and renounced his father's throne merely in the selfish interests of a handful of his subjects, his more sensible chiefs and ministers had to oppose him, albeit deep down in their heart of hearts they desired to love and respect him. Preferring flattery to good counsel, however, Mwanga prepared for himself the way to open rebellion, dragging with him many in his wake.

But what was really the cause of the trouble? We cannot overlook the testimony of Mwanga's own contemporaries. They knew not only their hero's failings and good qualities but also the peculiar circumstances and conditions of the time under which a new king with old ideas of government found himself on his accession to the throne. An entirely strange new form of government with its new code of laws which allowed liberty and freedom to everyone else except to the King alone, and which on that account, went directly against the old law whereby the King was accorded divine honor and was regarded as impeccable. And this is what struck Mwanga as wholly strange and disruptive . . . Before ending this chapter, would it not be fair and just for us to ask whether the young King was not, after all, mishandled by the unwise officials of Her Majesty's Government at the time, and whether or not the ill-treated King, for such he considered himself, was justified in the step that he took in self-defense and for the assertion of his natural rights.

DOCUMENT 42
'The king has fled' (III)

Reflections on the Kabaka's revolt, character and career by Hamu Mukasa, 'Do not turn back', III, pp. 75–6, 85–6. (See note on Document 5.)

NOTES FOR READING Lukiko = old informal council, now an official council of chiefs with legislative powers; Bazungu = Europeans; the two chiefs or Katikiros = Kagwa and Mugwanya.

Then those chiefs who were his friends told him that if Kagwa and Mugwanya wanted to become Kabaka he could leave them to do so. They told him to let them divide the country in two so that one ruled a part and the other another. This was better than being aggressed, they said. They were going to die for him they said. They said if expelling away boys from the palace was spoken of in the Lukiko, they were going to quarrel and see what was going to happen. The Kabaka asked them what they were troubling themselves for. He said leaving the country and leaving the Katikiros with their Bazungu was better. The Kabaka then told them to go back. He warned them not to say a thing they had talked about in case the two chiefs (should find out) . . .

(This is) what I tell you about this Kabaka. Some call him a bad Kabaka who had nothing good on him. See in the two ways, the bad and the good way he was. (1) Mwanga was not as hot tempered as his grandfather (Suna) of a long time ago. He would have killed very many times by the time he was thirty-four. (2) Kabaka Mwanga was very kind. He loved people. If he liked you he trusted you but what let him down was to like bad people who were speaking evils against their friends. If he took to heart all the evils they said he would have killed many. This kindness stopped him from doing this. (3) Kabaka Mwanga knew very well to judges cases. When he judged he did not judge according to the social status of the person. He used to judge right. But sometimes he was influenced. (4) Kabaka Mwanga used to like harder workers and he used to like promoting them according to what they were doing. But otherwise he was influenced by evil speakers. (5) Kabaka Mwanga liked very much visitors. He used to do them what he wanted, he did not make them sad. What spoiled him were evil-speakers . . .

What I have talked about is the ground on which I base not to call him completely a bad man. What I know that spoilt him was his weak spirit. He was not as hard-hearted as his father. There is nobody who has this and has not got spoilt by it in the goodness he may possess. This spoils Kabakas and chiefs. Among chiefs this spoils them not to control themselves and they just accept everything as people to whom things are done . . . It is like a boat on a small rope, it can be turned on any direction.

The revolt instigated by Gabriel Kintu and supported by King Kabarega of Bunyoro posed some real problems for the regime. By using guerrilla tactics and taking advantage of Britain's preoccupation with a mutiny of its Sudanese soldiers, Mwanga was able to hold out for two years. During this period of wandering, he wrote a number of letters, some of which are given below.

DOCUMENT 43
'Mwanga's letters from exile'

Mukasa, 'Do not turn back', III, pp. 92, 95, 182–5. See note on Document 5.

NOTES FOR READING Pilkington = CMS missionary; Andereya Luwandaga = prominent Protestant chief; Bazungu = Europeans; Gulemye = Kagwa; Mwanza = town on south of lake in what had become German East Africa.

My friends,

I have written this letter to tell you the reason which drove me off Buganda. Katikiro A. Kagwa wrote me a letter saying that I did not like them, that when I was deciding big things I decided alone and that I did not tell them. It went on that if I went on like this I was to see. This is the letter which drove me off because I saw it was very strong. I saw the Katikiros did not want what I said and they wanted Europeans. Are these my Katikiros any more? Are they not European Katikiros? That is why I left then their country.

Dear Mr. G. L. Pilkington,

I tell you that I am ready with a big army. I shall fight hard with Europeans because they have disliked me very much. I shall kill a lot of them and I shall kill every Christian so that I bring back old customs of my country. My country will then be cleaned. You have disliked me quite a lot.

Dear Mwanga Andereya Luwandaga,

I have greeted you like a man. I, Kabaka Mwanga, tell you that you know me from a long time ago. You were under a black Kabaka. The Baganda have a proverb which runs, It is difficult to take a wife whose husband is still alive. I also tell you that I shall not fail to come back in my country and fight. When you read in the book you see how the Kabaka is called Caesar. I am also Caesar. My country is my burial place. When I get brave Arabs know that I shall come back. You will hear. Goodbye. God keep you.

I, Kabaka Mwanga

Dear my friend Andereya Luwandaga, Kimbugwe,

I have written to ask you about this matter. If I come back will the Bazungu kill me or will they forgive me? Now my servant tell me. I cannot express the suffering we have here. We have no more strength. We are here just like that. Now, then, write to me soon.

I, Kabaka Mwanga

Dear Gulemye (Katikiro Apolo Kagwa),

How are you my friend? To live for long is wonderful, and to see your handwriting!! I saw what you wrote me. I wrote to you when I was in Mwanza but you did not answer me. I asked you for a village but you did not answer me. Later I saw Europeans wanted to arrest me. This frightened me and this is why I still think that you will treat me the same. Now you write and tell me before I go to the Arabs. These days routes are open to there. What you wrote me recently telling me how the country had settled and how beautiful the roads were and how many Europeans had come, I already know. Generations differ. When I see another letter I shall not fail to let you know many things and the suffering I have experienced in this country.

Now then goodbye.

I, Mwanga

In 1899 Mwanga was captured and deported to the Seychelles Islands, where he died in 1903. The British had already put his infant son, Daudi Chwa, on the throne, and appointed Kagwa, Mugwanya and one other chief as regents. In 1900 the British and the chiefs moved to a consolidation of the arrangements which had been operative for several years. The Uganda Agreement of 1900 confirmed their control and named Kagwa as Katikiro and Mugwanya as Chief Justice. Buganda now contained twenty counties, as against ten in 1890, because of its expansion under British protection at the expense of Bunyoro and other areas. Eleven of the counties were under Protestant leaders, eight Catholic and one Muslim. The Lukiko began to function as a legislature under the Katikiro. The most radical step of all was the division of vast areas of Buganda into private estates which were deeded to the Protestant and Catholic chiefs. The Uganda Agreement became the social and political charter of colonial Uganda.

AIDS TO UNDERSTANDING

Chronology

1840   Beginning of Zanzibari contact with Buganda
c. 1856   Death of Suna, accession of Mutesa
1862   Visit of Speke to capital
c. 1867   Mutesa begins enforced observance of Islamic practices
1872   Beginning of close Khedival Egyptian contact with Buganda
1874   Chaillé-Long's visit to capital
1875   Stanley's visit to capital
1876   Execution of Muslims
1877   Arrival of first Anglican (CMS) missionaries
1879   Arrival of first Catholic (White Fathers) missionaries
1884   Death of Mutesa, accession of Mwanga
1885   Killing of Bishop Hannington
1886   Execution of Christians
1888   (September)   Expulsion of Mwanga by Muslims and Christians

1888 (October) Expulsion of Christians by Muslims, followed by Muslim replacement of Kiwewa with Kalema
1889 (May) Mwanga joins forces with Christian exiles
1889 (October) Christians recapture capital, then lose it
1890 (February) Christians recapture capital, followed by Mwanga's agreement with German agent Peters
1890 (April) Jackson proclaims British protectorate of Imperial British East Africa Company (IBEA)
1890 (July) Anglo-German Agreement assigns Buganda to Britain
1890 (December) Lugard arrives at capital, signs treaty with Mwanga
1891 Lugard spreads IBEA hegemony to north and west of Buganda
1892 (January) Protestants and Catholics fight for control
1892 (April) Temporary settlement between the factions
1892 (June) Lugard departs
1893 Britain takes over Buganda as crown colony
1893 (April) Portal works out settlement with Catholics
1893 (June) Muslim revolt
1897 Revolt of Mwanga, installation of Daudi Chwa
1899 Capture and deportation of Mwanga
1900 Uganda Agreement

Glossary

Ahmed b. Ibrahim (Hamadi) = Zanzibari who gained influence with Mutesa
Ashe, Robert = CMS missionary
bagalagala = pages
bakopi = common people, peasants
baraza = meeting, assembly
bataka = clans
batangole = officials with diverse functions
bhang = marijuana
Brard, Father = White Fathers missionary
Dualla = Somali interpreter of Lugard
Emin Pasha = Austrian explorer and administrator in the service of the Khedive
Gabriel Kintu = prominent Catholic leader
Gabunga = head of the royal fleet on the lake and member of the Lungfish clan
Hirth, Bishop = head of White Fathers mission in Buganda
Kagwa, Apolo = prominent Protestant page, later Katikiro
Kalemba, Mathias = Catholic page killed in 1886
Kakungulu = prominent Protestant military leader
Katikiro = chief minister
Kibuka = god of war
Kitakule, Henry Wright Data = prominent Protestant leader

Livinhac, Father Leon = White Fathers missionary
Lourdel, Father Simeon = White Fathers missionary
lubare = gods and priests of the traditional religion
lubiri = palace
Luganda = language spoken by the Baganda
lukiko = advisory council to the Kabaka
Lunguja = Buganda name for Zanzibar and for the capital of the Muslim Kabaka, Kalema
Mackay, Alexander = CMS missionary
mbugu = cloth made from bark
Mengo = principal capital of Mwanga
Mugwanya, Stanislaus = prominent Catholic leader
Mujasi = head of the royal bodyguard
Mukasa = god of creation and health
Mukasa, Joseph = prominent Catholic leader killed in 1885
Mukasa, Katikiro = prominent official, then Katikiro under Mutesa and Mwanga
Mulondo = frontier post in Kyagwe county
Namasole = Queen Mother
Nende = second god of war
Nyonyintono, Henry = prominent Catholic leader killed in 1889
O'Flaherty, Philip = CMS missionary
Pearson, Charles = CMS missionary
pombe = drink made from fermented grain or plantain
Ramadan = Muslim of Baluchi origin at Buganda court
Selim Bey = Sudanese soldier in Khedival, later British forces; helped lead revolt of 1893
Sematimba, Michael = prominent Protestant leader
Tucker, Bishop Alfred = head of CMS mission in Buganda
Wilson, C. T. = CMS missionary
Wilson, George = British Sub-Commissioner for Buganda

An Essay of Questions
Sources and Interpretation

Buganda provides a wealth of data for the last two decades of the nineteenth century, but the material is very unevenly distributed according to perspective. How do the following facts about the documentation affect your ability to understand what is happening in Buganda: the abundance of accounts by missionaries with relatively profound knowledge of the society but highly partisan objectives; the abundance of accounts by European officials with relatively less knowledge of the society and with a concern to establish control or maintain order; the abundance of accounts by Baganda Protestants, given their identification with their party and the fact that they wrote their works some time after the events; the relative absence of Muslim, indigenous Catholic and traditionalist accounts?

In this case study literacy is as closely related to elite status, victory and the creation of a historiography as in the Sokoto instance, and the Baganda Protestants can in some ways be usefully compared to Uthman dan Fodio and his entourage. How partisan are James Miti and Hamu Mukasa? Can they, as well as missionaries like Ashe, Lourdel and Mackay, be used as sources of information about the *lubare*, the Muslims or the opposing Christian faction?

All of the other case studies are set in the first half or middle of the nineteenth century. Do you find the European authors in this section approach Africa differently? Are they more 'racist'; more 'ethnocentric'; more 'imperialist'? Do you discern important differences between French Catholic and English Protestant? How would you explain the contrasting impressions of Mutesa offered by Speke (Document 6) and Stanley (Document 8)? Do you find any significant differences between the perspectives and personalities of Mackay (Document 19) and Lourdel (Document 20) as they confront the crisis of 1885?

On two occasions we have given contrasting impressions of the same event. What insight can you gain from the accounts of Lugard and Hirth (Documents 33 and 34) on the events of January 1892; and from the accounts of Tucker, Miti and Mukasa (Documents 40–42) on the revolt and character of Mwanga? Compare their assessments of Mwanga with those given in Documents 15–19 and with your own impressions.

The Power of the Palace

The Kabaka was a strong ruler in a very centralized state at the beginning of this case study. By the 1890s his power had been drastically curtailed. How would you explain this change? What were the customary limitations on the power of the Kabaka? How dependent were the Kabaka and Buganda on continuing military expansion and the capacity to distribute booty and promotions? Why was the state sensitive to approaches from the north and east, but not from the south? What were the attitudes about taking human life, and how do they compare with attitudes in the other chapters?

Religion, Politics and Change

As in the other sections, religion and politics are inseparable in Buganda. The story here, however, is unusual in the aggressive way in which one king embraced foreign missionaries, even if he stopped short of permanently adopting their religions, and in the rapid formation of political factions around four sets of personnel and belief. How would you compare the Kabaka's relationship to Buganda religion with the situation of the Asante king? Was tolerance of religious difference incompatible with the organization of Buganda society?

How alert was Mutesa to the implications of his warm reception of Islam and Christianity? Compare his attitudes and actions to those of Moshweshwe and the Asante kings, Osei Kwame and Osei Bonsu. Did Mutesa need Islam and Christianity for something other than diplomatic and commercial gain? Did he have a personal quest? Was he looking for a new 'national religion'?

Muslims, Protestants and Catholics

How would you compare the situation and attitudes of Muslims in Buganda with those of their fellow believers in Asante and in Hausaland before the *jihàd*? Do they, and the other factions, change their policy depending upon whether they have majority or minority status? To what extent were the factions manipulated by their European or Zanzibari patrons? To what extent did they manipulate the patrons? Do you find analogies between Nafata's policies towards Islam (Chapter Four, Document 11) and the efforts of the Protestants to penalize conversion in the 1890s (Document 32 in particular)? Apolo Kagwa once said that the Baganda would not rebel unless they found a prince to serve as their leader. How do you explain the fact that the three 'revolutionary' factions always acted in the name of a king or candidate for the throne?

How would you explain Mwanga's behaviour and his failure to protect the power of the Kabaka—inexperience; bad advisers; the British; the Christian chiefs? How would you evaluate the various judgements of his character offered in Documents 15–19 and 40–42? What insight do you obtain from Document 43? Would you venture any psychological and sexual interpretations here, as some have suggested for Shaka? Do you perceive any significant changes in him between 1884 and 1899? Is he a hero at the end? Does your attitude towards him change?

Technology, Diplomacy and Conquest

This chapter is the only one set in the late nineteenth century and emphasizing the beginning of European colonial rule. Why was Buganda not able to use German and British competition to its advantage as Asante sometimes used the Anglo-Dutch rivalry? Compare Baganda perceptions of Europeans in Document 19 with Dingane's assumption that the Port Natal British would support his actions against the Boers. How do you explain the relative absence of resistance to British takeover in the 1890–93 period? Would you consider the revolt of 1897–99 a belated form of resistance? Compare the effect on Buganda of the financial dilemmas of the Imperial British East Africa Company with the impact of similar British concerns on Lesotho.

Buganda displayed an interest in guns and had entire regiments equipped with firearms by the 1880s. They were none the less no match for any European or European-trained force and avoided open confrontation wherever possible. Is this because the Baganda were not trained in the use of firearms, because weapons were changing at a rapid rate, because Buganda had no natural defences like Lesotho?

Conclusion

Scholars working on Buganda sometimes apply the expressions 'natural love of change' and 'revolution' to describe motivations and events in the late nineteenth century. Is 'love of change' what an analyst says when he cannot think of anything else, or does it represent 'Ganda character'? Is 'revolution' an appropriate term? If so, for what specific changes and under what definition?

Bibliographical Essay and Bibliography

For this chapter we have made extensive use of the works of Kiwanuka (1972), Low (1971 *Mind* and *History*), Rowe (1964, 1966, 1969 'Myth' and *Lugard*) and Wright, as well as the anthropological commentary of Roscoe (1911). Kiwanuka (1972) and Oded give general bibliography, while Rowe (1969 'Myth') and Twaddle (1974 'Historiography') provide detailed discussion and bibliography of Luganda writing. Langlands treats the European travellers of the late nineteenth century, while Perham (Lugard, *Diaries*, III) gives a series of thumbnail biographies of important Europeans and Baganda. Kiwanuka also provides a detailed evaluation of oral tradition and its contribution to Buganda historiography in his translation of Kagwa (1971). For visual impressions, see the published European primary sources, most of which contain sketches and photographs. The *Uganda Journal* (from 1934) contains a number of important articles.

For a treatment of Islam, see Oded. For suggestions about Muslim and Christian 'revolution', see Gray, Low (1971 *History*), Twaddle (1972) and Wrigley. The *Church Missionary Intelligencer* of the CMS gives a detailed if partisan commentary on events. *Les Missions Catholiques* is less amply documented. Taylor treats the growth of the Anglican church while Faupel and Thoonen dominate the 'martyr' literature emphasizing the Catholics who died in 1886. For an introduction to colonial Buganda and Uganda, see Kasfir, Low (1971 *History*) and Twaddle (1969; 1974 'Receptivity'). Kottak has dealt with the ecological variables of Buganda while Fallers and Southwold stress the bureaucracy. For an interesting retrospective see the book by Kabaka 'Freddie', who was deposed in 1966 and subsequently died in exile.

Historians are rapidly bringing the level of understanding of neighbouring states and societies up to that already possessed for Buganda. For Bunyoro, see Beattie and Nyakatura; for Ankole (Nkore), see Karugire; for Rwanda and Burundi, Lemarchand and Vansina; for the Alur and Lugbara people, Southall and Middleton respectively; for Busoga and eastern Uganda, see Cohen, Fallers and Vincent; for the Luo and Abaluyia, Ogot and Were.

Contemporary and Internal Accounts

Ashe, Robert, *Two Kings of Uganda*. 1889; F. Cass, London, 1970.
—*Chronicles of Uganda*. 1894; F. Cass, London, 1971.

Baker, S. W., *Ismailia*, 2 vols. Macmillan & Co., London, 1874,
Chaillé-Long, Charles, *Central Africa*. Sampson, Law, London, 1876.
—'Itinerary', In Egyptian General Staff, *Provinces of the Equator. Summary of Letters and Reports of H.E. The Governor General, Part I, Year 1874*. Cairo, 1877.
Church Missionary Intelligencer (CMS), Seeleys, London, 1881, 1885, 1886, 1892.
Faupel, J. F., *African Holocaust*. P. J. Kenedy, New York, 1962.
Gray, Sir John, 'The diaries of Emin Pasha'. *Uganda Journal* (1961–65).
Harrison, J. W., ed., *A. M. Mackay, Pioneer Missionary of the Church Missionary Society to Uganda, by His Sister*, Hodder & Stoughton, London, 1890.
Jackson, Sir Frederick, *Early Days in East Africa*. E. J. Arnold & Co., London, 1930.
Johnston, Sir Harry, *The Uganda Protectorate*. 2 vols. Hutchinson, London, 1902.
Junker, W., *Travels in Africa*. 3 vols. Chapman & Hall, London, 1890–92.
Kagwa, Sir Apolo, *Customs of the Baganda*. Columbia University Press, New York, 1934.
—*The Kings of Buganda*. Ed. Kiwanuka. 1971. (Copies Makerere College Library.)
Kagwa, Sir Apolo, and Kitakule, H., 'How religion came to Uganda'. *Uganda Notes* (Kampala, 1902).
Kasirye, Joseph, 'The Life of Stanislaus Mugwanya'. Mimeographed translation of Luganda publication. Kampala, 1963.
Kulumba, Sheikh Ali, 'The History of Islam in Uganda'. Manuscript translation of Luganda publication in 1953. (Copy Makerere College Library.)
Les Missions Catholiques. 1885, 1886.
Low, D. A., ed., *The Mind of Buganda*. Heinemann Educational, London, 1971; University of California Press, Berkeley, 1971.
Lugard, F. D., *The Rise of Our East African Empire*. 2 vols. 1893; F. Cass, London, 1968.
—*The Diaries of Lord Lugard*. Ed. M. Perham and M. Bull. 4 vols. Faber, London, 1959.
Mercui, Father J., *L'Ouganda, la Mission Catholique et les Agents de la Compagnie Anglaise*. Missions d'Afrique, Paris, 1893.
Miti, James, 'History of Buganda'. Typescript translation at SOAS, University of London, of unpublished Luganda work written in 1930s.
Mukasa, Hamu, 'Do not turn back'. Manuscript translation of the Luganda version, *Simuda Nyuma*. 3 vols. Vols I and II were published in Luganda in 1938 and 1942.
Nicq, Abbé A., *La vie du Reverend Père Simeon Lourdel*. Imprimerie des Missionaires d'Afrique, Algiers, 1906.
Portal, Sir Gerald, *The British Mission to Uganda*. E. Arnold, London, 1894.
Roscoe, John, *Twenty-five Years in East Africa*. Cambridge University Press, Cambridge, 1911.

Speke, J. H., *Journal of the Discovery of the Source of Nile.* 1863; Dent, London, 1969.

Stanley, H. M., *Through the Dark Continent.* 2 vols. Harper & Brothers, New York, 1878.

Thoonen, J. P., *Black Martyrs.* Sheed & Ward, New York, 1941.

Tucker, Alfred, *Eighteen Years in Uganda and East Africa.* Arnold, London, 1911.

Wilson, C. T., and Felkin, R., *Uganda and the Egyptian Sudan.* 2 vols. Stuttgart, 1882.

Secondary Sources

Apter, D., *The Political Kingdom in Uganda.* Princeton University Press, Princeton, 1961.

Fallers, L. A., 'Despotism, status and social mobility in an African kingdom'. *Comparative Studies of Society and History* (Mouton, the Hague, 1959).

—ed. *The King's Men.* Oxford University Press, London, 1964.

Fletcher, T. B., 'Mwanga: the man and his times'. *Uganda Journal* (1936–37).

Gale, H. P., *Uganda and the Mill Hill Fathers.* Macmillan, London, 1959.

Gray, Sir John, 'The year of the three kings of Buganda'. *Uganda Journal* (1950).

Kabaka, 'King Freddie', *Desecration of My Kingdom.* Constable, London, 1967.

Kasfir, Nelson, 'Cultural sub-nationalism in Uganda'. In V. Olorunsola, ed. *The Politics of Cultural Sub-Nationalism in Africa.* Peter Smith, Gloucester, Mass., 1975.

Kiwanuka, M. S. M., *Mutesa of Uganda.* East African Literature Bureau, Nairobi, 1967.

—'Kabaka Mwanga and his political parties'. *Uganda Journal* (1969).

—*A History of Buganda.* Longman, Harlow, 1972.

Kottak, C., 'Ecological variables in the origin and evolution of African states: the Buganda example'. *Comparative Studies of Society and History* (Mouton, The Hague, 1972).

Langlands, B. W., 'Early travellers in Uganda: 1860–1914'. *Uganda Journal* (1962).

Low, D. A., *Buganda in Modern History.* University of California Press, Berkeley, 1971.

Luck, Anne, *Charles Stokes in Africa.* East African Publishing House, Nairobi, 1972.

Oded, Arye, *Islam in Uganda.* Halsted Press for Israel Universities Press, New York, 1947.

Roscoe, John, *The Baganda.* Macmillan & Co., London, 1911.

Rowe, John, 'The purge of Christians at Mwanga's court'. *Journal of African History* (1964).

—'Revolution in Buganda, 1856–1900, Part I'. *Uganda Journal* (1966).

—'Myth, memoirs and moral admonition: Luganda historical writing, 1893–1939'. *Uganda Journal* (1969), 17–40, 217–19.

—*Lugard at Kampala.* Longman, Uganda, 1969.

Southwold, M., *Chieftainship and Bureaucracy in Buganda.* Buganda East African Institute of Social Research, Kampala, 1950, 1953.

Taylor, John V., *The Growth of the Church in Buganda.* SCM Press, London, 1958.

Twaddle, M., 'The Bakungu chiefs of Buganda under British colonial rule, 1900–30'. *Journal of African History* (1969).

—'The Muslim revolution in Buganda'. *Africa* (1972).

—'Ganda receptivity to change'. *Journal of African History* (1974).

—'On Ganda historiography'. *History in Africa* (1974).

Wright, M., *Buganda in the Heroic Age.* Oxford University Press, Oxford, 1972.

Wrigley, C. C., 'The Christian revolution in Buganda'. *Comparative Studies of Society and History* (1959).

Collateral Reading

Beattie, J. H. M., *Bunyoro: an African Kingdom.* Holt, Rinehart & Winston, New York, 1961.

—*The Nyoro State.* Oxford University Press, Oxford, 1971.

Cohen, David, *The Historical Tradition of Busoga: Mukama and Kintu.* Oxford University Press, Oxford, 1972.

Fallers, L. A., *Bantu Bureaucracy.* University of Chicago Press, Chicago, 1965.

Karugire, Samwiri, *A History of the Kingdom of Nkore in Western Uganda to 1896.* Oxford University Press, Oxford, 1971.

Lemarchand, René, *Rwanda and Burundi.* Praeger, New York, 1970.

Middleton, J., *Study of the Lugbara of Uganda.* Holt, Rinehart & Winston, New York, 1970.

Nyakatura, J. W., *Anatomy of an African Kingdom.* Doubleday, New York, 1973.

Ogot, B. A., *The Southern Luo.* East African Publishing House, Nairobi, 1967.

Southall, A. W., *Alur Society.* Heffer, Cambridge, 1956.

Vansina, J., *L'Evolution du royaume Rwanda des origines à 1900.* Brussels, 1962.

Vincent, J., *African Elite.* Columbia University Press, New York, 1971.

Were, G., *A History of the Abaluyia of Western Kenya.* East African Publishing House, Nairobi, 1967.

Chapter Four

The *Jihād* of Uthman and the Sokoto Caliphate

PLATE 4.1   *Kano in the 1850s (see Document 3)*

PLATE 4.2   *The Sokoto market in the 1850s*

PLATE 4.3   *Al-Kanemi of Bornu (see Document 23)*

PLATE 4.4   *Bodyguard of al-Kanemi*

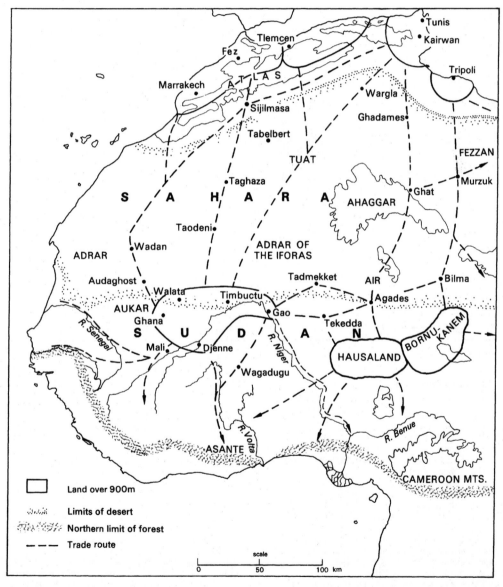

MAP 4.1   Trans-Saharan trading networks

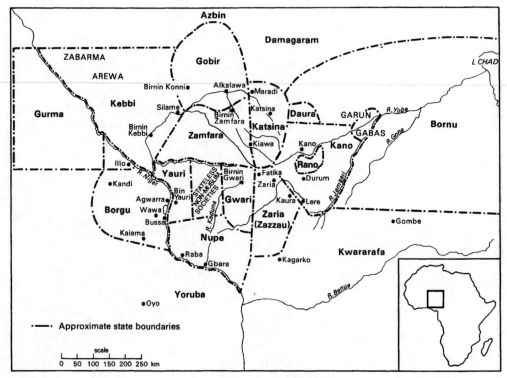

MAP 4.2   Hausaland c. 1750 with approximate boundaries of states

INTRODUCTION

The *jihād* or 'holy war' of Uthman dan Fodio took place in the early nineteenth century in what has become Northern Nigeria and resulted in the establishment of a Muslim regime called the Sokoto Caliphate. Although Islam had been present in the West African savanna for a thousand years in the form of traders, teachers and small communities, it had not spread very widely among the people nor had it become the governing basis of society until the eighteenth and nineteenth centuries. At that time several reform movements condemned what they called the syncretism and paganism in their societies and succeeded in replacing the old regimes with governments of their own making. The best documented, the most far-reaching and perhaps the most successful of these movements was the one led by Uthman.

The setting for this story is that part of the Central Sudan called Hausaland. The main actors are the predominantly agricultural Hausa, the predominantly pastoral Fulani and their respective leaders. For centuries the ancestors of these people had been living in medium-sized states organized around courts and market cities like Kano (Documents 1 and 3). The rulers or sultans of these states and capitals were Hausa. They exercised substantial control at the centre of their dominions but very little at the periphery, where many of the Fulani lived.

The states of Hausaland owed much of their prosperity to the Trans-Saharan and savanna trading networks. The market cities hummed with activity during the dry season, especially from November to April, when salt, cloth, guns and horses arrived from the desert and North Africa for exchange with the slaves, kola nuts, gold and ivory from the south. Hausa traders went south to the coast in Dahomey and Asante country along well-travelled routes (see Document 30 of this chapter and Document 7 of Chapter Five).

Several states tried to rule Hausa country over the years, but with little enduring success. Songhay exercised a great deal of influence there in the sixteenth century but never established control. Bornu was more successful, but had to keep coercing tribute from the local kings. The Hausa states themselves frequently fought one another and occasionally one, like Gobir in the mid-eighteenth century, might gain some advantage over its neighbours. No group maintained its hegemony for long, however, and basic loyalties and identities did not go beyond the individual state. In the eighteenth century the constant struggle for power tended to weaken the dynasties and make their subjects feel more acutely the burdens of taxes, military service and war.

The Hausa states and capitals were no strangers to Islam. Prestigious scholars had visited and resided there as early as the fourteenth and fifteenth century. The rulers were Muslim, at least in the sense that they considered themselves Muslim. They prayed, observed the Islamic festivals and patronized clerics (the *mallams* of the documents) at their courts—all without neglecting their specifically Hausa customs and obligations. Most of these court clerics, labelled 'venal *mallams*' by Uthman, were Hausa in culture and closely identified with the existing regimes. Another group of scholars, the Fulani teachers, tended to be much less tied to the towns, courts and the established order. It was among them that the long-standing tradition of Islamic reform (see Hiskett, 1962) took firm root and that the movement of Uthman was born.

The Fulani *mallams* did their teaching and judging of disputes in the countryside and villages at some remove from the control of the sultans. The *jamā'as* or communities of Muslims which formed around them had to pay taxes and could observe the burdens which the kings inflicted on the local farmers and pastoralists. They made the connection between those oppressive burdens and the 'mix' of Islam and 'paganism' at the courts. When the *mallams* and their *jamā'as* were able to persuade others of the validity of that connexion, they began to change the regimes of Hausaland.

The principal sources for this chapter are the Arabic materials written by Uthman and members of his family. European travellers visited Northern Nigeria in the 1820s, some years after the *jihād*, and a number of oral traditions from the late nineteenth century and early twentieth century are available. By comparing the different kinds of sources, searching for material composed outside of the Sokoto orbit, and analysing conflicts within Sokoto itself, it is possible to reconstruct the broad outlines and delineate the main issues of this period.

DOCUMENTARY NARRATIVE

The Setting in Hausaland

To set the stage for Uthman and the events in his state of Gobir in the next section (pages 130–43), we go back to a North African traveller, Leo Africanus. Born in Spain and raised in Morocco, Leo began to travel with his prosperous merchant uncle and visited the West African savanna between 1510 and 1515. Subsequently, he was captured by Sicilian corsairs on the Mediterranean and given to Pope Leo. He accepted conversion to Christianity, adopted his patron's name and began teaching Arabic to Europeans in Italy. He completed his *History and* *Description of Africa* in Italian in 1526, perhaps on the basis of an Arabic original. The English translation of the Italian manuscript was made in 1600.

DOCUMENT 1
'Gobir and Kano in the sixteenth century'

Leo Africanus, *The History and Description of Africa*, Hakluyt, Series 1, Vol. 94, (1896), pp. 828–30.

NOTES FOR READING   Gago = Gao; Guber = Gobir; Tombuto = Timbuktu; Cano = Kano; Zegzeg = Zaria; Casena = Katsina; Ischia = Askiya (title of the rulers of the Songhay Empire of the sixteenth century).

Of the kingdome of Guber.

It standeth eastward of the kingdome of Gago almost three hundred miles; betweene which two kingdomes lieth a vast desert being much destitute of water, for it is about fortie miles distant from Niger. The kingdome of Guber is enuironed with high mountaines, and containeth many villages inhabited by shepherds, and other herdsmen. Abundance of cattell here are both great and small: but of a lower stature then the cattell in other places. Heere are also great store of artificers and linnen weauers: and heere are such shooes made as the ancient Romans were woont to weare, the greatest part whereof be carried to Tombuto and Gago. Likewise heere is abundance of rice, and of certaine other graine and pulse, the like whereof I neuer saw in Italie. But I thinke it groweth in some places of Spaine. At the inundation of Niger all the fields of this region are ouerflowed, and then the inhabitants cast their seede into the water onely . . .

Of the prouince of Cano.

The great prouince of Cano stădeth eastward of the riuer Niger almost fiue hundred miles. The greatest part of the inhabitants dwelling in villages are some of them herdsmen and others husbandmen. Heere groweth abundance of corne, of rice, and of cotton. Also here are many deserts and wilde woodie mountaines containing many springs of water. In these woods growe plentie of wilde citrons and limons, which differ not much in taste from the best of all. In the midst of this prouince standeth a towne called by the same name, the walles and houses whereof are built for the most part of a kinde of chalke. The inhabitants are rich merchants and most ciuill people. Their king was in times past of great puissance, and had mighty troupes of horsemen at his command; but he hath since beene constrained to pay tribute vnto the kings of Zegzeg and Casena. Afterwarde *Ischia* the king of Tombuto faining friendship vnto the two foresaid kings trecherously slew them both. And then he waged warre against the king of Cano, whom after a long siege he tooke, and compelled him to marie one of his daughters, restoring him againe to his kingdome, conditionally that he should pay vnto him the third part of all his tribute: and the said king of Tombuto hath some of his courtiers perpetually residing at Cano for the receit thereof.

Contemporary accounts of eighteenth-century or 'pre-jihād' Hausaland are extremely difficult to find. One such source is the German explorer, Friedrich Hornemann, who began his journey towards the West African savanna from North Africa in 1797. He came to Hausa country and died there about 1801, but the only written reports which he left come from 1799 and the Fezzan area of the Sahara. Consequently, they are not first-hand impressions.

DOCUMENT 2
'The most intelligent people'

Hornemann's impressions of the 'interior of Africa'. Friedrich Hornemann, *The Journal of Friedrich Hornemann's Travels 1797–8* (1802), pp. 115–17.

NOTES FOR READING   Marabut = Muslim cleric or holy man; Asben = Air (Tuareg kingdom); Kashna = Katsina; Burnu = Bornu; Cabi = Kebbi; Nyffé = Nupe.

As to what the inhabitants themselves call Haussa, I had, as I think, very certain information. One of them, a Marabut, gave me a drawing of the situation of the different regions bordering on each other, which I here give as I received it. [See sketch on this page.]

The land within the strong line is Haussa; my black friend had omitted Asben.

These regions are governed by Sultans, of whom those of Kashna and Kano are the most powerful; but they all, (either by constraint or policy) pay tribute to Burnu, except Cabi or Nyffé, their districts being at too great a distance. Guber pays, moreover, a tribute to Asben. Zamfara is united with Guber; the Sultan of the latter having taken possession of it, killed the Sultan, and sold all the prisoners he could take.

The Haussa are certainly Negroes, but not quite black; they are the most intelligent people in the interior of Africa; they are distinguished from their neighbours by an interesting countenance; their nose is small and not flattened, and their stature is not so disagreeable as that of the Negroes, and they have an extraordinary inclination for pleasure, dancing, and singing. Their character is benevolent and mild. Industry and art, and the cultivation of the natural productions of the land, prevail in their country; and, in this respect, they excel the Fezzanians, who get the greatest part of their clothes and household implements from the Soudanians. They can dye in their country any colour but scarlet. The preparation of leather is as perfect as that of the Europeans, although the manner of doing it is very troublesome. In short, we have very unjust ideas of this people, not only with respect to their cultivation and natural abilities, but also of their strength and the extent of their possessions, which are by no means so considerable as they have been represented. Their music is imperfect, when compared to the European; but the Haussanian women have skill enough to affect their husbands, thereby even to weeping, and to inflame their courage to the greatest fury against their enemies.

In the nineteenth century European travellers visited Hausaland on several occasions. In 1824, one of them, Hugh Clapperton, recorded his observations of the Kano market. We are assuming that the realities of economic life were not altered that much by the Uthmanian *jihād* and that this description consequently holds in general terms for the late eighteenth century. Note that Kano was a centre of production as well as trade and that the control of the market was one of the most precious stakes of political competition.

DOCUMENT 3
'The Kano Market'

Hugh Clapperton, *Missions to the Niger*, ed. E. W. Borill, Hakluyt Series (1966), Vol. IV, pp. 650–5.

NOTES FOR READING   Sheikh = shaikh (here head of the market); soug = market; governor = the emir or sultan of Kano state; 8000 cowries = about £1 sterling; shambles = butcher shop; tobe = Arab dress; turkadee = cloth strip used for currency; cadi = judge; Felatahs = Fulani; Nyffuans = persons from Nupe; kafila = caravan; Tuaricks = Tuareg.

Kano may contain from 30,000 to 40,000 resident inhabitants, of whom more than one half are slaves. This estimate of the population is of course conjectural, and must be received with due allowance, although I have studiously under-rated

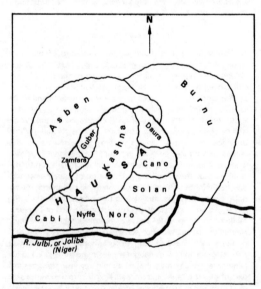

MAP 4.3   Hornemann's map of Hausa

my rough calculations on the subject. This number is exclusive of strangers who come here in crowds during the dry months from all parts of Africa, from the Mediterranean, and the Mountains of the Moon, and from Sennar and Ashantee. . .

The soug, or market, is well supplied with every necessary and luxury in request among the people of the interior. It is held, as I have mentioned, on a neck of land between two swamps; and as this site is covered with water during the rainy season, the holding it here is consequently limited to the dry months, when it is numerously frequented as well by strangers as inhabitants: indeed, there is no market in Africa so well regulated. The sheikh of the soug lets the stalls at so much a month, and the rent forms a part of the revenues of the governor. The sheikh of the soug also fixes the prices of all wares, for which he is entitled to a small commission, at the rate of fifty whydah or cowries, on every sale amounting to four dollars or 8000 cowries, according to the standard exchange between silver money and this shell currency. There is another custom regulated with equal certainty and in universal practice: the seller returns to the buyer a stated part of the price, by way of blessing, as they term it, or of luck-penny, according to our less devout phraseology. This is a discount of two per cent on the purchase money; but if the bargain is made in a hired house, it is the landlord who receives the luck-penny. I may here notice the great convenience of the cowrie, which no forgery can imitate; and which, by the dexterity of the natives in reckoning the largest sums, forms a ready medium of exchange in all transactions, from the lowest to the highest. Particular quarters are appropriated to distinct articles; the smaller wares being set out in booths in the middle, and cattle and bulky commodities being exposed to sale in the outskirts of the market-place: wood, dried grass, bean straw for provender, beans, Guinea corn, Indian corn, wheat, etc. are in one quarter; goats, sheep, asses, bullocks, horses, and camels, in another; earthenware and indigo in a third; vegetables and fruit of all descriptions, such as yams, sweet potatoes, water and musk melons, pappaw fruit, limes, cashew nuts, plums, mangoes, shaddocks, dates, etc. in a fourth, and so on. Wheaten flour is baked into bread of three different kinds; one like muffins, another like our twists, and the third a light puffy cake, with honey and melted butter poured over it. Rice is also made into little cakes. Beef and mutton are killed daily. Camel flesh is occasionally to be had, but is often meagre; the animal being commonly killed, as an Irish grazier might say, to save its life: it is esteemed a great delicacy, however, by the Arabs, when the carcass is fat. The native butchers are fully as knowing as our own, for they make a few slashes to show the fat, blow up meat, and sometimes even stick a little sheep's wool on a leg of goat's flesh, to make it pass with the ignorant for mutton. When a fat bull is brought to the market to be killed, its horns are dyed red with henna; drummers attend, a mob soon collects, the news of the animal's size and fatness spreads, and all run to buy. The colouring of the horns is effected by applying the green leaves of the henna tree, bruised into a kind of poultice. Near the shambles there is a number of cook-shops in the open air; each consisting merely of a wood fire, stuck round with wooden skewers, on which small bits of fat and lean meat,

alternately mixed, and scarcely larger than a pennypiece each, are roasting. Every thing looks very clean and comfortable; and a woman does the honours of the table, with a mat dish-cover placed on her knees, from which she serves her guests, who are squatted around her. Ground gussub water is retailed at hand, to those who can afford this beverage at their repast: the price, at most, does not exceed twenty cowries, or about two farthings and four-tenths of a farthing English money, estimating the dollar at five shillings. Those who have houses eat at home; women never resort to cook-shops, and even at home eat apart from men.

The interior of the market is filled with stalls of bamboo, laid out in regular streets; where the more costly wares are sold, and articles of dress, and other little matters of use or ornament made and repaired. Bands of musicians parade up and down to attract purchasers to particular booths. Here are displayed coarse writing paper, of French manufacture, brought from Barbary; scissors and knives, of native workmanship; crude antimony and tin, both the produce of the country; unwrought silk of a red colour, which they make into belts and slings, or weave in stripes into the finest cotton tobes; armlets and bracelets of brass; beads of glass, coral, and amber; finger rings of pewter, and a few silver trinkets, but none of gold; tobes, turkadees, and turban shawls; coarse woollen cloths of all colours; coarse calico; Moorish dresses; the cast-off gaudy garbs of the Mamelukes of Barbary; pieces of Egyptian linen, checked or striped with gold; sword blades from Malta, etc. etc. The market is crowded from sunrise to sunset every day, not excepting their Sabbath, which is kept on Friday. The merchants understand the benefits of monopoly as well as any people in the world; they take good care never to overstock the market, and if any thing falls in price, it is immediately withdrawn for a few days.—The market is regulated with the greatest fairness, and the regulations are strictly and impartially enforced. If a tobe or turkadee, purchased here, is carried to Bornou or any other distant place, without being opened, and is there discovered to be of inferior quality, it is immediately sent back, as a matter of course,—the name of the *dylala*, or broker, being written inside every parcel. In this case the *dylala* must find out the seller, who, by the laws of Kano, is forthwith obliged to refund the purchase money.

The slave market is held in two long sheds, one for males, the other for females, where they are seated in rows, and carefully decked out for the exhibition; the owner, or one of his trusty slaves, sitting near them. Young or old, plump or withered, beautiful or ugly, are sold without distinction; but, in other respects, the buyer inspects them with the utmost attention, and somewhat in the same manner as a volunteer seaman is examined by a surgeon on entering the navy: he looks at the tongue, teeth, eyes, and limbs, and endeavours to detect rupture by a forced cough. If they are afterwards found to be faulty or unsound, or even without any specific objection, they may be returned within three days. When taken home, they are stripped of their finery, which is sent back to their former owner. Slavery is here so common, or the mind of slaves is so constituted, that they always appeared much happier than their masters; the women, especially, singing with the greatest glee all the time they are at work. People

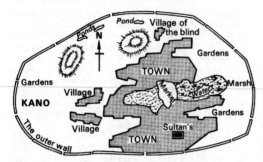

MAP 4.4   Clapperton's plan of the town of Kano

become slaves by birth, or by capture in war. The Felatahs frequently manumit slaves at the death of their master, or on the occasion of some religious festival. The letter of manumission must be signed before the cadi, and attested by two witnesses; and the mark of a cross is used by the illiterate among them, just as with us. The male slaves are employed in the various trades of building, working in iron, weaving, making shoes or clothes, and in traffic; the female slaves in spinning, baking, and selling water in the streets. Of the various people who frequent Kano, the *Nyffuans* [Nupes] are most celebrated for their industry; as soon as they arrive, they go to market and buy cotton for their women to spin, who, if not employed in this way, make *billam* for sale, which is a kind of flummery made of flour and tamarinds. The very slaves of this people are in great request, being invariably excellent tradesmen; and when once obtained, are never sold again out of the country.

I bought, for three Spanish dollars, an English green cotton umbrella, an article I little expected to meet with, yet by no means uncommon: my Moorish servants, in their figurative language, were wont to give it the name of 'the cloud'. I found, on inquiry, that these umbrellas are brought from the shores of the Mediterranean, by the way of Ghadamis.

A large kafila of Tuaricks, loaded solely with salt, arrived here from Billma. The Arabs told me it consisted of 3000 camels: at all events, the kafila was extremely numerous.

For impressions of the court and bureaucracy, we go to a Hausa source written down in the 1940s by two members of the royal family of Abuja, the kingdom formed by the Sultan of Zaria when he fled from the *jihādic* forces in the early nineteenth century. We are assuming (as does M. G. Smith, 1960, pp. 10–14) that this account is valid in general terms for nineteenth-century Abuja and eighteenth-century Zaria, and that it gives some indication of the nature of government of the Hausa states. Note the importance of the market, the military and the Islamic institutions.

DOCUMENT 4
'Hausa administration'

Alhaji Hassan and Mallam Shuaibu Ha'ibi, *A Chronicle of Abuja*, trans. F. Heath (1952), pp. 74–9.

NOTES FOR READING   Liman = Imam; Zazzau = Zaria; Alkali = judge. Emir was the nineteenth-century equivalent of Sultan or Sarkin. Bornu exercised some influence over Zaria and this is reflected in the bureaucracy. Zaria had a reputation as a slave-raiding state and this helps to explain the large numbers of slaves in the regime.

THEIR DUTIES

Almost all the old titles are still preserved in Abuja, but only one or two are anything more than honorary nowadays. They are usually given to people who hold some post of responsibility in the Native Administration or in local affairs. These were their duties in the old days:

THE CHIEF COUNCILLORS

The Madawaki.   He was next in importance to the Emir and was, under him, Commander of the Army to protect the land from enemies. He was in charge of one half of the town, the part built to the east of the Wuchichiri stream. He advised the Emir upon the appointment or dismissal of the title-holders; he replied to the Emir's address on Feast Days; he summoned the Chief Councillors and the Turbaned Councillors to their meetings. With the other Chief Councillors he chose the new Emir, but later, if any of these were themselves members of the Ruling Houses then he called upon the Kuyambana and the chief Malams to help him.

The Galadima.   He was always a eunuch, and was left in charge of the town when the Emir and the other chiefs went out to war. He arranged the marriages and naming of the Children of the Ruling Houses.

The Wambai.   He was always a eunuch and in addition to his duties as adviser, he took part in the naming of the children. He was also responsible for seeing that the private latrines and urinals of the Emir and his wives were kept clean.

The Dallatu.   When the Emir went to war, he was responsible for building his quarters in the war camp where, too, he performed all those duties which the Galadima performed in the town.

THE TURBANED COUNCILLORS

These were chosen from amongst the most important men in the town; even former slaves might hold these titles. Following the Madawaki were:

The Kuyambana.   He was the Madawaki's chief adviser in all matters.

The Sata.   He was in charge of the Household Servants and was responsible for seeing that the open space in front of the Emir's Compound was swept and the grass trimmed.

He also was the thatcher of the Entrance House of the Emir's Compound.

The Garkuwa Babba. At the war camp he kept watch over the enemy's movements. He led the foot-soldiers in the war dance before the Emir; originally, the Emir himself used to lead the dance.

The Makama Babba. He was responsible for the disposition of the troops in battle, and for sharing out the booty afterwards. With the Wagu, the Lifidi, the Shenagu and the Dankekasau he stood guard at the Entrance House of the Emir's Compound at feast times until the Emir came out to go to the prayer-ground of Idi.

The Lifidi. He was the Captain of the Shield-bearing Horsemen.

The Wagu. He guards the burial ground of the Emirs and keeps it clean. It is to him that the Dodon Wagu comes at the time of marriage in the ruling houses.

The Shenagu. He made the tethering ropes for the Emir's horses.

Following the Galadima were:

The Iyan Bakin Kasuwa. He was responsible for the markets in the town and in the satellite villages. . .

THE BODY SERVANTS

The Sarkin Fada. He was the chief official of the household. In time of war he helped the Makama Babba to divide the spoils; it was he who took the Emir's share and handed over the Madawaki's share to the Makama Babba. His followers were:

The Chinchina. He was the chief spy who would report on the state of the country and note any signs of unrest.

The Jagaba. He was chief of the heavily-armed foot soldiers. It was his duty to travel always one stage ahead of the Emir to see that all was well.

The Bakon Barno. Messenger to the Shehu of Bornu.

The Gwabare. He was responsible for the thatching of all houses inside the Emir's Compound. During the month of the Fast of All People he attended to the lamps for the evening prayers, at the end of which time the Emir would give him a robe.

The Magayaki. Assistant to the Jagaba.

The Jarmai. He was the chief warrior in the actual fighting; it was his special duty to come to the help of the Madawaki's forces if they were hard pressed. In times of peace he helped the Sarkin Fada in the household. His followers were. . .

THE IMAMS

The Liman Juma. He is the Chief Imam. He goes to the house of every ordinary family in the town where a death has occurred in order to say the prayers. He officiates at the service in the Mosque on Fridays. He was sometimes consulted in the choice of a new Emir.

The Salanke. He officiates at the prayer-ground of Idi, and prays at the death bed of all chiefs and title-holders; he was sometimes consulted about the choice of a successor to the Emir.

The Magajin Malam. The representative of the Shehu of Bornu. It is he who actually instals the new Emir.

The Magatakarda. The Chief Scribe and private Imam of the Emir's Household. He opens the Book at the Feast of the Month of Full Bellies. . .

THE EMIR IN COUNCIL

At dawn the Emir's Eunuchs entered the private apartments to greet him, and if he had any matter to resolve that day in council, he would tell them so, and when they had discussed it awhile amongst themselves, they would go out to the House of the Emir's Drums, which was the Council Chamber, the Makama Karami leading. Behind him went the Ma'aji, then the Sarkin Ruwa, next the Turaki, then the Fakachi, and after him followed the Sarkin Zana wearing a sword. Then came the Emir himself, and after him the Boroka.

When the Emir was about to sit upon his couch, two of these counsellors would stand in front of him holding out their wide robes so that no-one should see him in the act of sitting down. When they were all seated, the Turaki got up again and came before the Emir, and hiding his mouth with the sleeve of his robe, told him that the Sarkin Fada had arrived and was waiting at the door of the Entrance House. Being sent to fetch him, he went and, hiding his mouth with the sleeve of his robe, gave the message. Then the Sarkin Fada, the Jarmai, the Barde and the Hauni went through, and when they came to the House of the Emir's Drums they greeted the Emir two or three times before going in to sit down.

When they were all seated, the Makama Karami informed the Sarkin Fada of the matter under discussion and of the opinions already expressed. Then the Sarkin Fada would consult the Jarmai, the Barde and the Hauni who would either agree with the opinion of the others or else make their own suggestion. If it was clear that no agreement was likely without further consultation, the Emir sent the Turaki to summon the Chief Councillors, and the others would go out and leave them with the Emir. After a little time the Chief Councillors would usually go out and across to the old Entrance House of Zazzau where first the Kuyambana would be called, then all the other Turbanned Councillors, and the matter examined. Their opinion was then reported to the Emir by the Turaki.

Now the Emir sent for the Eunuchs and the Body Servants who came in, greeted him, and sat down. Then he told them what the Madawaki and his counsellors had advised. If all were agreed, the Emir announced the decision, but if they still could not agree, the Emir put an end to the argument by making the decision himself. Sometimes however, if it was a matter which they did not wish to become the subject of general discussion and gossip, the Madawaki and the Sarkin Fada would settle it privately.

Four times a year also, on the day of greeting in the months of Full Bellies and of the Birth of the Prophet, and at the Lesser and the Greater Feasts, the Chief Councillors and all the Turbaned Councillors would meet in the old Entrance House of Zazzau where, before going to visit the Emir, they discussed any matter that had arisen. When they were ready, the Madawaki went out first, the others following in order of rank. . .

JUSTICE

In olden times there was no Alkali, but anyone who had a complaint to make came before the Emir and told him of it. The Emir was always there in his Compound with the Sarkin Fada and the rest of the Body Servants, and anyone with a grievance would come and tell him his trouble. If the matter was of no great importance, not a question of murder or serious wounding, then the Emir would deal with it himself. But if it were serious, the Councillors were consulted; and though there was no Alkali, he would always seek the advice of the Chief Malams on questions of Islamic law. . .

TRIBUTE AND TAXATION

The Chiefs of all these towns and the Headmen of all the smaller places used to pay tribute to the Emir in money and in slaves. Each of them sent one slave or more to him, together with one hundred thousand cowries, or more; this they would pay once a year, or sometimes more often. To their representatives in Abuja they would pay one tenth as much as they paid to the Emir. The people would give a part of the produce of their home industries: the Kadara would give one hundred mats to the Emir and ten to their representative; the people of Gawu one hundred pieces of their woven cloth; the people of Kawu, one hundred lumps of iron ore; and so on.

All traders who came in with cattle, horses, sheep, goats, potash, salt, onions or whatever it was they brought, would take some of each kind to the Emir; and those who stopped in the Madawaki's or the Galadima's Ward gave them also a share. Besides this, the Emir received money from the Councillors and title-holders on their installation: from the Madawaki and the Galadima he had one million cowries each; from the Wambai and the Dallatu, five hundred thousand; from each of the rest of the Councillors about two hundred thousand; and from the other title-holders according to their position and means. A share of the spoil of any raid came always to their Emir and to the Madawaki; and when the Fulani were allowed to come, they paid a tax of ten thousand cowries on each head of cattle.

In return, the Emir had many obligations to his chiefs and people. When a new Madawaki or Galadima was appointed, he gave him a burnous, a robe, a turban and a horse; to the Turbaned Councillors he gave a robe and a turban; whilst to the rest of the title-holders he gave a robe.

Whenever the Chief of any town or district sent word that they were threatened by enemies, he would send warriors to help them fight; and he provided horses for his warriors and rewarded them for their bravery. If it was reported to him that any one was robbing or oppressing his people, he would send to seize the man and pass judgement on him.

He bought canoes for the big rivers so that the people might cross, and built bridges over the smaller streams. He helped needy strangers and destitute folk with clothing and with food; he helped the poor to provide for the marriage of their children and for the naming ceremony, and when death came he would give the winding sheet.

He provided gifts at the completion of the readings of the Koran; and when a young man had finished his first learning of the Koran, he was brought before the Emir who gave him a fez and a robe—but first he would see if the youth could read what was written on his writing board.

THE WEALTH OF THE PEOPLE

In olden days the prosperity of Abuja depended upon the slave trade. The Chiefs went raiding the pagan villages to capture slaves whom they brought into the town to sell to the well-to-do and the traders, obtaining in exchange money and fine robes. These rich merchants would take the slaves down into the Nufe or the Ilorin country and sell them there, buying with the proceeds all kinds of robes and garments, harnesses for horses, muskets and gunpowder which they would sell for further profit on their return. Sometimes the Nufe and Ilorin traders would come with their goods to Abuja and take back the slaves with them. A good slave, boy or girl, would fetch as much as two hundred thousand cowries, and therefore when the British came, those men who had been earning a rich living by this trade saw their prosperity vanish, and they became poor men.

Gobir, Uthman and the *Jihād*

In the eighteenth century Gobir acquired a reputation as one of the strongest and most aggressive Hausa states. The Sarkin or ruler renounced all obligations to Bornu and occupied much of Zamfara at mid-century. A few decades later, however, the state declined and suffered reverses at the hands of its neighbours in Katsina. The next document recounts the dynastic and military history of this period and comes from a European compilation of oral history collected in the early twentieth century.

DOCUMENT 5
'Chronicles of Gobir'

Our translation from the French account *Documents Scientifique de la Mission Tilho (1906–09)*, 2 vols (1911), Vol. II, pp. 471–2.

NOTES FOR READING   Gulbi N'Rima = Rima River; Gobirawa = the inhabitants of Gobir (the suffix -awa is Hausa for 'those of'); Birni-N'Katsina = the capital of Katsina. The dates given in the text are incorrect; Bawa died in 1789–90 and was succeeded by Yakuba who ruled until about 1794–95; Nafata then ruled until 1801–1802.

Finally Babari, son of Soba, came to power and ruled for thirty years, from 1734 to 1764. He was one of the most remarkable Sultans of Gobir.

He began by expanding his holdings to the southwest by conquering Zamfara. Then he transferred his capital to Alkalawa, on the banks of the Gulbi N'Rima. According to our Gobirawa informants, he also extended his authority into the Konni and Arewa areas and even into Sokoto, Kebbi and Dendi. In each case, the area submitted without being attacked and agreed to pay tribute as a vassal state. Some say he even occupied a part of Adar and imposed a tribute there.

Dan Gude, son of Babari, reigned from 1764 to 1771. He was attacked by the Sultan of Azbin, Muhammad El Rudala, who laid siege to Alkalawa. Pushed back the first time, he returned soon after with Tuareg support and attacked Zamfara. Dan Gude went to the support of his vassal but was completely defeated. He and many of his warriors were killed in the battle, which occurred in 1771 (1185 in the Muslim calendar) according to the Agades chronicle.

Bawa Jan Gorzo, son of Babari, succeeded him and reigned from 1771 to 1784. At the beginning of his reign the Zamfarawa wished to assert their independence but were defeated. Then Bawa directed his efforts against Birni-N'Katsina, but Agoragi, sultan of that city, defended it successfully and Bawa was killed.

His younger brother, Yakuba dan Babari, then came to power and reigned from 1784 to 1791. He continued the struggle against Katsina, but without any marked success.

Nafata dan Babari, his brother, reigned from 1791 to 1798. From the very beginning he was attacked by Agoragi. The two adversaries were on the point of fighting when the pious Mallam Uthman dan Fodio, who was accompanying Nafata, intervened. He succeeded in reconciling the two sultans without combat. Agoragi died before returning to Birni-N'Katsina and Nafata died soon after regaining Alkalawa.

Uthman dan Fodio was born in Gobir in 1754. He belonged to a group of Fulani known as the Toronkawa, known for their scholarship and originally from 'Toro' or 'Futa Toro' in Senegal. His paternal ancestors had emigrated from the west many generations earlier and had been living in Gobir for two hundred years before the reformer's birth. Uthman followed the educational pattern expected of a student and potential scholar, journeying from one teacher to another, staying with each teacher long enough to learn his specialty and becoming part of that teacher's community for that time. His first instructor was his own father, nicknamed 'Fodio' or 'teacher' (whence Uthman 'dan Fodio' or Uthman 'son of the teacher'). After mastering the Koran with Fodio, Uthman studied with his uncle and several other *mallams*. One of the most influential was Jibril ibn Umar, a sharp critic of the 'mix' of Islam and 'paganism' at Hausa and Tuareg courts. Uthman began his own career of teaching and preaching in about 1774 at his home in Degel. The next three documents describe his early career as a *mallam*.

DOCUMENT 6
'My heart burned'

A description by Uthman's younger brother Abdullah of the educational process. Abdullah dan Fodio, *Tazyin al-Waraqat*, trans. and ed. M. Hiskett (1963), p. 90.

NOTES FOR READING   Taqal = Degel; al-Suyuti and al-Bukhari = important Islamic scholars and authors. Jibril made the pilgrimage to Mecca twice. Abdullah was a close companion of his older brother and consequently this work, written in 1813, is one of the major sources for Uthman and the *jihād*.

Then after that my heart burned to visit our *Shaikh* Jibril b. 'Umar, may God be pleased with him, for a second time, for we had already visited him for the first time before our departure from our country of Taqal for the country of Zanfara at the time of his return from the pilgrimage again. We were with *Shaikh* 'Uthmān, may God be pleased with him, and we met (Jibril) who was at that time at his place called Qūdā...

We stayed with him for some days, and then our *Shaikh* 'Uthmān returned home and left me with him. I remained with him for about two months, and read al-Kawkab al-sāti' of al-Suyūtī according to his interpretation, listening to various books read by the students. Then I returned to my country, and found that *Shaikh* 'Uthmān had gone to al-Hājj Muhammad b. Rāj to read al-Bukhārī. I followed him, and found that he had not begun the reading. We went in together with him to the reading of al-Bukhārī, he reading and we listening to him. This was in A.H. 1201 (A.D. 1786); and God knows best.

DOCUMENT 7
'Itinerant preaching'

Abdullah, *Tazyīn*, p. 96.

NOTES FOR READING   Kabi = Kebbi; Kuwara = Niger.

Now when the *Shaikh* 'Uthmān had fulfilled his object in the country of Zanfara in mission work for religion, and (when) he saw that his community had become established there, and had become occupied with worldly matters, and fearing that on their account, he departed from the country of Zanfara and returned to his native country of Taqal, until such time as he set out from there on *hijra* with his religion, as will be told if God wills. After our return to him we travelled with him to teach religion, towards the west, and we wandered over all the country of Kabi, teaching religion until we reached with him the river Kuwārā which is the greatest river in our country. We entered it, and reached its west (bank) in a country called Ilū. We taught them religion, and (then) we returned to our own country. Then we travelled to the country of Zawma teaching religion until we reached the place of their *amīr*, at a place called Zaqū. Then we returned to our own country, and all had repented to whom God had ordained repentance.

DOCUMENT 8
'The Shehu's character and discourses'

Muhammad Bello. *Infaq al-Maisūr.*

NOTES FOR READING Muhammad Bello was Uthman's son and successor; he completed his manuscript in *c.* 1813. Extracts in this chapter (except for Document 23) are from a 'paraphrase and in some parts translation' by E. J. Arnett, *The Rise of the Sokoto Fulani* (1922). It is not always reliable but it is the only available published translation; and is hereafter called Bello (Arnett). This next document is taken from pp. 23–7. Shehu = Hausa for shaikh and the title applied to Uthman; Shari'a = Islamic law.

The Character of Shehu

It is known that Shehu as soon as he was grown up was a self restrained religious man, of a nature that won confidence and friendship. People came to him from East and West. He became a great Mallam. He upheld the banner of faith. He revived the law. He put an end to evil practices. He disseminated knowledge. He drove away unhappiness, he reformed the minds of men with his knowledge. He increased knowledge of the true law; he held public readings of the Koran before the assembled Chief Mallams and devout men. He put aside disputes and was steadfast in the truth. He made men to know things which it is difficult to know. He filled the countries of the West with knowledge and with seekers of knowledge. All the men of his time stood firm by his words. It became the custom for them to take counsel of him and question him about religious matters, and all both Mallams and those that are not Mallams paid honour to him. He became a preacher and very eloquent. He surpassed all men in nobility of character and charm of companionship. He was magnanimous and truthful. His manner of life was that of a saint. He was modest and had compassion on men and stood fast by the law. He was loved and honoured by men to a degree that is not often seen, so that you might have thought that men loved him more than they loved themselves. Men came to him in such crowds that they jostled each other. He showed them a smiling face and kindly nature and was glad with them. He was patient and had pity on Mohamedans. He found men obedient to him. Both men and spirits honoured him.

In truth God in his mercy to mankind revealed Shehu's work. God gave him power to become a king. God revealed to him wonderful things.

Know you also that I, Bello, used to see him when he was about to come out to the assembled people, he would stop and stand a little while in the open space of his compound, and he would say a few words which I did not hear. After that he would go out to the people. I asked him about this and he told me he was reviving his enthusiasm, he was making a promise to God that he would purify religion. Further he would pray God to make the people assembled here attend to all he told them. Then when he came before the people he would greet them so that everyone could hear. And when he had sat down upon his platform he would salute them three times. He looked pleased and smiled at them. Then he would call for silence. He was never wearied by them and never refused them. He was worried too by some who were badly behaved. When he told them to be silent, when he

stopped them asking a multitude of questions, they would not leave off asking.

Then he would begin his sermon to them in a loud voice. He felt no shyness in speaking before this assembly even though there were Mallams who hated him. Forthwith he preached his sermon to them all. He cared for none of them except that his words should be useful to them. His religion gave him strength and he feared no criticism. He gave his judgments with justice and never departed from the truth.

That is as much as we are able to tell you of his nature. If indeed we desired to tell all his nature we should need many books.

The Subjects of Shehu's Discourses

The subjects of Shehu's discourses to the people were five in number. The first was the perfect following of the Shari'a, that was the groundwork . . .

In the second he impressed on the people obedience to the Sunna of the Prophet. In the third he warned them against doubt [and sophistry] . . .

In the fourth part of his discourses Shehu spoke of the prevention of evil and the guarding against evil customs.

In the fifth part he taught the rules of the Shari'a. He explained what was in dispute and taught the usefulness of seeking fresh knowledge. In the fifth part he also uttered warnings to mankind, and these warnings form the greater part of the books he wrote. All that pupils may need is to be found in these teachings. Those that desire knowledge will find what they need. He expounded all questions that were in dispute and purified them by his knowledge. Moreover his teachings contained much that was new and increased our knowledge of important matters belonging to our times.

On the strength of his scholarly reputation and popular following, Uthman received an invitation to attend the 'Great Feast' of the Islamic calendar organized by Sarkin Gobir Bawa in 1786–87. As Document 9 shows, the young Fulani *mallam* interrupted the ceremonies to make several demands on Bawa: the freedom to continue his preaching, the release of illegally detained Muslim prisoners and relief for his *jamā'a* from some burdensome taxes.

DOCUMENT 9
'I give you what you ask'

Abdullah, *Tazyīn*, pp. 85–6, 88–9.

NOTES FOR READING qasida = Arabic poetic form (the 'other languages' here are Hausa and Fulani); *ulama* = clerics; Maghami = a site a few miles from the Gobir capital of Alkalawa.

Then we rose up with the *shaikh* helping him in his mission work for religion. He travelled for that purpose to the east and to the west, calling the people to the religion of God by his preaching and his *qasidas* in other languages and destroying customs contrary to Muslim law. Some of the people from the surrounding countries came to him, and entered his community while we were in his country which had become famous through him, and which was called after him, namely Taqal . . .

We travelled with him on one occasion to the country of Kabi. He called them to the reform of the faith, and to Islam, and good works, and to abandon customs contrary to them. Many of them repented, and travelled to him in groups, when he returned to his country, listening to his preaching, and God caused them to accept him for the first time.

Then he travelled to the towns until the community increased, and (its fame) spread. The *shaikh* was not in the habit of travelling to the kings, nor of having anything to do with them, but when the community grew larger about him, and his affair became well-known to the kings, and to others, he saw that he must go to them, and he travelled to the Amir of Ghubir, Bawa, and explained to him the true Islam, and ordered him (to observe it), and to establish justice in his lands. Then he returned to his own country, and he was enabled thereby to summon (people) to religion, because it came about that those who did not fear God, feared to deny his order because of his connection with the Sultan, (and thus it was) until we emigrated to the country of Zanfara, to summon its people to religion. We remained there about five years, and it was a land over whose people ignorance was supreme; the majority of its people had not smelt the scent of Islam. They used to come to the *shaikh*'s gathering mingling with their women. He segregated them, teaching them that mixing together was forbidden, after he had taught them the laws of Islam.

Then after this year, by one year or two, the Sultan of Ghubir, who was Bawa, sent word to all the *'ulama'* of his country, that they should gather together at his court during 'Id al-Adha, he at that time being in his place which is called Maghami.

We gathered together before him, and he said what he had to say, and gave much wealth in alms to the *'ulama'*. Then *Shaikh* 'Uthman stood up before him and said to him: Indeed I and my community have no need of your wealth, but I ask you this and this, and he enumerated to him all matters concerning the establishing of religion. The Sultan replied to him 'I give you what you ask, and I consent to all that you wish to do in this our country'. Then he praised God for that, and we returned to establish religion, and the rest of the *'ulama'* returned with their wealth.

Bawa's concessions gave Uthman a kind of official sanction and strengthened his movement. In fact, Uthman was not always so opposed to 'travelling to the kings' as Abdullah would have us believe, although he was careful to keep his support outside of the capital and 'established' Islam. His following grew rapidly in the decade after 1786–87, drawing particularly from western Hausaland (Gobir, Kebbi and Zamfara) but also from other parts of the Central Sudan. After studying with the master, Uthman's disciples returned home with copies of Uthman's works and his 'licence' to teach them and founded their own *jama'as* or communities. Some of these disciples later led the *jihad* in their own areas.

In the 1790s the growing Uthmanian community began to consider more militant action, as Document 10 reveals.

DOCUMENT 10
'Their desire to break away'

Abdullah, *Tazyin*, pp. 104–105.

NOTES FOR READING al-Mukhtar = leader of the Kunta family of the Timbuktu area who inspired a great revival of Islam in the late eighteenth century; Sharif = one descended from Muhammad; *Sunna* = orthodox or correct.

Now when these *'ulama'* rose up to help religion in our country, it increased in fame, and its followers became many, and the people came in crowds to *Shaikh* 'Uthman—may God be pleased with him—from east and west, from south and north, until (news of) his affair reached the country of the learned and upright *shaikh*, famous in the countries of the west and elsewhere, by the nickname of al-Mukhtar. And it was he, according to what we hear, who roused the people to follow what *Shaikh* 'Uthman said, until there came to us an Arab from his region, who told us that he was one of his students. He was called al-Sharif. We received him with great honour, and we questioned him about the circumstances of *Shaikh* al-Mukhtar, and he described his circumstances to us, until he made ready to return to *Shaikh* al-Mukhtar.

Then our *Shaikh* 'Uthman—may God perpetuate the glory of Islam through him—when he saw the greatness of the community, and their desire to break away from the unbelievers, and commence Holy War, began to incite them to arms, saying to them 'verily to make ready weapons is *sunna*', and we began to make weapons ready, and he began to pray to God that He should show him the sovereignty of Islam in this country of the Sudan.

By the time Nafata became Sarkin Gobir in 1794–95, Uthman's *jama'a* had become large and powerful. Faced with the threat of the Fulani *mallam* and the declining power of his own court, Nafata reversed the policies of his father. The next document describes this change as well as the growing strength of the Uthmanian community.

DOCUMENT 11
'Inherited religion'

An account of Uthman's activities and Nafata's ban. Bello (Arnett), pp. 47–8.

NOTE FOR READING zakka = alms.

When Shehu showed to the people the way of the Law they

perceived it and followed it. Moreover those that entered upon the way, entered upon it thoroughly and drove out the worldly people, the evil Mallams and the Chiefs. Their measure was diminished, their market broken, their greatness fell in the eyes of the people who obtained the Law.

But these evil Mallams and the Chiefs set to work to trouble the people of Shehu. They seized their property and robbed them on the roads, they harried them and blocked roads to all who were for approaching Shehu and his people. But Shehu himself and his people they did not touch. They considered that Shehu's people were not capable of anything against them because most of his followers were poor people and knew nothing of war at all. Unceasingly whenever a new Sarki was appointed in our towns he would attempt to hide the glory of Shehu. They made plans against Shehu and his people and plotted in secret to destroy them. On this point I said 'Take you my message to the Chiefs. Tell them if they ceased from wickedness, in truth they shall find good counsel. Speak out between us and let them listen to the message. If they harass us we will flee from them with our religion for the sake of God. In very truth every matter is in God's hands. Further I say of them I was watching them at the time that I know of. I was watching them at sunrise. If they attacked us in the morning we would fight with them till the fight grows severe. But God willed that they should die and they died one upon other.'

Again when they saw that Shehu did not cease from what he was upon and that his affairs only grew in strength and the multitude of his people was not diminished, but entered the faith in multitudes then they began to fear him on account of their actions. For their actions were not in accord with what he practised. In truth their authority was not in accordance with the Law. For so far as the Law is concerned they held to it in the measure of their washings and the fashion of their clothes: they said prayers and fasted and paid zakka and made the profession of faith. But in all this they knew not the Law thoroughly. And as for their judgments they followed the practice of their fathers who knew [not] Mohamedanism. Most of their judgments were contrary to the book so far as we are acquainted with them. And much of their speech and their actions were those of heathens only. In truth the revelation of religion and the maintenance of the Law could not be reconciled with their deeds. For this reason they began to make plans for war with Mallam Shehu and his people. They did not doubt that the victory would be with them because they saw that the followers of Shehu were poor and not fit for fighting. They gathered together and took counsel and said that the man must be prevented from calling to religion and from preaching in public and that every man must be commanded to return to what he had inherited from his father and grandfather.

There was nothing that caused us so much fear as the proclamation made by Sarkin Gobir Nafata. He proclaimed three things: First, that he would not permit any man to preach to the people except Shehu alone. Second, that he would not permit any man to be a Mohamedan except he who had inherited it from his father, and he who had not inherited Mohamedanism must return to what he had inherited from his father and grandfather. Thirdly, that no man henceforward must be seen wearing a turban and no woman veil her body.

This was the proclamation which he made in every market and these are the things he attempted to contrive against us. God sufficed us against his planning and his deceit. The Lord God willed that he should die shortly after his proclamation.

Nafata's declaration did not produce the intended results. Uthman continued to attract people to his standard and to 'convert' them away from their 'inherited religion'. He became more rather than less critical of the practice of Islam in Gobir. He elaborated on the differences between the sinful Muslim and the polytheist or unbeliever and attacked the 'venal *mallams*' and rulers who accepted the combination of Islam and 'paganism'. Many of Uthman's followers began to see him as the reformer who, according to prophecy, was to come in the thirteenth Islamic century (1785–1882 in the Christian calendar) to 'command what is right and forbid what is disapproved' (Hiskett, 1962).

When Yunfa became Sarkin Gobir in 1801–1802, Uthman still hoped to bring about a more Islamic society by persuasion and example. The new ruler had even studied with him and obtained his support for the position of Sarkin. None the less, relations between the *jama'a* and the court got worse rather than better and erupted in fighting in 1804. When the king's soldiers attacked, the Uthmanian community resolved the problems of distinguishing between sin and unbelief, Muslim and non-Muslim and persuasion and revolution. Now they were the true Muslims threatened by unbelievers, now they had to defend themselves and establish the law of Islam. The community moved away from the Gobir armies (the *hijra* or 'emigration'), constituted an embryonic state by electing Uthman as their leader (his first title was *imām*, later he became Caliph or Commander of the Faithful) and declared the *jihād* of the sword against the Sarkin Gobir and his followers. In this, Uthman and his supporters consciously imitated the pattern of Muhammad, who left a hostile Mecca for Medina, conquered Mecca and central Arabia and established the Islamic state (for the conscious comparison, see Document 18). The next three documents describe the events of the tumultuous year of 1804.

DOCUMENT 12
'The *Hijra*'

Abdullah, *Tazyīn*, pp. 107–109.

NOTES FOR READING   razzia = raid; Abd al-Salam = important Hausa leader in the jama'a (see Document 25); Umar al-Kammawi = important disciple of Uthman originally from Bornu; naphtha = gunpowder or gun; Qudu = Gudu (Uthman's 'Medina').

Now when the kings and their helpers saw the _Shaikh's_ community making ready their weapons, they feared that. Moreover, before that the numerousness of the community, and its cutting itself off from their jurisdiction had enraged them. They made their enmity known with their tongues, threatening the community with _razzias_ and extermination, and what their breasts hid was worse than that. They began to forbid what they heard concerning the dress of the community, such as the turbans, and the order that the women should veil. Some of the community feared their threats, namely the people of our brother 'Abd al-Salām, and they emigrated before us to a place in Kabbi called Ghimbana. Then the Sultān of Ghūbir sent word to them, that they should return, and they refused. Then that Sultān sent word to the _shaikh_, that he should travel to him, and we set out to (visit?) him. His intention was to destroy us, but God did not give him power over us, and when we went into his presence in his castle, he came towards us, we being three; the _shaikh_, myself, and 'Umar al-Kammawi, the _shaikh's_ friend. He fired his naphtha in order to burn us with its fire, but the fire turned back on him, and nearly burnt him while we were watching him; and not one of us moved, but he retreated hastily. Then he turned back to us after a while, and sat near to us. We approached him, and spoke to him. He said to us: 'Know that I have no enemy on the earth like you', and he made clear to us his enmity, and we made clear to him that we did not fear him, for God had not given him power over us. Then he said concerning that which God had ordained him to say, such as I am not now able to relate. God kept him back from us, and we went away from him to our house, and none knew anything of that (affair) other than we ourselves. And the _shaikh_ said to us, 'Both of you conceal this, and pray God Most High on our behalf that we may never again meet with this unbeliever'. He prayed for that, and we said 'Amen' to it.

Then we returned to our country, and (the Sultān of Ghūbir) dispatched an army after that against the community of 'Abd al-Salām, and it attacked them, and some of the Muslims were killed, and some were taken prisoner, and the rest of them scattered in the country of Kabbi. Now this increased him in pride and arrogance, and he, and those who followed him from among the people of his country, unbelievers and evil-doers, began to threaten us with the like of that until the Sultān sent word to the _shaikh_ that he should go away from his community and leave them for a far place, he together with his family, alone. The _shaikh_ sent word to him (saying) 'I will not forsake my community, but I will leave your country, for God's earth is wide' I Then we made ready to emigrate, and he sent word to the _shaikh_ that he should not leave his place. The _shaikh_ refused, and we emigrated to a place on the far borders of his lands, in the desert places, called Qudu.

DOCUMENT 13
'We made homage to Shehu'

An account of the creation of the new state and society. Bello (Arnett), pp. 48–53.

NOTES FOR READING Aliu or Agale = important Tuareg leader; Birnin Kebbi = capital of Kebbi; Waziri = minister or adviser; Zuru = important cleric at Yunfa's court. Some Tuareg supported Uthman but many sided with the Sarkin Gobir.

Shehu therefore made all speed and rose up and fled from the midst of the towns of Gobir. This was in the year of the Hijra 1218 [21st February, 1804 A.D.] in the month of Zulkiida and the tenth day. A Mallam of great renown and proved holiness Aliu, also known as Agàle, a Tuareg, a friend of Shehu, called on the Tuareg to assist Shehu in his flight, and defend him from what his enemies might do to him . . .

Then I went to Birnin Kebbi and scattered letters abroad and called the people together. I brought them back with me and when I reached Dagel, found the people there preparing for flight. We fled from the midst of the towns of Gobir and escaped safely. Mallam Agàle helped us with Mallam Mohamadu Gurdam and Aliu Jedu who was our war leader. With these and some others we reached Gudu.

The people gathered together and sought to ally themselves with Shehu. They came from the villages round about. Others also kept on coming for two months. After that Sarkin Gobir forbade them to join under penalty of losing their goods. This was in the month of Muharram. [Muharram 1219 A.H. = April, May, 1804 A.D.] The Gobirawa and Tuareg joined together and intercepted the roads by which the flight was taking place and seized the goods of our people. Those of the Tuareg who were near to them helped them to prevent our flight. In spite of this we did not desist. Some of our folk reached us with their families and their property. Others with their families and no property. Others again by themselves alone without their families or their goods.

Then Sarkin Gobir when he saw that he could not prevent the people from going, wrote a letter to Shehu to tell him to come back to his place at Dagel, and besought him to do so. Shehu replied in a letter that he would not return unless Sarkin Gobir repented and purified his religion as was right, and he, and all his people, turned to God and spread abroad righteousness and the true faith: also he must restore all the property he had looted and taken from the people, so that they should have security from him. Then only would Shehu return to Dagel.

The Messenger who took his letter was Shehu's boy Wodi, and he went with Wazirin Sarkin Gobir who had brought the letter to us. When they reached him, Yunfa had the letter read to him. Then he called his Waziris and Mallams and they came together and abused Shehu and his followers, and expressed their hatred.

Yunfa asked the assembled Mallams whether he and they were in the right way of truth or Shehu. They said to Sarkin Gobir, 'You are in the right. Shehu and his people are in the wrong.' The Sarkin Gobir was in the same position as the heathen of Mecca when they asked the Mallams of the Jews about the Prophet . . .

My relative Musharku Abul Hassan son of Ahmadu has told me that he was present when the letter of Shehu was read to Sarkin Gobir. Mallam Zuru was reading it and changed what was in the letter and read out what was not accurate with the intention of setting on Sarkin Gobir to attack Shehu and his people. And the Mallams who were there with Zuru before Yunfa assisted him. Abul Hassan remained silent. The Sarkin Gobir said to the messenger, 'Go. I will give you no guide. If God brings you to Shehu, tell him that I am preparing war against him, let him prepare against our meeting.' Then the messenger went forth and he was perplexed. He did not know what direction to take and found no one to guide him. Moreover the Soudanese people were killing any one going to join the Fulani . . .

Then in truth we knew that the peace was broken between us and the Gobirawa. In truth the Mallams of the Soudanese and Tuareg people who followed their way of life assisted them in their hostile operations against us. We had no supporters among the chiefs of these countries because they stood in together and declared themselves against us, and made a mutual undertaking of their intention to destroy us. Then we assembled and took counsel upon our affairs. We decided it was not right for men to remain leaderless and without a Sarki. Thereupon we made homage to Shehu and promised to obey him and follow him in prosperity and adversity. He accepted our homage and promised to follow the Book and the Law. This was on the evening of Wednesday. The first who did homage to him was my brother the Waziri Abdullahi. Then I, Bello, did homage to him. Then Wazari Umaru Mai-Alkammu and then the whole gathering of Mohamedans.

When God brought us to the next day Shehu set up his flag and we set to work on the ditches round the town. We said to ourselves, 'Truly but for God we should not have found any guidance, we should not be in the way of truth, we should not be making our prayers. May God shed His peace upon us. May God make our feet steadfast when we meet in battle.' 'The Gobirawa are oppressing us. If they think to punish us, we rebel against them.' Thus we talked while we dug the ditches as well as we were able.

DOCUMENT 14
'God broke the army of the heathen'

An account of the battle of Tabkin Kwotto in June 1804. Bello (Arnett), pp. 54–7.

NOTES FOR READING Tabkin = lake; Bedr = site of Muhammad's capture of a Meccan caravan in A.D. 624; Jibrile = Jibril ibn Umar, Uthman's former teacher; *Allah akbar* = God is great. The 'King' in this passage is Yunfa. Abdullah was in charge of the *jihādic* army and was second in command (as 'Waziri' or 'Chief Minister') to Uthman at this time.

The battle of Tabkin Kwotto was the greatest of all battles between us and the Gobirawa. It was like the battle which the Prophet fought with men of Mecca at Bedr. The manner of the battle was thus: when our messenger left the Sarkin Gobir, the Sarkin Gobir set to work to collect an army. He sent to all his villages and towns and wrote letters to his brother chiefs, Sarkin Katsina, Sarkin Kano, Sarkin Zazau, Sarkin Daura and Sarkin Asben. They all answered his letters and undertook what he asked of them, that they should help him and increase his strength to fight against all who allied themselves with Shehu. They sanctioned his war and each of them also prepared for war against all in their towns who allied themselves with Shehu. And when he had received their replies and their support in his undertaking and their promise to help him, he set out on a Sunday to his camp outside the city. There he halted two nights, or, some say, nine nights. Then he set out and going South halted for a night at Baure. Again he set out and halted at Ganba as we related at first. Thence he marched and halted at Makada. From thence again to Shara. Thence again to Jansarki. There he halted two nights and waited for the rest of his army. They arranged their affairs and reconnoitred with his army against us. No one but God knows how many there were. Most of the Tuareg were with him and they were eager to fight us.

Then news reached us and we set out on Saturday and made our camp not very far from our houses, Abdullahi the great Waziri, was our leader. We spent the day (Sunday 17 June) in camp, but heard no more news of the enemy at all. In the evening we returned to our houses and slept there. Then we went out at early dawn on Sunday to the camp where we had spent the previous day. Then the horsemen of our Fulani brothers came out from Sarkin Yunfa's army and crossed over to us. In truth they left their relatives in the dwellings of the heathen. . . . They informed us . . .

We returned to our houses and met Shehu who had come out. He called us together and prayed, and made us happy with his aid, and strengthened our courage against the heathen. Then he commanded us to go out at night when we heard the army had halted at Ayami. For Ayami was close to us, about a half day's journey. We went out at night and slept near our houses. All next day (Monday 18 June) we waited for them. We prepared our position between two rocks at a place called Maliba. We spent the day there and every time we saw dust whirl from afar towards us we sprang up to our places, or again, if we saw any smoke. When evening came we went back to our houses.

From our houses we saw the smoke of Sarkin Gobir's camp. We moved towards it. It was Thursday morning (Thursday, 21 June 1804 A.D., 1219 A.H.). We went quickly till we reached Gurdam. Then on again till we halted close to the water called the lake of Kwotto. The enemy were halted on the banks of the lake. We drank from the lake and then marched against them. In truth they perceived our movement and we saw their horsemen gather together. Mallam Agali went ahead with some of our horsemen. He drove their men away and captured some of their horses.

Then as we approached the enemy we marched in lines. The enemy, too, prepared and took up their positions. In truth they had put on chain and quilted armour about one hundred in number. They drew up in line with round shields, and square shields, and made their preparations. We formed our line of battle against them. We gazed at each other, and each man's eye looked into his enemy's. Then we shouted three times 'Allah akbar' and charged them. They beat their drums and charged to meet us. The lines met. Their right wing overbore our left wing and was mingled with our men and pressed them back into the centre. Their left wing also overbore our right wing and pressed our men back to the centre. Our centre stood firm. They shot their arrows, and we shot ours.

Our weapon at that time was the bow and arrow. Our horsemen did not exceed twenty but the Gobirawa had war horses not to be numbered except by God. When our centre held firm our right wing that had been driven back when it reached the centre also stood. So also our left wing when it reached our centre stood firm. The fight continued and the opposing lines were intermingled. God broke the army of the heathen. They fell back. They retreated, they ran and scattered. The Mohamedans pursued at their heels and killed them and took their property. Of those that were killed of them, God alone knows the number. Their King fled. His friend Baidu was killed and Magaji and some others.

Now when God gave the victory to the Mohamedans, they pursued the heathen all day and all night. Our Commander, Waziri Abdullahi, returned to the lake of Kwotto and halted there and we drank. Then we returned to camp and halted there and said the afternoon prayer. Then we went on to our houses and passed the night there, and gave thanks to God, the Lord of creation.

The rainy season followed on the heels of the reformers' victory at Tabkin Kwotto and forced a temporary lull in the fighting. Both sides took advantage of the rains to write to the rulers of other Hausa states for aid. The Uthmanians also began to broaden their appeal and formulate their programme or ideology, as the next two documents illustrate.

DOCUMENT 15
'Abdullah's appeal to the brethren'

Abdullah, *Tazyīn*, pp. 111–13.

NOTES FOR READING   Commander of the Believers = Uthman's title as head of the new Muslim state; Qubir = Gobir; Qurdam = actual site of battle of June 1804 near Tabkin Kwotto.

Then after this *qasīda* I composed another *qasīda* which I sent to my two brothers Dādi and Zayd when they did not emigrate with us, but remained among the unbelievers. I warned them about that, and informed them of what we had achieved, urging them to emigrate, and I said:

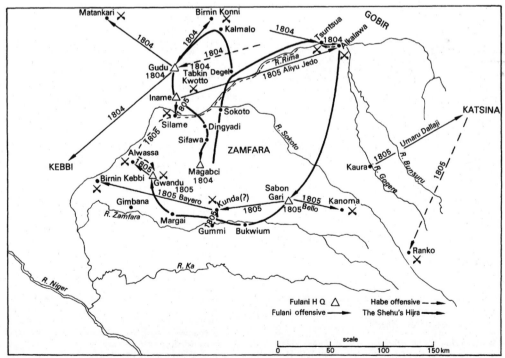

MAP 4.5   Main battles and offensives of the jihād *1804–5*

O who will convey from me to Dādi
And Zayd, and all who dwell in the towns,
Friends of the unbelievers, from fear of loss of wealth,
And from hope of security from the corrupt,
That there do not remain between the Muslims and you
The signs of love.
You deserted the army of Islam openly,
Content to help the foe.
You forgot what you had read in the Book.
For that reason you missed the straight way . . .
And indeed we are in a country in which
There is no rule other than that of God over (His) servants.
The Commander of the Believers is our commander,
And we have become, all of us, the people of Holy War.
We fight in the way of God, always.
And we kill the unbelievers and the obstinate.
Ask concerning us, the place where we clashed at Ghinghā
Matankari, Kunni in the days of the fighting.
Ask the scoundrel of Qūbir, Yunfa,
Was he not driven away from among the nomads
When he had collected armies to cut off religion
And cried out in the towns at every meeting place?
Upon them were ample suits of armour,
And beneath them excellent long-necked horses.
They came slaying, and taking the Muslims prisoner,
　　desiring corruption.
And we came upon them on Thursday
At Qurdam before midday, in the high places;
And they had spitted meats around the fire,
And gathered ready in tents
Fine vestments in a chest,
And all kinds of carpets, with cushions.
And do not ask about wheaten cake
Mixed with ghee and honey among the provisions!
Nothing frightened them as they slept in luxury
Save the tread of foot-soldiers and fine horses.
They rose up, and made everything ready for war.
Then they formed up in ranks according to size.
Our banner began to draw near to them,
And it seemed to them like an ogre in striped clothing.
We fired at them, and they fired naphtha.
Their fire became like ashes (and it was)
As if their arrows had no heads to them;
And as if their swords were in the hands of inanimate
　　things;
As if their lances were in the hands of the blind.
They turned in flight, without provision,
And their army was scattered, and they were thirsty,
Confused like young locusts.
We slew them, and collected all their wealth
Which they had left strewn in the valley . . .
And Yunfa fled headlong,
Running before his horsemen, who fled in disorder.
His clinging to the mane of his charger
Saved him from the death decreed.

DOCUMENT 16
'The manifesto of the *Jihād*'

Uthman dan Fodio, *Wathīqat Ahl al-Sūdān* ('Dispatch
to the people of the Sudan') trans. and ed. A. D. H. Bivar,
Journal of African History (1961), pp. 239–41.

NOTES FOR READING　Ibn Fudi = son of Fodio, that is,
Uthman; *ijma* = consensus of the learned community.
The manuscript was probably written in 1804–05.

In the name of God, the Merciful, the Compassionate. May
God bless our master Muhammad, with his family and his
companions, and welcome (them) with greetings.

Praise be to God who has bestowed upon us his dispensa-
tion of Islam, and guided us by our lord and master Muhammad, on whom from God the Exalted be most gracious
blessings and noble salutation.

After which, this is a dispatch from Ibn Fūdī, the Commander of the Faithful, 'Uthmān, to all the folk of the Sudan, and
to whomso God wills of the brethren in the (Hausa) States;
it is a dispatch advantageous in the present times. Thus speak
I, and success comes of God.'

Know then, my Brethren:

(i) That the commanding of righteousness is obligatory by
assent (literally 'according to the *ijmā*'');

(ii) And that the prohibition of evil is obligatory by assent;

(iii) And that Flight (*al-hijra*) from the land of the heathen is
obligatory by assent;

(iv) And that the befriending of the Faithful is obligatory by
assent;

(v) And that the appointment of the Commander of the
Faithful is obligatory by assent;

(vi) And that obedience to him and to all his deputies is
obligatory by assent;

(vii) And that the waging of Holy War (*al-jihād*) is
obligatory by assent;

(viii) And that the appointment of Emirs in the States is
obligatory by assent;

(ix) And that the appointment of judges is obligatory by
assent;

(x) And that their enforcement of the divine laws
(*ahkām al-shar'*) is obligatory by assent;

(xi) And that by assent the status of a town is the status of
its ruler: if he be Muslim, the town belongs to Islam;
but if he be heathen the town is a town of heathendom
from which Flight is obligatory;

(xii) And that to make war upon the heathen king who will
not say 'There is no God but Allah' is obligatory by
assent, and that to take the government from him is
obligatory by assent;

(xiii) And that to make war upon the heathen king who does
not say 'There is no God but Allah' on account of the
custom of his town (*bi-sababi 'urfi'l-baladi*), and who
makes no profession of Islam, is (also) obligatory by
assent; and that to take the government from him is
obligatory by assent;

(xiv) And that to make war upon the king who is an apostate
(*al-malik al-murtaddu*), and who has abandoned the
religion of Islam for the religion of heathendom is
obligatory by assent, and that to take the government
from him is obligatory by assent;

(xv) And that to make war against the king who is an
apostate—who has not abandoned the religion of

Islam as far as the profession of it is concerned, but who mingles the observances of Islam with the observances of heathendom, like the kings of Hausaland for the most part—is (also) obligatory by assent, and that to take the government from him is obligatory by assent;

(xvi) And that to make war upon backsliding Muslims (al-muhammalīn min al-muslimīn) who do not own allegiance to any of the Emirs of the Faithful is obligatory by assent, if they be summoned to give allegiance and they refuse, until they enter into allegiance;

(xvii) And that the anathematizing of Muslims on a pretext of heretical observances is unlawful by assent;

(xviii) And that the anathematizing of Muslims for disobedience (takfīr al-muslimīn bi 'l-mu'āsī) is unlawful by assent;

(xix) And that residence in enemy territory (fī bilād al-harb) is unlawful by assent;

(xx) And that refusal to give allegiance to the Commander of the Faithful and to his deputies is unlawful by assent;

(xxi) And that to make war upon the Muslims who are residing in Muslim territory is unlawful by assent, and that wrongfully to devour their property is unlawful by assent;

(xxii) And that to enslave the freeborn amongst the Muslims is unlawful by assent, whether they reside in the territory of Islam, or in enemy territory;

(xxiii) And that to make war upon the heathen to whom peace has been granted (al-kuffār ahl al-āmān) is unlawful by assent; wrongfully to devour their property is unlawful by assent, and to enslave them is unlawful by assent;

(xxiv) And that to make war upon the congregation of the apostates (jumā' at al-murtaddīn) is obligatory by assent, and that their property is booty (fai'un), and that in the matter of their enslavement there are two opinions, the widespread one being its prohibition, and the other that the perpetrator of this act does not disobey (the law) if he is following an authority which asserts its lawfulness;

(xxv) And that to make war on the congregation of the warmongers (jumā'at al-muhāribīn) is obligatory by assent, and that their property is booty, and that their enslavement is unlawful by assent;

(xxvi) And that to make war upon the oppressors (al-bughāt) is obligatory by assent, and that wrongfully to devour their property is unlawful by assent, for 'Use is made of their armour against them, and afterwards it is returned to them'; and their enslavement is unlawful by assent;

(xxvii) And that in the matter of the property of Muslims who reside in enemy territory there are two opinions, the sound one being that (its seizure) is permitted.

The manifesto and other writings helped produce widespread support for Uthman's cause throughout the Central Sudan (see the next section, 'The spread of the jihād', pages 143–8) as well as in Gobir, but not always for specifically religious reasons. Uthman's critique of the practices of the Hausa courts coincided with many of the grievances felt by the Hausa farmers and Fulani pastoralists, although most of them had little attachment to Islam. They tended to remain neutral in the ensuing struggle or to support the Shehu, thus enabling the new Muslim society to survive a difficult period of consolidation between 1804 and 1808.

After the victory of Tabkin Kwotto, the forces of Uthman lost a battle to the Sarkin Gobir at the end of 1804 (Tsuntsua). They withdrew to Kebbi in 1805 and made their headquarters there. Late in that year they suffered another reversal at the hands of the 'royalists' of Gobir and Kebbi and some Tuareg (at the battle of Alwassa). In 1806, however, they regained the initiative with a victory in Gwandu and then pressed the attack on the Gobir capital of Alkalawa. In 1808 they won a critical battle there, killed Yunfa and drove the survivors of the royal family into exile (see Document 26). Uthman's son Bello commanded the army at this time and gives us his narrative below.

DOCUMENT 17
'Victory at Alkalawa'

Bello (Arnett), pp. 94–5.

NOTES FOR READING Aliyu Jedo or Ali Jedo = Fulani leader who later became the official Commander of the Army; Jinns = spirits.

When spring (1223 A.H.—1808 A.D.) was come again I sent to all our towns and commanded them to prepare for war with Alkalawa. All the Moslems answered this call. In truth they were wrath with the heathen, the people of Gobir.

When autumn came we set out. Aliyu Jedo was in command of our whole force from the West. Namoda was in command of those from the East. The whole combined movement was in my hands. We set out and made our camp at Lajinge and spent some days there. On Sunday we advanced and camped close to Alkalawa. We passed the night there and at early dawn prepared for battle.

My comrade Namoda took the North of Alkalawa and fought there. We on our part took the East and fought there. Sarkin Katsina fought on the West and South. Then God opened Alkalawa to us. Like the winking of an eye the Moslems charged upon the enemy killing and capturing. Their Sarki Yumfa was slain. All his men were slain by his side. Thanks be assured to God. I sent a messenger to carry the news to Shehu but he found the Jinns had preceded him and had given Shehu news of all that we had done. Then Shehu came forth and blessed the people for all that they had done.

Some people relate that the Jinns went to Shehu with the news of the battle before the human messengers arrived. Others say that God revealed this matter to Shehu.

When God opened the city of Alkalawa to the Moslems, they were filled with very great joy, and the heathen on their part were greatly humbled. The Moslems in every part of the country were waiting to hear the result of the war with Alkalawa, and the heathen even where they saw their power assured saw it at the same time broken.

Thus it happened that in every town people were watching to see what would happen at Alkalawa, and when the capture of the city took place the traders went everywhere with the news and the heathen were downcast, and their backbone broken. Very many of them repented and became Moslems. Others again made peace. Our rule over the towns was assured to us and our outlying districts were at peace.

Although the Alkalawa triumph did not end the fighting in western Hausaland, it did shift the balance of power to the Uthmanian forces. The victors established a new settlement at Sokoto and subsequently made it the capital of the new Muslim state or Caliphate. While other scholars and soldiers were winning victories in other parts of the Central Sudan (see the next section, 'The spread of the *jihād*', pages 143–8), the Uthmanians began setting up an administration to conform to their ideals. It was during this period, from 1808 to about 1814, that Abdullah, Bello and Uthman wrote many of the essential documents of the new regime, including the *Tazyīn* and *Infāq* which have supplied the main narrative for this section.

What follows are two rather contrasting compositions by Uthman from this period. The first is a poem stressing the similarity between the reformer's life and that of the Prophet, thereby enhancing the legitimacy of the reform movement. It was initially written in the Fulani language and subsequently in Hausa, each time with Arabic characters. Uthman and his companions gave a great stimulus to writing the spoken languages and sought thereby to reach a larger audience beyond the community of scholars.

DOCUMENT 18
'The attributes of the Shehu'

An English translation of the Hausa poem by Uthman dan Fodio, *Sifofin Shehu*, by R. A. Adeleye and I. A. Mukoshy. *Research Bulletin*, Center of Arabic Documentation (Ibadan), Vol. 2, No. 1 (January 1966), pp. 26–7.

NOTES FOR READING Safar = second month of the Muslim year (the analogy is probably between Muhammad's battle at Badr or Bedr, mentioned in the notes to Document 14, and Tabkin Kwotto); spiritual power = mystical power or the power to perform miracles (*karama*; see Document 20).

In the name of God, the Beneficent, the Merciful; may God bless the noble Prophet.

I give thanks to God for the generosity he showed me,
  I give praise to Him, the Generous One.
I say, 'Peace be upon our prophet',
  Know that I have (obtained) many of his characteristics.

These will I mention in gratitude to Allah
  That Muslims may know them, East and West.
Know that prophecy was made of him before his coming,
  A similar prophecy was made of me, I am fortunate.
Know that he bore with the troubles of the people,
  Likewise am I known for this and for loving peace.
Indeed, he never angered anyone;
  For this too have people known me and for mercy.
After summoning people to the religion he made the *hijra*,
  When I made mine it cost me great effort.
At that place where the enemies came out
  As (they failed) against him, so also against me did they fail.
By making the *hijra* he was indeed saved (from them),
  I did the same and the same has been repeated.
He made it at the beginning of the sixth decade (of his life),
  Of a truth, mine is indeed (made at) the same (time).
No sooner had he made the *hijra* than he waged the *jihād*;
  Likewise did I, keeping the pattern.
Note that when *jihād* was begun for him, it was said to have been during Safar;
  Likewise was mine by the stroke of fate.
After he had fought five battles they (his enemies) did not get the better of him;
  As for my battles they were five and they (my enemies) suffered tribulation.
The five he fought brought victory;
  So it happened in my case. They repented.
The first fight against them supplied the evidence;
  Even so in mine (first fight) they saw these same signs.
Then, unfortunately, tribulation overtook the Muslims;
  So indeed was I affected when they retaliated.
Just as they surrounded his town with war;
  Thus often did they do to mine.
For they surrounded him, East and West;
  As over his town similarly over mine, they secured no hold.
Just as he was given control over it,
  So also was I, (given power) by reason of my spiritual power (*karāmā*) . . .

The second composition of Uthman, written between 1808 and 1813, provides instruction in the differences between 'pagan' and Muslim government, and recapitulates, in so doing, the grievances experienced by the reformers and their supporters.

DOCUMENT 19
'The book of the difference'

Uthman dan Fodio, *Kitāb al-Farq*, trans. and ed. M. Hiskett, *Bulletin*, School of Oriental and African Studies (1960), pp. 565–72.

NOTES FOR READING *khalifa* = successor or deputy (here in the sense of successor to Muhammad as ruler of the Muslim state); *qadi* = judge; *janghali* = cattle tax; *kurdin ghari* = tax levied on townspeople; *kurdin salla* = tax levied at the times of salla or great festivals; *wazir* = minister.

In the Name of God the Merciful, the Compassionate. May God bless our Lord Muḥammad, and his Family, and his Companions, and save them. The poor worshipper who is in need of the mercy of his Lord 'Uthmān b. Fūdī, may God cover him with His mercy, amen, says: Praise be to God who has favoured us with the favour of faith, and Islam, and has guided us by our Lord and Master Muhammad, upon whom from God Most High be most gracious blessing, and purest peace. As for what comes after; this is *The book of the difference between the governments of the Muslims and the governments of the unbelievers*. It comprises an introduction, four parts, and a conclusion.

The first part is in explanation of the way of the unbelievers in their government. The second part is in explanation of the way of the Muslims in their government. The third part is in explanation of the foundations of governments, and their ministers. The fourth part is in explanation of the different kinds of public treasury upon which depend the welfare of the Muslims, and its expenditure.

Introduction: I say:—and help is with God—it is incumbent upon the Commander of the Believers in the first place, to fear God, and to follow the habits of the Muslims in their governments, and avoid the habits of the unbelievers in their governments. It is incumbent on him to appoint someone to act for him in the towns if it is not possible for him to conduct all affairs himself. Ibn al-'Arabī says in *al-Ahkām* 'He must appoint deputies, and they are numerous and of three kinds; the first of them is the appointing of a deputy over the provinces either to take charge of general affairs, or to take charge of special matters. And whosoever he sets over special matters, and appoints (to deal with) a specific thing, shall let his gaze rest where it belongs. And whosoever he sets over general affairs then everything that is in the prpvince shall pass to him': (concluded). And that which befits the *Khalifa* in the first place is the appointing of a *sultān* in each of the provinces of his country to whom shall be referred back the laws of the emirs of all his provinces. Then he shall appoint a *qāḍī* in accordance with the *Sharī'a*, to be with him, to review under him the judgment of every (other) *qāḍī*. 'Abd al-Rahmān al-Suyūṭī said in *Tārīkh al-khulafā'* 'the *khalīfas* appoint the judge who supervises in their country the judging in all the provinces and towns which are under their rule. Then the judge in his turn appoints a deputy under his command in each province of each country, as he wishes, and for this reason he is customarily called "chief judge", and none shall be called thus except he who answers to this description, and any other than he shall be called "judge"/ only, and "judge of such and such a province", and the chief judge had greater judicial powers than the *Sulṭān* at this time': (concluded). Then he appoints his agents in all the provinces and assigns to each his portion, and (they have) nothing other than that . . .

The first part describing the way of the unbelievers in their governments; and I say—and help is with God—indeed the intention of the unbelievers in their governments is only the fulfilling of their lusts, for they are like the beasts. God Most High has said: 'they are but as the cattle; nay, they are farther astray from the way!'; 'they eat as cattle eat, and the fire shall be their lodging'. One of the ways of their government is succession to the emirate by hereditary right and by force to the exclusion of consultation. And one of the ways of their government is the building of their sovereignty upon three things: the people's persons, their honour, and their possessions; and whomsoever they wish to kill or exile or violate his honour or devour his wealth they do so in pursuit of their lusts, without any right in the *Sharī'a*. One of the ways of their government is their imposing on the people monies not laid down by the *Sharī'a*, being those which they call *janghali* and *kurdin ghari* and *kurdin sallā*. One of the ways of their governments is their intentionally eating whatever food they wish, whether it is religiously permitted or forbidden, and wearing whatever clothes they wish, whether religiously permitted or forbidden, and drinking what beverages (*ta'ām*) they wish, whether religiously permitted or forbidden, and riding whatever riding beasts they wish, whether religiously permitted or forbidden, and taking what women they wish without marriage contract, and living in decorated palaces, whether religiously permitted or forbidden, and spreading soft (decorated) carpets as they wish, whether religiously permitted or forbidden. One of the ways of their government which is well known, is that they bring presents which they call *ghaisūwā*. One of the ways of their governments is the devouring of the alms of women who are subject to their authority. One of the ways of their governments is to place many women in their houses, until the number of women of some of them amounts to one thousand or more. One of the ways of their governments is that (a man) puts the affairs of his women into the hands of the oldest one, and every one (of the others) is like a slave-woman under her. One of the ways of their governments is to delay in the paying of a debt, and this is injustice. One of the ways of their governments is what the superintendent of the market takes from all the parties to a sale, and the meat which he takes on each market day from the butchers, and they call this *tāwasā*, and one of the ways of their governments is the cotton and other things which they take in the course of the markets, and they call this *aghama*. One of the ways of their governments is the taking of people's beasts of burden without their permission to carry the *sultān's* (food) to him. Whoever follows his beast to the place where they unload it, they return it to him, but he who does not follow, his beast is lost, and they call this *kāmuwā*. One of the ways of their government is the evil things which the slave-girls of the *sultān* and their servants from among free-born women do in the towns, and they call this *jandūdu*. One of the ways of their government is to change the laws of God, and an example of that is that the *Sharī'a* decrees that the adulterer shall be flogged if he is not married, and stoned if he is married, and that the thief shall have his hand cut off, and that he who kills a person deliberately shall be killed, or if the killing was unintentional, shall be ordered to pay the blood money, which shall be divided among the heirs of the slain man. The *Sharī'a* also decrees that one who destroys one of the limbs of the body, a similar limb of his shall be destroyed. And for wounding it lays down retaliation in so far as retaliation is possible, and compensation where retaliation is not possible. They have changed all that has been mentioned, and turned it to devouring the property of the people. One of the ways of their government which is also well known is that whoever dies in their country, they take his property, and they call it 'inheritance', and they know that it is without doubt injustice. One of the ways of their government is to impose tax on merchants, and other travellers. One of the ways of their government, which is also well known, is that one may not pass by their farms, nor cross them without (suffering) bad treatment from their slaves. One of the ways of their government which is also well known is that if the people's animals go among their animals, they do not come out again unless they give a proportion of them, and if the *sultān's* animals stray, and are found spoiling the cultivated land and other things, they are not driven off. One of the ways of their governments is to compel the people to serve in their armies, even though they are Muslims, and they call it *gharghadi*, and whosoever does not go, they impose upon him a money payment, not imposed by the *Sharī'a*. One of the ways of their government which is also well known, is that if you have an adversary (in law) and he precedes you to them, and gives them some money, then your word will not be accepted by them, even though they know for a certainty of your truthfulness, unless you give them more than your adversary gave. One of the ways of their governments is to shut the door in the face of the needy. One of the ways of their governments is their forbidding to the worshippers of God part of that which is legal for them, such as the veiling of women, which is incumbent upon them, and turbans for men, which is *sunna* for them . . .

The second section is in explanation of the ways of the Muslims in their government. I say—and help is with God—the purpose of the Muslims in their governments is to strip evil things from religious and temporal affairs, and introduce reforms into religious and temporal affairs, and an example of stripping evil things from religious and temporal affairs is that every governor of a province should strive to fortify strongholds and wage holy war against the unbelievers, and the war-makers and the oppressors, and set up a military station on every frontier, and combat every cause of corruption which occurs in his country, and forbid every disapproved thing. An example of introducing reforms into religious and temporal affairs is that the governor of every country shall strive to repair the mosques, and establish the five prayers in them, and order the people to strive to read the Qur'ān, and make (others) read it, and learn knowledge, and teach it; and that he should strive to reform the markets and set to rights the affairs of the poor and the needy, and order the doing of every approved thing. These qualities which have been mentioned in this section are the qualities of the way of the Muslims in their governments, and he who follows them in his emirship, has followed the way of Paradise, which is the straight way. God Most High has said: 'and that this is My path, straight; so do you follow it, and follow not divers paths lest they scatter you from His path'. And he who follows the path of the Muslims in their governments, he has obeyed God and His Messenger and God Most High has said: 'whosoever obeys God and the Messenger, they are with those whom God has blessed, Prophets, just men, martyrs, the righteous; good companions they'.

The third section is in explanation of the foundations of government, and its ministers, and I say—and help is with God—the foundations of government are five things: the first is that authority shall not be given to one who seeks it. The second is the necessity for consultation. The third is the

abandoning of harshness. The fourth is justice. The fifth is good works. And as for its ministers, they are four. (The first) is a trustworthy *wazīr* to wake the ruler if he sleeps, to make him see if he is blind, and to remind him if he forgets, and the greatest misfortune for the government and the subjects is that they should be denied honest *wazīrs*. And among the conditions pertaining to the *wazīr* is that he should be steadfast in compassion to the people, and merciful towards them. The second of the ministers of government is a judge whom the blame of a blamer cannot overtake concerning the affairs of God. The third is a chief of police who shall obtain justice for the weak from the strong. The fourth is a tax collector who shall discharge his duties and not oppress the subjects.

The fourth section is in explanation of the kinds of treasury upon which the best interests of the Muslims depend, and their expenditures, and I say—and help is with God—the kinds of treasury are seven, and Ibn Jamā'a has arranged them (in verse) when he said:

The kinds of the public treasury are seven.
Their poets have written it in a verse:
The fifth and booty; land tax; poll tax; tithe
And inheritance; property whose owner is missing

And in the *Shurb al-zulāl*

The kinds of the public treasury are the fifth, the tithe
And poll tax and land tax; booty and surplus.
Then that the owners of which are not known,
And inheritance; property having no owner.
These seven constitute the public treasury
For him who wishes to make use of lawful things.

As for the account of the expenditure of the public treasury, Ibn Juzayy said in *al-Qawānīn*: 'the way of just *imāms* concerning booty and the fifth is that a beginning should be made by sealing off the dangerous places, and the frontiers, and with the making ready of weapons of war, and the pay of the soldiers. If anything is left over, it should go to the judges, and the provincial governors, and the building of mosques and bridges. Then it should be divided among the poor, and if there is any left over, then the *imām* should choose between dividing it among the rich, and keeping it against disasters (which may afflict) Islam. There is disagreement as to whether a person of sanctity should have preferential treatment in the award, and one who has precedence in Islam, or whether it should be apportioned equally to him and to others, and to the estates of the Caliphs. Then indeed the public treasury is not bound to be used up entirely for the buying of weapons for all Muslims, and other things which seem to the *imām* in the best interests of the Muslims, but if he wishes he may make all of it over to the Family of the Prophet—may God bless him and give him peace—and to others, or give some of it to them, and the remainder to yet others': (concluded) . . .

To conclude this section, we take an example of the popular miracle literature about Shehu Uthman which grew up in the nineteenth century and was transmitted in Hausa in both oral and written form. The following document is a variation of a story recorded in the early twentieth century and suggests the encouragement and expansion of trade (see the section, 'The conduct of the Caliphate, pages 148–54) which accompanied the creation of the Sokoto Caliphate.

DOCUMENT 20
'Shehu and the caravan captain'

H. A. S. Johnston, *A Selection of Hausa Stories* (1962), pp. 124–5.

NOTE FOR READING   This miracle is one example of the 'spiritual power' of Uthman cited in Document 18.

In the time of Shehu dan Fodiyo a trader was once making his way back from Ashanti with a caravan carrying a hundred thousand cola-nuts. The caravan came to the river Niger and the men and animals were ferried safely across. There remained only the caravan captain and the canoe put back to bring him over too.

As they were crossing a storm got up and the canoe rolled so much that it looked like capsizing.

'Shehu dan Fodiyo' cried the caravan captain 'come and save us.' No sooner had he said this than the figure of a man appeared in the middle of the river and seized the bow of the canoe and swung it round towards the shore. When the caravan captain reached dry land in safety he said: 'By God's grace when I reach Sokoto I shall give Shehu ten baskets of cola-nuts.'

Now at the time when the caravan captain called for help Shehu was in Sokoto. The disciples whom he was instructing noticed that he suddenly got up and went into his house and that on his return his gown was wet. When they pointed this out he said to them: 'In about twenty days from now you will learn the reason why it is wet.'

In due course the caravan reached Sokoto. Camp was pitched and the caravan captain measured out five baskets of cola-nuts. Next day he took them to Shehu's house and was admitted to an audience. After exchanging greetings, he related to Shehu everything that had happened when his caravan had been crossing the Niger.

Shehu asked him when these things had happened and he named the day and the time. The disciples then counted back and found that they had taken place on the very day and at the exact time when Shehu's gown had become wet.

The caravan captain now brought out the cola-nuts and said: 'Mallam, here are the alms which I promised to give to you if God delivered me from the storm.'

Shehu took the alms and thanked the captain. Then he smiled and said: 'You have fulfilled part of your promise but not all of it. You said you would bring ten baskets and I see you have only brought five.'

At this the captain was covered in shame. He went back to his camp and fetched another five baskets which he begged Shehu to accept. He also said that he repented of what he had done and asked for forgiveness.

Shehu said that he forgave him and took the cola-nuts and divided them all among his people. Then he prayed with the caravan captain and blessed him and sent him on his way.

The Spread of the *Jihād*

Uthman could hardly have anticipated the scale of response of Muslims and other discontented subjects in Hausaland to his *jihād* nor the possibilities of political integration that resulted from it. He was in fact well known and highly respected among the reformist and predominantly Fulani *jamā'as* scattered throughout the region. Consequently, when he emigrated and formed a community in opposition to the Sarkin Gobir in 1804, these *jamā'as* followed events closely and soon sent representatives to receive Uthman's blessing and the 'flag' of *jihād* in order to conduct their own movements. Hausa kings, anxious at the news from Gobir, clamped down on these reformers and provided new grievances in the process. By 1806 the new forces were fighting against the courts in several states and by 1812 they had established their control of the major states and capitals of Hausaland and some areas farther afield.

In Kano, as an example of what happened in the Hausa heartland, the *jihādic* forces concentrated on capturing the city and its vast bureaucratic and economic network. They succeeded in driving out the Hausa Sarkin by 1807, but faced a number of subsequent revolts and struggles, including divisions within their own ranks. The following account comes from an Arabic chronicle of Kano kings written in its final form in the late nineteenth century.

DOCUMENT 21
'The new regime in Kano'

From H. R. Palmer's translation of the 'Kano Chronicle'. H. R. Palmer, ed. and trans., *Sudanese Memoirs*, 3 vols. (1928), Vol. III, pp. 127–9.

NOTES FOR READING   Giddan Rimfa = palace; Habe = Fulani term for non-Fulani, Hausa or 'pagan'; *tawayi* = revolt or being in revolt; Osuman dan Hodio = Uthman dan Fodio. Much of the fighting after 1807 was between Fulani clan leaders, such as Dabo Dan Bazzo, Ibrahima Dabo (Galadima under Sulimanu) and Dan Tunku. The first two were among the original 'flag-bearers' of *jihād* for Kano. Ibrahima came from a different family than his predecessor Sulimanu and established his descendants as the ruling dynasty.

XLIII—MOHAMMA ALWALI, SON OF YAJI
A H. 1195–1222.   A D   1781–1807.

In Alwali's time the Fulani conquered the seven Hausa States on the plea of reviving the Muhammadan religion. The Fulani attacked Alwali and drove him from Kano whence he fled to Zaria. The men of Zaria said, 'Why have you left Kano?' He said, 'The same cause which drove me out of Kano will probably drive you out of Zaria.' He said, 'I saw the truth with my eyes, I left because I was afraid of my life, not to save my wives and property.' The men of Zaria drove him out with curses. So he fled to Rano, but the Fulani followed him to Burum-Burum and killed him there. He ruled Kano twenty-seven years, three of which were spent in fighting the Fulani.

XLIV.—SULIMANU, SON OF ABAHAMA.
A.H. 1222–1235.   A.D. 1807–1819

The forty-fourth Sarki was Sulimanu, son of Abahama, a Fulani. His mother's name was Adama Modi. When he became Sarkin Kano, the Fulani prevented him from entering the palace. He went into the house of Sarkin Dawaki's mother. One of the remaining Kanawa said to Sulimanu, 'If you do not enter the Giddan Rimfa, you will not really be the Sarki of city and country.' When Sulimanu heard this he called the chief Fulani, but they refused to answer his summons, and said, 'We will not come to you. You must come to us, though you be the Sarki. If you will come to Mallam Jibbrim's house we will assemble there.' Sulimanu went to Jibbrim's house and called them there. When they had assembled, he asked them and said, 'Why do you prevent me entering the Giddan Rimfa?' Mallam Jibbrim said, 'If we enter the Habe's houses and we beget children, they will be like these Habes and do like them.' Sulimanu said nothing but set off to Shehu-Osuman Dan Hodio asking to be allowed to enter the Giddan Rimfa. Shehu Dan Hodio gave him a sword and a knife and gave him leave to enter the Giddan Rimfa, telling him to kill all who opposed him. He entered the house, and lived there. All the Kano towns submitted to him, except Faggam, which he attacked. He took many spoils there. On his way back to Kano the chiefs of the Fulani said to him, 'If you leave Faggam alone, it will revolt.' So he divided it into two, and returned home. In his time Dabo Dan Bazzo raised a revolt. He dared to look for a wife in Sokoto and was given one. Sarkin Kano said, 'What do you mean by looking for a wife at Sokoto?' So Dabo was caught and bound. His relations, the Danbazzawa, however, came by night and cut his bonds, and set him free. He ran to Sokoto with Sulimanu following him. At Sokoto they both went before Dan Hodio. Dabo Dan Bazzo said, 'I do not wish to marry your daughters, but I wish for a reconciliation between myself and your Sarki Sulimanu.' So a reconciliation was made and they returned to Kano. Sulimanu sent the Galadima Ibrahima to Zaria to make war. Ibrahima conquered Zaria and took many spoils. He returned to Kano. Sulimanu was angry because of the Galadima's success, and had sinister designs against him when he died himself without having an opportunity of carrying them out. He ruled thirteen years.

XLV.—IBRAHIM DABO, SON OF MOHAMMADU
A.H. 1235–1262.   A.D. 1819–1846.

The forty-fifth Sarki was the pious and learned Ibrahim Dabo, son of Mohammadu, protector of the orphan and the poor, a mighty conqueror—a Fulani.

His mother's name was Halimatu. When he became Sarki he entered the Giddan Rimfa. Dabo made Sani Galadima. He,

however, immediately tried to raise a revolt and incite all the towns to disaffection. The country Sarkis assembled and became "Tawayi," from Ngogu to Damberta, from Jirima to Sankara, and from Dussi to Birnin Kudu and Karayi. Dabo said, 'I will conquer them, if Allah wills.' He entered his house and remained there forty days praying to Allah for victory. Allah heard his prayers. He went out to hasten his preparations for war, and made a camp on Dalla Hill. Because of this he got the name of 'The man who encamped on Dalla.' He spent many days on Dalla, and then returned home. He sent Sarkin Dawaki Manu Maituta to fight with Karayi. When the Sarkin Dawaki reached Karayi he sacked the town and returned to Dabo. Dabo said, 'Praise be to God,' and prepared himself to go out to war. He went to Jirima and sacked that town and afterwards sacked Gasokoli and Jijita. Hence he was known as 'Dabo, the sacker of towns.' After he returned home he kept on sending out men to raid towns. He went in person to attack Dan Tunku and found him at Yan Yahiya. They fought. The Yerimawa ran away, and deserted Dan Tunku, who fled to Damberta, and thence with Dabo following him, to Kazauri. When the Sarki reached the Koremma in pursuit he stopped, turned round again, and went back to Damberta, where he wrecked Dan Tunku's house. Dabo then returned home. Dabo was celebrated in the song:-

'The sacker of towns has come: Kano is your land, Bull Elephant, Dabo, sacker of towns.'

When he went to war the trumpets played:-

'The sacker of towns is mounting.'

He made war on Birnin Sankara and Birnin Rano, took the town of Rano, and lived in the house of Sarkin Rano. After this exploit he shaved his head. He never shaved his head except he sacked a town. When the Kano towns saw that Dabo would not leave any town unconquered, they all submitted to him, and his power exceeded all other Sarkis . . . These warriors of Dabo's time had no fear in war. When Dabo mounted to go to war no such dust was ever seen, so many were his horses. The dust was like the Harmattan. Dabo was called 'Majeka Hazo'. His was a wonderful and brilliant reign, but we will not say any more for fear of 'Balazi'. He ruled Kano twenty-seven years and three months and nine days, his reign ending on the ninth of Safar.

Beyond Hausaland the *jihād* sometimes took on overtones of an external Fulani conquest as well as an internal indigenous revolt. In Yoruba country to the southwest, the once vast and powerful Oyo kingdom was beginning to founder in the early nineteenth century. Its Kakamfo or military commander, a man named Afonja, seceded and established his own capital in northern Yoruba country at Ilorin. He granted freedom to all Hausa slaves in Oyo who would join him and enlisted the help of a powerful Fulani leader, Mallam Alimi. Picking up the story at this point is Samuel Johnson, a Yoruba clergyman of the Anglican Church born in Sierra Leone of freed slaves. He wrote his account on the basis of oral traditions extant in the late nineteenth century.

DOCUMENT 22
'The creation of the Ilorin Emirate'

S. Johnson, *The History of the Yorubas*, compiled by his brother O. Johnson (1921), pp. 197–8, 200–202.

NOTE FOR READING *Jamâs = jama'as.*

Afonja was now the sole power in the kingdom; the King and the capital were left to manage their own affairs by themselves.

The Jamâs were increasing in number and in rapacity, to the utter distress and ruin of the country. When there was no war in hand they usually scattered themselves all over the land plundering the people and committing outrages. They would enter any house, make it their headquarters, from which they would pillage the neighbourhood and surrounding districts. They fed upon the cattle of the house and led the rest away at their leisure and pleasure . . .

To further illustrate the gross licences of these Jamâs, slaves who had deserted their masters often returned to the same town, and even to the very house as a Jamâ, making their former master's house their headquarters for their rapine; masters who were kind to them formerly were now repaid by protection against the rapacities of their comrades; unkind ones were now treated with heartless revenge. These fellows were not regarded now as slaves but as the Kakanfo's servants.

Thoughtful men were now apprehensive of the evils to the nation which the unrestrained licences of these Jamâs portended, but no one was bold enough to remonstrate with the Kakanfo, or even to appeal to him against their rapacities.

But Afonja perceived his error when it was too late. Haughty and passionate, his very egotism was the cause of his fall. Fortune had carried him to such a high pitch of glory, he thought his fall was impossible; besides, he had unlimited confidence in his Jamâs, and was not aware of their growing disaffection and disloyalty towards himself. He thought he could put them down whenever he liked, and was sometimes very severe with any act of insubordination, openly threatening them with suppression and annihilation. This threat only served to increase their disaffection. Too late, he saw what Fagbohun had warned him against. He failed completely to check their ambition, rapine and lawlessness. His threats and warnings were not heeded. Long impunity had increased their boldness.

At last, the Kakanfo was resolved to give effect to his threats and to disband the Jamâs, but he miscalculated his own strength. By the death of his brother Agbonrin, and his head slave Lasipa he had lost his mainstay for these were men of power. He had offended all the powerful chiefs in the kingdom including his former friend and ally Solagberu of Oke Suna, and his priest Alimi by his high-handedness, lofty airs and haughty spirit.

Fearing lest these Jamâs should attack him suddenly if he were to delay their destruction, he sent a private message to the Onikoyi and other powerful chiefs in the country inviting them to make their appearance in Ilorin suddenly, and to assist him in annihilating these Jamâs.

But the secret was divulged to the Jamâs, and they, losing no time, being headed by Alimi the priest, rose up against him before he could obtain help from abroad . . .

Ilorin now passed into the hands of foreigners, the Fulanis who had been invited there as friends and allies. These being far more astute than the Yorubas, having studied their weak points and observed their misrule, planned to grasp the whole kingdom into their own hands by playing one chief against another and weakening the whole. Their more generous treatment of fallen foes and artful method of conciliating a power they could not openly crush, marked them out as a superior people in the art of government . . .

The distress caused by this calamity cannot be described. Aged people who could not be carried away were left to perish. The doleful lamentations of parents who had lost their children, and of thousands of widows and orphans were heartrending. Bereft of every thing, without money, or anything that could be converted into money in such hasty and sudden flight, they were reduced to abject misery and poverty among strangers, and could only support life by doing menial work by procuring firewood or leaves for sale and such like. A people who until recently lived in what for them was affluence and plenty, are now oppressed with want and misery brought about by the want of foresight, and the vaulting ambition of their rulers . . .

Alimi the Moslem priest, who was at the head of the foreigners at Ilorin died after the last war and was succeeded by his son Abudusalami, who became the first King, or Emir, of Ilorin. Ilorin now passes definitely into the hands of the Fulanis as rulers, and affords a home for the Gambaris (Hausas) from whom the Jamâs were recruited.

To the east of Hausaland lay Bornu and the Kanuri people, among whom Islam had an ancient tradition. The Mais or kings had adopted Islam as the religion of the state on much the same terms as the Hausa sultans. They exercised considerable influence and hegemony in Hausaland over the centuries and were considered a ripe target for *jihād* by some of their former subjects after 1804. Some Fulani chiefs of the Bornu borders obtained flags from Uthman and succeeded in capturing the Mai's capital in 1808. The Mai then called upon a nearby scholar and military leader named Muhammad al-Amin al-Kanemi to drive the Fulani out. Al-Kanemi succeeded and in the process reformed Bornu government along Islamic lines. He and his successors became the effective rulers of the state and remained a challenge to the Sokoto Caliphate, both in military terms and by demonstrating that reform could occur without *jihād*. What follows are two letters from the correspondence of al-Kanemi with Uthman and Muhammad Bello, written in the period 1808–1813 and contained in Bello's *Infāq al-Maisūr*. They raise all of the questions about the differences between sin and unbelief which the Sokoto leaders had wrestled with before the *jihād*. Uthman and Bello were correct that Bornu, in the period prior to al-Kanemi's control, had helped the Hausa kings against the reformers. Al-Kanemi was correct that the Fulani flagbearers had attacked Bornu, rather than the reverse. Compare the points made here with those of Documents 16 and 19.

DOCUMENT 23
'The great debate'

From correspondence between the Bornu and Sokoto leaders. Bello, *Infāq*. These passages are from Abdullahi Smith's translation in T. Hodgkin, ed., *Nigerian Perspectives* (1960), pp. 198–205.

NOTES FOR READING   *fiqh* = jurisprudence; *ulama* = clerics; *haram* = forbidden; *talaba* = students; Jahiliya = period of ignorance; *dar al-Islam* = world of Islam; *dar kufr* = world of unbelief.

Al-Kanemi: 'We love the Shaikh and the truth when they agree'

Praise be to God, Opener of the doors of guidance, Giver of the means of happiness. Prayer and peace be on him who was sent with the liberal religion, and on his people who prepared the way for the observance of His law, and interpreted it.

From him who is filthy with the dust of sin, wrapped in the cloak of shame, base and contemptible, Muhammad al-Amīn ibn Muhammad al-Kānamī to the Fulani *'ulamā'* and their chiefs. Peace be on him who follows His guidance.

The reason for writing this letter is that when fate brought me to this country, I found the fire which was blazing between you and the people of the land. I asked the reason, and it was given as injustice by some and as religion by others. So according to our decision in the matter I wrote to those of your brothers who live near to us asking them the reason and instigation of their transgression, and they returned me a weak answer, not such as comes from an intelligent man, much less from a learned person, let alone a reformer. They listed the names of books, and we examined some of them, but we do not understand from them the things which they apparently understood. Then, while we were still perplexed, some of them attacked our capital, and the neighbouring Fulani came and camped near us. So we wrote to them a second time beseeching them in the name of God and Islam to desist from their evil doing. But they refused and attacked us. So, when our land was thus confined and we found no place even to dwell in, we rose in defence of ourselves, praying God to deliver us from the evil of their deeds; and we did what we did. Then when we found some respite, we desisted, and for the future God is all-knowing.

We believe in writing; even if it makes no impression on you, it is better than silence. Know that if an intelligent man accepts some question in order to understand it, he will give a straightforward answer to it.

Tell us therefore why you are fighting us and enslaving our free people. If you say that you have done this to us because of our paganism, then I say that we are innocent of paganism, and it is far from our compound. If praying and the giving of alms, knowledge of God, fasting in Ramadān and the building of mosques is paganism, what is Islam? These buildings in which you have been standing on a Friday, are they churches or synagogues or fire temples? If they were other than Muslim places of worship, then you would not pray in them when you capture them. Is this not a contradiction?

Among the biggest of your arguments for the paganism of the believers generally is the practice of the amirs of riding to certain places for the purpose of making alms-giving sacrifices there; the uncovering of the heads of free women; the taking of bribes; embezzlement of the property of orphans; oppression in the courts. But these five charges do not require you to do the things you are doing. As for this practice of the amirs, it is a disgraceful heresy and certainly blameworthy. It must be forbidden and disapproval of its perpetrators must be shown. But those who are guilty of it do not thereby become pagans; since not one of them claims that it is particularly efficacious, or intends by it to associate anything with God. On the contrary, the extent of their pretence is their ignorant idea that alms given in this way are better than otherwise. He who is versed in the books of *fiqh*, and has paid attention to the talk of the imams in their disputation—when deviation from the right road in matters of burial and slaughter are spoken of—will know the test of what we have said. Consider Damietta, a great Islamic city between Egypt and Syria, a place of learning and Islam: in it there is a tree, and the common people do to this tree as did the non-Arabs. But not one of the *'ulamā'* rises to fight them or has spoken of their paganism.

As for uncovering the head in free women, this is also *haram*, and the Qur'ân has prohibited it. But she who does it does not thereby become a pagan. It is denial which leads to paganism. Failing to do something while believing in it is rather to be described as disobedience requiring immediate repentance. If a free woman has prayed with the head uncovered, and the time passes, but she does not repeat the prayer in accordance with what we know they say in the books of *fiqh*, surely you do not believe that her prayer is not proper because she has thereby become a pagan?

The taking of bribes, embezzlement of the property of orphans and injustice in the courts are all major sins which God has forbidden. But sin does not make anyone a pagan when he has confessed his faith. And if you had ordered the right and forbidden the wrong, and retired when the people did not desist, it would have been better than these present doings. If ordering and forbidding are confined within their proper limits, they do not lead to anything more serious. But your forbidding has involved you in sin, and brought evil on you and the Muslims in this world and the next . . .

Since acts of immorality and disobedience without number have long been committed in all countries, then Egypt is like Bornu, only worse. So also is Syria and all the cities of Islam. There has been corruption, embezzlement of the property of orphans, oppression and heresy in these places from the time of the Bani Umayya (the Umayyad dynasty) right down to our own day. No age and no country is free from its share of heresy and sin. If, thereby, they all become pagan, then surely their books are useless. So how can you construct arguments based on what they say who are infidel according to you? Refuge from violence and discord in religion is with God . . .

We have indeed heard of things in the character of the Shaikh 'Uthmān ibn Fūdī, and seen things in his writings which are contrary to what you have done. If this business does originate from him, then I say that there is no power nor might save through God, the most high, the most glorious. Indeed we thought well of him. But now, as the saying is, we love the Shaikh and the truth when they agree. But if they disagree it is the truth which comes first. We pray God to preserve us from being those of whom He said:

'Say : "Shall we tell you who will be
the greatest losers in their works?
Those whose striving goes astray
in the present life, while they think
that they are working good deeds." '

And from being those of whom he also said:

'But they split in their affair between them
into sects, each party rejoicing in
what is with them.'

Peace.

Muhammad Bello : 'The approval of paganism is paganism'

In the name of God, the compassionate, the merciful. Prayer of God be on him after whom there is no prophet. Praise be to God who has preserved the religion of Islam by the laws in his Qur'ān for the believers who seek guidance; who has wiped out that which Satan has put in the hearts of those who rule them oppressively, and in whose hearts there is sickness, the hard-heartedness of the idolators; who has preserved the laws in the Qur'ān by his saying:

'It is We who have sent down the Remembrance
and We watch over it.'

Prayer and peace on our lord Muhammad, lord of the prophets, the sayer who keeps the true knowledge from the false sayings of all its enemies, who preserves it from the alterations of the interpolators, the boastings of the triflers and the comments of ignorant people. Prayer and peace also on all his people and companions and on those who follow them in the better way until the day of judgment.

From Muhammad Bello ibn Amīr al-Mu'minīn 'Uthmān ibn Fūdī to al-Hājj al-Amīn ibn Muhammad al-Kānamī, peace and sincere greeting.

We have occupied ourselves with the letter which you wrote to those of our people who are your neighbours asking for an explanation of the true state of affairs. We have given it full consideration, and have understood from it what led to it. Briefly, we have understood from it that you desire us to follow the word of God, may He be exalted, when He says:

'If two parties of the believers fight,
put things right between them.'

Secondly you have put forward certain arguments . . . But, by God, I tell you, my brother, that, if the Lord is kind to you, and

you look on us with the eye of justice, it will be seemly for you to find that these are false arguments and mischief-making words, refutable contentions for the most part and worthless propositions. It is indeed seemly for me not to reply, but I am constrained to do so through solicitude for the ignorance of the *talaba*, so that they may not follow you because of your great conceit and mischief-making, and think that you are right in this way of acting. My intention is neither childishness nor quarrelling.

This is so that you will learn in the first place that what made it proper for us to permit our people neighbouring on you to fight Bornu was the continual receipt of news (of which we mastered the contents) from those who mixed with the people of Bornu and knew their condition, to the following effect. It was that they make sacrifices to rocks and trees, and regard the river as the Copts did the Nile in the days of the Jāhilīya. It was also that they have shrines with their idols in them and with priests. We have seen the proof of this in your first letter where you say: 'Among the biggest of your arguments for the paganism of the believers generally is the practice of the amirs of riding to certain places for the purpose of making alms-giving sacrifices there.' Then you explained that they do not wish by this to associate anything with God; nor do they believe that it has influence on events, the extent of their claim being that alms given in this way are better than otherwise. But it is not hidden from the meanest intelligence that this claim warrants no consideration. The verdict depends on what is seen. And God controls what is secret. Him whom we have seen sacrificing to rocks and trees we have charged with paganism. These matters are among those for which we have charged Bornu with paganism.

For what caused the Amir of Bornu (according to what has reached us) to inflict harm on the believers among the Shaikh's people near to you until they were obliged to flee? What caused him to begin to fight them, unless he were in alliance with the Hausa kings to assist them? It is manifest that he would not have risen to assist the Hausa kings had he not approved of their religion. And certainly the approval of paganism is itself paganism. To fight them is permitted, since the *jihād* against paganism is incumbent on all who are able.

May it be clear to you from what we have said of him that the Amir of Bornu has been known for his paganism. You also know that the law of a country is the law of its sultan. If he is a Muslim, then the country is *dār al-Islām*; if he is a pagan, then the country is *dār kufr*. Only those ignorant of the words of the *'ulamā'* will deny this . . .

If you had confined yourself to saying that the Bornuans had repented and desisted from what they were at, it would have been better than all this talk and clamour. For the latter is a weak argument for preventing the fighting to anyone who acknowledges the truth. But we did not know previously, and nothing reached us at all to show, that they had repented. However in the autumn of this year we received messages concerning you which indicated this. We have therefore sent our messenger to you in order that we may confirm this information, and so that he may bring back an account of the true state of affairs. If the matter is as we hear, then we shall despatch our messenger, Gidado Lima, to assemble our chiefs

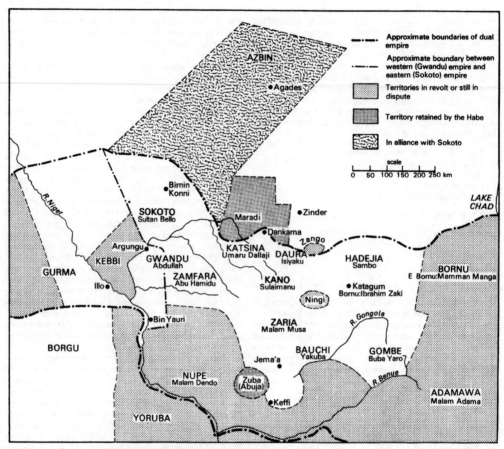

MAP 4.6   *The Fulani empires of Gwandu and Sokoto* c. 1812

of the east. You will send those whom you please to conduct your affairs and whom you trust behind your back; and a meeting will take place in Siko. And those assembled will make a treaty according to such bonds and covenants as they find mutually acceptable, and fighting will stop. Let peace be established. In this connection we have delayed raiding Bornu this year, though we intended to. If the matter is as I have said, namely that they have repented and desisted, then let the fighting stop, for it is repugnant to our relationship, and peace is necessary between us . . .

The Conduct of the Caliphate

Although the Caliphate had to deal throughout the nineteenth century with revolts from within and pressures from outside its borders, it maintained relatively orderly

conditions and achieved a level of political integration that Hausaland had not known before. The Emirs of the provinces, having obtained their flags from Uthman and succeeded in displacing the Hausa dynasties, continued to swear allegiance to Uthman and his successors as the Commander of the Faithful. They sent a portion of their tax proceeds to Sokoto and participated in the annual levy of troops to continue the *jihād.* They accepted the right of appeal to the Sokoto court and the Caliph's authority to confirm them and some of their subordinates in office. Their submission to Sokoto was by and large voluntary, not coerced, and can only be explained in terms of the close relations between Uthman and the flagbearers and through a shared commitment to an Islamic social order.

The goal of a reformed society was more difficult to achieve than that of political integration. The leaders of the *jihād*, both in Sokoto and the various emirates, made a serious effort to apply their understanding of Islamic law (see Documents 16 and 19) to their situations. The result was probably a more systematic and less arbitary regime. Some illegal taxes were still collected and the lot of most farmers and pastoralists probably did not change greatly. The new rulers tended to move into the palaces of their Hausa predecessors, form new dynasties and become increasingly Hausa in language and culture over time. The slave trade and slavery continued more or less as before. The region was probably more prosperous than in the eighteenth century. The bureaucracy was perhaps more efficiently run, at least as far as the Waziri or Chief Minister in Sokoto was concerned. He bore much of the burden of the administration of Sokoto province and the supervision of the other provinces. The bureaucracy was certainly closer to the Abuja pattern (Document 4) than to the simple version envisioned by Uthman (Document 19).

One of the problems faced by the Caliphate and the emirates was strife within the ruling families and classes. In Kano this took the form of a struggle among various Fulani clans (Document 21). In Sokoto it occurred as tension between Abdullah and Muhammad Bello, involving Abdullah's questions about the direction of the reform movement (Document 24) and his jealousy at the increasingly preponderant role played by Bello.

DOCUMENT 24
'Their inclination towards the world'

Abdullah's expression of disenchantment, set in about 1807–08. Abdullah, *Tazyīn*, pp. 120–1.

NOTE FOR READING   al-Qadawa = Alkalawa.

And when God had driven the enemy from us, we began to raid and to attack those who had rebelled against us, until we prepared, in the fourth years of our *hijra* to raid al-Qàdàwà. We set out at the end of Rajab, and the moon of Sha'bàn rose while we were on the road. Then there came to me from God the sudden thought to shun the homelands, and my brothers, and turn towards the best of God's creation, in order to seek approval, because of what I had seen of the changing times, and (my) brothers, and their inclination towards the world, and their squabbling over its possession, and its wealth, and its regard, together with their abandoning the upkeep of the mosques and the schools, and other things besides that. I knew that I was the worst of them, and that what I had seen from others would not deter me. I considered flight incumbent upon me, and I left the army and occupied myself with my own (affairs) and faced towards the East, towards the Chosen One—may God bless him and give him peace—if God would make that easy. I entered the wilderness with five of my companions, and we passed three nights without seeing anyone, nor the traces of anything other than the tracks of many elephants in that wilderness, until God made easy for us our arrival at the inhabited

places. Then there came to my mind, concerning that, [a poem] ... which I did not make known to anyone until we arrived at the city of Kano. (The people of Kano) prevented me from continuing, and sought from me that I should teach them how they should act in order to establish religion, for I found that God had driven the unbelievers from them, but their affair(s) had become confused among them because of their preoccupation with the world. I saw among them that from which I had fled in my own country, and I said to them, 'This that I see among you is that from which I have fled'. I even composed in my mind a *qasīda* concerning that, which I did not make known to anyone. They importuned me to make the *qasīda* known, and I wrote it down for them. Then I composed for them my book *Diyā' al-hukkām*, and I read to them all the commentary on the Qur'ān and they all repented, and put their affair(s) in order, and broke the instruments of diversion which I found with them, and made the wooden parts of their drums into containers for their horses' fodder, and God made clear to them what had not been clear to them before.

In 1812 Uthman withdrew from the active administration of affairs and entrusted the eastern portions of the Caliphate to Bello, based at Sokoto, and the smaller western dominions to Abdullah in Gwandu. Bello had the more important post and claimed the Caliphal Mantle in 1817 when Uthman died.

At that time, Bello and Abdullah encountered a common threat which helped to bring about their reconciliation. Abd al-Salam (Abdessalam in the following document; see also Document 12), an important Hausa leader in the movement, had become unhappy about the land and authority apportioned to him by the new regime. He took advantage of Uthman's death and of a defeat to Bello's forces to raise the spectre of revolt in Abdullah's area in 1817. This was especially serious since Abd al-Salam had an important following among the Hausa supporters of the *jihād*. After efforts at negotiation failed, Bello came to the aid of Abdullah.

DOCUMENT 25
'Abdessalam repudiated Islam'

An account of the Hausa revolt of 1817–18, written in the 1850s or 1860s. From our translation of O. Houdas' French translation of al-hajj Sa'id's *Tarikh Sokoto*, in Houdas, ed., *Tedzkiret en-Nisian* (1901), pp. 304–05.

NOTES FOR READING   Karo = Kware; Ali Jeit = Ali Jedo (Commander of the Army). Sa'id lived at the Sokoto court.

Then Abdessalam repudiated Islam ... All the country imitated him and repudiated Islam. Then the Commander of the Faithful [Bello] undertook constant expeditions against them for two months, although at first he did not believe the repudiation. It was only when Abdessalam threw himself on Tanjad [not identified], killed him and took all of his people prisoner that he [Bello] fully realized that he had repudiated [the faith]. It was then that he declared war and organized expeditions against him.

Then Namoda, the Sultan of Zamfara, joined his cavalry to that of the Commander of the Faithful and together they undertook an expedition against Abdessalam. When they drew close to the citadel of Karo, they chose 50 cavalry to advance towards the fortress and kept the rest in ambush. The inhabitants of Karo, seeing the small number of cavalry, went out to meet them. The cavalry then fled and dispersed. The Karo people pursued them and when they had gotten a good distance from the fort, the cavalry in ambush fell on them, cut off their escape and killed 10 000 men. This occurred at Lebbudo.

The people of Karo wished then to abandon their town, but Abdessalam prevented them and reassured them so well that they stayed. Then the Commander of the Faithful sent Ali Jeit and his troops against Karo. After fighting which lasting all morning, Ali Jeit entered the fortress and destroyed everything save the house of Abdessalam. Bello, who was at Sokoto, saw the smoke in the sky, mounted his horse and arrived while the fighting was still going on. 'Stop,' he said. 'We must make the sunset prayer. They [the soldiers] must come out now [to pray]. While they were praying, Abdessalam left the town. He was wounded as he was leaving by one of the men of Ali Jeit.

After part of the night had passed, the Commander of the Faithful asked if anyone knew what had happened to Abdessalam. 'Commander', replied the one who had wounded him, 'I shot him in the right shoulder. If you examine him and find no trace of my arrow, then you will know to believe no longer the word of a Fulani.' Abdessalam fled to Burma and died there. God preserve us from such an end!

The Hausa who supported Abd al-Salam continued to harass the heartlands of the Caliphate after their leader's death. Bello came to the aid of Abdullah again and in return received the allegiance of his uncle. Abdullah continued to govern Gwandu and some of the western and southwestern provinces with a considerable amount of autonomy in relation to Sokoto. For one view of the reconciliation of the two men, see Document 31.

In addition to the revolts of former followers, the Caliphate had to continue struggling against the displaced Hausa dynasties. One of the most difficult situations was in Gobir itself. The next document, from traditions extant in the early twentieth century, elaborates on one of the Gobir revolts.

DOCUMENT 26
'Butcher's knives'

An account of the revolt of Ali of Gobir. Johnston, *A Selection of Hausa Stories*, pp. 125–6.

NOTE FOR READING Ali was the son of Yakuba of Document 5.

When the Fulani captured the city of Alkalawa and slew Sarkin Gobir Yunfa the power of Gobir was utterly broken. The defeated Gobirawa either submitted to the rule of the Commander of the Faithful, Usuman dan Fodiyo, or else fled to the north beyond the reach of the Fulani.

Those of the Gobirawa who had retreated to the north lived in scattered groups on the edge of the desert. They did not acknowledge any one Chief, however, and they found it difficult to support themselves in that barren land. After about ten years therefore a party of them, led by a member of their former ruling house, came south and made their submission to Sokoto.

At that time Bello had just become Sultan. He accepted their homage and gave them land in that part of the Sultanate which had formerly been Gobir. They settled down there and Ali their leader was allowed by Bello to take the title of Sarkin Gobir.

But in the far north there were still many other Gobirawa who refused to be reconciled with the Sultan and who continued to attack and harry the Fulani whenever they could. These die-hards were outraged by the submission to the Fulani of Ali and his followers and were always taunting them for being cowards and traitors.

At first Ali paid little heed to these taunts but little by little they began to make an impression on his mind. At length, about fifteen years after his submission to the Fulani, an envoy arrived from the unsubdued Gobirawa in the north. Ali was in his audience chamber, surrounded by his courtiers, when the messenger was brought in. He was carrying a bundle and this, he said, contained a gift from Sarkin Gobir's kinsmen. Ali ordered the bundle to be opened and, when the wrappings had been taken off, the crowd in the audience chamber saw that the gift consisted of a set of butcher's knives.

For a time Ali did nothing but he was so stung by this insult that before long he decided to throw off the yoke of Sokoto. Having renounced his allegiance to the Sultan, he therefore marched north with his followers and joined forces with his own people and with the Katsinawa and the Tuaregs who were also in arms against the Fulani.

The news of Ali's revolt was quickly carried to Sokoto. Sultan Bello, then in the eighteenth year of his reign, gathered an army together and himself took command. They marched north-east, beyond the Rima, until at last they came up with the enemy at a place called Gawakuke.

On the following day a great battle took place. After fierce fighting the Tuaregs broke and their Chief, Ibra, galloped from the field. The Fulani then went on to crush the forces of Gobir and Katsina with great slaughter.

Among the thousands who fell in the battle was Sarkin Katsina Rauda and Sarkin Gobir Ali.

Muhammad Bello reigned as Caliph of Sokoto for twenty years (1817–37) and played a critical role in the consolidation of the new state. For some impressions of him, we go back to al-hajj Sa'id (see Document 25).

DOCUMENT 27
'Knowledge is preserved only by instruction'

Sa'id's impressions of Bello. Our translation of Sa'id, *Tarikh Sokoto*, trans. Houdas, pp. 318–19.

After his accession, this ruler (may God be satisfied with him!) lived twenty-two years (according to the Muslim calendar). Under his reign, Hausaland was flourishing. He spread knowledge and the scholars of diverse countries came here from all directions. He took very good care of them, favored them and gave them great gifts. When one arrived from the east, west, south or north, he was never welcomed by the ruler but with the greatest esteem. The ruler kept him close to him and was constantly preoccupied with him.

He devoted a great deal of time to composition. Each time that he finished one of his works, he announced it publicly and had it read. Then he began working on a new volume. He treated numerous subjects, usually answers to questions and controversies about the law. If someone submitted a question to him, he made that the occasion of writing a document. If he learned that such-and-such persons had some differences, he soon composed a treatise on the subject. He encouraged his children, brothers, and children of his brothers to study and, if they failed, he upbraided them sharply.

One day, I heard him say the following: 'The people of Hausaland are perverting our children when they tell them that their family is a family of saints and ascetics, they are turning them away from instruction. What they say is a lie, an illusion, an error and falsehood, for knowledge is preserved only by instruction and the *ulama* (clerics or learned ones) are closer to knowledge than anyone else.'

He gave each scholar his just due; he was evenhanded and modest. He ate only from the product of his own work, never supporting himself from the public treasury . . . He was good to the people, full of indulgence for all; calm, patient, unconcerned about the wealth that the people possessed. An able administrator, he checked on the *qadis* (judges), annulling the judgements which they had made in times of passion, insuring that they always remained alert.

Another description of Bello comes to us from the pen of Hugh Clapperton (see Document 3) after Clapperton's visit to Sokoto in 1824.

DOCUMENT 28
'Discussions with the Caliph'

Clapperton, *Missions to the Niger*, Vol. IV, pp. 676–8.

NOTES FOR READING   Boo-Khaloom = Fezzani merchant who joined a Bornu column against a Fulani force and was killed; bashaw = pasha; Denham = Clapperton's travelling companion for part of the journey; gadado = Gidado, the Waziri from 1817 to 1842.

March 17.—After breakfast the sultan sent for me; his residence was at no great distance. In front of it there is a large quadrangle, into which several of the principal streets of the city lead. We passed through three coozees, as guardhouses, without the least detention, and were immediately ushered into the presence of Bello, the second sultan of the Felatahs. He was seated on a small carpet, between two pillars supporting the roof of a thatched house, not unlike one of our cottages. The walls and pillars were painted blue and white, in the Moorish taste; and on the back wall was sketched a fire-screen, ornamented with a coarse painting of a flowerpot. An arm-chair, with an iron lamp standing on it, was placed on each side of the screen. The sultan bade me many hearty welcomes, and asked me if I was not much tired with my journey from Burderawa. I told him it was the most severe travelling I had experienced between Tripoli and Sackatoo, and thanked him for the guard, the conduct of which I did not fail to commend in the strongest terms.

He asked me a great many questions about Europe, and our religious distinctions. He was acquainted with the names of some of the more ancient sects, and asked whether we were Nestorians or Socinians. To extricate myself from the embarrassment occasioned by this question, I bluntly replied we were called Protestants. 'What are Protestants?' says he. I attempted to explain to him, as well as I was able, that having protested, more than two centuries and a half ago, against the superstition, absurdities, and abuses practised in those days, we had ever since professed to follow simply what was written 'in the book of our Lord Jesus', as they call the New Testament, and thence received the name of Protestants. He continued to ask several other theological questions, until I was obliged to confess myself not sufficiently versed in religious subtleties to resolve these knotty points, having always left that task to others more learned than myself. He now ordered some books to be produced which belonged to Major Denham, and began to speak with great bitterness of the late Boo-Khaloom, for making a predatory inroad into his territories; adding, in his own words, 'I am sure the bashaw of Tripoli never meant to strike me with one hand, while he offers a present with the other: at least it is a strange way for friends to act. But what was your friend doing there?' he asked abruptly. I assured the sultan, that Major Denham had no other object than to make a short excursion into the country. The books being brought in, proved to be the Nautical Almanack, two Reviews, Lord Bacon's Essays, and Major Denham's Journal; all which the sultan returned to me in the most handsome manner. Before taking leave, however, I had to explain the contents of each, and was set to read them, in order to give him an opportunity of hearing the sound of our language, which he thought very beautiful. The sultan is a noble-looking man, forty-four years of age, although much younger in appearance, five feet ten inches high, portly in person, with a short curling black beard, a small mouth, a fine forehead, a Grecian nose, and large black eyes. He was dressed in a light blue cotton tobe, with a white muslin turban, the shawl of which he wore over the nose and mouth in the Tuarick fashion.

In the afternoon I repeated my visit, accompanied by the gadado, Mahomed El Wordee, and Mahomed Gumsoo, the principal Arab of the city, to whom I had a letter of introduction from Hat Salah at Kano. The sultan was sitting in the same apartment in which he received me in the morning. I now laid before him a present, in the name of His Majesty the King of England, consisting of two new blunderbusses highly ornamented with silver, the double-barrelled pistols, pocket-compass, and embroidered jacket of the late Dr. Oudney; a scarlet bornouse trimmed with silver lace, a pair of scarlet breeches, thirty yards of red silk, two white, two red, and two Egyptian turban shawls, the latter trimmed with gold; four pounds each of cloves and cinnamon; three cases of gun-powder, with shot and balls; three razors, three clasp-knives, three looking-glasses; six snuff-boxes, three of paper and three of tin; a spy-glass, and a large English tea-tray, on which the smaller articles were arranged. He took them up one by one. The compass and spy-glass excited great interest; and he seemed much gratified when I pointed out that by means of the former, he could at any time find out the east to address himself in his daily prayers. He said, 'Every thing is wonderful; but you are the greatest curiosity of all!' and then added, 'What can I give that is most acceptable to the King of England?' I replied, 'The most acceptable service you can render to the King of England is to co-operate with His Majesty in putting a stop to the slave trade on the coast: as the King of England sends every year large ships to cruise there, for the sole purpose of seizing all vessels engaged in this trade, whose crews are thrown into prison; and of liberating the unfortunate slaves, on whom lands and houses are conferred, at one of our settlements in Africa'.—'What!' said he, 'have you no slaves in England?'—'No. Whenever a slave sets his foot in England, he is from that moment free.'—'What do you then do for servants?'—'We hire them for a stated period, and give them regular wages: nor is any person in England allowed to strike another; and the very soldiers are fed, clothed, and paid by government.'—'God is great!' he exclaimed; 'you are a beautiful people.'

In 1826 Clapperton visited Sokoto again, leaving the following impressions of life in the town and surrounding countryside.

DOCUMENT 29
'They go through the motions'

From Clapperton's journal of his visit to Sokoto in November 1826. Hugh Clapperton, *Journal of a Second Expedition into the Interior of Africa* (1829), pp. 207–08, 210–11, 213–14, 222–4.

NOTES FOR READING   Quorra = Niger; coozie = small guard house; gora = kola nut, which came principally from Asante country at this time (see Document 20); Fellatas = Fulani; Nyffé = Nupe; *Allahu Akber* = God is great; Rhamadan = Ramadan, the month of fasting in the Muslim calendar.

The city of Soccatoo stands on the top of a low hill, or rising ground, having a river passing at a short distance from the northern wall. It is formed of the united branches of the several streams, which take their rise to the south of Kashna, and flow past Zirmie. Having passed Soccatoo, it crosses the district of Cubbé in a southwesterly direction, and at the distance of four days' journey enters the Quorra. It is well stored with fish, which afford the poor people of Soccatoo a very considerable part of their food. The city is surrounded by a wall, about twenty-four feet high, and a dry ditch. The wall is kept in good repair, and there are eleven gates; seven having been built up at the breaking out of the rebellion. The clay walls which surround all African towns, clusters of huts, and even single coozies, give a deadly dull appearance to them all, whether negro to Mahometan. The only appearance of animation is given by the great number of slaves and others moving to and fro, or lounging, or lying in the shade at the doors of great men. A great part of the town within the walls might be taken for a number of ill-enclosed gardens . . .

The ordinary occupations of the higher, and indeed I may say of all classes of the Fellatas is, they rise at day-break, wash and say their prayers, count their beads for about half an hour, and then chew a gora nut, if they have any; which done, they sip a quantity of senkie, or furro-furrocoo. These articles are a preparation of half-boiled dourra flowers, made into balls of about one pound, mixed up with dry flour. Senkie is one of these balls, bruised and mixed with milk; furro-furrocoo is the same kind of ball mixed with water. About 10 A.M they have rice boiled, which they eat with a little melted butter. After this they pay visits, or lounge in the shade, hear the news, say prayers, count their beads, which employ them till sunset, when they have a meal of pudding, with a little stewed meat and gravy, or a few small fish; they then retire to rest.

During the spring and harvest the proprietors of estates ride out to their different slave villages to look after their grain, cotton, indigo, etc.; or to the place where they have their cattle. The occupations of the poorer class, who are not engaged in trade, are much the same as those of their superiors; their food is somewhat different, being principally confined to furro-furrocoo . . .

The domestic slaves are generally well treated. The males who have arrived at the age of eighteen or nineteen are given a wife, and sent to live at their villages and farms in the country, where they build a hut, and until the harvest are fed by their owners. When the time for cultivating the ground and sowing the seed comes on, the owner points out what he requires, and what is to be sown on it. The slave is then allowed to enclose a part for himself and family. The hours of labour, for his master, are from daylight till mid-day; the remainder of the day is employed on his own, or in any other way he may think proper. At the time of harvest, when they cut and tie up the grain, each slave gets a bundle of the different sorts of grain, about a bushel of our measure, for himself. The grain on his own ground is entirely left for his own use, and he may dispose of it as he thinks proper. At the vacant seasons of the year he must attend to the calls of his master, whether to accompany him on a journey, or go to war, if so ordered.

The children of a slave are also slaves, and when able are usually sent out to attend the goats and sheep, and, at a more advanced age, the bullocks and larger cattle; they are soon afterwards taken home to the master's house, to look after his horse or his domestic concerns, as long as they remain single. The domestic slaves are fed the same as the rest of the family, with whom they appear to be on an equality of footing.

The children of slaves, whether dwelling in the house or on the farm, are never sold, unless their behaviour is such that, after repeated punishment, they continue unmanageable, so that the master is compelled to part with them. The slaves that are sold are those taken from the enemy, or newly purchased, who, on trial, do not suit the purchaser. When a male or female slave dies unmarried, his property goes to the owner. The children of the slaves are sometimes educated with those of the owner, but this is not generally the case . . .

The next article is the white cotton cloth of the country, of which they make a considerable quantity, both for the home consumption and for exportation to Kano and Nyffé; what they export is principally made into tobes and large shirts before it leaves Soccatoo. They have also a cloth called naroo, which is something like our counterpanes; a few checked and red striped cloths, used as tobes, and some as wrappers or zinnies for the women. The weavers of the latter are mostly natives of Nyffé, as are also all their blacksmiths. They have shoe, boot, saddle, and bridlemakers. Another article of export is the civet; the animals that produce it are kept in wooden cages, and fed on pounded fish and corn. A few slaves are also sold out of the province to the merchants of Kano, Kashna, Ghadamis, and Tripoli. A young male slave, from thirteen to twenty years of age, will bring from 10 000 to 20 000 cowries; a female slave, if very handsome, from 40 000 to 50 000; the common price is about 30 000 for a virgin about fourteen or fifteen. The articles brought to Soccatoo for sale by the Arabs are the same as what are brought to other parts of Houssa, and are mentioned in another place. Salt is brought by the Tuaricks from Billma, and also by the Tuaricks of the west. The salt from the latter quarter is much better, being more pure, and in large pieces like ice. Ostriches alive and ostrich skins are brought by these people, but little is given for a skin, only from 4000 to 5000 cowries for the finest. They also bring horses which fetch a good price here; dates from Billma, and a small quantity of goods which they buy from the Arabs at Aghadiz. The articles they could export in considerable quantities, if there were buyers, would be elephants' teeth, bullocks' hides, which, when tanned, only cost five hundred cowries, equal to sixpence of our money. Goat skins, and the skins of antelopes, and other wild animals, might be procured in abundance, but, of course, would rise much in price if there was a great demand. Gum-arabic might also be procured in abundance. What they would take from us in exchange would be coarse scarlet cloths, which in all parts of the interior

bring a good price, say 10 000 cowries a yard; coarse yellow and green cloth; red tape; unwrought silk, of glowing colours; sewing needles, of the commonest kind; looking-glasses, no matter however small, at a penny or twopence each in England; earthenware with figures, plain ware would not pay; the coarsest kind of red camlet scarfs; jugs and hardware of the most common description, but stout; foolscap paper of the coarsest kind, if it did not let the ink through: beads, I think, are sold as cheap here by the Arabs as they are in England; sheets of tin; tin pots and cups; brass gilt rings for the fingers, arms, and ankles; as also ear-rings; copper and brass pots, the more figures the better; paper and wooden snuff-boxes of the commonest sort.

These Africans keep up the appearance of religion. They pray five times a day. They seldom take the trouble to wash before prayers, except in the morning; but they go through the motions of washing, clapping their hands on the ground as if in water, and muttering a prayer. This done, as if they had washed, they untie their breeches and let them fall off; then, facing the east, let the sleeves of their larger shirt, or tobe, fall over their hands, and assuming at the same time a grave countenance, begin by calling out, in an audible voice, 'Allahu Akber!' etc. kneeling down and touching the ground with the forehead. When they have finished repeating this prayer, they sit down, leaning over on the left thigh and leg, and count or pass the beads through their fingers. All their prayers and religious expressions are in Arabic; and I may say without exaggeration, taking Negroes and Fellatas together, that not one in a thousand know what they are saying. All they know of their religion is to repeat their prayers by rote in Arabic, first from sunrise to sunset in the Rhamadan, and a firm belief that the goods and chattels, wives and children of all people differing with them in faith, belong to them; and that it is quite lawful in any way to abuse, rob, or kill an unbeliever. Of the Fellatas, I should suppose about one in ten are able to read and write. They believe, they say, in predestination; but it is all a farce; they show not the least of such belief in any of their actions.

Clapperton died in Sokoto a few months later. With him at the end was his servant and companion, and an explorer in his own right, Richard Lander. Also present in Clapperton's last months was a Hausa from Gobir named Abu Bakr or William Pasko. What follows is Lander's account of the extraordinary career of Pasko, who seemed to have spent his life crossing the frontiers of states and cultures. Compare his story with the accounts of Abu Bakr al-Siddiq and Jan Nieser in the Asante chapter and Jacob Msimbiti in the Nguni story.

DOCUMENT 30
'Adopting the prevailing opinions'

Richard Lander, *Records of Captain Clapperton's Last Expedition to Africa*, 2 vols (1830), Vol. I, pp. 203–09, 212.

NOTES FOR READING   Gonja = the area north of Asante; Whydah = Dahomean port; Yariba = Yoruba; Borghoo = Borgu.

I had scarcely been in Kano a fortnight, when Pasko, our Houssa interpreter, absconded with a few articles of trifling value, and after a diligent and persevering search of three days, he was found concealed under a heap of yams, in the house of the mother to a female he had recently married. He was accompanied to our house by his better half, sobbing all the way, who begged me, with much earnestness, to forgive her husband for the offence he had been guilty of, which I consented to do, but not till after he had received a severe scolding, and promised never again to perpetrate a crime of a similar nature against me or any one else.

As this old man's history may not be altogether uninteresting, inasmuch as it shows, in a lively point of view, the ridiculous superstitions of his countrymen, imbibed in their infant years, which no circumstance or change of scene in their after life can wholly eradicate, I hope I may be excused for giving a short account of his adventures previously to his being engaged in the African mission, as repeated solemnly to me several times from his own lips, and after that period till his arrival with us at Kano, drawn from personal observation.

Pasko's native name was *Abbu Becr*, and although this is without doubt a Mohammedan appellation, he knew nothing more of Islamism than its name, being in reality a Pagan. He was born in the district of Goober, and was brother to the reigning prince of that country, who at the period of the subjugation of the neighbouring provinces to the yoke of Danfodio, Bello's father, ridiculed that wily conqueror's pretensions to sanctity, and rose with his people to dispute his further advances into Houssa. In an engagement with the Falatahs, in which Pasko distinguished himself, his brother was suddenly metamorphosed into a white elephant! . . .

The remainder of Pasko's history is entitled to a greater share of credence. A year or two subsequent to the above singular occurrence, as Pasko was dancing by the light of the moon, with several of his companions, he was kidnapped by a marauding party of Falatahs, and sold to a Gonja trader. This man not treating him with the kindness he expected, to be revenged Pasko took the liberty of robbing him of all his goods, and decamping in the night; he was, however, apprehended the next evening, in a state of intoxication, dancing with a dozen females, and taken back to his master, who re-sold him to a native of Ashantee. By this master he was taken considerable notice of, and sent, along with many others, to his own country (Ashantee); but no great while after his arrival thither he committed a second serious misdemeanour, for which offence he was driven to the sea-side, and sold to the master of a Portuguese schooner, then lying at Whydah. On her voyage to Bahia, the vessel was captured by an English sloop of war, and Pasko was liberated; but consented to remain with the British, and serve as an ordinary seaman. He was, however, taken from his employment by Mr. Belzoni, in order to accompany him in his attempt to reach Tombuctoo by way of Fez; but that enterprizing traveller dying of dysentery, Pasko returned to his duties in the British navy, where

he remained till engaged by Captain Clapperton, in the joint capacity of servant to Captain Pearce, and general interpreter to the mission.

Pasko was no more than five feet in height, with hands and arms disproportionately long: his face was open and expressive, if a mouth extending literally from ear to ear can impart an enviable cast of feature to the human countenance; and his cheek was furrowed with the tatto mark of the Houssa nation (eight deep scars, inflicted by a rude instrument during boyhood). His nose was excessively broad and flat, and his lips resembled, as nearly as possible, the famous German sausage ornamented; and these were, with large teeth, of pearly whiteness, which were generally exposed by a perpetual grin playing upon his countenance. But there was an undefinable expression of low cunning in his dark, wandering eye, and an habitual restlessness in his manner which induced one to suspect that there was more of evil in him than he was willing should be detected, and which he strove to disguise under forced stupidity and carelessness which in reality did not belong to his disposition. It is somewhat odd that Pasko, plain as his appearance most undoubtedly was, should have entertained the strange notion that almost every female who saw him, of whatever hue, nation, or religion she might be, could not help falling in love with him at first sight, imagining that his intellectual physiognomy possessed some peculiar attraction—an oil of rhodium,—which fascinated all beholders. Hence, secure of the affections of the softer sex, his behaviour to them was not always graced by that studied civility, and agreeableness of manner, which are the characteristics of most gallants; what others were obliged to entreat and sigh for as a favour, Pasko demanded as a right, and enforced his pretensions with an eloquence so commanding, that according to his own asseverations at least, his advances were never repelled by coldness or disdain. At the period of his engaging himself with the African mission, he might have been about sixty years of age, but looked considerably older; and the above unaccountable feeling of his had lost none of its intensity at so advanced a period of life . . .

Pasko never troubled his head much about religous matters, adopting the prevailing opinions about them in the various countries through which he might happen to pass: thus, he was a Christian in England, a Pagan in Yariba and Borghoo, and a Mohammedan in the Falatah empire; although the superstitious notions of his childhood clung like instinct to his manhood and declining years, evidently disposing him to lean towards Paganism, as the best and most convenient doctrine with which he was acquainted.

Epilogue

Despite its problems and the vast extent of its dominions, the Sokoto Caliphate remained the governing regime of Hausaland until the British conquest in the early twentieth century. The British chose to rule the area, designated as Northern Nigeria, through the ruling dynasties of the various emirates, with the Caliphal family playing a very prominent role. One member of that family, a great-grandson of Bello, became the leader of the Northern

Peoples Congress and was the most powerful single man in Nigeria when he was assassinated in the coup of January 1966—Sir Ahmadu Bello, Sardauna of Sokoto. This last document gives his reflections on his ancestors and the history of the nineteenth century.

DOCUMENT 31
'The instrument of destiny'

Sir Ahmadu Bello, *My Life* (1962), pp. 10–11, 14–16, 18–19.

NOTES FOR READING Western Empire = the part of the Caliphate under Abdullah and Gwandu; Lugard = the British officer who organized the conquest of the Caliphate and set up the administration of colonial Northern Nigeria (the same Lugard who appears in Chapter Three).

To those who are not fully aware of the history of this part of Nigeria, I must explain a little at this point. The Shehu Usuman was a Fulani leader born about 1744 in the country then called Gobir, north of the Sokoto River—an ancient kingdom. He was not only a leader but a great preacher and a man of the utmost piety. To quote a British parallel, he was a combination of John Wesley and Oliver Cromwell. He was among a people who were nominally Muhammadan: I say nominally, for the religion had become very corrupt and many pagan practices had crept in and had taken a firm hold even in the highest quarters.

The Shehu Usuman declared a Holy War against the polluters of the faith. In 1804 he started by attacking the Chief of Gobir, one of the worst offenders, in whose territory he was living. This local war went on for some time, and it was not until 1808 that the capital of Gobir was taken and destroyed; the kingdom of Gobir then disintegrated but by no means did it die. Meanwhile, to cleanse the religion, the Shehu had organised revolts in all the great Hausa states: the Fulani living in them rose and overthrew the Hausa kings. The Shehu appointed new rulers either from among the victorious generals or from among other important Fulani. Thus two-thirds of the present Northern Region came directly under the control of the Shehu and his son Bello, to whom he delegated more and more authority until he himself finally went into retirement . . .

This was too much for one man to deal with and so the Shehu divided it into two portions. One was based on the ancient town of Gwandu, a hundred miles southwest of Sokoto, but still in the Sokoto valley. This was given to Abdullahi, the Shehu's brother, as first Emir of Gwandu.

This Western Empire, as it was called, extended down the Niger and included the Nupe Kingdom, then based on Raba (not to be confused with my birthplace) and Ilorin. It was this section of the Fulani government that came up against the Yorubas, when the Emir of Ilorin was engaged in the endless wars of the last half of the nineteenth century.

The other Empire, the Eastern Empire, was based on Sokoto and included all the great Hausa states down to the Benue at Nasarawa, Muri, and Yola. This never came in physical contact with the people of the present Eastern Region, with whom our relations have usually been amicable in the last few years. Both Empires were liquidated when the British entered Sokoto, and the Emirates of Sokoto and Gwandu were confined to their home territories. The Hausa Emirates have continued to this day as they were founded by the Shehu.

Sultan Bello must have been a remarkable man, for he lived through twenty years of very testing time. The countries of Gobir and Zamfara, whose kingdoms had been destroyed by his father, revolted against him, but he subdued them finally after several campaigns. At the same time he had to control his vast empire and to advise and direct the Emirs of very distant places. It is difficult to describe how remote these places are from each other, even in these days of good roads and fast cars.

Then there were no roads at all. However important a man might be, the fastest way he could get about would be on horseback. By this method of transport it would take him nearly *forty* days to do the journey from Yola to Sokoto, travelling every day, and that takes no account of the difficulties and dangers of the route, the swollen rivers, hostile people and bandits, savage animals, sickness and accident to man and horse. And yet that is how it had to be done. Even Kano, the most important centre of the Empire then, as it is now, was twelve days' march away, and that lay across great waterless areas. The Sultan's control could not have been close or intimate, but it must have been effective.

Even at the start things were not at all easy. When the Shehu died in Sokoto in 1817 he expressed the wish that Bello should succeed him as Sarkin Musulmi, or Commander of the Faithful for the Western Sudan, while remaining as ruler of Sokoto in charge of the Eastern Empire. However, this was not known to the Shehu's brother Abdullahi, who was at Gwandu at the time and who thought he would succeed his brother as a matter of course. No sooner had he heard the startling news that the Shehu had willed otherwise than a rising broke out at Kalam Baina, near Gwandu, whose people had gone over to a rival. Things looked pretty bad, but Bello with generosity and promptitude sent men to his assistance and the revolt was crushed . . .

The two rulers met after the victory. Bello was on his great war-horse, Abdullahi on a mare, as befitted his position as a learned Mallam. Bello, being the younger man, made ready to dismount to salute his uncle, following strict etiquette; his uncle waved him to stay where he was and then bowed in his saddle and greeted Bello as Commander of the Faithful.

Thus by mutual tact the rift was closed. What might have been a disastrous breach was healed, and ever since then our two families have lived in perfect friendship and amity. This was just as well, as they both had their hands full in their own territories and mutual rivalry would have had serious consequences . . .

Looking at it all now with all my present knowledge I see that the constant fighting bore heavily on the people: that the Courts were just and carried out the law faithfully within their rights; that the taxation, though not unjust in principle, was sometimes unfair in its incidence, and, as has happened so often in all parts of the world at various epochs, the lowest class, being the least influential and unvocal, suffered more than it should have. Changes were bound, in the nature of things, to come; we could not have resisted external influences much longer and, even if some had wished to do so, the effect of education, which too must have come to us before very long, would have forced a general tidying up.

Whatever the rights and wrongs of the attack on Kano and Sokoto may be, the British were the instrument of destiny and were fulfilling the will of God. In their way they did it well . . .

They made no drastic changes, and what was done came into effect only after consultation. Everything went on more or less as it had done, for what could one Resident, an assistant and a few soldiers in Sokoto do to change so vast an area as Sokoto Emirate? . . .

Another matter which caught the imagination was that the incident which actually started the Shehu Usuman dan Fodio on the Fulani wars took place in 1803. A prophecy was made known that the Fulani Empire would last for one hundred years. No one then was greatly surprised when its end came on the grazing ground outside Sokoto almost exactly one hundred years later. Exactly fifty-six years later, to the very day, the Northern Region was granted self-government when the British Governor handed over power to me and my government on the balcony of gleaming Lugard Hall in Kaduna.

AIDS TO UNDERSTANDING

Chronology

1754   Birth of Uthman
1774   Uthman begins teaching
c. 1787   Great Feast at Alkalawa
c. 1794–5   Nafata accedes to throne of Gobir
c. 1801–02   Yunfa accedes to throne of Gobir
1804 (February)   *Hijra* of Uthman and his *jamā'a*
1804 (June)   Battle of Tabkin Kwotto
1804 (December)   Battle of Tsuntsua
1805 (November)   Battle of Alwassa
1806–12   *Jihād* in Zaria
1807   Kano Sarkin put to flight
1808   Battle of Alkalawa
1808–14   Struggles in Bornu, correspondence between Sokoto leaders and al-Kanemi
1809   Establishment of Sokoto
1812   Uthman divides empire between Bello and Abdullah and withdraws from administration
c. 1816–17   Afonja asserts independence of Oyo at Ilorin
1817   Uthman dies, Bello succeeds as Caliph
1817–18   Revolt of Abd al-Salam
1824   Clapperton's first visit to Kano and Sokoto
c. 1824   Afonja killed by Fulani and Hausa
1826   Clapperton's second visit to Kano and Sokoto

Glossary

Allah akbār (Allah akber) = Arabic for 'God is great'

cowry = small shell used as currency
— awa = Hausa suffix meaning 'the people of'
Degel (Taqal) = Uthman's home and base of operations until the *hijra*
Fellata = Fulani
hijra = Arabic for emigration, with specific reference to Muhammad's *hijra* (622 AD)
imàm = Arabic for 'the one who leads in prayer' and, by extension, leads the community or state
jamà'a = Arabic for community
Jibril = Jibril ibn Umar, a Tuareg scholar of the eighteenth century
jihād = Arabic for 'effort' and especially the effort to convert by force (holy war)
kafila = caravan
khalifa = Arabic for successor or deputy and applied to the head of an intentionally Muslim state
kola (gora) = fruit or nut of a forest plant chewed widely in the savanna
Kuwara (Quorra) = Niger River
naphtha = gun or gunpowder
Nyffé = Nupe
qāḍi = Arabic for judge (also appears as Alkali)
qaṣida = Arabic verse form
Sarki (Sarkin) = Hausa for king
Shaikh = Arabic for 'elder' and a scholarly title applied to Uthman
Sharī'a = Islamic law
Shehu = Hausa for Shaikh
Sunna = custom and precedent established by the Prophet and, by extension, 'orthodoxy'
'ulamā' = clerics
wazir = minister or chief minister (vizier)
zakāt (zakka) = Arabic for alms

An Essay of Questions

Sources and Interpretation

This case study differs radically from those on Asante and South Africa, where the European documentation occupies such a dominant position. Here we have no firsthand European accounts until twenty years after the *jihād* and the danger comes rather from the predominance of writings by the architects and elite of the new regime.

How would you analyse the nature of the literature written by the Sokoto leaders? What does that literature suggest about who their audience was and about the level and extent of 'learning' at the time?

How well did the training of Islamic scholars prepare them for writing historical narrative or historical analysis? Does the assumption that 'God willed this to happen' significantly affect the actor or the author? Or is it simply a justification for action after the fact?

In the Sokoto case, the principal actors and authors are the same and they acquire a strong vested interest in the new regime. One can none the less develop a critical commentary on the Caliphate by using the works of these leaders. With special attention to Documents 23, 24, 25, 27 and 31, formulate a critique.

It is usually difficult to find the voice of the 'losers' of a major historical encounter. Taking Documents 22 and 26 as examples of the perspectives of the victims of the *jihād*, what new insights emerge?

It is perhaps even more difficult to write the history of the 'less articulate,' be they on the side of the victors or victims. Taking Document 18, intended for a non-scholarly audience, and Documents 20 and 26 from the popular literature, what insights emerge about the attitudes of ordinary pastoralists and farmers?

European sources become abundant in the 1820s. To what extent do you find racism in this material, or ethnocentrism? Looking especially at Documents 28, 29 and 30, suggest what concerns are present in the European material but lacking in the Sokoto sources. At what points do these concerns and information assist in an evaluation of the *jihād* and Caliphate?

How does the European perspective here compare with that in Zululand in the 1820s; Asante in the 1810s; Buganda in the 1890s?

Compare Hornemann's map (Document 2), based on hearsay evidence, with Clapperton's (Document 3) drawn from first-hand observations.

On two occasions (Documents 3 and 4) we have 'extrapolated' insights from nineteenth- and twentieth-century material and claimed that they were relevant for the late eighteenth century. How justified was this in each case?

By comparing Document 31 with the rest of the case study, suggest what changes in the 'received' tradition about the *jihād* had come to be accepted by the 1960s.

Uthman and the Jihād

The 'indigenous' and 'incremental' qualities of the Sokoto *jihād* are very striking: it grew slowly and from within. Uthman took many years to form and train a community and remained committed to reform by persuasion for a long time. He and the leaders in the other provinces were native to their respective areas. How would you explain the eventual shift from persuasion to military action? How much responsibility for that shift in Gobir would you put upon Uthman and Yunfa and how much upon their respective supporters? Where would you put the 'turning point'? What factors would you assign to 'underlying causes' and to 'precipitating actions'?

The new movement was fortunate in the quality of its leadership, the co-ordination among the efforts in the various provinces and the willingness of all to accept the supremacy of Sokoto. Much of the responsibility for this goes to Uthman. What estimate would you give of his ability to teach and train; of his impact on pastoralists, farmers and the popular literature; of his 'charisma'? To what do you attribute his progressive retirement from the *jihād* and administration after 1804 and especially after 1812?

In military terms, the reformers' early triumphs over the numerous and well-armed forces of Gobir are astonishing. To what do you attribute them?

In the Songhay Empire of about 1500, a reform movement encouraged by Timbuktu scholars failed to significantly change Songhay society. Study the Hunwick articles (1966, 1971) on Songhay, and suggest what factors in Hausaland may have been critical to the success of the reformers there.

Bello and the Caliphate

Muhammad Bello, as the chief inheritor of the mantle of leadership of Uthman, became the chief spokesman and symbol for the success and achievement of the *jihād*. What impressions of the man emerge from Documents 27, 28 and 31, and from his own writings? What is your estimate of him as a political leader; a military leader; a scholar?

In the section, 'The Conduct of the Caliphate', we have suggested that the reformers achieved a new measure of political integration. Are increased spatial extension and political integration signs of significant achievement? Is the ability to endure one hundred years such a sign, or the ability to sustain a scholarly tradition, as the Caliphal and Waziral families have?

We have also suggested that it is very difficult to evaluate the nature of the 'reformed' society. How would you compare pre- and post-*jihādic* society in respect to prosperity; complexity and specialization; corruption; oppression; divisions into classes and between town and country? Were the problems of justice in post-*jihādic* society principally due to the insufficient application of Muslim law or to the content of that law itself? In sum, which society was more just and for whom? Clearly, there is no easy answer, perhaps no answer at all, to these questions, especially with the necessarily limited and impressionistic materials in the case study. None the less, wrestling with these issues does at least clarify the criteria for evaluating a major social change such as this. The following sets of questions represent efforts to approach the same fundamental issues from more limited and specific perspectives.

Abdullah expresses a sharp critique of the movement and its effects (Document 24). Do you dismiss this as personal grievance and jealousy or take it as a serious indictment? What do you make of the hesitant critique of Ahmadu Bello (Document 31)?

The debate of al-Kanemi and the Sokoto leaders (Document 23) was anything but 'academic' in spite of some of the language. Why was it so important? Who has the better of the argument logically, and theologically?

The differences between the 'sinful' Muslim and the 'unbeliever', between the 'venal' and the 'reformist' mallams, were critical in the minds of the Sokoto leaders and challengers like al-Kanemi. Did those terms correspond to real differences between individuals and between communities, or were they simply elements of debate and rationalization?

Abd al-Salam (of Document 25) and others might refer to the reform movement as the 'Fulani' *jihād*. Is this an appropriate designation? If so, does it mean that Uthman and Bello essentially failed in their goals?

Clapperton (Document 29) and Lander (Document 30) suggest that the overwhelming majority of Hausa and Fulani do not really understand the faith they practise or claim to practise. What is your estimate of the effect of the *jihād* on the practice and understanding of Islam among the people?

Many of the people of Hausaland in both the eighteenth and nineteenth centuries were slaves. Document 3 suggests that over half of Kano city was slave. Using especially Documents 3, 4, 22, 28, 29 and 30, what comments would you venture about the institutions of slavery and the slave trade?

In Documents 11 and 19 Bello and Uthman are critical of 'inherited religion' and 'hereditary right' in old Gobir. In Document 27 Bello expresses his anxiety about the effects of the privileged status of his family, while in Document 31 his great grandson implies an almost divine right of rule for the same family. Taking these sources and the rest of the case study, reflect upon the nature of social mobility, achieved and ascribed status, and the sense of social responsibility of the ruling elites in pre- and post-*jihādic* Hausaland.

Bibliographical Essay and Bibliography

For this case study we have relied heavily on the works of Adeleye, Hiskett and Last. Hiskett's biography of Uthman (1973) is a particularly good introduction to the Sokoto story and the Islamic culture of Hausaland. The book by Hogben and Kirk-Greene deals with each of the provinces or emirates of Northern Nigeria. Low analyses three of the eastern 'border states' while Paden concentrates on Kano. The articles by Lovejoy and the volume edited by McCall and Bennett provide an introduction to the economic realities of the eighteenth and nineteenth centuries.

Bivar, Hiskett, Hunwick, Last (1968) and A. Smith give introductions to the Arabic literature while Edgar, Johnston (1962) and C. Robinson give samples of the Hausa material. Bovill (1968) has provided a helpful summary of European exploration as well as annotated accounts of the voyages of Hornemann, Clapperton and others.

For other reform movements beginning in the late seventeenth century see Brenner for Bornu, Brown for Macina, Colvin for Cayor, Curtin for Nasir al-Din, Derman and Sow for Futa Jalon, Oloruntimehin and Willis (1967) for Umar, D. Robinson for Futa Toro and Willis (1971) for the Kunta. Of special interest is the reform effort of Songhay around 1500; consult Hiskett (1962) and Hunwick (1966 and 1971). For the Yoruba, see Akintoye and R. Smith in addition to S. Johnson. For Hausa life in the recent past consult M. Smith; for the present, see P. Hill. Adeleye (1971) and Muffett treat the British conquest of Northern Nigeria while Dudley, M. G. Smith and Whitaker deal with contemporary politics and history in the region.

For general introductions to Islam, Islamic law and the question of *jihād*, see the *Cambridge History of Islam* and the works by Khadduri and Schacht.

In the bibliography, we have listed the sources for Documents 4, 5, 20, 22 and 26 among the secondary materials because of the time when they were recorded.

Primary Sources

Abdullah dan Fodio, *Tazyīn al-Waraqāt*, trans. and ed. M. Hiskett. Ibadan University Press, Ibadan, 1963.

Clapperton, Hugh, 'The Bornu Mission' comprising vols II-IV of *Missions to the Niger*, ed. E. W. Bovill. Hakluyt series. Cambridge University Press, Cambridge, 1966.

—*Journal of a Second Expedition into the Interior of Africa*. 1829; F. Cass, London, 1966.

Hornemann, Friedrich, *The Journal of Friedrich Hornemann's Travels, 1797–8*. G. & W. Nicol, London, 1802. Also in Bovill, E. W., ed. *Missions to the Niger*. Vol. I, 1964.

Lander, Richard, *Records of Captain Clapperton's Last Expedition to Africa*. 2 vols. 1830; F. Cass, London, 1967.

Leo Africanus, *The History and Description of Africa*. Hakluyt series. 3 vols. 1896.

Muhammad Bello, *Infāq al-Maisūr*, written *c.* 1813. Trans. and paraphrased by E. J. Arnett, *The Rise of the Sokoto Fulani*, 1922. Excerpts translated by A. Smith in Hodgkin, T., ed. *Nigerian Perspectives*. Oxford University Press, Oxford, 1960, 198–205.

Palmer, H. R., ed. and trans., *Sudanese Memoirs*, 3 vols. 1928; F. Cass, London, 1967. Includes 'Kano Chronicle'.

Sa'id, al-hajj, *Tarikh Sokoto*, written in 1850s or 1860s. Trans. O. Houdas and appearing as an appendix to Vol. II of Houdas' *Tedzkiret en-Nisian*. E. Leroux, Paris, 1901.

Uthman dan Fodio, *Kitāb al-Farq*, written between 1808 and 1813. Trans. and ed. M. Hiskett, *Bulletin*, SOAS (1960).

— *Sifofin Shehu*, written before 1814. Trans. and ed. R. A. Adeleye and I. Mukoshy, *Research Bulletin*, Center of Arabic Documentation (Ibadan), **2**, 1 (January 1966).

—*Wathīqat Ahl al-Sūdān* ('Dispatch to the people of the Sudan'), written about 1804–5. Trans. and ed. A. D. H. Bivar, *Journal of African History* (1961).

Secondary Sources

Adeleye, R. A., *Power and Diplomacy in Northern Nigeria 1800–1906*. Longman, Harlow, 1971.

—'Hausaland and Bornu, 1600–1800', in Ajayi and Crowder. Vol. 1. 1971.

—'The Sokoto Caliphate in the 19th century', in Ajayi and Crowder. Vol. II. 1974.

— *See also* Uthman above.

Ahmadu Bello, *My Life*. Cambridge University Press, Cambridge, 1962.

Ajayi, J. F. Ade, and Crowder M., eds., *History of West Africa*. 2 vols. Longman, Harlow, Vol. I, 1972 and Vol. II, 1974; Columbia University Press, New York, 1972–3.

Al-Hajj, M., and Last, D. M. 'Attempts at defining a Muslim in 19th century Hausaland and Bornu'. *Journal of the Historical Society of Nigeria*, 3, 2 (Lagos, 1965).

Arnett, E. J., *See* Muhammad Bello.

Bivar, A. D. H., 'Arabic documents of Northern Nigeria'. *Bulletin*, SOAS (1959).

— and Hiskett M. 'The Arabic literature of Northern Nigeria to 1804: a provisional account'. *Bulletin*, SOAS (1962).

— *See also* Uthman above.

Bovil, E. W., *The Niger Explored*. Oxford University Press, Oxford, 1968.

See also Clapperton and Hornemann, above.

Documents Scientifiques de la Mission Tilho (1906–9). 2 vols. Ministère des Colonies, Paris, 1911.

Edgar, Frank, original compiler, *Tatsuniyoyi Na Hausa*. 1913. Trans. and ed. N. Skinner and published as *Hausa Tales and Traditions*. 3 vols. F. Cass, London, 1969.

Hassan, Alhaji, and Mallam Shuaibu Ha'ibi, *A Chronicle of Abuja*, trans. F. Heath. Ibadan University Press, Ibadan, 1952.

Hiskett, M., 'An Islamic tradition of reform in the western Sudan from the 16th to the 18th century'. *Bulletin*, SOAS (1962).

— *The Sword of Truth*. Oxford University Press, New York, 1973.

— *See also* Abdullah and Uthman above.

Hogben, S. J., and Kirk-Greene, A. H. M. *The Emirates of Northern Nigeria*. Oxford University Press, Nigeria, 1968.

Hunwick, J. O., 'The influence of Arabic in West Africa', *Transactions of the Historical Society of Ghana* (Accra, 1964).

Johnson, S., *The History of the Yorubas*, compiled by his brother O. Johnson. G. Rutledge & Sons, London, 1921.

Johnston, H. A. S., *A Selection of Hausa Stories*. Clarendon, Oxford, 1966.

— *The Fulani Empire of Sokoto*. Oxford University Press, London, Ibadan, 1967.

Last, D. M., *The Sokoto Caliphate*. Longman, Harlow, 1968.

— 'Reform in West Africa: the *jihād* movements of the 19th century', in Ajayi and Crowder, Vol. II, 1974.

— *See* Al-Hajj.

Lovejoy, Paul, 'Long-distance trade and Islam: the case of the 19th century Hausa kola trade'. *Journal of the Historical Society of Nigeria*, 5, 4 (Lagos, 1971).

— 'The Kambarin Beriberi: the formation of a specialized group of Hausa kola traders in the 19th century'. *Journal of African History* (1973).

— 'Interregional monetary flows'. *Journal of African History*, (1974).

Low, V. N., *Three Nigerian Emirates. A Study in Oral History*. Northwestern University Press, Evanston, 1972.

McCall, D. and Bennett, N. eds., *Aspects of West African Islam*. Boston University Papers on Africa. Boston University Press, Boston, 1971.

Paden, J., *Religion and Political Culture in Kano*. University of California Press, Berkeley, 1973.

Robinson, C., *Specimens of Hausa Literature*. 1896. Gregg International, Boston, 1970.

Smith, Abdullahi (formerly H. F. C.), 'Source material for the history of the Western Sudan'. *Journal of the Historical Society of Nigeria*, 1 (1958).

Collateral Reading

Akintoye, S. A., *Revolution and Power Politics in Yorubaland 1840–1893*. Longman, Harlow, 1971.

Boahen, Adu, *Britain, the Sahara and the Western Sudan 1788–1861*. Oxford University Press, Oxford, 1964.

Brenner, Louis, *The Shehus of Kukawa*. Oxford University Press, Oxford, 1973.

Brown, W., 'The Caliphate of Hamdullahi (Macina)'. Ph.D. Thesis, University of Wisconsin, 1969.

Cambridge History of Islam. Ed. P. M. Holt, *et al.* 2 vols. Cambridge University Press, Cambridge, 1971.

Colvin, L., 'Islam and the state of Kajor: a case of successful resistance to *jihād*'. *Journal of African History* (1974).

Curtin, P., '*Jihād* in West Africa: early phases and interrelations in Mauritania and Senegal'. *Journal of African History* (1971).

Derman, W., and Derman, L., *Serfs, Peasants and Socialists*. University of California Press, Berkeley, 1973.

Dudley, B. J., *Parties and Politics in Northern Nigeria*. F. Cass, London, 1968.

Hill, P., *Rural Hausa*. Cambridge University Press, Cambridge, 1972.

Hunwick, J. O., 'Religion and state in the Songhay Empire, 1464–1591', in I. M. Lewis, 1966.

— 'Songhay, Bornu and Hausaland in the 16th century', in Ajayi and Crowder, Vol. I, 1971.

Khadduri, M., *War and Peace in the Law of Islam*. Johns Hopkins Press, Baltimore, 1955.

Lewis, I. M., ed., *Islam in Tropical Africa*. International African Seminar of 1964. Oxford University Press, London, 1966.

Muffett, D. J. M., *Concerning Brave Captains*. Deutsch, London, 1964.

Oloruntimehin, B., *The Segu Tukulor Empire*. Longman, Harlow, 1972.

Robinson, D., 'The Islamic reform movement of Futa Toro'. *International Journal of African Historical Studies* (Boston University Press, Boston, 1975).

Schacht, J., *An Introduction to Islamic Law*. Clarendon, Oxford, 1964.

Smith, M., *Baba of Karo*. Faber, London, 1954.

Smith, M. G., *Government in Zazzau 1800–1950*. International African Institute, London, 1960.

Smith, R., *Kingdoms of the Yoruba*. Methuen & Co., London, 1969.

Sow, A. I., *Chroniques et Récits du Fouta Djalon*. Klincksieck, Paris, 1968.

Whitaker, S., *The Politics of Tradition*. Princeton University Press, Princeton, 1970.

Willis, J. R., '*Jihād fī sabīl-Allāh*. Its doctrinal basis and some aspects of its evolution in 19th century West Africa'. *Journal of African History* (1967).

—'The Western Sudan from the Moroccan invasion to the death of al-Mukhtar al-Kunti (1591–1811)', in Ajayi and Crowder, Vol. I, 1971.

Chapter Five

Osei Bonsu and the Political Economy of the Asante Empire

PLATE 5.1 *The Pra River, dividing the Asante heartland from the southern provinces*

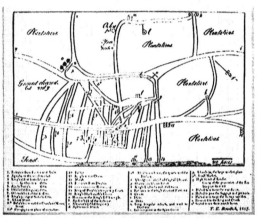

PLATE 5.2 *Bowdich's sketch of Kumasi (see page 165).*

PLATE 5.3 *Palace of the king's nephew and Dupuis' residence*

PLATE 5.4 *Asante priests invoking the national deities (see Document 24)*

INTRODUCTION

In this chapter we study the Asante Empire of West Africa during the reign of its king Osei Bonsu. We will not be looking at a period of state formation, as in the Zulu and Sotho chapters, nor an era of constitutional change, as in Sokoto and Buganda. Rather, our focus will be on Asante's political and economic responses to substantial challenges from areas near the fringe of the empire. In the north, the *jihād* of Uthman dan Fodio was making its influence felt in both commercial and religious terms. On the coast to the south, the British tried to abolish the transatlantic slave trade, a major part of the economy. Finally, strong independence movements emerged within the empire during Osei Bonsu's reign. These movements did not disrupt the fundamental stability of the heartland, but they did affect the implementation of imperial policy.

The Asante heartlands lay at a crucial crossroads of trade and production, near the southern edge of the savanna but still close to the coast. This part of the forest was rich in kola nuts, picked from a tree, and in gold, obtained by panning and by surface mining. Since the fifteenth century, traders had been operating along the routes connecting the goldfields and the Niger River. The gold they brought north stimulated the growth of the Songhay Empire and the trans-Saharan trade. At about the same time, Portuguese traders established commercial factories and forts along what became known as the 'Gold Coast' and began to divert some of the gold away from the northern networks. They and the other European merchants also dealt in slaves. The slave trade came to dominate other aspects of commerce until the British began their campaign against it in the early nineteenth century.

Prior to the middle of the seventeenth century the founders of the Asante state moved into the strategic area around Kumasi, close to the principal trade routes and markets. Like most of the inhabitants of southern Ghana and southeastern Ivory Coast, they were Akan people speaking the Twi language and following a matrilineal principle of succession to property and office. They formed six small city-states of which one—Kumasi—soon became dominant. The crucial period of transformation from a collection of settlements to a cohesive kingdom occurred in the last three decades of the seventeenth century, and the pivotal leader was a Kumasi prince named Osei Tutu.

As a young man he had learned the arts of government and war at the courts of two existing Akan powers, Denkyira and Akwamu. Later, Akwamu provided assistance to Osei Tutu in throwing off the yoke of Denkyira, which controlled the area occupied by Asante. In the process of establishing independence from Denkyira the Asante state was born and Osei Tutu became the first king or 'Asantehene'.

To consolidate his gains, seal the union of the six settlements, and establish the primacy of Kumasi, Osei Tutu developed the basic social charter of the state, a constitution which is called the 'Golden Stool'. The architect of the story and meaning of the Golden Stool was Okomfo Anokye, a priest and counsellor to the king. According to tradition, Anokye brought down from the sky a wooden stool covered with gold. He caused the stool to alight gently on the knees of Osei Tutu.

The story has long been accepted by most Asante as a way of portraying the primacy of Kumasi over the other five provinces, their 'stools' (offices), and chiefs. Kumasi's pre-eminence entitled the Asantehene to require the other leaders to provide troops for national campaigns and make contributions to the national treasury. He heard appeals from their courts and required their attendance at his annual festival—the Odwira—before they conducted their own.

As Osei Tutu founded the kingdom, so Opoku Ware (ruled *c.* 1720–50) expanded and transformed Asante into an empire. He conquered the tier of states to the south of Kumasi (Wassa, Assin, Akyem Kotoko, Akyem Abuakwa, Akwapim and Akwamu, in addition to the already-incorporated Denkyira). At several points he pushed through to the coast, opening up direct commercial relations with the Europeans. To the north, Opoku Ware extended Asante control and influence over most of today's northern Ghana (especially Gyaman, Gonja and Dagomba). By the time he died, Asante consisted of an area approaching 100 000 square miles, embracing 1–2 million people.

To administer these vast dominions, three of his successors—Osei Kwadwo (1764–77), Osei Kwame (1777–*c.* 1798), and Osei Bonsu (*c.* 1800–23)—established an extensive bureaucracy. They strengthened the position of Kumasi at the expense of the five other chiefdoms in the heartland, and the role of appointed officials at the expense of all hereditary leaders. The results were a capital city of about 20 000 people (see Document 3) and a highly centralized administration loyal to the Asantehene. The administration was divided into three principal departments; finance, political service, and provincial administration.

The Gyaasewahene (Opoku Frefre in the early nineteenth century, see Document 5) directed the finance section, the most elaborate part of the bureaucracy. He oversaw the collection of revenue from taxes of various kinds: tribute, road tolls, death duties and poll taxes. Both the form and amount of payments required varied depending on commodity values and the state's needs. Another major source of income consisted of profits from gold, ivory and kola nut enterprises. The financial department kept records both in the traditional system of cowries and in Arabic, with the assistance of the largely foreign Muslim community in Kumasi (see Documents 1, 5 and 26).

The political service handled the arbitration and negotiation of disputes (called 'palavers' in many of the documents). At the top echelon of the service were several 'linguists'; below them came a whole range of swordbearers, messengers, Muslim scribes and others. The linguists' most important responsibilities were to

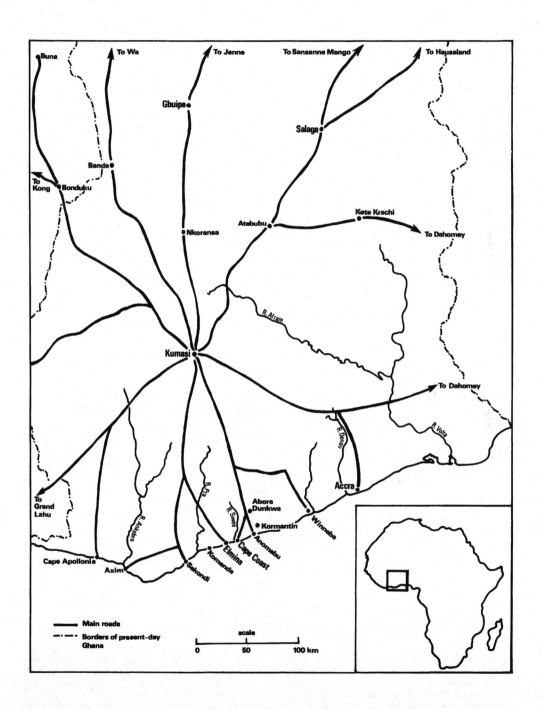

Buna

To Wa

To Jenne

To Sansanne Mango

To Hausaland

Gbuipe

Salaga

Banda

To Kong

Bonduku

Kete Krachi

Nkoransa

Atebubu

To Dahomey

R. Afram

Kumasi

To Dahomey

R. Densu

R. Volta

To Grand Lahu

R. Pra

Abora Dunkwa

Accra

R. Swee

Kormantin

Winneba

R. Ankobra

Anomabu

Cape Apollonia

Axim

Komenda

Elmina

Cape Coast

Sekondi

— Main roads

scale

·−·−· Borders of present-day Ghana

0   50   100 km

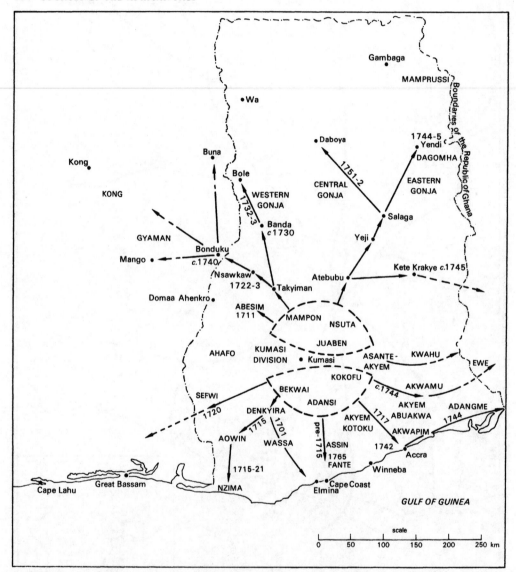

MAP 5.2   *The Asante Empire showing main directions of expansion in the eighteenth century*

negotiate acceptable solutions to problems in order to avoid warfare. When such attempts failed, linguists accompanied the Asante forces and worked on the peace agreements once military operations had ceased.

The provincial administration governed the non-Asante areas conquered by Opoku Ware and the other

rulers. It functioned in two ways. First, each subject chief was assigned a patron at Kumasi to serve as his inter-mediary at the court. Secondly, the king placed his own representatives at the courts of the subject chiefs to monitor their activities. These commissioners worked closely with the other branches of the bureaucracy,

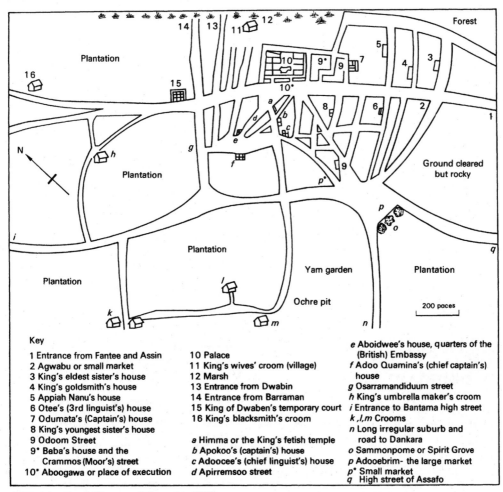

Key

1 Entrance from Fantee and Assin
2 Agwabu or small market
3 King's eldest sister's house
4 King's goldsmith's house
5 Appiah Nanu's house
6 Otee's (3rd linguist's) house
7 Odumata's (Captain's) house
8 King's youngest sister's house
9 Odoom Street
9* Baba's house and the
    Crammos (Moor's) street
10* Aboogawa or place of execution

10 Palace
11 King's wives' croom (village)
12 Marsh
13 Entrance from Dwabin
14 Entrance from Barraman
15 King of Dwaben's temporary court
16 King's blacksmith's croom

a Himma or the King's fetish temple
b Apokoo's (captain's) house
c Adoocee's (chief linguist's) house
d Apirremsoo street

e Aboidwee's house, quarters of the
   (British) Embassy
f Adoo Quamina's (chief captain's)
   house
g Osarramandiduum street
h King's umbrella maker's croom
i Entrance to Bantama high street
k,l,m Crooms
n Long irregular suburb and
   road to Dankara
o Sammonpome or Spirit Grove
p Adooebrim- the large market
p* Small market
q High street of Assafo

MAP 5.3 Bowdich's map of Kumasi in 1817

assisting finance in the collection of tribute and the linguists in settling disputes.

As Osei Bonsu took power in about 1800, the Asante Empire consisted of three geographic areas and three administrative levels. At the centre and top were Kumasi and the king's palace. It included all the major departments, whose heads formed an inner council which assisted the king in most of the tasks of government. The second tier consisted of the other Asante city-states. They controlled their internal affairs to some degree and participated intimately in the political, military and ceremonial activities of the capital. These two tiers con-

stituted the heartland. The last tier was the large group of non-Asante provinces which, unlike the heartland, were subject to tribute. Uniting all three levels and regions of the empire was the National Assembly. It consisted of representatives from the heartland and many of the provinces and met annually at the time of the Odwira festival to consider the most important decisions affecting the empire.

The main sources for Asante in the early nineteenth century come from European traders, travellers and administrators. Three of the accounts (Huydecoper, 1816–17, Bowdich, 1817, and Dupuis, 1820) are set in

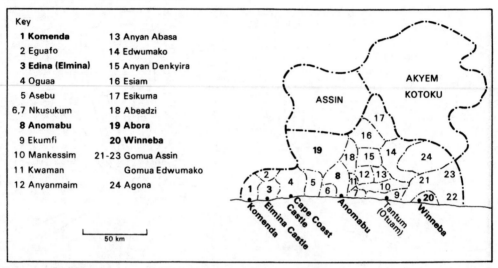

Key

1 Komenda   13 Anyan Abasa
2 Eguafo   14 Edwumako
3 Edina (Elmina) 15 Anyan Denkyira
4 Oguaa   16 Esiam
5 Asebu   17 Esikuma
6,7 Nkusukum   18 Abeadzi
8 Anomabu   **19 Abora**
9 Ekumfi   **20 Winneba**
10 Mankessim   21-23 Gomua Assin
11 Kwaman   Gomua Edwumako
12 Anyanmaim   24 Agona

50 km

MAP 5.4   The Fante states

Kumasi. In order to approach an Asante perspective, the historian should compare the nationality, vocation and experience of the European authors.

DOCUMENTARY NARRATIVE

The Accession of Osei Bonsu and the Clarification of Asante's Northern Policy

The last part of the eighteenth century marked a period of great prosperity for the rulers of the Asante Empire. Underlying their good fortune was the commercial policy of King Osei Kwame which emphasized Asante participation in the Muslim-dominated trading networks extending north to the Niger River. At this time, however, many Asante officials resented the king's apparent fascination with Islam, a fascination they believed endangered the Asante constitution. Tensions mounted until 1798 when Osei Kwame was deposed. The following account of Kwame's downfall comes from the journal of Joseph Dupuis, a British agent who visited Kumasi in 1820. Dupuis' knowledge of Arabic enabled him to gain a great deal of information from Muslims who served in the Kumasi administration, co-ordinated trade with the north, or represented their provinces at court. Document 1 is based in part on dynastic annals originally recorded in Arabic.

DOCUMENT 1
'A believer at heart'

Dupuis' version of the deposition of Osei Kwame in 1798. Joseph Dupuis, *Journal of a Residence in Ashanti* (1824), p. 245.

NOTES FOR READING   Sai Koamina = Osei Kwame; Bashaw = 'pasha', the title ascribed by Dupuis to Muhammed al-Ghamba, the head of the Muslim community of Kumasi.

[The origin of his deposition] was his attachment to the Moslems, and, as it is said, his inclination to establish the Korannic law for the civil code of the empire. Sai Koamina, according to the Bashaw, was a believer at heart; but the safety of his throne would not allow him to avow his sentiments. His name is handed to posterity as the most merciful of the race of kings. Towards the close of his reign, he prohibited many festivals at which it was usual to spill the blood of victims devoted to the customs; yet he could not be prevailed upon to relinquish the barbarous practice of watering the graves of his ancestors with human gore. These and other innovations were of a tendency to alarm the great captains; they feared, it is said, that the Moslem religion, which they well know levels all ranks and orders of men, and places them at the arbitrary discretion of the sovereign might be introduced, whereby they would lose that ascendancy they now enjoy. To anticipate the calamity they dreaded, a conspiracy was entered into, and he was deposed.

Asante struggled for several years against supporters of Osei Kwame who were concentrated near the empire's northern and northwestern borders in Gyaman, Buna and Gbuipe. A new Asantehene died unexpectedly in about 1800 and Osei Bonsu came to power. With the help of Adinkra, the loyalist ruler of Gyaman, the new king won a decisive victory in about 1801.

One consequence of that victory was the capture of several thousand Muslim prisoners, some of whom were sold into the transatlantic slave trade. One of them went to Jamaica and ultimately wrote a short autobiography in Arabic. His story provides impressions of the vast trading networks of the savannah and the forest as well as the perils of warfare.

DOCUMENT 2
'On that day was I made a slave'

From G. C. Renouard's translation of the autobiography of Abu Bakr al-Siddiq, 'Routes in North Africa by Abu Bakr es-Siddik', *Journal of the Royal Geographical Society*, vol. 6 (1836), pp. 102–07. Ivor Wilks has recently edited a new version of Abu Bakr's story in P. D. Curtin, ed., *Africa Remembered* (1967), pp. 152–63.

NOTES FOR READING Tumbut = Timbuktu; Jenneh = Jenne; Ghónah = Buna, one of the areas in conflict with Asante at this time; Misr = Egypt; Kashinah = Katsina; Bernú = Bornu; Kong = an important state west of Buna; *al-woda* = cowries; Buntukkú = Bonduku, the capital of Gyaman; Adingharah = Adinkra; Askumà and Ajimmakúh = towns on one trade route to the coast; Daghoh = Lago, east of Cape Coast.

'My name is Abú Bekr eṣ ṣiddík: my birth-place is Tumbut. I was educated in the town of Jenneh (Genneh), and fully instructed in reading and construing the Korán,—but in the interpretation of it by the help of commentaries. This was (done) in the city of Ghónah, where there are many learned men (ulemà), who are not natives of one place, but each of them, having quitted his own country, has come and settled there. . .

'Before all these things happened my father used to travel about (continually). He went into the land of Kashinah and Bernú. There he married my mother and then returned to Tumbut, to which place my mother followed him. It came to pass after this, that he remembered his brethren, repented on account of them and wept bitterly. He then ordered his slaves to make ready for their departure with him (on a journey) to visit his brethren, (and see) whether they were in (good) health or not. They, therefore, obeyed their master's orders, and did so; and went to the town of Jenneh, and from thence to Kong, and afterwards to Ghónah. There they abode and continued to serve their master, collecting much gold for him there. In that country much gold is found in the plains, banks of rivers, rocks, and stones. They break the stones, and grind them, and reduce them to dust. This is then put into vessels,

and washed with water till the gold is all collected under the water in the vessels, and the dust lies above it. They then pour out this mud upon the ground, and the gold remains in the vessels; and they spread it out to dry. After that, they try it (on a touchstone), and make such things of it as they are able. For money or exchange they use shells, called al woda', gold and silver; they also barter goods for goods, according to the measure of their value.

'My father collected much gold in that country, and sent much to his father-in-law; together with horses, asses, mules, and very valuable silk garments brought from Misr, with much wealth, as a present to him. He was my mother's father; his name was Al Háij Muhammed Tafsír, of the countries of Bernú and Kashínah, both inhabited by his family.

After this my father fell ill of a fever, and died in the city of Ghónah . . .

'About five years after my father's death, I asked my instructor, who taught me the Korán, to go with me to the city of Ghónah to visit my father's grave. He answered, 'Yea, Abŭ Bekr as-siddík, if it please God, I will do that thou dost desire." He then prepared himself, and sought for provision for the road: and he was followed by a large company of his disciples, who bewailed him. We reached the city of Kong, and afterwards went on to the city of Ghónah: and there abode a long time, reckoning that country as our own. We found protection in that country. Two years after our arrival in Ghónah, it entered into my teacher's heart to set out on the pilgrimage; and while he was making diligent inquiries from people who were going to perform the pilgrimage, some men told him of the business of Mohammed Keshín and his brother 'Omar, and Adam, of the land of Buntukkú. He then began to make inquiries of the people of Buntukkú, and they told him that Omar and Mohammed Keshín had departed, and had left Adam behind; that he was not (now) going, but wished to go. My master made haste to seek for him in some of the towns, and left me in the city of Ghónah with my uncle Mahmúd.

'At this time we heard the news of the business of Adingharah, Sultán of Buntukkú . . .

'Then was Adinkarah very wroth; and he ordered all his captains to gather all their soldiers together, and follow him to make war against Kujóh, and to kill him, that they might avenge the death of his servant Dikkí. When the Sultán of Ghónah heard that Adinkarah, Sultán of Buntukkú, and his army, had come against them to kill them, he and all his host together with Kujóh, rose up to meet them, and marched against them as far as the town of Bolóh, choosing to attack them there; and there they fought from mid-day till evening. Then they separated, and returned to their own places. Seven days afterwards, they again gathered themselves together, and engaged in battle, at the town of Amvighóh. It was a hard-fought battle, and many souls perished on that day. Thus did Adinkarah overcome the King of Ghónah, and take the town of Amvighóh. The people of Ghónah fled, and some of them passed on (as far as) to the city of Kong.

'On that day was I made a slave. They tore off my clothes, bound me with ropes, laid on me a heavy burden, and carried me to the town of Buntukkú, and from thence to the town of Kumásí, the King of Ashantí's town. From thence through

Askumá and Ajimmakúh, in the land of Fantí, to Daghóh, near the salt sea.

'There they sold me to the Christians, and I was bought by a certain captain of a ship at that town. He sent me to a boat, and delivered me to the people of the ship. We continued on board ship, at sea, for three months, and then came on shore in the land of Jamaica. This was the beginning of my slavery until this day. I tasted the bitterness of slavery from them, and its oppressiveness: but praise be to God, under whose power are all things, He doth whatsoever he willeth! . . .

'The faith of our families is the faith of Islám. They circumcise the foreskin; say the five prayers; fast every year in the month of Ramadán; give alms as ordained in the law; marry (only) four free women—a fourth is forbidden to them except she be their slave; they fight for the faith of God; perform the pilgrimage (to Mecca)—*i.e.* such as are able so to do; eat the flesh of no beast but what they have slain for themselves; drink no wine—for whatever intoxicates is forbidden unto them; they do not keep company with those whose faith is contrary to theirs,—such as worshippers of idols, men who swear falsely by the name of the Lord, who dishonour their parents, commit murder or robbery, bear false witness, are covetous, proud, insolent, hypocrites, unclean in their discourse, or do any other thing that is forbidden: they teach their children to read, and (instruct them in) the different parts of knowledge; their minds are perfect and blameless according to the measure of their faith.

'Verily I have erred and done wickedly, but I entreat God to guide my heart in the right path, for He knoweth what is in my heart, and whatever (can be pleaded) in my behalf.

'Finished in the month of August, on the 29th day, in the year of the Messiah 1834 (1835).'

Osei Bonsu launched a period of renewed prosperity and expansion. During most of his reign he controlled the bureaucracy and Asante chiefs and successfully negotiated the 'palavers' of the provinces. The following documents give first-hand impressions of Osei Bonsu and his capital as they appeared in 1816 and 1817. We assume that these accounts accurately portray the situation which existed several years earlier. Document 3 is from the journal of W. Huydecoper, a mulatto envoy who came to Kumasi on behalf of the Dutch in 1816. Huydecoper spoke fluent Twi, the language of the Asante. Document 4 is the work of T. E. Bowdich, a British representative from Cape Coast castle who journeyed to Kumasi in 1817. Unlike Huydecoper and Dupuis, Bowdich did not possess any special language skills.

DOCUMENT 3
'The glory of being a king myself'

From Huydecoper's diary, 22 May 1816. W. Huydecoper, 'The Journal of the Visit to Kumasi of W. Huydecoper, 28 April 1816 to 28 May 1817', mimeographed translation by G. Irwin (1962), pp. 24—6.

NOTES FOR READING   Important dignitaries were carried in hammocks or baskets; *sabeldragers* = sword-bearers; the umbrellas which protected the dignitaries were another sign of high office.

When I came into the town itself, what a sight met my eyes! The road was so full of people that neither sticks nor swords could keep them away from me. Many blows were rained on heads and backs before it was possible for my men to get my hammock through. We were in this stifling throng for more than an hour.

Orders then came through that we were to wait until further notice under a nearby tree, since the assembly was not in fact yet ready to receive us. And so we sat under this tree, but the people pressed closer and closer, streaming in from all sides in the hope of catching a glimpse of me. After we had been under the tree for a quarter of an hour, a house was pointed out to me as a possible refuge where we might be free of constant observation by the crowd. We therefore moved into this house and were able to enjoy a moment's peace.

At two o'clock I received orders from 4 more *sabeldragers* sent by His Majesty that I was to present myself at the capital, dressed in proper attire. With all eight *sabeldragers* leading the way, I set out, reaching the capital after half an hour's journey.

And what a tumult greeted me there! A king could not have expected more honour than was done to me today. There are more than 50 thousand people in this place. His Majesty has summoned all the lesser kings from the surrounding countryside for today's assembly. Every one of them was splendidly adorned with gold, and each had more than 50 soldiers in his retinue. There were golden swords, flutes, horns, and I know not what else in profusion. At the assembly I counted more than 50 large umbrellas (this figure does not include small ones).

When I saw all this, I felt very grateful for His Majesty's courtesy towards me. I got out of my hammock, and walked from person to person, shaking each by the hand until I came to the King. I bowed to His Majesty three times. No word was spoken during these proceedings. I must have shaken the hands of two hundred people today. Throughout the ceremony music was provided by drums, which were in position all around us, and the whole affair was marked by perfect order. Behind the King stood at least 100 men with muskets. They seemed quite as well disciplined on parade as European soldiers. 50 or 60 women were grouped around His Majesty, wearing golden ornaments of great value. But there was so much to see that I cannot now recall it all.

I also had to pay my compliments to the King's women. They were standing apart from the men. There were at least 200 of them, all handsome and decked with large pieces of fetish gold. I did not shake hands with them for it is not the custom.

His Majesty led me to a raised place under a tall tree where I sat to receive the appropriate return greetings from the King and from all his councillors, generals, captains and others. And now I experienced the glory of being a king myself, sitting in such majesty as I would have expected to find only in Europe. There was I, enthroned on a large Negro stool on a kind of platform, with my flag planted about 20 paces in front of me and all my men behind. Each king in turn came to greet me, to the accompaniment of loud music and great numbers of soldiers, and riding in a sort of basket under a great umbrella. The kings remained in their baskets until they were about 10 paces distant from me, when they dismounted with dignity and advanced towards me on foot. Each shook hands cordially three times and then three times again. These proceedings lasted from 3 o'clock until 6. Then His Majesty in full splendour came to greet me himself, sitting in a basket like the others, and accompanied by women carrying swords, golden basins, gold and silver water jugs, etc. He came up to me and shook my hand three times. For at least 5 minutes he stood looking at me, and then said, three times: 'Welcome! Welcome! Welcome!' and, laughing in a friendly way, added, 'You will do. I like you.' Then he said once again, 'Welcome!' and withdrew, accompanied by a vast throng of his followers. After this 10 other persons greeted me, all of them dignified by large umbrellas. It was past 7 in the evening before the ceremony ended. His Majesty's 'great linguist' approached, and told me that I should now follow him and he would show me my lodgings. He also offered me four jars of palm wine, which were a present from the King. I accepted these with pleasure, and set out for my house.

DOCUMENT 4
'The benevolence of his disposition'

Bowdich's estimate of Osei Bonsu. T. E. Bowdich, *Mission from Cape Coast Castle to Ashantee* (1819), pp. 246–8.

The King's private character is amiable; the children of his brothers share the fondness and indulgence which endear him to his own, and his few moments of recreation are the liveliest of theirs. The circumstances connected with the various instances which we witnessed of his generosity to others, justify me in ascribing it to the benevolence of his disposition. His admiration of ingenious rather than splendid novelty, has frequently imposed the appearance of a covetousness, scarcely culpable from his reverence for invention, and the amazement its extent excited . . .

He dismissed us twice with apologies for not proceeding to business, confessing, the first time, that he had been unusually irritated just after he sent for us, and had not recovered his calmness; the latter, that some agreeable news had induced him to drink more than fitted him to hear great palavers like ours. In his judicial administration, a lie always aggravated the punishment, and truth generally extenuated, and sometimes atoned of itself for the offence: he invariably anticipated the temerity of perjury, where convicting evidence was to be opposed to the accused. The King's manners are a happy mixture of dignity and affability, they engage rather than encourage, and his general deportment is conciliating though repressive. He speaks well, and more logically than most of his council, who are diffuse, but his superior talent is marked in the shrewd questions by which he fathoms a design or a narrative. He excels in courtesy, is wisely inquisitive, and candid in his comparisons: war, legislature, and mechanism,

were his favourite topics in our private conversations. The great, but natural fault of the King is his ambition; I do not think it has ever proved superior to the pledge of his honour, but it certainly has, and that frequently, to his sense of justice, which is repressed rather than impaired by it.

Bowdich spent a great deal of time observing the work of one of the king's most powerful officials, the Gyaasewahene, Opoku Frefre (Document 5). A man of rather modest origins, Opoku had received Osei Kwame's appointment as head of the financial department about 1790 and remained Gyaasewahene until his death in 1826. Opoku's rise to power in Asante was not anomalous. The career of Agyei, one of Osei Bonsu's linguists, presents another example of social mobility (Document 6).

DOCUMENT 5
'Exchequer court'

Bowdich's description of Opoku Frefre's activities. Bowdich, *Mission*, pp. 296–7.

NOTES FOR READING Apokoo = Opoku Frefre; Moorish = Muslim; Hio = Oyo, the Yoruba capital and kingdom; captains = officials.

Apokoo is the keeper of the royal treasury, and has the care of all the tributes, which are deposited, separately, in a large apartment of the palace, of which he only has the key. Numerous and various as the sums are, he disposes of them by a local association which is said to be infallible with him, for the Moorish secretary, (who resided some time at Hio,) only records the greater political events. Apokoo holds a sort of exchequer court at his own house daily, (when he is attended by two of the King's linguists, and various state insignia,) to decide all cases affecting tribute or revenue, and the appeal to the King is seldom resorted to. He generally reclined on his lofty bed, (of accumulated cushions, and covered with a large rich cloth or piece of silk,) with two or three of his handsomest wives near him, whilst the pleadings were going forward. He was always much gratified when I attended, and rose to seat me beside him. I observed that all calculations were made, explained, and recorded, by cowries. In one instance, after being convinced by a variety of evidence that a public debtor was unable to pay gold, he commuted sixteen ounces of gold, for twenty men slaves. Several captains, who were his followers, attended this court daily with large suites, and it was not only a crowded, but frequently a splendid scene. Before the footoorh or treasury bag is unlocked by the weigher, though it be by the King's order, Apokoo must strike it with his hand in sanction.

DOCUMENT 6
'From carrying salt to hard palavers'

Bowdich's description of Agyei's career. Bowdich, *Mission*, pp. 248–9.

NOTES FOR READING Agay = Agyei; Aquoomo = Akwamu; caboceer = chief; Amanqua = Amankwa, a general; Cudjo Cooma = Kwadwo Kuma, ruler of Akyem Abuakwa (see Document 10); Adoosee = Adusei, first linguist; Otee = Oti Panin, fourth linguist; take fetish = to swear.

Agay, when a boy, carried salt from Aquoomo to Coomassie for sale; he was afterwards taken into the service of Aquootoo, caboceer of that place, against whom the government had instituted a palaver, but wrongfully. Agay accompanied the caboceer when he was sent for to Coomassie for judgment. After the King's messengers had spoken, misrepresenting the case in preference to confessing the King to be in the wrong, and the caboceer was confused, this boy suddenly rose, and said, to use the words of the narrators, 'King, you have people to wash you, to feed you, to serve you, but you have no people to speak the truth to you, and tell you when God does not like your palaver.' The assembly cried out unanimously, that the boy might be hurried away and his head taken off; but the King said, 'No! let him finish'; and Agay is said to have spoken three hours, and to have disclosed and argued the palaver to the King's conviction, and his master's acquittal. He was retained to attend the King, but treated with no particular distinction. A serious palaver occurring between two principal men, it was debated before the council, who were at a loss to decide, but inclined to the man whom the King doubted; judgment was suspended. In the interim the King sent Agay, privately, to the house of each, to hear their palavers in turn, tête-à-tête; he did so, and when the King asked him who he thought was right, he confirmed his impression. 'Now', said the King, 'I know you have a good head.' Agay was then made a Linguist, and presented with a house, wives, slaves, and gold. Sometime afterwards, the King confessing a prejudice against a wealthy captain, his linguists, always inclined to support him, said, 'If you wish to take his stool from him, we will make the palaver'; but Agay sprung up, exclaiming, 'No, King, that is not good; that man never did you any wrong, you know all the gold of your subjects is your's at their death, but if you get all now, strangers will go away and say, only the King has gold, and that will not be good, but let them say the King has gold, all his captains have gold, and all his people have gold, then your country will look handsome, and the bush people fear you.' For this the King made him second linguist, and much increased his property. When Amanqua had the command of the army against Cudjo Cooma, the King asked him which linguist he would take, he replied, Adoosee or Otee; the King said, no! I will give you this boy, he has the best head for hard palavers. Amanqua urged that he was too young, the King told him he was a fool to say so. He then made Amanqua take fetish with him to report the merits of Agay faithfully, who distinguished himself so much, that he is always employed in difficult foreign palavers.

At the time of Osei Bonsu's accession, Asante's major northern trading exchange was in Gbuipe which, like Gyaman, was a centre of unrest. The Asantehene and his councillors decided to shift the emphasis of Asante's northern commerce to Salaga in eastern Gonja. Salaga was on the main route to Hausaland where Uthman dan Fodio's *jihād* had spawned a vast increase in the demand for kola nuts. These nuts (sometimes called 'Gooroo' or 'Boosoo' nuts in the documents) grew in abundance in the forests of Asante and were the only stimulant acceptable to the Muslim reformers (see Document 20 of Chapter Four). Document 7 presents a Gonja Muslim's account of the growth of the Salaga market.

DOCUMENT 7
'Then the market . . . was moved to Salaga'

Mahmud ibn Abdullahi's 'Qissatu Salaga' ('Story of Salaga'), trans. Mahmoud el-Wakkad, *Ghana Notes and Queries*, Vol. 3 (1961), pp. 24–8.

NOTES FOR READING Gufi = Gbuipe; Salga = Salaga; Kachina = Katsina; Malam = cleric or teacher; Baribari = Bornuese; Zugu = Zongo, a foreign quarter; Kilinga = trade centre to the northeast of Salaga.

Then the market of Gufi (Gbuipe) was moved to Salga after they had held it at Umfaha (Mpaha) for some time. Then war broke out at Kachina (Katsina) and they captured the village of Beno, where there was a notable called Malam Chediya. He came to Salga and was given land where he built (a house) and lived worshipping Allah. He had his people, and he built for them and for his guests (a compound) called 'The Learned Man's Compound'. He also built a Mosque there. It is the first Mosque at Salga.

He made Malam Musa, who was a native of Salga, its Imam. His descendents are there up till now . . .

Then (some) Baribari (Bornuese) came and asked for land. They were given land under a big tree. They built on it. They built a mosque. Their descendants are there up till now.

Then (came) a great shaikh from Zugu Kilinga (in northern Dahomey) . . . He was a pious man. His sole interest was to study and to worship Allah. He had many sons, who were all learned men. He settles there (i.e. Salaga). His descendants are there up till now, and they are learned men.

So Salga became a town with a population of different races. There is no big market except Salga. The first people treated kindly by the people of Gonja are the people of Salga. They never treat them unjustly.

The Hausa used to come to it (i.e. Salaga) with their belongings and trade in kola nuts.

Despite the restoration of order in Gyaman and Gbuipe and the demonstrated loyalty of officials such as Gyamanhene Adinkra (see Document 2), the king continued to channel trade through Salaga for the rest of his reign. In 1808 he emancipated a large number of Muslim slaves, a decision which probably strengthened commercial ties with the Sokoto Caliphate. Osei Bonsu's forthright stand against the northwestern dissidents apparently convinced the Asante council of his capacity to discriminate between

Muslim commerce and the Muslim creed. Although he employed Muslim record-keepers at court and maintained close ties with the Islamic community in Kumasi, Osei Bonsu was never accused of infidelity to the Golden Stool.

Consolidating Hegemony in the South

Significant Asante commercial interests also extended to the south, where European traders and trading companies had competed for gold, slaves and ivory since the sixteenth century. The merchants worked out of about forty forts and posts strung along the 350-mile coastline known as the 'Gold Coast'. Most were Danish, Dutch or British, whose respective headquarters were at Accra, Elmina and Cape Coast (see maps).

Between the Asante heartland and the European forts lay two tiers of small states. The tier closest to Kumasi and the coastal states in the vicinity of Accra and Elmina acknowledged Asante authority by paying tribute. The Danish and Dutch forts in these coastal areas also sent Kumasi annual payments (called 'notes' in the documents). However, the Fante states lying between Elmina and Accra resisted Asante rule. Their resistance coloured the attitudes of the British, whose forts were concentrated in this central section.

Fante areas were natural havens for those fleeing Asante justice. Document 8 recounts how the asylum given to two such dissidents ('Cheboo' and 'Quacoe Apoutay') by the Fante town of Anomabu ('Annamaboe') ultimately led to an Asante military occupation and the involvement of the British from the nearby fort.

DOCUMENT 8
'The confrontations of 1806–1807'

Henry Meredith, *An Account of the Gold Coast of Africa* (1812), pp. 132–5, 155–61.

NOTES FOR READING   Cheboo = elderly and blind ruler of the southern part of Assin; Quacoe Apoutay = deputy to Cheboo; Amoo = ruler of the northern part of Assin; cabbocier = caboceer or chief; Assecoomah = a northern Fante state; Appey Dougah = Apea Dunkwa, an Asante general; Abrah = Abora; Braffoes = Fante of the Abora state; the Muslim with the Koranic 'sentences' is from Katsina in Hausaland; Mr White = British Governor of Anomabu fort. The document is in two parts: the disputes of 1806 and the meeting of the British with Osei Bonsu following Asante's siege of Anomabu in June 1807. Meredith was an English trader who witnessed many of the events he describes.

The Assin country lies at the rear of the Fantee, and borders on the Ashantee country. It was divided into two states: the one governed by king Cheboo and Quacoe Apoutay; and the other by king Amoo. Apoutay, although not elevated to the dignity of king, held equal sway with Cheboo; but they were each subordinate to the king of Ashantee. A man of opulence died in Amoo's town; and, as is customary on such occasions, gold and other valuable articles were deposited with the body in the grave. On this occasion, one of Cheboo's people was present, and seeing what was done, watched an opportunity to rob the grave; which he effected, and escaped with the treasure. Amoo his neighbour sought redress of Cheboo and Apoutay; but without success: he then laid the affair before the king of Ashantee; who summoned all the parties before him, gave them an impartial hearing, and awarded in favour of Amoo. Quacoe Apoutay was detained as a hostage until restitution should be made: but he, in a short time, contrived to make his escape, and, when at liberty, refused to accede to the award made by the king of Ashantee. On this, Amoo attacked the town in which Cheboo and Apoutay resided, and routed his opponents: after this, at the instigation of the king of Ashantee, the parties met to settle the dispute; but Quacoe Apoutay, acting treacherously on the occasion, sent privately to Cheboo for an armed force to support him: and a battle was the consequence, which ended in the death of the man who had committed the theft, and the total defeat of Apoutay and his forces. At this crisis, the king of Ashantee, willing to bring about a peace again, interfered. He sent two gold manillas, the one to Amoo, the other to his adversary, directing them to cease all hostilities; to which both parties agreed, and took the manillas. Amoo obeyed the king; but Quacoe Apoutay attacked Amoo, and drove him in his turn from his town. Amoo, indignant at the repeated deceptions of Apoutay, obtained succours, and overthrew his treacherous opponent. The king of Ashantee, still anxious to reconcile his neighbours, and unwilling to draw his sword, presented two gold swords and an axe to Amoo, and recommended him to conciliate Quacoe Apoutay, and terminate their quarrels. Amoo consented to obey the king, but in the mean time was again attacked by his implacable foe, and totally defeated, and lost in the contest the golden sword and hatchet. His opponent committed ravages where-ever he came, killing messengers, and every man who fell into his hands, not sparing even the king of Ashantee's messengers! A war with the king of Ashantee followed hereupon: Quacoe Apoutay and Cheboo, dreading his vengeance, fled to the Fantee country: in consequence of which, the king sent a message to Acoom, the cabbocier or mayor of Assecoomah (a small state tributary to the king of Ashantee), accompanied by a present of twenty ounces of gold; stating the necessity of his pursuing his enemies to the Fantee country; but giving assurance of the king's pacific disposition towards the Fantees, and that his only object was to get into his possession Cheboo and Apoutay: the Fantees would not interfere, nor allow the Ashantee forces to come into their country. Upon this answer, Appey Dougah, the king of Ashantee's general, collected, by command of his master, a large force; and gave the enemy battle at Buinka, in Fantee: he displayed great gallantry, and defeated the two kings, in conjunction with the Fantee forces that had joined them. Next day, Cheboo and Apoutay having rallied their forces, and formed a junction with a fresh Fantee force, gave Appey Dougah battle; but were totally defeated, with the loss of many killed, and made prisoners: among the latter was Atia, the cabbocier of Abrah, the principal town of Fantee. A large sum was offered for his ransom, but refused;

and he was committed to the care of Acoom the cabbocier of Assecoomah, in whom the king had great confidence: but this person betrayed his trust, and liberated the enemy . . . In consequence of this conduct, Acoom became involved in the war: very shortly afterwards the king of Ashantee defeated him, and made rapid progress with his army towards the coast in search of Cheboo and Apoutay. The Fantees opposed his march, but were defeated in every onset; and the Braffoes were nearly extirpated by the Ashantees in their march. The Annamaboes, instigated by the remaining Braffoes, were impudent enough to receive and protect Cheboo and Apoutay: which proved fatal to them.

. . . .

Although these men proceeded to the Cape, it was found that nothing important could be transacted without an interview with the king; and for this purpose Colonel Torrane was obliged to go to Annamaboe, and a day was fixed for a conference. To give as favourable and as respectable an opinion as possible of the British, a number of articles as presents were sent to the king; and as many officers and soldiers as the service could afford, were assembled to attend the governor on the day appointed: but previous to these preparations, and a few days after the flag of truce was received by the king; Cheboo (one of the men who was the cause of the war) was secured by the governor at Cape Coast, and sent to Annamaboe, to be delivered up to the king, in expectation that any further effusion of blood would be prevented, and that it would be the means of saving the Fantees from entire destruction. These benevolent purposes were not realized: the king had proceeded so far in the war, that he could not recede without displeasing those auxiliaries he had with him, and who expected a vast deal of plunder; and besides, Apoutay and Acoom were again in arms, and collecting all the Fantees they could to oppose the king's progress. On the day appointed for the interview, the governor and his party were put in motion; and although the procession was not very numerous, it was arranged with taste, and made no despicable appearance. About twenty of the Company's artificers, habited in a neat manner, marched in front; a guard of forty men, and a band of music followed them; next walked the governor, followed by ten officers, two and two; and some gentlemen-traders (who were enticed from the Cape by curiosity), brought up the rear. When the procession had got a short distance, it was met by a principal man, who was sent by the king to conduct the governor, and to keep off the multitude, which was assembling in great numbers; some of whom had never seen a White man. Notwithstanding the authority of this person, and the exertions of his attendants, the curiosity of the people was so great, that every avenue was crowded; which, by preventing the circulation of air, augmented the natural heat of the day; and this inconvenience was farther increased by the putrid smell from the dead bodies, and the vast swarm of flies. The governor was obliged to visit each man of rank, before he could be received by the king; a ceremony that could not be prudently denied, and which occupied some time: for those men had their several courts, and collectively had formed an

extensive circle. Every one of them was seated under a huge umbrella, surrounded by attendants and guards, with young persons employed in fanning the air, and dispersing the flies which were numerous and troublesome. One of those men and his attendants excited some curiosity and attention: his dress and appearance were so different from those of the others, that it evidently proved, he must have come from countries situated a considerable distance inland. He was a tall, athletic, and rather corpulent man, of a complexion resembling an Arab, or an Egyptian. His dress was heavy, and by no means adapted to the climate. He wore a cap that came down below his ears; and, being made of yellow cloth, it did not contribute to diminish his tawny complexion. He was a follower of the Mohammedan religion, possessed much gravity; but was communicative, condescending, and agreeable. He had about him a great number of sentences from the Alkoran, which were carefully incased in gold and silver, and upon which he set a high value. He was a native of Kassina, a country that appears to be situated to the South of East from Tombuctou. He said, he had been at Tunis, and at Mecca; had seen many White men and ships; and described the method of travelling over the great desert. This person commanded a body of men, who fought with arrows, as well as muskets: four of the arrows were found in the fort; they were short and pointed with barbed iron. He had many persons in his train, who were of the same colour, but varied a little as to dress: they were all habited in the Turkish manner, but did not wear turbans. After the ceremony of visiting those persons was over, the governor was conducted towards the king, who was surrounded by a number of attendants, whose appearance bore evident signs of riches and authority: chains, stools, axes, swords, flutes, message-canes, etc. were either of solid gold, or richly adorned with that metal: those dazzling appearances, added to damask, taffety, and other rich dresses, gave a splendour to the scene, highly interesting. When the governor approached the king, and when an interchange of compliments had passed, the air resounded with the noise of musical instruments, such as drums, horns, and flutes. After some conversation, during which much politeness was observed in the behaviour of the king, the governor wished this ceremonial visit to be returned; which was agreed to, and a convenient place was found to receive the king and his train. The governor, his officers, and attendants, were formed in a half-circle, and seated under the shade of some trees; and a passage of sufficient breadth was formed by the soldiers for the king and his attendants to pass through. It was full two hours before his majesty was announced, so numerous was his train. Each man of rank, as he advanced, paid the necessary compliments agreeably to the custom of his country, and then filed off. It was previously directed, that the king should be received with arms presented and the grenadiers march when passing the soldiers. This mark of distinction and respect appeared to give him much satisfaction: he halted to observe the orderly behaviour and uniform appearance of the soldiers; and the martial air that was playing, seemed to produce the most agreeable sensations on his mind. The writer had an opportunity of seeing this man. He was of the middle size, well formed, and perfectly black, with regular features and an open and pleasing countenance. His manner indicated understanding and was adorned with gracefulness; and in all respects he exceeded the expectations of every person. His dress was plain: it consisted of a piece of silk wrapt loosely about him, a wreath of green silk ornamented his head: his with gold. He was not distinguished by any gold ornaments, as his attendants were. One man who was dressed in a grotesque manner, and who appeared to act the buffoon, was, literally, loaded with gold.

As this was a visit of ceremony, no business of consequence was transacted. The king politely enquired after Mr. White, and expressed a hope that he would soon be well of his wounds. He said he would move from Annamaboe soon, as his army felt ill effects from the water, and from the dead bodies. After this visit, every confidence was placed in the king and his army; and as the gates were now opened, a free admittance was allowed: various conferences of a favourable nature were carried on between both parties; but peace with the Fantees was considered impracticable. Apoutay had escaped the king's vigilance; and Acoom was at the head of a strong party, and marching towards Annamaboe to give the king battle. The king assured the governor, that after he had subdued his enemies to leeward, he would return to Annamaboe for the purpose of making arrangements relative to the future welfare of the country, and the regulations of trade.

It was agreed, that those residing under British forts, provided they observed a neutrality, should not be molested; and that every respect should be paid to the British flag. The governor likewise procured the release of those who sought refuge in the fort, although the king contested his right to them; for this reason, that as he destroyed the town, he had a claim to every person, and to every thing belonging to it.

Document 8 illustrates the relative weakness of the European position in relation to both Asante and Fante. The British willingly turned Cheboo over to Asante authorities. They knew the restoration of peace and commerce depended upon Fante recognition of Asante hegemony, but they could not force such recognition nor alienate the Fante, since they depended upon them for food and local trade.

Troubled by supply shortages and an epidemic, the Asante army left the south in 1807 without a resolution of the Fante problem. Cheboo was duly executed but Quacoe Apoutay and Acoom eluded capture. Apoutay, Acoom and their Fante supporters spent the next few years pressuring Asante's allies at Elmina and Accra. By 1810 the disruptions had turned into rebellion when a variety of local officials in three states north of the Fante (Wassa, Akwapim and Akyem Abuakwa) joined the Fante revolt.

DOCUMENT 9
'The confrontations of 1811'

Meredith, *Account*, pp. 164–9.

NOTES FOR READING   Warsaw = Wassa; Aquapim = Akwapim; Apakoo = Opoku Frefre of Document 5; Quaw = Kwaw Safrotwe; Crobo and Addah = small city-states east of Accra. Flindt, the Danish Governor, was a hostage of Opoku Frefre for several months in 1811; Tando, the Asante commissioner in Akyem Abuakwa, had expelled the Akyem ruler Attah.

When the Fantees considered themselves no longer in danger, and when they had recovered a little from the effects of the war, they formed plans of revenge on those who were neutral, or who in the least assisted the Ashantees against them. Being now reduced to a state of poverty, they were willing to embrace any means, whereby their condition would be amended, or a plausible pretext for plunder would be encouraged; and war offered them the most favourable means of carrying on their designs. War was accordingly declared against the inhabitants of Elmina and Accra.

From motives of policy, the Fantees did not think it prudent to declare openly against the Cape Coast people, who were perfectly acquainted with their intentions, and voluntarily came forward with a sum of money, and offered their assistance in the intended expedition against the Elminas. In this state were affairs in 1809 . . .

The Fantee forces were now divided into two bodies; one of them was joined by a strong party of Warsaws, and proceeded against Elmina; the other against Accra. Elmina was blockaded for nearly six months; and after many ineffectual attempts to take the town, the Fantees and Warsaws raised the blockade, and retired to their respective homes, in May, 1810.

The party which was destined to go against Accra, advanced towards that town in March, 1810; but meeting with a vigorous resistance, they retreated with precipitation, after losing about one hundred men. The Fantees having thus failed against both those places, did not deem it prudent to renew the attack immediately; and an unexpected change, unfavourable to the Fantees, soon followed, which will give us occasion again to introduce the Ashantees.

The king of Ashantee, hearing by a message sent to him by the governor of Elmina, how troublesome the Fantees were to their neighbours; and knowing that the preservation of Accra was of importance to him, being the only maritime state his subjects could trade to without interruption; was determined to give them assistance. He accordingly levied two armies for this purpose; one of them to proceed to the Fantee country, the other to Accra. The army that proceeded against the Fantees, and which consisted of only about four thousand men, routed them in every engagement. This body of Ashantees made their appearance on the coast on the 1st of March, 1811; but they did not long remain here; for, having supplied themselves with the different articles they were in want of, they returned with their prisoners and booty. The army which was marching towards Accra, met with an unexpected and severe check from the king of Aquapim, through whose country it had to pass in order to get to Accra. This man, it appears, was with the king of Ashantee in his first expedition; and not being rewarded, perhaps, in proportion to his wishes or expectations, took advantage of this occasion to be revenged. He watched an opportunity when the Ashantees were dispersed in small bodies, and surprized and destroyed numbers of them, before they could escape or collect for their defence.

This man, thus shaking off his allegiance, and becoming a formidable enemy, obliged the king of Ashantee to levy a strong force: twenty-five thousand were soon in arms under the command of Apakoo, the king's captain-general; and proceeded to be revenged upon Quaw, the king of Aquapim; who, like all others of the king's enemies, fled when he heard of this formidable force coming against him. He directed his route towards Crobo, a country eastward from Aquapim; but was soon followed by Apakoo at the head of twenty thousand men; having left five thousand to watch Quaw in case he should return to his country. When the Ashantee general got to the Crobo country, he heard that Quaw had fled to Addah: and he hastened in pursuit of him. But when he got to Addah, he was much disappointed in not finding his enemy. Quaw, by secret intelligence, diligently watched the movement of the Ashantees; and before they got to Addah, he was on his return by a private route inland.

Apakoo, in consequence of this unsuccessful and long march, was much enraged, and committed depredations against the inhabitants of Addah and Crobo, who, he suspected, had favoured the flight of his enemy: and when he turned his back, the king of Crobo declared himself against the Ashantees. Apakoo being in this manner diverted from his designs against the Fantees, got Mr. Flindt, the governor of the Danish fort at Addah, into his possession, and had him conveyed inland.

While these transactions were passing in this quarter, the Fantees were again suddenly awakened by an unexpected event in their favour: the king of Akim, who was in alliance with, or tributary to the king of Ashantee, suddenly withdrew his fealty; but not in so treacherous a manner as the king of Aquapim; and marched along the coast to the Fantee country, giving out, that he came to drive the Ashantees from the Fantee country, and exhorting every person capable of bearing arms, to repair to his quarters. He was joined by the inhabitants of Agoona, and other small districts, and soon found himself at the head of about three thousand men; with this force he wished to impress the Fantees with a great idea of his power, and succeeded so far, as to cause his name (Attah) to be dreaded and respected. This man, in conjunction with Tando, governed the Akim country, and was tributary to the king of Ashantee. He refused obedience to the king's orders, by not going against the Fantees: which produced a dispute between himself and Tando, who drove him out of Akim; and, being joined by a number of persons hostile to the Ashantee government, he became a respectable, an unsettled, and desperate warrior.

The southern conflict dragged on for several years, doing serious damage to the trade interests of the Asante and the Europeans. Attah died of smallpox, but two other influential ex-officials from Akyem Abuakwa—Kwadwo Kuma and Kofi Asante—helped Kwaw Safrotwe ('Quaw')

sustain the revolt. In 1814 Osei Bonsu gave the strongest possible charge to his leading general Amankwa: 'You must find these men: if they have jumped in the sea, you must swim after them; if they are in the ground, you must dig them up; if they are in the rocks, you must have them blown up; if they are under a fort which will not give them up, you must fight against it and take it, and bring these renegades to me.' (Daendels, 'Journal', p. 59). It took Amankwa until 1816 to accomplish his task. For an account of his campaign we go to a mulatto clergyman from Accra, Carl Christian Reindorf. He worked for the Basel Missionary Society in the late nineteenth century and wrote his history on the basis of oral evidence and written records.

DOCUMENT 10
'The smoked jaw-bones of victory'

Carl Christian Reindorf, *The History of the Gold Coast and Asante* (1895, reprinted 1966), pp. 158–61.

NOTES FOR READING Akyems = people of Akyem Abuakwa and Akyem Kotoko; Akuapems = people of Akwapim; Apea Dankwa and Apea Yanyo = Asante generals; Winneba = small Fante town and state, formerly containing a British fort; Adwumanko and Agona = small Fante states; Abora = important Fante town and state which served as headquarters for Asante activity in the south; fetish oath = religious oath with heavy sanctions; Ado Dankwa = relative of Kwaw Safrotwe. Reindorf does not explain how Kofi Asante was captured and killed. For Sir Charles MacCarthy see Documents 34–41 below.

The King of Asante made a great effort to crush the Akyems and Akuapems, whose revolt had lasted since 1811. He made another effort by collecting 20 000 men whom he placed under Amankwa. King Bonsu was determined to throw open the paths, to renew his communications with Akra, and to draw from thence his payment from the Danish Government which had not been paid since the last invasion. Amankwa was also ordered to receive the submission of Kwadwo Kuma and Kwaw Safrotwe, who, indeed, were expected to sue for peace on the approach of such a formidable force.

But to prevent any chance of their escape, Apea Dankwa was also sent at the same time with a small force in the direction of Winneba, to cut them off on that side. Amankwa moved towards Akuapem with his army; but when within a day's march of that place, one of his foregoing parties of seven men was cut off by Kwadwo Kuma, who the following day gave battle to the whole force at Adweso. The engagement lasted six hours, and ended in the defeat of the Akyems and their allies. Amankwa proclaimed his victory to the Akras by sending a jaw-bone and a slave to each of the towns, and soon following with his army, received the stipend from the Danish Government.

Kwadwo Kuma and Kwaw Safrotwe with their forces again fled to Fante for protection. Amankwa encamped at Onyase, eight miles north-east of Akra, remaining there nearly a year, to receive the submission of the Akyems and Akuapems . . .

Meanwhile the party under Apea Dankwa had encountered the Fantes several times. The Adwumanko and Agona people had been defeated with great loss; the towns of Winneba and Bereku were plundered and burnt, and the Fantes had been submitted to the most cruel punishments. Apea Dankwa died in Asen, and was succeeded as commander by Apea Yanyo. Opuro Tuata, Opuro Kwabena, Kofi Mensa of Berekuso, with a party from Akra, were commissioned to accompany the General and his forces to Fante. They united with Yanyo and his forces at Asikuma and marched together through Adwumanko, driving the Fantes before them. A large body of them had encamped at Abora, but took flight at the first onset. Crowds of people fled to the forts for protection; upward of 4 000 men, women, and children are said to have fled for protection to Cape Coast Castle. The Governor sent a flag of truce to the Asante General, to learn his intentions, but meanwhile the Asantes approached nearer and nearer to the Castle. On the 16th of March messengers arrived from the camp at Abora, and explained that the King of Asante's army had come to Fante in pursuit of Kwadwo Kuma of Kotoku, Kwaw Safrotwe, and Kofi Asante of Akyem Abuakwa. and with the intention of punishing all who sheltered them . . .

A meeting was held in the hall of the Castle at which it was proved that Kwadwo Kuma, Kwaw Safrotwe, and Kofi Asante were not in Cape Coast, and the headman took fetish oath to that effect. It was arranged that 100 ounces of gold must be paid by the Cape Coast people and the Fantes to purchase peace with the Asantes. This was done and their friendship cemented by a fetish oath. Soon after this the Asantes broke up their camp at Abora; they having now conquered the whole Fante country, and went in the direction of Akra in search of the prescribed men.

Kwadwo Kuma, having discovered that the Fantes could not protect him, fled from the country . . . [Some members of the Akyem royal family, who had been taken prisoner by Asante,] despatched eight messengers after Kwadwo Kuma, who was overtaken by them at Nkwantanan, and was urgently asked to return, as the Asantes had fled from the Fante country. They persuaded him to return, and then delivered him up to the generals at Nkum, while Osaka and Badua were released. Kwadwo Kuma and Amoako Hene were both beheaded, smoked, and brought to Kumase.

Kwaw Safrotwe was still a roaming fugitive and chief disturber of the public peace, whom no one could capture, although his own subjects as well as the Agonas were tired of him. The Akuapems sent a communication to the chiefs of Akra by Ado Dankwa, begging them to negotiate for peace in their favour; but the fees, demanded and paid to the Akras before they agreed to open the subject to the Asantes, were a puncheon of rum and 50 slaves. The General accepted the negotiation for peace on condition that 1 500 heads of cowries and 200 slaves should be paid, also that Kwaw and all the chiefs who had been in arms against the king should be surrendered. Kwaw Safrotwe had left the Fante country for Akuapem, and hidden himself in his own village at Amamprobi. Ado Dankwa, whom the General had promised to make Chief of Akuapem if he would deliver Kwaw into his hands, led a party

of Akras and Asantes to his hiding place at Amamprobi. Dankwa after placing an ambush around, entered into conversation with Kwaw. He advised him to kill himself, because it was impossible to escape from the Asantes' implacable vigilance; but Kwaw refused this friendly counsel, saying that he would wear out the king's patience. Without another word, Ado Dankwa left him; his doing so being the arranged signal for the party in ambush to fire and kill Kwaw Safrotwe. His body was smoked and sent to Kumase, Kwaw's two brothers, Opoku and Amankwa, shared his fate. . . .

All the chiefs of Fante, Akyem and Akuapem came to Akra; they admitted that they were tributaries to Asante, and an annual tribute was fixed for each of them. Thus by means of this peace, the Akras were able to occupy their own lands and villages unmolested by their enemies for twelve years, until Sir Charles MacCarthy persuaded them to break off their friendship with the Asantes.

The object of the war had been attained; the heads of Kwadwo Kuma, Kwaw Safrotwe, and Kofi Asante were now in the king's possession. Akyem and Akuapem had been reduced to a state of vassalage and King Bonsu's authority established throughout Fante. Asante residents were left in charge of the principal districts, whose duty it was to keep the Fantes in subjection and collect the king's tribute. In carrying out these orders, they were very tyrannical, and seldom without some pretext for their exactions. The mere suspicion of disaffection was enough to draw upon any Chief or Headman heavy fines. The Akras suffered in the same manner during General Amankwa's encampment at Onyase, several of whom became slaves and pawns. This caused the Akras to listen favourably when Sir Charles MacCarthy advised them to declare against Asante.

This expedition of 1814–16 resolved the outstanding problems in the south and established, at least momentarily, full Asante control. Residents were left in charge of the principal districts. The annual tributes from the southern states together with the 'notes' or ground-rents for the Anomabu and Cape Coast forts would now flow into the Kumasi coffers by right of conquest. Osei Bonsu was at the height of his power, for his policy—negotiation backed by force—had proved successful.

Two Missions to Kumasi (1816–17)

Following the Napoleonic wars, the Dutch, Danes and British gave some more attention to their lagging commercial interests on the Gold Coast. By 1814 all three had outlawed slave-trading by their subjects, and the British had stationed a naval squadron to police the West African coast. The three European powers sought to restructure the West African marketplace by supplanting the commerce in slaves with 'legitimate' trade in other products. Other nations, such as France and Spain, had not abolished the trade and there was continued demand for slaves in the Americas. As Document 11 indicates, economics rather than parliamentary fiat determined the nature of commerce along the Gold Coast.

DOCUMENT 11
'A mere act of the British legislature'

From an 1812 memorandum of London's African Committee to the Lords of the Treasury concerning trade on the Gold Coast. G. E. Metcalfe, ed., *Great Britain and Ghana, Documents of Ghana History, 1807–1957* (1964), pp. 23–4.

NOTE FOR READING 'that country' is the Gold Coast.

By the abolition of the slave trade, the commerce of Africa was rendered so insignificant that it may have appeared scarcely worth the maintenance of the settlements on the coast. But it must be recollected that those settlements which are supported at so trifling an expense, were originally formed with no view to the slave trade, which was then neither in existence nor in contemplation and that one of the chief arguments urged for the abolition of that trade was that on the adoption of that measure, a new, more desirable, and more extensive commerce would, in process of time, be established in Africa. We will not pretend to determine the precise extent to which these bright anticipations are likely to be realized; but that considerable progress has already been made will appear from the (fact) . . . that in the three years which have elapsed since the abolition, the average export to that country has been £830 325, and that the imports have rapidly increased until they amounted in the year 1810 to above half a million sterling, exclusive of gold, which has been imported in far greater quantities than during the slave trade.

It is a lamentable but certain fact that Africa has hitherto been sacrificed to our West India colonies. Her commerce has been confined to a trade which seemed to preclude all advancement in civilisation. Her cultivators have been sold to labour on lands not their own; while all endeavours to promote cultivation and improvement in agriculture have been discouraged by the Government of this country, lest her products should interfere with those of our more favoured colonies . . .

Before any material improvement can be expected to take place in any district of Africa, the slave trade must be completely annihilated, or at least driven from that part of the coast; for so long as any people carrying on that trade are in possession of a single fort in the same neighbourhood, their influence will be superior to ours, and we shall be considered as opposed to the interests of the natives and be regarded with feelings of enmity. It is, besides, unquestionable that the British trade will not be able to exist where the slave trade is carried on. Those engaged in the latter will monopolize the whole. Ships can always carry more goods than are required to purchase their complement of negroes, and with little additional expense and without loss of time, the surplus goods may be converted into gold, ivory, etc. whereas the British merchant must fit out his vessel expressly for the purpose of purchasing those articles.

The Commissioners complain that the forts, instead of preventing the slave trade, have permitted it to be carried on even in the towns under their walls, . . . which . . . we have stated to profess allegiance to us . . . But we have never asserted that the dominion of the forts was absolute, nor led the public to expect anything so absurd as that about 35 Europeans, with a handful of men, half soldiers, half slaves, dispersed in eleven weak forts, along a coast of 350 miles in extent, could combat, and with force oppose, the wishes and interests of surrounding nations, or even of the towns in their immediate neighbourhood. The allegiance professed by the towns is founded, not upon power, but upon mutual advantage and security, and has always been understood to leave them in full possession of their native rights and privileges, and of the usages of that country by which they are entitled to carry on every description of trade.

But the Commissioners are the more astonished at the inability of the forts to suppress the traffic in question because . . . the abolition is for the interest of Africa itself and . . . therefore the towns should be particularly willing to admit such interference as may be necessary to carry it into effect.

Can these gentlemen be serious in such an observation? Can the wildest theorist expect that a mere act of the British Legislature should, in a moment, inspire with wisdom and refinement the unenlightened natives of the vast continent of Africa, and persuade them that it is for their interest to contribute to, or even to acquiesce in, the destruction of a trade, not inconsistent with their prejudices, their laws, or their notions of morality and religion, and by which alone they have been hitherto accustomed to acquire wealth, and to purchase all the foreign luxuries and conveniences of life? . . .

So long as the vessels of other countries are allowed to frequent the coast, the forts will be unable to prevent the trade in slaves. Until, therefore, we can interdict such intercourse by foreign vessels, good policy would forbid our imposing the impracticable duty of attempting it by force, upon those whose prospects of success in the great work of introducing cultivation and civilization so essentially depend on their preserving the friendship, confidence and respect of the natives.

We are aware of but one mode by which the slave trade can be entirely abolished in this part of Africa, and that, we feel it our duty to recommend. It is the occupation by this nation of the whole of the Gold Coast, . . . stationing good and respectable garrisons in the most commanding situation, (and,) at the rest, establishments sufficient to mark our possession. The sole right of external trade or internal being thereby vested in this country, two or three small ships of war, with some troops or an extra number of marines on board, should be kept constantly cruizing on the coast, to prevent the approach of all vessels not British . . .

(The annexation of Holland by France makes it essential that we occupy the Dutch forts.) Great Britain, in the abolition of the slave trade, has made an immense sacrifice . . . of unparalleled liberality: but if the coast of Africa be allowed to remain in its present state, she will eventually feel that this sacrifice has been made, not to the cause of justice and humanity, but to France . . .

In 1815 the Netherlands West India Company appointed H. W. Daendels as its Governor-General at Elmina. Daendels was an aggressive official with experience in the Dutch East Indies. He sought to understand the alliances and antagonisms created by the recent unrest. The Wassa rebels had joined the blockade of Elmina town in 1809 (Document 9) and engendered an enduring Wassa–Elmina antipathy. The Dutch, situated in Elmina fort, were well liked in Wassa, which controlled the main trade route to Kumasi, and bore a deep distrust of the people of Elmina town and their leader—a mulatto trader named Jan Nieser. Shortly after Daendels' arrival Asante finally put down the Wassa rebellion and demanded reparations. In 1816 Daendels dispatched the Twi-speaking Huydecoper (see Document 3) to Kumasi with a plan for easing the political situation, re-opening the Wassa road and expanding Dutch 'legitimate' trade with Kumasi. Document 12 gives Daendels' instructions to Huydecoper while Document 13 shows how Osei Bonsu responded to the Dutch initiative.

DOCUMENT 12
'One king to another'

From Daendels' instructions to First Assistant W. Huydecoper on 25 April 1816. H. W. Daendels, 'Journal and Correspondence of H. W. Daendels, Part I, November 1815 to January 1817', mimeographed translation from the Dutch by J. T. Furley et al. (1964), pp. 92–100.

NOTES FOR READING   Kostgeld = an honorarium; Dinkera = Denkyira; Wassaw Caboceer = Wassa chief; Kong = state and area north of Asante (see Document 23); Moors = Muslims; Kachna = Katsina; Tombuctou = Timbuktu; Houssa = Hausaland.

Article 1.   He shall on Wednesday 24 April at 6 a.m. take the road to the Capital of the King of Ashantee to present our compliments to him, and assure him of our King's favourable disposition to his person, besides handing over to him the present:

1 Umbrella (large) with gold fringe and thread: 1 large cane with silver knob and chain:
1 hat with double lace point d'espagne: 2 pieces taft:
1 case liquour (with 6 large flasks), 4 cases of 6 flasks Genever:
1 3-piece flag:

Article 7.   Having come to the King's Court he must tell him how his special virtues and talents are well known in Europe, and that already for a long time the Powers have grieved that he has not been able fully to trade with the beach.

Article 9.   That the King my Master now ruling over a four times greater country and as many more inhabitants as Holland formerly possessed has ordered me to employ all possible means for the extension of Commerce and enlightenment and knowledge of the interior of Africa, and for that purpose I must address the King directly giving him the strongest assurance of his affection; wherefore I also make use of the first opportunity to send this my Embassy with presents, to the King; thanking him for the messengers sent to me, who have entirely responded to the intention of the King, and have behaved themselves very well. That they have received 1/2 ounce gold subsistence daily from me as well as the necessary presents, as well as the three 1st Generals of the army together with 24 ounces gold's worth in Powder for the King, this being the 'Kostgeld' ('note' or rent) for the whole of the current year, which in future will always be paid by me in gold's worth, and not in merchandise: while all the arrears have been sent to him to Accra in merchandise, in accordance with the old practice.

Article 10.   That the English Government, most closely allied with the Netherlands, entertains the same sentiments about this as our King, and that I do not doubt that the King will receive the same information from that quarter.

Article 12.   That I propose that the King make a great road, 24 feet broad, from his Capital to Elmina, so that one can see merchants transported along this road by beasts of burden, such as camels, tame elephants, and bullocks, which surely are to be found in the great Kingdom of Ashantee; and in places where there may be turbulent inhabitants, to establish small Forts, the creation of which could be directed by our engineers, and placing in them an Ashantee garrison under a Dutch Commandant in order to provide escort, and a secure night resting place for the traders.

Article 16.   The General desires to meet the King himself about this great project, and will be most highly honoured to be able to pay his respects to him; that to that end he proposes a meeting with the King on the 1st September next in Dinkera (Denkyira) or at such other place as the King shall please.

Article 18.   The Wassaw Caboceer (chief) with whom we are now good friends and who takes much goods from us, must be notified in passing, that we wish to live in peace with him, but that the least hostile intention will end in the destruction of his territory.

Article 22.   Besides gold and ivory Africa can deliver to Europe prepared green, red and yellow leather-work, wax, gum, dye wood, palm- and other oils, drugs and medicinal articles; while trade itself will cause more articles of export to be discovered.

Article 23.   That this commerce will not be confined to the Kingdom of Ashantee, but that the Ashantee caravans would carry European goods over the great Kong mountainrange, and supplant the caravans of the Moors, who now transport merchandise more than a thousand hours through sandy wastes on camels and horses.

Article 24.   That the General has himself constructed in Asia a road of 60 feet breadth at least, which was 260 hours in length: so that with the help of the King he could very easily construct good roads to Kachna (Katsina), Tombuctou (Timbuktu), and Houssa (Hausaland), and make the King ride in Coaches which are as comfortable as the softest beds.

Article 26.   That very little expense would be caused to the King and to the Government for the whole of this establishment: and that the tolls which the King will impose on the great road, which must be small in order not to burden trade, and to be careful that our goods were always cheaper than those of the Moors, would quickly make it up.

Article 27. But that the General would propose other ways and means to the King, which were profitable and not oppressive for the inhabitants, in order to provide him with considerable and vast revenues, by pointing out to him a lasting work in the cultivation of products, a portion of the produce of which would be allotted to the King.

DOCUMENT 13
'The Wassaws must make apology'

From Huydecoper's entry for 19 June 1816. Huydecoper, 'Journal', pp. 41–2.

NOTES FOR READING Opoko = Opoko Frefre of Documents 5 and 9; Kwakye Kofi and Adum Ata were important senior officials of Osei Bonsu's court: terregentes = aristocracy.

About 7 o'clock this morning General Opoko came to request, in the King's name, that I accompany him to the palace, because the King was holding a council and wished me to be present. I set out at once with Opoko, and on arrival at the palace found assembled the most senior generals. Kwakye Kofi and Adum Ata, and the three linguists, with the King at their head. I took my seat next to Opoko's.

[The King] proposed ... to begin constructing the road from his capital through Dinkira and Wassaw at once, on the one condition that I wrote by express post to the General to settle a small dispute which had arisen between Ashanti and Wassaw. This dispute had not been caused by Ashanti, but rather by the people of Elmina.

Some time ago the Elminas had sent envoys by sea to Accra and thence overland to Ashanti, bringing a request from the chief of Elmina and his *terregentes* that the Ashantis should be sent to fight the Fantis and the Wassaws. The grounds were that these two nations were hoping to murder the chief and *terregentes* of Elmina, and burn their town. He had been putting off sending his soldiers to punish the Fantis and the Wassaws, since it was by no means his wish that these nations should suffer so grievously at the hands of an enemy, but now the situation had changed. The Wassaws had recently confiscated some presents the Elminas were sending to him, as King of Ashanti, and had turned the Elmina envoys back, refusing to allow them to come to see him. He was therefore somewhat angry with the Wassaws.

There were, however, no other important palavers outstanding and, in order that everything might be arranged conveniently and without delay, he wished me to send a letter as soon as possible ... to the General. This letter is to state that if the General wants the road built quickly then, on receipt of the letter, he is to send someone to the Wassaw caboceer to discuss the whole matter. The caboceer is to be asked if he has any other palavers with the Ashantis and, if the answer is, Yes, whether such palavers can be dealt with by the General. The Wassaws must make apology to the Ashanti King, and drink an oath in the presence of the King's representatives. This oath will bind the Wassaws to settle all matters peacefully with the

King. They must further swear that, when the envoy has returned [from this mission], the King will be able to begin the construction of the road without any interference, and all parties may then live and trade in peace one with another. If these things are duly sworn, the King will immediately begin preparations for making the road. All the materials are ready, and the men to do the job have been assigned. The King hopes to start on the road this month. It is only the matter of the assurances that must be obtained from the Wassaws that is delaying him, since without these he cannot allow the work to proceed.

Daendels started the Wassa mediation in July. In Kumasi, Osei Bonsu's councillors continued to debate the efficacy of negotiation versus military reoccupation. Meanwhile, the Asantehene sent an official named Tando, who once served as provincial commissioner in Akyem Abuakwa (see Document 9), to secure the release of Asante citizens being held captive in Wassa. Daendels encouraged Tando to take over the general settlement negotiations. Tando, Daendels and Wassa officials reached an agreement in November, but when the enterprising Tando returned to Kumasi he discovered that the king and his council were unhappy with the settlement and his show of initiative. Tando's fate offers a striking contrast to the fortunes of Agyei (Document 6).

DOCUMENT 14
'No man must dare to do good out of his own head'

Bowdich, *Mission*, pp. 123–4.

Our Accra linguist pointed out a man to me named Tando, whom he recollected to have visited the Coast some years, in great pomp, never going the shortest distance, but in his taffeta hammock, covered with a gorgeous umbrella, and surrounded by flatterers, who even wiped the ground before he trod on it. This man had now scarcely a cloth to cover him. He had been retired from his embassy to Akim, in consequence of a dispute with Attah, then the king of that country; for though Attah was adjudged to be in fault, after the palaver was talked at Coomassie, the Ashantee government thought it politic to displace Tando, though he had become disagreeable to the other, only for his vigilance and fidelity. After a long interval of the most luxurious life the capital could afford, he was instructed to proceed to Elmina, to talk a palaver for the King; but thinking it would be a coup d'éclat much more important and agreeable, if he could settle the Warsaw palaver as well, he visited the country on his return, and persuaded them to conciliate the King, and avert their ruin, by carrying a considerable sum of gold to Coomassie, and agreeing to pay twenty-four slaves for every Ashantee subject killed or injured by one of Warsaw. Deputies returned with this man for this purpose; but the King dismissed them contemptuously; and to the disappointment and surprise of Tando, declared that no man must dare to do good out of his own head, or perhaps he would find he did bad, as Tando had done, in spoiling a palaver which he and his great men meant to sleep a long time. Tando was immediately stripped of all his property for his presumption, and from a noble became a beggar.

In addition to the Wassa palaver, Osei Bonsu focused his talents on resolving the Dutch dispute with the people of Elmina. The highly partisan Huydecoper blamed the trouble on Jan Nieser and some of his allegations are contained in Document 15. Like Huydecoper, Nieser was the descendant of a European father and African mother. Slaves constituted a substantial part of his lucrative trade with Asante and Nieser vigorously opposed European abolition efforts. Some of Nieser's agents were in Kumasi at the time of Huydecoper's visit and their attempts to subvert the mission (Document 16) prompted an extraordinary response by the Dutch envoy (Document 17).

DOCUMENT 15
'A thorn in the flesh'

From Huydecoper's entry for 2 May 1816. Huydecoper, 'Journal', pp. 8–9.

NOTES FOR READING *terregrandes* = principal supporters; Government = Dutch Government at Elmina; *onderkoning* = sub-chief; Commany = Komenda, a coastal village and British fort near Elmina.

(2 May 1816.) I hear from many people that Appiah is definitely resolved to attack Commany. This action on his part, if it is to happen, will be solely at the instigation of the Elmina chief, Jan Nieser, and his *terregrandes*. Other Ashantis say that Appiah has no orders to do anything other than fetch Cudjo Koema and the rest of the Fantes who are in hiding at Commany. Could I have a few words with Appiah in the name of General Daendels, urging him to abandon his resolve. The matter was handled secretly. Everyone should seek to advance the interests of his master and supress an unlawful chief whenever this is possible.

This Jan Nieser has often been the cause of disobedience on the part of the people of Elmina against the Government. His constant inciting of the population and his numerous villainies were the cause of his being thrown out of Accra, though this banishment does not seem to have taught him much of a lesson. This wicked man, this root of all evil, who has long been a thorn in the flesh to us, is now in a fair way to bring down the Government of Elmina itself. He spreads wickedness which all know about, but none dare speak of. I myself make no bones about saying that this man is not only overweening and ambitious but a ringleader and a trouble-maker, and if he is not watched carefully by General Daendels, he will be Emperor of Elmina yet. The man Adam knows him well, and much may be learnt from Adam by means of soft words. He is trustworthy, moreover, and will say in Nieser's presence anything the Governor wants him to say. I have often

heard him describe how Jan Nieser talks: 'Now I am king over all. The white men dare not do anything to me. They have to come to me if they want anything.' I have also many times heard how the *onderkoning*, by name Aboe, says to his master (for he is Nieser's slave), 'You are our lord. We want no one over us but you,' at which the 'Emperor' laughs in great glee so that his belly shakes.

DOCUMENT 16
'Some very serious rumours'

From Huydecoper's entry for 3 July 1816. Huydecoper, 'Journal', p. 47.

NOTES FOR READING The Dutch for 'bush black' is *wilde neger*; Hogenboom = Acting Governor-General at Elmina who was killed by a mob in 1808 (there is no evidence of Nieser's involvement).

I have to record that some very serious rumours have been circulating here these past three days. They are being spread by certain Ashantis who have returned from the coast. Some soldiers among them affirm that Mr. Jan Nieser and the Elmina *terregentes* told them (giving it out as positive truth) that General Daendels was a very bad man, who had been sent out from Holland to make a dupe of the King of Ashanti; that General Daendels proposed to murder the whole Elmina population with guns; that he had not come here to trade, but to mislead the peoples of Africa; that he had sent me as his envoy to trick the Ashanti King into building a great road through the Wassaw country; that, when this road has been finished, the General would be able, together with the Wassaws, to plunder the goods and murder the men and women of the Ashanti nation; and many similar incitements and villainies. In all this Mr. Nieser, bush black that he is, is in alliance with the foolish, dim-witted elders of Elmina, men who constantly oppose the Government and always seek to set themselves above it, and who are unable to realise that in time of war it is only the Government that can keep an enemy away from them and protect them. In connexion with these unworthy rumours, I take leave to observe that Mr. Nieser is a bad servant to the Government, and has long deserved to be brought to book. He is a gallows-bird (though he may well die in his bed as an honest man), and on one pretext or another is very likely to be killed sooner or later by his own people, just as he himself made away with President Hogenboom.

DOCUMENT 17
'This my oath will surely kill me'

From Huydecoper's entry for 31 July 1816. Huydecoper, 'Journal', pp. 62–3.

The King was now convinced that lies had indeed been spoken. He therefore had the oath brought in a copper basin. Once more he asked the Elminas if they had anything further to say against me which could be washed away by the drinking of this oath. They, however, remained silent.

Addressing myself to the King, I swore my oath in these words:

'I swear that the General, my master, sent me to you in all sincerity and without any hidden plans in his mind; I swear that all the power, shot and firearms which my master has brought with him are for no other purpose than to be sold impartially to all merchants who care to buy; I swear that my master is a most sincere friend of the Ashantis and will never show any enmity towards their King; I swear that the King of Holland is the best friend the King of Ashanti has and that he sent the General to Africa to bring peace and unity; I swear that everything I have said in his name is the absolute truth . . .

I swear that the General and the King of Holland intend to trade with all men as brother, without choosing one side or the other or making war, and that trust may always be placed in them; I swear that I was not sent here to spy on the King of Ashanti or to assess his military might with a view later on to making war on him . . .

I swear that everything the Elminas have come here to tell the King is untrue, and damnably untrue, that everything they say they have been told to say by someone else, and this if one single word of all that they have said is true, this my oath will surely kill me.'

When I had spoken these words, the oath was administered to me three times, and I took it with the greatest satisfaction. The King and his nobles all praised me for this act, and congratulated me on having won my contest against the Elminas, whom they now looked at out of the corners of their eyes. All the Ashantis were convinced of the unshakeable truth of my cause.

Nieser's people had earlier requested Osei Bonsu to send a force to punish the English fort at Komenda ('Commany'), just to the east of Elmina. Daendels had urged the Asantehene to hold back his army in the interests of peace and commerce. Osei Bonsu complied and offered his compliance as an example for Daendels' conduct toward the Elminas.

DOCUMENT 18
'Be at one with the Elminas'

From Osei Bonsu's letter to Daendels, written 29 November 1816. Daendels, 'Journal', p. 281.

NOTES FOR READING   Commany = Komenda, a coastal village and British fort near Elmina; General = Daendels.

Then the Elmina people sent messengers to me to ask me to give them people to go and fight English Commany. To this I replied that the General had already asked me not to do this. So I refused the Elminas, on your account; and that I acknowledged you as my King above the Elminas, and I

will not reject what you say to comply with the requests of your subjects.

The messengers being afraid of you, came here without your knowledge and out of fear have told me some foolish things which I have not accepted; and I have therefore let Mr. Huydecoper drink oaths to clear you from everything. As then it has appeared that your affairs are cleared, so I request you, my dear master and friend to forgive these people, as I forgive the Commanys and the Wassas (Wassaws) according to your wish, and entrust everything to you. Be at one with the Elminas, for if you are at one with your subjects, you are also my good friend, for these people are all my slaves and subjects: and if they offend you let everything be settled calmly: and if it is all too difficult, let me know and I will settle it for you.

If you are good friends with the Commanys and the Wassas without being so with the Elminas also, there is nothing good between us, for these people are mine.

Huydecoper finally returned to Elmina in May 1817 without the type of trade agreement sought by Daendels. The Governor-General died the following year, leaving his grandiose scheme without application. None the less, an Asante agent continued to reside at Elmina, supervising his government's contacts with the Dutch. Asante–Dutch commerce remained profitable for many years.

As Huydecoper was returning to Elmina, a British delegation made its way to Kumasi. British relations with Asante were much less cordial than those of the Dutch and Danish. Osei Bonsu had resident commissioners at Elmina and Accra who supplied him with information and resolved disputes. He had no such contact in Cape Coast and associated the British with the rebellious Fante and the active effort to end the export of slaves. None the less, the king expected to establish better relations since he had conquered the Fante and taken over the ground-rents for the Anomabu and Cape Coast castles (for the Anomabu 'note' or ground-rent, see Document 28).

For their part, the British had suffered a significant loss of trade, especially during the several recent Asante invasions of the coast. Consequently, the African Company of Merchants authorized a mission to Kumasi in 1817, hoping to regularize British–Asante relations. Governor John Hope Smith of Cape Coast appointed Frederick James, Governor of the English fort at Accra, to lead a group consisting of William Hutchison, writer, Henry Tedlie, assistant surgeon, and Smith's nephew, T. Edward Bowdich, scientific investigator. For an account of the stormy beginnings of the mission, and how Bowdich came to replace James at the head of it, we go to Bowdich himself.

DOCUMENT 19
'They come to put shame upon my face'

Bowdich, *Mission*, pp. 46–51.

We were sent for to the King's house; he was only attended by his privy counsellors; he expressed much delight at the camera obscura and instruments. He said, 'the Englishmen knew more than Dutchmen or Danes—that black men knew nothing.' He then ordered our people to be dismissed, said he would look at the telescope in a larger place, that now he wished to talk with us. He again acknowledged the gratification of Tuesday, and desired Mr. James to explain to him two notes which he produced, written by the Governor in Chief at the request of Amooney, King of Annamaboe, and Adokoo, Chief of the Braffoes, making over to Sai, King of Ashantee, four ackies per month of their company's pay, as a pledge of their allegiance and the termination of hostilities. The impression seemed instantly to have rooted itself in the King's mind, that this was the Governor's individual act, or that he had instanced it; his countenance changed, his counsellors became enraged, they were all impatience, we all anxiety. 'Tell the white men,' said the King, 'what they did yesterday made me much pleasure; I was glad we were to be friends; but today I see they come to put shame upon my face; this breaks my heart too much. The English know, with my own powder, with my own shot, I drove the Fantees under their forts, I spread my sword over them, they were all killed, and their books from the fort are mine. I can do as much for the English as the Fantees, they know this well, they know I have only to send a captain to get all the heads of the Fantees. These white men cheat me, they think to make 'Shantee fool; they pretend to make friends with me, and they join with the Fantees to cheat me, to put shame upon my face; this makes the blood come from my heart.' This was reported by his linguist with a passion of gesture and utterance scarcely inferior to the King's; the irritation spread throughout the circle, and swelled even to uproar.

This much was inevitable; it was one of our anticipated difficulties; it was not a defeat, but a check; and here originates our charge against Mr. James, whom we declare to have been deficient in presence of mind, and not to have exerted those assurances and arguments which, with a considerate zeal, might at least have tended to ameliorate the unjust impression of the King, if not to have eradicated it. Mr. James said, 'the Governor of Cape Coast had done it, that he knew nothing about it, that he was sent only to make the compliments to the King, that if the King liked to send a messenger with him, *he was going back and would tell the Governor all that the King said.*' This was all that was advanced, 'Was this enough for such a Mission to effect?' the King repeated, 'that he had expected we had *come* to settle all palavers, and to *stay* and make friends with him; but we came to make a fool of him.' The King asked him to tell him how much had been paid on these notes since his demand—that he knew white

men had large books which told this. Mr. James said he had seen, but he could not recollect. Nothing could exceed the King's indignation. 'White men', he exclaimed, 'know how many months pass, how many years they live, and they know this, but they wont tell me; could not the other white men tell me.' Mr. James said, 'we never looked in the books.'

Mr. James's embarrassment had not only hurried him to extricate himself as an individual at the expense of his own dignity and intellect, but, which was worse, he had thrown the whole onus of this invidious transaction on the shoulders of the Governor in chief, against whom the King's prejudice would be fatal to all, and whose interest in his honour was most flattering to the King, most auspicious to us, and the hopes of the Mission; not only the future prosperity, but the present security of the Settlements hung upon this, and the dagger was at this moment suspended from a cobweb. Mr. Bowdich urged this in the ear of Mr. James, urged the danger of leaving the King thus provoked, the fatal sacrifice of every object of the Mission, the discredit of the service, the disgrace of ourselves; Mr. James replied, 'he knew the Governor's private sentiments best.' The Moors of authority seized the moment, and zealously fanned the flame which encircled us; for the King looking in vain for those testimonies of British feeling which presence of mind would have imposed, exclaimed, as he turned his ear from the Moors, 'I know the English come to spy the country; they come to cheat me; they want war, they want war.' Mr. James said 'No! we want trade.' The King impatiently continued, 'They join the Fantees to put shame upon my face; I will send a captain to-morrow to take these books, and bring me the heads of all the Fantees under the forts; the white men know I can do this, I have only to speak to my captains. The Dutch Governor does not cheat me; he does not shame me before the Fantees; he sends me the whole 4 oz. a month. The Danes do not shame me, and the English 4 ackies a month is nothing to me; I can send a captain for all; they wish war.' He drew his beard into his mouth, bit it, and rushing abruptly from his seat exclaimed, 'Shantee foo! Shantee foo! ah! ah!' then shaking his finger at us with the most angry aspect, would have burst from us with the exclamation, 'If a black man had brought me this message, I would have had his head cut off before me.' Mr. James was silent ... Not a moment was to be lost; Mr. Bowdich stood before the King, and begged to be heard; his attention was arrested, the clamours of the council gradually abated: there was no interpreter but the one Mr. James brought from his own fort, and no alternative but to charge him promptly in the Governor's name, before reflection could associate the wishes of his master, to speak truly. Mr. Bowdich continued standing before the King, and declared, 'that the Governor wished to gain his friendship more than he could think; that we were sent, not only to compliment him, but to write what he had to say to the Governor, and to wait to tell his answer to the King, and to do all he ordered; to settle all palavers, and to make Ashantees and English as one before we went back. That the Governor of Accra was sick, and in pain, and naturally wished to go back soon, but that himself, and the other two officers would stay with the King, until they made him sure that the Governor was a good friend to him. That we would rather get anger, and lose every thing ourselves, than let the King think the Governor sent us to put shame on him; that we would trust our lives to the King, until we had received the Governor's letter, to make him think so; and to tell us to do all that was right, to make the Ashantees and English as one; and this would shew the King we did not come to spy the country, but to do good.'

Conviction flashed across the countenance of the interpreter, and he must have done Mr. Bowdich's speech justice, for the cheerful aspect of the morning was resumed in every countenance. The applause was general; the King (who had again seated himself) held out his hand to Mr. Bowdich, and said, 'he spoke well; what he spoke was good; he liked his palaver much.' The King's chief linguist came forward and repeated his commendations with the most profound bows; every look was favourable; everywhere there was a hand extended.

Despite Bowdich's efforts to restore British credibility, Osei Bonsu sent a delegation to Cape Coast in an attempt to verify Governor Smith's intentions. The king and his inner council debated the proposed treaty draft over a period of several months, but could not give a decision until the Asante National Assembly met in September during the Odwira festival. While waiting, Bowdich recorded his observations of the Asante economy, including Asante perceptions of the potential dangers of an enlarged merchant class and the fact that war was a favoured form of investment despite the apparent drop in the value of slaves.

DOCUMENT 20
'The Asante economy'

Bowdich, *Mission*, pp. 332–3, 334–7.

NOTES FOR READING   Inta = Gonja; Dagwumba = Dagomba; Boossee and Gooroo were names for the kola nut.

Most of the slaves in Coomassie, were sent as part of the annual tribute of Inta, Dagwumba, and their neighbours, to Ashantee; very many were kidnapped, and for the few who were bought, I was assured by several respectable Ashantees, 2000 cowries, or 1 basket of Boossee was the greatest price given; so full were the markets of the interior. I have brought some pods of the Boossee; it is astringent, and the natives chew it to excite a flow of saliva, and allay the sensation of hunger . . .

'The preference of the Ashantees for the Dagwumba and Inta markets, for silk and cloth, results not merely from their having been so long accustomed to them, but because they admit of a barter trade. The Boossee or Gooroo nut, salt, (which is easily procured, and affords an extravagant profit,) and small quantities of the European commodities, rum, and iron, yield them those articles of comfort and luxury, which they can only purchase with gold and ivory from the set-

tlements on the coast. Gold they are all desirous of hoarding; even those less covetous than is generally their nature, that they may be prepared for the purchase of guns and powder to a large extent, on any sudden war, and thus ingratiate themselves with the king and the government. Were the Ashantees a commercial people, they might be the brokers between the interior and Europeans, or, purchasing supplies more adequate to the demands of their neighbours for European commodities, which would be bought with avidity, realize large properties. But they have no idea of buying more of the various articles than will supply themselves; and leave a small residue to barter for the cloth, silk, and tobacco in the Inta and Dagwumba markets. They are as little commercial as the Romans were in their infancy, and their government would repress rather than countenance the inclination, (believing no state can be aggrandized but by conquest,) lest their genius for war might be enervated by it, and lest, either from the merchants increasing to a body too formidable for their wishes to be resisted, or too artful from their experience to be detected, they might sacrifice the national honour and ambition to their avarice, and furnishing Inta, Dagwumba, or any of their more powerful neighbours (who have yielded to circumstances rather than force) with guns and powder (which are never allowed to be exported from Ashantee), break the spell of their conquests, and undermine their power. The chiefs are fed bountifully by the labours of their slaves, and sharing large sums of the revenue, (the fines their oppression has imposed on other governments,) with incalculable fees for corruption or interference, refine upon the splendor of equipage even to satiety, and still possess a large surplus of income daily accumulating. Were they to encourage commerce, pomp, the idol of which they are most jealous, would soon cease to be their prerogative, because it would be attainable by others; the traders growing wealthy, would vie with them; and for their own security, stimulated by reflections they have now too little at risk to originate, they would unite to repress the arbitrary power of the Aristocracy; and even if they did not, inevitably (as the chiefs conceive) divert the people's genius for war.

It will occur that even to furnish the necessities or luxuries of the Ashantees alone, in cloth, silk, etc. would, considering the extent of the kingdom, considerably augment the returns of our commerce in this part of the world; and therefore it would be well to wean them, gradually, from the markets of the interior, by inducing their cultivation of cotton, which grows abundantly, is of a superior quality, and which, offered in quantities, in addition to the ivory, would lessen the balance of trade now in our favor, and by enabling them, in some degree to purchase with produce instead of gold dust, remove the present comparative disadvantage in trading with Europeans entirely. This occurred to me, and I explained the view not only to the king, but to the more enterprising and reflecting natives: but they had no idea of a quantity, and immediately concluded cotton to be so desirable to us, that 40 or 50 lbs. would be received in barter for twenty times its value; and they required one tokoo and a half per lb. for it, (say one shilling,) even in gold, and on the spot. When I urged that they must clear the ground, form plantations, and superintend the labours of their slaves; they replied, that the

Boossee or Gooroo nut grew spontaneously, and required no labour, that salt was brought to their frontier by poorer nations, and sold for little without the trouble of fetching it; and these articles, with the value, their prevention of all intercourse but their own with the water side nations, attached to a little rum and iron in the interior, furnished them with silks and cotton cloths at a much easier rate, pattern and quality.

In early September the National Assembly met and approved the proposed treaty. The most important articles of the Asantehene's copy appear below, while additions found only in the Cape Coast Governor's copy are given in parenthesis. The contents and interpretation of the treaty played an important role in subsequent relations, despite the British failure to ratify it.

DOCUMENT 21
'The Treaty of 1817'

Articles 4–8 taken from the Asantehene's copy, from Dupuis, *Journal*, p. cxix. With additions from the Governor's copy, from Bowdich, *Mission*, pp. 126–8.

4th. In order to avert the horrors of war, it is agreed that in any case of aggression on the part of the natives under British protection, the king shall complain thereof to the governor-in-chief, to obtain redress; and that he will in no instance resort to hostilities (*even against the other towns of the Fantee territory*) without endeavoring, as much as possible, to effect an amicable arrangement (*affording the Governor the opportunity of propitiating it, as far as he may with discretion*).

5th. The King of Ashantee agrees to permit a British officer to reside constantly at his capital, for the purpose of instituting and preserving a regular communication with the governor-in-chief at Cape Coast Castle.

6th. The King of Ashantee pledges himself to countenance, promote, and encourage the trade of his subjects with Cape Coast Castle and its dependencies, to the extent of his power.

7th. The governors of the respective forts shall at all times afford every protection in their power to the persons and property of the people of Ashantee, who may resort to the water side.

8th. The governor-in-chief reserves to himself the right of punishing any Ashantee guilty of secondary offences, but in case of any crime of magnitude, he will send the offender to the king, to be dealt with according to the laws of his country.

William Hutchison stayed on as resident in Kumasi until February 1818 and his diary bears witness to the unresolved Asante–British problems. The biggest issue was probably the slave trade. Asante sold slaves to obtain guns and other European products and to get rid of surplus people obtained in tribute and war. One of the traders who helped Asante to continue exporting slaves was Sam Kanto Brew, a mulatto grandson of an Irish trader and—like Jan Nieser to the Dutch—a 'thorn in the flesh' of the British. In what follows Hutchison gives us some Asante perceptions of the slave trade and Brew.

DOCUMENT 22
'Too many slaves in the country'

From Hutchison's diary for 26 September, 11 and 15 October, and 24 December 1817. Bowdich, *Mission*, pp. 381–2, 390, 392, and 413.

NOTES FOR READING Dahomey = large state east of Asante; Buntokoo = Bonduku (see Document 2); Cudjo Cooma = Kwadwo Kuma of Akyem Abuakwa, whose patron at court had been Opoko (see Document 10); Adoosee = Adusei, important senior official at the court; Brue = Brew; Apokoo = Opoko Frefre, who uses 'slave' both in the sense of property and subject.

September 26. After we left the palace this morning, Apokoo invited me home to take some refreshment. He entered into a long conversation concerning the slave trade: he heard, he said, that an English vessel had arrived at Cape Coast, and had brought out a letter from the King of England to the Governor-in-Chief, ordering a renewal of the slave trade, and asked me, if I had received any letter. I said I had not, but if such a thing had taken place, I thought I should have early accounts. He enquired what were the objections we had to 'buy men?' I told him what I conceived to be proper; he laughed at our ideas, and enquired if the king of Dahomey had not sent a 'book four moons ago to Cape Coast, inviting the English to trade again, in his kingdom.' I replied there was a message sent, but I could not say exactly in what words . . . 'England', he said, 'was too fond of fighting, her soldiers were the same as dropping a stone in a pond, they go farther and farther': at the same time he described an enlarging circle with his hand, and shook his finger and head significantly at me. He was anxious for me to write a 'proper book' on the slave trade, many slaves, he told me, had revolted, and joining the Buntokoo standard were to fight against them; there were too many slaves in the country, (an opinion I tacitly acquiesced in), and they wanted to get rid of some of them. There might be a deal of trouble from them; he alone had one slave, who had 1000 followers at arms, and he might trouble them as Cudjo Cooma did, who was a slave of his when he revolted, and whose adherents alone were 10 000, independent of runaways, etc.

Saturday 11 [October]. The King sent for me, and on going to the palace I found them in full council talking palavers. Adoosee was ordering a messenger to go to Quamina Bootaqua, to make him proceed to Cape Coast, and inform the Governor that Payntree had sworn by the King and had broke his oath, Bootaqua having sent word to the King of it; but they did not mention any thing to me. After this, Adoosee informed me, that messengers have gone from Amanfoo, sent by Sam Brue, to complain that the Cape Coast people had come armed against him to kill him. After hearing a long statement of grievances, they told me I must write to the Governor about it; I said I would, at the same time I assured the King that Sam Brue was a slave trader, and not to be tolerated at Cape Coast, his conduct was so infamous; they then called on his messenger to know what reason Sam had to leave Cape Coast; he entered at great length into the grievances experienced by Brue from the Governor-in-Chief and officers, because he owed eight ounces of gold; I was called in to reply, which I said I could not condescend to do, until I heard from the Governor-in-Chief, as they had sent messengers to complain to him . . .

Wednesday 15 [October]. . . . I was told by a Fantee man, that Sam Brue had procured 200 guns and a quantity of powder for the King, for slaves he had sold to the Spaniards now on the coast.

Friday 24 [December].   Baba called, and began an oration about Sam Brue, hinting that he should like if I could get Brue, the slave trader, back to Cape Coast. He was my good friend, I was his friend, the Governor was my friend, Brue was his friend, and a long genealogy fit to puzzle a Scottish or Welch family herald. I told him no person must interfere in such affairs. He had that morning received from Brue, powder, guns, and cloth for slaves he had sent down; he brought me a piece of the cloth to shew me, it was very coarse with large red figures on it. I told him when he washed it, he would need to take his staff and put on his sandals to hunt after the colours; he told me he had found that out; for he had washed a piece, and he could not tell what colour it was. He then began a dissertation on the *good* the slave trade did them, and what changes he had seen since he came here; he thought God intended to change the power of white men, and give it to the blacks and Moors.

Towards a More Militant Policy

After 1817 the Asante government began to respond more aggressively to challenges to its authority. Revolt came first in Gyaman. Gyamanhene Adinkra had fought on behalf of Asante against Gyaman and Gbuipe rebels after Osei Kwame's downfall (see Document 2). However, he later grew to resent Kumasi's authority, perhaps as a result of Gyaman's loss of economic importance following the installation of the Salaga market. By 1815 Adinkra and his supporters had decided to pay tribute to the state of Kong instead of Kumasi. Protracted negotiations followed, but by the time of Bowdich's mission in 1817, Adinkra's subjects were in full revolt (see Document 22) and the council at Kumasi pressed for action.

DOCUMENT 23
'Get the King of Gaman's head'

Bowdich, *Mission*, pp. 244–5.

NOTES FOR READING   the sister of the king of Gyaman probably held the position of Queen Mother; benda = two ounces.

The King had sent to demand the royal stool of Buntooko or Gaman which was thickly plated and embossed with gold; it was given up by Adinkara, the King, from fear; his sister, a woman of masculine spirit and talent, and the soul of the government, being absent. On her return, she reproached her brother severely, and ordered a solid gold stool to be made to replace it. That being also demanded, as the right of the superior, with a large gold ornament in the shape of an elephant, dug out from some ruins, the sister, receiving the ambassadors, replied, that the King should not have either, and added, impressing it with more force than delicacy, that her brother and she must change sexes, for she was most proper for a King, and would fight to the last rather than be so constantly despoiled. The King of Ashantee sent word that she was fit to be a king's sister, and a strong woman, and he would give her twelve months to prepare for war. Several embassies have been sent however to negotiate; two during our stay, the latter, it was said, with an offer of 400 Bendas, (£3200.) but the aristocracy were obstinate, and urged to the King, that his other tributaries would laugh at him, if he did not get the King of Gaman's head. The small pox was raging in Buntooko.

A declaration of war followed and Osei Bonsu led the expedition which left Kumasi in 1817. Document 24 describes the preparations made before departure, illustrating the close link between the military and religious spheres in Asante, and recounts an important event which transpired while Osei Bonsu was away.

DOCUMENT 24
'The necessary orgies to insure success'

Dupuis, *Journal*, pp. 114–16.

NOTES FOR READING   the governess = Queen Mother; Bouromy = Bron, a province in the eastern part of the empire; Ouso Cudjo = a military commander.

When the king was about to open the campaign against Gaman, he collected together his priests, to invoke the royal Fetische, and perform the necessary orgies to insure success. These ministers of superstition sacrificed thirty-two male and eighteen female victims, as an expiatory offering to the gods, but the answers from the priests being deemed by the council as still devoid of inspiration, the king was induced to *make a custom* at the sepulchres of his ancestors, where many hundreds bled. This, it is affirmed, propitiated the wrath of the adverse gods. The priests then prepared a certain Fetische compound, which they delivered to the king, with an injunction to burn the composition daily in a consecrated fire pot within the palace; and upon no account to neglect the fire, so as to suffer it to go out; for as long as the sacred flame devoured the powder, he would triumph over his foes.

When the king joined his army he commissioned his eldest sister (then governess of the kingdom), to attend strictly to the sacred mystery, telling her that his crown and life both depended upon her vigilance, and the fulfilment of his order. He selected also three wives to whom he was more attached than the rest, to watch by turns over the mysterious rites, in conjunction with his last-mentioned sister.

During the King's absence, this arbitress of his fate formed a connexion with a chief of Bouromy, whose ambition suggested a plan to seat himself upon the throne.

In this conspiracy, seventeen of the king's wives and their families are said to have joined; the fire pot was broken to pieces, and the chief commenced arming his party. But the king, added my informer, who had sustained heavy losses in the early part of the war, *and was unable to account for the audacity of the enemy*, performed an incantation over a certain talisman, which gave an insight into what was transacting in the capital. He therefore dispatched a body of men under Ouso Cudjo, who, after an impotent struggle on the part of the enemy, effectually crushed the rebellion. When the king returned home, he called a council to deliberate upon the punishment due to the offenders, and it was finally decreed that his wives should suffer death by decapitation. His sister, to prevent the profanation of spilling royal blood, was ordered to be strangled. The chief, her paramour, and all those of his party, were doomed to the most cruel deaths at the grave of the king's mother. These sentences were carried into prompt execution, and it is affirmed that above seven hundred people were sacrificed, or fell in resisting the royal forces.

A significant number of northern Muslims supported Adinkra's revolt. Many others, however, sought to disassociate Islam from the rebellion. Document 25 is a letter to Osei Bonsu, probably written by a Muslim figure of Gbuipe. Note that the writer uses the term *jihãd* to describe the actions of Asante, not Gyaman.

DOCUMENT 25
'May Allah give you victory'

N. Levtzion's translation of a Muslim letter to Osei Bonsu. The original document is in the Royal Library in Copenhagen; the translation is from Levtzion, 'Early nineteenth century Arabic manuscripts from Kumasi', *Transactions of the Historical Society of Ghana*, vol. 8 (1965), pp. 110–11.

NOTES FOR READING   Osei Kwesi = Osei Bonsu; Dinkira = Adinkra; mithqal = weight or measure of gold.

Oh, great Sultan Osei Kwesi, nicknamed (*walaqabuhu*) Bũsu. Oh, sympathiser of the Muslims, who is not afraid of anything, but Allah. May Allah give you long life. What is attributed by hearsay and deceit, nothing will happen to you, for the sake of the Holy Qur'ãn. But you have to give in present: a woman

with a child, a man, a horse, five *mithqal*, a new gown—all of what you like yourself and a white goat. If you give this, nothing will harm you, never will the town spoil, and no bad disease will come. As for the consequences of the *jihãd*, no town will be spoiled or put in fire. Oh, Sultan Osei Kwesi, Dinkira was (or will be) killed one day; and all countries were (or, will be) surprised. The present for the outcome of the *jihãd* against Dinkira: a black male slave, a black gown, everything eatable, a bowl, a gun and a fowl. Oh, Sultan of the Muslims, have pity on the Muslims; may Allah give you long life, and bless you all your life. May Allah give you victory, and raise you over enemies. May Allah fulfil all your needs, and reward your goodness.

The Muslims of Kumasi were obliged to 'bless' and participate in the Gyaman campaign: the king wanted Islamic as well as 'fetish' power working on his behalf. These men were accustomed to such expeditions; but, as Document 26 shows, this one posed a dilemma, since they would be supporting an unabashedly 'pagan' power against an army containing fellow believers.

DOCUMENT 26
'His character as well as his life were at stake'

The account of Muhammed al-Ghamba, 'Bashaw' or head of the Kumasi Muslims (see Document 5), and his associate, the trader Abu Bakr ('Abou Becr'), as told to Dupuis in 1820. Dupuis, *Journal*, pp. 97–9.

NOTES FOR READING   Salgha = Salaga (see Document 7); Talb = Arabic word for pupil or believer; Moraboth = teacher or holy man; Cady = judge; Sarem = savanna country; Dagomba = province in the northeast; Ghunja = Gonja; Kaffar = infidel.

When I was a young man,' said the Bashaw, 'I worked for the good of my body. I traded on the face of God's earth, and travelled much; as my beard grew strong I settled at Salgha, and lastly removed to this city. I was still but an indifferent Talb, when, God be praised, a certain Moraboth from the north was sent to me by a special direction, and that learned saint taught me the truth; so that now my beard is white, and I cannot travel as before; I am content to seek the good of my soul in a state of future reward. My avocations at Coomassy are several; but my chief employment is a school which I have endowed, and which I preside over myself. God has compassionated my labours, and I have about seventy pupils and converts at this time. Besides this, the king's heart is turned towards me, and I am a favoured servant. Over the Moslems I rule as Cady, conformably to our law; I am also a member of the king's council in affairs relating to the believers of Sarem and Dagomba; and I trade with foreign countries through the agency of my friend Abou Becr.'

This confession was in some points open to a prejudicial construction, inasmuch as it looked ostentatious; but from the general conduct of the man, his modesty and urbanity, I could not bring myself to think so uncharitably.

In adverting to the religious opinions of the Ashantees, the reply was, that they were poor wandering heathens; but that many of the chiefs were bigotted infidels, not excepting the king himself; although that monarch would sometimes give ear to the law, (of Mohammed) and never opposed the believers of Ghunja; but on the contrary was a friend on whom they could always rely for protection. Although the king, added my informer, was a misguided infidel, he was yet superior by far, to many other sovereigns, and particularly to the king of Dahomy, his eastern neighbour, who was an infidel of infidels (Kaffar ben al Koufar).

This sovereign a short time back was an avowed enemy to the religion of Islam, and actually put a number of the 'Prophet's children' to death in his country. God, however, they said, had changed his heart, and now the brethren of the true faith travel even to the sea side in safety, and gain numbers of proselytes in his dominions. Reverting again to the king of Ashantee, they asserted that with the exception of many barbarous practices, such as the libations of human blood at sacrifices, and the horrid cruelty of his wars, he was a good man, and wholly undeserving the name of tyrant. The character of true believers, they added, stood very high with the king, for he consulted them upon many important occasions, where the interests of their nation were concerned; and moreover, he never engaged in any warlike enterprize without their society.

In the case of the recent war of Gaman, they informed me that they both accompanied the king.

Subsequently I learned that the Bashaw deserted from the army, the evening after the great battle of the Tando river, and returned to Coomassy. This conduct enraged the king, who swore that had he not been a holy man, he would have put him to death. After I became acquainted with this little history, I took a favourable opportunity to insinuate its contents to the chief, who, in reply, admitted the truth; but alledged in his defence, that his character as well as his life were at stake; for in regard to the former, he could not without deserving to be stigmatized as infamous, witness the horrid butcheries in the camp, so contrary to the tenets of his religion, and what would it have booted him in the world to come, had it pleased God to have destroyed him in the ranks of the infidels, when he was not fighting for the faith, but against it.

It was the bloodiest campaign they had ever witnessed, for many thousands of Moslems perished in the war, as Ghobagho and Kong (both Mohammedan countries,) had united their forces with Dinkera, king of Gaman, who had cast off his allegiance to the king of Ashantee, and transferred a tribute which he formerly paid him to the Sultan of Kong. In describing some of the characteristics of the war, they declared they had actually witnessed the massacre of ten thousand old men, women, and young children, besides numbers of chieftains, who were put to death by tortures the most revolting to humanity. The Ashantees, they affirmed, were, as enemies, the most terrible of mankind, and in war, were justly dreaded even by the true believers.

This political conduct on the part of the king appearing to me a little enigmatical, and as it did not tally with what I had been previously told of the respect entertained for Moslems, I suggested the question as an apparent inconsistency. But I was readily informed that his majesty's affection for true believers was limited to the more eastern districts, and to Talbs or priests of all nations, but more especially those who came from Egypt, or any part of the Holy Land. His western wars were strictly political. Yet the prisoners he took in battle, if Moslems, were never put to death like infidels; on the contrary, they were well used, and generally transferred to the eastern division of the empire, particularly to Bouromy on the Volta. If they fell in battle against the king, it was considered their 'blood was upon their own heads.'

During the Gyaman campaign, Osei Bonsu levied soldiers from all of the southern provinces. When certain Fante areas refused to supply men, the Asantehene considered it an act of aggression and sought redress under Article 4 of the 1817 Treaty. Document 27 recounts the conclusion of the Gyaman struggle and gives an account of Asante's reaction to the Fante and British challenge in the south.

DOCUMENT 27
'He applied to the Governor for redress'

Reindorf, *History*, pp. 165–7.

NOTES FOR READING Governor = the same John Hope Smith of the time of the Bowdich mission; for the Articles of the 1817 Treaty, see Document 21.

Adinkra was beaten and killed; and his son, Prince Apaw, cut off his father's head, and opening the belly of a woman with child, put the head inside and sewed it up. The battle raged for several days. Apaw was taken prisoner and brought before Osei Bonsu, who, by promises and kindness, induced him to assist in finding the body and head of his father. When this was found, the Asantes stitched the dead kin's head on his body, dressed and seated him, then held a court in which Bonsu brought his charges against Adinkra. The Elders, after discussing the question, brought in a verdict of guilty. Adinkra was then, according to the Asante custom, beheaded by the executioner. Immense treasures and numerous prisoners were taken to Asante. The Kong army arrived after the death of Adinkra, and returned home with the Princess . . .

All the tributary kings of Akyem, Abuakwa, Kotoku, Akwamu, and Akuapem had either joined personally or appointed forces in this war; only the Fantes kept aloof. Encouraged by rumours of disasters said to have befallen the invading army, they grew insolent and began to insult and beat Asante residents, and among these was Koso (Osoko) a court-crier of King Bonsu, whose gold-cap, the sign of his office, was lost in an affray. Reports of this were brought to the king in camp, and on the strength of the late treaty, he applied to the Governor for redress.

The Governor refused; and when other messengers came, he received them with great indignation, presenting them with a ball cartridge to show that he was ready for war.

When the king received the message, his nobles demanded to be led to the Coast. But the king could not reconcile the conduct of the Governor with British good faith, believing that there must be some mistake, and the Governor had been imposed upon, because the treaty had stipulated clearly that in the event of any aggression on the part of the protected tribes he was to seek redress through the Governor rather than take the matter into his own hands.

The king, therefore, sent Owusu Dome, a messenger of high rank, with a numerous retinue. A little previous to this date, the British Government had sent out Dupuis as Consul to Asante, and he was waiting at Cape Coast to proceed to Kumase, when Owusu Dome arrived. The Governor appeared to have been extremely jealous of Dupuis' appointment, and determined to thwart him. When the ambassador of the king appeared in the Council Chamber at Cape Coast, he begged that the treaty might be read aloud, and laid much stress upon the fourth article, already given, and the seventh, which provides that 'The Governors of the respective Forts shall at all times afford every protection in their power to the persons and property of the people of Asante who may resort to the water side.' The envoy then, with much dignity, said, that redress must be given at once, or the king would appeal to arms.

The envoy was then informed of Dupuis' presence and of the nature of his appointment. At the close of his address, he had tendered to the Governor, the parchment on which the treaty was written. At Dupuis' intercession, he consented to retain possession of it till he had received new instructions from King Bonsu. A relative of the king was next sent as ambassador, who abated nothing of his demands, but insisted on a payment of 1600 ounces of gold from the inhabitants of the Gold Coast, and a like sum from the British Governor. Upon this demand Dupuis went to Kumase.

Joseph Dupuis had a formidable assignment when he finally went to Kumasi in January 1820. The British Government had appointed him consul to Asante in 1818 and he arrived on the Gold Coast the following year. London had not clarified his relationship with Governor Smith and the two men quickly came into conflict. Dupuis saw himself as a mediator between Cape Coast and Kumasi; Smith considered Dupuis an unwelcome intruder. Before Dupuis left for Kumasi, Smith instructed him that Asante demands for 1600 ounces of gold from the British were not to be discussed and that he should try to reduce the amount demanded of the Fante.

Osei Bonsu was also in a difficult situation. His preference for negotiation was being subverted by what he considered Governor Smith's bad faith. The British had neither respected the 1817 Treaty nor kept the Fante in line. Furthermore, Governor Smith had assigned inflated values to the items constituting rent (the 'notes') for the Cape Coast and Anomabu forts. When Dupuis presented these goods, Osei Bonsu became angry (Document 28). Some of the king's most important advisers now favoured a show of force (Document 29).

DOCUMENT 28
'Is this treating me like a friend and a king?'

Osei Bonsu's reactions to the rents offered by the Governor. Dupuis, *Journal*, pp. 119, 123–5.

NOTES FOR READING sixteen ackies = one ounce (see Document 19); White was Governor of Anomabu fort (see Document 8).

The goods that were sent to the king under my charge in payment of the notes were subjected to a rigid scrutiny, after which his majesty demanded to know their respective prices, as they stood valued upon the list. When these charges were read over, he affected the greatest astonishment, mingled with anger. 'What,' said he, 'is it thus the governor shews his friendship for me, charging me an ounce of gold for an anker of rum, or a keg of powder; six ackies for a romal, an ounce for a piece of taffety silk, and all the other goods at the same high prices? Is this treating me like a friend and a king? Truly, I see he makes this extravagant profit, *because I would not receive the notes at four ackies a month*. This is not proper conduct in white men towards the blacks. The great God gave them much sense, and they make books that ought to speak truth; but this book is not true, for the governor puts down whatever he chuses, because he knows I cannot read. This is shameful, for when I made the book (treaty) with the other white men, I was too happy, and I sent all the trade to the governor's warehouse as he told me, and I sent him a present of gold and slaves, and a present of slaves to the governor of Annamaboe. When I do good in this manner, how can the white men say, I wish to quarrel and make war? I like all white people, for God has made them better than the blacks, and they hold my heart. Mr. White was a good man; he always told me the truth, and never quarrelled with me or cheated me; but this governor proposes to be my friend, and when I accept his offer he deceives me, and shames me before my captains and the Fantees. When I went out to fight against Dinkra, I sent to Cape Coast for fifty kegs of powder and some lead to make shot, because I liked Englishmen best; but the governor sent my messengers away, because they had not gold enough; they then went to El Mina, and the Dutch governor gave them the powder and shot, and sent my gold back. Which was the best friend? Suppose I make an alliance with a king and he wants gold; I give it him: if he wants me to help him, I must go and fight for him too; and then he knows I have a true heart, and love him like a brother.' God made white and black men: he loves all men; he does not say they must not be friends because they differ in colour. White men read books, and know the great God, therefore the blacks say, these are strong people; their fetische is good. This is true, but then they must not do evil. Now when I sent gold to Cape Coast to buy goods, and the governor does not know it, so I buy powder at two and three kegs to the ounce, and three ankers of rum to the ounce, and seven ackies for the best guns, and I get one hundred bars of lead for two ounces. The Dutch governor always pays me fairly, he same as if I buy in the town, and I get good things; but when the governor of Cape Coast sends me articles, they are bad;—the rum is watered, and the powder is all dust, like charcoal. I think a white man cannot do this; therefore I say to my captains, See what the Fantees do; they cheat me, and dishonour the English governor. Then my captains take up the sword, and swear they must march to the water side, and live in the towns. But I do not want to kill old men and women and children for their gold, as my soldiers do, I prefer friendship.

Anomabu 'note':

'Cape Coast Castle, April 1, 1817.

'Zey Tooto Quamino, King of Ashantee, at 160s. per month.
(Signed) 'JOHN HOPE SMITH,
'Governor in Chief.' L. S.

'This note was held by Amoney, Caboceer of Annamaboe, but in consequence of the conquest of the Fantee country was claimed and transferred to Zey, king of Ashantee, by the consent of the former owner.'

Goods	Paid to ultimo, July, 1817. (Signed) W. SMITH.		8oz.
10 Anders Rum, 1oz.	Paid to ultimo, December, 1817, in W. S		10
24 Kegs powder	Paid to December 31, 1818, in W.S.		24
66 Lead bars	Paid to December 31, 1819, in oz.	2	1
4 Ankers Rum		4	0
4 Kegs Powder		4	0
13 Cottons		1	10
1 Ditto Bandanoe		0	8
2 Taffeties		2	0
5 Glasgow Danes		1	14
1 Fathom Scarlet		0	8
8½ Pieces Long Cloth		4	4
3 Romals		1	2
5¼ Manchester Toms		2	1
		oz. 24	0 W. S.

DOCUMENT 29
'Ashantee is mighty in war'

Opoku Frefre's views on the Cape Coast 'palaver'. Dupuis, *Journal*, pp. 91–2.

NOTES FOR READING Apoko = Opoku Frefre; the previous 'white captain' = Bowdich; Sai = Osei Bonsu; for Apoutay and Cheboo, see Document 8; great king = King of England. Note that 'book' can refer to any written document.

Apoko took up the scimiter in turn. It was not unknown to me that the political sentiments of this chief, whose influence was powerful, were hostile to the Fantees. His rank in the army rendered his voice in the cabinet the most important, perhaps, in the list of caboceers. It should be recorded, however, that although he and his party were adverse to a reconciliation with the natives of Cape Coast, they did not openly implicate the governor and council in the quarrel, unless as accessaries to the conduct of the Fantees. The king of England, Apoko one day said, could not know the truth; for, as the governor had at least taken a secondary part in the quarrel, and had broken the law (treaty), he would not surely write a true book to the great king. The sentiments of this man, to be gathered from his speech, were naturally interesting at this crisis.

'Chief of the white men,' said he, 'that book is good, the king likes it, and we all like it. Sincerity appears in your face. The great god you serve knows what is in the heart; but I think you cannot tell a lie. I see the great king sends good things to Sai, because he thinks he is a true friend, and will take care of his forts, and the white men, and make a good trade. But the white captain, who came up before, told the king lies; because he made a book of friendship, and then cheated the king. Sai is a true king, I am only a captain. If he say—Make war, and kill the people, I must do so. If he say—Be friends, then I certainly cannot fight. Now I hear the words of that book (the commission), I like it, because the great king wishes to make Ashantee and England all one. Sai knows I tell him what I think is good for him; because I cannot sit here when I see people insolent, and hear them say he is not the king. I fought in Fantee and Assin, with Apoutay and Cheboo. If Sai be not king, as the Fantees pretend, why does the white king now send him a true captain, and presents? But they lie! and it is their deceitfulness; because they do not wish him to see the king. The white men know very well that Ashantee is mighty in war; and it is not right for the governor to say to the people, "Make a wall, and fight the king." That is not like a true friend, according to the book. This palaver, Captain, (addressing me) is what is in my heart: I think it very shameful in the governor; but let that pass. I swear the king's oath, that what he says, I will do; and if he say, fight for the great king, I will kill all his enemies, so that all the people shall serve him here as in the white country. Sai is our master, and the great king is our master too.'

Dupuis and Osei Bonsu deliberated about a possible treaty, discovering in the process an important misunderstanding about the 1817 agreement. They also discussed the merits of the abolition of the slave trade.

DOCUMENT 30
'The other white men cheated me'

Dupuis' account of a discussion at the court. Dupuis, *Journal*, pp. 131–3.

NOTES FOR READING Tantum and Apollonia = British forts; Abroah = mulatto linguist from Cape Coast sent by Governor Smith; 'my nephew' refers to a member of the royal dynasty (either Adu Brade or Owusu Dome) who served as an intermediary with the British at the coast.

The king resumed the argument, and in an animated tone declared he never could or would relinquish his right of sovereignty from the conquest of Fantee, over the whole country. Elmina Town, which for wealth and population, greatly exceeded Cape Coast, acknowledged his supremacy; and the Dutch governor compelled the people to obey him, for that reason he was the friend of the Dutch. The natives themselves were his friends, and he never had any palavers there. Danish Accra, English Accra, Tantum and Apollonia never disputed his title; the people never gave him any trouble, and therefore if his power was acknowledged so far to the east as Accra, and so far to the west as Apollonia, he must surely be the master of Cape Coast which lay in the centre. The king of England, he added, was his great master, he would do all in his power to give him pleasure; but he could not think that a poor black town was an object worthy his notice. 'I don't want war', said the king emphatically, 'I want the people to serve me, and serve white men. It is true I told the governor he must pay me gold, but now I see your face I am willing to relinquish that. Cape Coast, however, must give me gold, for they are my people, and if they will be insolent I must punish them: for unless I do so, all these countries will laugh, and say, What kind of king is this? The governor knows I am right, for he now sends word the people are unable to pay 1600 ounces, and that if I will abate something it will be paid. What I tell you,' added the king, noticing my surprise, 'is very true: here is the messenger,' pointing to the man who brought the message up. This man confirmed what the king said, and concluded with an observation which he affirmed the governor had made, that the object of my visit was merely to convey some presents to him from the king of England. The linguist Abroah was pointed out as a witness, who interpreted the very message in the castle hall. 'Do I speak the truth,' said the messenger emphatically, 'or do I tell a lie before the king and the white captain?' The linguist confirmed his statement. 'Then,' said the king, addressing his conversation to me, 'I must be paid. I shall look to you, to the governor, and to my nephew: but it is the governor who must see to it, for he now says he will settle that palaver with me.'

The arguments with which I opposed those of the king palliated the alleged offences of the Cape Coast people as far as it was practicable, although it would have been impossible to deny what in substance the king had related. I retorted, however, that the sixth article of the old treaty had been violated, in which the king pledged himself to encourage the trade of his subjects with the Cape. This article I maintained had been infringed upon, by the act of cutting off the communication between his capital and the settlements. In reply, the king said 'Yes, I made that book, it speaks true now; but that is not my fault; Cape Coast did the first wrong: they sold some Ashantees off the Coast, and seized their property. Fourteen traders went to Tantum, and the Fantees stole all their gold and ivory, and sold them for slaves to a ship. Another time they seized two Ashantees, and killed them for the Fetische. When the traders heard these things it made them stay at home, for they were frightened; and so those who wanted trade went to Elmina, because the Dutch governor takes care of my people. If the traders will not go to Cape Coast, I cannot help it. I did not break the law, the governor broke it.'

I desired to know upon what grounds the king had thought proper to demand gold of the governor. The reply was laconic, 'For breaking the law.' This, I maintained, was illegal and unjustifiable, either upon the face of the treaty, or by the laws of nations. The answer was, 'I made that book (clause) with the white men; they told me if I broke the law, I was to pay

gold; and if the governor broke it, he must pay it. Now all the people know it was the governor who broke it; for when Cape Coast was insolent, he would not hear my palaver; but told them to give the gold to him, and fight the king. Here is the book,' added his majesty, handing me the treaty to peruse. 'You will find the gold mentioned in it.' Upon inspection, I assured him that no such clause was to be found. 'No!' said the king, musing as he spoke, 'then true it is the other white men cheated me. Here are my captains, they will speak true; and here,' pointing to one of my own servants, 'is a Fantee who came up to Coomassy with the white men the other year, he must tell true.' This man, whose name was Coffee, declared he was present when the treaty was read over, and that it was explained to the king precisely as he had stated. I then told the king that I would neither dispute his word, nor the evidence; but certainly I knew that neither Mr. Bowdich nor his uncle were authorized to agree to pay money on account of the king of England, in a case of that kind; for when my master was forced into palavers, nothing but war could settle the dispute.

DOCUMENT 31
'If they think it bad now, why did they think it good before?'

Osei Bonsu's comments on the slave trade. Dupuis, *Journal*, pp. 162—3.

NOTES FOR READING   Braffoes = Fante of Abora; Sarem = savanna country; great king = King of England; Crammo = Muslim; great water = Niger River.

'Now,' said the king, after a pause, 'I have another palaver, and you must help me to talk it. A long time ago the great king liked plenty of trade, more than now; then many ships came, and they bought ivory, gold, and slaves; but now he will not let the ships come as before, and the people buy gold and ivory only. This is what I have in my head, so now tell me truly, like a friend, why does the king do so?' 'His majesty's question,' I replied, 'was connected with a great palaver, which my instructions did not authorise me to discuss. I had nothing to say regarding the slave trade.' 'I know that too, retorted the king; 'because, if my master liked that trade, you would have told me so before. I only want to hear what you think as a friend: this is not like the other palavers.' I was confessedly at a loss for an argument that might pass as a satisfactory reason, and the sequel proved that my doubts were not groundless. The king did not deem it plausible, that this obnoxious traffic should have been abolished from motives of humanity alone; neither would he admit that it lessened the number either of domestic or foreign wars.

Taking up one of my observations, he remarked, 'the white men who go to council with your master, and pray to the great God for him, do not understand my country, or they would not say the slave trade was bad. But if they think it bad now, why did they think it good before. Is not your law an old law, the same as the Crammo law? Do you not both serve the same God, only you have different fashions and customs?

Crammos are strong people in fetische, and they say the law is good, because the great God made the book; so they buy slaves, and teach them good things, which they knew not before. This makes every body love the Crammos, and they go every where up and down, and the people give them food when they want it. Then these men come all the way from the great water, and from Manding, and Dagomba, and Killinga; they stop and trade for slaves, and then go home. If the great king would like to restore this trade, it would be good for the white men and for me too, because Ashantee is a country for war, and the people are strong; so if you talk that palaver for for me properly, in the white country, if you go there, I will give you plenty of gold, and I will make you richer than all the white men.'

Advisers favouring a demonstration of force pressed Osei Bonsu for action. In mid-March the king made a firm decision (Document 32). The resulting treaty deferred the reparations question; but it settled other outstanding issues including the problem of who ruled the Fante. The crucial articles are included in Document 33.

DOCUMENT 32
'His plan of negotiation'

Dupuis, *Journal*, pp. 147–8.

NOTES FOR READING   For Bashaw and Abou Becr, see Documents 1 and 26; the 'war' and 'peace' advocates were all influential members of the court, and included Opoku Frefre (Apoko) and Adusei (Adusai), the first linguist.

March 18.   The forenoon passed away in anxiety, for no messenger came from the palace. My Moslem friends paid me a visit in the interval, and from them I learned that the king was engaged in close conference with his ministers; that Apoko, Ado Quamina, Agampong, and the whole of the army interest were implacable in their resentment at what they termed the presumption of their vassals, who had dared to stipulate for the price of their own insolence; and that a very great majority in the assembly of chiefs loudly cried out for war. Yet the king was averse to it. He, Adusai, Amon Koitea, Kankam, and Ado Matta, opposed the torrent. 'We have just given our opinions,' said the friendly Bashaw, 'to the king in private, that a war will ruin him in the land of the whites, and perhaps your Sultan will send a great army to conquer the country. We should not be sorry,' said he, in a laughing whisper, 'to see white men here; but we have told the king what we believe to be the truth, for that is our duty, and he has been good to me. The Bashaw sent Abou Becr again to the palace to get information.' At his return I learned that the king threatened every opposer in the council, and insisted upon an unconditional submission to his plan of negotiation.

DOCUMENT 33
'The Treaty of 1820'

Articles 3–7, from Dupuis, *Journal, cxx–cxxi.*

3d.   The claim recently made by the King of Ashantee, on the governor of Cape Coast Castle, amounting to one thousand six hundred ounces of gold, or £6400 is hereby acknowledged to be relinquished; and it is agreed that there are now no differences or palavers existing between the King of Ashantee and the Governor, or between the king and any other of His Britannic Majesty's subjects, collectively or individually.

4th.   The King of Ashantee agrees and binds himself to support and encourage the commerce of this country with Cape Coast and its dependencies, by all the means in his power; and pledges himself not to allow any differences that may occur to interrupt the trade with the English merchants on the Coast.

5th.   The King of Ashantee claims the Fantee territory as his dominions, which the consul, on the part of the British government, accedes to, in consideration and on the express condition that the king agrees to acknowledge the natives, residing under British protection, entitled to the benefit of British laws, and to be amenable to them only in case of any act of aggression on their part.

6th.   After the final adjustment of the present claims upon the natives of Cape Coast, the King binds himself to submit all future complaints to the Consul only, and on no account whatever to make war with the natives, at any of the English settlements, without first allowing the consul an opportunity of settling such differences.

7th.   The consul, on the part of the British government, guarantees all the protection in his power to the subjects of the king of Ashantee, who may have any commerce with the British Settlements on the Coast.

Osei Bonsu's distrust of Governor Smith spurred him to order a delegation of Asante officials to accompany Dupuis to England and to present the 'great king' himself with the treaty. However, the British navy denied passage to the embassy. Smith refused to discuss the agreement with Dupuis, who left for London where he tried but never succeeded in gaining British government ratification.

The Death of Osei Bonsu and the Clarification of Asante's Southern Policy

In 1821 the British Parliament, expressing dissatisfaction with the failure of the Company of Merchants to effectively supplant commerce in slaves with 'legitimate' trade, abolished the Company and assumed direct control of the Gold Coast settlements. The Crown's authority was given to Sir Charles MacCarthy, who was already the Governor of Sierra Leone. MacCarthy arrived at Cape Coast in March 1822 and thereafter alternated between his Gold Coast and Sierra Leone assignments.

The Governor immediately adopted a militant pro-Fante, anti-Asante posture. Throughout 1822 and 1823 he and his subordinate officers pressed the coastal people to renounce Kumasi authority. Document 34, which was written by a Scottish merchant and magistrate who first came to the Gold Coast in 1834, presents a description of MacCarthy's sentiments and activities. This and Document 35 give impressions of the strength of anti-Asante feelings generated by the MacCarthy–Fante alliance. Finally, Document 36 presents one example of why many coastal leaders, who were otherwise neutral, ultimately supported the Governor.

DOCUMENT 34
'The mention of his name'

Brodie Cruickshank, *Eighteen Years on the Gold Coast*, 2 vols (1853), Vol. I, pp. 145–6, 148.

The Gold Coast became a dependency of Sierra Leone, and was placed under the government of Sir Charles M'Carthy. He arrived at Cape Coast Castle in March, 1822, and gave life and energy to the drooping spirits of the people. It does not appear that he made any attempts to establish amicable relations with the king. He seems to have at once assumed (no doubt influenced by the representations made to him) that negotiation was hopeless, that he had to do with a state of confirmed hostility, and that there was no other way of establishing peace except by the sword. There is now good reason for believing that the king, at this time, would have been willing to listen to terms of accommodation, and it is to be regretted that Sir Charles did not at first make overtures of this nature. But he had no ordinary difficulties to contend against. The servants of the African Company, almost to a man, refused to take office under him, and withdrew themselves from any participation in the management of affairs.

The new governor was thus left to grope his way as he best could, exposed to the machinations of interested and designing men. His noble and generous nature sympathised deeply with the sufferings of the oppressed Fantees, and led him to conclude that their independence alone could give them relief, and restore tranquillity to this long-distracted country. His measures, therefore, were all calculated to this end. He had frequent intercourse with the most influential chiefs. He laid before them his views of the policy which he desired them to adopt. He endeavoured to give unanimity and decision to their counsels, and assisted them largely with all the munitions of war. So thoroughly did he identify himself with the struggle, that the Fantees soon hailed him as their deliverer, and gave themselves entirely up to his guidance . . .

His majestic figure, towering a foot beyond the tallest of his staff, as he passed along the ranks, smiling encouragement to all; his frank, courteous, and gallant bearing; his lavish, almost reckless, expenditure of money; and his un-

shaken confidence in the result of the impending struggle, inspired all ranks of society with the most enthusiastic and flattering anticipations.

Even at this distance of time, it is astonishing to observe the effect of the mention of his name, which seems to act as a potent spell with the Fantees. Anecdotes of his power, generosity, and benevolence, are treasured up with a species of sacred regard, and transmitted from father to son. The very spots where he had given a few pic-nic parties with all the *éclat* of rich English uniforms, and a military band, are still pointed out with a lingering fondness, while his name is perpetuated in the corrupted form of Karté bestowed by many a parent upon his child.

DOCUMENT 35
'MacCarthy must defeat O'Saii'

Excerpts from poems published in Gold Coast and Sierra Leone newspapers in 1823. The first is from *The Royal Gazette and Sierra Leone Advertiser*, 12 July 1823; reprinted in Ivor Wilks, *Asante in the Nineteenth Century* (1975), p. 169. The second is from *The Royal Gold Coast Gazette*, 25 October 1823; reprinted in *Asante Seminar '76*, No. 5 (Northwestern University, November 1976), p. 22.

NOTES FOR READING   'O'Saii' and 'O'Saii Tootoo' = Osei Bonsu; Brew = Sam Kanto Brew of Document 22.

Lets drive from this country, the trait'rous Brew,
And down with the power of O'Saii Tootoo;
Shou'd he send to demand his customs' arrears,
He'll get a *discharge* from our brave Volunteers . . .

. . . .

Awake from your slumbers ye Fantees who fear,
Arouse now to vengeance . . . MacCarthy is near.
O bright be thy visions, thou land of the Sun,
Thy fetters are broken, thy freedom begun.
Bid the *'Tyger drum'* beat, bid the conchs blow!
Strike one for your freedom, or kneel to the foe,
For bloody the day, and sleepless the night,
When free men and despots commingle in fight.
The Oracles tell, and the Prophets proclaim,
Despair to the *Tyrant* confusion and shame,
The Minstrels may chant, and the children may sing,
Defeat to the *Despot*; and woe to the King!
Behold where you cowards retire in fright,
When the warning cannon resounds in the night;
The Banners of Occan floats o'er thy floods,
The call of the Bugle resounds through thy woods.
Remember the *Towns* by the Tyrant o'erthrown,
The Sons who have bled, and the Captives that groan,
O think of those wrongs in the bloody affray,
The war cry 'MacCarthy!' . . . must defeat! 'O'Saii!'
Awake from your slumbers, ye Fantees who sigh
Arouse now to vengeance, MacCarthy is nigh
Bid thy solitudes cease, and thy wild echoes ring,
Till nations exult in the fall of the King.

DOCUMENT 36
'The quantities fixed by him are unreasonable'

From a memorandum of Major Chisholm to Governor MacCarthy in Sierra Leone, 30 September 1822. Metcalfe, *Documents*, p. 78.

NOTES FOR READING Annamaboe = Anomabu; 'He' = the British Colonial Secretary attached to the Gold Coast mission who attended this meeting of southern Akan officials in mid-1822.

He saw at Abrah representatives from the Elminas, Accras, Wassaws, Assins and some other states tributary to Ashantee. The caboceers of Annamaboe were invited to join them, but they had declined doing so. It was understood that this assembly was convened to receive the commands of the King on various important points. One was said to be a demand of an additional tribute, and an alteration in the mode of payment. The slave trade was at its height when these states were brought under the Ashantee yoke, and the taxes imposed on them were receivable in slaves. The great reduction in the value of human beings and the want of purchasers for them of late years, have determined the King not to take them in payment hereafter. He requires gold or European goods in their stead, and as the quantities fixed by him are unreasonable in the extreme, the people have no hopes of being able to pay them, and consequently cannot be prevailed upon to accede to the proposed change.

MacCarthy's agents used a range of coercive tactics in addition to propaganda. In 1822 they detained Agyei, the linguist for 'hard palavers' (Document 6), deported the slave trader Brew (Document 22) and murdered a number of Asante merchants. News of MacCarthy's activities and the collapse of the 1820 treaty strengthened the hand of the advocates of a more aggressive policy in Kumasi.

Asante–British polarization was symbolized in an incident which occurred in May 1822 at Anomabu between an Asante trader and a Fante sergeant in the British service. Following an altercation, the merchant invoked the jurisdiction of Osei Bonsu by pronouncing the Great Oath of Asante.

DOCUMENT 37
'By Cormantine and Saturday!'

From the memorandum of Major Chisholm to Governor MacCarthy in Sierra Leone, 30 September 1822. Metcalfe, *Documents*, p. 79.

NOTES FOR READING James Swanzy = lieutenant in the Royal African Corps; captains = Asante officers or chiefs.

You were here when the dispute at Annamaboe occurred and the particulars were made known to you by Mr. James Swanzy, but so ridiculous and unworthy of consideration must they have appeared to you that I conclude they have long ere this escaped your recollection, and I therefore proceed to detail them. The Ashantee trader, having got into an altercation with some person in Annamaboe fort, and the noise he made being very great, the serjeant desired him to be more ruly, observing that he was instructed by his master (meaning the officer) to preserve order and tranquillity, and that he could not permit him to violate these orders. The Ashantee immediately damned his (the serjeant's) master and said he did not care whether he was pleased or otherwise. The serjeant retorted in the same language, and his words being understood to apply to the King of Ashantee, the matter was made known to two of his captains then at Annamaboe. Mr. Swanzy heard of the affair and he caused it to be signified to the captains that a regular investigation would take place on the following day. They intimated it to be their intention to assist at the inquiry and accordingly attended at the appointed hour. The statements on both sides having been heard, the Ashantee was declared by all parties to be in fault, and being greatly irritated at the decision, he swore by the terms 'Cormantine and Saturday' that the serjeant was guilty to the extent he had asserted. The Ashantee chiefs, as if terror-struck by these expressions, declined to interfere further, saying that none but their King could now settle the business.

In November 1822 the sergeant was kidnapped; in the following February he was executed. The next two documents approach these events from different perspectives. One comes from Reindorf, writing at the end of the century but with access to an abundance of oral and written traditions. The other is taken from the work of a contemporary of the events, a captain in the Royal African Corps who was stationed on the Gold Coast and consequently swept up in the atmosphere surrounding MacCarthy.

DOCUMENT 38
'In spite of the king's objections'

Reindorf, *History*, p. 72.

NOTES FOR READING Abora = Abora Dunkwa, Asante headquarters in the south; chyle = thick white lymph fluid.

When Sir Charles returned to Sierra Leone, leaving Major Chisholm in command, he left affairs in this dangerous state. A few months later, the same sergeant, who had spoken badly of the King of Asante, was sent by an official to Agya, a small town about three miles away, when he was seized by some Fante chiefs, and delivered to Kwame Butuakwa, Amon Bata, and Apentento, the Asante residents at Abora, in whose custody he remained for four or five months; after that time he was cruelly put to death, and his head and hands sent to the king. This cruel execution and the man's confinement for four or five months, strengthen the evidence of the following narration: 'The Sergeant, after his capture, was sent, under escort, to the king, who personally desirous of living in peace with the British Government, raised objections to the sergeant's being brought to Kumase, and released him . . . , but punished the accusers with death. The chiefs and captains of Asante then took the responsibility upon themselves, and authorised Butuakwa to kill the Sergeant in spite of the king's objections. Before carrying out the order, Butuakwa was reported to have said: 'How often I have tried to keep together the powerful kingdom of Asante by my eloquence, but they will not have it.' Some chyle being found mixed with the blood of the sergeant, bystanders exclaimed: 'The world has given the white clay (sign of justification); and the slain on the field of battle will be numerous.' These words were proved in the future to be indeed prophetic!

DOCUMENT 39
'In breach of the treaties'

From the account of Captain H. I. Ricketts. H. I. Ricketts *Narrative of the Ashantee War* (1831), pp. 13–15.

NOTES FOR READING   Donquah = Abora Dunkwa, the Asante headquarters in the south; MacCarthy was in Sierra Leone from May to November 1822.

Such was the state of affairs on the Gold Coast when Sir Charles MacCarthy, agreeably to instructions from his majesty, took upon himself the government of that part of the coast. He sailed for Sierra Leone about the 12th of May, leaving particular instructions to cultivate and cherish a good understanding with all the natives around, to fulfil the treaties by the due payment of customs, and to impress on their minds that Great Britain had no other object but to encourage their commerce and industry. Sir Charles, with the impression that he should at his next visit find the country in the full enjoyment of peace, was with the most bitter feelings of disappointment informed in November following, that the chief of the Ashantees, after receiving by his messengers the usual presents, had, in breach of the treaties entered into with Mr. Bowdich, and afterwards with Mr. Dupuis, and in defiance of the established usages of the country during peace, without any application whatever to Major Chisholm, the commandant of the Gold Coast, employed his agents to kidnap a mulatto man, (a serjeant in the royal African colonial corps) who was on duty at Annamaboe; the unfortunate man was carried a prisoner to Donquah in the Fantee country, fifteen miles at the back of Annamaboe fort, and there detained in irons. This atrocious violation of the existing treaties was said to have been occasioned by a dispute which had taken place between an Ashantee trader, and the serjeant inside of Annamaboe fort in the month of May preceding . . .
   On the 2nd of February, it was ascertained that a son of the late king had been sent down by Osai from Coomassie, with one of his executioners, to put the serjeant to death, and to send the jaw-bone, skull, and one of the arms of the victim to him . . . This murder was committed on the 1st of February. His excellency now considered it to be his duty to punish the perpetrators of such an atrocious act.

In the wake of the sergeant's death, MacCarthy's men worked swiftly to consolidate the drive for southern independence. They took their campaign beyond the Fante states to provinces like Wassa and Denkyira which were indisputably subject to Asante authority. In Kumasi those advocating an aggressive southern policy now dominated the deliberations. Osei Bonsu fell ill, withdrew from government business and died in 1823. One of those who mourned his passing and what it portended was Dupuis, who continued to receive letters in England about events in the Gold Coast.

DOCUMENT 40
'The king . . . was no more'

Dupuis' observations upon hearing of the death of Osei Bonsu. Dupuis, *Journal*, p. 215.

NOTES FOR READING   Sai Quamina = Osei Bonsu; the new monarch was Osei Yaw.

About the month of March last (1824) further accounts were received from the Gold Coast, but they were in no way important, except as it was stated in a private letter, the king— the inflexible, the hospitable, the celebrated, the friendly, the distressed *Sai Quamina*, was no more; having, as it would appear, departed this life in grief and vexation, bequeathing to his successor the kingdom and the palaver together, as Mr. Smith had already resigned his share of it to the interest which succeeded him. The successor to Sai, the same accounts stated, had commenced his reign by an *edict* against the British, wherein they were accused (whether justly or not it is the reader's province to decide) of perfidy, infractions of treaties, violations of public faith, treachery, cruelty, etc. To revenge which, and to appease the shade of the departed conqueror, in the region of spirits, the new monarch vowed eternal war against the British until he had obtained satisfaction; declaring (in the form of the great oath of his predecessors) that he would not cease from hostility until he had watered the grave of the departed Sai Quamina with the blood of white men, etc.

Osei Yaw, the new Asantehene, immediately formulated plans for the reoccupation of the southern provinces. He ordered his generals to restore order among the rebellious subjects, but to avoid any direct engagement with the British. MacCarthy interpreted such restraint as weakness and led a small force into the hinterland. In January 1824 the Asante mistook MacCarthy's contingent for a group of rebels. For what transpired we return to Ricketts, the Governor's chief of staff for the expedition.

DOCUMENT 41
'Headless trunks'

Ricketts, *Narrative*, pp. 82–3.

NOTES FOR READING Assamacow = Nsamankow in Wassa; Williams and Ricketts were among the few survivors.

It appeared by Mr. William's statement, that he left the field of action in company with Sir Charles MacCarthy, Mr. Buckle, and ensign Wetherell, and, after proceeding a short distance along the track to Assamacow, they were suddenly attacked by a part of the enemy, who fired and broke one of Sir Charles's arms; and that he immediately after received another wound in the chest and fell. They then removed him under a tree, where all remained awaiting their fate, which they perceived to be inevitable. Immediately after, Mr. Williams received a ball in his thigh, which rendered him senseless; previous however to his falling he saw Ensign Wetherell, who appeared also to have been wounded, lying close to Sir Charles, cutting with his sword at the enemy, as they were tearing the clothes off his friend and patron. Mr. Williams, upon recovering his senses, perceived that some Ashantees were attempting to cut off his head and had already inflicted one gash on the back of his neck; luckily however, at this crisis an Ashantee of authority came up, and recognizing Mr. Williams, from whom he had received some kindness in the African company's time, withheld the hand of the savage: on Mr. William's recovering his senses, he saw the headless trunks of Sir Charles Mac Carthy, Mr. Buckle, and Ensign Wetherell. He was then taken prisoner and marched to Assamacow, where the Ashantee army was encamped.

Asante maintained its armies in the south for much of 1824, then withdrew because of logistical problems and the ravages of smallpox and dysentery. In 1825 Osei Yaw persuaded his reluctant councillors to authorize a new campaign. A year later his armies moved into the south and encountered a British-led force at Katamanso, north of Accra. This time the Europeans won a decisive victory, killing several Asante leaders including Gyaasewahene Opoku Frefre. The campaign cost Kumasi at least one year's revenue. Moreover, the military levies prevented the kola nut harvest of 1825 and stopped trade at Salaga for an entire year. In this context, Kumasi returned to the policy of negotiation. When George Maclean took charge of the British settlements and succeeded in persuading a Fante force to abandon its blockade of Asante trade, he prepared the path to the Treaty of 1831 – the first to be ratified by both sides. In exchange for peace and guaranteed access to the coast, Asante renounced its administrative and political control over Denkyira, Assin and most of the Fante states. The agreement would govern British–Asante relations for the next thirty years.

AIDS TO UNDERSTANDING

Chronology

c. 1798 Osei Kwame deposed
c. 1800 Osei Bonsu accedes to throne

c. 1801 Battle of Koka in which Abu Bakr is captured
1803 Denmark abolishes slave trade for its subjects
1806–07 Major Asante campaign in the south
1807 Great Britain abolishes slave trade for its subjects
c. 1808 Asante establishes Salaga as main northern market centre
1809 Fante put pressure on Elmina and Accra
1811 Major Asante campaign in the south
1814–16 Major Asante campaign in the south
c. 1815 Gyaman ceases paying tribute
1816 (April)–1817 (May) Huydecoper's mission to Kumasi
1817 (May–September) James' and Bowdich's mission to Kumasi
1817 (September) 'Bowdich' treaty ratified by Asante
1817–18 Asante campaign against Gyaman
1820 (January) Asante demand for reparations from Fante and British
1820 (January–March) Dupuis' mission to Kumasi
1820 (March) Dupuis' treaty ratified by Asante
1820 (April) British officials on Gold Coast refuse to give hearing to treaty or take Asante embassy to Great Britain
1821 (February) British raid Asante group at coast, Asante begin blockade of central coast
1821 (March) Great Britain transfers Gold Coast settlements to crown control
1822 (April) Governor MacCarthy arrives at Cape Coast
1822 (May) Dispute between Asante trader and Fante sergeant
1822 (November) Sergeant kidnapped; linguist Agyei detained; British initiate attacks on Asante traders in south
1823 (February) Sergeant executed, British attack Abora
1823 (May) Sam Kanto Brew deported, dies on board ship
1823 (*c.* June) Osei Bonsu becomes ill
1823 (*c.* November) Osei Bonsu dies, Osei Yaw accedes to throne
1823 (December) Asante army moves into the south
1824 (January) Battle of Nsamankow where MacCarthy was killed
1824 (August) Asante army withdraws
1826 (August) Battle of Katamanso where Asante defeated
1831 Peace Treaty

Glossary

Abora (Abora Dunkwa) = Asante headquarters in Fante area
Abu Bakr = Timbuktu Muslim captured in slave trade (Document 2); prominent Muslim trader in Kumasi (Documents 26 and 32)
ackie = one-quarter of £1, one-sixteenth of an ounce
Accra = coastal town containing a number of European forts, including the Danish headquarters

Adinkra = ruler of Gyaman
Adum Ata = senior official of Asante
Adusei = first linguist of Asante
Agyei = second linguist of Asante
Amankwa = Asante general
Anomabu = British fort and Fante town
Apea Dankwa = Asante general
Apea Yanyo = Asante general
Apute (Apoutay): see Kwaku Apute
benda = 2 ounces
Bonduku = capital of Gyaman and important trading centre
book or note = usually refers to ground-rent paid by Europeans to presumed owner of land occupied by fort
Brew, Sam Kanto = mulatto trader operating in Fante areas
caboceer = captain, chief
Cape Coast = British for (headquarters) and Fante town
Cheboo = a chief of Assin
Elmina = Dutch fort (headquarters) and coastal town
fetish = religious artifact or ritual or the whole traditional religious sphere
Gyaman = province northwest of Kumasi
Katsina = important trading centre in Hausaland
Kong = important town and state northwest of Kumasi
Kwadwo Kuma = ruler of Akyem Abuakwa
Kwaku Apute = a chief of Assin
Kwaw Safrotwe = ruler of Akwapem
Muhammad al-Ghamba (Baba, 'Bashaw') = head of the Muslim community of Kumasi
Nieser, Jan = important mulatto trader of Elmina
Opoku Frefre ('Apoko', 'Apokoo') = Gyaasewahene and a leading general of Asante
ounce = unit of measure equal to 16 ackies or £4
palaver = problem, issue to be discussed
stool = office and the physical stool that symbolized it
Tando = Asante official in the political service and provincial administration
Torrane = British Governor at Cape Coast (1805–07)
Tsibo: see Cheboo
White = British Governor of Anomabu in 1807

An Essay of Questions

Sources and Interpretation

Most of the materials available for the study of Asante in the early nineteenth century come from European sources. Some are set in Kumasi, some on the coast. None gives the perspective of persons outside the forts or the Asante capital. How would you evaluate the following factors in terms of their contribution to the insight and objectivity of the author: eyewitness observation; knowledge of Twi; knowledge of Arabic; familiarity with Kumasi and the Asante court; Dutch perspective; British perspective; the perspective of someone accustomed to

the slave trade (e.g. Meredith) as opposed to someone intent on abolishing it (e.g. MacCarthy)?

We have relied heavily on the three Europeans who visited Kumasi and wrote accounts of their visits. How would you evaluate the relative insight and objectivity of Huydecoper, Bowdich and Dupuis? How do you explain the differences in perspective among them? Was it important, for example, that Bowdich was the nephew of Governor Smith, or that Dupuis only spent about one month in Kumasi? Do you find the travellers' quotations of Osei Bonsu's words helpful in judging the king's character?

The chapter contains no missionary accounts but it does include perceptions by persons for whom Asante customs were strange and—in the case of human sacrifice, slavery, and the slave-trade—inhumane. Was it possible for a European to understand Asante? Is it possible today for a student of history? How do these issues of human sacrifice and slavery affect your ability to perceive? Was it easier for the northern Muslims, who accepted and participated in slavery and the slave trade, to understand Asante society?

We have given several accounts of the Gyaman campaign (Documents 23–27) and two versions of the kidnapping and execution of the sergeant of Anomabu (Documents 38 and 39). What contrasts do you perceive in the different presentations and perspectives?

Identity, Literacy and Views of History

The 'social charter' called the Golden Stool played a very important role in Asante life, as demonstrated by the Gyaman campaigns of 1817–18. Do you find any comparable charters of established authority in your own society? Why did Kumasi react so strongly to Adinkra's actions (Documents 23–27)?

Was it possible for an Asante citizen also to be a Muslim? Were Muslims and Christians basically identical from an Asante perspective (cf. Document 31)? Was Islam incompatible with Asante identity since it was a 'leveller' of status (Document 1)? On all these issues, compare Asante with Buganda.

What do you understand by the stereotypes of black and white that come out in the Kumasi discussions? Did Osei Bonsu believe that 'black men know nothing' (Document 19)? What colour or ethnic identity would he have assigned to himself? What does he mean when he says that the 'great king' is his master (Document 30), or that the Englishmen know more than the Dutch and Danes (Document 19) or that he likes Englishmen 'best' (Document 28)?

How do you understand the Great Oath (Document 37) and the part it played in the Asante 'constitution' and identity; Huydecoper's oath and the process of which it was a part (Document 17)? Did Huydecoper believe in the process; did the Elminas; did the king?

The chapter contains a number of references to 'books' and literacy. Did the knowledge of writing give Europeans or Muslims advantages over the Asante? Did it provide a different sense of time (cf. Document 19)? Was the king at a disadvantage because he could not read (Documents 28 and 30)? To what extent did Osei Bonsu use the skills of literacy in his administration?

A number of people in the case study cross cultural and racial frontiers. Compare the situations of Abu Bakr (Document 2), Jan Nieser (Documents 9, 15–17) and Sam Kanto Brew (Document 22) with those of Pasko in the Sokoto chapter and Jacob in the Zulu chapter.

The Asante State

Kumasi was the capital of a highly centralized and intricately organized state. What similarities and contrasts would you posit between Asante and Buganda? What insights do the careers of Opoku Frefre, Agyei and Tando (Documents 5, 6, and 14) provide about the bureaucracy and promotion? How did political and economic considerations figure in the decisions of the court? How important was prestige? Was Asante a 'country for war' (Document 31)? Did 'war' and 'peace' parties exist at the court?

What do the accounts of the Gyaman struggle of 1817–18 say about the religious dimensions of the Asante state? Was the Asantehene a 'divine king'? In what ways did the religious dimension of his office increase or decrease his power, or his freedom to innovate? Was the bureaucracy a secular domain where the king had greater capacity for change? How would you compare the 'sacredness' of the positions of Asantehene and Kabaka, or the Islamic initiatives of Mutesa with those of Osei Kwame and Osei Bonsu?

Asante encountered problems in administering non-Asante territory, especially in the northwest and south central areas. Was this due to faulty methods; logistical difficulties; disease; excessive demands; too much or too little control; or outside agitators such as Fante chiefs, mulatto traders, British officials or Kong Muslims?

Osei Bonsu

What sense do you obtain of the character of the man who filled the office of king from 1800 to 1823? Compare the estimates of Documents 4 and 26 with the decisions made during those years. How would you compare Osei Bonsu with Muhammad Bello; Mutesa; Dingane? Compare the king's interest in and use of European technology with that of Moshweshwe. Compare his curiosity about the outside world with that of Moshweshwe, Mutesa and Muhammad Bello.

Economy and Foreign Policy

Many secondary sources maintain that Africa produced little more than subsistence economies in pre-colonial times. How would you describe the Asante economy? How was Asante activity in the production and exchange of kola nuts, gold, slaves and ivory organized? What can

you tell about sources of supply, and methods of production, distribution, investment? What principles governed market activity; supply and demand; profit maximization; status; redistribution of wealth? What constraints affected the development of the Asante economy: high transportation costs; size of the consumer population; attitudes towards the growth of a merchant class; slavery?

How would you explain Asante participation in the slave trade? Was Asante dependent upon it? How did the state obtain slaves? What do the documents reveal about the impact of abolition on the slave trade (cf. Documents 11, 20, 22 and 31); on the Asante economy; on the value of exports (kola, gold, ivory, and slaves; cf. Document 36); on Asante stability? How did Asante respond to these changes?

The documents are full of examples of protocol (hammocks, umbrellas, 'linguists', 'notes', palm wine, etc.). What were the functions of these? How would you compare the Dutch and the British as regards comprehension of Asante protocol? How do you explain the differences in the two copies of the 1817 Treaty (Document 21) and in Osei Bonsu's understanding of it (Document 30)? What observations would you venture about the freedom and restraints affecting Fante and mulatto traders, about the durability of their power and wealth, about their ability to influence Asante or European decisions?

The sources provide some examples of adulteration, inflation and other forms of cheating in trade (cf. Documents 19, 22, 28, and 29). Do you perceive any operative standards of commercial morality? How might such standards have been enforced? How does Asante compare with Sokoto in this regard? Several documents (especially Documents 22 and 31) discuss the slave trade. Was the British effort to stop the exportation of slaves a 'moral' stand in an 'immoral' or 'amoral' society? Did abolition improve the lot of slaves in this part of Africa?

The Asante and the British clashed on several occasions in the 1820s. Do you understand their confrontation as competition for scarce resources, or the result of competing ideologies, or of misunderstanding? How wide was the technological gap between European and African here, in comparison to that faced by Moshweshwe, or by Buganda in the late nineteenth century?

Like Lugard in Buganda, MacCarthy took action very soon after his arrival in the Gold Coast and had a major impact on events. How would you compare the two men in terms of independence of judgement; partisanship; wisdom?

Bibliographical Essay and Bibliography

In preparing this chapter we have relied greatly on the work of Ivor Wilks. Arhin and Fynn also treat the foundation and functioning of the Asante state. Rattray describes the society as it appeared to him in the 1920s. Daaku portrays the coast in the seventeenth century while Johnson analyses the mechanisms of trade. Lever treats Jan Nieser and Priestley describes the Brew family. Metcalfe's book on Maclean deals with the period after Osei

Bonsu's death; his collection of documents and those of Crooks and Newbury contain a great deal of important official material. Tordoff deals with Asante in the late nineteenth and early twentieth centuries. For overviews of the early nineteenth century, Claridge and Ward are helpful. For a geographical introduction, one should consult Dickson. For Islam and northern Ghana, consult Levtzion (1968). For visual impressions of life in Kumasi, see the elaborate drawings and paintings in Bowdich and Dupuis.

Some of the themes presented in this chapter can be pursued in other contexts. For the transatlantic slave trade, start with Curtin's *Census* and use his bibliography to move to other works. For long-distance trade and trading communities in the interior, see Meillassoux for West Africa, and Gray and Birmingham for Central and East Africa. For comparisons of Asante political structures with other African kingdoms, consult the Lloyd article. For comparisons with other coastal and foreign polities, see Akinjogbin for Dahomey, Smith for the Yoruba, Ryder for Benin, Dike for the Niger Delta and Vansina for Kongo and Angola.

Contemporary and Internal Accounts

Abu Bakr al-Siddiq, 'Routes in North Africa by Abu Bakr es-Siddik'. Trans. and ed. G. C. Renouard. *Journal of the Royal Geographical Society* (J. Murray, London, 1836). A recently annotated version appears in Curtin, 1967.

Beecham, John, *Ashantee and the Gold Coast*. 1841; Dawsons Pall Mall, London, 1968.

Bowdich, T. E., *Mission from Cape Coast Castle to Ashantee*. 1819; F. Cass, London, 1966.

Crooks, J. J., *Records Relating to the Gold Coast: Settlements from 1750 to 1874*. 1923; F. Cass, London, 1973.

Cruickshank, Brodie, *Eighteen Years on the Gold Coast*. 2 vols. 1853; F. Cass, London, 1966.

Curtin, Philip D., ed., *Africa Remembered*. University of Wisconsin Press, Madison, 1967.

Daendels, H. W., 'Journal of Correspondence of H. W. Daendels: Part I, November 1815 to January 1817'. Mimeographed translation from the Dutch by J. T. Furley *et al*. University of Ghana, 1964.

Dupuis, Joseph, *Journal of a Residence in Ashanti*. 1824; F. Cass, London, 1966.

Freeman, T. B., *Journal of Two Visits to the Kingdom of Ashanti*. J. Mason, London, 1843.

Hutton, W., *Voyage to Africa*. Longman, Hurst, London, 1821.

Huydecoper, W., 'The Journal of the Visit to Kumasi of W. Hudecoper, 28 April 1816 to 18 May 1817'. Mimeographed translation from the Dutch by G. Irwin. University of Ghana, 1962.

Levtzion, N., 'Early nineteenth-century Arabic manuscripts from Kumasi'. *Transactions of the Historical Society of Ghana*, Vol. 8 (Accra, 1965).

Mahmud ibn Abdullahi, 'Qissatu Salga'. Trans. Mahmoud el-Wakkad. *Ghana Notes and Queries*. (Accra, 1961).

Meredith, Henry, *An Account of the Gold Coast of Africa*. 1812; F. Cass, London, 1967.

Metcalfe, G. E., ed., *Great Britain and Ghana. Documents of Ghana History, 1807–1957*. Nelson, London, 1964.

Newbury, C. W., ed., *British Policy towards West Africa. Select Documents, 1786–1874*. Oxford University Press, Oxford, 1965.

Reindorf, C. C., *The History of the Gold Coast and Asante*. 1895, reprinted 1966.

Ricketts, H. I., *Narrative of the Ashantee War*. Simpkin & Marshall, London, 1831.

Secondary Sources

Arhin, Kwame 'The structure of Greater Ashanti'. *Journal of African History* (1967).

—The financing of Ashanti expansion, 1700–1820'. *Africa* (1967).

Asante Seminar '76. Northwestern University, Evanston, 1976.

Boahen, A. A., *Topics in West African History*. Longman, Harlow, 1966.

Claridge, W. W., *A History of the Gold Coast and Ashanti*. 2 vols. 1915; F. Cass, London, 1964.

Collins, E., 'The panic element in nineteenth-century relations with Ashanti'. *Transactions of the Historical Society of Ghana* (Accra, 1962).

Coombs, M. D., *The Gold Coast, Britain and the Netherlands, 1850–1874*. Oxford University Press, London, 1963.

Daaku, K., *Trade and Politics on the Gold Coast, 1600–1720*. Oxford University Press, New York, 1970.

Dickson, K. B., *A Historical Geography of Ghana*. Cambridge University Press, Cambridge, 1971.

Feinberg, Harvey, 'There was an Elmina Note, but...'. *International Journal of African Historical Studies* (Boston, 1976).

Fynn, J. K., *Asante and its Neighbours, 1700–1807*. Longman, Harlow, 1972.

Johnson, Marion, 'The ounce in eighteenth-century West African trade'. *Journal of African History* (1966).

—'The cowrie currencies of West Africa'. *Journal of African History* (1970).

Lever, J. T., 'Mulatto influence on the Gold Coast in the early 19th century'. *African Historical Studies* (Boston, 1970).

Levtzion, N., *Muslims and Chiefs in West Africa*. Oxford University Press, Oxford, 1968.

McCaskie, T. C., 'Innovational eclecticism: the Asante Empire and Europe in the nineteenth century'. *Comparative Studies of Society and History* (Mouton, The Hague, 1972).

Metcalfe, G. E., *Maclean of the Gold Coast*. Oxford University Press, Oxford, 1962.

Priestley, M., *West African Trade and Coast Society.* Oxford University Press, London, 1969.

Rattray, R. S., *Ashanti.* Clarendon, Oxford, 1923.

—*Ashanti Law and Constitution*, Clarendon, Oxford. 1929.

Reynolds, E., *Trade and Economic Change on the Gold Coast, 1807–1874.* Longman, Harlow, 1974.

Tordoff, William, *Ashanti under the Prempehs.* Oxford University Press, London, 1965.

Ward, W. E. F., *A History of Ghana.* Allen & Unwin, London, 1967.

Wilks, Ivor. 'Aspects of bureaucratization in Ashanti in the nineteenth century'. *Journal of African History* (1966).

—'Ashanti government'. In D. Forde and P. Kaber, eds *West African Kingdoms in the Nineteenth Century.* Oxford University Press, London, 1967.

—'Asante policy towards the Hausa trade in the nineteenth century'. In Meillassoux, 1971.

—'The Mossi and Akan states, 1500–1800'. In J. F. Ade Ajayi and M. Crowder, eds. *History of West Africa.* Vol. I. Longman, Harlow, 1972.

—*Asante in the Nineteenth Century.* Cambridge University Press, Cambridge, 1975.

Collateral Reading

Akinjogbin, I. A., *Dahomey and its Neighbours, 1708–1818.* Cambridge University Press, Cambridge, 1967.

Curtin, Philip D., *The Atlantic Slave-Trade. A Census.* University of Wisconsin Press, Madison, 1972.

Dike, K. O. *Trade and Politics in the Niger Delta, 1830–1885.* Oxford University Press, Oxford, 1956.

Gray, R., and Birmingham, D., eds., *Pre-colonial African Trade.* Oxford University Press, Oxford, 1970.

Lloyd, P. C., 'The political structure of African kingdoms: an exploratory model'. In M. Banton, ed. *Political Systems and the Distribution of Power.* Tavistock Publications, London, 1965.

Meillassoux, C., ed., *The Development of Indigenous Trade and Markets in West Africa.* Oxford University Press, Oxford, 1971.

Ryder, A. F. C., *Benin and the Europeans, 1485–1897.* Longman, Harlow, 1969.

Smith, Robert, *Kingdoms of the Yoruba.* Methuen, London, 1969.

Vansina, Jan, *Kingdoms of the Savanna.* University of Wisconsin Press, Madison, 1966.

Index

A

age groups, 3–4, 8, 43
agriculture, 42, 124
  adoption of new crops, 67
  crops, 2, 66, 127, 152, 182
  crops destroyed, 13, 49, 74, 75, 81, 106, 125
  famine, 7, 13, 44, 45, 49
alcohol, 54, 67–8, 70, 85, 89, 169
assassination, 9, 22–3, 34, 155

B

bureaucracy:
  advance within, 85, 102
  corruption, 113–15, 138, 142
  decision-making within, 14, 16, 87, 93–4, 100, 129,
    182, 190
  description of: Baganda, 81–4, 107; Hausa, 128–30;
    Islamic, 140–2; Zulu, 13–14
  growth and establishment of, 11, 81–4
  loss of control over, 92, 96
  removal and replacement of advisers, 9, 23, 85, 104,
    106–7
  reorganization of, 106–7, 111–12, 148
  see also social mobility

C

cannibalism, 13, 45, 47, 48
capitals, *see* political organization
cattle, 14, 125
  as fines, 62, 63–4
  as wealth, 46, 85
  raiding for, 15, 32, 44, 47, 68, 75
  ritual use of, 53
  see also agriculture, economic organization,
    pastoralism
childhood, 86
  Moshweshwe, 44
  Mwanga, 97–8
  Shaka, 7–8
  see also initiation, education
Christianity:
  African views of, 51–4, 67, 74, 97
  commercial aspects, 94
  conversion, 52, 53–4, 67, 68, 70, 92, 96, 99, 125
  political aspects, 67, 70, 92, 100–1, 102–7, 107–12
  recruitment, 92, 94–5, 99
  resistance to, 52–4, 93–4
  response to, 91–2, 95
  schisms within, 92, 106, 107–12
  see also missionaries, religion, religious change
civilization, *see* Christianity, custom, economic
  organization, identity, ideology, Islam, law, political
  organization, social organization, warfare
climate, 2, 42, 49, 61, 66, 81, 137
colour, 31, 69, 76
  'black', 30, 51, 59, 117, 187
  'white', 30, 35, 51, 54, 59, 68, 92, 116, 172, 181, 187
commerce, 11, 49, 67, 71, 126–8, 177
  Asante–British, 180–4
  Asante–Dutch, 177–80
  cloth, 86–7, 124, 153, 182
  commercial morality, 26, 68, 127, 141, 187
  gold, 124, 162, 167, 169, 171, 176, 177, 182, 186–7
  ivory, 17, 20, 26, 86–7, 104, 113–14, 124, 171
  kolanuts, 124, 143, 170, 182–3
  'legitimate', 175–6, 190
  regulation and control, 5, 28, 67–8, 113–14, 126–8, 189
  salt, 124, 153, 182, 183
  trade routes, 5, 17, 90, 123, 124, 130, 143, 166,
    167–8, 170, 171
  transatlantic, 167–8, 171
  trans-Sáharan, 124, 128, 167–8
  weapons, 29–30, 69, 72, 86–7, 124, 182, 187
  see also economic organization
communications, 12, 15, 46, 99, 155, 178
  access to state secrets, 100, 103, 104, 109, 145
  interpreters, 25–7, 92, 154
  'linguists', 170, 181
  messengers, 12, 15, 46, 129
  spies, *see under* military organization
custom, 6, 7, 8, 9, 16, 17, 128–30
  burial, 21, 52–3, 171
  challenge to, 52–4, 88, 90, 93–4, 103, 113

D

demography, 3, 5, 17, 20, 49, 50, 56, 60, 65, 67, 81,
  85, 126, 168